William Penn

William Penn

by

HARRY EMERSON WILDES

Macmillan Publishing Co., Inc.

NEW YORK

Collier Macmillan Publishers

LONDON

Macmillan Publishing Co., Inc.
866 Third Avenue, New York, N.Y. 10022
Collier-Macmillan Canada Ltd.

Library of Congress Cataloging in Publication Data

Wildes, Harry Emerson, 1890–
   William Penn.

    1. Penn, William, 1644–1718.
F152.2.W46   974.8'02'0924 [B]   73–1857
ISBN 0–02–628570–3

FIRST PRINTING 1974

Printed in the United States of America

WITH HEARTFELT APPRECIATION OF THE

LIFELONG DEVOTION GIVEN BY

Dr. Albert Cook Myers

TO THE DISCOVERY AND PRESERVATION OF

ALL MATERIALS RELATIVE TO INCIDENTS

IN THE LIFE OF WILLIAM PENN,

TOGETHER WITH DEEP GRATITUDE

TO THE OFFICERS AND STAFF OF THE

CHESTER COUNTY HISTORICAL SOCIETY

OF WEST CHESTER, PENNSYLVANIA

FOR MAKING THE MYERS COLLECTION

AVAILABLE FOR THIS BIOGRAPHY.

Contents

INTRODUCTION: MAN OF PARADOX

For a gentle, quiet man, William Penn the Quaker stirred up an amazing amount of controversy. Few people during the exciting era of the Puritan upheaval, the Cromwell Protectorate, the Stuart Restoration, and the Glorious Revolution understood him; in many ways he remains a mystery until this day.

The uncertainty extends even to his appearance. Four or five so-called portraits exist, but there is no solid proof that any of the supposed likenesses were painted during Penn's maturity or by anyone who knew him well. Neither of the two best-known portrays Penn as we would expect. The portrait of a young man in armor is not the picture of a dedicated pacifist, while the scene of a treaty signing with the Indians shows a fat and stodgy-looking old man in a costume of a hundred years later. While the armor portrait does have youth and freshness, and the treaty picture reflects friendliness and benevolence, neither shows how vibrant and dynamic Penn was.[1]

Penn was probably big-boned and inclined to portliness, but there is no certainty whether he was tall or of medium height. His father was five feet eight, and both parents were stout. His hair was flaxen, though scanty throughout life, the result, he assumed, of a smallpox attack when he was three—but there is no agreement whether his eyes were blue or gray.[2]

Penn was not a secretive man, but his personality is as much in doubt as is his appearance. Although a prolific letter writer and the author of scores of publications, he shed but little light upon his own feelings or experiences; even the details were not invariably precise. In recalling an event years later, time may have played tricks upon him, perhaps leading him, in all innocence, to write down what might have happened, rather than what actually did occur.

There being at no time any question of Penn's integrity, many biographers uncritically accepted everything he wrote, including details of visions as Penn recalled them. Nor could they refrain from treating old tradition as trustworthy authority.

His reticence served him ill; he would have been better understood, then and now, had he been more open. His aims were lofty and his services great; he accomplished far more of value to his fellowman than did many others of wider renown. His contributions, however, presented quietly through his writings, his sermons, or his conferences, attracted less attention than did the words and deeds of more flamboyant contemporaries. His influences on American colonial government and on the subsequent development of the United States have been less publicized than those of other early statesmen.

Penn was both complex and contradictory. A bookish man who would have been happier in ancient Rome than in brawling seventeenth-century London, he founded three American colonies, one of them, Pennsylvania, the greatest ever planted by a private individual. A man who always thought of himself as poor, he owned more land than any other commoner in history. A modest, retiring man, he moved at ease among pushing, sophisticated courtiers. A sincere man who believed others to be as honest as himself, he was easily deluded, yet, by his frankness, he countered the devious. An upright, thoroughly moral man, he was the victim of suspicion, slander, and vicious persecution. A man who abhorred conflict, both physical and intellectual, he argued incessantly, both by speech and publication, and even fought a duel. A man who respected authority, he attacked the Established Church and challenged the divine right of kings by insisting upon the divine right of popular government. Against strong pressure for centralized control, he demanded and, to large degree, won colonial autonomy; of all the proprietors of American colonies, he alone retained control for himself and for his family until the Revolution.

Penn's naïveté concealed his complexity. His candor and frankness bewildered those who suspected trickery. Straightforward yet evasive, tolerant yet inflexible, he was a dreamer who could be intensely practical. No wonder that a book formerly credited to Benjamin Franklin said that Penn joined the subtlety of the serpent with the innocence of the dove.[3]

William Penn's ideas were far in advance of his time. His chief concern was for freedom, particularly the right—indeed the duty—of each individual to think for himself, especially to worship God as each thought best. Unfortunately, he campaigned for religious tolerance in an era when conformity was accounted virtue. He demanded equality in an era of aristocracy, justice in a period when fair-mindedness could be accounted heresy, if not treason.

Penn stood firm for what he regarded as the fundamental and historic rights of Englishmen: the rights of life, liberty, and property; the right to government by popular consent; the right to trial by independent juries. These rights, stemming from ancient custom and guaranteed by such solemn compacts as the Magna Charta, were not to be infringed upon by any overlord, regardless of his rank or power.

But Penn was more than just a political reformer. He worked for free and general education, not only for the clergy or the lawyers or any other privileged class, but education to improve the status of the common people. He recognized the need for better food and housing, for health services, for protection of the weak against exploitation. He planned garden cities, pioneered a type of zoning, demanded conservation of natural resources, insisted that the gifts of nature were intended not only for one's own time but for generations to come.

Penn's program for social betterment, beginning with eugenics, included campaigns against child labor and for shorter working hours, against exploitation of workers and for government-run employment agencies and mediation offices. He urged minimum- rather than maximum-wage laws, condemned profiteering, and insisted that employers plan and operate their businesses in cooperation with their workmen. Far in advance of his time, he recognized the evils of slavery and tried to limit, if not to abolish, its injustices. Convinced that all men, of whatever race or color, were the children of God, he pleaded for equality of treatment.

Since many variables enter into the appraisal of one human being by another—differences of time, circumstances, accuracy of information, psychologies and points of view among scores of others—the estimates of Penn's character varied widely. His enemies thought him vain, hypocritical, scheming, and untruthful—charges his friends hotly denied. William I. Hull, an ardent admirer, spoke for Penn's defenders: "Of the nearly 100 human virtues listed in *Fruits of Solitude* Penn exemplified nearly half; of the score or more of vices excoriated in *No Cross, No Crown*, he avoided or overcame nearly all."[4]

Differences of opinion among contemporaries are inevitable and, if the reasons are sound, forgivable; what is unpardonable is obvious fabrication or distortion of fact. Penn, more than most men of his time, suffered from the uncharitableness of thought that characterized the seventeenth century. He himself was not immune from the vice of writing or speaking intemperately about those who crossed him. All too often he dubbed such men "the greatest of villains," "the vilest of men," "a pack of brutish spirits," "presumptuous and blasphemous wretches" even, in the case of a former good friend, George Keith, a man with "stomach enough to lick up vomit."[5]

That such crudities were common enough in his time, or that the epithets hurled back at him were worse, does not excuse Penn's indelicacies, but at least he did not resort to the downright lies invented by his adversaries. There seemed no limit to some people's credulity. The more absurd the fantasy, the readier were fly-by-night newsletters to publish it or for some readers to accept it as truth. Alarm sounded in 1690 that England was about to be invaded. William Penn had fled to France (another version said Scotland) bent on returning with thirty thousand veteran French soldiers. His traitorous purpose? To restore his friend James II, the Stuart exile, as a French and papal puppet on the English throne. So realistic and detailed was the "revelation" that a century and a half later no less a historian than Thomas Babington Macaulay suspected that the rumor might really have been true.

Those who distrusted Penn asserted that his true purpose had never been to help his fellowman but just to aid the French. Nearly everyone in England and certainly everyone in America would recall, the detractors said, that whenever English colonists were endangered by French intruders and their savage Indian allies, Penn's province often refused to send a single soldier or to spend a shilling for the common defense. The dangers, they admitted, were always far from Penn's settlements, and sometimes his province did agree, reluctantly, to provide a few pounds sterling, but only, Penn's enemies pointed out, "to feed the hungry" or "to clothe the naked," which meant, it was asserted, to help the Indians and not the Englishmen. Even then the relief was often long delayed or never arrived at all.

The truth was, said Penn's slanderers, that the man had always been pro-French. Had he not gone to school in France at a place he called Saumur? Of course, he carefully explained that Saumur was a Protestant college near Tours, but was it not, if the truth were known, really St. Omer, the Jesuit seminary near Calais?

Francis Bugg, a tireless anti-Penn pamphleteer, even "exposed the secret reason" why Penn had gone to Pennsylvania in the first place: to avoid being shot by a jealous Irish husband; according to Bugg, moreover, Penn had never given up philandering. When, years later, he returned to London, he locked himself behind barred doors in a fourth-story refuge. Why? Because, Bugg explained, Penn had been consorting with a certain haberdasher's wife but had thrown her aside when her charms faded. The reporter did do Penn a sort of justice by admitting that he had pensioned off the lady at £40 a year, but her hurt had not been healed; her jealousies were kept alive by his alleged attentions to a rival whom he was visiting "twice or thrice a week."[6]

Scandalous reports, built in every case on flimsy and questionable foundations, long continued to circulate. An otherwise well-accredited scholar, in a doctoral dissertation, speculated that Penn's constant pleas of poverty indicated that someone with a knowledge of a skeleton in Penn's past had been blackmailing him. A writer for the official journal of the University of Pennsylvania, presumably in a clumsy attempt at humor, "exposed the fact" that Penn named his capital city for a lost love who had been christened Philadelphia; he supported his argument by pointing out that in later Penn generations at least two baby girls had been given the same unwieldy first name.[7]

Despite such rumors, Penn's reputation, like that of the Quaker movement generally, grew steadily. The high-mindedness of the Friends and their evident sincerity as evidenced in their good works appealed to the hearts and minds of men and women who, hungering for justice, peace, and righteousness, saw that Quakers were obeying the word of God in their personal and public conduct.

It was inevitable that, to balance the libels and slanders about so eminent a figure as William Penn, an overblown praise should also circulate. During Penn's lifetime and down to the present time, Penn's words and deeds carried such conviction that his followers and especially his biographers, in seeking to explain his extraordinary influence, conjured up for him an aura of saintliness. Just as Francis Bugg and other inveterate enemies presented William Penn as a hypocrite, a traitor, a lecher, and a liar, unthinking adorers drained him of humanity.

Indeed, the well-meaning eulogies may have harmed Penn more than the lying caricatures. The overstatements of his enemies, being so palpably untrue, caused little harm; the godlike wisdom, purity, sanctity, and absolute perfection ascribed to him by his admiring friends were equally incredible, and Penn thereby became unreal, almost mythic—a highly superior being much too good to be true.

Just as in his biographies he has never really been alive, so has he never really been young. Even as a child, Penn comes into view fully grown in aspect, action, and mentality. No biography lets him grow; he is invariably mature. Not a single schoolboy friend is mentioned; at college he associated not with classmates but with John Locke, twelve years older than himself, a lecturer in Greek, science, and philosophy. He did not play but kept his nose stuck deep into dusty books.

The flattering biographies carefully omit any human weakness. Not for William Penn any munching of a bun as he strolls the streets of a strange city, not for him a kite-flying experiment in a thunderstorm, certainly no dalliance with complaisant ladies in Parisian settings, not for him even the suggestion of an unbecoming anecdote. The wildest story told of Penn is that once, on a First Day morning, he stopped his horseback ride to carry a tired little girl to meeting; even so, we do not know how she managed to retrace those seven miles back home.[8]

No, unhappily, William Penn's admirers failed to make him human. Even in his own city of Philadelphia, Benjamin Franklin is better known and, what is worse, probably the object of more heartfelt admiration. Even today many Quakers, thinking of William Penn, see him only as a well-fed, beaming man in a broad-brimmed hat, with no human foibles. Franklin is almost always "Ben," but who, even in his childhood, ever called the founder "Bill"? (Oddly enough, the big bronze statue atop Philadelphia's City Hall is almost always identified as "Billy" Penn, the nickname given to his wastrel son but never to the father.)

True, Anthony A. Wood, who wrote a short sketch of Penn's Oxford years, says that Penn excelled in many sports, particularly rowing. A Philadelphia Quaker lady swore (or rather, affirmed) that when Penn made that famous treaty with the Indians—a treaty grossly misrepresented both in story and in art—he outran and outjumped a score of competing Indians, but the lady was recalling what she thought that she had seen some seventy or eighty years before.[9]

Since Penn himself specifically asserted that he had never, even in his youth, wasted time or effort in what he called "carnal entertainment," it is unlikely that he could have competed successfully against tribal chiefs, even those as old as he, for while he had been sedentary for many years, they were outdoorsmen who would have been in excellent condition.[10]

The old lady may have been overenthusiastic about Penn's prowess as an athlete, but was it not praise enough that she also said that William Penn was the handsomest man that she had ever seen?

It is now impossible to recover trivia about William Penn, too late to learn much about his youth. The slanders are forgotten and the more obviously swollen praises lanced, but imagination still conjures up legends. One especially hardy perennial asserts in detail how Cotton Mather, of all people, plotted to hijack Penn and his party on their way to America in order to sell them all into West Indian slavery. Though the story has been exploded time and time again, it continues to be revived, in more or less responsible publications, every five years or so.[11]

More incredibly, as late as the Christmas season of 1973, two presumably literate Philadelphians seriously argued whether anyone named William Penn ever existed. A local newspaper, one disputant declared, had published an article saying that "Penn" and Benjamin Franklin were one and the same person.

To settle the dispute they appealed to the Historical Society of Pennsylvania. Still unconvinced when "the slightly startled assistant director" of that august institution dismissed the idea as "completely wild," the doubter of Penn's existence combed through the files of Philadelphia newspapers for the alleged statement. The search was, of course, wholly unproductive.[12]

The people of the Bahama Islands had no such doubts of Penn's existence. In 1973 their postoffice department issued a commemorative stamp bearing Penn's portrait—something that the United States postal authorities have so far failed to do.

1

SELF-REARED CHILD

WILLIAM PENN'S ORIGINS ARE NOT EASY TO TRACE. THE NAME PENN, DERIVED FROM A WELSH OR CORNISH WORD MEANING "HILL," OCCURS IN NINE OR TEN ENGLISH COUNTIES, SOME, IF not all, of these families may be related, especially as several bear the same coat of arms (three white plates on a black horizontal band), but genealogists have discovered no convincing proofs.[1]

Penn himself once told a questioner that his ancestors were Welsh and that his grandfather was a John Tudor of Penmurith who assumed a new name when he moved to London, but this must have been a jest, for Penn knew better. He also professed himself descended from a Norman knight, one de la Penne to whom William the Conqueror gave a Buckinghamshire estate.[2]

The line of William Penn the Quaker stems from William Penn, yeoman of Minety in Gloucestershire, who died in 1592. Little is known of this great-great-grandfather except that he possessed a considerable estate and that he lies buried in the chancel of Minety chapel. Even less is known of his son, William, a law clerk, who predeceased his father the yeoman, but not before siring six children.

Giles Penn, one of the law clerk's younger sons, was the grandfather of William Penn the Quaker. A sea captain sailing out of Bristol, he traded with the Spaniards, the Moors, and probably with Algerian pirates. Blessed with a natural talent for making friends, Giles won the confidence of the Moors and learned their language—while, at the same time, he curried royal favor by supplying the English court with Arab horses and hunting falcons. Later he became the official agent for ransoming English captives.[3]

In an era when giant overseas-trading companies were being formed,

Giles planned to exploit the western Mediterranean. As English consul at Salé, he was in a position to control, if not to monopolize, the commerce of North Africa and Spain. By establishing his older son, George, as a resident merchant at Seville, he could make money in the lucrative Spanish wine trade. A second son, William, would captain a vessel to take the goods to Bristol, where the influential merchant Thomas Callowhill would sell the cargoes and supply a return consignment. The profits would be enormous.

Giles's scheme worked well for a time, but suddenly everything went wrong. Because of some charge never fully explained the Spaniards annulled George's marriage to a Spanish girl. George thought it had something to do with his Protestantism, but, oddly, neither George nor the lady seem to have raised an objection. Then the persecutors arrested George, confiscated his property "down to a nail in the wall," threw him into a dark dungeon, and for weeks fed him on nothing but bread and water. They also beat him regularly with a knotted whipcord.[4]

Then William left the trading company. Craving excitement, he joined the Royal Navy. When Giles pointed out that merchant shipping offered larger and quicker returns, William answered in words that his son, the founder of Pennsylvania, might well have spoken: "Gold to me is dirt; 'tis the goodness of the cause that hath only to put me on, and nothing shall take me off the service."[5] Nothing did. William the Sailor remained a naval officer all his life.

During a shore leave in London in 1643, William met and fell in love with Margaret Jasper Vanderscure, a gay, party-loving widow some years older than himself. Not much is known of her background except that she was born in Rotterdam and that her parents, John Jasper, a merchant, and his wife, Marie, may have been of Dutch, English, Irish, or even French descent. In her early teens Margaret had married one Nicasius Vanderscure, of whom even less is known, and soon thereafter she, with her husband and parents, moved to Ballyease, County Clare, Ireland, where they prospered as traders.

How long Margaret's marriage lasted, whether it was happy, whether there were children (probably not), or how Nicasius died no one can now tell. We do know that Margaret and her parents, having lost all their property because of riot, rebellion, confiscation, and theft, fled to England, where they lived more or less in poverty. A certain John Baptist Jasper, who may have been her grandfather, was a merchant in the Strand; other Jaspers lived eight miles out of London at Wanstead, in Essex. Indications are that it was at Wanstead that William met the sprightly widow.

Old Giles had taught his sons to cultivate the company of superiors who could further their careers, and William had learned the lesson well. As a bachelor he was ineligible to secure lodging in the Navy colony of

Tower Hill, where influential naval officers resided, but during his leaves he frequented one or another of the three taverns they patronized. A genial young man, he gained their friendship, for he was convivial and charming, able to tell a story well, to sing pleasantly—often bawdily —and to flatter his elders by deferring to them gracefully. Two of the more important, admirals both, invited him to visit their country homes at Wanstead, the red-brick village on a hill where everybody knew everyone else. Two such young people as Margaret and the young officer could not have escaped each other's notice, and Margaret Jasper Vanderscure and William Penn the Sailor were married June 6, 1643, at St. Martin's, Ludgate.[6]

The Penns, intent on furthering their position, immediately took lodgings on fashionable Tower Hill. Their two rooms, one above the other, in George Court, on the east side of Trinity Square, were much too cramped for entertaining notables, but William and the energetic, extroverted Margaret were welcome guests at various parties. Thus they widened their acquaintance to include such dignitaries as Algernon Percy, Earl of Northumberland, and Sir Harry Vane, recently returned from governing Massachusetts and now the Navy treasurer. Those powerful new friends joined the Wanstead admirals in seeing to it that William received a captaincy.

The commissioning of the twenty-two-year-old Captain Penn over the heads of older men caused criticism in the wardrooms. Jealous rivals spoke, and with much justice, of favoritism; others, with less cause, alleged that Captain Penn was unfit for the honor. He came, they said, from humble origins: a common sailor, one scoffed; a cabin boy, another sneered. The favoritism charge was correct, but Giles's son had never been a foremast hand or a menial.[7]

Captain Penn, not being the only officer to enjoy special favor, shrugged off the grumblings of his rivals; he knew that he was at least as skilled a sailor as any of his rivals. What hurt him were the indirect attacks whose sources he could not always identify, insinuations of imaginary shortcomings, the magnifying of minor flaws, the gossip that he drank too much, hints of inaccuracy in his accounts, of ill-treatment of seamen, questions of his courage. No one really took the rumors seriously, but their cumulative effect was certainly not favorable, nor did they ever cease.

Neither did Margaret's personality, however pleasing to the men, sit well with certain ladies on Tower Hill. Theophila "The" Turner, wife of a Navy bureaucrat and cousin of Samuel Pepys the diarist, paying a courtesy call on the new arrival, was shocked by what she thought Mrs. Penn's bad manners. The bride, "The" Turner said, was "slattery," one of the sourest women that she ever saw, "a dirty slattern with her stockings hanging round her heels." Nevertheless, Mrs. Turner, being, by her own admission, considerate and helpful, undertook to correct Margaret's shortcomings and to introduce her to other ladies of the Navy circle.[8]

"The" Turner's unkind comments, reported by Pepys, cannot be uncritically accepted, for Pepys, for one reason or another, heartily disliked the whole Penn family and was very sparing in his praise of them. Unfortunately, few other opinions of Margaret are discoverable. Even her grandson, in writing a biography of William the Sailor, gave Margaret no more than one short sentence, and that only toward the close of the second volume. Early Penn biographers ignore her, though in the sugary sentimental fashion of early Victorianism, later writers describe her as the conventionally soft and gentle, all-wise, retiring, and patient Christian mother.

While Margaret was being coached in good deportment, her husband was facing a dilemma. By conviction pro-Anglican and royalist, Captain Penn's allegiance as a naval officer was to Cromwell's Commonwealth. Some officers, in such circumstances, resigned and others deserted with their ships, but Penn placed his country above his personal preferences. The Navy, England's safeguard, must, in a period of Civil War, protect the nation against marauding French and Spanish privateers. He joined a squadron preparing to defend the Irish coast against possible invasion.

Though the decision reflected Penn's sincere loyalty to England, detractors were quick to notice that it also served his private interest. The lands lost by Margaret and the Jaspers lay along the western Irish coast near Limerick, close to the famous Bunratty Castle, the stronghold of a prominent insurgent. A successful naval assault upon that rebel fortress would benefit the English cause and simultaneously improve Penn's family fortune.

During the summer of 1644, while Captain Penn was busy fitting out his ship by day and hobnobbing with the other officers at night, he was also scouting for better living quarters. The two rooms on Tower Hill had served their purpose by enabling Penn to meet leaders who could help him, but to leave Margaret there alone would be a grave error. The breeziness and high spirits that made her popular with young officers would fail to charm the ladies; the catty Mrs. Turner could rip Margaret's reputation to shreds.

There was, moreover, a second, very compelling reason for a move. Margaret was pregnant. After the baby's birth, due sometime in October, it would be much better both for her and for the child to live away from the crowded unhealthful city.

Wanstead was the best locality. The presence of Jasper relatives in that pleasant neighborhood would ease Margaret's loneliness. The fact that the top two commanders of Penn's expedition lived at Wanstead would, if Margaret toned down her exuberance, advance Penn's social and professional position. His two superiors helped him find a house and saw that he was promoted to admiral; their ladies, who moved in a society above the Turner circle, found Margaret delightful.

Throughout the late summer and early autumn of 1644, Admiral Penn lived under constant tension. Though eager for active service, he hoped earnestly that departure would be delayed until after the child arrived. When at last, in mid-October, the waiting ended, he simultaneously received two calls; to sail for Ireland and to hurry home to Margaret.

As on so many occasions in Penn family history, high-placed friends solved the difficulty. Sir Harry Vane suggested that though, as a good officer, Penn must weigh anchor, there was no reason why, while his ship stood down the Thames, the Admiral could not be rowed ashore, ride back home, stay with his wife until assured of her well-being, and then gallop south a hundred miles or so to resume command.

Early in the morning of October 14, 1644 (O.S.), a son, yet another William Penn, was born. Twelve days later, with the father still present, the boy was baptized, the Reverend Edward Layfield performing the Anglican ceremony at the charming medieval Church of All Hallows Barking on the far side of Tower Hill.[9]

He was a strange child. One might expect the son of a convivial sailor and a hearty, zestful mother to be rollicking, but William Penn of Wanstead was in no sense an extrovert. On the contrary, the son of Admiral William, the great-grandson of William the law clerk, and the great-great-grandson of William of Minety, was from his earliest years quiet and introspective, a boy who later in life declared that he had never wasted time in play.

The difference in temperament between William and his parents may be partly attributed to his being reared in a predominantly feminine household. During his first seven impressionable years young William saw almost nothing of his father, who returned home for only brief visits from patrolling the Irish coast. The presence, now and then, of various male relatives—of Uncle George, now freed from captivity on the condition that he never return to Spain, of Grandfather Jasper, then on church relief rolls, and of some others, vaguely described as cousins— afforded some masculine influence, but the men were either sickly or ineffective and were, to William's childish mind, ancients from another world.

Female domination, normal for most small children, would not necessarily suppress an active little boy, but William was not by nature active, and because of special circumstances, Margaret was exercising a stronger discipline than she would have imposed at Tower Hill. The fun-loving bride had calmed; she was trying to recast herself in a new image. To win approval from the Wanstead matrons, most of them older than she, Margaret was striving to become what we would today describe as a typical suburban housewife and to make her son a polite, self-effacing little gentleman.

As a housewife, Margaret was not spectacularly successful. Years later, the unfriendly Samuel Pepys still pictured her housekeeping as messy. Her cooking, said Pepys, with his customary delicacy and charm, "stank like the very Devil." His professed revulsion did not prevent his dining there frequently, perhaps because it was there that he first ate a melon or tasted tea. Margaret, however, did accomplish her major purpose. She won a place in Wanstead society, the better to promote her husband's career.[10]

Where young William acquired his interest in religion and study, the two chief concerns of his life, is not apparent. No Penn ancestor in either line is credited with having read, much less owned, any book other than a business ledger. Religion was, of course, a common concern in Cromwellian times, but the Penns, while nominally Anglicans sharing an All Hallows Barking pew with Pepys, were showing only token interest in church affairs. None of the family had played an active role in ecclesiastical matters, save for a certain William Penn, a century and a half in the past, who became a monk at Glastonbury—and even his interest was flawed, for rumor alleged that he was popularly known as Lewd William.

In March 1652, when little William was seven, the Admiral came home on leave. Actually, it was the first real opportunity the boy had ever had to know his father well, for though there had been occasional brief visits, the Admiral's last long leave had been five years before when the child was ill with smallpox.

The omens were unfavorable. On the very day of the Admiral's return the sun was shadowed and the skies were dark, sure proof to superstitious minds that disaster lay ahead. If it should come the ill fortune would not have been unusual, for though the Admiral, in patrolling the Irish coast and in chasing enemy ships about the Mediterranean, had captured a few blockade runners and had taken some prisoners, his successes had been relatively minor. He had failed to recover the Jasper estates and, through accident, had lost or seriously damaged three ships. Nor was this all; persistent reports charged that the Admiral, like so many other commanders, had taken for himself an undue share of booty found on captured enemy ships. Formal investigation acquitted him but, from time to time, ill-wishers revived the accusation.[11]

The imputation never ceased to irk the Admiral. Instead of retaining treasure, he declared, he had been singularly honest, so strict in fact that when Margaret admired a Spanish gold piece he would not allow her to keep it unless she added its value in sterling to the prize money he was turning in to the Navy Office. The coin, bearing the likenesses of Ferdinand and Isabella, was then made into a pendant which she wore about her neck for years and which, when her son was married he gave as a present to his bride.[12]

The Admiral's shipboard experiences had not been particularly happy. Fellow officers, resenting the favoritism that had promoted him over their heads, were, he suspected, spreading exaggerated stories of his supposed pro-Stuart and anti-Commonwealth sympathies. Even if such reports had not prejudiced Cromwell against him, Admiral Penn still worried over his having in some way disappointed the Protector. Why else, he wondered, would the Navy Office continue to hold up his forty shillings daily pay owing him these last three years? And why had Cromwell failed to recompense him, as the Protector had rewarded others, by gifts of land confiscated from Irish rebels?

Happily, the fears proved groundless. When his leave expired, Penn returned to active service and, taking a leading part in a naval war with the Dutch, received honors from the Protector: a gold medal and chain worth £100, a new title (General-at-Sea), and command of an expedition against Spanish-held Hispaniola. The dire events predicted by that solar eclipse on the day of the Admiral's return for leave were slow in their arrival but, to the superstitious, the omens were at length fulfilled. Through no fault of the General-at-Sea heat, hunger, and disease brought failure to the Hispaniola expedition. As an alternative, Penn launched an unauthorized attack upon undefended Jamaica, but though he took the island, he lost a ship and at least a hundred men when fire broke out in a powder magazine.

In 1652, Penn returned to England only to be jailed, ostensibly because he had come back before receiving orders to do so, though perhaps, as some thought, because he may have offered to turn over his whole fleet to Charles II. The imprisonment was brief, but the General-at-Sea, in his prime at thirty-one, went most unwillingly into forced retirement. During his rustication he pressed Cromwell for payment of that long withheld salary, plus compensation for Margaret's loss of land; the least the Protector could do, the brooding sailor suggested, was to assign Irish lands that would bring in the £700 yearly rentals Margaret had lost.[13]

Cromwell paid the salary arrears but postponed granting lands. It was, William the Sailor believed, a sorry sequel to a message Cromwell had written bidding him to "bee not shye and let me know wherein I may express my love and you shall find mee your very true friend." But later, after Cromwell had assured Penn that the Hispaniola expedition was under the General-at-Sea's exclusive command, "full entire to yourself, nothing interfering with it nor in the least lessening you," Penn had made the mistake of not appointing Cromwell's nephew second-in-command, even after the Protector had promised the young man the appointment. Cromwell's revenge for that mistake was to delay until

1655 giving the land-grant bonus already received by other public servants.[14]

Whatever Penn, now again an admiral, may previously have thought of Cromwell and the Commonwealth, the Protector's delay in bestowing an estate was unforgivable. Thereafter, though Admiral William Penn played no open role in furthering a Stuart Restoration, he hoped for Charles II's return and may have plotted secretly toward that end.

Retirement to be sure, yielded great advantages. However galling the inaction, however deep the indignation against the ingrate Cromwell, the Admiral at least enjoyed more home life than he had known since boyhood. During thirteen years of marriage he had been home, all told, no more than a few months. He did not really know his family. Margaret had changed her appearance; like most women of her years she was putting on weight, and there were those who said that she was more flirtatious. He knew even less of his youngsters, William, now eleven, four-year-old Peg, and baby Richard, whom he was now seeing for the first time. They, in their turn, knew him only as a big, jovial man in an admiral's red cap and blue scarf who sometimes played with them.

2

LONELY VISIONS

BY MODERN STANDARDS WILLIAM PENN HAD VERY LITTLE FORMAL
SCHOOLING, LESS, HE RECALLED, THAN FOUR FULL YEARS IN ALL.
OBVIOUSLY, THE STORY OF HIS EDUCATION IS INCOMPLETE. FUGI-
tive and untrustworthy reports suggest that William attended a small
private school on Tower Hill; if so, its very existence is forgotten. There
may have been some tutoring by highly skilled instructors. No evidence
exists that Margaret or any other relative was a skilled pedagogue, yet by
the time he was eleven, Penn was not only reading and writing English
but had acquired sufficient Latin to understand it and to speak it; he also
had the rudiments of French. Apparently he was reading avidly and over
a wide range of subjects beyond the capacity of most lads of his age, but
where and how he found the books and who, if anyone, guided his
choice remains a mystery.

With such a background young William must have been a cut above
the average student at Chigwell Free Grammar School, four miles from
Wanstead, where he began attending at eleven. A safely Anglican institution, Chigwell held as its chief goal the "stirring up of the buds of
virtue" in its students; its two-man faculty, both men over twenty-seven
who neither smoked nor drank, were "poets . . . of grave behavior."[1]

The description is misleading. That they were poets does not imply
that either the English master or his Latin colleague wrote verses; it
merely indicates that they were university graduates. Certainly they were
not modernists; they taught no secular writings since those of the ancient
Romans. In consequence, though William later read much history and
legal theory, he seldom, if indeed ever, quoted any popular author after
Chaucer, and Chaucer only because "his manner and not his poetry
heartily affects me." Even so, he credited Chaucer with having written

[15]

William Lackland's *Piers Plowman*. When, to be sure, he came to America he owned a copy of Milton, but that was a quarter-century after his schooldays.[2]

Life at Chigwell was not easy. Classes began early and ran on for ten straight hours in summer and eight in winter, broken only by a brief lunch period and by a psalm-reading in the afternoon. Recitations were in Latin, with the masters instructed to whip or slap any boy who inadvertently let drop a word of English; the instructors were also to reprove in the same way any lad who swore or lied or used any word the masters considered filthy. The Chigwell boys had one consolation, however; the master who struck more than thrice or who punched anyone in the face paid forty shillings fine for each illegal blow. The fine was heavy for the times and the school retained the money. The rules had been laid down in 1629 by Chigwell's founder, Archbishop Samuel Harsnett.[3]

Sunday brought little relief; chapel attendance was lengthy and compulsory, nor was there any preaching, for Chigwell rules forbade professional sermonizing.

As for Chigwell's lighter side, there was none. This would not have bothered Penn for, as he described himself, he was "a sedulous person after religion, and of a retired temper," who, as he also said, "could never join, though a child, with any of their carnal professions." Even had he not been quiet and sober-minded, the unremitting drive of schoolwork, together with his four-mile walk to and from his classes, would have calmed any exuberance.[4]

No record survives that William Penn had any school acquaintances, much less any chums. The boy's social life, such as it was, was with his elders, and these, with the exception of his parents, were grave and, for the most part, reverend. Convincing evidence is lacking, but it is not unlikely that, next to his family, William's closest, if not his only, friend at Chigwell may have been Edward Cotton, the Latin master.[5]

Cotton, then beginning his seventeenth year at Chigwell, was not a happy man. Events had not worked out well for him. He had already buried two wives, and nearly all his children also lay buried in Chigwell's churchyard. As one reported to have had High Church leanings, he would have been dismayed that certain nonconformist ideas were being enforced at Chigwell. Just before William's enrollment, for instance, a vicar had been evicted for reading prayers with his back to the congregation and for having kissed the altar twice in every service.

Cotton himself could not take orders lest by Chigwell's strict rules he, too, be ejected "as if he were dead," but a sincere and dedicated lad like William, not only eager for his Latin lessons but properly brought up in orthodox religious ways, might develop into an acceptable substitute.

There was precedent for such a development in William's home town

of Wanstead. Some years before, a mystical writer named John Saltmarsh
had been publishing a long list of theological pamphlets. They were
not the type to please Cotton, for Saltmarsh was not an Anglican and
he was a rebel in politics. He had been demanding complete religious
liberty and unrestricted freedom of the press for any writer with the
courage to sign his name to the books he wrote. But Saltmarsh had
gone further; though he was himself a minister, he condemned those of
his fellows who, instead of preaching sound doctrine, had relied upon
their black gowns and their university degrees for acceptance as divines.
For such criticisms, and for his refusal to doff his hat in the presence of
his betters, Wanstead called him crazy.[6]

Nevertheless, if Wanstead could produce a writer and an author,
albeit one of whom Cotton disapproved, why could not an omnivorous
reader like William Penn, who had been so well brought up at home and
at All Hallows Barking, become a writer, and perhaps a preacher, able
to counter Saltmarsh in the interest of sound Anglicanism? Wanstead had
laughed at the silly arguments of crazy John Saltmarsh who wrote such
tortuous prose; the town would welcome the more lucid and much
sounder publications that young William Penn would write.

William was not as dedicated to High Church as Cotton would have
wished. Just as Chigwell professed a desire to steer a middle course between papacy and nonconformity, so William, even in his boyhood,
entertained mild doubts concerning certain rites and ceremonies, that
of kissing the altar, for example. He spent long hours with his Bible,
meditating so intensely that, as he later said, he frequently "was ravished
by joy and dissolved into tears." No wonder that, while deep in thought,
he was visited by "an external glory" that convinced him that God
existed and that man was capable of "enjoying communion with him."
These were not, of course, the words he would have used when he was
eleven, but they expressed his belief that he was called upon to lead a
holy life.[7]

There may have been other such experiences. In letters written
between 1668 and 1674 he dated his preoccupation with religion as
beginning in 1656 or 1657, and says that he constantly suffered for it; he
hinted that further revelations followed.

A stronger influence was exerted by Isaac Penington the Younger,
who frequently came down to Wanstead to visit his parents and his stepsister. It was an interesting family that certainly would have attracted
attention at any time in any village. Sir Isaac, the father, was a former
lord mayor of London who had been one of the judges who tried King
Charles I, though he had refused to sign the death warrant. The son, an
able pamphleteer, proclaimed the right of every individual to freedom of
conscience. William, as a Chigwell schoolboy, may not then have appreciated the full implications of the younger Penington's talk about a new

sect, the Quakers, who were insisting that all men were free and equal because all people were the children of God, but being a thoughtful lad, he would have mulled it over. Penington was not then a Quaker, but in time he would join the Society of Friends.[8]

If Penington's talk had exerted no other influence, it would at least have inoculated William against the gibes and jeers of those who either hated or laughed at those queer Quakers who would not fight or swear an oath and who, even in the presence of their betters, refused like Saltmarsh to doff their hats.

Isaac Penington the Younger was by no means the only dynamic figure of the household. Mary Springett Penington was, for her times, extraordinary, for she not only founded and conducted a cottage industry producing herbal medicines but, according to contemporary report, practiced eye surgery with such skill that patients came to her from distant parts. Given the instruments and especially the antiseptics of the period, she must in serious cases have had at least as many failures as complete cures, but there must have been some solid basis for her reputation.[9]

And then, by no means least from William Penn's standpoint, there was Gulielma Maria Springett, Mrs. Penington's daughter by an earlier marriage. Guli, as everyone called her, was an heiress in her own right, holding estates in England and in Ireland that Wanstead believed yielded £10,000 a year. She roused the envy of every other Wanstead child by riding up and down the lanes in her own little coach, attended by a footman and her maid. History does not state whether Guli, eight months older than William, ever invited him or any other boy or girl to ride with her, but being the amiable little lady that she was, it is unlikely that she rode alone.

William liked her and would spend much more time with her in later days. He showed a romantic interest by using the same word Guli, short in his case for the latinization Gulielmus, in signing letters to her.[10]

It would be an exaggeration to suggest that in his Chigwell days the Penington examples convinced William that all individuals were equal, that tolerance was a basic right, and that women were capable in business matters, much less that Quakerism was final truth. The seeds of such convictions were, however, firmly planted in very fertile soil.

William left Chigwell before his twelfth birthday. How well he had profited by the teaching is debatable. Certainly, under the guidance of the poets, his English, his Latin, and his knowledge of the ancient had been, from time to time, available, but they were not dynamic, writings were increased, but a lifelong weakness in mathematics betrays that he had not completed—perhaps not even begun—the school course that, according to the curriculum, would have taken him "as far as the accountancy."

He left in 1656 because the family moved to Ireland. The Admiral, at thirty-five unwillingly retired again and pensionless, depended for an income on rentals from the Irish lands that Cromwell had at last assigned him. These rentals, far less than the Admiral thought he deserved, could only be collected by someone living there.

The estate, Macroom, twenty-six miles west of Cork, gave the elder Penn higher social status than he had previously enjoyed; in addition, he exercised the powers of a minor magistrate and the command of a small force of cavalry and foot. Here, in his three-story stone castle, whose fifteenth-century square tower stood high above a swiftly flowing stream, the Penn family, their Negro, Anthony, and their pet parrot dominated a small circle of relatives and sea captains who had served with the Admiral on his expeditions.[11]

Yet, despite this added prestige, the elder Penn was bored and uncomfortable. Missing the excitements of London, conscious that he was unwelcome in a rebellious land, he sought solace in alcohol.

For his son, life at Macroom offered compensations, such as the masculine companionship the quiet, introspective lad needed. True, his Uncle George and Grandfather Jasper had been available from time to time, but they were not dynamic. The Admiral was a man's man, bluff, hearty and decisive. Three William Penns—the Admiral, his elder son and Uncle George's boy—roamed about Macroom.

The Admiral liked to talk, and the two boys—William and his cousin, Uncle George's son, also named William—were an appreciative audience. He had fantastic tales to tell of battle and adventure, of the Spaniard he had lashed to a mast in retaliation for the way in which Spain had mistreated George, of Jamaica and of the great New World that lay beyond that distant island. His son would not have liked the anecdotes of warfare, but, inspired by Penington's ideas, he would have thought of the New World as a place where vanities and corruptions were unknown and where oppressed people might find a haven.

A few years later, perhaps after hearing Josiah Coale, a Quaker missionary, praise the soil, the climate and, above all, the friendliness of that New World, he had another vision, an "opening of joy." The vision may have owed its origin quite as much to his father as to the missionary.

A shaky tradition clings to Macroom Castle. The Admiral, it is said, heard of a street-corner Quaker preacher in Cork who was attracting large crowds. With an open-mindedness not previously detected nor later witnessed in him, the Admiral invited the evangelist, one Thomas Loe of Oxford, to visit Macroom.[12] "Let us," the father urged, "be like the noble Bereans," referring to the biblical people who "received the Word with all readiness of mind."

Loe came, after having ridden from Cork over exceedingly bad roads, and preached so effectively that everyone, from Anthony, their Negro, to the Admiral himself, broke into tears. Young William was so impressed that he thought it would be well if all the world could hear the message.

The story is so well composed that it should be true, but it is based upon remarks made by Penn some forty years after the supposed event and, even then, was not published for another thirty years. From all that is known about Admiral Penn, it seems unlikely that he would have opened his doors to an itinerant evangelist, one of a sect whose members were believed to be mentally unbalanced, blasphemous, and quite possibly seditious. If he was moved to tears, the effect must have been short-lived, for only a few months later William reported that his father had thrown him out of the house for accepting Quakerism.[13]

Unlike his son, the Admiral had never experienced the presence of an external glory and certainly never had felt called upon to lead a holy life; his interests lay in more mundane matters. The boy could not have been unaware that his father was unhappy, that he was grumbling, not always to himself, against the Protector's ingratitude, the Commonwealth's tightfistedness and suspicion that he was plotting treason.

If any basis for suspicion existed, the adolescent was unaware of it. Now and then the Admiral went up to Dublin, perhaps for consultation with Stuart sympathizers; at times a friend or two visited Macroom. If on these occasions the Admiral talked about the possibility of a Stuart restoration, his son knew nothing of it.

From the Admiral's table talk and from what could be seen of his methods, young William learned lessons that would serve him well. He saw that it was well to please people in authority, to defer to the important, to yield on minor matters as a means of winning more important goals. Above all, the Admiral's career showed that a clever man must make himself the center of a tightly organized, smoothly operating circle of relatives and friends, particularly those holding high positions. He must, however, do this quietly and without seeming to be pushing himself forward.

The Penn relatives and former colleagues in the Macroom area satisfied some of these requirements and practiced the approved techniques. They did not yet hold high positions, nor did they attract unfavorable attention from Cromwell's officers, but they had hopes that, should the Stuarts ever regain power, they would be in a strategic position to push themselves ahead.

That moment came at last. After four long years of rustication for the Admiral, and even longer for King Charles, word reached Macroom that restoration was impending. Though no elections had been held nor any voters consulted, Admiral Penn was to represent Weymouth in Parliament; he was also to go to Holland to escort Charles on his return to the throne.

Fifteen-year-old William Penn went along. In this, his first entry into public life, the boy who in twenty years would found a democratic Quaker commonwealth was, in 1660, an Anglican supporter of a divine right monarch.

For whatever secret work the Admiral had done, Charles proved his gratitude. His first official action aboard the ship en route from Holland to England was to make the Admiral a knight; he then appointed Sir William a Navy commissioner at £500 a year. Nor was this the sum total of royal generosity. Charles dismayed his new commissioner by restoring Macroom to its former owner, a stanch royalist, but more than eased the hurt by conferring upon Sir William a larger estate, at Shanagarry, south of Cork in the barony of Imokilly. The new lands yielded larger returns. The Admiral also had other perquisites: the governorship of Kinsale, then a thriving port and market town, and the command of a larger military force. Together these posts were estimated to be worth £2000 a year, a very tidy fortune for the times.[14]

The income was real enough, but at no time after his appointment did the Admiral ever spend much time on his property. He moved his relatives and friends from Macroom to Shanagarry and made them his deputies, while he remained for the most part in London.

It may have been just as well. The Kinsale company of foot of which he was the absentee commander and his nephew William Penn the ensign would have shocked the strict disciplinarian. It was a raggle-taggle outfit, very far from smart, and, worse still, its strength was almost nil. Not one man was properly equipped. Only two-thirds of them had muskets, most of which could not be fired, while many of those whose weapons were in good condition possessed no ammunition.[15]

What Shanagarry did have was plenty of tradition: legends of blessed wells where, if one had faith enough, ague could be cured; legends of saints who singlehandedly raised strong towers overnight; a legend even of the time when Jesus Christ had sought refuge there against his persecutors. No one could refute those legends; Irishmen had for years recited them, and so they could not be otherwise than absolutely true.[16]

Not that Sir William, who had a sailor's love for yarns that taxed credulity, would have challenged them. Nor would he have wondered much about those megaliths that proved that ancient man had been a giant. He would have joined his Irish tenants in putting down any skeptic, especially a Quaker, who dared question cherished tradition.

No member of the Penn family, however, seems ever to have taken even the faintest interest in local folklore. The lad, having reached the age when he and other members of his class could buckle on their ornamental swords, was looking forward to going up to Oxford. Sir William was cementing his alliances with high Navy officers, and his wife, now addressed as Margaret, Lady Penn, was under no obligation to cater to the conventional old ladies of the retired Wanstead set; she was preparing to assert herself.

Readjustment was easier because the Penns, the better to facilitate the Admiral's return to active life, had moved back to Tower Hill. The new house, less spacious than the Wanstead mansion but far better than the two-room apartment of earlier days, lay on the south side of Crutched Friars Road just east of Seething Lane, close by the houses of other Navy bureaucrats.[17]

Social life on Tower Hill could not have pleased teen-aged William. The naval officers, now staunchly royalist, felt none too secure, for most of them, after twenty years of civil war and the Protectorate, had some record, open or secret, of something said, done, or written that they did not wish recalled. Each lived in fear that amid the jealousies, power struggles, and treacheries of the time, someone might denounce him as having been disloyal to the Stuarts. Because they dared not speak of serious affairs, they frittered away time in childish games, in playing silly practical jokes upon each other, and in drinking much too heavily. William was old enough to share in the frivolities, but this was not the holy life to which his vision called him; he fled upstairs and even to the attic where, away from the uproar of the parlor, he found sanctuary for his reading and his meditations.

Downstairs, his mother and the other ladies romped about wearing men's wigs or, blackened by soot and candle grease, shrieked boisterously; the raucousness deepened his disillusion with the world. Had he realized the duplicity and hypocrisy of some of the revelers, his pessimism might have been more intense. Samuel Pepys, the Navy secretary who lived next door, continued to detest the whole Penn family, thinking Lady Margaret a fat frump, young William a pretentious fop, little Peg a conceited show-off, and the Admiral a tricky rascal. He did not air these opinions; on the contrary, he pretended, "out of great and necessary discretion," to be friendly, joining the Admiral in theater and tavern parties. He confessed, however, to his diary on July 5, 1662, "I hate him with all my heart."[18]

Young William clung to one illusion. Even if all the world had surrendered itself to empty-headed foolishness, there yet remained a hope for one who yearned for close communion with the Lord. Knowledge, not only of the Bible, which he had been studying for years, but of the wisdom of the ages was the key to holy living. Some of this knowledge he had already gained, with or without the help of tutors, but he needed more, especially that which was to be acquired at the university, where learned professors and dedicated students like himself would help each other become worthy citizens. Oblivious as possible to the din and tumult on the lower floor, he worked hard to prepare himself for college entrance.

However much the Admiral disliked the boy's bookishness and his almost monastic mode of living, he thoroughly approved of his son's desire to go to college. Not, to be sure, because the university, once a training school for priests, was still supposed to be "a nursery of piety," but for a more material reason. By going to college, the boy would meet a group of very fashionable young nobles; they would not only knock the bookish nonsense out of William's head but would introduce him into court life and help him win high social and political position. On this supposition the Admiral willingly paid his son's "cautions," the deposit that would be forfeited in case the boy misbehaved himself, and settled back contentedly now that his son's future seemed assured.

3

SCHOLAR AND GALLANT

TWO WEEKS AFTER HIS SIXTEENTH BIRTHDAY, IN LATE OCTOBER 1660, WILLIAM PENN MATRICULATED AT CHRIST CHURCH COLLEGE, OXFORD. HE HAD SPENT LESS THAN A YEAR AT CHIGWELL, FOLLOWED BY FOUR years' absence from any school whatever. Technically, he was not a student, that term being reserved at this institution for those whom other colleges called fellows; he was a gentleman scholar, one of a special group of twenty aristocrats who paid higher fees but from whom little was expected beyond the glamor of their names.

Christ Church College was not the proper title; the official name was Aedes Christi, or House of Christ, which undergraduates shortened to just "the House," or, if speaking to outsiders, "the Old Church." William was not in the least discouraged that the House was one of Oxford's smallest colleges, having only about a hundred students, and he was overjoyed to find that its library, one of the largest of the Oxford complex, held more than two-thousand volumes. Most of these, of course, were theological, as Cardinal Wolsey, the founder, would have preferred, but the library held books on more secular matters, such as law and medicine, even some poetry and drama.[1]

Nothing indicates that young Penn at any time dipped into Shakespeare, Edmund Spenser, or Beaumont and Fletcher. Such books disgusted him. Except for works on law, theology, history, and science, reading, he would later say, was "an oppression of the mind and extinguished the natural candle," which explained the existence of "so many senseless scholars."[2] To Penn's disappointment, many of his fellow scholars were intent on picking flaws in what others firmly believed; they argued endlessly over trivialities. The more he saw of college life, the more he was repelled by the vain quiddities, the pedantry, the sophisticated syllogisms that passed for learning.[3]

Despite a conviction that an inordinate thirst for knowledge merely worsened man's condition, Penn read incessantly. This involves no contradiction. Penn, in his teens, was neither critic nor polemicist; he read not to question teachings but to store up information, to prove the truths already known. The Bible and the Christian fathers, he firmly believed, had already set down everything necessary for human guidance; all else was unessential. He was trying to understand what God had wrought, not how or why He had performed His miracles. Penn would not then have hesitated to swear his belief in the Thirty-nine Articles of Anglican faith.

Aloof as Penn remained from undergraduate activities, his very name brought him an invitation to play a small, and insignificant, role in college life. During the first month of the term, Henry, Duke of Gloucester, the twenty-nine-year-old brother of the King, died of smallpox. The University, to show its grief, its loyalty to the Stuarts and, by implication at least, its adherence to the Established Church, published Latin elegies, under the title *Epicedia Academiae Oxoniensis*. Penn's six-line contribution was one of the shortest, and it was buried near the middle of the pamphlet—though at the top of its page—but his flattery of the unfortunate prince was among the more fulsome tributes. The eulogy did not pass unnoticed; soon thereafter Penn received an invitation to attend a court function where the King and his brother James greeted him with what Penn thought was special warmth. He would have assumed that this show of friendship stemmed from the Admiral's support of the Stuarts in their exile and from the tutoring in seamanship given by Sir William to James when the heir presumptive was a boy.[4]

Also, to his father's delight, he was asked to join the little group of restless, aristocratic playboys who shunned the classroom for gayer pleasures. The future earls of Rochester and Sunderland were William's classmates and may have been his sponsors; they were certain to become prominent and influential.

William was friendly with the rollicking aristocrats—all his life he would associate more with the titled and the rich than with the common people—but he felt no urge to join them; he had seen quite enough of their kind on Tower Hill. Certainly he disapproved of the public brawls in which some of them engaged.

New University regulations, issued, it was said, by royal order, set off other riotous demonstrations. All students were required to attend chapel and, what to the few nonconformists was much worse, to wear the wide-sleeved surplices that were meant to show that they were, in theory at least, candidates for holy orders. To most people the surplices were meaningless symbols, but to the nonconformists, the garments smacked of popish services, especially when worn to compulsory chapel where set prayers were recited and where organs were played. Protestors ripped off the surplices from other boys, and some teen-agers joined the

free-for-all more as a roughhouse than as a religious protest. William
Penn could tolerate no such rowdyism; certainly he did not help the
hoodlums who stole the surplices from their storage place and stuffed
them down a privy.[5]

William did, however, enter the small group of undergraduates who
trooped out of Oxford on Sunday mornings to attend religious services
at Dr. John Owen's country home. Owen, a flute player, an athlete, and
a prolific pamphleteer, had once been vice-chancellor of the University
and a dean of the Old Church, but the restored Stuarts had dismissed him
because of his unorthodox religious opinions. A few earnest young men
who disliked High Church formalism considered that the inspiration they
could gain from Owen outbalanced the confiscation of their caution
money for failure to attend official services.

Penn's presence in the Owen circle was not owing to his religious
feelings. Though vaguely uneasy because he had not found scriptural
authority for certain Church of England rites and practices, he had no
quarrel with basic Church beliefs. He went to Owen's meetings through
family connections. Owen was a friend of Robert Boyle, the Oxford
professor of chemistry and physics, and Boyle was a relative of the Earl
of Orrery, one of the Admiral's Irish cronies. Whether Sir William suggested to Orrery that Boyle look after the young man, or whether Boyle,
hearing that young Penn was at Oxford, asked Owen to take an interest
in the student, is immaterial; Penn became an Owen protégé.

Owen helped stabilize Penn's thinking. The former dean reawakened
and reinforced the Penington stress on tolerance; he let William see that
doubts about certain ceremonies and symbols were quite legitimate; as a
tireless writer on religious matters he may have, consciously or unconsciously, encouraged Penn to become a publicist. Owen, who was writing
a voluminous history of religion, "from the creation to the Reformation," may have taught young Penn how to organize his knowledge and
how to synthesize what he knew.[6]

None of this implied any sharp break with orthodoxy. Penn's mind
was boiling with thoughts, but as yet he was unaware of where they
might lead him. His association with Owen may, in fact, have postponed
for a year or two any such realization. By coincidence, only a couple of
months after William arrived at Oxford, Thomas Loe returned to the
university city. Had Penn been less preoccupied with Owen, he certainly
would have become aware of Loe's intense evangelism; as it was, in spite
of Loe's supposed visit to Macroom, Penn failed even to mention Loe's
presence. Concerned as Penn always was with the sufferings of martyrs
for conscience's sake, it is unthinkable that he would have been silent
about Loe's being jailed had he known of the injustice to one who, he
later professed, had been a hero of his childhood.[7]

Another of Penn's revelations may have occurred about this time.

Both in 1677 and in 1681, he recalled a certain "opening of joy" about America which, he said, had come to him at Oxford. Since he did no more than mention the event, without supplying any more details, efforts have been made to reconstruct its nature.[8] The usual guess has been that Penn referred to the possibility of a Quaker settlement along the Susquehanna River. The recently converted Quaker explorer, Josiah Coale, of whom Penn may have heard at Wanstead, had made two visits to this undeveloped Indian country, now part of north central Pennsylvania and western New York, and he was enthusiastic about it. His second visit in 1660 was intended to scout the possibility of such a settlement where persecution would be unknown. If Penn had been associating with Oxford members of the Society of Friends, he could have had an "opening of joy" concerning it, but no evidence exists that Penn had met any local Quakers.[9]

The "opening" reflected Penn's disillusionment with Oxford. Far from being a nursery of piety and learning, he found it "a signal place for idleness, loose living, profaneness, prodigality and gross ignorance." Listening to John Locke's lectures on science or watching dissections in an anatomy clinic was educational enough, but the quiddities, the corruption of religious principles, the hooliganism disgusted him. Oxford was, he said, "a den of hellish ignorance and debauchery."[10]

Even after allowances for the usual Restoration exaggeration, the condemnation was excessive. The Restoration, certainly, was notorious for profligacy; its cultural polish was superficial; its courtesy was routine and insincere; and colleges enrolled too many callous, sensual youths. But some students, at least, must have been as sensitive and as civilized as William Penn. He himself was not so responsive at that time as he would later become to the plight of the poor or to the suffering of those oppressed for other than religious reasons, but debauchery and sin disturbed him deeply. That fellow students would not heed good counsel seemed to him a personal affront, a bitter persecution bearable only through the Lord's special grace.

The distaste Penn felt for the Oxford climate bothered his father. Sir William would have accepted as quite normal a sowing of wild oats, but to question opinions held by all right-thinking people was a serious fault; even worse was daring to criticize the private lives of the nobility. Yet the Admiral tried to be fair-minded. Because his boy had been well reared, he could not have gone wrong on his own initiative. Some evil influence must have led the boy astray, most probably that spread by the ejected dean, John Owen. To withdraw William from that malignant source would be the wisest course. He asked neighbor Samuel Pepys whether Cambridge would be the better university.[11]

William did not wait to be transferred. In February 1662 he left Oxford and came home. His explanation was dramatic: the University had banished him. Some seventeen years later, elaborating on the incident, he added that the House had thrown him out because "the priests" disliked a book that he had written.[12]

Memory played him false. The story was too highly colored. If any such book or manuscript ever did exist, "the priests" destroyed all traces of it. One would suppose that even if all copies had been destroyed, there yet would remain rough drafts or notes from which the work could be rewritten, but for eight or ten years after his leaving Oxford, no book appeared that might have been in any way identified with the missing Oxford publication. Nor, for that matter, do official college records, which list the names of many expelled students, include that of William Penn.

After all, what "crime" had he committed? He himself, and he is the only source, alleged nothing more than the censored book and the failure to attend compulsory chapel. Other students who cut chapel to worship at Dr. Owen's house were not dismissed. Only a very brave administration would have dared expel the son of a prominent official, a royal favorite and a nominal Churchman, for attending private services while other students did so with no punishment beyond being fined.

Fifteen years later, in recounting the ordeals endured by early Quakers, he mentioned the horrid persecution that he underwent at Oxford. Of this there is no record other than his loss of caution money. He also cited the bitter treatment he received when, after leaving Oxford, he went home to be beaten by his father and then turned out of doors.[13]

This may have happened. The Admiral had a quarter-deck mentality; he spoke impulsively and acted roughly. Probably his temper flared when his high hopes for his son collapsed. He may have shouted something that the sensitive boy took to be a disowning by his father but which the Admiral certainly did not intend as a final dismissal. In any case, the anger was short-lived and the exile a matter of but a few hours at the most. It may, however, have opened a breach between the two.

Conflict was inevitable between Sir William and his son. Different personalities and generations were bound in time to clash. They had been differently reared; each held strong, inflexible opinions. Thus far the conflict had been postponed, partly because of wartime separation, later because the son was still gripped by a small boy's love, awe and admiration of his father. But now, at eighteen, the adolescent, while still full of love and admiration, was struggling to establish his independence and to assert his own identity. The Admiral remained oblivious to any change. He only knew that the young cub was too argumentative, too given to spouting crazy ideas, and much too certain that he knew it all. Sir William simply could not realize that his small son was becoming an adult.

The fact was that young Penn was uncertain both of himself and of his opinions. He had read widely, and his memory was retentive, but the scraps of learning picked up from the Bible, from Penington's conversation, from John Owen's talks and perhaps, though this is doubtful, from Loe's sermon of six years before, lay only half understood and almost wholly undigested in his mind. He did not know just what he thought, but he did know that something was amiss in the religion in which he had been reared.

Five uncomfortable months passed, during which the strained relationship between father and son became evident even to outsiders. Pepys, with unaccustomed insight, admitted that while superficially everything seemed quite all right, something, he knew not what, was quite wrong. The boy was grave and did not look at all well; his father was unusually testy.

For William's solemnity and absorption in religious research there was a remedy as sovereign as it would have been for an unworthy infatuation, had he been so afflicted. A stay in France would round off his education. Moreover, since the Admiral was obliged to go to Ireland to look after his estate, a trip abroad would prevent any association with John Owen while Sir William was away.

In July 1662, therefore, William Penn crossed into France. Reports declare that he traveled in company, though no details are given, with "several persons of rank." One of these may well have been Robert Spencer, later Earl of Sunderland, though Penn states rather strangely in a letter, twenty years later, that he first met this old college classmate in Paris after he had left the University.[14]

When authenticated personal details of Penn's life were missing, enthusiastic biographers have often filled in the gaps by having him excel in those activities in which a regular fellow would have taken part. Just as at Oxford where, without a shadow of solid evidence, he is said to have been an avid sportsman so in France he has been represented as an outstanding young courtier at Versailles. In sharp contrast to everything that is known about the teen-ager's personality, preferences, and habits, he is said to have become suddenly a gay young gallant, able, with equal facility and charm, to flirt with the ladies and to revel with the gentlemen, to be equally at home turning a light compliment or holding his own in cultural discussions in a coterie familiar with the writings of Corneille, Racine, Molière, and La Fontaine. Perhaps he did, though no contemporary seems to have noticed his participation. Penn himself said later that he led the gay life and wore fine clothes to please his parents.[15]

However this may have been, the social triumph, if ever it existed, did not last. One evening, as he recounted eight years later, when he was walking to his lodgings down a badly lighted street, an angry voice demanded that he defend himself. A stranger complained that he had taken off his hat to Penn, but that Penn had insulted him by not returning the salute. William explained politely that he had meant no slight, that he simply had not seen the man, much less seen the gesture. The answer did not erase the stain upon the unknown man's honor; he demanded satisfaction. William drew his sword in self-defense and, either because he was more skilled in fencing or because his challenger was drunk, he disarmed his adversary. He returned the man's sword with a polite bow and went his way.

The incident disturbed him. "I ask any man of understanding or conscience if the whole round of ceremony was worth the life of a man." For once, it is interesting to note, Penn had a witness to one of his experiences; a servant of the Earl of Crawford had seen the confrontation.[16]

Abandoning the idleness and pleasures of court life in France, William Penn went back to school. As a substitute for Oxford he chose a small Protestant seminary at Saumur, in Touraine on the Loire, about 150 miles southwest of Paris.

Why Saumur? Certainly not for routine college work, for Penn, by independent research, had already assimilated much of what Oxford had to offer. Nor did he go to Saumur on the recommendation of any of his Versailles associates; they would have approved of the town's cavalry school, and they might have known that it was one of the places visited by Jeanne d'Arc, but they would not have endorsed an institution that promoted liberal Protestantism.

It is even more unlikely that the Admiral or any of his friends suggested that the young man study at Saumur; Sir William's revulsion against John Owen's teaching would have been mild in comparison with what he would have thought of Saumur's influence. For Saumur's best-known professor, Moïse Amyraut, held unorthodox views. A lawyer who had turned to teaching, he declared that the laws of God live in the hearts of men and that anyone might learn the truth by heeding his own conscience. It was a concept close to what Quakers called the Inner Light, and Amyraut, by teaching it, excited repeated charges of heresy, though he survived them all.[17]

None of Penn's correspondence from this period is extant, but it seems probable that he learned of Amyraut through his good friend John Owen, there being few other persons of his acquaintance, except possibly Isaac Penington the Younger, who would have approved either of the college or of Amyraut, and Penington, unhappily, was now in jail for nonconformity. Whatever the source, Penn went to Saumur and, although he did not formally enroll, he became a member of the Amyraut household on the rue de Ste. Jeanne. The fact that he was so honored indicates that someone high in Amyraut's esteem, a fellow theologian with not too dissimilar ideas, had sponsored him.

If that sponsor was John Owen, it may well be that William Penn, always considerate of his father's easily ruffled sensibilities, may have overlooked mentioning in his letters home a too detailed account of Amyraut or of his host's unconventional teachings. There would be no point in rousing the Admiral's ire, to say nothing of a possible cutting off of remittances from home.

In any case, young Penn, to use one of his own expressions, must have cut an odd figure on the rue de Ste. Jeanne. Saumur, a quiet provincial town, was unaccustomed to Versailles gallants in slashed doublets, pantaloons, silk stockings, and high-heeled shoes, much of the costume tricked out with embroideries and laces.[18] Amyraut was a plain man who detested ostentation but, tolerant in principles and in practice, he probably raised no eyebrow at his guest's display. Penn's ornamental sword, which he had so skillfully used in his nighttime encounter, clashed with Amyraut's idea that fighting and the love of Christ were incompatible. The differences, however, were very far from basic; the sixty-seven-year-old Amyraut found William, now free from youthful brashness, both willing and receptive.

From Amyraut, Penn learned new interpretations of teachings that he had misunderstood. He now saw that God predestined men to happiness if only they had faith, that the universality of grace brought freedom to all who truly believed, that the Sabbath, instead of being the burden that the Puritans had made of it, was, in reality, a day of rest, and that, instead of unremitting labor as a fulfillment of His purpose, God prescribed such healthy recreations as walking, preferably in meditation, in the open fields.

Most important of all, perhaps, was that the injunction to fear God, heavily stressed as long as man could recall, really meant to reverence Him, not to tremble with the thought that somehow, inadvertently, some sin had been committed that would draw down an awful wrath.

Penn learned much in these Saumur discussions, these seminar sessions in which the two men subjected historical events, classic writings, and religious ceremony to the test of Biblical authority. Inevitably, such study seriously disturbed the neat, and once comfortable, package of belief inculcated at All Hallows Barking and at Chigwell; it intensified the doubts raised in his early youth by Penington and stirred again when he was more mature by Owen at Oxford. He was moving away, as he himself must have realized, from the High Church but, though more influenced by the nonconformists than he suspected, he was not yet prepared to break with the established faith. What would have resulted had Amyraut lived is speculative, but early in 1664 the old man died, and Penn left Saumur.

Penn seems to have gone up to Paris, where he fell in with Robert Spencer, who was about to travel through France to Provence and thence to Italy. Apparently without consulting his father, Penn went along. He enjoyed the journey. The beauty of Provence, its soft climate, the quality of its wines and, above all, its tradition of religious liberty left such a strong impression upon him that for years thereafter his highest praise of a region would be its similarity to southern France and especially to the area about Montpelier, famous for its interest in medicine and education.

Sir William, for some reason, was not so pleased; he may have heard, belatedly, from Lady Penn's friend Sir Joseph Williamson, a Saumur alumnus, about the nature of Saumur teaching, and so he sent a letter to William at Turin, advising an immediate return. War with the Dutch, said Sir William, was about to break out.[19]

If, as may well have been the case, the Admiral's purpose was to save his son from Saumur's influence, under which, of course, William had already fallen, the result was to bring the young man into contact with what to Sir William were even more undesirable ideas. While returning, in accordance with his father's demands, William fell in with Algernon Sidney, a republican noble in exile whom Royalists such as Sir William unjustly considered as a possible traitor in foreign pay.[20]

Bishop Gilbert Burnet, the historian of the period and, incidentally, a churchman so eminent that he was offered four bishoprics before he was thirty, considered Sidney the most outstanding student of government that he had ever known. He was not, however, the most popular or the most approved, for Sidney was a strong believer in equality and freedom and in what Rousseau would later call the social contract. Convinced that the strength and welfare of England rose from, and was dependent upon, the maintenance of its people's ancient rights, he opposed both the Commonwealth's military dictatorship and the Stuart doctrine of divine right. Popular consent, he argued, was the only authority for exercising power; unless a ruler governed well, that is, by known and accepted law, he might and should be ousted.

Since many of these convictions paralleled what Penn had himself gleaned from his studies, as well as from such men as Penington, Owen, and Amyraut, the two men struck up a lasting friendship.

4

WORLDLY GLORY FADES

To ALL APPEARANCE, WILLIAM PENN, ON RETURNING TO LONDON IN AUGUST 1664, WAS A MODISH FRENCHMAN. NOT ALL HIS LOYAL BIOGRAPHERS ACCEPT THE BIASED SAMUEL PEPYS' SNEER THAT THE young man displayed affected mannerisms of speech and gait, but they admit that the twenty-year-old flirted so often, and so expertly, with the diarist's half-French wife that Pepys grew jealous, especially when he failed to understand the French that they were using. Whether William's poetic effusion "Ah, Tyrant Lust, could I thy power stay . . ." belongs in this period, and the mystery as to who, if anyone, evoked it, might well become the topic of a doctoral dissertation.[1]

In any case, Pepys, chafing under Penn's criticism of his French as being too provincial, grumbled in August 1664 that the upstart was insufferable, a bore who chattered incessantly about his trip abroad. Pepys complained that he had adopted too much of the vanity of the French garb.

No outward evidence revealed that, when not chattering or flirting, Penn seethed with unorthodox opinions. His European sojourn had filled him with "French humors," but it had also taught him a little tact. In approaching maturity he was learning not to air too openly anything that might disturb the peace of mind of his superiors or elders.

Sir William, as a matter of fact, was very pleased; his strategy in sending the boy abroad seemed successful. Apparently the Owen influence had been outgrown and the heresies of Amyraut—if the Admiral had heard of them—had fallen on infertile soil. The boy was almost ready to take his proper place in London's court circles.

He needed, however, just a little brushing-up; Saumur's Spartan life had somewhat dimmed the Versailles gloss. To restore a perfect ease of manner, to perfect his etiquette, the Admiral decided, it would be well to enroll the young man in one of the several Inns of Court. No one, least of all the Admiral, expected William to become a lawyer, but the Inns of Court were more than law schools; they were graduate schools of gentlemanly culture.

For this finishing polish the Admiral chose Lincoln's Inn, an institution famous for producing "not gudgeons and smelts but the platypuses and leviathans, behemoths and the giants of the law."[2] Sir William cared nothing for its efficiency in training lawyers; his interest lay solely in its social status. James Scott, the King's illegitimate son, lately created Duke of Monmouth, was already enrolled there; to hobnob with that rising star was in itself well worth the Inn's £25 tuition fee. The chaplain, a young cleric named John Tillotson, would later become Archbishop of Canterbury.[3]

No one can charge Lincoln's Inn with unduly taxing its students' minds. Oxford, where class attendance had been optional and where only one student in a hundred ran any risk of being examined, had been easy enough, but Lincoln's Inn was a lazy man's paradise. Not only was attendance never checked, but all work could be done by proxy; the Inn, with full knowledge and consent, allowed hired substitutes to do the small amount of work required while the student employer received full credit for it. When the day's chores were performed—by others—the students assembled for their dinners and, in all likelihood, fell asleep directly afterward, for each boy's daily ration included six pounds of England's justly famous prime roast beef.[4]

William did not long expose himself to this travesty of education. He missed all but eight days of the first term, but he was conscientious. Though Lincoln's Inn lay a good two miles from Tower Hill, he was at the school library by eight o'clock and he stayed until late at night. Throughout the two-month winter recess he read prodigiously.[5] His chief interest lay in what was then called municipal law, a misleading title; the subject matter was neither county legislation nor town ordinances, categories then of only slight importance, but English common law or equity in contrast to what remained of the Roman civil law.

Actually Penn did not complete a full semester. Just before classes were scheduled to begin, war with Holland finally broke out, Sir William, restored to active service with the unique title of Great Captain Commander, took his son with him on his flagship.

The situation was peculiar. Despite that impressive title Sir William had little real authority and his son, nominally a volunteer assistant, no authority whatever. Supposedly the naval operation was directed by James, Duke of York, brother of the King, but as James had enjoyed only limited naval training, the Great Captain Commander was assigned to do the work, to "advise" the Duke, and, if things went well, to praise him for being a naval genius, but, if anything went wrong, to shoulder all the blame without complaining. The Great Captain Commander had no objection; whatever the outcome, he was again storing up a moral debt for the Stuarts to repay by marks of special favor.[6]

In his eagerness to curry still more favor, Sir William made a move that eventually affected the future not only of his son, but of America and of the Society of Friends. The lad enjoyed naval life, and apparently the Duke of York was pleased with him. Had young William remained as a guest aboard the flagship, he probably, instead of having just gone along for the ride, would have received some sort of naval assignment and so have become the third of his line to go to sea. Backed by the Duke of York, there is no doubt that if he had remained a sailor he too would have been made an admiral. William, however, chose to return to Lincoln's Inn, where classes were about to resume. His father and the Duke of York sent him back to London with dispatches for King Charles.

The envoy sailed for Harwich and rode down to London, arriving at Whitehall just before daybreak. The King was still asleep, but as the dispatches might be of importance, his aides awakened him. Charles came out of the bedroom, clad only in gown and slippers, greeted William and, apparently without bothering to read the messages, talked with Penn for half an hour. In the course of that conversation, as Penn reported it, the King asked three separate times about the health of the Great Captain Commander but, if William's report is complete, did not inquire at all about the Duke of York.[7]

William considerably thanked his father for the pleasure given by the brief naval service. He regretted that exigencies of war would keep the Great Captain Commander away from home.

"As I never knew what a father was until I had wisdom to prize him," William wrote, "so can I safely say that now, of all times, your concerns are most dear to me. 'Tis hard meanwhile to lose both a father and a friend." The letter does not sound at all as though his father had ever whipped him and driven him out of doors.[8]

By the time William reported for classwork at Lincoln's Inn, not only were the holidays over, but all but two weeks of the second term were lost. After a three-week vacation, when the third session, Trinity term, was about to begin, the Great Plague was raging, so that, after only five days' work, all classes were suspended.

So to measure the amount of Penn's study at Lincoln's Inn would be misleading. For students such as William Penn, class lectures and even the moot courts that were sometimes held were not the chief means of learning. His library research continued and those vacations, seemingly a time for play, were for him, times of independent study. Thus he anticipated one of the best modern learning techniques. William, almost wholly self-taught, never regretted his lack of formal training. He felt toward Lincoln's Inn exactly as he had felt toward Christ Church College. The Inns of Court, he declared, "now and then afford us a few able lawyers but the generality are like the man of old who returned home seven times worse than he went out."[9]

Sir William's carefully worked out plans did not develop in accordance with his expectations. The stay at Lincoln's Inn was too short to permit William to cement a close friendship with the Duke of Monmouth, and if the Great Captain Commander had any thought of reviving the idea of a naval career for his son, disappointment lay ahead. Everything seemed rosy at the moment because, off Lowestoft in Sussex in June 1665, the English fleet had decisively defeated a larger Dutch force, the Great Captain Commander directing operations for which the Duke of York prepared to take the bows.

England did not respond in proper fashion. The victory, critics said, was very welcome, but it should have been much greater. If only the Duke of York had chased his beaten enemy, the whole Dutch fleet could have been wiped out. Why had there been no pursuit? Because the Duke of York was not a competent commander; he had shortened sail and given up the chase.[10]

Sir William rose gallantly to the occasion. James Stuart, brother of the King, he replied, was highly skilled in naval matters. Did not everybody know that the Duke had published a manual on naval operations? The question was unfortunate. Too many people were aware that though James's name appeared as author, the book had been ghost-written by the Great Captain Commander. The catty Mrs. Turner also challenged the Duke's authorship; by her account Sir William had stolen the manuscript from her husband before giving it to James.[11]

The critics, not daring to deal too harshly with the King's brother, the heir-presumptive to the throne, turned on Sir William. Where had he been while the battle raged? Two answers circulated, both highly unfavorable and neither of them true. Reviving old slanders, some said that, being a coward, Sir William was probably hiding in a coil of rope, others declared that he was down below dead drunk.[12]

James should have cleared the loyal Sir William, but he did not; he remained silent. While on his recommendation King Charles rewarded various noble officers for less valuable services, he put off Sir William with renewed promises that, if all went well, he might some day become Earl of Weymouth. Meanwhile, he retired the Great Captain Commander from the active service that he enjoyed by giving him desk duty at the Navy Office.

Callous as the conduct of the Duke of York appears, James did show some signs of gratitude. While allowing Sir William's reputation to remain besmirched, he did small favors for the Admiral throughout the latter's life and, at Sir William's request, continued to be a friend and patron for the son. King Charles recognized the relationship. The charter later given William Penn for his American province specifies, in fact, that the grant was made in recognition of the Admiral's "discretion with our dearest brother James."

With hope, William lived at home for several months. Sir William, understandably embittered, suffering from what he called gout and drinking much too heavily, failed as an inspiring companion. For William home life was uncongenial, a house filled with noisy practical jokers including Lady Margaret, Peg absorbed in her new clothes, and brother Dicky, quiet enough but not yet in his teens. The household's reputation for hospitality meant little to William Penn. As before, he withdrew into an intellectual seclusion.

The retreat brought great, and badly needed, comfort. For all his dandyism and his persiflage, William Penn had never really enjoyed sophisticated court life; its rigid formalism was not conducive to meditation, nor did many of the courtiers waste time on serious study. Certainly he was not at home on rollicking Tower Hill, where quickness of wit and skill at turning a phrase went unappreciated amid the uncharitable backbitings and the spiteful tittle-tattle that passed for cleverness. Neither at court nor on Tower Hill did people credit others with good intentions. Individuality and initiative were suspect. Nonconformity in thought and deviation from accepted codes were frowned upon.

Quakers, members of that Society of Friends to which Thomas Loe and, latterly, Isaac Penington the Younger belonged, were special targets. Few on Tower Hill had ever known a Quaker, but they were convinced that all adherents of that sect were madmen, witches, or fanatics. Sir John Robinson, Lieutenant of the Tower and a good friend of the Admiral, voiced the general opinion when he blurted out that Quakers were all either fools or knaves and that all of them should be locked up.

> Keep them out of their [meeting] houses, and, if any of them preach, send them to Newgate for six months or for the King's pleasure. Some knaves are rich and there's no way to proceed against them but to indict them—seize their estates or imprison them. If this rule was generally followed and kept close to, it would break them without any noise or turmoil.[13]

Young Penn's personal acquaintance with the Friends could not have been much wider than Sir John's, but in spite of all the stories he had heard of their eccentricities, he could not think that they should be condemned en masse. Amyraut and Owen, and latterly his friend Sidney, had taught him that, within the bounds of decency and public order, each man should be free to profess such political or religious opinions as his conscience dictated.

William, as he neared maturity, was reaching the point where scattered bits of knowledge could be fused into some consistency, using truths learned in one field, say religion, to reach valid conclusions in another, for instance, statecraft. He was very far from being ready to publish, as Amyraut, Owen, and Penington had done, but he had attained a certain proficiency in synthesis. He was becoming more and more convinced that not only Anglicanism, his boyhood faith, but all organized religions had strayed from Scripture to follow false courses.

The Admiral did not share his son's uncertainties (the Berean mood, if it ever had existed, had long since disappeared), but he admired certain facets of his son's character. The boy applied himself to every-thing he undertook; though too inclined to bookishness, he thought clearly, if often mistakenly, and he showed ability to analyze and evaluate. The results, of course, were not always to Sir William's liking, but this could be ascribed to immaturity; more knowledge and experience would give the lad more wisdom. After all, Sir William noted, his son mixed well with other people, even with those whom young William found distasteful. The Admiral wished that the boy showed more of the bub-bling spirit of his seafaring ancestors, but, all in all, everything boded well for a successful career in business or public life.

There was work that he could do in Ireland, a mission where, as Admiral Sir William knew, failure was impossible. There was a lawsuit to be quashed. Although the King had more than once confirmed the Penn title to Shanagarry, a certain Colonel Wallis, the former owner, was stubbornly contending that the land should be returned to him. The claim was futile, for royal decrees were surely arguments enough to confirm Sir William's ownership, but if more authority were needed, Roger Boyle, Earl of Orrery, the Lord President of Munster, and James Butler, the Lord Lieutenant of Ireland, were close friends of the Admiral and, if only because of personal friendship, would surely rule against the luckless Colonel Wallis. The business, therefore, did not take much time. Nor did a second commission, the persuasion of Shanagarry tenants to pay their rent bills, pose greater difficulty. William's offer of unexpectedly low charges, backed by his well-known influence in Irish official circles, quickly calmed the rent disputes.

Flushed with success, William then went up to Dublin to cultivate the acquaintance of leaders in social and political life. All doors swung wide for the young, good-looking, fashionably dressed Londoner with the continental manners. The sophisticated set, a literary and artistic group calling itself the Society of Friendship, enthusiastically welcomed him.[14]

"The glory of the world was with me," Penn reported, "and I was ever ready to give myself unto it."[15]

He did not elaborate the theme, but members of the Society of Friendship, not confining themselves to criticizing music, literature, and art, were far from averse to exchanging tidbits of social gossip. Penn's polite attentions to another charming young lady did not pass unnoticed. Somehow, perhaps through the aid of Lord Shannon, Orrery's young brother, word reached Wanstead that not all young William's time was spent in soothing unhappy tenants. The Admiral, pleased as he was by William's progress in the social world, wondered whether it was really necessary for the boy to spend so much time in Dublin when his missions had been accomplished. The boy should finish his assignments and come home.[16]

For one who, according to young William, was addicted to beating the boy and then turning him out of doors, the Admiral displayed a surprising fondness for "Sonne William"; Sir William worried that the boy was being spoiled.

"I think I should be the gladdest person to see you, notwithstanding any expectation you might have from flattering women, and certainly it will neither be honorable or honest to leave the work you have until it be strongly perfect and then come, in God's name, the sonner [*sic*] the better."

He signed the somewhat incoherent recall letter "Your very afft. father."[17]

While the military and civilian officials pursued pleasure in their Society of Friendship, the troops were muttering. At Carrickfergus, just east of Dublin, common soldiers mutinied because, they said, their officers embezzled army funds. Four companies of loyal troops rushed to put down the uprising. William, who had never spent a single day at soldiering, and who, at Saumur, has listened eagerly to arguments that war was most un-Christian, volunteered to go along as an officer.[18]

The campaign against leaderless mutineers was short and successful. William so distinguished himself that Lord Lieutenant Orrery, whose son commanded the expedition, suggested that the Admiral resign the Kinsale captaincy in William's favor. What William had done to merit the honor was never explained, nor even hinted at. The commendation was probably just a courtesy, but the Admiral declined to step aside. He thanked Orrery for the suggestion, but coldly suggested that he "respite his favors for the present"; he urged William to be careful "lest your youthful desires outrun your discretion."[19]

Apparently, William was disappointed; it was at this period that the portrait in armor was commissioned. It is interesting, however, that years later, when his own son was offered a commission as captain of a company of Irish Foot, William Penn, by then a pacifist, angrily rejected the idea. His refusal did not spring from indignation that his son was being asked to fight; the offer was beneath the youth's dignity and merits. "He shall dig potatoes first," said William Penn.[20]

Why William should have thought of entering military service, much less considered it as a career, is difficult to fathom. His nature, reinforced by Amyraut's instruction, would have seemed sufficient to have turned him from the army. The £400 salary as captain of Kinsale's Foot might possibly have been tempting, but his father had already put him out of any need for outside income.

Whatever the reason, William Penn did seek a military post. When the captaincy was denied him, he sought to become commissary agent for the rag-tail Kinsale company, the same type of position that the Admiral had held for the entire Royal Navy. He failed, for some reason, to obtain the post; it went, instead, to his cousin, William Penn, the son of his Uncle George.

Both for the sake of history and for William Penn himself it was well that his ambition was unsatisfied. The itch for military service was just a final flare-up of his immaturity. As an army officer his career would have been very brief, for just a few weeks later he went through an experience that would have caused him either to resign or to be cashiered from the service.

Only a short time after the Carrickfergus expedition he entered a shop in Cork and found, to his surprise, that the owner was a woman he had known ten years before. In chatting about old times at Macroom, Penn mentioned that he had heard a man named Thomas Loe who preached with great persuasion.[21]

"I will never forget him," William said in effect. "If only I knew where he was I would go a hundred miles to hear him again."

"There is no need to go so far," she answered. "Thomas Loe is here in Cork. You can hear him preach tonight."

William went. Loe preached upon the text "There is a faith which overcomes the world and a faith which is overcome by the world." The sermon must have been extraordinarily powerful, for the text does not seem particularly inspiring, but Loe's logic, eloquence, and sincerity convinced William Penn that he, too, must become a Quaker.

The story may be as highly colored as that describing his first meeting with Thomas Loe, for Penn, in first recounting it a generation later, may unconsciously have streamlined the details, but there is no doubt that it was in 1667 that he first became a Quaker, and that the active agent was Thomas Loe.

To give to Thomas Loe full and exclusive credit for the change in William Penn would be a naïve distortion of the facts. Penn's convincement was no blinding revelation on the road to Damascus, no sudden shift from a life of guilt and sinfulness to one more spiritual, no vision of a New Jerusalem or sound of angel voices. Penn's change was both gradual and steady. For at least half his twenty-three years he had been slowly shifting his beliefs, from the High Church Anglicanism of All Hallows Barking to the Low Church stressed at Chigwell, from the modified nonconformity of John Owen to the eclecticism of Moïse

Amyraut. He had been a dilettante and, to slight degree at least, a social butterfly, but he had not been a sinner. He had been a sailor briefly and a soldier too, but was not by any means a military man. None of these pursuits had brought him inner peace. He knew he had been unhappy with sterile forms and, to him, useless ceremonies, but he had not realized how fundamental were his differences with either the religious or the political establishment. His soul was calmer than in his school years, but he was as yet unaware that the quiet meant that many of his doubts and uncertainties had been resolved.

Everything lay in its proper place for recognition when William Penn entered the meeting house to hear Loe speak. He was in a receptive mood to hear a call from on high, to hear the Word with all readiness of mind.

If we knew whether William Penn went to that meeting alone, or in company with others, whether prior to the meeting he had spoken with Thomas Loe, or whether Loe even knew that Penn was in the congregation, we might be better able to assess Loe's impact; but we can only guess that Loe's sermon gave the final nudge that made Penn realize that he was, indeed, a Quaker. At all events, the subsequent alliance with the Society of Friends was not a sudden and dramatic action; it was the culmination of a progress that had begun in early youth, perhaps as a result of that schoolboy vision, and because of that slow and steady progress, the alliance was ever strong and lasting. From the summer of 1667 until the last day of his life, William Penn never deviated from Quakerism.

The acceptance in no way guaranteed that henceforth William Penn would invariably be calm in utterance and nonviolent in attitude. The fervor of a recent convert showed itself in speech and action. Only a few days after the Loe meeting, Penn's warrior spirit broke out when a soldier disturbed a Quaker meeting. Seldom had William used force but on this occasion he started from his seat as though to throw the soldier out; only the intervention of cooler heads restrained him.[22]

The incident was not over. Constables arrested Penn and eighteen other Quakers for holding what was said to be a riotous assembly. Mayor Christopher Rye threw the Quakers into jail, all except Penn, for the mayor could not think that a gentleman like Penn could possibly be a member of the Society of Friends.[23]

William would not accept his freedom. In a letter to his father's crony, the Earl of Orrery, now the Lord Chief Justice, he complained that the mayor had maliciously insulted him and all other Quakers. He drew upon his legal training to declare that the mayor had acted on a "dead and antiquated order" whose validity had been repudiated by the highest authorities in Ireland.[24]

The letter expressed for the first time William Penn's lasting conviction that religious toleration was the prime necessity for political and social freedom. It is, he told the Lord Chief Justice, "an infallible observation that diversities of faith and worship contribute not to the disturbance of any place." Only when freedom of conscience is allowed, he insisted, can peoples prosper.

Whether because of the letter, family friendship, or simple justice, Orrery freed Penn and his fellow Quakers. At the same time word reached the Admiral that son William, the intellectual, the gay man about town, the would-be Army officer, had turned, of all things, Quaker.

Sir William had supposed his son cured of adolescent fancies. To learn that his son had joined a fanatical and blasphemous sect whose members would not fight was more than Admiral Penn could tolerate. He dashed off a hasty, angry letter, closing with the sentence, "I charge you and strictly command that you come to me with all possible speed."[25]

William, ever the dutiful son, heeded the summons, but could not leave at once, for there was estate business to be concluded, and, if a letter from Lord Shannon, Orrery's younger brother, is to be taken seriously, a young lady from whom he must part. In late December 1667, he headed back toward London.[26]

He did not go alone. Realizing that the interview with his father would be strained, if not painful, William enlisted Josiah Coale, the Quaker missionary of Susquehanna fame, as a companion.

What actually happened when William met his father is anybody's guess. A highly imaginative version relates that William angered the Admiral by keeping on his hat and speaking in Quaker plain-talk, a supposition that is reasonable enough, but then the tale relates that the Admiral prayed that God cause the lad to give up the Quaker nonsense, while William, throwing open a window, threatened to jump out unless his father quit the praying. No one knows what might have followed had not a passing nobleman stepped in to calm them both. Whereupon, and this is even more incredible, all hands had a glass of sherry and everything went well between father and son. It is a moving story, but quite out of character for either man.[27]

Then, too, there is the customary account, based on next to nothing, that the Admiral once again ordered his son to leave the house. This would have been a highly melodramatic gesture, for it would have meant that the errant lad was thrust outdoors in the heavy snow that covered London, but apparently there was no such eviction. What really seems to have occurred was that his disappointed and indignant father fumed and doubtless swore. At all events, if William was exiled, the separation was brief, for, only a few days later he was invited to the christening of his sister Peg's baby boy.[28]

An unrepentant William did not attend.

TOWER PRISON

THE YEAR 1668 WAS VERY TRYING FOR ALL THE PENNS. THROUGHOUT A WINTER OF GREAT COLD AND HEAVY SNOWS FEW MATTERS WENT WELL FOR ANY MEMBER OF THE FAMILY, ESPECIALLY NOT FOR LADY Penn, who had to bear the brunt of everything.

Peg was a problem. She was safely married, to be sure, but the neighbors chattered about her: the airs she puts on, how recklessly she spends money on new coaches and her clothes, how she plasters her face with beauty patches and how quickly she strips them off when she comes near home where her father might see her. And that husband of hers, that Anthony Lowther from somewhere up in Yorkshire: who knows anything about him? How much older he is than Peg, and did you know he had been married before? Mr. Pepys says he's much too good for Peg but then, you know, Pepys doesn't like Peg; he thinks her stupid and already bad-looking. Wonder why he's changed his mind; he used to make a fuss over her; took her to dinner and the theater once or twice.

Margaret could avoid the neighbors, though doing so cut down the social life she loved, but home life was little more agreeable. Sir William was unhappy, and not being a man to suffer in silence, he unburdened himself to his wife. He was, he complained, most unfairly criticized. Through no fault of his own, a Dutch squadron had sailed up the Thames, surprised a negligent English garrison, and burned three warships. For this, just because it was he who had designed and supervised the building of defenses, he was being blamed. That fellow Pepys was at the bottom of all that, for the diarist was accusing Sir William of neglect of duty.[1]

Then there were revivals of old rumors that the Admiral had been not only remiss but cowardly in battle, and that he had taken for him-

[43]

self from captured ships valuables that he should have shared with his officers and men. The charges were either groundless or highly exaggerated, but they led to his impeachment. Although he was completely cleared of guilt, no member of the family felt comfortable while the case dragged on.[2]

Naturally, the neighbors talked again. The Admiral could escape with his cronies to the theater or the tavern and young William to the attic with his everlasting books, but Lady Penn had no such recourse. She caught snatches of gossip: how, if the Admiral was innocent, could he have paid that £15,000 dowry that Peg took with her? Why, if he was so rich, were the Penns reduced to borrowing their plates and even their cooking utensils from Mrs. Pepys?

All this was quite enough for Margaret to bear, but to make matters even worse, her husband came down with his gout, which often kept him housebound. The seclusion, added to the pain, made him extremely testy.

His chief target was his son. Something had got into the boy. Instead of mingling like a gentleman in high society, as he used to do, he was consorting with those miserable Quakers, the fools and knaves whom Sir John Robinson was always saying ought to be locked up. The boy was forever preaching, telling people that they must not enjoy themselves by going to the theater, by wearing fashionable clothes, or by cracking jokes. He was even picking on the clergy—young William called them "priests" —because, he said, they preached a dark, unscriptural, filthy doctrine. All this was so out of keeping with what he had been doing before he went to Ireland that the boy had probably gone crazy. Why, young William, who only a few months before had been wanting to join the army, was now actually saying that war was always wicked and that everyone should love his enemies. Could anything be more absurd?

Margaret was in a quandary. She, too, worried about her son, and although she knew that, deep in his heart, the Admiral loved him too, she could not bear to hear her husband find such fault with him. It was all the more difficult because neither father nor son was noted for restraint in voicing his opinions. Young William, with the intolerance of the newly converted, would not have been above lecturing his father for wasting precious time watching Nell Gwynn's acting or at frivolities like *Flora's Vagaries*. If he should continue to commit such impertinences, the Admiral more than likely might, figuratively at least, boot him out of the house.

What was Lady Penn to do? She could not bear to see her son ill-treated, no matter how greatly he deserved such treatment. Yet if she defended the boy, the Admiral would turn on her.

Even the heavens seemed hostile. Spring came early, but a brilliant comet presaged what the fearsome said foretold another London fire as

well as personal catastrophe. Only a few weeks later, a falling star reinforced the certainty of doom. It was as long as a church steeple and so
bright that one could read by it, if one stayed calm enough to read. And
then came rains, heavy rains that were really inundations. Lady Penn was
not superstitious in the least, but just the same, one really was compelled
to think that maybe all this had some meaning.

William did not think of portents; he was too preoccupied in starting
out in missionary work. Having discovered truth he saw himself as the
agent chosen to detect false doctrine and to save others from falling
into error.

It was a dangerous decision. The first Restoration decade was an era
when interest ran high in matters of government and religion, when
advocates of many causes battled for acceptance. Few propagandists
tolerated opposing views; all rivals were heretics, rebels, foreign agents,
or maniacs. For safety's sake, therefore, careful publicists avoided direct
criticism of high authorities or of specific issues of key importance;
they wrangled instead over exact interpretation of Bible texts, the purpose of a symbol, the value of a ceremony. Torrents of argument gushed
forth on knotty philosophical or highly technical details.

While such discussion might be intelligible and even welcome to an
educated public, the great majority of listeners simply could not understand what they were hearing. They did, however, appreciate and relish
personal attacks. As long as the King and his immediate family were
spared and top Church dignitaries exempted, one could safely charge a
rival with such nonpolitical shortcomings as ignorance, hypocrisy, or
lack of ethics, or describe his actions as evil, wicked, and corrupt, unparalleled in filth and vileness. In frenzied oratory or in the paper
bullets of the press the first and greatest casualties were truth, honesty,
fair play, and elementary good manners. No obligation existed to concede
any opponent a single redeeming quality.

In July 1668, just after one of his father's severe gout attacks and
following the warning of that shooting star, William started off on a
preaching tour in company with Loe and Coale. His sermons warned
against four chief evils: pride, lust, avarice, and vanity. He was particularly vehement in condemning "the vain fashion mongers of this shame-
less age." Only much later did he admit that he had shared the worldliness of Dublin and Versailles. Instead, he wrote:

How many pieces of ribbon, feathers, lace bands and the like had
Adam and Eve in Paradise or out of it? What rich embroideries,
silks, points, etc. had Abel, Enoch, Noah and good old Abraham?
Did Eve, Sarah, Susanna, Elizabeth and the Virgin Mary use to curl,
powder, patch, paint, wear false locks of strange colors, rich points,
trimmings, laced gowns, embroidered petticoats, shoes and slip-slaps

[slippers] laced with silk or silver lace and ruffled like pigeon's feet, with several yards, if not pieces, of ribbons? How many plays did Jesus Christ and his disciples recreate themselves at? What poets, romances, comedies and the like did the apostles and the saints make or use to pass away their time?[3]

Away with such time-wasting, said William Penn. Recreation, as Amyraut had said, is good for man, but the best recreation is to do good. Men and women should be diligent in work, frequent the assemblies of religious people, visit sober neighbors to be edified and wicked ones to reform them. They should carefully teach their children, be exemplary to their servants; they should relieve the needy, see the sick, visit prisons, promote peace, and study, though moderately, such commendable and profitable arts as navigation, arithmetic, geometry, husbandry, handicrafts, medicine; and they should read the best reputed histories of ancient times.

And women? Let them spin, sew, knit, weave, garden, preserve (and follow) other housewifely and honest employment and often, in private retirement from all worldly objects, enjoy the Lord by secret and steady meditations on the divine life and heavenly inheritance.

One wonders what the doughty Lady Mary Springett Penington, a practicing oculist, manufacturer of patent medicines, and mother of Penn's childhood friend Guli, thought of this rather naïve advice! It should be remembered, however, that Penn was reflecting the ideals of the late 1660s. He was also reflecting, to large degree, the thoughts of his favorite classics, the belief, common in all ages, that the distant past was a period when men were happier and life more pleasant, a Golden Age existing before man's depravity corrupted the world. Everyone would be happy again if only we could return to that state of bliss.

Such was the message he preached on this missionary tour where he first met other Quaker luminaries, men like Thomas Ellwood, neighbor and secretary of John Milton, a half dozen energetic Bristol Friends, and, though neither made note of it at the time, George Fox, founder of the Society of Friends.

Tradition states that Penn, his conscience uneasy because he, a pacifist, was wearing a sword, asked Fox about the propriety of a Quaker's going armed. "Wear it," Fox is reported to have advised, "as long as thou canst." William's tolerance was brief; he unbuckled the weapon and never again put it on. (Unfortunately for the antiquity of the legend, Henry J. Cadbury, after diligently searching for the source, could find no record prior to 1852 of the incident.) [4]

While on the missionary circuit Penn renewed his acquaintance with Gulielma Maria Springett, whom he had last seen as a child riding around Wanstead in her little coach. Guli had matured into striking beauty and, like her stepbrother Isaac, had become a Quaker. Guli was impressed by the handsome and intense young man who preached so eloquently; William was attracted by her piety and charm. They began a correspondence that, though more frequent and more personal on William's part than on hers, brought happiness to both.

After finishing the tour, Penn, with Coale, Loe, and George White-head, another of the more prominent Quaker evangelists, twice went to Whitehall to plead for the release of Quaker prisoners. Their lobbying methods varied widely from those to which Restoration courtiers were accustomed. Whitehead preached, Loe and Coale prayed earnestly, and Penn, the former dandy, now hatted and in plain garb, exhorted the officials to return to the toleration which he supposed to have been practised by Norman and Saxon predecessors. The court officials listened politely, for, after all, Penn was the son of a royal protégé, and they promised to do whatever they could, but, to no one's surprise, no liberation followed.[5]

Penn now set himself up, first as a voluntary, later as official, defender of Quaker interests. In answering a flood of anti-Quaker libels, he too launched personal attacks, less vehement and less libelous than those of opponents of the Society of Friends but more severe than would be tolerated today. He used the style taught at Saumur by Amyraut: the copious citation of Bible passages, excerpts from patristic writings, and all the classical precedents that he could find. It was the beginning of a lifetime task of exposing falsehoods, of rebutting critics, and of clarifying the truth about Quakerism.

Penn did not confine himself to defensive labors, however. In vigorous rebellion against frivolity and worldliness, he crusaded for more godly modes of living. Earnestly he appealed to Quaker youth to avoid wickedness and to meditate upon the joys of eternity. The virtuous person must not waste time and energy in "idle talking and vain jesting."[6]

Later, in October 1668, Penn's easily aroused anger flared when he read two papers hostile to the Friends. One, by Jonathan Clapham, *A Guide to True Religion*, proclaimed that Baptists, Quakers, and certain other nonconformists were beyond redemption. The young enthusiast would have taken the reference to Baptists and others with equanimity, but the slur against the Friends was unforgivable. Thomas Loe was seriously ill, and Penn was deeply worried. To have Clapham condemn Loe as unfit for Heaven must have affected him deeply at such a time. Disregarding his oft-repeated advice to youth not to "enter into many reasonings with opposers," he dashed off a reply in which, in Penn's words, he confuted Clapham's religion, "exposed his hypocrisy, reprehended his aspersions and compared his contradictions." As for Jonathan Clapham, said Penn, he was peevish.[7]

To make matters worse, Thomas Vincent, a nonconformist preacher

and a fellow alumnus of Christ Church College, inflicted new hurts, all
the more serious because Vincent had himself been persecuted and was a
man with an enviable reputation for work among plague sufferers. He
had, moreover, been personal chaplain to Robert Sidney, Earl of Leicester and father of Algernon Sidney, a man of strong liberal tendencies.
Yet, according to Penn, Vincent was anything but a model clergyman.
His pulpit language, Penn reported, on hearsay evidence, was so filthy,
so full of "carnal observations, will-worship and vain conversation," that
many of his congregation had defected to Quakerism. Evidence of the
secession was unconvincing, since loyalists of the Vincent congregation
listed only two who had seceded, a woman and her daughter, but whatever the number may have been, Vincent was said, again by Penn, to
have declared that he would rather have lost them to a bawdyhouse than
to a Quaker meeting.[8]

Following a common practice of the time, Penn challenged Vincent
to debate but, while Vincent accepted, on condition that the meeting
take place in his own chapel, Penn was outmaneuvered. By the time he
and George Whitehead arrived, an hour before debate was to begin,
Vincent had so packed the chapel that only a few Quakers could get in.
Vincent may have lost many of his flock, but those who remained were
a raucous lot, who laughed and hissed at the Quaker handful, shoving
them about, striking them, and calling them "impudent villains and
blasphemers." Vincent himself was rude and mocking.

The maltreatment continued. Vincent spoke first, and talked, Penn
reported, for hours, not stopping until after dark; another report said
that he kept on talking until midnight. Then "he rose from his knees"
(had he been praying all this time?) and strode from the church, calling
on his faithful parishioners to follow. Somewhere the Quakers found
candles, so that Penn could preach to the few people who remained, but
Vincent came back, blew out the candles, and ordered everyone to leave.

All this was bad enough, but Vincent went further; he alleged that
William Penn was not really a Quaker but was, in fact, a secret Jesuit.
He offered no firm evidence, hinting merely that someone, unidentified,
had told him that Penn was corresponding with the Vatican. For corroboration Vincent pointed out that young Penn was unmarried. Were
not all Jesuits celibates? Moreover, if he were not a Jesuit, why did he
firmly refuse to swear to abjure the Pope? The accusation was ridiculous
and the "proof" absurd, but in the all-pervasive state of fear then prevalent, many people readily accepted the slander.

The charge, moreover, was worse than ridiculous; it was brutal, for
Vincent implied, none too indirectly, that William Penn was a rebel
against both Church and state. Neither by word nor by deed was Penn
able to stifle the nonsense; for at least a generation there were Englishmen who, echoing Vincent, branded Penn as a conspirator and, in all
probability, a traitor.

All this, of course, is the Quaker version of what had happened at the one-sided debate, for each participant had rushed to the printing press to present his own case. Vincent's *The Foundations of God Standeth Still* was the first to appear; it failed to mention any mistreatment, spoke of Vincent's calm, judicious, and tolerant behavior, noted the Quaker "rantings," and regretted their obtuseness.

Penn's answer, *Sandy Foundations Shaken*, was a three-part pamphlet. Readers found the first part, his story of what had happened at the chapel, more vibrant than the usual Penn writing, probably because he composed it in anger. Interest bogged down in the second section, the speech which Penn had planned to give, and vanished entirely in the complexities of the final division, wherein Penn laboriously tried to popularize theologic philosophy. Those readers who enjoyed knowing about quarrels but who had no special taste for doctrinal disputes approved the book. Samuel Pepys, for instance, rated it well done, though "too good for him to have writ it." The diarist warned, however, that the pamphlet was not fit for everyone to read.

It may, as a matter of fact, be questioned whether Pepys, or many other readers, understood such chapters as that treating of "The Notion of the Justification of Impure Persons by Means of an Imputative Righteousness," or indeed whether they ever reached that point in the book.

Sandy Foundations Shaken was, to large degree, an unfortunate production. It won few friends for Quakerism but instead created enemies. The fault lay in Penn's methods. He must have known that every word, to say nothing of its context, would be closely scrutinized for its precise meaning; yet, following the initial delay, he sent in copy piecemeal to be typeset; worse still, he sometimes stood by the printer's side extemporizing important passages.[9] Thus, editing and copy-reading suffered and the way lay open for misunderstandings. Superficial readers of the published work, as well as those who knew *Sandy Foundations* only by hearsay, gained the impression that William Penn had challenged the doctrine of the Trinity. Pepys's fellow diarist John Evelyn was not the only one who thought so. The Right Reverend Humphrey Henchman, Archbishop of London, may have believed Penn guilty.[10]

Penn suffered for the carelessness that caused the misunderstanding. Belief in High Church circles that Penn denied the Trinity could lead to possible conviction for blasphemy, a crime which, until only a few months earlier, had been a capital offense. Few were astonished, therefore, when, after publication in the *London Newsletter* that he had issued "an infamous and blasphemous pamphlet," he was thrown into the Tower.[11]

Libel laws applying to the press being as weak and as poorly enforced as were the laws against slander in debate, the *Newsletter* further vilified William Penn, describing him as having "passed through all degrees of looseness and extravagance." It implied that he had run away, but a week later the *Newsletter* announced triumphantly that "the author of that horrid and abominable piece against the Holy Trinity" was safely under custody.[12]

The cause for the arrest was clear enough, but public interest in so prominent a man as the young son of Admiral Sir William Penn was not satisfied with simple and easy explanations. Some people, mostly Penn's friends, suggested that the real reason was that he and the printer, John Darby, had made the mistake of not asking the Bishop for leave to print, a request that supposedly was standard practice but which was frequently ignored with absolute impunity. If, however, failure to obtain clearance had been the reason for arrest, why should Penn have been sent to the Tower while Darby languished in the common jail?

More imaginative people, always alert to unmask plots, conjured up fantastic explanations. A story ran that, by what can only be described as a well-planned "accident," an unknown enemy had dropped a letter containing treasonable material. A court official, apparently a party to the suspected plot, picked up the letter, saw Penn's name mentioned therein, and so arrested him. The whole yarn rested only on gossip, neither letter nor official ever having been identified nor any evidence ever been produced, and the story may be dismissed as sheer invention.[13]

So may the absurd suggestion that young Penn was arrested because his father wished to spare him from a charge that would have been more serious, though what offense could have been more perilous than heresy and blasphemy is difficult to imagine.

Still another guess suggested that someone, possibly Henry Bennett, Lord Arlington, a principal secretary of state and an enemy of Sir William, struck at the Admiral by arresting the latter's son.

That many of these "explanations" gained currency points up the credulity and suspicion of the time. Penn's own explanation is not entirely free of imaginative embroidery. He held, and is undoubtedly correct, that Archbishop Henchman scented heresy and blasphemy, but he also believed that Thomas Vincent, the scandalous preacher, had egged on the good Archbishop. Penn failed to make it clear why a high cleric of the Church of England should have been influenced by a non-conformist, especially by such a man as Penn supposed Vincent to be.[14]

That blasphemy was the major accusation was borne out when Darby, from his prison cell, sent his wife, Joan, to Lord Arlington with a petition for release. Darby, the petition read, was wholly guiltless. To be sure, he had printed what Penn required, but copy arrived in such confused fashion that he did not recognize its "dangerous and pernicious" content. Intent as a good workman should be in "setting the letters" as Penn dictated, "he knew not the poison therein contained."[15]

The arrests shocked the Society of Friends, few if any of whose members saw any harm whatever in Penn's book, and certainly no serious threat against the state. The indignation of those whom the orthodox decried as a poor, sullen faction grew when a none too accurate rumor revealed that he was being held unfed during that cold December in an unheated cell. He was, they understood, incommunicado, no one, not even a barber, being allowed to visit him. There was no consolation in the thought that a prison guard, whose duty was to stay with the prisoner day and night, was suffering the same privations.

Whatever may have been the situation, Sir John Robinson, Lord Lieutenant of the Tower, was obeying orders. A literal-minded man, whom Pepys characterized as a "talking, bragging, buffle-head," he so detested Quakers that he would have granted them no favors, even if he could have done so, not even to a son of his close companion and Tower Hill neighbor, the Admiral.

For more than a week Penn remained incommunicado, but on Christmas Eve—a day of only slight significance to William Penn—his servant, Francis Cooke, came to visit him. The call gave little solace, for Cooke carried no message from Sir William, who was ill, nor apparently any from Lady Margaret. He did, however, deliver a communication from the Archbishop, a curt ultimatum saying, in effect "Recant or stay in prison till you die." This ultimatum may have existed only in Cooke's imagination, for there is no record of it in the Archbishop's archives, but in any case, Penn refused; he sent back word through Cooke that he could not be intimidated. "My prison shall be my grave before I will budge a jot, for I owe my conscience to no mortal man."[16]

Cooke delivered the message, and then, by pleading Penn's need for food and fuel, borrowed £40 from one of William's friends. Instead of buying these necessities, he ran off with the money. At the time Penn knew nothing of the loan, but when he learned of it, he paid it off with his apologies for Cooke.

What the Archbishop replied to the message Cooke delivered is not known, but, having failed to frighten Penn, Henchman now changed his tactics. He sent the Reverend Dr. Edward Stillingfleet, the royal chaplain, to talk William out of heretical opinions. The choice was excellent, for Stillingfleet was only a few years older than Penn and had already won a name for himself as an advocate of compromise among rival sects. He and Penn struck it off well together and became lifetime friends, but Stillingfleet could not change Penn's convictions.

Three months went by with no one admitting any change in his position. The situation remained at a standstill, the Church upholding its dogma of the Holy Trinity and William Penn defending his right to liberty of conscience. (In this mood he wrote to Guli: "Be watchful that thy mind be not darkened nor thy light extinguished—wait for the Day Star to arise and be a child of the Son." He signed it "Thy Loving

Master, William Penn."[17]) Sir William, though a professed Anglican, was less interested in doctrine or in forms of worship—he believed whatever the Established Church deemed proper—but he was deeply concerned with his status as a parent; that his son was a notorious nonconformist and, worse, a rebel against family discipline argued a faulty upbringing. Naval officers, moreover, were unaccustomed to rebellious subordinates. He loved his son and in a way admired him, but to write to a prisoner in the Tower would seem a weakness. Displaying anger by staying aloof argued strength of character.

Yet, despite the show of firmness, Sir William was the first to yield. Quietly, and without informing his son, while keeping the pose of indignation, the Admiral drew a will, bequeathing to his son his most prized possession, the gold chain and medal bestowed upon him for his naval service. Nor was this all; William was to inherit the major portion of the estate and was, in addition, to act as the executor.[18]

Two months later the Admiral gave in completely. Perhaps after conferring with his good friend the Duke of York, he petitioned the Privy Council to release his son. "His late failings by his departure from the Protestant religion," said Sir William—momentarily setting up the Church of England as the only Protestants—"has been, and is, a great affliction." The Admiral assured the Council that heresy certainly did not reflect the teachings by which young William had been reared. He went on to promise that if his son were freed, the offenses would not be repeated, for young William had given "reasonable satisfaction to those worthy persons appointed to examine him." The assurance seems to reveal that in private discussions with Stillingfleet, Penn, too, had softened sufficiently to clarify, if not disavow, controversial beliefs.[19]

Rumors of such an agreement had already circulated, only to be hotly denied. On one occasion Penn had authorized Stillingfleet to disabuse the King himself of any misconception. "Thou mayst tell the King that the Tower is the worst argument in the world to convince me. Whoever is in the wrong, those who use force in religion can never be in the right." He wrote Lord Arlington that force may make hypocrites but not converts.[20]

Finally, when general agreement had been reached as to the wisdom of his release, he wrote an application to Lord Arlington, pointing out that, though he was a trueborn Englishman, he had not received an Englishman's right to a fair trial before imprisonment, but had been kept in jail merely at the whim of the Archbishop. He appealed to Arlington to have the King release him.

"I beseech thee to entreat the King on my account not to believe any man to be his enemy that cannot shape his conscience to the narrow forms and prescripts of man's inventions."[21]

At the same time he produced another pamphlet, *Innocency with Its*

Open Face, subtitled *An Apology for Sandy Foundations Shaken*. This was a volume, prepared in conjunction with Stillingfleet, to make it very clear that *Sandy Foundations* was in no way an attack upon the Church of England, but was, if anything, a defense of the Established Church against the teachings of Thomas Vincent's Presbyterians.

The work is, as it was supposed to be, an admirable propagandist volume. Even the subtitle was skilfully chosen, for the word "apology" could be construed both as an explanation, which of course it was, or as a recantation. A Philadelphia jurist went so far as to declare that *Innocency* was, in reality, a lawyer's appellate brief, cleverly marshaling arguments and precedents to support the author's case just as an attorney cites precedents and statutes. It was the first of a series of arrangements— the unkind might call them "deals"—whereby conscience accommodated itself to irresistible official pressure. In any case, it served its purpose, both parties to the difficulty claiming victory. On July 28, 1669, Penn went free. He had been in prison for seven months and a half.[22]

The misunderstandings did not cease. The *Newsletter* informed its readers that the extension of the King's grace had been granted only on condition that young William Penn leave the country.[23] The fact that he shortly thereafter set out on a mission to Ireland was seen by many as confirmation of the rumor. Yet the *Newsletter* item was just another of the innumerable exaggerations voiced by both sides in Restoration disputes. Few, if any, statements of the time can be accepted without considerable linguistic discount. Just as any adversary was ipso facto a selfish and corrupt scoundrel, so one's own partisans were invariably and incontrovertibly high-minded. Downright lies, such as the report of Penn's exiling, called for neither retraction nor apology.

6

LOVE AND DUTY

QUAKERS, TOO, EXAGGERATED. UNDOUBTEDLY THEY WERE UNJUSTLY PERSECUTED AND CRUELLY MISUSED, AND IT IS QUITE UNDERSTANDABLE THAT FOR ALL THEIR CHARITY AND FORBEARANCE THEY looked upon their oppressors as inhuman. They credited few, if any, enemies with honesty or benevolence and set down virtually all as wicked, malicious, heartless, and spiteful. Reports of Quaker tribulations, "taken from official records and authentic accounts," list cruel punishments inflicted for no ostensible cause other than "speaking to a priest." Nothing indicates just what was said, but official skins were thin and tempers short. Despite the Quakers' restraint and their laudable efforts to love their enemy, it is unlikely that the "speaking" was limited to pleasant salutations. Similarly, prison conditions, unquestionably bad, could not have been as intolerable as has been reported, else how could George Fox and William Penn, shut up, as they reported, in filthy, crowded quarters with the scum of the earth, without food, drink, heat, or sanitary facilities, have managed not only to write long letters but, in Penn's case, complete books?[1]

For it was in the Tower that Penn wrote, or at least blocked out, one of his best books, *No Cross, No Crown.* The catchy title derives from Francis Quarles, a former student of Christ Church College and of Lincoln's Inn. His poem "Hadassah," written in 1621, contained the couplet, "The way to bliss lies not on beds of down/ And he that hath no cross deserves no crown."

Penn was no devotee of poetry, though, like many another young man, he had tried his skill at it, but the couplet was popular and appears to have been known to Thomas Loe. When Loe lay dying, Penn, though himself ill with fever, had hurried to Loe's side. The sick man took him by the hand and said, "Dear heart, bear thy cross. Stand faithful to God and bear thy testimony in thy day and generation and God will give thee an eternal crown of glory that none shall ever take from thee."

"Then," Penn added, "he passed away in a great stillness."[2]

Penn's biographers of the Victorian period insist that he wrote *No Cross, No Crown* entirely from memory, without the aid of reference works. Since the complete volume includes quotations from at least a hundred classical authors, together with as many more later rulers, philosophers, and churchmen, the claim has very properly been challenged.

No Cross, No Crown exhorted degenerate modern man to return to the virtuous simplicity of early Christianity. This had been Penn's text on preaching missions. Persistently he hammered home his plan of an end to pride, avarice, luxury, frivolity, and injustice. Penn demanded sweeping reforms, a complete change of heart. Man must choose a spiritual and righteous life, end all persecution, show love and charity toward all, abandon all false distinctions among fellow human beings, for as God made all peoples of one blood and one family, there can be no nobility save that of virtue.

William's rejection of false and flattering titles must have particularly struck home to Admiral Sir William Penn. A father who cherished the hope that the King would someday name him Earl of Weymouth, a title to be passed down to his descendants, would certainly not have approved of abolishing titles.

Had Penn rested content in simply urging moderation and justice in human relationships, as so many other preachers did, *No Cross, No Crown* would have been ineffective. While he refrained from criticizing individuals, he did not spare either church or state. No kingdom in the world, he said of England, "is more infested with cheating mountebanks, savage morris dancers, pickpockets, profane players and stagers."

As for the priests, too many of these pretended servants of the Lord were really nothing but agents of the devil. What need was there for carnal, formal, pompous, and superstitious practices, for stately buildings, images, rich furniture and garments, choirs and music, costly lamps, candles, and perfumes? By all this, men had made God a being as sensual as themselves. True worship springs only from the heart, prepared by God's holy spirit.

"Choose the good old paths of temperance, wisdom, gravity and holiness," Penn pleaded.

When people have first learned to fear, worship and obey their Creator, to pay their numerous debts, to alleviate and abate their oppressed tenants, but, above all outward regards, when the pale faces are more commiserated, the pinched bellies relieved and naked bodies clothed, when the famished poor, the distressed widow and helpless orphan are provided for, then, I say, if then, it will be time enough to plead the indifferency of your pleasures.

It was an extraordinary appeal, nonetheless eloquent because it was a common plaint of Quaker preachers, expressed in something less than perfect prose, but all the more effective coming from a man of standing, one who had been welcome in the highest social circles. Chigwell should have been pleased that the buds of virtue had been thus stirred.

When a man writes some one hundred and fifty books and pamphlets, his style varies widely. Penn can be, and often is, sharp and sententious as in the opening chapters of *No Cross, No Crown*, or in a later book of maxims that he entitled *Fruits of Solitude*. He is capable of careful phrasing, as when he describes himself in an embarrassing moment as standing "with my finger in my mouth," tells of a plotting parson as "plotting and piping with a pirate," or complains that to own a colony without the power to control it is to "have the ring without the stone." Even so savage a commentator as Francis, Lord Jeffrey, of the *Edinburgh Review* was moved to praise by a letter that Penn once wrote to his wife and children. After complimenting Penn on the "affectionateness and patriarchal simplicity of the testament," Jeffrey praised Penn's diction: "The language appears to us to be one of the most beautiful specimens of that soft and mellow English which, with all its redundancy and cumbrous volume, has, to our ears, a far richer and more pathetic sweetness than the epigrams and apothegms of modern times."[3]

Unfortunately, when Penn passes from the clear and vivid paragraphs in which he condemns man's fall from the high standards of a golden past, he grows dull and wordy. Instead of slashing away at crucial issues, he wanders in the dark thickets of theological polemics. His bold crusade against pride, avarice, luxury, and injustice becomes a series of skirmishes against matters of ephemeral importance. The Penn who can, and so very often does, capture and grip attention becomes difficult to read.

The same dichotomy showed itself in conversation. Satiric Jonathan Swift, who lampooned the same type of evil as Penn did, found that the Quaker spoke very agreeably and with much spirit, but Bishop Gilbert Burnet, who did not care for Penn, described him as talking tediously.[4]

Tedious or not, Penn seemed at last to be standing in his father's good graces. Sir William's success in persuading James, Duke of York, to procure William's release from the Tower somewhat relieved the father's unhappiness. Though still only in his early forties, the Admiral was aging rapidly, plagued by aches and pains. He was, as he must have realized, drinking too much and, what was worse, doing it in solitude rather than in tavern conviviality; he was, moreover, becoming more and more short-tempered. The realization that, in spite of all this, he still had influence with the Duke buoyed his spirits and, together with the discovery that his son was willing to write *Innocency*, which the Admiral construed as a retraction, brought him more happiness than he had enjoyed for months. He was even able to crack a mild joke after reading *No Cross, No Crown*. "If you are ordained to be a cross to me," he told William, "God's will be done and I shall arm myself as best I can against it."[5]

It was not, to be sure, much of a joke, but it did indicate at least a grain of tolerance for a younger generation whose ways he could not understand and for which he had never shown much sympathy. It testified to the strong family ties and to the love that surpassed the constant disagreements.

As a mark of confidence, the Admiral sent William back to Ireland, again to supervise the Shanagarry estate. Matters there were not as muddled as before, but tenant problems remained and readjustments were required. Ill as he was, the Admiral had at last decided to resign the governorship of Kinsale and the command of the cherished company of Foot. William had once coveted that post, but now that he was a Quaker, he shrank from bearing arms. As Cousin Richard Rooth was willing to pay £400 for the captaincy, William was instructed to turn over the leadership to him. William was also to hire a manager for the Shanagarry estate.[6]

William's departure, in September 1669, two months after leaving the Tower, seemed to many a proof that his release had been conditional on his quitting England. Not until his return, nine months later, was the misconception corrected.

Penn's task of hiring a manager was not difficult. He already had a protégé, Philip Ford, to whom he was advancing money. In the light of subsequent developments this first appearance of Ford merits special attention. For over forty years Ford and his wife, the former Bridget Gosnel, played a leading part in Penn's financial affairs. According to an affidavit filed a generation later in the Court of Chancery, Ford was an itinerant peddler of laces on the London streets on whom Penn took pity and whom he set up, first as an elementary schoolteacher and, after his marriage, as a dry-goods merchant. The venture did not prosper because, said Penn, the Fords charged "dear and extortionate prices" for the hoods and scarves they made and sold.[7]

Actually, Ford had been well known in Quaker circles. He had been jailed in 1665, along with eleven other Buckinghamshire Friends, for refusal to take oaths. Even in jail he had been persecuted, for when the Society of Friends sent him a bed to ease his discomforts, the warden had stolen it from him. Almost immediately upon his release he had been again imprisoned for a further refusal to swear oaths.[8]

Why the Admiral approved the nomination is inexplicable, unless Sir William was so ill that his judgment was impaired. He did, however, hire Philip Ford at a salary of £40 per annum. It was extraordinarily high pay for an unsuccessful shopkeeper said by Penn to have been hawking laces on the London streets. Actually, the salary was misstated, for Ford received £12 at first but £80 within three years.[9]

William sent Ford on the way to Ireland and, a day or two later, followed, but instead of taking the main highway west, as Ford had done, Penn took a longer, more indirect road. He went through Buckinghamshire, the land, as Penn believed, of his ancestors. He was not, however, seeking relatives, real or imagined, but visiting fellow Quakers. Isaac Penington the Younger, free again after months of imprisonment, was living near Amersham in a house that he had turned into a Quaker hostel. Attending Quaker meeting in the red-brick Penington house by the clear-running Misbourn stream was a solemn duty and a precious privilege more important to William than the mission entrusted by his father.

The privilege may have been all the more special because of the presence in the Amersham house of pretty Gulielma Springett, whom he had known at Wanstead and to whom he had been reintroduced at Bristol while on his first preaching tour. The two had been exchanging letters since even before his imprisonment. By the standards of the time, Guli, now all of twenty-five, a few months older than William, was an old maid, but her spinsterhood was due to choice rather than to lack of opportunity. There had been suitors aplenty, among them the noble lord who had sold the Admiral the Wanstead mansion, but none of them had caught her fancy; some of them, she suspected, courted her because of her £10,000 yearly income. She had other attractions: skills taught her by her mother in medicine and even in surgery.[10]

Before renewing her acquaintance with William Penn, Guli's closest, perhaps her only, male companion had been Thomas Ellwood, another childhood playmate and, more recently, tutor of the Penington children. Ellwood, if local gossip can be credited, had unsuccessfully proposed marriage time and time again, but Penn roused a warmer interest. Though they had met infrequently since their reunion at Bristol, and only for short periods, acquaintance developed into friendship and then into love.

Letters between the two at this period do not survive, but Penn's literary wooing must have been effective. Had he not already signed one of his messages "Thy Loving Master"? Nor was there much time at Amersham for intimate conversation, since he arrived on September 16, spent the evening at meeting, and planned to leave early next morning to meet Philip Ford on the Bristol road.

Luck came, as it so often did, to William's aid. On arriving at the place of rendezvous, he learned that Ford had not yet come. Penn, far from being cast down, turned his horse about and spurred back ten miles to Guli's home.

Such impetuosity was so uncharacteristic of William Penn—on few other occasions, if indeed ever, did he act so hastily—that one wonders whether he really had intended to proceed to Bristol. The Amersham household showed no surprise at his return; everyone acted as though he was expected.

William and Guli spent the next day together, in no other company. They took a horseback ride (let us hope Penn rode a Penington horse, for his own must have been quite tired) ostensibly to visit the village of Penn, named for William's namesake. But though the settlement was only six miles away, the journey took all day. They returned to Amersham to dine and, in keeping with Quaker custom, spent the evening in worship.

Apparently he had proposed and had been accepted, not only by Guli but by all the Peningtons, for when morning came, everyone went off on a gala picnic to William Russell's recently remodeled house two miles away. Russell's place, Old Jordan's, a brick building a story and a half high conveniently located at a crossroads, claimed, even in 1669, a romantic history. A secret chamber, it was said, had often sheltered dissenters against persecution. Some of the timbers, a few believed, together with the oaken beams of the nearby barn, had come from the bark *Mayflower*, which had taken the Pilgrims to America; a carved door panel and a peculiarly mended beam proved the authenticity of the legend. To Friends, however, Old Jordan's was more important as a meetinghouse.[11]

On the twentieth, William, who does not seem to have shown the slightest concern about missing Philip Ford or about delaying the business on which he had been sent, resumed his journey toward Ireland. In contrast with his lone ride three days before, a retinue accompanied him, the Peningtons, Ellwood, and Guli riding with him for several miles. Eventually, of course, they turned back, while William rode on to Bristol. Philip Ford was waiting for him there. William and Guli, now officially engaged, were not to see each other again for almost a year.

Whatever William's parents may have thought of his engagement to a Quaker girl, the stepdaughter of a troublemaker only recently released from jail, the Admiral was far from pleased at his son's slothfulness in fulfilling his assignment. It was bad enough that William was a Quaker preacher who wrote questionable books and who was about to be allied to a Quaker family, but to have him idling about when he should have been settling Shanagarry's affairs was unforgivable.

William continued to delay, however. Arriving at Bristol nearly three weeks late, partly because of very muddy roads, he learned that city officials and local Quakers were at odds. He spent more time in settling the dispute and then lingered longer to talk with George Fox who had just come over from Ireland. William made one concession for his father's sake; he did not stay to attend George Fox's wedding.

Arriving at Cork, October 26, almost six weeks after leaving London, he learned to his astonishment that every local Quaker was in jail. The Mayor, Matthew Deane, Penn heard, had imprisoned them because he envied their prosperity.

Penn took up their cause. Going straight to the Mayor, he demanded their release. When Deane refused, William appealed to higher authority, as he had done in a similar situation several years before. He rode to Dublin, covering two hundred miles of bad road in four days' time, only to find that here, too, a large proportion of the Quaker population was in jail.

Once more luck favored William Penn. Not many members of the Society of Friendship, the intellectual coterie to which he had once belonged, remained in high position, but John, Lord Berkeley, the new governor, was an old Navy Office associate of Admiral Sir William and, though never a close family friend, was predisposed to favor his old colleague's son. He had, moreover, liberal and tolerant tendencies. A co-proprietor, with Sir George Carteret, of plantations overseas, notably in New Jersey, he had conceded freedom of conscience to his settlers. He listened sympathetically to Penn's appeal; within a month all Irish Quakers were set free.

On the assumption that Philip Ford was doing his work well at Shanagarry, William spent much time at Dublin attending Quaker meetings and investigating the status of various land claims, especially those of his mother and of the Peningtons and Guli, too. Here, again, he was fortunate, for the chief surveyor, Sir William Petty, was, like Berkeley, an ex Navy Office man. Petty, too, favored toleration; he used to argue that to allow freedom of conscience would increase productivity by 50 percent, though he was never clear just how that desirable result would be achieved.

Petty was willing enough to extend what help he could, but as he explained, the Shanagarry award included compensation not only for Macroom but also for Margaret's claims. As for Guli's land, it was worthless; the soil was so poor that only about ten acres were of any value.

The Petty report was not particularly favorable, but it did have one satisfactory result. Penn wrote home. Thus far he had sent so few letters to his parents that Margaret was beginning to worry whether the news was so bad that her husband was keeping William's letters from her.[12] The fact was that William, a compulsive writer who spent hours daily composing books, pamphlets, and even letters on theological matters, was singularly inept in reporting much about himself; he could, on occasion, complain bitterly about injustices done to him, but he simply could not express other types of personal feelings. If Guli hoped for love letters she must have been disappointed, for while during that month-long stay in Dublin, Penn sent her a number of notes, all were couched in stilted style. He was obviously in love, but his warmest endearments were no more than "my o.d.f." or "o.b.f." meaning, apparently, my own dear friend or my own beloved friend. To a girl in love the abbreviations undoubtedly carried much more meaning than they would to a neutral observer.[13]

Before leaving Dublin, William indulged in a bit of harmless vanity that Guli may possibly have suggested. Embarrassed by a growing baldness, which he now laid to his imprisonment, he had a barber cut off the hair to be made into a wig. It could not have been his first. If, as Penn once supposed, the baldness was due to smallpox, he would have worn a wig at Versailles, if not at Oxford, and the portrait in armor, painted almost four years earlier, shows him with curly hair descending to his shoulders.[14]

Resort to the wig caused some surprise among the strictest Quakers, some of whom later accused Penn of being "a periwig man," guilty of un-Quakerlike pride. Fox, however, came to Penn's defense. Penn had worn a wig, said Fox, before convincement, but after becoming a Quaker, he:

> endeavored to go in his own hair but when kept a close prisoner in the Tower, next the leads, with no barber suffered to come at him, his hair shed away. Since, he hath worn a short, civil thing, and he hath been in danger of his life after violent heats in meetings and riding after them, and he wears them to keep his head and ears warm and not for pride—He is more eager to fling it off if a little hair come than ever he was to put it on.[15]

Unfortunately for the "short, civil wig" explanation, Sewel, in his history based on consultations with Penn, says that when Penn was in Ireland in 1669 he was wearing "a great periwig," and, a few years later, Penn himself mentions his "periwigs," plural.

At the end of November 1669, William took horse for Shanagarry. He rode more slowly than on his hurried ride to Dublin, not reaching Shanagarry for about a week. He spent a long, hard winter leasing land at a flat rate of four shillings sixpence per acre yearly, a charge that Penn regarded as below the market rate. By leasing only half the estate he provided the Admiral a full £1,000 yearly.

With Ford as manager doing most, if not all, the routine chores at Shanagarry, Penn led an idyllic existence, puttering about the estate, exploring the countryside, getting lost in the mountains in midwinter, and in reading various pamphlets about religion. Apparently a rumor in London about the fashion-following and frivolity of an unnamed "little friend" was also on his mind, for he wrote a *Letter to the Young Convinced,* pointing out that "lightness, jesting and a careless mind

grieves the Holy Spirit." Far better, he admonished, to "deny all ungodliness and worldly lusts and live soberly, righteously and godly."[16]

As the letter had a general appeal, again warning youth to shun all
sports, plays, and entertainments, he had it printed, but though the
message seemed innocuous enough, Penn, mindful of the aftermath of
Sandy Foundations Shaken, had the printing done secretly and without
a title page. The end of the last page carried a notation, "Your little
brother and fellow traveler in the Kingdom and patience of Jesus Our
Love, W.P."

Soon after publication, Penn received a letter from his father demanding to know why, now that the land-ownership and rental missions
had been finished, William was staying so long in Ireland. The situation
at Wanstead, the Admiral declared, was growing worse; his mother was
worrying, and he himself was suffering not only from gout but from
dropsy as well. "I find myself in decline," Sir William wrote, urging
his son to return at once.[17] The news saddened Penn, but the recall
pleased him. "My parents, who had disowned me—had come to love
me above all."

At a matter of fact, William was already planning to return. Ten days
before his father wrote the letter, he had laid in ten gallons of usque-
baugh, the Irish whiskey, surely not all for personal consumption but, it
may be, as a present for his father.

Misfortune delayed him. Word reached him from Cork that many
Quakers were in prison. When he went to visit them, "the wicked and
malicious mayor, the worst who had ever been in office," raided his
lodgings and carried off some books. William protested, only to be
called a coxcomb, a jackanapes, and a fool. So, for the third time, Penn
went over a mayor's head, appealing to his old friend Orrery, now
governor of the area.[18]

The response was only half satisfactory. William recovered his books,
but nothing happened to the mayor except a reprimand for using ill
language to a person of Penn's quality. The Quakers stayed in jail.[19]

Then came further delay: a bout of fever. It was not until two
months after receiving the urgent summons that Penn was able to take
ship for England.

7

FOR ENGLISH RIGHTS

ENN'S PARENTS, IGNORANT OF HIS ILLNESS AND OF HIS DIFFICULTIES
WITH THE MALICIOUS MAYOR, COULD NOT UNDERSTAND WHY HE HAD
WAITED SO LONG TO RETURN. NEITHER COULD GULI, WHO WROTE HIM
over the signature "thy friend in lasting friendship."[1]

Twenty-six-year-old William, expecting to find a household of love
and peace and happiness, found it filled with discord and regret. The
Admiral was quite as critical and even more short-tempered than before.
Sick both in body and spirit, he felt callously deserted. Richard, his
younger son, was off in Italy, sowing, some suspected, his wild oats. Peg,
the social climber, had gone to Yorkshire with her husband, but while she
was bombarding her father with suggestions that he and Margaret
come up to live with them, her husband was demanding that the Admiral pay the promised dowry.

The once gay Margaret, beaten down by the ailing and petulant
Sir William and by neighbors who disapproved of her son's Quaker
activities, could not, for the life of her, understand why William had
sent her no letters and why he set such store by trivial things like keeping
on his hat even when speaking to his king. While doing the housework
in a mansion much too large for the Admiral and herself, helped only
by two maids, both of them invalids needing constant nursing, she
illogically blamed that Quaker girl to whom William was engaged for
adding to her problems.[2]

The truth was that William, saddened though he was by his father's
illness and his mother's grief, was more affected by the sufferings of his
fellow Quakers. His parents were in distress, but the sufferings were in
their bodies, not in their souls; their troubles were physical, not
spiritual. What was happening to them was by the will of God, not due

to the tyranny of priests or despots. William Penn had to defend civil liberties, to safeguard the historic rights of Englishmen, to assure to everyone freedom of conscience. In comparison with these responsibilities, Wanstead's transitory troubles were as nothing.

Much of the harassment of Quakers was traceable to loosely written laws. Legislators, panic-stricken by irrational fear of Jesuit plots, were in a state of hysteria. A new statute, the so-called Conventicle Act, hastily drawn to limit nonconformist meetings, could be construed to punish almost any group whatever. Witch hunters, professional informers, and spies, whom the Quakers called "pettifogging caterpillars" or "the Devil's nut-hooks," denounced guilty and innocent alike in order to reap the bounties offered for uncovering subversives. Judges and jurymen uncritically accepted accusations made by scaremongers and *agents provocateurs*.

Much of the Quaker leadership was in prison. George Fox and William Russell, the owner of Old Jordan's, had been convicted on false charges; the accuser, Penn was told, was a villain, a cattle thief who had narrowly escaped the gallows. Another professional informer was "a fellow egregiously wicked and debauched—a man tenfold more a child of the Devil—a savage brute more a monster than a man."[3]

Wild rumors were afloat that George Fox and Margaret Fell, his wife, believing themselves the reincarnations of Abraham and Sarah, were expecting a messiah to be born to them. Why an anonymous "North Country Gentleman" wrote to William about this, or just what Penn was supposed to do about it, was not suggested, but the silly fabrication had to be dispelled.[4]

What, in any case, could he do at Wanstead? He had no use whatever for the billiard table where the Admiral liked to play; while he enjoyed gardening, he had no time to tend his mother's elaborate boxwood maze. Though his parents would have enjoyed hearing of his adventures, William would not loll about in Wanstead's luxurious turkey-work chairs chattering about inconsequentials. Sir William and Lady Penn would have been only too happy to give great dinner parties, not so much to honor their son as to show off Wanstead's fifteen dozen tablecloths, twenty-two pairs of sheets, and its three-hundred pounds of pewter tableware, but William, though he liked to eat well, would not cooperate.[5]

After only a week at Wanstead, William Penn moved to London. His purposes, with so many leaders imprisoned, were to help direct the Society of Friends and, more important, to defend fundamental English freedoms against repeated encroachments by the Stuarts or by the Established Church. He had no quarrel with either the monarchy or the clergy, for the King had every right to rule, provided that he listened to the people's will, and Anglicans had every right to worship as they pleased, provided that they accorded that right to others. Neither church nor state, however, could be allowed to change, much less to cancel, divine rights guaranteed by scripture nor human rights sanctified by law or ancient custom. Most important of these rights was that of every man to worship God in accordance with his individual convictions, assuming, of course, his form of worship violated no moral law and did not interfere with anyone else.

In Penn's view, both church and state were guilty of infringement upon man's liberty of conscience. He had no quarrel with those who fined, jailed, or even executed violators of laws firmly based upon the Ten Commandments, the Golden Rule, and any other scriptural revelation, but he demanded freedom of conscience as a God-given right, and such other privileges as life, liberty, and the enjoyment of property as were guaranteed to Englishmen by ancient precedent. Those basic rights were everlasting and unassailable; for overlord or priest to interfere was tyranny.

To challenge church persecution and royal tyranny, Penn deliberately invited a court test of an Englishman's rights to free speech, free assembly, and freedom of worship. On August 14, 1670, he and two associates, Captain William Meade, a recently converted London dry-goods dealer, and Thomas Rudyard, a Quaker attorney, attempted to hold a religious service. As this was to be a Quaker meeting, not an Anglican service, and conducted in violation of the Conventicle Act, without official permission, constables blocked the doors of the meeting-house on Grace Church Street, near Penn's old home on Tower Hill. When Penn's group, unable to enter, gathered in the street, constables arrested Meade for something he had done two months before and Rudyard and Penn, the Quakers said, on some vague and flimsy charge.[6]

In order to set up a clear-cut case of denial of freedom of worship, all three submitted peacefully. Unfortunately, a minor scuffle in the crowd of three-hundred people, for which none of the arrested men was responsible, changed the excuse for the arrests from violation of the Conventicle Act, which would have brought them before a summary court, to conspiracy to incite a riot, which required a jury trial. Thus, a test case intended to examine the legality of religious freedom widened into an examination of the jury system.[7]

The proceedings that ensued were, by present standards, incredible. Rudyard, for some reason, was not brought up for trial as yet, but Penn and Meade appeared at the Old Bailey wearing hats. As they were about to enter the courtroom, a bailiff snatched off the offending head-gear only to clap the hats back on again by order of the Lord Mayor, Sir Samuel Starling, the presiding judge. As soon as this was done, Starling fined both Quakers £5 each because hat-wearing in court constituted an act of contempt.[8]

Penn, who acted throughout the trial as though expecting to be convicted by a highly prejudiced court, protested the fine. Both heads were bare, he pointed out, when he and Meade had crossed the court-room threshold. If anyone was to be fined for wearing a hat in the presence of the judge, it must either be the bailiff who had replaced the hats or else the person who had ordered the replacement to be made; in other words, Starling should really fine himself. Starling retorted, with some degree of justice, that the defense was frivolous, since obviously the Quakers had fully intended to wear their hats, and so the fines should stand. Though both defendants refused to pay the fines, Starling ordered the trial continued, "for all you are Penn's son who starved the sailors."

For a man who had received some slight legal training, Penn's manner, as his own attorney, was peculiar. Not only did he expect conviction, but he actually seemed to invite it, quite possibly in order to set up an appeal to a higher tribunal. He had no respect whatever for the law for whose violation he was being tried, and he had every justification for his disrespect, but his manner at the trial was such that had he been acquitted, he might still have been guilty of contempt of court. When the recorder, John Howell, read the indictment and called upon the defendants to plead guilty or not guilty, Penn answered with what the court considered impertinence. "The question," said Penn, "is not whether I am guilty under the indictment but whether the indictment is legal." Howell retorted that, regardless of the indictment's legality, both Penn and Meade were guilty under the common law.

"But what is common law?" Penn asked. "That law which is not in being is so far from being common that it is no law at all."

"It is unwritten," Howell explained. *"Lex non scripta,* that which men have studied thirty or forty years to know, and would you have me tell you in a moment?"

"If it is so hard to understand," Penn countered, "it is far from being very common."

The repartee was quick and sharp and in its elements of humor revealed an entirely new side of William Penn; moreover, Howell had incautiously let himself in for it, but it could be considered by an unfriendly court as verging on contempt. In any case, the quibbling was not the type of argument to appeal to judges whose minds were already made up.

Further proceedings gave Penn even more ground for protest. After hearing witnesses for the prosecution, but denying Penn the right to cross-examine, and after refusing Penn the right to subpoena witnesses for the defense, the judge asked the jury for a verdict. While the jurymen considered the one-sided evidence, Penn and Meade were to be locked up. Again Penn objected: "Must I be taken away," he shouted, "because I plead for the fundamental rights of Englishmen?"

To everyone's amazement, the jury brought in a verdict acquitting Meade and finding Penn guilty of nothing but speaking in the streets. This would have been enough in itself, under existing law, to send him to prison, except that the prosecution had charged the defendants with conspiracy to incite a riot. By convicting one man only, and that on a charge for which he had not been indicted, the jury had really found Penn guilty only of conspiring with himself, which obviously was impossible. As for the accusation of incitement to riot, for which either man, or both, could have been found guilty, that charge would have collapsed because no witnesses, pro-prosecution though they all were, had testified about anything that either Penn or Meade had said or done.

Starling lost his temper. The verdict, he declared, was against the weight of evidence, as certainly it was, since the defense had not been allowed to present any witnesses whatever. For what the judge considered a miscarriage of justice he blamed the jury's foreman, Edward Bushell. Recorder Howell, echoing the judge, added that Bushell, that "scheming, canting fellow," was a worse offender than either of the defendants and was, in fact, worse than any other person who had come before the court that day. Starling sent the jury back to reconsider; they were to remain locked up without food, drink, or toilet facilities until they found both Penn and Meade guilty as charged.

The action was a clear violation of the English jury system. The jury rebelled. Even the four men who reputedly had voted on early ballots for conviction resented Starling's attempt to intimidate them. The twelve men remained imprisoned for two full days, undergoing what must have been a difficult, if not painful, ordeal, before coming back with a new verdict. Instead of convicting Penn and Meade, they now declared both men innocent!

Starling ordered the men to think again, and to think as he commanded them to think, else he would have them watched day and night to find some excuse on which to arrest them. Howell went further: it was a shame, he said, that England did not have something like the Spanish Inquisition to deal with such stubborn people; at the very least their noses should be slit. And when, in spite of this attempted coercion, the jurors stubbornly refused to change their verdict, Starling fined every one of them because, he alleged, they had broken their oaths to return an honest verdict. The jurymen, as stiff-necked as Penn or Meade, refused to pay, so everyone was sent to jail. Sharing quarters with Penn and Meade, all were to stay until they paid their fines.

Admiral Sir William, then on his deathbed, heard of this travesty of a trial and urged his son to pay the fine imposed for wearing the hat and so regain his freedom. Quaker William refused; his conscience, he replied, would not permit him to yield.

"I could not suffer on a better account or by a worse hand," he explained, "I am truly grieved to hear of thy present confinement," he added, "I desire thee not to be troubled by my present confinement."[9]

Nevertheless, someone, probably the Admiral, paid the fine for Penn and Meade, but the courageous jurors remained in jail for two long months, despite the hundred or more demands they made for their release. Eventually, in November, they went free on writs of habeas corpus, and four years later Chief Justice John Vaughan, ruling on Bushell's claim for compensation for false arrest, confirmed for all time a jury's freedom from coercion by the bench. His decision, famous in British law as the Rule in Bushell's Case, affirmed the innocence of all those whom Starling had imprisoned in the Penn-Meade trial and upheld all the jurymen's contentions, but, oddly enough, condemned Bushell for asking redress; his bringing suit for false arrest, said Vaughan, was a worse offense than anything committed by Samuel Starling.[10]

Meanwhile, ten days after William's release, Admiral Penn died at the age of forty-nine. In accordance with the pious fictions then thought proper, he was credited with having delivered a deathbed speech commending his soul to God, exhorting his children to live righteously, and approving, in elaborate detail, his son's devotion to Quaker principles. He may, indeed, have spoken words that could have been thus construed (such action would have been greatly to his credit), but the speech as reported was lengthy, intricately phrased, and full of sentiments never before expressed by him. It concluded with a hope that King Charles II and his brother James, the presumptive successor, would show kindness toward his eldest son. The appeal would explain many of the Royal favors William was later to receive.[11]

William buried his father in St. Mary's Redcliffe Church in Bristol, the city of the Admiral's birth; he also composed a memorial to be erected to his father's memory. Anyone who ever believed that Sir William had misused his son would have been disabused by seeing a letter to the Admiral's colleagues of the Naval Commission in which the son professed his earnest desire to hold sacred even the smallest relic of his father's achievements.[12]

Less than a fortnight after the funeral, Penn and Rudyard set to work and compiled a Bill of Exceptions to the biased and prejudicial actions of Lord Mayor Sir Samuel Starling in the Penn-Meade trial. To this was added a Rudyard treatise on the rights of juries. The two articles appeared as a pamphlet, The People's Ancient and Just Liberties Asserted.

Starling replied by an immediate and vehement Answer to the Tedious and Scandalous Pamphlet in which he called William "this wild, rambling colt" and went on to condemn the Admiral as a "renegade worse than three Turks."

Stung by this gratuitous attack which had nothing to do with the lawsuit, William published Truth Rescued from Impostors, subtitled

A Brief Reply to a Mere Rhapsody of Lies, Follies, and Slanders, a spirited defense of the Admiral against all the false gossip that had circulated about Sir William's naval career.

War by pamphlet was not sufficient for Sir Samuel Starling. He enlisted the aid of Sir John Robinson, now a fellow judge, a neighbor and supposed friend of the Penn family, but Penn's jailer in the Tower. The two laid traps for both Penn and Rudyard. The first step was to raid Rudyard's house in the middle of the night and to throw him into jail on charges of inciting riot and sedition. Freed by a writ of habeas corpus, Rudyard was rearrested for obstructing justice. Acquitted of this charge, he was again arrested for having been present at the Grace Church assembly; found guilty, he was sentenced to Newgate prison.[13]

Penn, meanwhile, was continuing his letter writing, telling Pepys of his unhappiness at being "misrepresented by some and wonderfully misunderstood by others," complaining to the Vice-Chancellor of Oxford, whom he called "a poor mushroom," against persecution of Quakers in that university, and asking Parliament to substitute solemn averments, affirmations, promises, or attestations in the place of oaths.[14]

But Starling and Robinson continued their quest for vengeance. Hearing through spies, Penn supposed, of a scheduled religious meeting for which no permit had been issued, they drafted a warrant in advance and sent constables to arrest Penn as soon as he should begin to speak.[15]

Again the proceedings were extraordinary. Robinson, the presiding justice, should, by legal ethics, have disqualified himself as judge because of his long association with the Penns, but instead he pretended not to know William when the case came up before him. Penn, acting as his own attorney, again quibbled. The Quaker meeting was not, he contended, a religious gathering, hence the Conventicle Act under which he was rearrested did not apply to him. Reminded that laws forbade dissenting clergymen from speaking in certain areas, he admitted having been in a restricted area, but though one of the cherished Quaker beliefs was that every Friend was a minister of God, he denied being a clergyman. Strictly speaking he was correct, for there had been no specific ordination ceremony, but the denial did not convince Sir John Robinson.

Robinson, like Recorder Howell, committed the error of bandying words with William Penn. Following the hair-splitting on the meaning of the word "clergyman," Robinson pointed out that scholars, as well as clerics, were barred from those restricted areas, to which Penn answered that he was no scholar. Then Robinson fell back upon the argument that the laws prohibited unlawful assembly, upon which Penn argued that no one had ever defined the implication of those loose words. William further infuriated Robinson by challenging Sir John's judicial methods; the judge, he said, was patching together isolated scraps of law taken from all sorts of sources.

Tired of the pointless wrangling, Robinson resorted to the infallible device used by anti-Quaker judges; he demanded that Penn take the oath of allegiance, and when William predictably refused, sent him to jail. In sentencing Penn, Robinson added gratuitously, "You have been as bad as other folks, abroad and at home, too."

Penn seized an opportunity. "I make a bold challenge to all men, women and children on earth, justly to accuse me of ever having seen me drunk, heard me swear, utter a curse, or speak one obscene word.— I trample thy slander as dirt."

"Well, Mr. Penn," Robinson answered, "I have no ill will toward you; your father was my friend. I have a good deal of kindness toward you."

"Thou hast an ill way of expressing it," commented William.

This time Penn went to Newgate, a prison not intended, like the Tower, for political offenders, but for those whom Thomas Ellwood called "the veriest rogues and meanest sort of felons and pickpockets—if they come in bad they do not go out better, for they instruct one another in their art." Thomas Rudyard, who was already there, would have rented accommodations in what was called the Master's Room, but William refused preferential treatment as undemocratic. Instead, he entered the Common Room, crowded with upwards of a hundred convicts of all sorts, ages, conditions, and degrees of health. The stink that pervaded the jail was such, Ellwood reported, as to spread sickness. Penn, however, was luckier than Ellwood; he did not see the dirty buckets filled with the quartered bodies of executed criminals, nor meet "the nasty sluts" who, Ellwood says, thronged the Common Room.[16]

Here, in a jail so filthy after four hundred years of constant overcrowding that Penn said the Lord Mayor would not use it for his pigs, Penn remained six months. If Charles and James were in any way moved by the Admiral's deathbed plea that they befriend his son, they, too, had an ill way of showing their concern, for they could have pardoned him or set him free without conditions.

In the midst of the discomfort, dirt, noise, and wild debaucheries of Newgate, Penn somehow managed to complete a surprising amount of writing. Even if, as during the incarceration in the Tower, wardens had special instructions to accord him some measure of privacy, his ability to concentrate under such conditions as well as to ward off curious fellow prisoners while he worked was amazing.

The output ran a gamut. Penn wrote to the English sheriffs complaining about insulting jailers and their stinking prisons. He assured Parliament that Quakers denounce all plots and conspiracies as "horrible impiety." He answered a Catholic who protested that Penn was too severe in criticizing papist tracts. He attacked persecutors who were hounding Quakers on the Isle of Ely. He composed a testimony to Josiah Coale, "a faithful servant of the Lord," a tribute that concluded, "And therefore woes to the dark, hellish, sin-pleasing, persecuting priests, professors and profane of the whole earth." In collaboration with George Whitehead (one wonders how the two men, one free, the other a prisoner, managed to confer), he wrote *A Serious Apology for the People Called Quakers*, exposing "the malicious aspersions, erroneous doctrines and horrid blasphemies" of Thomas Jenner and Timothy Taylor.

William even wrote a poem "An Holy Triumph," which he sent to "Dr. G. M. Springett"; the salutation doubtless stood for "dear" or "darling."

> Your gaols and prisons we defy
> By bonds we'll keep our libertie
> Nor shall your racks and torments make
> Us, e'er our meetings to forsake.
>
> . . . .
>
> And overturn for evermore
> False prophet, dragon and the whore.

Upon his release, Penn, after seeing George Fox embark in August 1671, for America, went abroad himself to organize meetings in the Netherlands and Germany. This was an important mission, for another purpose was to win over to Quakerism the members of a Dutch commune that taught a doctrine akin to that of the Society of Friends. The Bible, the members declared, could be properly interpreted only by the light shed upon the soul by the Holy Spirit.[17]

The leaders of the Cloister of the Evangelic Church at Amsterdam were interesting people. Jean de Labadie, a Jesuit-trained rector of a French university, who had turned against Catholicism and been hailed in Geneva as "a second Calvin," believed that "within the church" all goods should be held in common; he also held that prophecy was not confined to Biblical times but was continuous, and that Sabbaths, too, should be continuous. His co-leader, Anna Maria van Schurmann, a Dutch bluestocking reputed to know eleven languages including Arabic, Syriac, Ethiopian, and Chaldean, was a pioneer advocate of women's rights. Both were classicists, but not of a school that would have delighted William Penn, for she, at least, professed that only Homer and Virgil were worth reading, the other ancients being nothing more than "poisonous drink."[18]

On arriving in Holland, Penn argued with de Labadie, but found him "airy and unstable," nothing more than "a sect master." Anna Maria also was light-minded, placing great store by singing and dancing. Evidently the authorities thought so too, for they ordered the Labadists to "prove their spiritual joy" more quietly.

Penn therefore left the Netherlands for Westphalia in Germany to meet Princess Elizabeth, the Protestant Abbess of Herford. She was the granddaughter of James I but was more renowned in Europe as the favorite pupil of Descartes. She gave Penn a warm and friendly reception but could not be persuaded to accept Quakerism.

Back in England in the autumn, Penn resumed his desk duties, having become, in the absence of George Fox, the acting director of Friends' activities. He was hale, hearty, and very hard at work.

FREEDOM TO THINK

REEDOM OF CONSCIENCE, FOR ALL WHO BELIEVE IN GOD AND FOLLOW
SCRIPTURAL PRECEPTS, WAS IN PENN'S MIND THE MOST IMPORTANT
HUMAN RIGHT. CONVINCED OF ITS NECESSITY WHILE STILL A CHILD, AND
strengthened in that conviction by the teachings of Penington, Owen,
and Amyraut, he never deviated from its advocacy. In private conversation, in speeches, and in publication, in a stream of letters to statesmen
and rulers in England and on the Continent, he demanded complete
liberty of religious thought.[1]

Denial of what he considered this basic human right was for William
Penn the most flagrant form of tyranny. Beginning, immediately after his
convincement, with his protest to the Earl of Orrey against persecution of
Quakers by the mayor of Cork, Penn waged campaigns for toleration
for almost half a century.[2]

There would be no point in listing all the many occasions when
William Penn argued for toleration of nonconformity. His thesis remained unchanged: man's conscience belonged to God alone. Neither
mortal rulers nor human institutions were privileged, or even qualified,
to dictate to it or to attempt control. Man's communion with his God
was an area that none other might invade.

No government agency, Penn would have said, could be as abhorrent
to the Lord as that Spanish Inquisition for which Recorder Howell
yearned at the Penn-Meade trial. Establishment of an official religion,
Penn contended, had no scriptural authority; moreover, it violated the
best traditions of the past. Nothing in Penn's reading revealed that the
great classical empires, not Persia, Greece, or Rome in its days of freedom,
forced their subjects into the strait jacket of an established church; on
the contrary, they welcomed foreign gods, admitting them into their

[73]

pantheons. More significantly, some nations, fearful lest an alien deity had unwittingly been overlooked, had gone so far as to erect shrines to "the unknown god." Of course, he admitted, there had been persecutions, bloody mistreatments, as of the Christian martyrs in imperial Rome, but here there were two matters to be considered: those persecutions had not begun until after the high ethical and moral standards of the republic had been weakened, nor did the empire long survive after the persecutions began. Socrates had been forced by "the priests" to drink the hemlock, but not for worshipping in some unconventional manner; his alleged offense, a trumped-up charge, was corrupting the youth.

But why go back to ancient Greece and Rome? Hospitality to gods and to one's own variety of worship had characterized the wandering Germanic tribes; the Saxons who had come to England had been as fond of liberty, freedom, and toleration as were the classic empires. The security of person, property, and religious freedom existed among Britons long before the Norman Conquest. Those rights, Penn declared, flourished in England long before the Church itself.

No one need fear ill effects from religious toleration, Penn insisted. A diversity of beliefs and forms of worship actually strengthens the established church, he said, for open competition allows it to know its opponents and to defend itself more efficiently than it could against a secret enemy. So, too, is the king safer, for his people rest more easily. Diversity in religious practice, far from weakening religion, really strengthens it.

While Penn's historical deductions may be questioned (he sometimes mistook peace in religious affairs as proof of tolerance rather than of an absence of rival sects), he held steadfast to the principles they taught him. "I owe my conscience to no mortal man," he had said in 1668, and from that conviction he never strayed.[3]

Nor did he believe that others should dare invade a realm that belonged exclusively to God. In protesting the maltreatment of Quakers in Poland he reminded King John Sobieski that a predecessor, Stephen (Istvan) Bathory, had refused to limit freedom of conscience. "I am king of men, not of conscience," Stephen had said, "king of bodies, not of souls."[4]

To his infinite credit, Penn defended the right of every other individual to an equal right to worship as he pleased. "I have bowels for mankind," he told Dr. Tillotson, the cleric appointed to reason with him in the Tower. "I dare not deny to others what I crave for myself, I mean liberty for the exercise of my religion."[5]

"I deplore two principles in religion," he said on another occasion, "obedience upon authority without conviction and destroying them that differ with me for Christ's sake."[6]

Penn's rejection of authorized persecution of those who did not accept established church practices by no means implied that he was indifferent to beliefs and ceremonies of which he disapproved. His demand that others enjoy the same freedom he wished to enjoy did not bar him, nor, he would have admitted, should it bar others, from making strong, impassioned and, to modern ears, too fevered criticism of other religions, but that did not justify persecution.

During his stay in Ireland he read, just before New Year's 1671, a Jesuit tract that so angered him that within two months he wrote and published *A Seasonable Caveat Against Popery*. His fear and dislike of Catholicism was ingrained. There would be further attacks upon Romanists. He warned voters to be on their guard against papists who might run as "disguised Protestants ready to pull off their masks when the time serves." Elect only sincere Protestants, he advised.[7]

It speaks well for the tolerance of Charles II, who leaned toward Catholicism, and later of his brother, James II, a confessed communicant, that despite Penn's open opposition to the Roman faith, he remained welcome at Whitehall. There may well have been, as some supposed, a political motive for their continued patronage of William Penn, in that his pleas for toleration benefited Catholics quite as much as they favored Quakers, but the two monarchs, with every reason for showing anger against Penn, remained his friends. The attitude could not have been wholly due to Admiral Sir William's deathbed wish.

Even more remarkable is the fact that, despite those anti-Catholic pamphlets, many Englishmen seriously believed that William Penn himself was one of the masked Catholics against whom he warned. No one with even the sketchiest knowledge of Penn's personality, his mode of life, his writings, or his preachings could credit such a rumor; yet once Thomas Vincent put the gossip into circulation, there were Englishmen gullible enough, or fanatical enough, to believe it. The obvious fact that Penn was engaged to be married, that no one had ever seen him in a Catholic church, nor in company with any prelate, failed to convince those who wanted to believe him hypocritical. The very lack of proof, they contended, in a sort of twisted logic, showed only that he was indeed a Catholic. His anti-papal utterances, they maintained, were a common Jesuitical deception. Those monks were trained to lie and to deceive; they carried dispensations absolving them for anything that they might say or do in getting the better of a heretic. The real, incontrovertible proof of Penn's Jesuitism was his repeated, brazen, and scandalous refusal to lay his hand upon the Bible and swear to uphold the King of England and to renounce the Pope.

Oh yes, the anti-Quaker publicists conceded, Penn always quoted the Scriptures in declaring that he had been ordered by the apostle James, even by the Lord Jesus Christ Himself, to swear no oaths at any time, to anyone, on any matter whatsoever. He had even contributed to a symposium entitled *A Treatise on Oaths*. But what was his refusal to swear allegiance to the king but a flat confession that he wished the Pope and not the rightful Stuart king to rule the English people?

Foremost among the verbal and literary snipers were two indefatigable pamphleteers, John Faldo and Francis Bugg, against whom Penn contended for years. Faldo disliked the Society of Friends; like Vincent he considered Quakerism "a near approach to Popery." In abusing Penn and his associates, Faldo, as even his apologists admitted, was colorful, unrestrained, and sometimes downright offensive. In these years of dueling by pamphlet Francis Bugg was the more persistent. Originally a Quaker, after being fined £15, Bugg made peace with the conformists. Some say that in consideration of his becoming an informer for the authorities he recovered a portion of the fine. He showed his gratitude by reporting that his aunt, one of the highly esteemed Quaker ladies, was "a most notorious liar," and by continuing over a twenty-year period to publish books attacking Penn.

There were constant "revelations" of Penn's supposed depravity. That Quaker soft-talk that everyone should throw away his weapons, turn the other cheek, and never raise a hand against a fellow human being—all that was a damnable trick to disarm the unwary. Penn was not a pacifist at all, nor had he ever been; had he not, like his father, the Admiral, fought in Ireland? Actually, said the sensationalists, he was a military man and there was a portrait in armor to prove it.

Hypocrisy was not the only alleged Penn failing. The strait-laced preacher who so constantly argued for righteous living, who said so often that plays and games and all amusements were evil and that light talk and jesting were to be deplored, had been, by his own admission, a willing participant in the corrupt court orgies at Versailles, frittering away his time in the vain, and doubtless loose, worldly entertainment that he would deny to others.

All this was unjust and greatly overdrawn, to say the least, but there was more to come. Penn talked, with evident emotion and seemingly with sincerity, about forgiveness of the shortcomings of others, for the absolute necessity that all men should love one another. These sentiments were beautiful and heartfelt, but unfortunately they were only too easily perverted by his ill-wishers. Who, his enemies asked, knew better how to enjoy love? Who was a better authority than William Penn on love, if not the love of all mankind, then, certainly of the private, unconventional, and unsanctified variety? What about that young lady in Ireland whom Lord Shannon, Orrery's brother, twitted him about? Or the "little friend" in London "who thinks you mad"? Not all the tales told about the antics of Dublin's Society of Friendship dealt with such high-minded matters as musical and dramatic criticism.

The whisperings, the misunderstandings, and the downright lies could be endured because they were so obviously false; what was more serious was the uncertainty whether Lady Penn was happy with her son's plans for his future. For more than two years, he and Guli had been, as Thomas Ellwood put it, "reserved for one another," but as yet approval of their engagement had not been sought from the Society of Friends. The reason for the delay is none too clear. During much of the time he had been away from home, either abroad on business for his family or for the Quakers or in prison, but even allowing for these interruptions, there had been plenty of time to ask the Society's approval. Yet though all their intimates knew of their intentions, William and Guli had not applied for the Society's consent.

The best guess is that Lady Penn was unenthusiastic about the match. No evidence exists to show displeasure at her son's desire to marry a Quaker, but Margaret had little sympathy with Quaker beliefs, activities, or associations, and though Guli and the Peningtons were rich and of good family, the marriage would not further the hopes that she and the Admiral had cherished for William's career. It is possible that the public announcement had been postponed in hopes of winning her consent.

Whatever the reason for delay, on February 7, 1672, William Penn of Walthamstow and Gulielma Maria Springett of Tyler's Green asked approval of Jordan's Friends Meeting for their intended marriage.

The unusual addresses seem to imply that William was not living with his mother at Wanstead nor Guli with her relatives at Amersham, but neither implication is correct. Both William and Guli lived slightly beyond the legal boundaries of their villages and so were registered, or would have been had they been Anglicans, in parishes other than those of their towns.

In accordance with Quaker custom, Jordan's Meeting appointed two members to inquire into the propriety of the match, one being Ellwood, once Guli's suitor but now happily married. To no one's astonishment, all reports were favorable, and on April 4, 1672, a full month after receiving the Society's permission, William and Guli were married.

For some reason the ceremony took place not in Guli's home, nor at Jordan's, but in the low-ceiling, stone-flagged great hall at King's Farm, a fourteenth-century structure near Amersham. Ellwood, all the Peningtons, and Margaret and Richard Penn signed the certificate as witnesses. Penn's sister Peg was conspicuously absent, probably because her Yorkshire home was distant, but maybe because her brother William had not attended the christening of her baby. Baptism, said William, was a pagan ceremony.

Leaving the Wanstead mansion to Margaret and Richard, the newlyweds rented Basing House, a two-story red-brick building near Rickmansworth, not far from Jordan's or Amersham but twenty miles away from Wanstead. It was a pleasant residence, with a walled garden, a lawn and great linden trees. It also had a history. An earlier house, built on a site commanding the main road from the western counties to London, had been the seat of Sir John Paulet, fifth Marquis of Winchester, a monarchist who on every windowpane had scratched with a diamond the words *"Aimez loyauté."* In the Civil War it was still a royalist stronghold which the Cromwellians had besieged for three months before it was leveled to the ground.[8]

The new mansion was in a fashionable neighborhood, and some of their neighbors must have told them of the Basing House history, but politically Rickmansworth could have been dangerous. Nearby, at Moor Park, once Cardinal Wolsey's county seat, lived James Scott, Duke of Monmouth. The tall, handsome, illegitimate son of Charles II was unhappy at being passed over as the successor to the throne. He would, in time, lead a rebellion; other malcontents lived nearby.

Though Penn lived apart from his neighbors, he was far from being in retirement. With George Fox still in America, though his return was momentarily expected, Penn's supervision over established meetings and the creation of new Quaker centers led him, through an oppressively rainy summer and autumn, to take many trips. Penn's frequent absences from Guli because of his missionary work, and his absorption with his writing while at home, aroused considerable speculation among his neighbors. One current legend, wholly unsubstantiated, alleged a love affair with a mistress of the Duke of Monmouth. The story gained such currency that it remained in circulation for many years.[9] Yet Penn had no time for dalliance; on one swing through Kent and Sussex he attended twenty-one meetings for worship in as many days.

When at home he was equally busy, reading Quaker manuscripts for prepublication approval, directing Quaker activities, drafting appeals to various officials as far distant as Bremen and Danzig, who were unfairly treating Quakers. He pleaded with Lord Baltimore, proprietor of Maryland, as previously he had pleaded with the King, not to consider Quakers disloyal just because they had conscientious scruples against swearing oaths.[10]

Philip Ford, his work at Shanagarry finished, headed Penn's Basing House staff. He was now receiving £80 a year for duties that consisted, in large part, of managing Penn's financial interests. For Penn, now very well off with the income from Sir William's estate and from Guli's £10,000 rent roll, had surprisingly little interest in financial matters. To care for his revenues, drawn from estates in Ireland, which Penn described as his "principle verb," from landholdings in England and from small commercial ventures recommended by Ford, would have been troublesome and time consuming. To manage them properly would have detracted from his more important activities for the Society of Friends.[11]

Ford lifted the burden from Penn's shoulders, recruiting Philip Theodore Lehnmann, born in Saxony but later a Bristol schoolteacher, as Penn's private secretary. Though Lehnmann worked fourteen years for Penn, beginning with odd jobs at ten shillings each, Penn never mastered the man's name, referring to him indiscriminately as Lehman, Lemon, or Le Main. Ford solved the difficulty by calling him Philip the German.

Ford took money matters entirely into his own hands, receiving rents and other income, settling bills, large and small. He paid burial expenses for the Admiral (£56 8s), which Penn had left unpaid for a year and a half; he gave the clergyman and the sexton fifteen shillings in fees. Ford also paid the expenses of William's eighteen-year-old brother Richard, who was receiving twice as much per year as Ford was paid.[12]

To list prices is misleading, for costs have risen astronomically since the 1670s, but the Penn family was buying shoes in dozen lots at an average cost of 3s 3d per pair. For what may have been a special shopping binge Ford settled Lady Penn's purchase of 2½ yards of silk, 18 yards of staying tape, and 17 dozen buttons, all for less than ten shillings. Guli was buying bombazine at two shillings per yard, one of Ford's hoods at fifty shillings, and an £8 cloak.

Ford even carried Penn's pocketbook for minor expenses. Scrupulously he listed every expenditure, down to a penny for "gully-pot," whatever that was. When Penn met "a poorman" on the road and wished to be generous, he had Ford give him sixpence; a luckless fellow whose house had just burned down received five shillings, about a fifth of the amount that Ford had just paid for oysters.

The account books reveal how completely, and how carelessly, Penn relied upon Ford's honesty. The confidence seemed well placed, for Ford, despite his business failures, enjoyed an admirable reputation among the Friends. His marriage, in 1672, to Bridget Gosnel was as glittering a social event as Quaker custom would permit, with Penn, Whitehead, Ellwood, and John Fenwick, later of New Jersey, signing as witnesses.

Ford was, however, under strong temptation. With so much money passing through his fingers, with freedom to set his own figures as to costs and with virtually no supervision (for Penn usually approved accounts without really looking at them), the temptation to tamper with the petty cash called for a treasurer of exceptional honesty. Penn trusted him completely.

Rickmansworth gave Penn a very welcome freedom to meditate, to write, and to plan for the Society of Friends. Guli's household efficiency, Ford's business management, and Lehnmann's secretarial help allowed him to concentrate on the public services that he performed so well. The few years at Rickmansworth were full of happiness. Unfortunately, they were not to last. Tragedy struck. In the midst of an extremely cold winter a baby girl was born, only to die within two months. Exactly a fortnight later, William's eighteen-year-old brother Richard also died.[13]

Richard's death raised a problem about which nothing was written and perhaps little said but which must have caused considerable concern. He and his mother had been living in the great Wanstead mansion, but with Richard gone, the widowed Lady Penn was left alone. Whether William and Guli suggested that she move into Basing House or whether she preferred to stay where she had lived so long is not known, but remain she did, in a town where she must have had many friends; in Rickmansworth or in Yorkshire with her married daughter she would have been a stranger.

Things were changing for the Penns, though they may not have sensed it at the time. Word came at last, in July 1673, that George Fox had landed at Bristol, after a transatlantic passage so remarkably swift that Fox believed that God Himself had filled the sails. William and Guli, with other Quaker leaders, hastened to join him there. There was much to talk about. Quakers, as a rule, wasted little time on small talk, but Penn and his companions must have told Fox that the heaviest floods in history were ruining the crops and that a plague of flies was punishing England for its sins. Penn reported on his trip to Holland, where the Labadists had been so obdurate, and to Germany, where the Princess Elizabeth had been so kind. Fox would have heard, while still in America, that the English and French were allied against the Dutch and that, in consequence, to assure a united front at home, King Charles had allowed dissenters to worship freely; he may also have heard that, in consequence of that action, some five hundred prisoners, many of them Quakers, had been freed from jail. He may not have known, however, that Parliament, indignant at the King's assumption of the right to suspend laws, had forced him to repudiate his action, and had passed a Test Act requiring all officials to swear allegiance to Anglicanism.

Penn must also have told Fox about the numerous verbal and literary arguments, especially with an inveterate Quaker enemy, one Ludovici Muggleton, who had called the founder "a great, old fat fox" and Penn "a young spruce serpent" who, according to Muggleton, "knows less than a coach horse." William had retorted in the same vein, using epithets that Fox himself would have employed; he had called Muggleton a "presumptuous and blasphemous wretch" whom God would surely blast.[14]

There was better news to be told, that Charles II was not really hostile to Quakerism, if only because, after a disastrous battle, a young Quaker had once carried him on his back to safety. Penn said, too, that James, Duke of York, regarded Friends as "quiet and industrious people who led good lives."

If the monarch and the presumptive heir to the throne were tolerant, many other Englishmen were not. It was not a time of tolerance. After years of violent quarrels over governmental abuses and religious disputes, complicated by hysteric fears of treason and sedition, passions were running high. Englishmen were everywhere quite as suspicious of their neighbors as they were of foreigners. Morbid fears ran rampant. Anyone who in the slightest degree strayed from rigid conventional behavior, whose ideas varied from those socially, religiously, or morally accepted, who failed to conform to the folkways and mores of his class, was shunned as dangerous. Inevitably, all Quakers, more than other dissenters, were bound to be suspect. Their peculiar customs, traced by the Quakers to biblical precepts, were grievously misunderstood. Their plain talk not only set them apart from the rest of the community but offended many. Their refusal to doff their hats insulted those who, rightly or wrongly, claimed high social status or exalted official position.

There were worse misunderstandings. Quaker refusal to take up arms must mean that they were disloyal to their country. Their refusal to swear allegiance to the King "proved" that they were traitors bent on revolution. Their avoidance of Anglican church service "testified" either to their atheism or to their Jesuitism.

Freed as he now was from routine administrative duties by the return of George Fox, Penn set himself to the seemingly unending burden of correcting misconceptions about the Society of Friends. His task, self-imposed at first but soon an official duty, of reading and refuting anything that might be published or even spoken against Quakerism, kept him continually at his desk.

OVERSEAS OPENING

GEORGE FOX RETURNED FROM AMERICA FIRED WITH THE HOPE OF ESTABLISHING A QUAKER SETTLEMENT. TWO YEARS OF WANDERING THROUGH THE MIDDLE ATLANTIC COLONIES, THOSE VAST, FERTILE, undeveloped areas that so reminded him of western England, excited his desire to found an overseas utopia where his Quakers, the Society of Friends, could live in peace, worshiping as their consciences dictated, without annoying their neighbors or being persecuted by them.

The idea was not new. Both Fox and Penn had thought of establishing a religious haven. Penn's opening of joy at Oxford, the teachings of Amyraut and Owen, and possibly Sir William's talk about Jamaica and the New World that lay beyond, all nurtured the same thoughts in William's mind. Josiah Coale's enthusiastic reports about the upper Susquehanna, like Fox's praise of the seaboard and the river Delaware, proved that there were wide areas, unoccupied by white men, available for the erection of an ideal community where church and state would not invade each other's private sphere and where true Christian brotherhood might flourish. Fox and Coale envisioned a tolerant Quaker community in America; Penn made the dream come true.

He was not the first, to be sure, to plan a free, tolerant community in the New World, for Roger Williams in Rhode Island, the Calverts in Maryland, while John Berkeley and John Locke in the Carolinas had drafted basic plans for the Carolinas. Quakers were foremost, however, in urging a large-scale exodus of their people for the express purpose of worshiping in their own fashion. In conjunction with Anthony Ashley Cooper, Earl of Shaftesbury, they had been considering moving to the Carolinas, for Shaftesbury had promised that if they would settle, within five years, a town of thirty houses and one-hundred people, he would let them have twelve-thousand acres.

The Shaftesbury connection fanned a mild unrest that was beginning to appear against Penn among some members of the Society of Friends. Penn's critics, by their constant reiteration of his supposed Jesuitism, had caused Quakers to suspect his sincerity. But though the Society as a whole valiantly defended Penn, the gossiping, whisperings, and misrepresentations exerted some slight effect. For one thing Penn was criticized for becoming involved in politics, thus confusing spiritual and material affairs. Penn was growing increasingly pessimistic about the future of civil liberty in England, and just about this time he ran across an account by Sir Bulstrode Whitelocke, a former ambassador to Sweden, of how Gustavus Adolphus had planned a sanctuary for the oppressed. Whitelocke reported that Gustavus Adolphus wished to establish in America a home where "every man should have enough to eat and toleration to worship God." That haven was to be at Zwaanendael, near Cape Henlopen on the lower Delaware. The free colony had never been founded, for one reason or another, but the plan made a deep impression on Penn; a few years later he wrote a biography of Sir Bulstrode.[1]

Wanstead had also talked excitedly and, one fears, not too charitably about a former neighbor, Sir Edmund Plowden, who had received a patent for Delaware Valley land to be called New Albion. His goal was not so much philanthropy, for he proposed setting up an aristocratic state; nor were his people pacifists, for instead of seeking to be helpful to one another, they mutinied while on the ocean, marooned Sir Edmund far from New Albion, and never did succeed in making a firm settlement.[2]

Yet a third effort at establishing a tolerant colony had been made. On July 28, 1663 a Dutch Mennonite, Peter Cornelis Plockhoy, had settled with forty others on the very site that Gustavus Adolphus had chosen. Plockhoy, unlike Plowden, did promise peace and toleration, but to Penn's disappointment, he limited those blessings; reputedly, his colony was not to harbor "usurious Jews or English stiff-necked Quakers."[3]

The reputation was probably slanderous. Plockhoy, like the Quakers, cherished religious freedom and, while not renouncing war, recognized the right of anyone to be a conscientious objector. Like Penn, he too planned a utopia. He had no wish that "servile slavery should ever burden the people." He frowned upon private wealth. Each of his twenty-five adults was to labor six hours daily at some useful occupation, the profits of the toil to be divided equally among all persons in the community over twenty years of age. His people would be honest and charitable, but to guard against the corroding influence of money, all public funds were to be kept in a strong box locked by three different keys, one in the hands of each of the three public officials.

Two years after the founding of his settlement, Plockhoy's experiment became a casuality of the Anglo–Dutch War, ravaged by the English "to a very nail," precisely the same description given to the Spanish wreckage of George Penn's property. Plockhoy escaped, returning, thirty years later, blind, hungry and in rags. He eked out some sort of existence on a piece of vacant land.[4]

The stories differ, however, concerning his reception. The local court, according to one version, offered him two building lots provided that, within a year, he would build himself a dwelling acceptable to local standards. If he failed to meet the requirements of this early zoning ordinance, he would lose his lots, be fined £10 and, apparently, be obliged to resume his travels.

Presumably, he fulfilled the requirements. Sixteen months later the court announced that Plockhoy had sworn allegiance to the King of England and fidelity to William Penn.

The second version, according, oddly enough, to an official brochure of the city of Lewes, declares, however, that Plockhoy went up to Germantown, which also offered him sanctuary, but without requiring a fine or mentioning the type of house he must construct.[5]

Though none of the projects had been successful, Penn, Fox, and the Quaker leaders in London knew that still another settlement was being made, this one with far better prospects of success. As far back as 1664, a year after Plockhoy's attempt, James, Duke of York, on the authority of his brother the King, deeded to Sir George Carteret and John, Lord Berkeley, Penn's Dublin friend, the land between the Hudson and the Delaware. The new proprietors named their province Nova Caesarea or New Jersey.[6]

Like so many early land grants, the gift was poorly worded. The patent set New Jersey's western boundary as the Delaware River but failed to specify whether this meant the middle of the stream or of the ship channel, or if, as the State of Delaware was later to contend, merely the low-water mark on the river's eastern shore. The oversight would lead in time to disputes between Penn's colony and the Crown as to who policed the waterway.[7]

Agents of the Crown, the Duke of York, and the Berkeley–Carteret partnership showed incredible carelessness or indifference. Charles II had granted his brother, the Duke, the right to govern the territory between the Hudson and the Delaware, but in transferring the area to the proprietors, the Duke had conveyed title only to the land, not to its government. Yet for years thereafter, the proprietors and their successors usurped the right to rule, unquestioned by the Duke, who held the legal right, or by the Crown, whose formal consent would have been requisite for a transfer of authority.

Announcement of the grant to Berkeley and Carteret, already proprietors of the Carolinas, closed off the last stretch of open seacoast to Quaker ownership. For a time, moreover, there seemed a distinct possibility that Quakers might be pushed still farther back into the interior. Almost as soon as they received their grant, Berkeley and Carteret dickered with the Duke of York for an exchange of territory whereby they would return to him the northern section of New Jersey, thus allowing him complete control over the excellent harbor of New York, if he would give them land extending twenty miles inland from the west bank of the Delaware. Fortunately, the trade was not effected, since the Duke possessed no title to that western land.[8]

Although hope seemed lost for a Quaker-controlled colony with access to the sea, Penn was enthusiastic over the Berkeley-Carteret policies. The proprietors were liberal-minded for the times, their sales terms were not exorbitant, though they did require an annual quitrent even after purchasers had bought and paid for acreage, and they had no intention of uniting church and state. George Fox had reported favorably on the climate and on the fertility of the soil.[9]

Neither Berkeley nor Carteret was democratically minded in any modern sense, but in order to attract settlers, they did offer special inducements to people who might be restless under England's strict authoritarianism. Calling again upon John Locke for his assistance, they redrafted in 1665 his Carolina frame of government, which neatly balanced proprietary privilege with popular participation. A colonial assembly of landowners and proprietors (they were called freeholders) was to enact the laws, but the proprietors reserved the right of veto; at the same time the frame guaranteed that no tax could be levied without the assembly's consent. Debates upon projected legislation were to be conducted in secret, but the general public was permitted to enter when voting on the proposed legislation was about to begin.

From the Quaker standpoint, and, for that matter, from the standpoint of nonconformists generally, New Jersey was to have complete liberty of conscience, together with the enjoyment of all basic English rights. This, of course, was the goal toward which William Penn had long been striving; he thoroughly approved the long steps thus projected toward political and social freedom.

Berkeley and Carteret, however, foresaw considerable opposition to their proposals. Charles II, like other Stuarts, was asserting the divine right of kings to rule; the New Jersey proprietors feared that the King and his advisors might think the plans too liberal, or even revolutionary. The proprietors, therefore, presented the project not as specific laws to be immediately effective but as concessions graciously handed down by them as overlords to their subject peoples. If the King or his courtiers should think that the liberties had been exacted by popular pressure, the program would certainly be vetoed by the King.[10]

To the Society of Friends the promise that in New Jersey everyone might worship as he pleased offered hope that here might be the longed-for religious refuge, but Penn, well acquainted with both Berkeley and Carteret, had more ambitious thoughts. Knowing that both men were in financial straits and that neither was especially interested in the province, he thought it might soon be possible to buy out one of the proprietors, if not both. His anticipations were well founded. Through circumstances that have never been made quite clear, Berkeley suddenly offered his lands for sale. Through arrangements that could have been neither accidental nor spontaneous, Berkeley suggested that a close friend, one Edward Byllinge, a London brewer and a Quaker, buy out his half of New Jersey. He offered to sell his four-thousand square miles for £1000 cash.[11]

Byllinge did not at the time have £1000, nor, had he possessed as much, would he have dared admit the wealth, for teetering as he was upon the brink of bankruptcy, his creditors would have attached the money. Providentially, however, Major John Fenwick appeared, money in hand, to lend Byllinge enough to buy the land.

Nothing whatever indicates that Fenwick, a rather undistinguished Cromwellian and for the last nine years a Quaker, would have been interested in overseas acreage. He had been in the livestock business, on a reasonably large scale, but he had always pastured his cattle and sheep on rented land. Thus far in his fifty-six years he had taken no part in colonial matters, nor, except for thirteen months' imprisonment for his Quakerism, had he been notably active in the Society of Friends. He had, however, a distant family relationship with Guli Penn, and at one time had rented land near her estates at Worminghurst in Sussex, but that was when Guli was only eight years old.[12] Nevertheless, on March 18, 1674, Fenwick, in association with Edward Byllinge, bought Lord Berkeley's half interest in New Jersey.

The purchase caused some speculation. Byllinge insisted that the money came from his own pocket, but that he had employed Fenwick, whom he may or may not have known before the transaction, in order to prevent creditors from demanding the money for themselves. Fenwick strenuously declared that he had lent the money to Byllinge on condition that he receive both a commission and interest on the loan.

There were those who doubted both stories, suspecting that Byllinge and Fenwick were straw men and that the real purchaser was a group of leading London Quakers. Just before Fenwick produced the £1000, they noted, Guli had sold some of her Sussex land, while Penn, hitherto well off, had borrowed £300 from a beneficial society set up by Quaker women "for the relief of distressed Quakers." Penn would scarcely have seemed eligible, but then a manager of the fund was Bridget Ford, wife of his business agent. The question rose whether Penn had raised the cash that Fenwick had lent to Byllinge.[13] Something, certainly, was amiss, else Penn would not have chided Fenwick for an unexplained action which "reflects on you both, and, what is worse, on the truth." Penn hoped that all would work out well to "hide your shame."[14]

As both Byllinge and Fenwick were Quakers, the Society of Friends, through London Monthly Meeting, stepped in to settle the dispute, choosing William Penn as arbiter. For all Penn's wide and deserved reputation for fair-mindedness, it is difficult to imagine that, had there been complete freedom of choice, Byllinge would have accepted a distant kinsman of his opponent as impartial. Yet any hope Fenwick may have entertained for special favor proved misplaced. Penn listened patiently to Fenwick's complaint that Byllinge had defaulted. His so-called partner, Fenwick said, had promised to reward him with a tenth of Berkeley's New Jersey land but had never done so, never even surveyed it, nor, for that matter, never indicated just where the promised tenth might be. When both sides had presented their respective cases, Penn decided against Fenwick. Fenwick should have his promised tenth, some four hundred square miles of land, but he must pay £100 for it. Instead of recovering £1000 he should get back only £900.[15]

Fenwick objected. The decision, he protested, gave him neither commission nor compensation for the use of his money. While he was happy to receive four hundred square miles at a cost of a penny per acre, he considered himself ill used, but there was nothing he could do to change the arbiter's award.

In course of time, regardless of the justice of Penn's decision, the settlement gave a windfall to Major Fenwick. Much of the land proved to be barrens, swamp land, or sand, but the rest was highly fertile and included the best harbor on the east bank of the Delaware.

Credence is lent the supposition that Edward Byllinge, as well as John Fenwick, was a straw man by his immediately placing what was left of his half of New Jersey into the hands of three Quaker trustees; William Penn, the mediator, together with Gawan Lawrie and Nicholas Lucas. As a reward for the use of his name in buying the land, the trustees appointed Byllinge governor and, through sales of the property, paid off his debts.[16]

Thereafter the portion of the Jersey peninsula which he had bought, really the southern half, was called West Jersey, while Carteret's half, in the north, was East Jersey.

The proceedings complicated the existing legal tangle. Though the land transfers were entirely valid, there being no doubt that Berkeley could sell to Byllinge and Fenwick and that Byllinge could place his share of the property in trust, the ethics, if not the legality, of bypassing creditors left much to be desired. As Penn and at least two of the principal creditors were members of the Quaker directorate which, to say the least, masterminded the deal, the issue was not pressed.

Nor, for some years, was the question raised of who held the reins of government. Since Berkeley had never officially received the right to rule, he could not pass it over to Fenwick nor to the Quaker trustees, but by some oversight or, more likely, indulgence that has never been explained, all at one time or another exercised the right. Not until November 1683, nine years later, was the situation clarified by the King's signing an official confirmation that the New Jersey proprietors did hold the right to govern, subject of course to Royal veto.

Fenwick had not waited for clarification. Conflicting ambitions moved him to action. He was sincerely anxious to erect a Quaker colony, but he also desired through sales of land to recover his £100 and to collect additional profits. Not least in his mind, perhaps, was a desire to equal the status of his father, the lord of a manor in Northumberland, by building manors in New Jersey, complete with such feudal append-ages as courts leet and courts baron.

Fenwick, though described by his biographer as the "victim of injustice, deceit, brazen gall and dire threats," plunged wholeheartedly into the business of selling land. Presumably with Penn's permission and that of the London Friends, he described his holdings, which he had never seen and of whose exact location he was ignorant, in most en-thusiastic terms. A contemporary publication by John Ogilby, self-entitled "King's Cosmographer and Geographic Printer," had given him a most appealing recommendation: "If there be any terrestial happiness to be had by any people, especially of any inferior rank, it must certainly be here."[17]

Fenwick offered to sell at £5 for each thousand acres, a rate which, if he sold but twenty lots, would return him his £100, while leaving him with more than 90 percent of the area he owned. In addition, he expected an annual quitrent of a penny an acre which, in the unlikely event that he sold off all his land, would yield him more than £1000 a year.[18]

Quakers, their hunger for a settlement of their own enhanced by the glowing promise of the prospectus, subscribed in such numbers that early in 1675 a shipload was ready to embark for America. Mrs. Fenwick, his second wife, remained in England, but the Quaker major, with three daughters, two sons-in-law, five grandchildren and ten servant workers for house and farm, boarded the *Griffin* for the Delaware.[19]

The passage was an ordeal, as voyages in small ships under sail invari-ably were. Men and women crowded together in small and stuffy holds sweltered in the heat of the tropics at night and had but slight chance to exercise by day. Rations were small, the ordinary fare being peas and salt meat on four days of the week, while on the other three a piece of raw fish was given each passenger to cook for himself with the quarter pound of butter he was allotted weekly. Drink was more generous; four pots of beer and two jugs of water daily.[20]

Unfortunately there was scandal aboard the *Griffin:* One John Spooner was found guilty of what was considered rashness. Unhappy with the arrangements, Spooner completely lost control of himself, cursing the ship, together with the men, women, children, and even the dogs that were aboard by such wicked expressions as calling down the plague, or the pox upon them. For this he was, of course, properly rebuked both by Fenwick and Robert Wade, one of the principal colonists, but Spooner, cautioned by a Friend of less stature, compounded his offenses by calling his critic "thou rascal."[21]

On arriving in America, the Quakers sailed up Delaware Bay and River until they reached a sharp bend in the stream, where on the eastern side they saw a hospitable-looking bay. Here they landed, at a point which, "from the delightsomeness of the place," Fenwick called Salem. Less romantic people dubbed it Swamptown.[22]

Perhaps because the rigors of the passage had frayed men's tempers, minor disagreements rose. Wade, who had helped discipline Spooner, complained that Fenwick's "aim was altogether for his own exaltation, not the public good." Another passenger alleged that Fenwick "would only sell to those who signed such papers as he drew up, which would have been to ensnare us."[23]

The criticisms were too harsh. Fenwick was neither selfish nor a sharper seeking to ensnare. He respected the rights of the Indian inhabitants and of those few Swedes who were living in the Salem neighborhood. If anyone were defrauded, it was John Fenwick himself, for though the chiefs of those same Indians had already twice sold the neighborhood to Europeans, Fenwick bought out their claims again, paying for them with eight knives, two pairs of scissors, two rough woolen cloaks, and sixty gallons of rum.

Fenwick was delighted with his purchase. He sent back word to Penn and the other trustees that West New Jersey was a "terrestrial Canaan," with not more than six weeks of winter, and marvelously productive, all the fruits that England grew and more, fish and waterfowl bigger and better than at home, "extraordinarily fat and good in great plenty." In short, "there is nothing wanting that can reasonably be desired for the delight and sustenance of man."[24]

Penn and his fellow trustees did not care for the site chosen by Fenwick for his own; they may have heard the nickname Swamptown. They preferred to build their capital much farther up the Delaware, as far as a vessel of a hundred tons could sail. From that point they desired to have a road across the colony to salt water at Sandy Hook, for this would enable them to unload cargo without the need of shipping it a couple of hundred miles farther around the New Jersey peninsula. Someone from West New Jersey, they suggested, should go down to Maryland, to the Labadist settlement at Bohemia Manor, to see if Augustin Herrmann, the well-known geographer and map maker, could be engaged to survey the route of that new road.

Meanwhile the Byllinge forces were enrolling emigrants, the recruiters being especially active in London, whose monthly meeting had inspired the purchase of New Jersey, and in Yorkshire, where Byllinge had many friends, among them many creditors. In the spring of 1677, some 230 colonists had sailed for America in the *Kent*.

Doubtless for the same reasons that caused dissension in the *Griffin*, the voyagers aboard the *Kent* were not entirely harmonious, the group separating into two factions, Londoners versus Yorkshiremen. By the time they reached the Delaware, the former were ready to secede. Instead of sailing up to the head of navigation, they asked to be disembarked at an attractive site then called Arwamus, where the Dutch had built Fort Nassau, but either because of Penn's instructions or because they were outnumbered by the Yorkshiremen, they were overruled. The *Kent* sailed on upstream to the head of navigation. There the travelers founded a town which they called Bridlington, after a town in Yorkshire. The name was soon corrupted to Burlington.[25]

The houses were neither elaborate nor attractive, being almost all of them log cabins, with clay floors, bark roofs, and chimneys that had an annoying habit of catching fire. Inside were two rooms, a combined kitchen and living room, and a sleeping room for husband, wife, and daughters. Boys slept with the hired men in the attic. There were, of course, no carpets, no glass windows, nor any stoves, an open fireplace providing the only heat.

Unhappily, the rift between the two Burlington factions did not quickly heal. All settlers lived in virtually identical houses on the one street that stretched between the river and the nearby woods, with the Yorkshiremen housed on the east side while Londoners took the river front. Two bridges spanned the several creeks that crossed the town site, but by common consent segregation was so stringent that for at least two centuries after the founding, one bridge was always known as the Yorkshire, the other as the London, Bridge.

Unlike Fenwick, who gave personal attention to the development of his Salem colony, Byllinge did not cross the ocean, a circumstance that lent color to the belief that he had acted not in his own interest but in that of the Society of Friends. While he may have been, and probably was, consulted in decisions made in London concerning the Burlington settlement, actual local administration was entrusted to Samuel Jennings, its first deputy governor and, after his replacement, for thirty years Penn's agent in West Jersey.

Gawen Lawrie, Nicholas Lucas, and Penn, the last by far the most important, owned no Jersey land at the outset of their trusteeship, but they directed and supervised the management of the colony, and since no mention is made of any salary or commission received by them, it is probable that they, too, were commissioned by the Friends.

10

COME, YE OPPRESSED

THE SOCIETY OF FRIENDS SET ITSELF TO ESTABLISHING IN NEW JERSEY A GOVERNMENT THAT WOULD BE FREE, TOLERANT AND, FOR ITS TIME, DEMOCRATIC. AS THE 120 FENWICK COLONISTS, AS WELL AS THE 230 Burlington settlers, were Quakers and, as such, fair-minded people accustomed to settling problems by ascertaining, and abiding by, the sense of the meeting, the task of drafting a basic constitution did not seem too difficult, especially as there already existed as a guide the very liberal concessions already proposed by Berkeley and Carteret. All that was really needed was implementation of that framework and the arrival of more people.[1]

As a beginning Penn issued a warning, probably the first and perhaps the only one of its kind ever voiced by land salesmen to prospective customers. You will be very welcome, he said in effect, and the more of you the better, but before you commit yourselves to sailing for America, please consider very carefully just what purpose you have in mind. The climate of our terrestrial Canaan is, as we have told you, equitable and pleasant, the health conditions excellent, the Indians friendly, the soil fertile, and the food is good, cheap, and plentiful, but you should not go for material or selfish betterment alone. What should be sought in America is spiritual freedom, a place to worship God in peace, and solace for your souls. In other words, though neither brusque nor impolite, William Penn said, in effect: "If you are emigrating out of curiosity or out of restlessness, if you are seeking adventure or material gain, please stay home."[2]

Despite what seemed discouragement, colonists flocked to New Jersey. By 1680, there were six thousand people, representing ninety-five trades and occupations. To Penn's delight only three were haberdashers or goldsmiths and only one a lawyer. The lack of attorneys especially pleased Penn, for despite the bit of legal training he himself received, he regarded lawyers with suspicion. With the exception of his own legal advisor, Thomas Rudyard, soon to become vice-governor of New Jersey, he distrusted all such people; he thought them, together with "priests," unnecessary in a properly run community.[3]

Penn and his fellow trustees did their work well, so well that they withdrew, leaving Byllinge to govern the property. Not only had they cleared the former major of debt, but they had made him so solvent that he was able to indulge one of the more important Quaker virtues, charity to the less fortunate. As a good Quaker, he had resented and resisted paying tithes to an established church of which he disapproved, and he had been imprisoned for his refusal, but immediately after the retirement of his trustees, he voluntarily offered a large block of West Jersey land for the relief of impoverished Quakers. Each of a hundred indigent families in England, with equal numbers in Wales and in most of the countries in western Europe, would receive a hundred acres of farmland, not precisely free of charge, but certainly not at an exorbitant rate, for the rental would be but one wheat grain per year, and that only if demanded.[4]

Fenwick had enjoyed similar good fortune. He, too, had sold land, though, since surveys had been delayed and deeds unskillfully drawn and worse recorded, the titles that he conveyed were not unclouded.

From the very beginning of the New Jersey Quaker settlement, Penn's partners willingly left to him the drafting of a frame of government, it being assumed that a widely read Oxford man, bred to the law, would be well fitted for the task. They may not, as a matter of fact, have been overly concerned with the exact provisions to be included. Quakers were profoundly interested in such essentials as freedom of worship and of conscience, liberty of the individual and preservation of the historic rights of Englishmen, but not so much with practical details. Because of their refusal to take the required oaths of allegiance to the throne and of abjuration of the Pope, only a small proportion of England's fifty thousand Quakers possessed the right to vote or to hold public office, and many who by some loophole or another did possess the franchise seldom exercised it. Every member of the Society of Friends had, however, suffered, in greater or less degree, from persecution or prejudice. As long as Penn made sure that freedom of religion was guaranteed, and nothing was more certain than that he would do so, the remainder of the basic law was of less importance.

For Penn the opportunity to write a charter of freedom was the culmination of his long campaign for the historic rights of Englishmen. Never before had he been asked to marshal the conditions that would assure free men their rightful liberties, and never before had he been so filled with fervor to set down those conditions.

The moment was extraordinarily propitious. With youthful enthusiasm (he was only thirty-three) Penn set out, if not to reform the world, at least to transform his terrestrial Canaan into a model of righteous living that would lead to changes elsewhere. He was at the peak of optimism, ready to devise a perfect state that would work perfectly with perfect people. Never before had he been able to make his dreams come true; never again would he be free from the dull routine of managing the day-to-day operations of governmental machinery.

He may not have anticipated complete success, for after all, New Jersey was not wholly Quaker. The population was diluted with Dutchmen, Connecticut Yankees, and Scots in East Jersey, as well as Englishmen dating from the Berkeley–Carteret regime, and with Swedes and pre-Quaker English in the West. Nevertheless, despite the absence of a large Quaker majority needed for the perfect state, New Jersey was an excellent laboratory in which to try out new plans. Penn, therefore, worked like a graduate student preparing a dissertation, except that he was unguided and unsupervised. Concerned with theory rather than with practice, drawing upon his studies and interpreting them in the light of his hopes, he was not bound by need to justify his proposals nor would he be held responsible for their successful operation.

Penn never completely disclosed the sources of his theories of government, if indeed he had any other than the Bible and the concessions already granted by Berkeley and Carteret. He had read many books and, being the type of man he was, had meditated long and earnestly upon their contents, but he gave no clues as to just what authors or what volumes had influenced him, nor at what period his thoughts had turned in such directions. Usually, it is assumed that Penn's interest in government began while he was browsing through the Oxford library, perhaps because of Henry Stubbs. There could have been no earlier date, for despite his precocity, neither he nor any other pre-teenager, would have had the patience, much less the understanding, to wade through such volumes. Guesses have been made that since the Christ Church College library contained copies of James Harrington's *Oceana*, Thomas Hobbes's *Leviathan*, and Thomas More's *Utopia*, Penn may have followed their ideas. He failed to note any such influence or even to mention that he had then known about any of the three. He may well have seen all three volumes, for Penn had an insatiable curiosity about books, but it is more than likely that he devoted virtually all his free reading time to the writings of the church fathers and historians.[5]

Actually, at that period Penn was undisturbed by political questionings; then, and for some years thereafter, he was a staunch Stuart partisan, content with the divine right concept, and undisturbed by politics. Both at Oxford and at Saumur, his extracurricular researches reflected John Owen and Moses Amyraut rather than any political scientist.

His awakening, when it did come, was a by-product of his legal studies. His stay at Lincoln's Inn had been brief and interrupted first by his few days of naval service and then by the outbreak of the plague, but it was long enough to kindle an interest, not so much in the practice as in the philosophy of law. Run-of-the-mill cases failed to intrigue him, nor did the thought of cajoling juries appeal to him, but the history of law and the theory of justice did challenge his attention. As usual, he read everything he could find, but he preferred the classics, writers like Sir Edward Coke, champion of the common law, or Henry de Bracton, the twelfth-century legal historian.

Coke and de Bracton, together with a host of other authors, blended with the classicists to strengthen Penn's conviction that just as God's word, as revealed in the scriptures, was all the authority needed in religion, so those same sacred writings proved that God meant the king to be supreme in secular activity. He would, of course, concede that no king could thereby rule despotically or irresponsibly, for the divine commission required that the laws of God must be obeyed, that he must deal justly with the people, and that if the king betrayed his trust, the people might dethrone him. Implicit, though unexpressed, in Penn's thinking was the theory that the king ruled by popular consent, that the divine right to rule inhered in the people, the king being their visible agent.

Had Penn been called upon, prior to being involved in the New Jersey situation, to state succinctly his political belief, he might have answered that in a perfect state the ideal government was no government whatever. Such a community would be moral, conscientious, and moved by charity; it would need no control over it. The people would be free, as God intended them to be, free to think, to act and, above all, to worship God as their consciences decreed and as the primitive church had shown to be God's will. No man in an ideal community would interfere with, much less restrain, the equal rights of others. Government was needed, Penn would have explained, to protect good people from the wicked, but in an ideal community no one would be wicked.[6]

Penn's less spiritually minded associates did not share his views. Algernon Sidney, the republican, reversed Penn's theory. It is not free men, said Sidney, who produce good government, but free government that produces free men. He agreed with Penn that it was essential to regain the civil liberties that both men believed prevailed among the ancient Britons; but while Penn preached that the best method was through peace, Sidney, a former army colonel, saw virtue in successful war. "That is the best government," said Sidney, "which best provides for war." The former colonel was also convinced that certain peoples, Africans and Asians, were "slaves by nature," a judgment that William Penn could not accept.[7]

Penn's political theories sprang less from any ideological synthesis, and more from a fundamental belief in mankind. To Penn, any system would work well if the people were good; any system would fail if they were not. It was a theory of government admirably suited to the idea—and the practice—of the social contract.

To attract those good people Penn resorted to advertising, producing a series of leaflets that combined every type of appeal he could think of. Unlike England, the land was cheap, "generally fertile and devoid of stones"; he said nothing about pine barrens or sandy tracts. Easily cultivatable, "with much smaller labor than in England," it produced any kind of grain, vegetable, and garden truck, all of excellent quality; there was ample pasturage, wildlife, and "fish in great plenty and easy to take."[8]

In chanting the praises of that "terrestrial Canaan," even now nicknamed the Garden State, Penn carefully avoided the excesses of a former publicist, one "Beauchamp Plantagenet," who alleged that New Jersey was filled with music because "angels in the guise of birds sing matins, prime and evensong," but he minimized no selling point. Consider, he suggested, the case of Richard Hartshorne, who came to New Jersey and within six years piled up enough profit to own thirty cows, seven mares, and all the horses his family needed to ride about. (Penn did not stress the advantage Richard might have enjoyed in being the brother of one of the twelve chief persons in the province.)[9]

But what, someone might ask, of the savage Indians we hear about? No problem, Penn implied; they are few and they are friendly. Loneliness? Not at all; there are already "seven considerable towns, well inhabited by a sober and industrious people." Most of those towns have as many as a hundred houses, and even the smallest has forty. What is more, there are plans afoot to erect a principal town, "probably at Ambo Point on the Raritan, a sweet, wholesome and delightful place." In short, what more could anyone desire? Transportation, too, was cheap, only £5 for adults and 50 shillings for children under twelve, "sucklings free."

Penn assured prospective purchasers that New Jersey would be renowned for liberty, equality, and tolerance, a trio not too different from that proclaimed by French philosophers a century later. To promise this brotherhood of man was easy enough, but to couch the guarantees in words that no court would declare invalid posed great difficulty. Penn knew exactly what he wished to achieve, but he lacked the insight into human nature, the patience to deal with knotty details, and quite possibly the skill to write legal prescriptions.

For Penn's world was simple. In an agrarian society where everyone loved God and, except for helping the unfortunate, minded his own business, there was but one path to pursue. Not for William Penn were there differences in social or political philosophies nor any alternatives

from which to choose. Those who knew the Truth, the will of God, and
the clear teachings of the Scriptures would infallibly choose aright. All
else was error. For William Penn there were no honest differences of
opinion on such matters.

In a perfect state government would be more passive than dynamic.
The public, entrusted with universal male suffrage, would annually
select for office by secret ballot men "of most note for their virtue,
wisdom and ability." The office would seek the man, for to put one's
self forward as a candidate would betray an unbecoming egotism that
would stamp him as unworthy. So strongly did Penn believe that political campaigning was degrading that he frowned upon the formation of
political parties (he called them "factions.") He would later impress
upon his sons that they must not meddle in governmental affairs. Such
activity was unbecoming; it was also unnecessary, for if people loved
one another, worked together for the common good, helped, comforted
and were considerate of their neighbors, a consensus would arise as to
what was desirable for the community.

Penn completed his draft of the *Concessions and Agreements* on March
3, 1677, and saw it adopted unanimously by those who had bought land.
The document, a constitution for the province, varied little from its
predecessor, but it reaffirmed human rights and civil liberties. A popularly elected assembly was to make the laws and choose executive
officers. As was only to be expected in a fundamental law drafted by
William Penn, no fine, imprisonment, or punishment was to be inflicted except after a fair and open jury trial. Juries, entirely free of all
control, were to interpret the laws and to return verdicts that could
not be questioned. The assembly, meeting at the call of the governor or
on its own initiative, was to have complete freedom of debate, with
power to adjourn at will, and to have exclusive tax-levying rights.
Members were to be paid a shilling for each day they were in session.

Judges were to be elected for two-year terms. Imprisonment for debt
was prohibited. All land deeds were to be recorded in record books
open for public information.

Another important provision guaranteed orphans the right to an
education at the cost of the colony. An interesting sidelight on the New
Jersey zeal for education was a grant to the town of Burlington of an
island in the Delaware whose land, or the revenues therefrom, was to be
used "for educational purposes forever." The Burlington schools continue
to this day to draw income from this source, the oldest endowment of
the kind in the United States.[10]

Penn and his fellow trustees thereupon created a West Jersey Company and, with *Concessions and Agreements* as an alluring prospectus,
invited purchasers to buy stock at £350 for each hundred shares. Not
all the shares, however, were put on the market; ten went to Fenwick,

in accordance with the arbitration award, and twenty more to pay off the Byllinge creditors. The remainder would, it was hoped, be bought by Friends anxious to migrate to a community of saints.

The trustees were overoptimistic; only about half the available shares were sold immediately, though the buyers were, as had been hoped, almost all members of the Society of Friends. Of the 120 subscribers to whole, or partial, shares, five-sixths were Englishmen, seventeen were Irish, Dubliners or Shanagarry neighbors, and three were Scots. The Quaker response pleased Penn; he was not so happy when he learned that only about a quarter of the subscribers planned to emigrate, while the rest, if not land speculators, were planning to be absentee landlords.[11]

The difference in purpose led to confusion. The original stock-holders, the proprietors, disagreed both with tenants and with buyers for whom they subdivided their estates. The proprietors, while insisting that *Concessions and Agreements* was a firm compact as far as their relation with the trustees was concerned, would not agree that the terms of that document applied to those who did not buy directly from the Penn trusteeship. In consequence *Concessions and Agreements* never went into complete effect; the spirit of the constitution was upheld by some, but there was constant argument about its validity for all.

11

SQUIRE IN SUSSEX

EANWHILE, AT RICKMANSWORTH, PENN, IN HIS EARLY THIRTIES, WAS LEADING A BUSY AND, DETRACTORS MIGHT SAY, A VERY CONTENTIOUS LIFE. EXCEPT FOR VISITING QUAKER MEETINGS HERE AND there and for entertaining various Quaker dignitaries who dropped in from time to time, he spent all day at his desk.

It is possible that Penn's activities were welcomed by the authorities. While he was still in Newgate he had assured the English sheriffs and, for that matter, Parliament itself that he was completely loyal to the government and to its laws, excepting those limiting free worship. He had not only denied complicity in any plots whatsoever but had denounced conspiracy as horrible impiety. In return he had asked relief from persecution, and this had been tacitly granted him. Since no one but a few fanatics or extremists ever questioned Penn's integrity and since granting him a measure of immunity would, to some degree, split the nonconformist movement and so weaken its impact, government officials were quite willing to concede a bit of leeway to one with friends at court.[1]

Though he was tranquil, his writings on non-military matters were not particularly peaceful; those whom he opposed may, with some justice, have thought him belligerent. In warring against ideas that he considered false, dangerous or heretical, he lashed out against their advocates as vile, filthy, wicked, or blasphemous. Judging only by his writings or by his speeches he showed little tolerance or open-mindedness.[2]

Yet such harsh judgment would be unfair. He firmly believed that everyone must have the right to worship and to speak as his conscience dictated but this freedom, while it forbade persecution or suppression as long as the rights of others were not denied and no divine command-

[98]

ments were broken, did not preclude criticism or rebuttal of the views expressed.

Penn's comments were pointed and severe. Because he assumed that those with whom he associated would be just, sincere and honest, he seldom praised; his tributes were for the most part expressed in funeral ceremonies, such as those for Loe, Coale or Fox. His praise was restrained, but he struck hard blows on those of whom he disapproved.

Nor was he consistent in fitting his practice to his teaching. No sooner had he counseled his friends against entering into arguments than he embarked upon a series of debates. Though he assured his readers that "Truth often suffers more by the heat of the defenders than from the arguments of the opposers," his arrows of criticism were sharp; his enemies would have said that they were poisoned. With the zeal of a recent convert and in the brashness of youth he attacked older men of established reputation whose writings, in his opinion, ran counter to the ideals of the Society of Friends. One man he classed as wanton and debauched, another as a cowardly skulker in holes, several were put down as hypocrites, blasphemers, ungodly enemies of Christianity. The words of Thomas Hicks, who Penn said was a scurrilous perverter and forger, were nothing more to Penn than vomit. Ludovici Muggleton, who boasted of having received "an inward illumination that opened to him the meaning of Scripture"—an experience not unlike that of the Quaker Inner Light—was called a presumptuous Antichrist whom God would surely blast. Penn rejoiced that Muggleton's cousin, John Reeve, who had died a dozen years before, lay rotting in his grave.[3]

During the eight years ending in 1676 Penn condemned no less than a dozen adversaries, some from the platform, others by pamphlet. All were, he said, hypocritical cutthroats, purveyors of dirty, bitter stuff, vice and malice. One of them, at least, was guilty of "biting before barking, the sign of a cur."[4]

John Faldo came off little better. It was bad enough that he had written a pamphlet entitled *William Penn, a Counterfeit Christian,* that he had "wickedly insinuated lies," that he had affronted Penn "in opprobious names" before Penn's relatives, but he had accused Admiral Sir William of dishonesty and had gone on to allege that Penn had a private income of £2000 a year. "If he, John Faldo, will make that report good," said Penn, "I will give him a year's rent."[5]

Penn's disclaimer, while technically correct, was splitting hairs. His income was in fact considerably more than £2000 a year. However the greater portion of the amount was not his personal income but was derived from Guli's lands.

Despite their verbal violence Penn's retorts implied no real hatred. While still arguing hotly with John Faldo, Penn sent his adversary a note sincerely wishing him prosperity. The good wishes contained a barb, however, for Penn also hoped that Faldo would acquire "a disposition to candor and quiet."[6]

Penn also wrangled publicly with Richard Baxter, the highly respected Puritan author of *Saint's Everlasting Rest*. The intense young Quaker, still in his mid-twenties, charged that Baxter, a man of twice his age, had condemned members of the Society of Friends as "little more than lost people." In a debate that began at ten in the morning and ran on until five in the afternoon, Penn rebuked Baxter for "virulent and imperious behavior," motivated by envy and strife into a "clamor wrapped up in terms fit only for the Divvil." Baxter retorted, less colorfully, that Penn resorted to raillery, slander, interruptions, and "dirty reflections."[7]

Penn would have liked to hold a second debate but Baxter, though professing willingness, stipulated that the meeting should not last another seven hours. Penn then complained that Baxter, "a perverter, traducer, forger," was trying to avoid discussion. He signed his letter "Thy friend."[8]

After 1676 Penn's combativeness somewhat subsided. More active field work for the Society of Friends and the supervision of colonial activities kept him fully occupied. He was as quick as ever to resent criticism and anti-Quaker libel but, in his greater maturity, he was disciplining himself to follow his advice to others that difference of opinion should be settled privately.

Perhaps Penn's willingness to keep the peace sprang from the fact that he and Guli were having to make certain adjustments in their private life. While thoroughly happy together, neither William nor Guli was particularly pleased with Rickmansworth. The climate, they believed, was atrocious, the coldest, wettest winter in a dozen years; moreover, it was unhealthy. In February 1674, Guli had borne twins, sickly babies, William and Margaret, the one living but three months, the other just under a year. Three children had thus been born at Rickmansworth, and all three had died in infancy. Guli, expecting a fourth in 1676, suspected that the three streams that flowed nearby, though they watered lovely meadows, promoted some sort of swamp fever.[9]

Regardless of Guli's unfounded fear of malaria, it may have been just as well that the Penns left Rickmansworth; people would soon be thinking that the neighborhood was deteriorating. A few years later Sir George Jeffreys would build a house among these Chiltern Hills, a mansion whose bricks, it would be said, owed their color to the blood shed in his infamous assizes. Then, too, an eccentric, Francis Dashwood, Lord de Spenser, would landscape an estate to the form of a female body; his notorious Hell-Fire Club would outrage the community by its orgies and black masses. A happier note would be sounded, though much later, by the establishment, at nearby Chequers, of a country home for Britain's prime ministers.

William and Guli yielded to their fears before any of these developments affected them. Guli had a fondness for Sussex, where she owned ancestral estates, charming places where, from the hilltops, one could look south across a lake and wooded valleys, while on the north lay wide, undulating pastures where, whether Guli remembered it or not, John Fenwick had pastured his sheep. Near Ringmer, three miles north of Lewes, was the manor of Lord de la Warre, whose name was given to the American river of which Fox spoke so glowingly. At Ringmer, too, were 1500 acres owned by Guli, and at Ringmer, though Penn probably never knew of it, nor would have cared had he known, John Harvard had found his bride.

Fifteen miles from Ringmer, near the old Saxon village of Washington, about forty-six miles from London, the Penns found a two-story, slate-roofed brick house set high upon a hill amid tulip trees and Spanish chestnuts. Worminghurst, its ancient manor—now spelled Warminghurst—had once been owned by the Benedictine fathers of Fécamp, inventors of the liqueur, and later by the Shelley family, ancestors of the poet; they had acquired it from Henry VIII for £391.[10]

Americans seeking links between the Penn country and their own colonial beginnings have tried in vain to connect the village of Washington with the family of the Revolutionary leader. They take some consolation, however, in the discovery that for some years Tom Paine collected taxes here while keeping a tobacco shop, and that the area was long the home of various Lees. Those Lees, by one report, were "all honest cottager folk," but, alas, local legend, embodied in a couplet, is less flattering: "There was never a Lee in Worminghurst/ That wasn't a gypsy, last and first." The word "gypsy," unfortunately, was formerly used to describe a cunning rogue, the slang term "to gyp" being a survival thereof.

The Penns might have been ready to move to Worminghurst early in 1676, but the departure was delayed because on January 25 Guli gave birth to another son, a healthy-looking little boy whom the Penns named Springett. Apparently he brought good luck, for after dreary weeks of unusually cold rain and snow, the weather turned mild and remained so for the rest of the winter.[11]

On June 3, the Penns moved down to Worminghurst. They had agreed to pay £4982, approximately thirteen times as much as the Shelleys had paid a century and a half earlier, but the terms were easy; 3 percent to be paid within six months and the balance another half-year later. They had hoped to raise about half the cost from the sale of Basing House, but the buyer used so many legal maneuverings to put off payment that the Rickmansworth transaction was not concluded for seventeen years.[12]

Life at Worminghurst was strictly regulated. Everyone rose at five on summer mornings, at seven in the winter, and at six in other months.

After morning worship and breakfast, the family attended to its various household chores before assembling at eleven for Bible reading and noon dinner. Five hours of uninterrupted work filled the afternoons. After another religious service at six and supper, everyone reported the progress he had made, received his assignments for the following day, and went early to bed.[13]

Two admirable precepts governed family activities. The first, easy to observe in those early days at Worminghurst when there was only one small child, and he a quiet infant, forbade "loud discourse or any troublesome noise." The second, surely unnecessary in the Penn household, required that all domestic grievances or quarrels be resolved before bedtime; no one was to nurse his anger overnight.

It was just as well that the Penns had as little social life at Worminghurst as they had had at Rickmansworth, Sussex being as politically dangerous as Hertfordshire. The Duke of Monmouth had come down, though not with Penn, to cut a vivid figure as he rode about in scarlet suit and cloak. Algernon Sidney, the rebellious opponent of absolutism, was still in exile, but his Sussex partisans were expecting his early return.

A third man was quite as dangerous. The Reverend Titus Oates, curate of his father's church at Hastings, to the southeast, a curious fellow whose low forehead and oversized chin placed his mouth almost in the center of his face, had little to commend him. Though a clergyman, from Penn's point of view he was a self-seeking schemer, a liar, and a person of repulsive habits. The full force of his virulent bigotry had not yet developed when Penn first came to Worminghurst, and Oates was soon to leave the district to serve as chaplain aboard a ship commanded by Penn's cousin, Richard Rooth.

In 1678, however, Oates returned to Sussex and soon startled England by alleging, without even the faintest proof, that the Jesuits were plotting to make England a Catholic country by murdering Charles II and Catherine of Braganza, his queen, in order to crown James, Duke of York, in their stead.

Many of the more gullible Britons not only credited this fabrication of a Popish Plot but also, because Penn had been a neighbor of Titus Oates and was, moreover, a relative of Capt. Rooth, associated Penn with the supposed conspiracy. Had not Oates briefly attended St. Omer, the Catholic seminary where Penn was popularly supposed to have studied? Had there not been persistent gossip of Penn's supposed correspondence with the Vatican?

Neither William's caution in avoiding embarrassing entanglements nor his absorption in his work saved him from suspicion. Someone in Chester wrote a letter accusing "cursed Penn the Quaker" of persecution. The anonymous letter, obviously the work of a crank, might have been ignored had it not accused both the King and Queen of illegitimate birth. The nervous authorities badgered Penn to explain something of which he knew absolutely nothing. Though the investigators discovered no evidence whatever of any wrongdoing on Penn's part, they continued for years to look with suspicion on everything he did.[14]

Despite this renewal of governmental mistrust, Penn was finding pleasure in his life at Worminghurst. Happy in the conviction that air on the Worminghurst hilltop was more salubrious than that of Rickmansworth, the Penns spent much time mapping out the career that little Springett was to follow. Early in his babyhood it was decided that the boy should follow the family tradition of the sea. He was not, however, to sail ships as his great-grandfather and his grandfather had done but, rather, to build ships for others. Until he reached fifteen or so he should be tutored at home, instead of wasting time at an English school or college; after this he should go to Holland to broaden his general culture, to acquire a second language, and to be taught the shipwright's arts and crafts. In Holland he would see, and learn to appreciate, the blessings of a free country where tolerance was accorded everyone. In their enthusiasm, they seemed to overlook a basic principle—that Springett should have freedom of choice.[15] In the meantime, as a step toward the development of Sussex economy and, quite possibly, to allow Springett an employment close to home, Penn urged the Lord Lieutenant of Sussex, a former patron of Nell Gwynn, to encourage a ship building industry in that country.[16]

Penn was also again concerned with the preservation of harmony within the Society of Friends. John Story and John Wilkinson, two Quakers of the northern counties, were creating a serious division. Some of their complaints were basic, such as their fear that a hierarchy was developing within the Society, and their strong objection to allowing women to preach. Others were minor, as, for instance, their contention that no records should be kept of those incurring reprimands; they also thought that too many meetings were marred by noisy or impolite behavior. Ordinarily such matters would have been settled by the intervention of George Fox, but with Fox in jail, the task of restoring harmony fell upon William Penn.[17]

Failing to reconcile the objectors, Penn used what he called "heavenly discipline," or a series of condemnations by various Quaker meetings. This, too, failed. Wilkinson and Story, instead of seeing anything heavenly about the method, regarded the rebukes merely as additional proof of bias, illegality, and autocracy. Again Penn tried conciliation, and this time he succeeded. He managed to extract from the dissidents something that George Fox considered an apology. The solution was not final, but it did ease an uncomfortable situation.

With the Wilkinson–Story controversy cooled, Penn returned to the defense of the fundamental rights of Englishmen. These he construed as what Thomas Jefferson would describe a century later as the inalienable rights of life, liberty, and the pursuit of happiness. Based upon morality,

justice, civil liberties, the Golden Rule, and the laws of Jehovah, these
rights, inherited from an idealized past, were not "concessions," as Locke
and Berkeley had thought them, but essentials of human freedom. Since
to Penn an acid test for freedom was absence of persecution, he combed
through history to find instances of rulers who had allowed people to
speak and worship according to their consciences. The list was impressive; partly because as usual Penn did not invariably distinguish between monarchs who had allowed dissent and those in whose realms
no dissent existed.

Penn demanded freedom in government as well as in religion. In no
sense a revolutionary, he did not question the monarchy nor leadership
by those best qualified to rule. Existing English methods pleased him,
but they must be pursued by wise, honest, and God-fearing rulers. He
demanded an end to arbitrary, capricious, and despotic rule, for he had
himself seen too much cronyism and too much bribery to consider judges
and other officials perfect; equally, he deplored reckless and unbridled
criticism. He was not an unqualified libertarian; it was, he considered,
right and proper for men of property and special skills, men of probity
and wisdom, to hold the reins, but he insisted upon justice, even, if
need be, against the King himself. Much, if not all, of this had been
assured, he contended, by ancient English custom and by agreements
between the people and their sovereigns. Though William Penn never
used the term "social contract," his interpretation of history closely paralleled the theories later voiced by Jean Jacques Rousseau.

As at Rickmansworth, Penn propagandized actively. Whenever any
critics spoke or wrote against Quakerism and freedom of conscience or
of worship, or if they challenged basic English rights, he counterattacked
promptly and vigorously. Not all his replies were effective, for William
lacked the spectacular mass appeal possessed by certain other Quaker
leaders. More at home in his library than on the public platform, more
persuasive in conversation than in his writing, he could not always
sense the temper of an unsympathetic meeting. Occasionally he might
grip an audience, but usually his closely reasoned, legalistic arguments,
heavily laced with classic precedents, went over the heads of listeners.

If Penn's great magnetism was not always strong with the general
public, his influence with the intellectuals was greater and more lasting
than was that of more emotional evangelists. Though only a handful
of his sermons have come down to us, his writings are still effective.
These important books, brochures, and pamphlets increased in numbers
as Penn entered his mid-thirties. Angered in 1675 by decrees that all
participants in legal or official affairs must swear upon the Bible that
they were loyal and truthful, Penn had declared in the *Treatise on
Oaths* that such requirements deterred no one. Any rogue would glibly
swear to anything he pleased. Only the God-fearing would take oaths
seriously, and they were the very people who needed no oaths to guaran-

tee their honesty. But—waiving the ridiculousness of requiring oaths—what right had the King of England or any other mortal being, even a bishop, to disobey the direct command of Jesus in the Sermon on the Mount specifically forbidding anyone to swear? As though it were not enough to show the silliness of oaths, and their impiety, or to say trenchantly, "Good men may be ensnared by oaths but oaths never yet caught a knave," Penn added no less than 120 quotations from great men in ancient and medieval times who had denounced such requirements.

Other political developments called forth Penn's *England's Present Interest Discovered*, one of his numerous pleas for freedom of conscience and for justice in government. Characteristically, he appealed to precedent. The king of kings in Persia, Jewish monarchs, the tsars of Muscovy, all, Penn contended, had from time immemorial admitted, by actions or by words, that sovereignty over human conscience belonged to God alone. His history may have been somewhat sketchy, his estimation of some ancient rulers overgenerous, but no one could question his sincerity. The right of everyone to worship as he pleased was sanctified, he was convinced, by time, custom, and authority; it antedated not only Stuart kings and Anglican prelates but Christianity itself.

The twenty-five or thirty writings of this period reveal Penn as a collector rather than as an inventor of ideas. A critic determined to be captious could easily find him guilty of selecting only such precedents as proved his case. Yet, in contrast to certain others who demanded toleration for themselves while denying it to rivals, Penn's concern was very real.

Penn did not have the same tolerance for certain rites and ceremonies as he had for the words and phrases of which he disapproved. Words and phrases were often dangerous, and they might be evil but with proper reasoning, they could be corrected. Rites and ceremonies, however, were symbols that, if not useless because of their emptiness, promoted paganism and idolatry. Like other Quakers of his time Penn viewed the costumed priests who used them—the incense-swingers, the altar-kissers, the genuflectors, and those who turned their backs upon the people as they prayed—not as servants of the Lord but as agents of the devil; their practices were filthy travesties of worship.

Despite Penn's vehemence against the prevalence of customs he thought perilous, he was at this stage of his life an optimist who believed that the heart of man is fundamentally sound; he had only to point out what was unacceptable and good men would at once accept the truth. Later he would become disillusioned and would think that human beings, perfect in Eden, had degenerated since that golden age when they scrupulously observed the laws of God.

The plain fact was that William Penn invariably relied too heavily upon man's innate goodness and integrity; he never really knew the world. Though schooled in court diplomacy and adroit with the bureaucracy, he had only slight acquaintance with ordinary people. Except for ideologically minded individuals, bookish men, and dedicated missionaries, he was always more at home with imaginary folk of bygone ages, with the people of the Bible or of Augustan Rome, than with the men and women whom he saw on London streets. He had warm, unlimited, and very real compassion for the poor and the oppressed; but except for those who suffered for their Quakerism, his knowledge of their plight was secondhand at best. No record indicates that except for conversations with fellow prisoners he ever talked at length with any ordinary citizen other than laborers on his own estates or worshipers in his own meetinghouses; he never seems to have penetrated deeply into a festering London slum, visited an almshouse or an orphanage, or even chatted at taverns as his father would have done. A man who much preferred the library to the village inn, the meetinghouse to the marketplace, he easily confused the shepherds of Worminghurst with those of the Judaean hills.

The survey of Penn's activities up to his mid-thirties, if not indeed until even later years, can easily mislead. Rural life at Shanagarry and at Worminghurst would suggest a familiarity with farming problems were it not known that actual management lay largely in the hands of such agents as Philip Ford. The possession of greater than ordinary wealth and its expenditures on projects beyond the scope of ordinary men would seem to imply at least a modicum of business experience; yet William Penn, throughout his life, was careless and indifferent about money matters. Legal training, such as it was, should indicate some skill at the bar; yet aside from clever, and very irritating, verbal exchanges with a judge or two, Penn made little use of what he knew.

Inexperience in practical affairs could readily have been counterbalanced had William Penn been canny in his employment practices. He showed, however, a surprising inability to read character. All too often his criteria for choosing agents and assistants were nepotistic: relationship to Guli or himself, service in his father's squadrons, and, above all else, proven Quakerism. Ability and experience did not seem to matter.

The science of personnel management had not yet been invented nor, in simple justice to William Penn, can it be said that official appointments were more efficient elsewhere, but he paid only slight attention to possible efficiency. Those whose concept of government was based on little more than fear of the Lord, good will toward men, and strict observance of the Ten Commandments could face the future bravely. In a staunch Quaker community, a settlement of saints, where everyone was free and equal and regardful of the rights of others, no vice, crime, or injustice could possibly arise.

12

CRUSADE FOR EUROPE

GOOD NEWS FROM NEW JERSEY AND OPTIMISTIC MESSAGES FROM QUAKER MISSIONERS IN EUROPE COMFORTED FRIENDS WHO WORRIED OVER SIGNS THAT PERSECUTION WAS REVIVING. OPTIMISTS TRUSTED that just as nonconformists half a century earlier had found freedom in Holland and America, so Quakers could find haven in New Jersey or in Europe. The hope that Quakerism might spread to Germany and Holland, perhaps even to Poland and France, did not reach the astonishing heights of a decade or so earlier, when Quakers had seriously suggested that the Emperor of China, the legendary Prester John, and even the Pope himself might be won over, but the feeling was strong that parts of Europe were ripe for convincement. In 1677, therefore, the London Yearly Meeting planned a missionary campaign. Penn was to organize and lead a task force of evangelists into Germany and Holland.

When the meeting ended, Penn invited half a dozen leaders to go down with him to Worminghurst to map out plans. There, in what must have been a supreme test of Guli's domestic arrangements, since apparently before the Yearly Meeting there had been no suggestion of a conference, the Friends conferred for about a week.

In preparation for the "refreshment" of Quakerism on the Continent, Penn spent much time at his desk. He wrote a message *To the Churches of Jesus Throughout the World* and again pleaded with the King of Poland for toleration in that relatively unknown land. He assembled a number of pamphlets explaining Quaker principles and practices for translation into Dutch and publication in the Netherlands. He sent word to Benjamin Furly, a prominent Quaker merchant in Rotterdam, to make all necessary advance arrangements. Penn was particularly anxious again to meet, and to endeavor to convince, Princess Elizabeth, Robert Barclay's cousin, who, Barclay said, was now ready to turn Quaker.

On July 22 Penn began his journey. Riding through Horsham and St. Leonard's Forest, to Gatwick and Croydon, where the airports now are, he came at last to London. After attending to some little business for the Society and for himself, he called at Wanstead to see his mother, and then went on to Colchester,[1] Furly's home town and the site of the imprisonment and death of the Quaker boy martyr, James Parnell. From there Penn rode on to take ship for Holland.

A party of eight awaited him, including two women and two "servants," (a secretary and a guide); the rest, among them Fox and Isaac Penington, were missioners like Penn. Neither Guli nor Margaret Fox was a traveler, the one because year-old Springett was too young to travel, the latter because she was needed to care for Swarthmoor, the Fox estate in Lancashire.

None of the group spoke either Dutch or German with any fluency, though Penn knew a little of the latter tongue and may have picked up a few Dutch words from his mother. Furly would act as their spokesman until the party reached Holland, where everyone would have his own interpreter.

To their surprise, the group received special treatment aboard ship, not because they were Quakers but because the skipper had served under Admiral Sir William. (What the captain may have thought when William Penn, the son and grandson of professional sailors, became seasick is not recorded.) Good fortune lasted only until the ship arrived off the Dutch coast. The captain, nearing Rotterdam after dark, decided to lay to for the night, but William, certain that Furly would be anxiously waiting, asked to be set ashore. Though the skipper knew that by Dutch custom all port officials would have gone off duty at sunset, he yielded to Penn's pleas and ordered six men to row Penn and Fox three miles to a landing place.

Furly, however, had gone home, intending to return at daybreak, and the town gates were securely locked. Penn and Fox, having dismissed the oarsmen, spent the night in a fishing boat they found drawn up on shore.

When the gates opened in the morning, Furly escorted the visitors to his comfortable mid-city home. Here William must have been sorely tempted to linger, browsing in Furly's well-stocked library; but after having some meetings in Rotterdam; possibly arranging for the publication of *A Tender Visitation*, one of the manuscripts he had brought with him, he moved on two days later to Amsterdam. Fox then went off to make the rounds of Dutch meetings, while William and Furly set out to call upon Princess Elizabeth and the Labadists.

The Princess was most hospitable. When Penn and Furly arrived, bringing with them George Keith, then wholly orthodox, and Robert Barclay, her cousin, she met with them at seven in the morning. The Friends preached to her for five straight hours, then, declining for some incomprehensible reason to stay for noonday dinner, went to their inn for lunch. By two o'clock, however, they were back and, resumed talking for five more hours. For four full days they maintained this exhausting schedule, though after the first day the Princess, pleading the press of business, begged off from morning sessions. Her absence, she said, would allow "the more inferior servants" of the house an opportunity to hear the Quaker testimony. They might be reluctant, she said, to present themselves before her.

The afternoon meetings steadily became less formal, the Princess not hesitating to argue with her guests. The talk grew more personal. William told her of his Chigwell vision, of the persecutions he said he had endured at Oxford and of the consolations he received, but apparently he did not mention either Preacher. Loe or the Berean precedent. The Quakers, now more at home, stayed for evening meals; after the tables were cleared Penn and his companions continued their sermons for several hours. The Princess listened attentively but remained unconvinced. Penn did not report on what effect the morning meetings had upon the servants.

After the verbal wrestlings, which everyone enjoyed though no opinions were seriously changed, the party moved on, taking with them an enthusiastic invitation to return. For a month they rode cross-country in wagons, floated down the Rhine, or walked, visiting fifteen communities. Receptions were mixed. Some towns were "dark and popish," but on the whole western Germany was hospitable. No spectacular convincements were recorded, though at one meeting a hysterical young girl was reported as having cried out, "It will never be well with us until persecution come and some of us are lodged in prison." The cry seems an unlikely one to have been called forth spontaneously, but the fault may lie in the translation rather than in the content. A few individuals, however, went forth convinced, persuaded others, and so built up a number of centers from which the Quaker message spread. Only a few years later the results showed themselves by a movement to America of very desirable emigrants from the Palatinate.

Some reports by Penn contemporaries asserted that while on the Continent William met Princess Mary of England just before her marriage to William of Orange, and that she praised Penn as a man of the highest gravity who spoke "in the most exquisite terms." She would not, however, hear him preach, suggesting instead that he listen to sermons by some very good preachers whom she could recommend.[2]

There were less happy incidents. William heard of a noble girl, young and beautiful, whose father was mistreating her "because she was too pious." Using the local schoolmaster as a go-between, Penn asked for an audience and was told that if he kept the appointment secret, she would meet him at her minister's house. The appointed place was six miles distant, but Penn began to walk. While on the road he met her father, the count, who asked, none too politely, who he was and where he was going. Penn began to reply—one wonders what answer he would have made—but the count, insulted because William, following Quaker custom, failed to remove his hat, broke in, "We need no Quakers here. Get off my land." His soldier escort marched Penn away and, toward dusk, left him in the midst of a dark forest. William could not find his way out until ten o'clock, by which time the town gates were shut. He spent the night in a marshy field. He was lucky, the townsfolk said in the morning, that the count had not loosed his dogs upon him.

Penn had equally bad luck, though without the threat of dogs or armed force, in trying to renew his acquaintance with the Labadists whom he had met six years before. De Labadie was dead, but his successors refused to let him see Anna Maria van Schurmann; she was too old, they said, too weak and was taking physic. When, despite their objections, he did manage an appointment, he made no progress, she having been warned against Quaker teachings, "lest the brightness of the testimony be obscured among the poor, illiterate and simple." The warning does not seem to make much sense, but apparently, it was an effective inoculation against Penn's teaching.

Nor were the remaining days of the journey more productive. Each day the Quakers, traveling by cart, suffered agonies because fellow passengers either talked vainly or profanely or else sang Lutheran hymns. Daily meetings at towns along the road, or at Princess Elizabeth's on a return visit, yielded few recruits. On October 7, Penn returned to Amsterdam. Here George Fox, who had been evangelizing in the north, rejoined him. The two arranged a public debate with Galenus Abrahams, a Mennonite who, Penn said, rejected Quakerism because it had produced no miracle workers. Unfortunately Fox came down with what seems to have been bronchial asthma, so William, for two full days, argued with Abrahams, a man "high and shy." Neither convinced the other, but Penn felt that he had planted good seed; two months later, he reported, Abrahams, mulling over what he had said, became "very loving and tender."[3]

After eighty-nine days on the Continent, covering, as he estimated, some three thousand miles of difficult traveling, holding meetings in fifty-three different towns, Penn turned back to England. His troubles were not over; he became so seasick that he vomited blood.

The long ride back to London in an unseasonable heat wave was a hardship. Penn was not feeling well and the news that greeted him was most distressing. Persecution was again upon the rise, a persecution as irrational as it was severe. Two justices of the peace were making his life so uneasy because of his nonconformity that Penn appealed to the authorities for protection. In addition, a former Quaker was publishing diatribes inspired by "degeneracy and sour grapes."[4]

Nor had Penn time to rest and recuperate. London Monthly Meeting summoned him to meet Lord Baltimore to see what could be done to ease the Quaker lot in Maryland, where Friends were being persecuted not because of their beliefs but because they would not swear to defend the government. Penn did manage to persuade Lord Baltimore then that Friends were in no sense rebels and that their affirmations were quite as trustworthy as were other men's oaths.[5]

Despite this success and despite what Penn considered the generally favorable outcome of his mission to the Continent, Penn's morale was low. Something undoubtedly was amiss, because for him dejection and pessimism were far from usual. Quite possibly he was ill or harboring some disappointment; if so, he kept the matter to himself.

The weather, following his return from Europe, was unusual and unpleasant. The great heat wave that had greeted him after he crossed the Channel had been succeeded by weeks of rain and fog. Many people, Penn perhaps among them, were pent up in their houses where many of them sniffled with colds or fought influenza. December was so bleak that a surprising thunderstorm with lightning flashes, followed by a fall of hailstones, was almost welcome because it broke the dull monotony. Then came January cold, which like the December wetness put a damper on the spirit. Ordinarily the sedentary Penn would have passed the time in study or by writing, but for once he felt no urge to work.

The lethargy was so unusual that something quite serious must have been bothering William Penn. His call upon the authorities for protection might have been construed as a plea to be spared from political or religious persecution, but sometime later, when Penn, who never showed any interest in household pets, bought himself a mastiff, he seems to have betrayed a need for some defense against personal attack. It is pleasant to record that the purchase was either effective or, more likely, unnecessary.[6]

That Penn gradually renewed activity did not mean that he was once more cheerful and optimistic. He remained despondent, owing, one may suppose, to his very deep belief that divine retribution was about to fall upon England. Degeneracy had become, in his view, so outrageous that he was convinced God would soon destroy the nation as He had punished Sodom and Gomorrah.[7]

13

CHARM A DEAF ADDER

U NLESS BETTERMENT CAME IMMEDIATELY, ENGLAND'S CONDITION WAS HOPELESS. IT WAS, SAID PENN, A COUNTRY OF "MANY ABOMINATIONS AND GROSS IMPIETIES," A NATION MARRED BY "LUSTS, PLEASURES, wantonness, drunkenness, whoredoms, oaths, blasphemies, envies, treacheries and persecutions of the just." In a jeremiad very similar to the writings of his early evangelical career, a call to action so fevered as to border on hysteria, he warned that Quakers must "stand in the gap" to save England from "the overflowing scourge of God's wrath . . . just ready to break out." The metaphor was mixed but the concern was deep.[1]

Since only the Society of Friends truly obeyed the laws of Jehovah, its members alone could save England from annihilation. They, therefore, must go forth to spread the Word of God. "To thy tents, O Israel," he pleaded.

The Quakers did not connect Penn's prediction of an overwhelming scourge with the heavy rains that poured down soon after the publication of his warning, nor did they embark upon an intensive campaign of national reform. Instead, they listened to persistent rumors about his supposed Catholicism. His withdrawals into semi-retirement, his occasional absences from meeting, and the air of mystery that surrounded him were misconstrued. London Monthly Meeting, which certainly should have known better, "being conscious of the great scandal cast on William Penn, and that his absence casts upon the same," went so far as to ask one of its members to investigate the situation. The prober found nothing, simply because there was nothing to be found.[2]

Other investigators, not so partial to Penn, were not so sure. Some time previously Penn had been summoned before a Parliamentary Committee on the Penal Laws to testify on behalf of freedom of religion. He had then declared, "I am far from thinking it fit that Papists should be whipped for their consciences' sake because I declaim against the injustice of whipping Quakers. . . . We must give the liberty we ask."[3] The anti-Quaker pamphleteers seized upon the passage, tore it from its context, shortened it, and presented what was left of it as incontrovertible "proof" that William Penn was indeed a Jesuit.[4]

All this combined to create what Penn called a "sickly time" when "the discovery of plots and plotting goes on despite all arts to smother it." High among these discoveries was the hysterical "revelation" by Penn's former neighbor, Titus Oates, of a non-existent Jesuit plot to murder the King, crown the Duke of York, and restore England to the Catholic fold. Although the plot existed only in Oates' fertile mind the authorities were alarmed, and some gullible private citizens suspected that Penn might be implicated.[5]

Sussex County needed no more proof. In compiling a list of Popish recusants, Catholics who refused to attend Church of England services, the authorities included the name of William Penn of Worminghurst.[6]

The news did not seem to cause Penn any great anxiety; possibly he could not spare the time, for Guli had just been delivered of a baby girl. The Penns named her Letitia, shortened in ordinary conversation to Tish or Tishy. William was so delighted with his little daughter and so solicitous of Guli's care that he took little heed of the Sussex County action.[7]

Though the leadership of the Society of Friends valiantly defended Penn, the gossipings, whisperings, and misrepresentations were bound to have some effect upon the credulous. There may have been some, indeed, who were moved by Faldo's ironic tribute in *Quaker Quibbles*, which praised Penn only to impugn his orthodoxy: "I do really own that thou, William Penn, hast a voluble tongue and a strong voice and clear, a grateful utterance and, I believe, good lungs—an excellent rhetorician, but this doesn't make thee a Christian."

Others continued to think it unseemly that Penn should have so much to do with worldly matters, thus confusing spiritual and material affairs. His friend the Earl of Shaftesbury had been arrested on charges of criticizing Parliament, and Penn had gone, with Rudyard and Byllinge, in company with the Duke to Buckingham to talk with the prisoner. Failing to gain entrance to the Tower, Penn organized a protest movement to free Shaftesbury. Though Penn did not join a group that set bonfires in the London streets that night to demonstrate against the arrest, he circulated a petition for Shaftesbury's release. In seeking signatures at Bull and Mouth Meetinghouse he approached Francis Bugg, but Bugg refused to sign. "Glad am I," said Bugg later of Penn and the Penn associates, "that I was made sensible of their evil intent." Bugg, who would later develop into one of Penn's most virulent opponents, went on to brand

Penn's group as an evil generation devoid of charity[8] and Shaftesbury was completely cleared and restored to both royal and parliamentary favor.

Soon after, Algernon Sidney visited Penn, bringing with him as a present "the best and warmest robe" that was to be found among traders with the Indies. The reunion was pleasant, but it had unfortunate results, for Sidney was in official disfavor, partly because of what would today be called his leftist ideas, more because he was suspected of being a former, if not a current, pensioner of the King of France. Those overly suspicious Sussex authorities who considered Penn a recusant branded both Penn and Sidney as persons dangerous to law and order. Neither man took effective steps to dispel the misconception. Sidney rode over frequently to Worminghurst to talk with Penn about his hopes of making England an ideal community and possibly curtailing royal power. As a preliminary step he planned to run for Parliament.[9]

His enthusiasm was infectious. Friends, as a rule, steered shy of practical politics but they never shrank from promoting basic principles of liberty and justice. Penn produced, therefore, a brochure, *England's Great Interest in the Choice of a New Parliament*, a statement of principles which might well have been one of the earliest drafts of a party platform. He signed it "Philanglus," a hybrid name his Chigwell and Oxford tutors would have disapproved, but one so catchy that half a dozen others besides Penn published under the same pseudonym. Few of these later Philanglus productions could have been by William Penn; certainly not the hostile *Letter to the Quakers*, which may have been written by Francis Bugg, and there were those who doubted whether *England's Great Interest* was a Penn pamphlet. Oddly enough, though William Penn, of all people, stood in no need of a ghost writer, some suspected that Sidney had written it, allowing Penn to take the credit; others named the Earl of Shaftesbury or Benjamin Furly.

Today, the chief planks of this unconventional Whig platform seem not only desirable but essential; no one now questions the need for security of life, liberty, and property, for trial by independent jury, or legislation by a popularly elected parliament. To Royalists of the time, however, the broad recommendations implied a great deal more than their literal meaning; court circles scented radicalism, perhaps revolution. Recommendations for punishing plotters against the throne were all very well, but were not those suggestions, written by authors suspected of that very design, merely intended to divert suspicion from themselves? To oust "the evil councillors of the King"—a standard sentence in any criticism of a tyranny—implied danger not only to the advisors but to the governmental system.

Because Penn, like other Quaker leaders, had never voted nor played any role in practical politics, certain sections of the manifesto do not echo his usual style nor voice his usual sentiments. Penn could not sink to the level of routine politics. He disliked what he termed "the envy, malice and incharitableness" of political campaigning, "the corruption and drunkenness of the polls," and so he floundered when trying to appeal for votes.[10]

Sidney was to stand for Guildford, a parliamentary district about twenty-five miles northwest of Worminghurst. Penn wished to help, but his ideas of campaigning were peculiar. Instead of appealing to the Guildford electors, he buttonholed high court officials and half a dozen powerful lords for their support, his lack of practicality being shown by his asking Royalist help for an anti-Royalist candidate. Not unpredictably, he failed to get it. In those days of very limited suffrage electioneering speeches were of little value, but Penn proposed to take the stump. One may seriously question whether, in any case, his speeches would have won over many voters, but the matter was never tested; the Guildford officials, thinking him a Jesuit, demanded that he take an oath abjuring papacy. Penn, realizing that the purpose was not only to prevent his speaking but also to jail him for refusing to swear, questioned the legality of demanding an oath at such a time. The officials responded by banishing him from the district.[11]

Sidney fared no better. When he went to the mayor to announce his candidacy, that official told him it would be a useless waste of time and money for him to contest the seat. It was the custom of the district, the mayor said, for the voters to accept the choice made by the mayor and aldermen; since they were already committed to the candidacy of one Thomas Dalmahoy, Sidney could not possibly win the election.

From a modern point of view the Guildford procedures were incredible. When Sidney persisted in campaigning his opponents challenged his eligibility because, they said, he was not a freeman registered in the district. This was, for Englishmen, an odd argument, because residence had never been a requirement of candidacy, but Sidney asked to be registered. The mayor promised to arrange it, but neglected to tell Sidney whether he had succeeded or even if he had tried. Next, the Dalmahoy forces, in full command of the election machinery, refused to tell Sidney when the voting was to take place. Then, at midnight, they announced that balloting would begin at nine in the morning. This snap election, intended to take Sidney voters by surprise, was to be held on a market day, "a thing never known before."

When the town recorder, the official in charge of the election, opened the polls some Sidney supporters were challenged because in this open oral voting they mispronounced Sidney's name. Others were "threatened with loss of money benefits." One man who was owed £300 was told that if he voted for Sidney he would not be paid. Supporters of Sidney in other areas, Charcoal Barn Chapel, for instance, and Black Horse Lane, otherwise known as Sidney's Alley, were flatly refused any chance to vote.

Nevertheless, Penn contended that Sidney had carried the election. If so, he was refused certification because the mayor had failed to certify him as a freeman. Dalmahoy was declared elected. His victory was brief; within two months the King dissolved Parliament and called for new elections.

Sidney was ready to try again. Realizing that Guildford was hopeless, he pitched upon Bramber, a one-street town only five miles distant from Worminghurst. In making the choice, he and Penn displayed a lack of political knowledge, for Bramber, even for those days of political dishonesty, was notoriously corrupt. Two rival families, with their numerous in-laws, made up three-quarters of the electorate; between them they monopolized the public offices. After campaigns that were invariably marked by violence and bribery, the results were always contested because of overt irregularities. Nevertheless, Penn and Sidney were confident that Sidney could win.[12]

The two rival families united against the stranger. First they pretended that Algernon's brother Henry had already been accepted as a candidate, whereupon Algernon, unwilling to run in opposition, withdrew his name. Penn then learned that Henry was in Europe, with no intention of returning home, that he knew nothing of the scheme, and was almost wholly unknown in the district. On hearing this, Algernon became, as it was delicately understated, "slightly disgusted." When Penn suggested that Algernon reenter, he refused to do so on the ground that it would be undignified. He stood instead for Amersham and was, he believed, elected, but the result was contested and Parliament denied him the seat.[13]

Sidney's failures disappointed William Penn; they undermined his faith in the political wisdom of the ordinary voter. He still believed that left to themselves, the people would select as their leaders upright men of wisdom and integrity; but if such men, other than Sidney, would not come forward to contest elections, what good would be attainable? "There is no hope in England," he declared. "The deaf adder cannot be charmed."[14]

The realization bewildered him. He construed the political setbacks as forecasts of the future. Freedom of conscience, he thought pessimistically, was to be denied. He had tried, in every way he knew, by publications, by personal appeal, and by example to persuade Englishmen that toleration served both God and state, yet all his efforts had been fruitless.

Why could not all the world apply the Golden Rule? Why could not everyone accommodate differences quietly, be kind to everyone, especially to the unfortunate, to all be helpful and to all be inoffensive? Himself neither fanatic nor doctrinaire, he tried to understand the thinking of those who differed with him. Though firmly convinced that Quakerism embodied Truth, he sincerely admired upright and godly men of all denominations. Bigotry appalled him. Why could not others be as generous as he? Yet when, acting on those principles, he conceded that there could be good in those who disagreed with him, his enemies cried out that, like Admiral Sir William, he was a compromiser and a trimmer. Not satisfied with calling him vacillating, they said he was a self-seeking hypocrite.

Certainly from time to time Penn changed his mind on many matters. As conditions changed, as new information became available, as he matured, as he thought more clearly, he sometimes saw matters in a different light. No one, for instance, could have been more averse to authoritarianism than he when, in *England's Great Interest*, he argued that Parliament alone should make or repeal laws ("All else is tyranny"). But to further toleration, he once or twice condoned a king's arbitrary nullification of existing laws. Usually he trusted people to be wise, yet after Bramber, he despaired of them.

To condemn Penn for inconsistency would be very easy, but it would also be grossly unfair. He clearly saw the goal of human happiness for all who feared God and were good neighbors; but the road to that happiness being neither smooth nor straight, he stumbled now and then or found himself obliged to retrace his steps. Like everyone else, he made mistakes, but unlike most of us, he had the courage to confess an error and to correct it.

Many in his position would have given up the struggle and sunk themselves in comfortable retirement. The mature Penn was not, however, the youth who played at soldiering nor the young man who hobnobbed with courtiers and social butterflies. The dilettante of Dublin's Society of Friendship had disappeared; he was now afire with evangelical zeal. If Guildford and Bramber showed that England was hopeless, why then the western wilderness lay open.

14

PASSPORT TO PEACE

A S A FIRST STEP TOWARD HIS HAVEN OF PEACE AND TRUTH, ON JUNE 1, 1680, PENN FORMALLY ASKED FOR A GRANT OF AMERICAN LAND WEST OF THE DELAWARE AS FAR AS MARYLAND RAN AND NORTHWARD from that province "as far as plantable." This width, he suggested, might be five degrees of latitude.[1]

Purposely he made a vague request. Neither he nor anyone else could define precisely just what territory was available. Few Englishmen were well acquainted with the terrain, for not many traders or adventurers had penetrated the unknown Indian country. Not being trained observers and certainly not skilled geographers, they had brought back only sketchy maps and not wholly trustworthy accounts. Penn knew that he wanted the Delaware, primarily as an access to the sea; beyond that he had little idea of what else should be included, provided only that he should have good land, good water routes, good climate, and good neighbors. All these, provided he received the Delaware, would be available, for the land accorded him would lie between tolerant Maryland and the Dutchmen living in what was now being called New York. Lord Baltimore, he understood, had some sort of shadowy pretension to the mouth of the river, a claim that Penn did not recognize, but most of the rest of the land was unsurveyed. Some of the riverfront, he knew, was thinly settled by Finns and Swedes and Dutch, even by a sprinkling of pioneering Englishmen from Connecticut, but none of these were expected to cause trouble.

The proposed width of five degrees, however, as Penn must have been aware, was unrealistic. The Maryland northern boundary was in dispute but, wherever it might be, a reach of five degrees farther north would run across western New York well into Canada. Subsequently, Penn would be offered three degrees, a suggestion he accepted, only to find that this, too, would take in Western New York and also Canadian territory, almost as far as Ottawa or Montreal. Eventually, Penn would be allowed a province that would run only to the New York line. And not even this reduction prevented overlapping titles. Connecticut, by virtue of its charter, claimed territory extending as far as the Pacific, except, of course, that area belonging to New York. In early days the conflict of title over the entire northern part of Pennsylvania caused no difficulty; but in the late eighteenth century, battles would ensue, the three Pennamite Wars, until a court decision in 1792 set aside the Connecticut claims. These problems were unforeseen at the time of Penn's petition, partly because of the absence of adequate maps, but more because both the Crown and Penn were really more interested in the patent's issuance than in its accuracy.

Penn's petition came at a moment so opportune for the King and his brother that it is quite possible that they or their advisors encouraged the request. The royal brothers were under heavy criticism. Religious quarrels were causing much discussion. James, Duke of York had been an avowed Catholic for eight years, and, though his two daughters were being brought up as Anglicans, it seemed obvious that he intended upon his accession to bring England back to the Roman faith. Penn's friend, the Earl of Shaftesbury, was heading a movement to bar James from the throne. Thus, there was conflict, with fears on both sides that religious persecution would intensify. If, then, a grant were made to Penn, a nonconformist, King Charles might blunt the edge of Protestant hostility by showing that the Stuarts were not bigots.

Other motives lay deeper. King Charles, in common with most other Englishmen, regarded Quakers, except a few like William Penn, as downright nuisances. He and his brother James knew better than to credit the ridiculous rumors that many members of the Society of Friends were secret papists or that they plotted to overthrow the monarchy; they realized that Penn and his associates were patriotic, loyal Englishmen. No demagogue could have led them into military action, since they would not resort to violence; no radical could possibly incite them to rebellion. Nevertheless, neither the Stuarts nor many other Englishmen yearned for Quakers as neighbors. To ship malcontents and eccentrics overseas, however peaceful they might be, would make everybody happy.

Penn himself, while publicly explaining that he looked upon his expected province as compensation for an unpaid debt owed his father, privately believed that Charles wished to get the Quakers out of England. "The government," he said, "was anxious to be rid of us at so cheap a price."[2]

If this was really the King's reason for approving Penn's petition, he did not think it politic to say so. Instead, he advanced three other explanations. He cited Admiral Sir William's "discretion with our dearest brother James," a very indirect reference to Sir William's tact in assuming blame for the naval blunder committed by the Duke of York. He mentioned Penn's "commendable desire to enlarge the British Empire and to promote such useful commodities as may be beneficial to the King and his dominions." He touched delicately upon religious matters by suggesting that Penn's influence would "reduce the sav-- age nations by just and gentle manners to the love of civil society and the Christian religion."[3]

Nor was Penn crude enough to suggest that he and his co-religionists were aching to get out of England to a more tolerant land; he steered clear also of emphasizing that only by receiving colonial land could he hope to get the Crown to settle its just debt.[4]

The debt was an old one. While serving Charles II on active sea duty, the Admiral was paying from his own pocket for the food furnished His Majesty's Navy. Charles had not reimbursed him at the time but had, in fact, declared a moratorium on paying bills. During this delay, the so-called closing of the Exchequer, and thereafter, the debt had swollen, with interest, to about £16,000. Penn was willing to accept cheap land in exchange for a debt that was obviously uncollectable. He had no idea whatever how much such land might bring upon the open market, if actually it would be salable, but assumed that a fair price might range somewhere close to the £16,000 figure. Years later when he learned that the land granted him had been offered by some unknown official to some anonymous possible purchaser for only £1,200, Penn complained that instead of receiving a bargain, he had been cheated.[5]

Penn's petition began a tortuous and leisurely course through bureau- cratic channels. Favorable consideration was virtually assured, not only because of the reasons publicly assigned but also for the unpublicized arguments. In addition to the King and to the Duke of York, Penn possessed an influential group of friends in office, a lobbying team that included the Earl of Rochester, the Duke's brother-in-law, the Earl of Halifax, a privy councillor, Chief Justice Francis North, and Wil- liam Blaythwaite, influential secretary of the Council on Trade and Plantations.

Even so, progress was extremely slow, for bureaucrats dragged their feet. Some wished to create the impression that deep thought was being given to a decision; others lagged in hopes of receiving "gratuities" to hasten their action. It was necessary, too, to consult various individuals whose interests might be affected, the chiefs of neighboring provinces or their London agents, the bureaucrats managing court affairs, eminent lawyers, influential statesmen and the like.

Penn killed time while waiting by editing a collection of his father's papers, which, with an eye to flattery, he dedicated to the King. His peti- tion crawled along, thanks to the influence of Penn's friends and to his generous gratuities. The Duke of York, if not a sponsor of the petition, certainly favored it, though it took his slothful office four full months to say so. Lord Baltimore, though anticipating no dangers or difficulties about having a pacifist province on his northern frontier, withheld immediate approval awaiting better information concerning boundaries. Meanwhile, he contented himself by suggesting, most unnecessarily, that Penn promise not to sell arms or ammunition to the Indians.[6]

Not until November, five months after Penn's application, was even a draft patent ready for the Crown's consideration. The period had been filled with frequent conferences between the bureaucrats and Penn over the precise wording of the provisions to be included. Though the project was primarily designed as a philanthropy for the Society of Friends, London Meeting contributed little more than its good will and its blessing. Certainly it donated nothing toward defrayment of costs for those gratuities. That expense, Penn declared, ran as high as £10,577, an enormous figure for those days, equal to a full year's income from Guli's rich estates.[7] In only one instance did Penn explain to whom he paid out these gratuities, which were disbursed not in plebean shillings or even in pounds sterling but in the professional men's guineas.

He proposed that his province should be named Sylvania, because so much of it was forested. The King, however, whether in honor of the Admiral or because he suspected that such a name would attract few immigrants, ordered that the prefix Penn be added. Though certainly not without his share of self-esteem, William protested that for the province to bear his family name would be presumptuous and conceited. He sought out Sir Leoline Jenkins, the secretary of state, whose task it was to draft the patent, and offered him twenty guineas to omit the prefix, but Sir Leoline would not consent to overrule the King.[8] Thus rebuffed, Penn modestly explained that Pennsylvania was a hybrid invention, like Philanglus. "Penn" as a prefix, he declared, was just a Welsh word meaning hill. Thus, Pennsylvania did not mean Penn's Woods but just High Forest, something akin to the High Wycombe near which he had lived at Rickmansworth.[9] It is extremely doubtful that anyone accepted the explanation or, for that matter, believed then, or remembers now, that the prefix honors Admiral Sir William.

Not all the delays in drafting the patent need be laid at the door of men greedy for bribes. The machinery, and to some extent the form, of English administration was undergoing transformation. Royalists, disturbed because too many rights and privileges had been carelessly thrown away, were busily engaged in strengthening and extending the power of the central government, particularly in its control over its colonial possessions. The powerful Council on Trade and Plantations, more royalist than the King, was intent on concentrating power in the monarch's hands. To that end the committee paid more attention to retaining royal

authority and, if possible, to recovering some rights that had been carelessly lost, than it did to marking out carefully the precise area Penn was
to receive. In comparison with paragraphs dealing with Penn's rights and
duties, those locating the area were rather casually drawn; they would, in
time, lead to confusion, argument, and bitter enmity between Penn and
his neighbors.

The committeemen, while very well disposed toward Penn, looked out
more carefully for Royal interests; almost every special privilege given
Penn had a stout string attached to it. He and his heirs were to govern
Pennsylvania, either in person or through a deputy, but no lieutenant
governor or other high official could be appointed except with Royal
approbation. Proprietary courts could indict and try suspected violators
of the law, but convictions might be overruled by higher English tribunals. As perpetual governors, Penn and his heirs could pardon most convicted offenders but not those found guilty of first-degree murder or of
any offense within the broad category of treason or sedition.[10]

Penn's province was further restricted in matters of taxation. It could
levy and collect taxes, provided that, as in England, the freemen, through
a popularly elected legislature, gave approval; but alone among American proprietary colonies, Pennsylvania might also be taxed by King and
Parliament. London's reservation in this matter explains why, years
later, Pennsylvanians were less disturbed than their neighbors about such
measures as the Stamp Act.

The Provincial Assembly, which was to be elected, held all lawmaking
power, subject, of course, to a gubernatorial veto, except that if emer-
gencies occurred during a recess, the governor or his deputy could issue
special ordinances. In any case, emergency included, all regulations, ordinances, and statutes must harmonize with English law and custom. The
requirement was, of course, no hardship; the principle was precisely that
for which William Penn had long contended.

The lords composing the Council on Trade and Plantations trusted
Penn to govern wisely, honestly, and well; but, in cases a successor should
be less upright, the lords insisted that Pennsylvania, alone among the
American provinces, forward copies of all legislation for London's inspection. This regulation, however, like the boundary lines, was somewhat
carelessly drawn. All legal measures were effective upon assembly passage
and gubernatorial signature, but they need not be bundled up for ship-
ment to England until five years after becoming effective. A bad law
might thus be enforced for years before the Privy Council or the Lords of
Trade and Plantations sent back word of its rejection.

The time span thus nullified the lords' attempt to guard against what
they might consider unwise legislation. Clever manipulators could cir-
cumvent London's disapproval. If any measure seemed likely to incur
Royal opposition, it would only be necessary to repeal it four years
after it had become effective and to reenact it a few days later.

Tight restrictions governed Pennsylvania's industry and commerce. England, very conscious that it was establishing an empire, looked upon its colonies as suppliers of raw materials and as consumers of English products. Trade laws and the Navigation Acts required colonials to give preference to English merchants, to avoid competition with the mother country, and to transport freight and passengers in English-flag ships plying between English ports. Special care was to be taken lest even Scots attempt to break the English monopoly.

All this was very clearly explained to William Penn. He was obliged to promise (other provincial governors swore) that Pennsylvania would strictly observe the Navigation Acts and the trade laws. He was also required, when he was not personally in England, to maintain a London agent to whom orders could be given and from whom reports could be received. Furthermore, as additional assurance, admiralty officials and Royal customs collectors were sent to watch the province. If less imperialistically minded officials suspected that the patent provisions requiring the stationing of special agents as watchdogs for the Crown might lead to jealousies and conflicts between provincial and Royal officials, they held their peace.

Others active in the drafting tinkered with the wording. Chief Justice North and Attorney-General Jones, noting that the draft said nothing about defense, advised provisions permitting Penn, the pacifist, to form and train an army for his protection against "pirates, thieves or invading barbarians." This was strange language, inasmuch as Pennsylvania, an inland province, would seem unlikely to have much to do with offense committed on the high seas, crimes which, in any case, would be matters for the Royal Navy. Nor was it quite clear just who was meant by "invading barbarians," unless, perchance, it referred to Indians coming in from Maryland, New Jersey, or New York.[11]

Henry Compton, Bishop of London, contributed two bright ideas. Though Penn had for years been insisting on freedom of worship, the Bishop thought it necessary to require him to allow Anglicans to worship in their own church. He also felt that, in simple justice, William Penn should compensate the Indians for lands that he was settling. That Fenwick's Quakers had already taken just such steps, as had the Swedes and Dutch and various groups of Englishmen before him, seems not to have been known to the good Bishop. Penn had never thought of slighting the red men in any way, but ever the gentleman and the tactful diplomat, he thanked Compton for the suggestion and gave him credit for suggesting that Pennsylvania buy out Indian titles.[12]

On January 28, 1681, the Committee on Trade and Plantations approved the amended draft patent. Although in all respects the document met the King's wishes—the clauses giving Penn warmaking powers having been omitted—Charles took his time about accepting it, but on March 4 he added his signature.

William Penn was now the "True and Absolute Proprietor" of the province of Pennsylvania. Except for some small acreage held by Swedes and Finns who had already acquired titles, he now owned about forty-five thousand square miles of unsurveyed and largely unexplored territory, an area greater than that ever before possessed by any other private citizen in Western, or probably in world, history. For a province richer in natural resources than was any other American proprietorship, he was to pay to "the castle of Windsor" a token tribute of two beaver skins a year, if demanded, plus one-fifth of any gold and silver that the province might yield. A month later the King called upon all inhabitants of the province to obey their new overlord.

Penn soon discovered that it was one thing to receive a patent but quite another to decipher just what it really meant. The bureaucrats had been instructed to draft a transfer of title and this, with the aid of the gratuities, they had done; but, whether by ignorance, carelessness, accident or design, they had filled it with uncertainties, contradictions, and cleverly concealed restrictions on Penn's privileges.

The real weakness of the document was its imprecision. Geographical inaccuracies were understandable because the American interior was still underexplored, but there was no valid excuse for trained lawyers uncritically accepting slipshod reporting as proved fact or for their including in Penn's grant land that might have been already conveyed to others. Interpreting the patent's wording and correcting its errors caused great and long-lived confusion. Not for almost a century were Penn or his successors completely certain of just what land the patent conveyed. The eastern and western boundaries seemed clear enough for all immediate needs, the former being the river Delaware and the latter the same approximate line as that of Maryland, but even these were inexact. Sir John Werden, he whom the Spaniards called Juan Diablo, was quick to notice that the patent excluded from Pennsylvania any islands in the Delaware. Confusion on this score was for the most part minor, since Penn and his associates controlled all of West Jersey and could make satisfactory arrangements about those islands. A few years later, however, when a new province was created on the west bank of the lower Delaware, the ownership of the stream would cause considerable controversy.[13] The western line of Pennsylvania also failed to meet the patent's provisions. Owing to boundary conflicts between Maryland and Virginia, Lord Baltimore's west frontier would be found to lie some fifty miles east of that of Pennsylvania.

Penn's southern boundary caused the worst confusion. The uncertainty sprang from the loose wording of the patent for Maryland granted in 1632 to Cecil Calvert, second Lord Baltimore. That patent described Maryland as beginning at a place called Watkins Point, assumed to be on the thirty-eighth parallel, and extending northward a certain number of miles, which it was believed would bring it to the fortieth. The description was inexact. Watkins Point was not at the thirty-eighth, the number of miles supposedly between degrees was incorrect, and the fortieth parallel was not where it was supposed to be. All this led to bitter argument between Penn and various Lord Baltimores who disputed for decades in council chambers, law courts, and Royal offices. On one or two occasions, armed conflict was only narrowly averted.[14]

Actually, the argument was probably unnecessary. Both participants professed to be satisfied with the fortieth parallel as a dividing line, but for one reason or another, neither seemed overanxious to pinpoint its location. Every ship captain sailing to America possessed a sextant by which he determined latitude, and it is unthinkable that in all those years no one took observations to settle disputes once and for all. But, probably because each side overstated its case and did not care to admit errors, no scientific findings were accepted.

Almost immediately after receiving his patent Penn had resigned as one of the West Jersey trustees. If his motive had been to avoid conflict of interest the gesture was in vain, for almost immediately the affairs of Sir George Carteret, who had died a few months earlier, were found to be in such chaotic condition, and his debts so heavy, that it was necessary to auction off his East Jersey holdings. Again, the London Society of Friends intervened, enlisting Penn, Rudyard, and ten other leading Quakers in a syndicate to buy the East Jersey proprietorship. After winning the auction, by a bid of £3400, the twelve men added a dozen others to the syndicate. Since eight of the new men, largely Scots and Irishmen, were already members of the West Jersey proprietary board, the result was to unify the Jerseys and to give the Friends complete control of the seacoast from New York harbor to Cape May.[15]

Unfortunately, the purchase failed to solve the problem of how to win for Pennsylvania an unrestricted access to the sea. Though the Jersey coast had numerous inlets from the ocean, some of them deep enough and large enough to accommodate overseas traffic, the shoreline was so paralleled by sand bars and shallows that navigation was unsafe. The one good outlet for Pennsylvania remained the Delaware, whose eastern shore was wholly Quaker-owned; but Lord Baltimore still insisted that his 1632 patent, almost half a century senior to that of William Penn, gave him ownership of the lower reaches of the western riverbank.

The real point at issue was not so much the entire line of the fortieth but the precise locations at which that parallel crossed Pennsylvania's two major rivers. Penn's great concern was for a deep-water harbor, one that would give him safe and easy access to the sea. The Delaware, Penn had learned, was an excellent stream, "as broad as the Thames at London," but by his best estimates, the fortieth crossed it at a point ninety or a hundred miles short of the Atlantic. Its one good port then in use, a harbor which the Dutch called New Amstel, lay south of the important parallel. To reach the ocean his ships must sail past western shorelines which might conceivably someday be hostile. True, the eastern bank was firmly in Quaker hands, but its one good harbor, Fenwick's Salem, was much too far downstream to meet Pennsylvania's needs.

The Marylanders maintained that the fortieth crossed the second river, the Susquehanna, at a place called Susquehanna Fort, and the Pennsylvanians hoped that, if all else went wrong, the Susquehanna might just possibly provide an outlet to the sea. The hope was not a bright one, for the Susquehanna lay a hundred miles to the west, and a trackless forest lay between, so that it would be most inconvenient, if not impossible, as a harbor. To make matters worse, there was at least one other Indian town by the same name and there might be more. No one was certain whether Susquehanna Fort lay on an inland stream, which might not be navigable, or at the head of Chesapeake Bay. Even if it did lie on the bay, traffic from that port would be at the mercy of the Marylanders and, at the mouth of the bay, of the Virginians also.[16]

The west bank of the Delaware, therefore, was essential for Penn's use if his province was to thrive. Somehow, therefore, he must win title to that western bank. It had been Swedish and it had been Dutch, but in 1668 the English had taken it, together with New Netherlands, and King Charles had given it to his brother James. As the western shore of the Delaware was of minor size compared with New York and was, moreover, isolated from that larger holding, Penn hoped to persuade James to add it to the Pennsylvania grant which it adjoined. If this could be done, Penn in his own right, or in company with his Quaker friends of New Jersey, would own the entire basin of the Delaware River. Thus, Penn's free access to the sea would be assured and his harbor problems solved. He would have no neighbors for at least a hundred miles to the north and west. Many of the eastward people were his fellow Friends, while, if Maryland people on the south should unaccountably turn hostile, there were but few of them and they, too, lived far away from the capital he planned to build. As the province would be more nearly safe against invasion than any other in America, he would need neither troops nor fortifications. There was no better place in all England's American possessions to build a pacifist community.

All things considered, Penn and the Society of Friends were well satisfied with their patent.

15

FREEDOM FOR THE ASKING

WHILE PENN'S PATENT WAS INCHING ITS WAY TOWARD APPROVAL, PENN WAS CONSIDERING THE BASIC PHILOSOPHY FOR THE PROVINCE HE WOULD EVENTUALLY RECEIVE. THE WORK WAS MOST congenial, the type of activity for which his temperament and studies had prepared him. He acted very cautiously, taking great care to offend no one lest he antagonize some high official who could block the patent's progress. His conscience would not permit him to cease his appeals to free Quakers from injustice, but most of the officials responsible for persecution were small-time functionaries who would have no power to delay the patent. As long as Penn moved carefully at court, holding himself aloof from national politics, he would offend no one of importance.

It was not surprising, therefore, that in December 1680 the French ambassador reported to Versailles that though William Penn, "a man of great parts . . . and very rich," favored Algernon Sidney's hope for the creation of an English republic, he was giving the scheme no public support. Like his old friend Dr. John Owen, Penn allowed Sidney and the Duke of Buckingham to stand in the forefront.[1]

From what Penn had seen of the legislative process, how executives administered the laws and the tortuous manner in which courts interpreted the wording of the statutes, he realized that for ordinary governments lawmaking would be difficult. For his own province, however, he expected no such problem, for his people would be different from ordinary colonists; they would be honest, God-fearing people dedicated to the common good, each eager to help all others, everyone anxious to promote the general welfare. There would be little need for government. Laws would be virtually unnecessary. The leaders, chosen conscientiously for their wisdom, qualification, and ability, would invariably act correctly. The province that he would build would be a haven of righteousness; in Penn's own words, a "Holy Experiment." For such a state the basic law would be more an ethical than a legal matter. Actually, it could be brief: the Golden Rule, the Ten Commandments, and the Sermon on the Mount would suffice to insure a perfect government where freedom and equality, justice, peace, and toleration would necessarily prevail. Yet, since others besides members of the Society of Friends would filter into the community, and since in England not all Friends were perfect, some friction might possibly arise. A set of laws must therefore be adopted. For the transition period in Pennsylvania, until the two thousand Swedes and Dutch already resident could be joined by the expected Quaker influx, the existing code, known as the *Duke of York's Book of Laws*, could remain in force, together with the English common law. During the interval the Quakers could be preparing a better system.

The King's order in April, 1681, that all Pennsylvanians must immediately obey William Penn as "True and Absolute Proprietor" seems to have taken Penn by surprise. While he had, of course, looked forward to the grant of territory, he may not have anticipated that his responsibility for governing would come so soon.[2]

No one seriously objected to a continuance of the Duke of York's laws, but a delay in conferring those special rights and privileges of which he had talked and written for so many years might engender in England charges of hypocrisy. A government set up by popular consent of residents already in the province would not be Quakerish but Dutch–Swedish; a new government created by Penn and a few advisors would be autocratically imposed. Neither could be regarded as an embodiment of English democracy nor as ratified by a popular assembly.

Not, to be sure, that the province would protest, for, as a matter of fact, it had no expectation of being asked for its approval. Except for a very small minority, the people of Pennsylvania had little knowledge of William Penn nor of what he had been advocating. Actually, neither Penn nor the provincials dependent upon him had much information about the other. Such news as reached them was neither trustworthy nor unbiased. The small handful of Friends already living in Pennsylvania had certainly heard of Penn, both from Quaker sources and from such Jersey neighbors as they may have met. These, no doubt, testified to his piety, his humanity and his tolerance, but colonials were not likely to have gained much specific data about his ideas of needed legislation or of his views on economics, government, and social welfare.

Similarly, Penn's information about his province must have been more impressionistic than reliable. While publications had appeared about Massachusetts and Virginia, the writers had devoted very little space to areas other than their own, and when they did, they were not apt to waste praise upon their neighbors. Even a seventeenth-century

European broadminded enough to credit the savage Indian with simplicity of soul and kindness of heart seldom extended that charity toward a stranger who was white. Quakers such as Coale, Fox and Thomas Thurston had visited parts of Pennsylvania, though briefly and usually hurriedly; but while they had met a few other Quakers and English-speaking Indians, they had encountered only a handful of non-Quakers whom they considered friendly. Penn had talked with such travelers but had learned much more about the soil, the climate, and the crops than about the people living there. The accuracy of what knowledge he gained may perhaps be judged from his assurance to Jonathan Swift that the province lacked the shelter of mountains, "which left it open to the northern winds from Hudson's Bay and the Frozen Sea which destroyed all plantations and trees and was even pernicious to all common vegetables."[3]

Since Penn envisioned his province as a Quaker community, made and kept so by preponderance of numbers rather than by special favors to the Friends, he thought it best to wait until a sufficient number of English Quakers were committed to the colonization project. A group of the better qualified of these so-called First Purchasers would then meet in London to draft proposed legislation. The plan seemed, on the surface, to deny the Dutch and Swedes much share in determining their own future, but Penn avoided this discrimination by requiring a ratification of the proposals by a popular assembly to be chosen by all Pennsylvania landowners. Thus, with both Quaker and Dutch–Swedish approval, the colonial administration would be satisfactory to everyone.

Such general acceptance was essential at a time when neither Englishmen living in the colonies nor their London overlords put any great amount of confidence in each other's integrity. Lack of knowledge colored all opinions. Colonials judged the London bureaucrats in terms of the agents sent out from London to supervise the provinces; and as these agents often combined customs, rents, and tax collections with private trading opportunities, the provincials thought of the officials as tyrannical and corrupt. Similarly, London viewed the provinces as nests of smugglers, trade law violators, and, very frequently, of pirates or malcontents ready to go over to the French, Dutch, or Spanish enemy.

Characteristically, Penn began his governmental revision by offering reassurances. About a month after becoming True and Absolute Proprietor he dispatched a letter to his colonists. "It has pleased God in his Providence," he said, "to cast you within my lot and care. It is a business that though I never undertook before, yet God hath given me an understanding of my duty and an honest desire to do it uprightly."[4]

Technically, the letter was correct. Though Penn had been actively involved in organizing and directing the government of New Jersey, he had not borne the sole responsibility. By the King's patent, it had now fallen upon him to do so in Pennsylvania. Instead of being obliged to consult with a score of partners, as in New Jersey, the burden was his alone. He intended, however, to allow Pennsylvanians a powerful and, indeed, a controlling voice in determining their own future. "You shall be governed by laws of your own choosing and live a free, and if you will, a sober and industrious people," he promised. "I shall not usurp the rights of any or oppress his person. . . . Whatever sober and free men shall reasonably desire for the security and improvement of their own happiness I shall heartily comply with."[5]

Then, lest the people worry about what might happen in the future, he added reassurance. "I propose that which is extraordinary: to leave myself and my successors no power of doing mischief, that the will of one man may not hinder the good of a whole country."[6]

The Stuarts and their partisans could have considered such promises, if taken literally, so subversive of divine right as to warrant committing the author to the Tower. Penn was reasonably safe, however. His formula was simple and effective. He had written precisely what he meant to say, confident that the bureaucrats, themselves adept at masking their real intentions by using weasel words, would not suspect that every word he wrote was true. He had said nothing that could not have been cynically accepted by almost any English king since Magna Carta. Were not all English statutes, in theory at least, endorsed by a Parliament in which the people were represented? Did any English monarch ever admit that he was exercising any power that he did not think his own? Had any monarch ever refused his people anything that he considered reasonable? Every English ruler would have been quite certain that, no matter what his subjects might have thought, he was performing his duty uprightly and honestly.

Penn was familiar enough with Whitehall's theories and practices to anticipate how courtiers would misread any honest, straightforward pronouncements; they would disregard whatever was spoken plainly and sincerely and search for the hidden meanings that, from their experience at court, they were certain must lie below the surface. He was careful, therefore not to say too much about any specific plans. "To publish these things here and now would not be wise."[7]

Penn's advisors were not so helpful as they might have been in planning the administration of the new province. Except for John Locke, whose ideas had been tested in the Carolinas and in New Jersey, they were, for the most part, theorists wedded to their own pet programs; they often were contemptuous or hostile to suggestions voiced by rivals. Penn himself, while more amenable, dredged from his memory proposals put forward in books he had read. From James Harrington's *The Commonwealth of Oceana* (1656) he recalled that to avoid tyranny and confusion it would be well if basic laws were available to everyone in published form. History had shown that latifundia could easily develop into a land-owner oligarchy, that open oral voting might lead to violence by terrorists against reform-minded or independent citizens, and that frequent elections were desirable lest officials long in office become dictatorial. He approved of Thomas Hobbes's praise of pacifism in *Leviathan* and of Sir Thomas More's report of the religious freedom in *Utopia*, though he would not have accepted the authoritarianism of the former nor the communism advocated by the latter. Unfortunately, Henry Stubbs, whose comments on Harrington and Hobbes might have helped Penn, had died in 1676.

Penn and his colleagues all agreed that Pennsylvania must be a Christian community that would not become a theocracy nor recognize any one sect, not even Quakerism, as its state religion. All avowed their faith in liberty, toleration, and the rights of man, but they differed in their interpretations. They were less in accord with his idea that government was a social service agency concerned with promoting health, welfare, and education as well, of course, as the furtherance of religion, morality, and peace. They upheld the principle that the people should rebel against an unjust monarch, though in view of what some of them had seen in England's recent history, they voiced their opinions guardedly. All of them, including Penn, realized that much more was needed to assure a perfect state than a resolve to live by God's eternal laws. It was, they learned, far easier to crusade for freedom and justice than to write laws to guarantee those privileges. Each advisor, convinced that he and he alone possessed the magic key, became impatient with his colleagues.

Though Penn's cabinet of advisors did its best to prevent news of disagreements from leaking to outsiders, rumors spread that William Penn, the Proprietor, was no longer calling quite as insistently for a social and political Utopia. Ill-wishers, scandalmongers, and loose-tongued busybodies, remarking Penn's constant attendance at court, professed to notice changes in Penn's attitude. Though as a rule their criticisms were poorly based, it was nevertheless true that Penn was viewing solutions to his problems from a somewhat different point of view. The realization that he was now responsible for the lives and happiness of thousands of trusting colonists induced a trend, not previously evident, toward conservatism. Ownership of vast estates, however distant and undeveloped, rendered him more cautious. Penn was invariably a man of sober thought, but he was now more careful in his thinking and even more so in his utterance.

Idealism and practicality were clashing. Penn still proclaimed his love of liberty, but he was coming to understand that too sudden bestowal of too great freedom invited license. He stood, as always, for manhood suffrage, yet he was realizing that not everyone was ready for self-government. He continued to trust in man's inherent rectitude, but he was becoming aware that in all too many instances that trust might be tragically misplaced. Surely, he had supposed, his people would be renowned for probity and wisdom, but he realized that many of them would be ordinary human beings, moved quite as much by selfish interest as by altruism, people who instead of being grateful for favors received would demand more and more concessions as their proper due. He was quite certain that the common people should be allowed to accept or to reject proposed laws, but he doubted if they were able to draft them.

Scarcely had Penn received his patent before certain of his intimates asked for special privilege. James Claypoole, an importer who, in partnership with his brother Edward in Barbados, was conducting a thriving business in slaves, sugar, and tropical goods, thought himself entitled to favored treatment. A Quaker in excellent standing, close friend of Fox, Rudyard, Meade and other leading Friends, co-author of the *Treatise on Oaths*, he was publicly enthusiastic about the Holy Experiment while privately warning his friends against investing too hurriedly. As a first purchaser he subscribed for five thousand acres but only after trying to strike a bargain; he willingly offered the full down payment but asked to be relieved from any need to pay the fifty shillings annual quitrents required of other buyers. To his surprise, the discount was not granted.[8]

The rebuff did not cool his confidence that he might yet win special treatment. From his experience as a businessman he was aware that overseas settlements were quite as hungry for capital as they were for immigrants. Penn was complaining to his friends about how much the province was costing him. Conventional financiers, none too anxious in the first place to put money into a Quaker colony, were holding back from taking chances on an undertaking that was losing money. In point of fact, Claypoole was himself advising his close friends to "forebear" buying land there until prospects brightened.[9]

Meanwhile, confident that Penn was in such dire need for cash that he must soon agree to make concessions, Claypoole was forming a syndicate to trade on a large scale with Pennsylvania. "Penn is so much my friend," said Claypoole, "that I can have anything in reason I desire of him."[10]

Either independently or in conjunction with Claypoole, Thomas Thurston, a Maryland Quaker who had suffered greatly and who had been Coale's fellow explorer, presented an attractive suggestion. Less than two months after Claypoole's request, Thurston promised that if Penn would grant him the exclusive right to trade with all the Indians between the Delaware and the Susquehanna, Thurston would pay Penn £6000 outright and, in addition, guarantee him a 2½ percent commission on all the profits.[11]

It was, said Penn, "a great temptation," but he refused. "I never had my mind so exercised by the Lord about my outward substance. I would not abuse His love nor act unworthy of His providence and so defile what came to me clear."

Neither Thurston nor Claypoole abandoned hope. Believing Penn's constant pleas of poverty, they were certain that his resolution must sooner or later disappear. Meanwhile rumors of the temptations had unfortunate consequences. Disregarding the facts that Penn had rejected favoritism and that he could not be bought, some of Penn's associates worried over what might happen in the future. Algernon Sidney was so disturbed that rumor spread that he and Penn had quarreled. When well-meaning, or perhaps inquisitive, friends repeated the rumor to Penn, he dismissed it as absurd, but "when I denied it and laughed at it, they told me I was mistaken." In his anxiety to patch up any breach that might have occurred, he dashed off a letter more notable for its concern than for its wording: "I would pray one for the truth of the fact, for the injury it hath done me already is nothing to the trouble it will give me if I have deserved it, and, if I have not, of losing a friend through a mistake."[12]

Unfortunately the rumors were all too true. Sidney, disappointed because Penn had not wholeheartedly accepted the Sidney plan of a province ruled in a manner something like the ancient Roman republic, all too hastily turned against him. A contributory factor had been a loose remark by Penn that while his primary purpose in Pennsylvania was to establish freedom, he was not averse to reaping a financial profit. This, in conjunction with the Claypoole and Thurston episodes, revived the old cry of hypocrisy, as convenient an explanation for mundane matters—and as untrue—as that of Jesuitism in the religious field.[13]

It is quite possible that Penn was himself unaware of what was being said by his detractors. He was, as it happened, overwhelmed by important work that demanded immediate attention. To write a constitution for Pennsylvania—he called it a Frame of Government or a Charter of Liberties—was only one of the demands upon his time; he also had to write land sales brochures, to canvass for colonists, to select a staff of colonial officials, and to wind up his interests in New Jersey. All this while caring for an ailing Guli, who had just borne a second son, William, always to be known as Billy.[14]

16

PLANNING PERFECTION

Though Penn became sole owner of the largest land area ever held by any private citizen in history, less than 2 percent of the estate was, for the present, either useful or accessible to him. He lacked good waterways. Unlike New York or Maryland, where ocean vessels could sail well into the interior, the settlement of Pennsylvania was limited, until good highways could be built, to ribbons of land along the Schuylkill and the Delaware. Even so, the rivers flowed from the north, and as the greater portion of Penn's land lay to the west across high hills, they gave little access to inland regions.

A second handicap, though one that could be soon removed, was a general ignorance about the province. Not many people knew precisely where it was and fewer still what it was like. A few Quakers, of course, had sketchy information, but the great majority of people knew only that Pennsylvania was a forest wilderness inhabited by roving Indians.

Penn's task was to convince the people, especially the unfortunate and the oppressed, that happiness lay in an unknown land. He wrote a land sales broadside, *Some Account of Pennsylvania*, aimed primarily at members of the Society of Friends but extending to all others wishing equality, peace, and opportunity. He pledged liberty of conscience and abolition of discrimination, guaranteeing all the civil and political rights of any Englishman. Even those who did not emigrate would profit, he declared, for the province would provide good markets for English manufactures and hence more work for English labor. "How many thousands of blacks and Indians may be accommodated with clothes?" he asked.

Though not specifically saying so, Penn held forth the hope, indeed the certainty, that the factors causing poverty, disease, and to a large degree unhappiness in the Old World could not exist in his new province.

[134]

Why live in poverty in crowded English cities, he implied, when vast acreages of fertile land are available to everyone at extraordinarily low rates? Why starve in England, when anything that grows there flourishes more luxuriantly and costs less in Pennsylvania? Why risk the high death rates of London, especially for your babies, while people live to ripe old ages in the clean open air of Pennsylvania's countryside?

He was not seeking to stampede his readers. Though he did not go to the extremes of warning against rash emigration as he had in his New Jersey writings, he did urge that no one should go overseas "without seriously considering the hardships to be met." Those hardships would be minor, for crops grew with less labor than in English fields, but still there would be problems to solve. No one should emigrate without the permission, "if not the liking," of his near relatives.

Though Penn's Royal patent gave him a clear English title to Pennsylvania, he sincerely believed that he was in honor bound, if not legally required, to buy out Indian rights to that territory as the Swedes, the Dutch, and his English predecessors had done. Yet it is interesting that, in spite of that honest conviction, Penn began offering land for sale as soon as he received the patent. On March 22, 1681, when the patent was only three weeks old, Penn sold ten thousand acres to Dr. Nicholas More. There was, indeed, a sale recorded to one William Smith of Wiltshire dated March 1, 1681, the very date of the patent, but it is possible that the year was entered 1681 by error for the more accurate 1681/2 that would have been customary. At any rate, the sale to More, and later to others, antedated Penn's efforts to quiet any title the Indians may have possessed.[1]

Penn's next step was to set up a sales organization. Philip Ford, his manager and treasurer, whose previous experience, according to Penn's probably incomplete account, had been an utter failure, revealed unexpected talent as attorney Thomas Rudyard's co-worker in the London sales office. Robert Turner canvassed Irish Quakers, other agents worked in Wales and Scotland, and Benjamin Furly, aided a few months later by Francis David Pastorius, enlisted Dutch and Germans.

Penn, who never forgot that pleasant but aborted trip through Provence, felt confident that many Frenchmen would transplant their silk and winemaking experience to Pennsylvania. He was certain they would succeed, for Pennsylvania, he believed, had a climate like that of Naples or of southern France. He overlooked the fact that Naples was three hundred miles farther south than Languedoc, as far as Philadelphia from southern New Hampshire.

Penn's account of Pennsylvania, added to that already published for New Jersey, contained so much information on the soil, climate, fauna, flora, and native people that John Houghton of the Royal Society proposed him for membership in that scholarly group. On November 9,

1681, the Society, citing Penn's "keen and comprehensive observation" of a province he had never visited, elected him to membership. Penn marked his entry by presenting the Society with a map of Pennsylvania based upon Augustin Herrmann's map of Maryland and its environs. As only the second person to be so honored for colonial services (he had been preceded eighteen months earlier by Governor John Winthrop of Connecticut), Penn was proud of the distinction, but his attendance at meetings was somewhat sporadic. Though he is said to have contributed further papers from time to time on Pennsylvania developments, the Society records are incomplete.

Meanwhile he was selling land. The beginnings were modest; he hoped to find one hundred purchasers, each of whom would pay £100 to buy five thousand acres. The hope was not extravagant. In 1681 some fifty thousand Quakers, many of them prosperous businessmen, were living in the British Isles. If, in the first campaign, he attained his goal, he would thus part with five hundred thousand acres, about eight hundred square miles, for which he would receive £10,000. The amount would be less than the gratuities he had distributed, and in addition, he must bear the cost of selling the land and of paying whatever employees he would need. He would retain 98 percent of the forty-five thousand square miles allotted him. Much of that reserve would not be arable, and he might wait an indefinite time before the rest of it became valuable. He would in time, however, be able to sell large tracts, together with any minerals that might be found, at an extremely handsome profit.[3]

To his disappointment a full year's sales campaign yielded only forty-one of the projected hundred subscribers. Total sales for the first two years netted only £6379 9s. Partly the cause was an unexpected apathy among the wealthy, but a contributory factor may have been overpricing, for Penn was charging considerably more than had been asked for New Jersey land. Fenwick had asked £5 for one thousand acres. There was also the issue of the quitrent.[4] The amount was small (a shilling each year for every hundred acres bought from Penn, and payment of even that sum was deferred until after 1684), but the necessity of paying it was irritating. Similar exactions had already caused resentment in New Hampshire, Connecticut, and New Jersey, and together with the fact that colonial land could be purchased more cheaply in other areas, may have put off some non-Quakers who might otherwise have invested in Pennsylvania.

Transportation costs had also gone up since Fenwick and Byllinge sent colonists to America. Penn charged £5 10s for each adult, 10 shillings more than the Jerseymen had paid; but while the rate for children was the same 50 shillings, "sucklings free," a child in Penn's interpretation was anyone under seven, while Fenwick set the topmost age at twelve.

Except for the financial disappointment, it was just as well that the five-thousand-acre subscriptions fell short of expectations. For a hundred owners to monopolize eight hundred square miles of the most accessible parts of Pennsylvania would have had unfortunate results. Five-thousand-acre holdings, even if they had been split up, as Penn wished, into smaller tracts, would either have encouraged land speculation or have led to large-scale plantations that could only have been farmed by slaves or by indentured servants. With the exception of whatever area would have been occupied by a seaport, the entire Pennsylvania riverbanks would have been taken up by huge estates, leaving nothing for the small investor except isolated forest tracts among the hills.

Penn may have foreseen the probability of an economy dependent upon bound labor. Even before his good friend Robert Turner landed at Philadelphia with seventeen "servants," Penn promised that any "master" who paid a cut rate of £5 passage money for an indentured laborer would, at the expiration of the bondage period, receive fifty acres for the servant and another fifty acres for himself.[5]

Other perils than latifundia and relegation of small farmers to the interior were implicit in Penn's plan. He had promised that if five-thou-sand-acre purchasers planted substantial settlements within three years, they could hold their acreage as semi-private townships over which they could exercise local political control similar to that allowed the landed gentry of England. Thus, Pennsylvania stood in danger of establishing a hundred "rotten boroughs," enough to constitute a formidable bloc in any provincial legislature.

If the large-scale purchasers were relatively few, the smaller buyers more than compensated for them. Four hundred and thirty investors raised the total acreage sold to about 5 percent above the quota Penn had set. The average small purchaser in this first year bought seven hundred and fifty acres.

The type of purchasers took Penn somewhat by surprise. Although he might have known from Fenwick's experience that urban artisans and small businessmen would respond to his offers, he had expected that a majority would be yeomen like his Sussex neighbors. Instead, they were craftsmen, carpenters, brewers, shoemakers, representing—or so it was said —eighty different occupations. A small sprinkling of professional men came, a couple of teachers and three medical men, and, surprisingly, seven single women. To Penn's delight there were no lawyers, no literary men, no artists, and, save for one or two Quakers who might be classed as preachers, no priests.

Again to Penn's surprise, about two-thirds of the subscribers to large tracts waited a year or two before leaving for America, and some never came at all; but he was pleased that a large majority of those buying less than one thousand acres emigrated almost immediately.[6]

Obsessed by the idea that his investors in this first year, the so-called

First Purchasers, would consist for the most part of well-to-do rural gentry, the leading citizens who would come into town to transact official business, Penn offered a bonus of ten-acre city lots for the average buyer, with larger tracts to five-thousand-acre subscribers. On these they would build townhouses, mansions set back from the road amid gardens, lawns and orchards. Thus, his city would always be a green country town that would not only be beautiful and comfortable but also safe and healthful. He was anxious to avoid the squalor and congestion of Old World cities, their vice and dirt and crime and, especially, the hazards of such fires as had ravaged London in his youth.

The City Beautiful plan went further. No home was to be closer than a quarter of a mile to the waterfront, a provision intended to assure two riverfront park areas. Nor were these to be the only open spaces, for two main avenues, High (later Market) and Broad, each one hundred feet wide, would lead to a ten-acre central "square." Each quarter of the city, moreover, was to have a slightly smaller square. All these were to assure breathing spaces for the general public. Luckily, they still remain, all except the center square, now occupied by the Philadelphia City Hall on which Penn's statue stands. Smaller streets, each fifty feet wide and tree-shaded, paralleled the two main highways. All were to be straight, identified by numbers if they ran north and south or named for trees if they ran east and west.

The plan was beautiful but unrealistic. The numerous mansions, each set in its private park, would have eaten up too large an area. Neither was there provision for housing craftsmen, tradespeople, workmen, or servants. To satisfy such requirements, with no provision for future growth, would have required, according to some estimates, at least ten thousand acres, or about fifteen square miles, a much larger area than Penn anticipated. Penn therefore, soon reduced the size of the land bonuses. He set up what he called "backward streets" for the less affluent, at the cost of introducing a certain amount of the urbanization and congestion that he had wished to avoid.

After a lapse of time, legends sprang up about the city's origin. Odd stories began to spread about the early Philadelphia days. Myths circulated that Philadelphia derived its name from the Bible, from an ancient Near East city called Philadelphia, now known as Amman in Jordan, from an Egyptian Pharaoh, Ptolemy Philadelphus, or, most romantically, from that imaginary first love, the young lady named Philadelphia.[7] A street, honoring the Bristol shipping firm of Callowhill for whom Giles Penn carried cargoes, was said really to refer to a nonexistent place called Gallows Hill where criminals were hanged. Some one invented the legend that Penn had decreed that a space within the city should be left forever vacant so that visiting Indians might have a place to camp. And yet another story, fathered by an Orientalist from Penn's own college, "revealed" that Philadelphia's famous gridiron street plan was taken over bodily from ancient Babylon. Though the Orientalist was once a tutor in the family of one of Penn's Irish friends, there are no indications that Penn ever even heard of the assertion.[8]

Years later legends would arise that not only had Penn copied his gridiron street plan from ancient Babylon but that he chose oaks and mulberries for planting along the streets, the one to provide timber for a shipbuilding industry that would keep warm the memory of his son Springett, and the other to feed the silkworms that he hoped would be brought over from France. For Penn cherished the thought that a sizable French immigration would soon appear to give his province both a silk and a wine industry. The shipbuilding project flourished for a century, though because of forest oaks and Pennsylvania iron and steel rather than because of curbside trees. There was a brief flurry, though not because of Frenchmen, in silkweaving, but Pennsylvania wineries were never too successful.

Unfortunately Penn himself contributed to a failure to maintain a riverbank mall. Early in the city's history, businessmen, with whom Penn was in partnership, erected unsightly warehouses, wharves, and dockyards along the waterfront; in addition, Penn allowed a council session to pass an ordinance requiring all slaughterhouses to be moved away from the city center to the riverbanks so that "the garbage and gore" could be washed away by the tides.[9]

QUO WARRANTO THREAT

F EW WORSE MOMENTS COULD HAVE BEEN CHOSEN FOR WILLIAM PENN
TO RECEIVE HIS PATENT THAN THE ALMOST TROPICAL SPRING OF 1681.
HIS PROBLEMS WERE NUMEROUS AND SERIOUS; BOTH HIS WIFE AND HIS
mother were ill; his own health was undermined; his finances were shaky;
and his enemies, and even some Quakers, still harped on that absurd
charge of Jesuitism. All this came at a time of unremitting work for the
Society of Friends.

Doubtless the concrete proof of Royal favor cheered Penn, but he must
have known that he was on the losing side of a power struggle within
court circles. Not all the King's advisors had been in favor of the patent's
terms; some even resented its issuance. Taken as a group the courtiers
were not averse to William Penn whom, personally, they liked. A powerful clique, however, was striving hard to strengthen the throne, especially
by centralizing London's control over the American dominions, and this
Pennsylvania grant was weakening that control. Penn's patent was, in a
sense, anachronistic, the last example of the type of land grant that the
clique was trying to abolish. At the very moment that Charles II was
handing Penn his patent as Proprietor, his advisors were exerting every
effort not only to block the granting of such patents but to cancel those
which, in their opinion, earlier Stuarts had too carelessly given away.

A legal process called quo warranto, after the first two words of a writ
of inquiry, provided an excellent device for recovery of the crown's lost
privileges. Under this writ, first issued in 1535, the King's Bench called
upon the holder of any office or the executor of any function to explain
by what authority he held that office or executed that right. If the victim
could not prove his strict performance of every minor detail of operation
of his duties (and contrary to English custom, the burden of proof was

upon him), he could be ejected from office or deprived of his privileges. Quo warranto was a perfect instrument for those determined upon centralization. Some minor flaw or loophole could be discovered by clever lawyers or found by a complaisant court in almost every case to justify canceling the charter against which they were proceeding.[1]

The agency most hostile to proprietors of American provinces was the Council on Trade and Plantations, usually known as the Lords of Trade, a group within the Privy Council. Though Penn had warm friends on this committee, such men as Shaftesbury and Rochester, he was only too aware that their loyalty was to the King and to the strengthening of Royal power rather than to him as an individual. He was conscious of their activities and was disturbed that, within three months of the issuance of his patent, they were busily engaged in attacking the Royal charter that had been granted to Massachusetts. He had no wish to be their next target.

The Lords of Trade, in their campaign for recovering Royal control over colonies, had as their chief agent one Edward Randolph, the newly appointed inspector general of customs, who had for years harassed New England merchants and administrators. Technically, Randolph's authority did not extend as far south as Pennsylvania, but the people along the Delaware did not escape his vigilance. They were, he said, carting tobacco from the eastern shore of Maryland, packing it into barrels, and shipping it to illegal destinations "under the guise of fish" or flour; moreover, they were grossly understating weights, thus cheating His Majesty of customs duties. To remedy these abuses he advised the use of quo warranto, the revocation of patents and the imposition of strict Royal control.[2]

Penn felt obliged to remain in London to answer the complaints that he was certain Randolph would soon be sending about real or fancied violations of the Navigation Acts. He must also have an alert deputy in Pennsylvania to prevent any reason for such complaints. Penn's choice for the position revealed a flaw in his administrative skill: while he certainly disapproved of cronyism—he had seen too much of that at court—he was confident that people whom he knew and liked would be trustworthy and efficient. If, in addition, they were Quakers, relatives, or former associates of his father, they certainly must be people of good character and well fitted for any position.

Such a man was available. Captain William Markham, Penn's first cousin, a forty-five-year-old navy veteran, had been a protégé of Admiral Sir William. Unfortunately, he was not a member of the Society of Friends, but to appoint a non-Quaker as deputy governor would show that Pennsylvania was, in truth as well as theory, a colony of tolerance. Actually, little was generally known of Captain Markham other than that while he was at sea his young wife, the former Nan Wright, had been one

of the vivacious set of Tower Hill. Nan had died, however, and her husband, when not at sea, had been living quietly on the Penn estates in
Ireland.[3]

Penn attached little importance to Markham's lack of experience
except as an authoritarian naval officer. Markham himself may have had
some qualms against taking office as a deputy, or lieutenant governor,
but he accepted the position on Penn's promise that, in a year or two, he
could command a ship.[4] With supreme confidence that Markham would
be successful, Penn assigned him missions for which Markham had no
preparation whatsoever. As deputy, Markham was to name a temporary
provincial council as his chief legislative agency, which was to care for
the interests not only of the Proprietor and the recent land-purchasers
but also of the older residents. Six men represented such English settlers
as had preceded the Quakers, two others were leaders of the Swedish
community, men born and reared in the Delaware valley, and one was a
Scot who had lived there for nearly twenty years. Until such time as a
popular assembly could be elected to draft new laws, the Duke of York's
code would be retained, together with the Duke's officials, with Markham acting as chief resident authority.

In addition to routine governmental matters, Markham had a wide
range of responsibilities. He was to cultivate the friendship of the Indians, to iron out boundary disputes with Lord Baltimore, especially that
knotty problem of who owned the mouth of the Delaware, and to see that
the Swedes, the Dutch, and the English, both Anglican and Quaker,
cooperated harmoniously. He was to search out a suitable site for a
capital city, to be called Philadelphia, and another for a country estate
for William Penn; he should also build, presumably after designing personally, a proper mansion for the True and Absolute Proprietor. Penn
would also deeply appreciate frequent and detailed reports from Deputy
Governor Markham on Pennsylvania's Indians, on local personalities, on
the flora, fauna, soil, resources, climate, productions, and commerce.[5]

For all this Markham was to receive £200 per year.

Having set up his council, Markham proceeded to inspect the province. The more he saw of Pennsylvania, the more delighted he became.
Everything, he thought, was wonderful; the views were superb. Near New
Castle, the town which the Dutch called New Amstel, then the main port
on the west bank of the Delaware, land was flat and very fertile; farther
north, in what unquestionably was Pennsylvania, the country, wooded for
the most part, reminded him of western England. Game was plentiful and
very cheap; a whole deer cost only a trifle more than a shilling. In England
quail was a luxury; in Pennsylvania such fowl were so numerous and so
tame that you could knock them off the lower tree boughs with your
walking stick. Peaches, as luscious as any in the world, grew so abun-
dantly that branches broke beneath their weight; farmers, after making

all the brandy they could drink—excellent brandy, too—shoveled the excess fruit into troughs for their pigs to eat. The rivers were not only beautiful but so alive with shad and sturgeon that one hesitated to cast a net into the water lest the weight of fish break through the meshes. To row a skiff was hazardous; so many huge fish leaped into the frail craft that unless the oarsman was extremely cautious they would sink the boat. A healthy country it was, too. "Some people live to be a hundred years old."[6]

By July 1681, the province was beginning to thrive. New settlers were coming in: sturdy, reliable people, the country folk Penn had hoped for, yeomen out of England, Scotland, and Ireland, an increasing number of Pietist Germans, but, to Penn's disappointment not many of those Frenchmen on whom he had counted for wine and silk industries. They were cooperating beautifully, helping each other to give the colony a firm, solid foundation. Judged only by the looks of the people, their houses and their farms, everything was highly satisfactory. The Holy Experiment seemed headed for outstanding success.

Markham reported optimistically that the beginnings were smooth. He had organized a provincial council, with ample representation for the minorities. In lieu of an elective popular assembly, he had arranged for mass meetings of all the citizens if need should arise for a referendum, though that contingency had not yet occurred. The framework of a democratic government had thus been built.

Markham had also located what he believed an ideal site for the capital city, a large, level, and well-wooded tract where the Schuylkill joined the Delaware. He may or may not have mentioned that there were two tiny Swedish villages already there, Wicaco on the Delaware and Passayunk on the Schuylkill, but that he hoped to relocate the Swedes on larger and perhaps better tracts beyond the city limits so that the entire area would be available for Philadelphia. Lasse Cock, the leading Swedish merchant, whom Markham and most Englishmen usually named Lacey Coxe, would, Markham thought, assist in carrying out this plan. For Cock, a long-time resident and head of the Swedish community, was an influential figure in early Pennsylvania. Fluent in the local Indian dialect and in English, he was invaluable in developing the colony. He served at various times as assemblyman, councilman, court interpreter, and as a judge; he was a principal advisor both to Markham and, later, to William Penn himself.

Even before Markham's reports began to arrive, Penn, realizing that he had burdened his cousin too heavily, sent him some assistance, a three-man advisory commission. Its duties were somewhat vague, which was just as well, for none of the appointees was outstandingly qualified. The chairman, "Cousin" William Crispin (really an uncle) was, like Markham, an Irish neighbor who had been one of the Admiral's captains. As with so many of Penn's appointees, the choice was peculiar, for as far as any records show, Crispin, who was to be chief justice, had never been exposed to even an hour of legal training. His ability, however, was never tested, for the seventy-year-old Crispin died at Barbados while en route to Pennsylvania.[7] Of the other two nominees, one seems to have cut no figure whatever, while the third went into private trading; his chief mention in provincial history was that he once sold a slave for six hundred pounds of beef.[8]

Markham knew nothing of their appointment or of their intended sailing for America; but as soon as he named his provincial council and picked the site for Philadelphia, he set out upon his most uncongenial and certainly his most difficult task, that of trying to reach a boundary agreement with Charles Calvert, third Lord Baltimore. It was not a meeting to which Markham eagerly looked forward. He had no desire to ride 120 miles over bad roads to southern Maryland in hot and muggy August weather to discuss topics with which he was unfamiliar. A chief subject, to be sure, was geographic, the exact location of the fortieth parallel, which was to be the common frontier for the two proprietorships, and on this Markham was highly competent. There were other matters about which he had neither knowledge nor interest—problems of historical backgrounds, of legal definitions, of the precise meanings of Royal charters half a century old. Since the London press and James Claypoole, too, had reported confidently a month or two earlier, that Penn was about to sail for America, he preferred to postpone the meeting until the True and Absolute Proprietor should arrive. Nevertheless, he was under orders to treat with Lord Baltimore and, as a well-disciplined navy man, he embarked upon his journey.[9]

The conference opened auspiciously. Markham introduced himself and then handed Lord Baltimore the Royal proclamation, dated April 1681, informing Pennsylvanians that they must obey Penn's orders, the term "Pennsylvanian" being applied to all persons living from twelve miles above New Castle as far north as the forty-third degree of latitude. Baltimore listened politely and said that he would, of course, obey all Royal commands, though these certainly were not addressed to him. He added that the King's advisors were in error, that instead of Pennsylvania's southern line running twelve miles north of New Castle, the true distance was really twenty. Markham demurred, and the meeting ended with little more than routine exchanges of courtesies. The conference, it was agreed, would be resumed in a day or two.[10]

No further sessions were then held in Maryland. The weather being more sultry than that of Pennsylvania, Markham came down with fever, a sudden "dangerous illness" which kept him abed in Baltimore's house for three long weeks. When he recovered, in September, he hastened back to Pennsylvania, though not before agreeing to meet again on October

16 in New Castle. Markham was confident that by that time Penn would have arrived to conduct his own negotiations. He lost the gamble. When the meeting day drew near with no sign of William Penn (the news items about Penn's intended voyage probably referred to Crispin's departure), Markham sent word that he must go to New York and must therefore postpone the meeting for two weeks. He hinted that, as he owned no sextant, he would borrow one in New York so that he and Baltimore could make joint observations. When, even after this delay, Penn did not appear, Markham again fell sick. He was suffering, he said, from "a tertian quartan ague," a type of malaria, and must reluctantly put off any conference until the spring.

Meanwhile, William Penn was, to some degree, relaxing. His troubles in England were continuing, but he had been told (surely not by Markham) that the all-important fortieth crossed both Delaware and Chesapeake Bays about thirty miles south of New Castle, instead of twenty miles north of that line. The mistaken "news" comforted him; it implied that he owned the port of New Castle, both banks of the Susquehanna, and considerable land frontage on the Chesapeake.

Without waiting to check the accuracy of his information, or to hear what results might have flowed from the Markham–Baltimore meeting, Penn wrote to Augustin Herrmann and to other landowners in the upper part of Maryland's Eastern Shore warning them against paying taxes to Lord Baltimore. It was an ill-timed move, since it could not possibly arrive until the 1681 taxes had been paid and long before any call for 1682 taxes would have been made. Moreover, it was tactless, since its only immediate result would be to antagonize the Maryland leaders whose friendship he was courting. Nor was this all; the usually considerate William Penn hinted, none too delicately, that his influence at court was stronger than was that of Lord Baltimore. He closed with the hope that everyone—obviously, in this instance, the Marylanders—would always do "the thing that is just and honest," if only because "it is always wise so to do." The tone of the letter, even more than its wording, widened and deepened the breach between the two Proprietors.[11]

When by mid-May 1682, Markham had made no further mention of a meeting, Lord Baltimore invited him to come in June to Augustin Herrmann's plantation, that same Bohemia Manor claimed by both participants. Though new rumors were circulating that Penn would soon come to America, Markham accepted the invitation. On the appointed day, however, neither participant appeared. Lord Baltimore's agents explained that he had been called away to suppress an uprising near the Potomac. Markham sent no message.

The Marylanders took the initiative. In June they went up to New Castle, having, they said, "a curiosity to see that town." Markham was not there but apparently by sheer luck, a sloop had just come in from

New York bringing not a sextant, the surveying instrument of which Markham had spoken some months earlier, but a sextile. "With some difficulty and many entreaties they persuaded the master of the sloop to permit them the use of it." One wonders what hint of bribery or force lay concealed in the euphemisms.

After Lord Baltimore quelled the Potomac uprising, he too went to New Castle where he heard about the sextile, and was told that it determined latitudes. Since Markham had not yet returned, Baltimore went to Upland, the present Chester, and installed himself in Markham's lodgings there to await the Deputy's return.[12]

When Markham eventually came back, with what the Marylanders described as "a disordered countenance and an odd behavior," Baltimore asked to be allowed to use the sextile. Markham answered that it was not in working order, that it lacked lenses. Apparently it had been in proper condition at New Castle; but whether Baltimore's men had damaged it, whether Markham himself had removed the lenses, or whether the excuse was well-founded does not appear. At any rate, Baltimore persisted in requesting its use, eventually received it, found it operational, and determined the Upland latitude as 39 degrees 47½ minutes. There was some talk of taking other observations; but when Baltimore triumphantly pointed out that thus far everything he had said about the location of the fortieth had been verified, Markham called off further meetings.

Instead, fearing that Baltimore would attempt to take both Upland and New Castle, the non-Quaker Markham, who always kept his arms in readiness, waited until Baltimore had returned to Maryland and then summoned all males between the ages of sixteen to sixty to be prepared to mobilize at an hour's notice.[13]

Just what he expected his men to accomplish is far from clear. Maryland had one or two tiny "warships" and some soldiers with experience in Indian skirmishes, but the Lower Counties had only a few volunteer militiamen, none of whom had been in the field for at least sixteen years, while pacifist Pennsylvania had no fighting men whatever. There were, to be sure, several cannon at New Castle, but they were rusty and unusable relics of the Dutch regime. The Maryland force could scarcely have been classed as crack troops, but even a small detachment, perhaps even a platoon, could have taken over the towns that Baltimore claimed.

This conduct would certainly have distressed and displeased the Proprietor; but Penn, still in London, knew nothing of the recent developments. Having now cleared up much of his basic work about the founding of his province, he was planning to leave for America.

He may, as a diversion, have been intrigued by discovering somewhere an old letter from Morocco. One Mahomet Benison Nicasis, Governor of Tetuan, had written to "General" William Penn, the Founder's father, inquiring about "my ancient friend, Captain Giles Penn, who so long a time was consul in this city." (Actually, Giles, who had died in 1664, had been consul at Salé, two hundred miles distant from Tetuan, though he may have served both regions.) The interesting point was the Governor's name, Nicasis, which may possibly have had some connection with the name of Lady Margaret Penn's first husband, the rather mysterious Nicasius Vander Schure.[14] The letter may also have reminded Penn that when, in 1654, his father had petitioned Cromwell to indemnify Lady Margaret for the loss of her Irish lands, he had told the Protector that she was the daughter of the Vander Schures.[15]

18

DRIFT TO THE RIGHT

PENN'S ASSURANCE THAT HIS PROVINCIALS WOULD BE FREE, THAT THEY WOULD LIVE UNDER SUCH LAWS AS THEY THEMSELVES REASONABLY DESIRED, AND THAT NO FAVORITISM WOULD BE SHOWN TOOK HIS PEOPLE by surprise. To seventeenth-century Dutchmen, Swedes, and non-Quaker Englishmen such liberties went far beyond their experience with governments, far beyond their concepts of democracy. Accustomed as they were to strong central government, most of them did not grasp the implications of Penn's words. Those few who did, even Quakers who knew Penn's reputation for truthfulness, construed them as a politician's paper promise. Only a handful really believed him. Their doubts and cynicisms deepened when weeks, months, and even a year went by without significant betterment of their conditions. The old laws of the Duke of York remained effective; the deputies sent out by William Penn, the chief among them a non-Quaker, spoke fairer words but were not notably more efficient administrators than their predecessors.

The delay was not due to any change of heart in William Penn, however. He had not, as some may have supposed, forgotten his intentions, but he was discovering that to throw out present evils and to inaugurate a brilliant future by returning to a golden—and imaginary— past required more thought and skill than merely pasting up the Ten Commandments and the Golden Rule in a statute book. He had counted on assistance from various advisors on how to form a central administration and to what matters its powers should extend. In this expectation he was far from disappointed, for the response was overwhelming. Unfortunately, not all the proposals were feasible, many were contradictory, and some were undesirable. Moreover, when he did not enthusiastically accept every suggestion, authors became angry. In his cheerful optimism, Penn had failed to allow for human frailty, for the rivalries, jealousies, and conflicts of opinion among those who considered themselves experts and authorities. He had to summon all his diplomacy and tact to calm ruffled feelings and to prevent open opposition.

Other heavy pressure centered upon Penn from businessmen, even from Quaker businessmen, some from his circle of close acquaintances. High among them, if not their chief, was James Claypoole, he who had sought special discount in buying land. From listening to Penn's customary talk of financial stringency he realized that Penn was himself in no position to supply the necessary funds and that conventional financiers would not risk their money in a Quaker colony. Claypoole, therefore, undertook to form a consortium of well-to-do merchants, for the most part Quakers, to exploit Pennsylvania's resources and, not in the least incidentally, to reap a profit from them.[1] Working in cooperation with Robert Turner, a Dublin linen merchant, with Robert Barclay, a New Jersey Proprietor, with Benjamin Furly of Rotterdam, and with Philip Ford, all of them close friends of William Penn, in March 1682, Claypoole organized a stock company, the Free Society of Traders, to conduct diversified activities in Penn's province.

Claypoole's plans were as ambitious and as far-reaching as those of a modern conglomerate. The Free Society of Traders, the FST, would buy twenty thousand acres as a company, plus ten-thousand-acre tracts for several of its leaders, in return for recognition as a sort of semi-official agency. It would, Claypoole suggested, engage in mining, farming, fishing, and manufacturing; conduct an import-export business; establish factories (which then meant trading posts for the Indian trade) ; operate a whaling enterprise; and encourage colonization. Catering to Penn's prejudice against granting monopolies, it did not ask exclusive rights, but an organization of such size would not need such help; no minor business would be able to compete.[2]

Claypoole relied, successfully as it turned out, on Penn's humanitarianism and his gratitude. Mindful of Penn's interest in the welfare of ethnic minorities, Claypoole offered FST aid to any Indians who might care to settle in the cities; the company would help them and guide them in any way it could. The company would hold slaves, of course, for slavery was not yet illegal, but it would free its slaves after only fourteen years of service; moreover, it would give land free to all the slaves it manumitted, provided only that the free Negro would repay the FST by giving it two-thirds of all crops raised upon that land.

Whether Claypoole suggested that Penn show his gratitude in any concrete form is doubtful, but Penn did grant concessions. Somehow he was moved to cut quitrents to one shilling a year for the entire grant, to allow the FST exemption from tolls or customs duties, and to grant it manorial rights, which meant freedom in minor matters from local court controls.

As Proprietor of the province Penn refrained, as did Guli, from buying shares of FST stock, but their children were put down for generous purchases. Six-year-old Springett invested £400, becoming one of the largest shareholders; three-year-old Letitia and her younger brother Billy each chipped in £300. Before Richard's death the Proprietor's brother had acquired £100 worth before his death, as did Penn's attorney, Thomas Rudyard, and Cousin William Markham.[3]

One of the more interesting investors was Penn's business manager, Philip Ford. In two separate purchases the former street pedlar acquired stock valued at £400. Since the transactions must have cost him five full years' salary, there may have been considerable speculation concerning the source of his wealth; if so, neither Penn, the Society of Friends, nor the highly respectable organizers gave any public heed to it. The FST, in fact, appointed Ford its London land sales agent, the same post he was currently holding for William Penn.

Ford, by now accustomed to handling large sums of money, was an excellent choice, but the conditions under which he was to work contrasted rather sharply with those under which he had worked for William Penn. The FST organizers were sharp businessmen who closely supervised commercial operations. Penn, on the other hand, disliked routine details; he had allowed Ford complete freedom, seldom scrutinizing the financial reports that Ford submitted. He did not read Ford's statements on acreage sold, subscription money received, nor expenses incurred, but signed whatever papers Ford placed before him.

Penn was more interested in developing a favorable image of the province than in commercial matters. For some time past he had been gathering materials for brochures that would set forth the advantages to be enjoyed by emigrants who would go to New Jersey and to Pennsylvania. Thus, while Ford and Claypoole created a development company, he would publicize the merits of the provinces.

By unhappy coincidence, he was distracted for several weeks from active participation in Pennsylvania affairs in the early part of 1682. His mother, the widowed Lady Penn, died in her late sixties. William, while always reticent about his personal feelings, had said little, and had written less, about his relations with his mother; but the connection had apparently been close, for the news of her death threw him into an emotional shock.[4]

This was unfortunately just the time when Claypoole's syndicate was putting the final touches to its charter and when Penn was supposedly finishing his suggestions for the basic constitution of his province. He was unable, in his distraught state, to give these documents the close examination they deserved.

No changes had occurred in his philosophy of government; he still trusted in the goodness of his associates; he still believed that what mattered was not the form of government but the hearts and consciences of the people who lived under it. The character of a government, Penn asserted, depends upon the nature of its citizens. "Governments, like clocks, go from the motions men give them. As governments are made and moved by men so by them are they ruined, too. Wherefore governments rather depend upon men than men upon governments. Let men be good and the government cannot be bad; if it be ill they will change it. But, if men be bad, let the government be never so good, they will endeavor to warp and spoil it. Though good laws do well, good men do better."[5] Governments, then, should not control the people; the people should control the government.

Penn, whose forte was theorizing rather than the conversion of theory into practice, entrusted the writing of both the Frame of Government and the FST charter to his associates. Doubtless, in his simplicity and trust, he was not as alert as he should have been in sifting the many suggestions offered him. It is quite possible that, following his practice with the Ford accounts, he signed his name to documents without careful scrutiny. At any rate, for whatever reason—grief for his mother, financial pressures, the responsibility for property and lives, greater maturity, or the smooth talk of businessmen who took advantage of his innocence— the final versions of both documents revealed a strong tendency toward conservatism.

The 1682 Frame of Government, the first of three constitutions proclaimed for Pennsylvania during the colonial period, however, was by no means reactionary; it withdrew no privileges but conferred some that were new. There were protests against it, chiefly from extremists whose suggestions had been ignored—Furly, for example, was indignant because neither slavery nor the slave trade had been prohibited. To a large degree its scope was limited by the provisions of the Royal patent. Necessarily it recognized the Proprietor as chief executive with power to act personally or through a deputy; it guaranteed that his privileges would be hereditary.[6]

The title of True and Absolute Proprietor was, however, somewhat misleading; Penn could not govern autocratically. The patent stipulated, certainly with Penn's enthusiastic consent, that he must work in conjunction with a legislative body elected by all resident taxpayers except any landowners who had failed to cultivate at least one-tenth of their holdings.

Looking back from the vantage point of three centuries of social change, the charter seems loosely written. The rather sketchy definition of voting eligibility, though it did grant the franchise to the landless, failed to specify that electors must be English citizens by birth or naturalization. By a strict construction that no one in any country would have thought of at the time, all aliens, even any Indians subject to taxation, were immediately eligible to vote. The matter was, at first, purely academic since, by act of December 7, 1682, all foreigners, meaning of course the two thousand Dutch and Swedish residents, were admitted to citizenship; as new taxpaying immigrants arrived, under the terms of the Frame, each would automatically acquire both the franchise and the right to hold office.[7]

Theoretically, some few Indians might have benefited. Not many of them owned land in their own individual right and few paid taxes; but, as Penn consistently regarded Indian chiefs (he called them "kings") as sovereigns holding title valid enough to sell land, a strict interpretation of the Frame might conceivably confer voting rights upon the chiefs. The question never arose, but one wonders how Penn, invariably moved by a sense of perfect fairness, would have answered it.

The same wonder applies to the status of women. Nowhere does the Frame limit voting rights to males. There were a few women taxpayers and, in one Delaware county instance, an all-female jury trial, but no test case was ever held on votes for women. Neither, until that December 7, was there mention of an age qualification for electors. On that date the franchise was limited to those over twenty-one who believed in Jesus Christ as the Son of God and the Savior of the World. This would have excluded almost all Indians whether or not they paid taxes. Here, again, was confusion, for freedom of conscience was thereby denied to Jews and, quite possibly, to some Christians as well. The laws barred from the voting places any persons convicted of ill-fame, or those of unsober or dishonest behavior—Penn's word was "conversation." If the provisions had been strictly enforced, moreover, certain members of the legislature who were fined for drunkenness could have been expelled and disfranchised, together with a number of respectable merchants accused, properly, of cheating the Indians in business dealings.

The Frame created a bicameral legislature. A provincial council of seventy-two persons, elected to this upper house as "of most note for their wisdom, virtue and ability," was to be, with the Proprietor, the real administrator. Together they would execute the laws, care for public peace and safety, create and settle towns, manage finances, control trade and manufactures, and establish and operate schools. They were also to set up courts and the Council was to nominate lists of candidates from which the Proprietor would choose judges, sheriffs, coroners and other public officials. In addition the councilmen, each with one vote (the Proprietor had three), would draft all legislation for consideration by a five-hundred-member provincial assembly.

The lower house, the Assembly, was virtually powerless. It could not originate, amend, or repeal any measure whatsoever unless the Council had previously approved such action. In the earliest days at least, it could not even debate whatever the Council chose to send it. Only after an ingenious assemblyman construed a "leave to confer with one another" as meaning the right to discuss were Assemblymen allowed the privilege of speaking in their sessions on what they were voting upon. Previously they had been allowed merely to vote Yes or No on Council proposals.

The powerlessness of the Assembly, a restriction that may have been slipped by Penn during his period of distraction, shocked Penn's more radical supporters. Furly called attention to the differences between the preliminary versions of the Frame and its final form: "I wonder who should put thee upon altering them for these," he said, "and how much thou couldst ever yield to such a thing. . . . Who has turned thee aside from these good beginnings to establish things unsavory and unjust?"[8]

Penn could have answered that his seventy-two-man Council was a democratically elected body. He could also have pointed out that close and exhaustive examination of legislation would be next to impossible in a five-hundred-member assembly. He held his peace, however, even when the short-tempered Algernon Sidney angrily condemned the arrangements. The system was, he said, "the basest on earth, not to be endured, or lived under. . . . The Turk is not more absolute."[9]

Markham, who was far from being a radical, said nothing at the time, but he had an answer to Furly's wonder. "I know very well," he said some years later in talking about the Frame, "that it was forced upon him by friends who, unless they received all that they demanded, would not settle in the country." Actually, the Frame, as the name implied, was no more than a rough beginning in creating the machinery of government. The lawmaking bodies thus established were to enact specific legislation.[10]

As Penn purposed to allow his people complete freedom to select the type of laws that they preferred, he imposed no code upon them. He did, however, name a committee of thirteen major purchasers of Pennsylvania land to recommend the type of legislation that they hoped the province would adopt. All but two of these, Dr. Nicholas More, a London physician, and Herbert Springett, Guli's uncle, a lawyer, were members of the Society of Friends. Three were shareholders in the New Jersey proprietorship. All were wealthy men, identified in one way or another with the Claypoole project. All of them, too, were strong supporters of free and humanitarian government.

As the FST had won, through its charter, the scope and freedom of action it desired, commercial pressures were absent; the Society of Friends met no opposition in suggesting a remarkably progressive program. The committee, meeting near Penn's old home on Tower Hill, where Thomas Rudyard had his offices, drafted a number of recommendations which, when ratified by the Council and Assembly, were to be "forever fundamental." Their forty suggestions, misnamed *Laws Agreed Upon in England*, included ideas far in advance of any other contemporary legislation.[11]

There were, of course, no denials of any basic liberties, the age-old civil rights of Englishmen, for which Penn had long contended. Courts must be open to all and must be conducted in plain English. As was only to be expected from a participant in the Penn–Meade trial, juries, whose members might be challenged for cause by both prosecution and defense, must be absolutely free from any dictation by the judge. Their verdicts could not be questioned. No person should be held prisoner unless legally charged. Those arrested should be allowed freedom on bail unless accused of capital offense. Convicted prisoners should not be required to pay for food, lodging, heat, or wardens' fees. While in jail, they should, if possible, receive whatever proper correctional treatment was available. Workhouses should be established for vagrants and loose or idle persons. Every child above the age of twelve should be taught a trade or skill. All persons wrongfully prosecuted should receive double indemnity from the informer or prosecutor responsible for their having been detained. Not all these revolutionary suggestions for penal reform could be fully implemented, of course, but they did create a climate of reform in penology that, for years thereafter, put Pennsylvania in the forefront of humanitarian legislation.[12]

The civil liberties of Englishmen were guaranteed to everyone, though regrettably some restrictions remained on non-Christians; lying and scandalmongering were also forbidden. In words that today might easily be misunderstood, the committee proposed that "all scandalous and malicious reporters, backbiters, defamers and spreaders of false news . . . shall be severely punished as enemies to peace and concord." So, too, were certain amusements specifically forbidden.

> All such offenses against God as swearing, cursing, lying, prophane talking, drunkenness, drinking of healths, obscene words, incest, sodomy, rapes, whoredoms, fornications, uncleanness . . . all treasons, misprisons, murders, duels, felonies, seditions, maims, forcible entries and other violences to persons and estates, all prizes, stage plays, cards, dice, may-games, masques, revels, bull-baitings, cock-fightings, bear-baitings and the like, which excite the people to rudeness, cruelty, looseness, and unreligion shall be respectively discouraged and severely punished.

In addition, First Days were to be devoted to religious services and to rest.

If these recommendations were approved by the Provincial Council and Assembly, as it was certain that they would be, the committee thought it would be well to hang copies of the formal laws in public offices and to require the entire code to be read each year at the first openings of Council sessions, meetings of the Assembly, and court sessions.

19

RULE BY AMATEURS

A FULL YEAR HAD PASSED SINCE PENN HAD RECEIVED HIS PATENT, BUT AS YET, ALL THAT HE KNEW OF HIS PROVINCE HAD COME TO HIM THROUGH HEARSAY, AND MUCH OF THAT INFORMATION WAS QUESTIONABLE. Quite naturally, the Proprietor wished to see his land, to know his people, to set its government into operation. Events had conspired against him. The death of his mother and his subsequent feeling of depression, the need to take time to settle her estate, the delays in drafting the Frame and in planning the progressive legislation he hoped to introduce, and the worries arising from the talk of possible quo warranto proceedings all had prevented his taking ship.

The one encouraging note was the seeming success of the Free Society of Traders, whose stock was selling well. Investors, encouraged by reports that the East India Company was so prosperous that it was declaring a 100 percent stock dividend, were certain that the FST would be equally successful. Unfortunately, the Free Society of Traders would discover, all too late, that those same subscribers, after more mature deliberation, would suspect that they had been too eager in speculating. Many of them would default in their payments. The company that started operations with such bright prospects would, in a very few years, face financial difficulties.[1]

Penn, in addition to his other commitments, had more work to do for the Society of Friends. Quakers in the Worminghurst neighborhood, who had been worshiping in each others' homes, asked him to look about for a good site on which to build a meetinghouse. Penn and a friend did so and they found an old abandoned building that they believed could be remodeled. Though it was described as being "eight miles from anywhere," it was well located for serving Horsham, Coolham, Thakeham, and Worminghurst.[2]

With the British genius for inventing local history, the old house acquired an instant tradition. Though it antedated Penn's arrival in Sussex—some said by 270 years—the story ran that it was built from the timbers of a Penn ship, a legend reminiscent of that *Mayflower* barn at Old Jordan's. That ship, the story said, had boasted a blue figurehead that, for some reason they did not bother to explain, was of Buddha. Obviously, therefore, the structure was known as the Blue Idol. Less imaginative neighbors rejected the explanation. The name, they said, should be not the Blue Idol, but, because the building with its faded blue paint had stood so long unused, the Idle Blue. Whatever the reason for the name, Horsham Meeting acquired the property, though it did not raise the money for remodeling for a dozen years thereafter.

Penn took time from this transaction to dispatch help to overburdened Deputy Governor Markham. Informed that Crispin, the designated chief justice, had died and that Crispin's two colleagues had not been notably active, Penn sent a new man, and a better one. Captain Thomas Holme, yet another of Sir William's naval veterans and Irish tenants, was not a relative, but he did have a history of persecution for his Quaker beliefs. A surveyor in his late fifties, he was commissioned to help Markham choose a site for a capital city, "high, dry and healthy," where water was deep enough for ocean-going vessels to tie up at docks, thus avoiding lighterage. He was to test the riverbeds to see that the bottoms were not swampy, a precaution designed to help the settlement escape the fevers traceable, as was then thought, to marsh vapors. Thus, the capital would avoid the afflictions that had decimated Jamestown and Plymouth.[3]

Holme was not to take over Crispin's assignment as chief justice, perhaps because by this time Penn had remembered that the most important court official should know at least a little law, but Holme was to make friends with the Indians. In doing so he was to behave with gravity and dignity, to be, in Penn's words, "tender of offending them for they love not to be smiled upon." He was to buy land from them but he should previously inspect and, if possible, survey that land. He must also be careful not to repurchase land already bought by white men or land that the Indians with whom he would be dealing did not really own.[4]

For though Penn trusted people and believed their words, especially the words of such nature's children as the Indians, he was not a man to be imposed upon. He respected the rights of Swedes and Dutch and Englishmen who had already acquired permission to live along the riverfronts, and quite possibly he had heard reports that Fenwick, for example, had repurchased lands Indians had already sold to Europeans.[5]

Not that he considered those Europeans who had preceded him to be above reproach, for they, or some of them at least, had cheated the aborigines after having, as Penn put it, "learned them drunkenness." If any whites should try such tactics against the Quakers, or be "hard or grasping, taking advantage of our circumstances," Penn told Holme, "give them to know they will hurt themselves." As for Indians who mis-behaved, Penn said, "You must make them keep their word. If they see you use them severely when they are roguish and kindly when just they will demean themselves accordingly."[6]

On the other hand, to reassure the Indians, Penn gave Holme a letter addressed to the "Emperor of Canada," pledging that the Quakers would always live in peace and harmony and that Penn would "never allow any of my people to sell rum to make you drunk." Just why he sent the letter to people with whom he had no frontier nor precisely whom he meant as "Emperor" was not made clear.[7]

Holme suffered no unfair treatment from the Indians; his only com-plaint was that a certain Englishman had overcharged him. Holme had gone upriver a mile or two to meet with some Indians and, with his four children, had lodged in the Englishman's house. Everything had gone well until, when the council ended, the landlord presented a bill for £50 which, Holme implied, was for board and lodging. The amount, by the standard of the times, was certainly exorbitant, amounting, as it did, to half the yearly salary of a skilled artisan; but it may have covered a longer period than just the duration of the council and may have included other items than just the board and lodging. There was, in addi-tion, a further charge of £3 which Holme said was for horse hire and the landlord's fee for serving as a guide. Penn did not pay the bill for nineteen years.[8]

Both Markham and Holme carried out their missions as best they could and, for the first few months at least, succeeded, in the main, in pleasing the Proprietor. They worked, however, under handicaps, for they were three thousand miles away from London, performing tasks new to them and under unfamiliar conditions. They may, moreover, have been piqued. Penn, their personal friend and, in Markham's case, a rela-tive, seemed to be bypassing them. Instead of communicating with them directly, he was, more and more often, introducing popular rule by work-ing through the local Council of Pennsylvania residents. True, the Coun-cil, at the outset in August 1681, had not been elected by the people but had been appointed by Markham. Nevertheless, the Deputy Governor, and perhaps Holme too, may have felt that their authority was being undermined. If Penn's innovations succeeded, the Council would take the credit; if the plans failed, it might shift the blame onto Holme and Markham, for the province was not without its share of people who would write complaining notes to William Penn. Those complaints would have their effect, because at least six months would elapse before the two men would hear of them and explain the circumstances. Meanwhile, the Proprietor would have been prejudiced against them.

As a matter of fact, Penn was already beginning to worry about the quality of his administrators. Disaffected colonists, some of them anti-Quaker, others critical of the Markham–Holme activities, were sending disturbing reports to London. The two men, the critics said, were much too bureaucratic. Markham was lazy, unreliable and, some added, profligate. Holme and certain others "move slowly in their offices" unless coaxed into action by gifts of wine, by "treats" or by other favors. One man complained that it had cost him £10 just to induce an official to listen to him.

The accusations were usually vague, with little concrete evidence submitted, and probably much of the libel was spitework. Penn did indicate, to be sure, that criticism of Holme was not unexpected. Such complaint, he said "grieves me to hear, knowing his infirmity. . . . He is a man I love and wish well . . . but his infirmities and follies have cost me dear in trouble of spirit and my reputation." Penn did not clarify just what the infirmities might have been, nor how he had been injured, but whatever the weaknesses, they do not seem to have unduly interfered with either the scope or the efficiency of the man's activities. Whatever systems of perquisites and gratuities existed in Pennsylvania was probably less than that in London's governmental circles, but Penn was dismayed that any such evils should exist in the Holy Experiment.[9]

However exaggerated the complaints may have been, their currency was dangerous. Those London officials who looked to quo warranto as a method for enlarging Royal power would file them with Edward Randolph's letters as proof of Quaker mismanagement. They would ignore the fact that only the disaffected would have been the authors of the criticisms. Nor, not knowing the individuals who sent the letters, would they have realized that jealousies, disappointments, and piques would have prompted many of the messages.

The fact was that the Provincial Council, designed in good faith by William Penn as an advisory group representing all segments of the population, was already vying with the Deputy Governor for leadership. The rivalry was unavoidable, for the members were almost all men of affairs, well versed as administrators and executives. Much better trained in such matters than the inexperienced Captain William Markham, they knew precisely what they wanted. They knew also how to gain their ends.

One of these men, Dr. Nicholas More, headed a powerful Free Society of Traders bloc within the Council. He was not a Quaker (there may have been an unwritten policy against naming Quakers to high office in the nonsectarian province), nor was he the man whom Penn would have chosen to head Markham's advisors. A short-tempered, sharp-tongued autocrat, he railed against a political system "wherein every Will, Dick and Tom govern." He thoroughly disapproved of popular government; more than once he cautioned Pennsylvania legislators that liberal policies might lead to trials for treason. If such policies were followed, he warned, "thousands will curse you and your children after you." Surprisingly, Penn did not hold such outbursts against Dr. More. Indeed, they may not have been reported to him. Instead, though More obviously lacked a judicial temperament and though he had no more legal training than Crispin had received, Penn named him chief justice. As such, and in presiding over tribunals of less stature, More acted remarkably like Sir Samuel Starling.[10]

In addition to Penn's natural desire to see his province, a continued flow of criticisms, great and small, about the quality of local leadership and of injustices to minorities made him anxious to view the situation for himself. He believed that his presence would not only smooth out difficulties among his own people, but would also clear up that Maryland boundary dispute which Markham had been unable to settle with Lord Baltimore. The problem would be solved for Penn if somehow he could gain possession of the English-held west bank of the Delaware between the fortieth degree of latitude and the sea. That area, colonized continually since 1638 by Dutch or Swedes, had been conquered in 1664 by English troops and had been entrusted by King Charles II to his brother James, Duke of York. According to the Marylanders, it belonged to them. The gift to James infringed upon the patent granted in 1632 to Charles Calvert for all land between the thirty-eighth and fortieth parallels except that cultivated by any Christian peoples. Maryland had not claimed its rights for a quarter of a century. In 1659, a Maryland colonel appeared there to demand submission. Ignoring the Dutch authorities, lest this constitute some sort of official recognition of their right to rule, the colonel went from house to house "to seduce the inhabitants to a revolt." If they did not yield, he warned, "the whole province of Maryland would come and reduce them and they then would be plundered and their houses taken from them."[11]

The doughty Dutchmen did not panic. Either they did not believe the colonel's threat that the entire Maryland population would descend upon them "with arms and fire and sword" or they did not fear the consequences. Besides, they pointed out, Hollanders had been in the region in 1631, a full year before the Marylanders had received their charter. As this land had actually been cultivated by a Christian power, the patent did not include the lower Delaware.

The colonel withdrew in some discomfiture, but the Marylanders were not convinced that their claim was ill-founded. For at least a century a semantic quarrel raged over the translation of a Latin phrase. In that charter of 1632 did the words *hactentus terra inculta* deny to Maryland only those lands *continually* cultivated until the present time, i.e., 1632, as Lord Baltimore insisted; or, as the Dutchmen argued, all lands that *ever* had, at any time, been cultivated by any Christian power, no matter how short a time that cultivation had been continued? A tiny Dutch settlement, Zwaanendael, near Cape Henlopen, held the key to the dispute. It had been established in 1631 by twenty-eight families prior to the Baltimore patent and thus had certainly been cultivated, but the colony had been destroyed and its people massacred before the issuance of that charter, and so was not in existence when Maryland was founded.

The matter was highly important to William Penn. Probably he had never heard of Zwaanendael nor of the *hactentus terra inculta* controversy prior to the grant of his own patent; seizing upon the Dutch interpretation, he begged the Duke of York to transfer to him the entire west bank of the Delaware from the fortieth degree south to the ocean. Thus, he would assure himself a good harbor, the Dutch port of New Amstel, and a safe passage to the open sea.

The Duke went through the motions of compliance. Though he himself had not yet actually received title to the land, he transferred to Penn control over the area Penn had asked. In fact, he did so doubly, first by leasing the territory to Penn for a period of ten thousand years and then by deeds of feoffment which presumably gave Penn title subject to the payment of one rose a year, if the Duke or his heirs should demand it, plus one-fifth of any profits Penn might receive.

As though the situation were not sufficiently complex, other complications were introduced. For various legal reasons the Duke did not execute one lease or one deed to Penn but had written two of each, one set for the region south of New Castle, the old New Amstel, the other for the land north of that port.[12] Nor was this all; he set the upper limit of that northern part as an arc supposedly representing part of a circle drawn at a twelve-mile radius from New Castle's courthouse. Why such a boundary was prescribed was never made quite clear, though it was supposed that the purpose was to protect New Castle merchants and shippers from the competition of Pennsylvanians.

Whatever the actual reason may have been, this northern portion of the so-called Twelve Mile Circle still survives as the boundary between Pennsylvania and what is now the State of Delaware. It also gave the latter exclusive jurisdiction over the waters of the Delaware River included within the area of that circle. Since there had been no settlement by any Christian power on land within the Twelve Mile Circle to the west, the grant did not affect any portion of Maryland.

For almost a century following the Duke's grant to Penn of lands south of Pennsylvania, the areas so conveyed possessed no special name, being identified only as Penn's "Territories" or as the Three Lower Counties of New Castle, Kent, and New Deal, soon after renamed Sussex. These Three Lower Counties held a somewhat peculiar relationship to the three Pennsylvania counties, Philadelphia, Bucks, and Chester, being under the same deputy governor and enjoying equal representation in the Pennsylvania legislative body. This arrangement continued until 1704, when the Three Lower Counties seceded from Pennsylvania. The area did not officially receive the name Delaware until the American War of Independence.

The circle boundary, unique in America except for three or four Tennessee counties, was the subject of litigation between Delaware and New Jersey for more than two centuries. Delaware contended that the deeds to Berkeley and Carteret extended only "to the river," which to Delaware meant the eastern bank. By this interpretation, all fishing and navigation rights within that portion of the river included within the Twelve Mile Circle belonged to Delaware. Eventually the United States Supreme Court upheld the Delaware contention.[13]

There was yet another problem. Did the Duke of York really own the area he had leased or deeded? No one denied that Charles II had in 1664 given his brother all of New Netherlands, but there were those who insisted that the lower west bank of the Delaware had been owned by the Dutch West India Company or by the City of Amsterdam and had never been part of New Netherlands. If so, the King had not actually given it to York. The doubt was so strong that the King mended York's title by a new deed in 1683, thus pointing up the possibility that the Duke had given property to Penn that he did not own. James, in his turn, fully intended to give Penn new and valid deeds but, for one reason or another, put off making Penn's title good. The patent was eventually drafted, but in the confusion caused by the Glorious Revolution, James fled from England leaving the deed, unsigned, behind him.

A week after receiving the leases and the deeds of feoffment, Penn sailed for Pennsylvania. He was very well aware that among his first tasks in America must be to come to some agreement with Lord Baltimore about these boundary disputes.

20

WESTWARD TO UTOPIA

By SUMMER 1682, ALL WAS READY FOR PENN'S DEPARTURE. HE RESERVED PASSAGE IN CAPTAIN ROBERT GREENAWAY'S THREE-HUNDRED-TON BARK, "WELCOME." IF HE DID NOT GIVE FIFTEEN HUNDRED ACRES OF Pennsylvania land to Greenaway in lieu of passage money he at least refunded the purchase price. In any case, Penn did not pay Greenaway the price of his passage directly, for he apparently had a psychological block against paying bills in cash. In his lifelong fear of poverty, a condition only relative in his case because of his own and Guli's ample resources, he disliked spending money; it was less painful to have his secretaries or his managers pay out whatever was owing.

The practice caused hardships for his more important American agents. His first deputy worked nine years without receiving any pay, while a successor, Penn's most trusted aide, served five years without remuneration. One of the more important colonists, a man who described himself as a lackey who responded to Penn's very whistle, waited nineteen years before complaining. Penn answered this "poor but weak man" by explaining that he, Penn, was "one of the poorest men in the province" whose purpose was "neglect of himself and not selfishness." The man waited thirteen more years for his pay. Philip Ford, Penn's estate manager and land sales agent, was less patient; he resorted to what Penn's friends called unsavory tactics to collect what he claimed his due. The effort started just before the *Welcome* was about to sail for America.[1]

In early July 1682, Ford submitted a bill for £2851-7-6, which represented, Ford said, an indebtedness running back at least two years. The circumstances surrounding the claim were so confused and the statements concerning them so contradictory that, at this late date, it is quite impossible to state the facts either clearly or concisely. Moreover, neither

Penn nor Ford made public mention of the matter until many years later, when the specific details were no longer sharp even in the minds of the central figures. In attempting to recall them for use in chancery after years of bitter argument, anger and disappointment warped their views.[2]

Ford alleged that Penn had shipped overseas four different consignments of goods valued, Ford said, at £1503-15-9, but had not paid for the goods. In addition, Ford asserted, Penn had borrowed from him enough money to bring the total up to more than £2851. There were also hints that Penn was in arrears in paying Ford's salary and that the Proprietor had failed to pay his agent commissions on amounts received or spent as Penn's financial manager, on fees due for land sales to 450 persons Penn had referred to him.

Penn admitted that he owed Ford money, but he did not specify either the amount or the reason for the debt. He denied any borrowing. He may have wondered, though he did not lay any charges, how so poor a businessman as he insisted that Ford always was could amass any money to lend on so low an annual salary or where Ford had procured the money to buy £400 of FST stock. He did not seem to question why Ford, in collecting Irish rents or receiving money on land sales, did not deduct commissions that might have been due him before remitting the proceeds to his employer. Incidentally, he overlooked telling the Lord Chancellor that for the ten years prior to 1682 he had been paying Ford £80 instead of the original £40.

Ford might have answered in his turn, though apparently he did not, that none of his colleagues in the land sales offices or in Quaker circles generally had found him inefficient, nor had his integrity been questioned. Had such questions been raised, however, members of the Society of Friends would have explained that Quakers did not dispute with each other in public, but always sought to compose their differences quietly and unobtrusively so that all participants would be assured of justice.

Penn, as he himself admitted, was careless throughout life about his money matters. He was not a miser nor was he niggardly but a rich man who, despite his constant plaint of poverty, always had access to money; he simply could not comprehend that a creditor might really be in need of cash. One who pressed for payment was, in Penn's view, not only clamorous and rude but guilty of outrageous behavior. Of one such individual Penn said sadly, "I wish I had nothing more to do with him," but he did not end the relationship by paying what was rightfully owing.[3]

In Ford's case, Penn confessed, he had been in the habit of relying implicitly upon his financial agent. Ford regularly submitted statements that Penn routinely signed as correct without, Penn said, taking time to read the entries. Yet oddly enough, twenty-one years later, when Ford's heirs brought suit in equity for payment of this 1682 debt and for other indebtedness, Penn was able to cite dates and amounts of payments he had made in 1682 to his business manager.

It is impossible to declare with certainty just who, if anyone, was really at fault in this dispute or to what point the guilt extended. All that is certain is that, as in so many other cases, Penn pigeonholed the bill without having read it and then, presumably, thought no more about it until Ford protested.

Three months later, when Penn's ship was almost ready to sail, Ford jogged his memory, only to receive the vague reply that the matter would be settled in a day or two. Ford, who by this time must have been skeptical of such assurances, returned, only to be again put off. This time, however, Ford had come prepared. He presented a paper for Penn to sign acknowledging the debt and agreeing that unless settlement was made within forty-eight hours Ford would receive, in lieu of money, three hundred thousand acres of Pennsylvania land free of all charge except an annual quitrent of four beaver skins.[4] Ford may have still expected, in the face of all indications to the contrary, that he might receive payment in cash; he may have wished to protect his own estate in case he should die before Penn's return.

Penn, as he later confessed, signed this document also without bothering to read it; he was pressed for time, he said, and besides he had full confidence in Philip Ford. He let the deadline pass.

Contemporary comments on the situation are lacking, but later critics were not generous in judging Ford's motives. They doubted his honesty and declared that Penn had certified the debt only because he had not read the papers. One early biographer not renowned for accuracy, referred to Ford as "a sleek and subtle" swindler, "one of the vilest scoundrels that ever ruined a trusting client." A Columbia University professor, suggested that Ford was using blackmail, perhaps because he had "knowledge of some incidents in the Proprietor's life that he wished to keep concealed."[5]

Whatever Ford's purposes may have been they did not deter him from publishing, six months after Penn sailed, a spirited *Vindication of William Penn* against irresponsive rumors that the Proprietor was dead and that he had confessed himself a Jesuit. The libel, Ford said, was invented by Thomas Hicks, who "has been openly proved a notorious forger, slanderer and defamer." Ford described himself as writing "in sincerity by him who is a lover of truth but a hater of falsehood." Nor did Ford take any steps to foreclose his mortgage or to renew his claim in any other way until after Penn had finished his business in America and had returned to England.[6]

Penn gave less attention to Ford than to Guli's last-minute decision not to go overseas. She was again expecting, this time a seventh child, and she was fearful that, despite the presence of those three physicians already in Pennsylvania, and of the services of Dr. Thomas Wynne, a Welsh physician booked for passage on the *Welcome,* the undeveloped province would not be safe for a newborn infant. Her solicitude was justified; but when in March 1683 the baby daughter was born, "a mighty, great child," Guli was suffering from erysipelas, St. Anthony's Fire, her face being so swollen that she could not see. Guli recovered, but the baby became infected and died within three weeks.[7]

Penn concealed his disappointment at Guli's decision to remain behind but responded by a touching letter, "A Testament" for Guli and the children. "My love, which neither sea nor land nor death itself can extinguish or lessen toward you, most endearingly visits you with eternal embraces and will abide with you forever. . . . My dear wife, remember thou wast the love of my youth and much the joy of my life; the most beloved as well as the most worthy of all my worldly comforts. . . . God knowest, and thou knowest, it was a match of Providence's making."[8]

As befitted a good father and an active Quaker minister, Penn showered his wife and children with advice. Watch ever for good, the Testament urged, be diligent in holding daily meetings. Live sparingly until all debts are paid. Guard against flatterers and encroaching friendships. . . . Live in the country rather than in town; a decent mansion with £100 per annum is better than £10,000 in a city such as London. Teach children to be obedient, humble, kind, and to love one another.

The children were too young to profit at the moment by their father's injunctions, but they would grow up. They should study his *No Cross, No Crown*; it would guide them in avoiding the appearance of evil. They should be temperate and plain living, speaking no evil, meddling not in other peoples' affairs. They should study, preferably with a tutor, for in schools too many evil impressions are commonly received. Penn recommended such useful subjects as building ships or houses, surveying, navigation, "dialing," by which he apparently meant clockmaking, and agriculture, the last being, he said, "especially in my heart."

For his part Penn was embarking upon an experiment unique in history, the testing on a large scale, with the lives of human beings at stake, the feasibility of establishing an earthly paradise. He trusted in three firm supports: the help of God, the guidance of the Scriptures, and the innate goodness of sober, righteous men. With these supports he could not fail.

None of the hundred or so London and Sussex Friends accompanying William Penn expected the voyage to be pleasant. As was the usual custom, Greenaway sold only transportation and bare wooden bunks in stuffy cabins; each passenger brought along his own food to be prepared and cooked as best he could. If all went well, the transatlantic passage might require six weeks, but to be on the safe side, since storms or headwinds might cause delay, it would be better to provide supplies to last three months.

Though the bark was trim, her decks were cluttered. One man, for instance, loaded such live food as thirty-two chickens, seven turkeys, eleven ducks, and two hens. He also carried six dried codfish, and a box of eggs, capacity unspecified. He brought a box of spices, another of dried herbs, and a "pot" of tamarind. In the absence of fresh vegetables, something would be needed to prevent scurvy, so he shipped a barrel of Chinese oranges, five of those pear-shaped grapefruit just recently imported from Polynesia by a Captain Shaddock, and six bottles of citrus water. For dessert or between meals, he had eighteen coconuts and a large keg of candied fruit and nuts. And since drinking water would certainly go bad, especially if the *Welcome* were blown into the tropics, he provided himself with a keg of rum, a larger keg of wine, four bottles of madeira, five dozen of ale, nine pints of brandy, and six balls of chocolate.[9]

Penn carried more. In addition to food, clothing, and bedding, he took along three thoroughbred mares and a fine white riding horse, together with some work animals. All these traveled on deck, limiting the open space where passengers might take the air or exercise; he packed the hold with furniture and fittings for the mansion that he planned to build, including carved doors and window frames, as well as two complete mills, one for sawing lumber, the other for grinding grain.[10]

As usual, sickness raged, not the ordinary ship fever or typhus, which was to be expected, but smallpox. The infection spread. Almost every man, woman, and child fell ill. Penn, himself immune because of his brief touch when he was three, nursed the sufferers; but despite all that he or anyone else could do, at least a third of the passengers died. Such was the severity of the epidemic that for half a century people remembered it as one of the worst in early colonial history.[11]

When the smallpox passed an opportunity appeared, as one passenger put it, to profit by Penn's good conversation. The gentleman, whose name does not appear upon the passenger list, reported that Penn borrowed £30, though for what purpose aboard ship is far from clear. When asked to repay the debt, Penn offered in exchange a choice building lot in the city he planned to create.[12]

"You are very good, Mr. Penn," the creditor, obviously not a Quaker, replied, "and the offer might be advantageous but the money would suit me better." In any case, city building lots were selling at a much cheaper rate.

"Very well," Penn replied, "thou shalt have thy money but canst thou not see that this will be a great city in a very short time?"

On October 24, ten days after Penn's thirty-eighth birthday, eight weeks out of Deal, he sighted West Jersey. Telescopes revealed the long sandbar island on which Beach Haven and other seaside resorts now stand. The *Welcome*, with its ten-foot draft, could not ride in close to shore because of shallow water, but inlets were visible leading to what seemed to be a thickly wooded mainland. None of the whales of which the sales propaganda had spoken were visible, but Penn later learned that the waters teemed with fish and that oysters and clams were so plentiful that the beach was littered with shells from Indian feasts.

Greenaway steered the *Welcome* sixty or seventy miles southward until he reached the mouth of Delaware Bay. Here, for the first time, Penn saw land that he owned, not through relatives or by purchase like Worminghurst, nor in partnership as in the Jerseys, but as an original proprietor. He had the Duke of York's deeds and leases in his pocket. He knew the region, though only by hearsay.

The bark sailed upriver another sixty miles. Other than a glimpse of Fenwick's huts near Salem, there was little to attract attention. The newly acquired land on the left, the Three Lower Counties, and New Jersey on the right were low, flat, and often swampy. There were numerous creeks and little rivers, excellent places, Penn would be told, for smugglers and pirates to hide. Few ships, however, were seen and surprisingly few people, Indians or whites. At last, above the head of the bay, where the stream bent sharply to the right and where a hostile nation would have built a fort, the town of New Castle came into view.

To the Friends aboard the *Welcome*, the tiny settlement had a strange appearance, though Penn recognized its dikes and windmills as authentically Dutch. It had been Swedish and it had been Dutch and at least one of its leading citizens, Jean Paul Jaquette, had been of French extraction; but at this time, most of its three hundred people were English, some of them former Jerseymen. As the largest and best port on the west bank of the Delaware, its possession was of great importance to William Penn. Though the papers in his pocket from the Duke of York certified Penn's ownership, he was very well aware that he must defend his rights against Lord Baltimore.

Penn arrived about dusk on October 27. Though accounts of his arrival assert that local officials had long awaited his appearance, it is highly doubtful that they knew him as their new chief and governor. He had left England within ten days after receiving those additional deeds and leases, and no ship had outsailed the *Welcome*.

According to certain unscholarly chroniclers, the town officials, after seeing Penn's credentials, proclaimed a general holiday to begin in the morning. At that time the entire population crowded to the dock to meet their new overlord.[13] A pleasant ceremony ensued, planned by someone with a well-developed sense of the dramatic. As Penn appeared, "with noble mien," his usually somber clothing adorned by a light-blue silken sash, which apparently he intended as a badge of authority, the local dignitaries presented him with symbols of his ownership—a bit of turf, a twig, and a bowl of river water. Penn told his plans for popular government. Until it could be instituted, he asked the incumbents to remain in office as his personal representatives.

According to one report, following his speech the populace called upon the Proprietor to "reign over them in person and to annex them to Pennsylvania that they might have one county, one parliament and one ruler." Penn promised that he would consider the request. If the call was actually made, which may be doubted in view of the region's independent spirit and of the fact that Quakers were in a minority, the people soon repented of it, particularly of the absorption into Pennsylvania.

Penn did annex the region to Pennsylvania but as "the Territories," not as an integral part of the older province. The Lower Counties then asked, but did not receive, a guarantee that they would always have as many representatives in the common provincial Assembly as did Pennsylvania.

On the next day, the twenty-ninth, Penn sailed in the *Welcome* sixteen or seventeen miles north to Upland, where Markham had established his headquarters. He was now in Pennsylvania.

Upland, a log cabin settlement of about a hundred people, was the largest Pennsylvania community. Small though it was, it had pretensions to greatness; as provincial capital, ruling over about two thousand people, it contained a courthouse, a jail, the gubernatorial mansion where only recently Lord Baltimore had stayed, and, Penn was glad to note, a meetinghouse, a fine brick structure facing Robert Wade's residence.[14]

Wade, disillusioned with John Fenwick's Salem settlement, had crossed the river into Pennsylvania. With him came his wife, the energetic former Lydia Evans, and together they had begun what might be described as America's first salon. Here they entertained everyone of importance who was traveling in the region. Barely a month had passed since Lord Baltimore had been their guest while the Marylander was taking observations to determine the latitude. Markham had been using the house as his official residence. Earlier still, in November 1679, when the Dutch Labadist Jasper Dankaerts had been touring the colonies to locate a suitable place for a settlement, the Wades had entertained him. Now the True and Absolute Proprietor was to be their guest.

Doubtless the Wades were too tactful to tell Penn that when Dankaerts had been there, a fellow guest had been a lady of some notoriety in Quaker history. This was Mrs. Hannah Stranger Salter, an eccentric who had been an active supporter of one James Nayler, whom orthodox Quakers regarded as a troublemaker. After that she had migrated to America, had lived in New Jersey and in Bucks County, Pennsylvania, and was, at the time of Jasper Dankaerts' visit, a farmer, land dealer, and prophetess in the Lower Counties. The Wades would have remembered her well, for during dinner she suddenly began to groan and tremble, causing the table to shake and making a noise so loud that she could be heard far off.[15]

Penn had probably forgotten about Hannah—he had been quite young in Nayler's period—but he was concerned with another matter. He saw no reason why the capital of his province should bear a Swedish name, Upland being a corruption of Optland, a Swedish province from which many of the first settlers had come.[16] A legend states that, while still aboard the *Welcome*, Penn had asked a fellow passenger, Thomas Pearson, ancestor of Benjamin West the painter, what to name the town and that Pearson had suggested Chester, his own native city. Regardless of the accuracy of the legend, the suggestion was taken, though for decades after the renaming of the town many people continued to refer to the village as Upland. A Chester suburb retains the name.

21

SEEDS OF UNREST

IMMEDIATELY UPON ARRIVING AT NEW CASTLE AND INTRODUCING HIMSELF
TO HIS PEOPLE, PENN HAD TAKEN A QUICK, PRELIMINARY LOOK AT HIS
PROVINCE AND THEN SENT WORD TO HIS FRIEND LORD BALTIMORE,
to ask his health but in reality to suggest a meeting at which he could
display the deeds given him by the Duke of York entitling him to possession of the west bank of the Delaware. Baltimore, who in all probability
had not yet heard of the deeds, answered politely, suggesting that the
conference, which he assumed would be merely a social visit, be scheduled
for December.[1]

The delay played into Penn's hands. It gave him an opportunity to
know something of his people, to pay his respects to "my Royal patron"
by making a formal call upon his neighbor, the Duke's governor in
New York, to have a brief look at New Jersey, which he had helped to
found and where he still owned land, and, perhaps more important, to
give the mature freeholders time to elect representatives to a constituent
assembly. This body, to be composed of "persons of most note for wisdom, sobriety and integrity," would adopt a constitution or a fundamental law under which a legislature would be chosen. Ideally, it would
also ratify the *Laws Agreed Upon in England*.[2]

Little is known of the details of Penn's traveling except that he
visited New York, journeyed over to Long Island, as George Fox had
done, to inspect Quaker meetings, and on his way back to Pennsylvania
stopped over in East New Jersey. He found, to his delight, that his old
friend and attorney, Thomas Rudyard, had just arrived to serve as deputy
governor. As a landowner in both Jerseys, Penn was, of couse, vitally
interested in promoting good relations with that Quaker community, and
Rudyard's appointment guaranteed cooperation. The presence of his

friend was to produce another dividend, for Rudyard would later strike up a close relationship with the new governor of New York, Thomas Dongan, who would rely heavily on Rudyard's legal advice and so assure New York's friendship with Pennsylvania.

Penn returned to his province, probably by way of Burlington, where he could see how the feuding Londoners and Yorkshiremen had softened their antagonisms. From there he crossed the Delaware into Bucks County to inspect the site, thirty miles north of Philadelphia, which Markham had selected for Penn's country estate. The land was part of a forty-five-thousand-acre purchase for which Markham had given the Indians, twenty guns, forty pounds of shot, two barrels of powder, two hundred knives, forty axes, forty pairs of scissors, and two thousand one hundred feet of wampum, together with some liquor and some cloth.[3]

Penn approved the site improbably described, though not by Penn, as "a treble island, the Delaware running three times around it." It was heavily wooded, though the river frontage was clear and suitable for converting into a lawn. Markham was to build a house at the top of a rise so that it would stand above marsh vapors such as had proved so fatal at Rickmansworth. There was an exceptional supply of sand and gravel that would be useful for building and for grading roads.[4]

The Proprietor then rode down to the site Markham had chosen for Philadelphia at the confluence of the Schuylkill and the Delaware. This too pleased him, for it was high, not too heavily wooded, and accessible to the sea; the channel being deep enough for ships of the day to tie up at piers.

Penn was in good spirits when he finished this tour and prepared to confer with the representatives whom his people had chosen to make plans for their new government.

To Penn's surprise, he met a mild rebellion when he returned to New Castle to open his first assembly. Only half the elected delegates were on hand, and they, an assertive lot, were in a somewhat belligerent mood. Though Penn had assured the provincials that the people were to be allowed to make whatever laws they wished, within the limits of reason, Nicholas More of the FST had told them that the laws were already drafted, the so-called *Laws Agreed Upon in England*, and that the elected delegates were expected to approve them without debate.[5]

Almost all Pennsylvanians were in the dark about the content of those projected laws. They had been agreed upon in London six months before, but only by anticipated colonists and nonresident land purchasers, and thus by only a handful of resident Pennsylvanians. Few ships had since arrived from London, none of them known to have brought copies of the agreement.

The general ignorance of the proposed laws may explain why only half the delegates appeared. There were, of course, other reasons. Representatives from the Three Lower Counties had no experience whatsoever with an elective assembly. They may not have understood just what the meeting was supposed to do. Pennsylvania's delegates were either mostly Quakers to whom Penn's wish would be law, or members dominated by More and his Free Society of Traders. Neither group would be enthusiastic about traveling all the way to New Castle merely to rubber-stamp agreements already made and to arrange for a full session of a provincial council and an assembly that was not to meet until March.

The early arrivals, gathering in the local tavern which Penn had vetoed as a meeting place, demanded the rights which they believed that William Pen had granted them. They were not hostile to Penn nor to the Free Society; in fact they chose Nicholas More their chairman, but they did think they had a right to know the contents of those laws before accepting or rejecting them. They desired not only to know precisely what the proposals were but also to have the right to discuss them thoroughly before voting on them.

Penn faced a dilemma. The proposed procedure certainly followed the English precedents that he invariably supported. Yet if he approved the demands, the government might begin in chaos. If he refused, however, he would not only be denying an essential English freedom, but he would be repudiating his pledge to grant whatever sober and free men might reasonably desire.

He took refuge in a technicality. He did not really believe that a lower house of parliament, though democratically elective, should own the right to debate, or to amend proposals; these were functions of an upper elective body. His denial of the right to debate was, in fact, one of Sidney's reasons for describing Penn's proposals as "worse than the Turk." Yet, after all, this Chester group was not a parliament but only a group to confer legal powers on a legislature. The limitations he had set on initiating and debating proposals need not, therefore, apply to this first meeting, but would apply to the actions of the lower house which it would authorize. The quibble averted a crisis for the moment but, for twenty years thereafter, the same problems would be threshed out in Penn's province.[6]

After the caucus in the tavern won the right to debate, the members made little use of it. Inexperienced as they were in creating governmental machinery or in planning legislation, they showed slight interest in mundane affairs. No real differences of opinion marred the official sessions so far as such details were concerned. No delegate questioned the high principles of the basic documents Penn laid before them. Every member cherished the same desire for peace, justice, and the welfare of mankind; the only points raised were whether the methods proposed would procure the ends desired. This was the harmony Penn had expected; he had never anticipated serious opposition.

The newly won right to debate was, however, invoked for questions of theological interpretation. Was Penn correct in asserting that Almighty God was "the only Lord of Conscience, Father of Lights and Spirits and the author as well as the object of all divine knowledge, faith and worship"? Presumably Speaker Nicholas More could, under the rules, have applied cloture; but seventeenth-century assemblages relished such types of argument, and so free speech continued until, by formal vote, the delegates approved the wording. Was it against the will of God to refer to days of the week and months of the year by their common, and pagan, names? It was, indeed, improper to do so. Should there be freedom of conscience in the province? Most certainly there must be, but only those who believed in Almighty God and in Jesus Christ, His Son, should be permitted to hold office. Not until within the memory of living men were professed atheists allowed to hold high political office in Pennsylvania.[7]

Once these vital matters were settled, the assembly moved quickly and decisively. Despite the pre-session clamor in the tavern, no close, thorough or independent study could have been given to the Frame, the forty *Laws Agreed Upon in England,* or to the twenty-nine additional sections added thereto, since the assembly debated on all its topics, spiritual and mundane, for only four days. Nevertheless, a comprehensive and, for the times, a remarkably progressive set of principles, the Great Law, was blocked out and agreed upon by the Assembly.[8]

The Great Law required every resident to declare his fealty, though not by formal oath, both to the King and to William Penn. It also declared that all persons then resident in Pennsylvania and the Lower Counties were admitted to citizenship. The voting franchise, and presumably the right to hold office subject to the religious test, was extended to all freeholders of one hundred acres, to all servants, meaning indentured workers who had served their terms, and to all urban taxpayers. All England's basic civil liberties were guaranteed to everyone in Penn's provinces. The right of free speech, however, was not to extend to those who "speak slightingly or carry themselves abusively against any magistrate in person or in office under penalty of 20 shillings fine or 10 days' hard labor." To guarantee that the legislature would always hold the reins to control the executive, the Great Law forbade any tax to be levied for more than one year at a time.

The Great Law gave Pennsylvania and the Lower Counties the most humane legal code of any American colony. The Duke of York's laws, hitherto operative, had been as good as could have been expected in the seventeenth century, but they listed eleven capital offenses; the mother country had two hundred! The Great Law prescribed death only for first-degree murder, though treason was later added. Drunkenness, lying, swearing, sex crimes, and other felonies were to be punished by hard labor or by lashing. The whipping post persisted in Delaware, the former Lower

Counties, until its abolition in July 1972, though actual lashings had been abandoned some time earlier.

Pennsylvania was also noted for its humanitarian prison system. Each jail was to be a workhouse, rather than merely a detention building; it was to try to rehabilitate prisoners, to teach them useful trades, and to free them from the exploitations characteristic of the English prisons.

Finally, the Great Law widened the scope of social legislation. It transferred lawsuits dealing with domestic relations or morals offenses from ecclesiastical to regular courts. It abolished primogeniture, that feudal system whereby an eldest son, to the exclusion of his brothers and sisters, inherited the entire estate of anyone who died without leaving a valid will. By a provision soon to be modified, and several times amended, it forbade the sale of liquor to Indians. It recommended the establishment of vocational and technical schools not only to train prisoners for careers after their release but also for all children above the age of twelve.

The Great Law was not perfect. Though remarkably progressive for the times, it could not possibly reflect the more advanced social thinking of later generations. Necessarily it contained shortcomings due to current philosophy and to inexperience with the proposals being advanced. When even the largest colonial villages consisted of only a few score houses no one recognized the need for such innovations as home rule for cities. Too much authority, therefore, was vested in the county courts. They were to levy taxes, to manage roads and bridges, to provide charity toward widows, the needy elderly, and the poor. They were also to have a measure of control over prices in order to prevent extortion and to supervise wage scales; not for the purpose of guaranteeing a living wage, but rather to prevent payments from mounting too high.

It was important that court procedure be conducted in plain English and that the right to trial by impartial jurors be guaranteed. Even with the addition of the new duties imposed upon judges by the Great Law, no one foresaw that judges should be elected, much less that possibly they might be recalled by popular vote.

On December 7, 1682, the last day of the session, the Constituent Assembly also voted to unite Pennsylvania and the Three Lower Counties into one government. The union was shaky from the start. The people were of different stock, the Lower Counties being more Swedish, Finnish, and Dutch than was Pennsylvania. Quakers were less numerous and because of the region's vulnerability to pirates, the other residents were anxious for military defense, while Pennsylvania, safe from attack, remained pacifistic. The people of the Lower Counties, moreover, accounting themselves the senior partners because of their longer history, insisted on equal representation in the government, a concession that Pennsylvania, larger in area and growing more rapidly in wealth and population, was increasingly unwilling to permit. If it had ever been true that the New Castle residents, welcoming Penn on his arrival, had cried out with one voice for a merger with the northern counties, they soon repented of the action, for the rapid growth of Philadelphia as a metropolis and as a seaport was reducing New Castle's importance.

Dissatisfaction spread throughout the Lower Counties. Complaints were voiced that the Proprietor was spending too much time in Pennsylvania and so ignoring his southern counties; that because he was a pacifist, he would not allow the lower Delaware to defend itself against pirate raids; that he considered the Lower Counties as "the Territories," not as an integral part of the province. A movement to break the union developed and steadily gathered strength.

HOW TO TREAT MINORITIES

ENN TOOK PAINS TO CULTIVATE GOOD RACE RELATIONS. IT WAS A MATTER DEAR TO HIS HEART. OTHER AMERICAN PROVINCES HAD MIS-TREATED THEIR INDIANS, NOT BECAUSE OF VICIOUSNESS OR HOSTILITY, but through ignorance and misunderstandings; naturally, the Indians had responded in kind. Penn, in common with other well-meaning leaders, laid the cause of conflict to failure to recognize that all men, as children of a common God, were, or should be, brothers. The Holy Experiment, he believed, must show the way to peace, harmony, and cooperation.

Himself a member of a minority group whose unusual customs were misinterpreted and distrusted by the authorities, Penn was determined that no one in his province, whatever his race, religion, or background, should suffer discrimination or persecution. All Pennsylvanians, whatever their origins, were to be equally protected by laws passed by a free legislature democratically elected. This did not necessarily imply that everyone was to be wholly equal to all others, for certain rights, suffrage for example, must be exercised only by those capable of wise and mature judgment, but any limitation imposed applied equally to everyone. No free white citizen should own a privilege denied a black man of equal status. No Quaker should possess a power denied on religious grounds to any other Christian. A fully naturalized Frenchman should stand on precisely the same footing as a citizen of English birth. Wholly unrestricted manhood equality had not yet dawned in any country, but Pennsylvania under William Penn came closer to that goal than any other region in his day.

Penn came to America with rather sketchy ideas about the Indians. Certainly he had listened to George Fox and to Josiah Coale, perhaps also to others, as they talked about their travels in America. As a frequenter of the court he would have met officials returned to report on colonial conditions. He may have known, or at least have seen, an Indian or two. His insatiable appetite for ransacking libraries would have led him to inform himself about Sir Walter Raleigh's ill-fated settlement at Roanoke, as well as about the luckier adventures in Virginia, Carolina, New England, and, of course, New Jersey. None of the sources, except the very recent Quaker experiences, were beyond criticism. Officials would have had axes to grind. Indians, in whom Penn would have been far more interested, would not have commanded sufficient English to discuss the topics with which Penn would have been most concerned.

From what Penn had read or heard or seen of Indians, he had formed a highly favorable opinion of them. They were quiet folk, much like typical Quakers, serious, reserved, and taciturn, qualities Penn admired. They were dignified, not frivolous, nor were they given to vain jesting as were so many people of the world. They prized their honor and never forgot a discourtesy, but they were more considerate than European snobs, for never would an Indian act rudely to another. Penn did not use the term "nature's gentlemen" to describe the Indians, but he would have approved of it. Since he was no devotee of poetry, he may not have read John Dryden's lines about noble savages running wild in the woods, but he would have accepted the description.[1]

Penn, shocked and dismayed by the wickedness that he believed lay all about him, saw in unspoiled America man's best, perhaps his only, hope for earthly redemption. He looked upon the Indian almost as a man of Genesis, living in an isolated world untouched by civilized corruption. In this naïve belief he broke new ground. According to general report, the Indians were rude and barbarous, benighted, and perhaps subhuman. Some said they were thievish, treacherous, and murderous. Penn, willing enough to believe that white men of his generation were decadent, had a higher opinion of the aborigines. Europeans had been corrupted by the evil institutions of their times; they had rejected the good teachings of ancient days and had drifted from the paths of virtue, but the Indians remained unspoiled.

No one could argue that Penn understood the Indians. All the evidence was against him. But secure in his faith that the Indians might very possibly be pursuing some form of the ancient laws of Jehovah, as they interpreted those laws, he thought it possible that those Indians might really be survivors of the Ten Lost Tribes of Israel. All those derogatory rumors stemmed from the casual and unreliable reports of chance visitors, some of whom, at least, had been seeking only adventure, profit, or rich land that would cost them nothing but would yield enormous wealth. Virtually none were high-minded scholars looking for the truth. Penn intimated that few indeed had ever tried to understand the Indian's social structure, his psychology, or his ethics.[2]

Penn envied the Indian's simplicity and his freedom from the corruption of the supposedly civilized world. Theirs was the way of life that God intended man to live, a life close to the heart of nature, where everyone was free and equal, each willing and anxious to help his fellows, to share the good and to work together to avoid the evil. Theirs was not the selfish world where men thought only of private gain. They did not practice cutthroat competition, seek public office to exact gratuities, or cheat each other. They did not draw up lengthy contracts, swear solemn oaths that they would perform what they promised, and then tear up the agreements if thereby they could save a shilling or two. The Indians were honest men who needed no police, no lawyers, and no jails. Apparently they had never heard of taxes.[3]

Though the Indian religion left something to be desired, it did hold promise. To a Quaker mind it was unilluminated, but there were faint gleams of light. Their beliefs and practices were far from being as "dark" as Penn considered some European forms of worship. The Indians did not recognize the One True God, at least not by that name; but with a little coaching, they would come to realize their Great Spirit's true identity. They were not fanatic; they did not demand conformity. Certainly they did not punish those who disagreed for conscientious reasons.[4]

Their simplicity and innate goodness extended even to their speech. Indians avoided verbosity, restricting their talk to a Quakerish Yea-Yea or Nay-Nay; but when they did speak they were fervent and eloquent, their sentences notable for imagery and charm. Penn resolved that he would learn their tongue.

William Penn was not maudlin in his admiration, however. The Indians had faults, though some of them could be excused. "They live by their pleasures," said Penn, but he was quick to add, "I mean hunting and fishing." Unhappily, they drank too heavily; this vice was not entirely their own fault, for they had been a temperate people corrupted by the Swedes and Dutch and, to Britain's shame, by English traders who had dealt with them. They did not always keep their word, but maybe this was due to ignorance. Indian chiefs had "sold" the same lands over and over again, but white men must remember that Indians knew nothing of European systems of land titles. What had really happened was that foreigners had "bought" something that the Indians had never sold: not the exclusive ownership of any territory but merely an equal right to live and hunt and farm together with the tribesmen.[5]

Reared in a monarchial and aristocratic culture, Penn did not realize that primitive tribesmen had little concept of a stratified society. Quite understandably he assumed that Indian spokesmen were kings or at least noblemen with powers similar to those of English monarchs: the right, for instance, to make binding treaties, to commit their people to specific actions, to barter away the tribal land.[6] Thus, Penn undertook to purchase territory, not realizing that the price that he would pay would not be used for tribal benefit but would be accepted as presents to the "kings" to be used for their personal enjoyment. As such prices were usually paid in goods rather than by cash, it was indeed strange that neither Penn nor others connected the transfer of so many articles of clothing, so many pairs of shoes, or so many blankets; so many axes, knives, or scissors; so many guns or so many rounds of ammunition; even so many gallons of liquor, with the number of chiefs attending the conferences at which the goods were given.

Penn's misconceptions were not peculiar to him; they were shared by virtually every European who had done business with the Indians. Each wave of immigrants had bought and paid for the land on which the people settled, and each, after the first arrivals, had been dismayed to learn that the same land had been previously sold, sometimes several times, to others. The Indians, however, had not been guilty of fraud; rather, they had been hospitable, freely admitting strangers to equal enjoyment of the land.

Though Penn, like others, anticipated exclusive possession of farm and residential tracts, he had no thought of exploitation of the Indians. He assured the red men of his firm intention to avoid the harassment to which other foreigners had subjected them; he expressed his anxiety to avoid animosity by treating them with kindliness and justice. If disputes should occur, the conflicts would be resolved by fair trials before impartial courts. "If anything should offend you or your people," he promised, "you should have a full and speedy satisfaction for the same by an equal number of just men on both sides."[7]

He, no more than any other European, ever stopped to wonder whether Indians had any real idea of precisely what he meant, and the Indians were too polite to request an explanation. It was exactly what he had told his European colonists, and it was said for exactly the same reasons. Penn well understood that his province, unlike most of the others and to a greater degree than any, was polyglot, with peoples of various stocks, whose backgrounds, languages, and customs varied widely. His plans of settlement, he suspected rightly, would entail inconveniences, some relocations, and perhaps serious culture clashes; unless the matter was delicately handled, strong antagonisms might arise. In fairness and justice the disputes must not be arbitrarily settled by any one group, however overriding that group's authority might be, but must be ended by mutual agreement. The Swedes, Hollanders, and non-Quaker English should have as strong a say as should the Friends and, unusual as the practice might be, so should the Indians.

Penn therefore instructed his officials, when dealing with the Indians, to treat them as equals and not to assume that because a chief might happen to understand a few words of broken English he could negotiate in that alien tongue. Everything that might be said to Indians,

Penn insisted, should be translated by just such a competent interpreter as Lasse Cock, his own interpreter.[8]

Early in November Penn, with a small group of Friends, rode up to Shackamaxon, a mile or two north of the city where a few Quakers had already established a meeting. His major purpose was to attend services at the home of Thomas Fairman, and as Shackamaxon was a favorite Indian council grounds, he hoped to meet some of their people. He would transact no business on a First Day, but the acquaintances would be helpful at further conferences.[9]

As usual, Penn was lucky; it so chanced that Chief Tamamend of the Lenni Lenape, who American Revolutionists later adopted as Tammany, the patron saint of the young democracy, was visiting the council grounds. According to legend, Penn here pledged to Tamamend and to leaders of tribes from as far west as the Susquehanna, that Indians and Quakers would always live side by side in mutual harmony and perpetual peace. The legend apparently originated with John Oldmixon, author of English histories, who possibly misread the date of a letter in which Penn described a later conference held on the same grounds or who may have confused Penn's Shackamaxon meeting with an earlier meeting there by Markham.[10] Whatever the cause of the error, Shackamaxon in November 1682 has long been commemorated as the occasion when Penn and the Indians, standing under a giant elm, concluded a solemn treaty pledging that Indians and Quakers would remain forever friendly. Penn said:

> The Great Spirit who made me and you, who rules the heavens and the earth and knows the inmost thoughts of man, knows that I and my friends have a hearty desire to live in peace and friendship with you. It is not our custom to use weapons. . . . We are met on the broad pathway of good faith and good will . . . all is to be openness, brotherhood and love. . . . I will not do as the Marylanders did, that is, call you children and brothers only, for parents are apt to whip their children too severely, and brothers sometimes will differ. Neither will I compare the friendship between us to a chain, for the rain may rust it, or a tree may fall and break it, but I will consider you as the same flesh and blood with the Christians and the same as if the one body were to be divided into two parts."

Whether Penn actually delivered such a speech, translated into Indian by Lasse Cock, is immaterial; there is no question that he would have endorsed every word of it. Nor is it important whether, when the speech was ended, Penn did or did not join the Indians in feasting on roasted acorns and hominy. It is questionable, however, whether he then played with them, "hopping and jumping higher than any of them" (as the legend has it), for that sort of activity, which he would have termed "carnal frivolity," was not in his character.[11]

The famous Benjamin West painting, wherein Penn, clad in anachronistic costume, stands between Deputy Governor Markham and West's ancestor Robert Pearson, is historically incorrect. Certainly the Penn of the portrait, fat and pudgy at thirty-eight, would have offered no athletic competition to the lithe young Indians of the background, nor, if the picture were accurate, could the ancient lady half a century later have described the Proprietor as "the handsomest man she had ever met."[12]

As Indians were averse to indoor gatherings, the sharp frosts of a Pennsylvania winter prevented further conferences until spring. Penn did not find the cold too severe; he was pleasantly surprised that it was no worse. At a season when, in England, he would have seen the Thames frozen, with thousands of people on the ice, booths and huts erected upon it, and even some enterprising merchants roasting oxen on the frozen surface, Pennsylvania, he assured his London friends, was reasonably comfortable. Once in a while, he admitted, there might be ships caught in the ice, but there were no coaches rolling up and down upon the river such as he would have seen upon the Thames. Even though the temperature might be low, there was none of the "foul, thick, black weather the northeast winds bring to England." The climate might be "dry, cold, piercing and hungry, yet I remember not I wore more clothes than in England."[13]

After "a sweet spring, no gusts but gentle showers and a fine sky," Penn and his entourage, including Lasse Cock, met the Indians again at Shackamaxon on June 23, 1683. Because this was a formal occasion, the conclusion of a treaty of lasting peace and friendship, the one that was never sworn to and never broken, Penn dignified the occasion by wearing the impressive sky-blue sash he had worn at New Castle. The Indians arrived in full regalia, Tamamend crowned by a chaplet and carrying a small horn as a symbol of authority. Addressing Penn as "Onas," which they explained was Indian for a pen or quill, they presented him with a wampum belt showing a hatted man holding an Indian by the hand. Both the belt and the sash are preserved at the Historical Society of Pennsylvania.[14]

Thus the Indians again welcomed Penn's colonists to residence while Penn, in return, distributed useful European articles. These were the usual household articles, the customary knives, axes, fishhooks, needles, and other steel goods, together with such woolens as blankets, knee-length stockings, and the long mantles which were then called matchcoats. It is doubtful that Penn included rum or other grog in this list of gifts; himself a moderate consumer of wine and beer, he was far more careful than other colonial leaders about supplying liquor to the Indians. In buying some New Jersey land, Fenwick, for instance, had paid two matchcoats and forty gallons of rum. Penn, however, realized that Indians were particularly susceptible to hard liquors, unknown to them before the coming of the white men. The Indians when drunk, Penn saw, were easily cheated; for sixpence worth of liquor they would part with furs that they would not sell for five shillings' worth of any other commodity. Penn would have liked to impose total prohibition on the sale of rum to red men, and one or two chiefs, even before Penn's arrival, had proposed as much to Lasse Cock, but white men would not cooperate. Indians then proposed that drunken Indians suffer the same punishments as drunken Europeans, but this scheme proved unworkable because Indians had no cash to pay the five-shilling fine imposed. Law enforcement broke down entirely when a sheriff, hunting through the woods to find some culprits, became hopelessly lost and had to be rescued, apparently by the very Indians he had been sent to arrest.[15]

Despite the tokens of friendship distributed at Shackamaxon, the tribesmen were not entirely happy in their new alliance. Tamamend, realizing that the white men acted as though Indians no longer had the right to hunt on the land, was quoted as having threatened to burn their houses. "He has played the rogue," Holme reported. Tamamend had contended that the Indians had never parted with any land and so the whites should move away.[16]

Penn did not hear of this development until after he had returned to England, but he took a firm stand. He had given Indians, he said, the equivalent of at least £1000. "Tamine [*sic*]" he told Holme, "sold all and if the Indians do not punish him we will and must." Apparently Chief Tamamend needed no chastisement. For the rest of Penn's life no further misunderstandings developed.[17]

Actually, the conflict had been exaggerated, for only three days after Tamamend's threat, a Hollander, writing from Germantown, assured his friends in Europe that Indians were friendly. "We live together with them very quiet and peaceful. We travel day and night through the forest without the slightest fear." The testimony reinforced German assurances. "The so-called Indians or savages," a leading German reported, "are kind-hearted, honest folk who, upon a time, in that great day of judgment will stand up with those of Tyre and Sidon to shame the false-mouthed Christians."[18]

White conduct toward the Indians was not above reproach. The common trader practice of making the tribesmen drunk, the easier to cheat them, was bad enough but certain scoundrels went farther. Arming themselves with bottles of rum the young Europeans, identified only as the "servants" of a prominent Philadelphian, visited nearby Indian villages, invited the natives to drinking parties and then not only lay with the squaws but, afterward, beat up both men and women. When the red men complained the Provincial Council took appropriate action; it ordered that the laws against *selling* liquor to Indians be strengthened and enforced. Though the Indians identified the culprits no punishment was inflicted.[19]

23

BALTIMORE CONFRONTATION

FOUR DAYS AFTER THE ADJOURNMENT OF HIS CONSTITUENT ASSEMBLY,
PENN, IN COMPANY WITH HOLME AND CHRISTOPHER TAYLOR, WAS ON
HIS WAY TO MEET HIS OLD ACQUAINTANCE CHARLES CALVERT, THIRD
Lord Baltimore and, since 1675, the second Proprietor of Maryland. The
two proprietors could scarcely be described as close friends, but they had
much in common. Both owned large tracts in America and both had
Irish backgrounds, Baltimore by virtue of his birth and Penn because of
his land ownership there. By stretching a point or two, they might even
be described as neighbors, not only because their provinces adjoined but
because the Baltimore Irish holdings, near Cape Clear, were only thirty-
five or forty miles from Shanagarry. Since, however, travel in Ireland during "the troubles" was neither safe nor easy, there is no evidence that
the two men had met in youth. Both men frequented court circles, though
Baltimore, Governor of Maryland since 1661, when he was only twenty-
four, was not often in England in the days when Penn was most active at
Whitehall. Finally, both proprietors were undergoing similar annoyances
from bureaucrats and courtiers striving to undermine the charters given
them by kings whom the Royalists thought too generous.

Certainly the two men knew each other. Late in 1676 London Quakers received reports that Lord Baltimore, who had succeeded to the proprietorship the year before, was harassing Quakers who could not swear
an oath of allegiance. The Friends were being punished because refusal
to take the oath smacked of treason or of possible rebelliousness. To ease
the Quaker situation, the Society of Friends, in December 1676 and again
in the following November, asked Penn to meet Lord Baltimore to
explain the Quaker principles and to seek an understanding. Penn had
done so and had reported that Baltimore had agreed to submit an affirmation for an oath of fealty.[1]

In his anxiety to settle the boundary disputes, Penn went to some inconvenience. "I did incontinently take a long journey in a cold and unpleasant season." He and his two companions rode from New Castle to Bohemia Manor in Maryland, the home of Augustin Herrmann, the geographer, and his Labadist associates. Quite possibly they traveled with some apprehension. None of the Pennsylvanians knew Maryland well, and ugly rumors were circulating about the inhabitants of that region. It was a good country, the legends reported, "but 'tis possessed by a debauched, idle, lazy people. All that they labor for is only as much bread as services them for one season, and as much tobacco as will furnish them with clothes." This raising of tobacco as a cash crop was generally regarded, especially by Royal customs collectors, as an illegal trade because, according to reports by Edward Randolph, the Eastern Shore people not only mislabeled the contents of the tobacco kegs, but understated weights and, whenever they could, conveyed the tobacco past the customs gates by night. "I believe," said one critic, "it is the worst improved country in the world, for the Indian wheat is what they trust to and if that fail they may expect to starve."[2]

If Penn's party actually entertained such ideas, which is extremely doubtful, for they were intelligent people, the brief stay at Augustin Herrmann's and the ride thereafter through Maryland's Chesapeake countryside would have disillusioned them. Later, in reviewing his travels through New York, Long Island, New Jersey, and Maryland, Penn praised the country in the highest terms. "Here is what Abraham, Isaac and Jacob would be contented with. How sweet is the quiet of these parts, freed from the associations and troublesome solicitations, hurries and perplexities of woeful Europe."

He said nothing about the generality of people; but had they been as shiftless as reported, he would not have spared his condemnations. As it was, he did not mention that inland Pennsylvanians referred to Marylanders as "the hominy gentry."[3]

At Colonel Thomas Taylor's plantation in Anne Arundel County (named for Lord Baltimore's mother), the Maryland Proprietor was awaiting Penn. A veteran of Indian troubles, of trade and boundary disputes with Virginia, and of ownership problems with New York over the Three Lower Counties, Baltimore was inured to difficulties. He had successfully combated charges by Titus Oates of complicity in the fictitious Popish Plot and, by guaranteeing liberty of conscience, he had managed to rule a largely Protestant people as a Catholic province.

Baltimore's concept of his northern boundary clashed with that of William Penn. By the terms of his 1632 charter Baltimore claimed, and Penn admitted, that Maryland was to lie "under the 40th parallel." They differed on the precise location of that parallel and on what was meant by "under" it. Baltimore contended that "under" it meant up to the line itself. He knew, however, that eleven days before the *Welcome* had left Deal, the King had ordered him to "set down your northern boundaries by a measurement of two degrees," a distance of 120 miles, "from Watkins Point." As such a measurement would leave a neutral zone between Maryland and the fortieth parallel, Baltimore hoped to convince the King that a degree was more nearly seventy than sixty miles wide.[4]

Penn, insisting that "under" the fortieth meant that Maryland must not impinge upon that important line of latitude, professed surprise that Lord Baltimore should venture to question the Royal "compasses," particularly as the existence of the buffer zone gave Pennsylvania a chance to acquire the upper Chesapeake, and more of the lower Delaware as well. If, by any chance, the *hactentus inculta* clause was not enough to protect this latter region from falling into Baltimore's hands, Pennsylvania might gain New Castle by acquiring an ownerless strip between the two provinces. Such were the matters that the two proprietors settled down to discuss.

Opinions differ widely as to what happened at the conference. According to Baltimore, Penn readily admitted that, except for New Castle, the Marylander's claims were just (a skilled negotiator would scarcely have begun a parley by admitting that his opponent was right!) and, for that reason, asked that proceedings should be kept secret. Penn then said that discussion need not be concerned with land, of which Penn had plenty; what Pennsylvania really needed was a waterway. Because he had no bay or river west of Philadelphia, said Penn, his hinterland was really nothing but a great lump of clay, wholly useless without water transportation. He then asked Lord Baltimore to sell him land at the upper end of the Chesapeake. Just 1 percent of Maryland's water frontage, said Penn, was vital to the welfare of 99 percent of Pennsylvania. If Lord Baltimore, like a good neighbor, would sell him a port, Penn would pay well, whatever Baltimore might ask, in return for the favor. Baltimore replied that he thought the request reasonable but that first he must consult his council.[5]

This version does not agree with the Pennsylvania report. Far from admitting Baltimore's claim, the Pennsylvanians said, Penn produced Maryland's own map of 1635 which showed Lord Baltimore's northern limit, the mysterious fortieth, as lying just short of the head of the Chesapeake, so that Pennsylvania really was entitled to an outlet there. Nevertheless, to keep the peace, Penn offered to buy the land, only to be rebuffed by Baltimore.[6]

As for the secrecy request, Baltimore had agreed but then had broken his promise. Unbeknownst to the Quaker, the Marylanders had stationed a clerk behind a door to take notes on what was said. Baltimore admitted the presence of the clerk but denied the pledge of secrecy. He had offered Penn a transcript of the clerk's notes, said Lord Baltimore, but the Pennsylvanian would not wait to receive it. He was in too much of a hurry to visit the Quaker meetings which George Fox had founded twenty years before.

Aside from the disagreements and the accusations, the conference seems to have been harmonious. The two proprietors planned a further parley in the spring. Then, as though loath to part company, Lord Baltimore mounted a horse and rode with the Quaker party for several miles, turning away only when Penn was drawing near the first Friends meetinghouse. The accusations and recriminations, it appears, did not begin until the writers of the reports were compiling their formal records.

After Lord Baltimore turned back, Penn crossed the Chesapeake to attend Quaker meetings on the Eastern Shore, where he discovered, to his surprise that his congregations included a number of prominent citizens.

It was a good time to travel, that December of 1682, for the weather had so improved that it was much like an English spring. Penn would have liked to sail down the Chesapeake, as Fox had done, to visit Thomas, Lord Culpeper, Governor and co-proprietor of Virginia, but he did not have the time to spare. Instead, he wrote a friendly letter, reminding Culpeper that they were relatives by marriage ("my wife's great-grandmother was thy great aunt"). He could not have known too much about his Lordship, else he would not have committed the *faux pas* of boasting to a man notorious for an unsavory life that he, Penn, was "a man of Christian decency." Nor would he have told Culpeper, whom Virginians detested and who had taken up his post only at the King's command, that "I am like to be an adopted American." All that Penn really knew about Culpeper was that, like himself, he wanted an elective assembly which should have only the option of accepting or rejecting whatever the governor and his council submitted to it. Penn completed his visits and returned to Pennsylvania just in time to attend the opening session of his first formal legislature. He was to preside over the sessions of the all-powerful Provincial Council.[7]

Pennsylvania's first popularly elected Provincial Council and Assembly organized on March 12, 1683. It was a smaller legislative organ than Penn had originally contemplated. On mature deliberation he had come to realize that a seventy-two-man council and an assembly of five hundred, a number roughly equal to one-tenth the male population, would not only be unwieldy but impracticable: where, in a community of no more than one hundred small houses, could so many out-of-towners be housed? He had, therefore, asked each of the six counties to send nine delegates, the three with the most votes in each county to be councilmen and the others assemblymen.[8]

There may be some question whether the fifty-four successful candidates represented the wisest, soberest, and most virtuous of all the residents; only three days later a councilman was fined five shillings for being drunk. (This, as it happened, was sheer favoritism, for the Great Law provided that drunkards should be lashed or put to hard labor.) Nor was he the only culprit. Charles Pickering, another legislator, was arrested for counterfeiting. Despite his fervent plea that his coins contained more silver than the official shillings, he was fined forty shillings, in addition to redeeming each of his counterfeits by honest money. Apparently his conviction did not affect his standing either in the legislature or in the community, for he continued as a lawmaker and as an influential citizen.[9]

In spite of these peccadillos, there is no doubt that the great majority of those elected were imbued with a commendable spirit. They were sincerely anxious to promote the general welfare. It is also certain that they and their constituents approved and shared Penn's high ideals. Nevertheless, neither they nor Penn himself had very clear ideas about how to convert those high ideals into good legislation. The Proprietor, for all his experience at court, trusted that righteous and religious men, representing people of good will, would invariably act properly. He had no suspicion that his province could be corrupt or moved in any way by gratuities or by personal considerations. Such influences, he supposed, could not flourish in the Holy Experiment.

Few if any of the elected representatives and their constituents had political experience, and the general public was politically illiterate. Only a small fraction had been educated above the elementary grades. There were, of course, distinguished exceptions, physicians, lawyers, teachers, clergymen, or other professional people; but taken as a group, they formed a small percentage of the population. These, with the wealthier and better-known traders, were those most likely to have been picked for public office.

Under such circumstances surprises were inevitable. The Assembly's first action almost upset the Proprietor's plans. He had assumed that Friends would control the government; yet when the Assembly balloted for speaker, the non-Quaker delegations from upcountry and from the Lower Counties almost exactly equaled the number of Friends. Only because two rural members failed to arrive on time was the Quaker candidate chosen and then only by a one-vote margin.[10]

At the outset the Assembly was cooperative. Either because it wished to please the Proprietor, who, after all, knew best, or possibly because it supposed that it was acting as the Frame directed, it agreed that all measures should be prepared by the Governor and Council, and that the Assembly should accept or reject, without debate, whatever the Council proposed to it. The subordination, however, was short-lived. The Assembly, realizing that it had voted away the powers exercised by the earlier Assembly, asked for the rights to initiate, to debate, and, if necessary, to amend Council proposals; unless it possessed such powers, the Assembly protested, the Council, elected at the same time and by the same voters as itself, would be a dominating and aristocratic upper house. When Penn denied the request, as contrary to the Frame, the Assembly agreed that he might veto a Council action, but not a decision of the Assembly.[11]

The unrest, especially in the Assembly, would widen and deepen. For the most part everybody meant well, but in the prevailing ignorance about what should be done or the proper way to do it, the various groups were jealous of their dignities. Everyone suspected his colleagues' motives. Hurt pride was very common and the seventeenth-century propensity to regard all dissidents as filthy, base, and vile raged unrestrained. Penn felt, for instance, that he was undervalued by his people, that his critics were undermining his position, and that they were ungrateful. As he would later express it, they were not only playing "the great game of 'Cheat the Governor'" but were "cutting great collops" out of his property. The Provincial Council, not satisfied by his voluntary surrender of two of his three votes, and smarting under the taunts of being an aristocratic body, seemed bent on reducing the Proprietor to the status of just ordinary citizen. The Assembly charged him with hypocrisy. He had nobly promised that the people might live under laws of their own choosing; even before the popular Assembly was created, he had reduced the people's voice to impotency.[12]

One of the few things upon which everyone agreed was that the original Frame was faulty and a new one should be drawn.[13]

Though the opinions of the general public were not expressly sought, and though little was recorded about their feelings at the time, some may have fretted over what seemed Penn's propensity to quibble. He had allowed the Constituent Assembly to debate and to amend, but he had refused the same privileges to the popularly elected General Assembly. He had split hairs over the forms to be used in the qualification of officials. He had not forced them to take oaths, "except for such as could swear," but he substituted an attestation: "You solemnly promise in the presence of God that you will justly try and deliver in your verdict," a subtle distinction in which non-Quakers saw no difference.[14]

That some sort of dissatisfaction was rife seems evident, for a few months later one Anthony Weston received ten lashes on each of three successive days for having drawn up proposals "of great presumption and contempt for the Governor and the Provincial Council."[15] Certain freemen who had signed Weston's petition were put under bond to keep the peace. What the proposals may have been is unknown, for Council sessions were secret, no prying newspapermen probed for leaks, and the carefully edited *Minutes* shed no light. The matter must have been seditious if the Council thus punished the exercise of the rights of petition and free speech.[15]

However sensitive the Council may have been, Penn did not call for lashes for those who attacked him. In response to a critic who rebuked him for not working hard enough to assure Quaker dominition, he dispatched a letter of pained protest. "I am night and day spending my life, my time, my money, not a sixpence enriched by this greatness, to say nothing of my hazard and the distance I am from a comfortable estate, and, which is more, my dear wife and poor children." He closed with a burst of temper. "Thy conceit is neither religious, political nor equal and, without high words, I disregard it as meddling, intruding and presumptuous."[16]

Due to the absence of a dynamic and forceful Assembly leader, a second Frame of April 2, 1683, failed to give that body much more power. It did gain the right to initiate and to debate, even though, at first, it had to do so indirectly by petitioning the Provincial Council, but it still remained relatively impotent.

Penn's power was reduced. He was not, by this new Frame, permitted to perform any public act without the advice and consent of the Provincial Council, though to balance this retriction, he assumed that he, in turn, could veto any Council action. Penn was also to be allowed, as long as he lived, to appoint judges and minor officials, provided that he chose them from a list of nominees submitted to him by the Council. The right was not hereditary. He was relieved of the necessity of paying government expenses from his own pocket. Though many landowners had supposed that this practice was the reason for the quitrents, justices were empowered to levy taxes for government needs and, in addition, all males between the ages of sixteen and sixty were saddled with a poll tax. The change was not popular among the people![17]

With unexpected generosity the legislators then offered to the Proprietor the proceeds of an excise tax on liquor: two shillings per gallon on all rum, wine, and brandy imports and a penny per gallon on foreign cider. He was also to have twenty shillings out of every £100 of all customs duties except those on molasses. Though Penn had been insistently complaining that the province was bleeding him white, he graciously declined the offer. Ill-wishers said that as no cider was imported, as Pennsylvanians made their own rum from the tax-free molasses and brandy from their peaches, and as the other imports were negligible, his gesture cost him nothing. Twenty years later Penn, forgetting that he had voluntarily waived the gift, complained that a former friend, in collusion with a "few selfish spirits," had canceled the law without Penn's consent. The action, Penn declared, "has been the cause of all my troubles and inability to support myself."[18]

The one setback Penn received in the new Frame was the refusal to require that the Pennsylvania statutes be made required reading in the schools. Instead, the Provincial Council voted not to publish the laws.[19]

Perhaps this was just as well. Though the Frame had specified that laws should be posted in public places, it might have been dangerous for London to read them before the mandatory five years had expired when the legislation must be sent for bureaucratic perusal. There was nothing in the least revolutionary about the Frame, nor about any of the laws, but London was on the lookout for anything that might serve to justify the invoking of quo warranto.

⟨ 24 ⟩

LOVING TENANTS

WHEN THE TROUBLESOME ASSEMBLY AT LAST ADJOURNED PENN REOPENED NEGOTIATIONS WITH MARYLAND. THOUGH HE PROBABLY WAS NOT AWARE OF ANY PRESSING NEED, IT WAS HIGH time that he did so. Lord Baltimore had just instructed Colonel George Talbot, his cousin, "to press and employ" two carpenters to build a small palisaded fort within the Lower Counties at Christina (Christiana) Bridge near New Castle. Talbot was then to garrison this stronghold with three able-bodied soldiers.

The fort, to be located within the Twelve Mile Circle granted William Penn, would serve a multiple purpose. It would assert Baltimore's claim to the Lower Counties, protect it against possible incursion from pacifist Pennsylvania, and defend the region "against outrage and violence by Indians and other thieves." The bridge, said Lord Baltimore, "has afforded too great a conveniency to escape to Pennsylvania where they have been protected." In times of peace the fort would be useful as a trading post.[1]

Baltimore further ordered Talbot to run a line from the upper limit of the Twelve Mile Circle westward to the mouth of Octorora Creek, the place which Marylanders assumed to be the site of Susquehanna Fort. Such a line would be slightly south of the fortieth degree of northern latitude.

While Marylanders were thus active in trying to define and defend their boundaries, the Pennsylvanians were apparently neglectful. Even Markham, the sea captain experienced in shooting the sun, is not on record as having tried to fix the latitude. Though he had borrowed the sextile and had been with Lord Baltimore when the latter took observations at New Castle, Markham does not seem to have checked the Marylander's conclusions. It is inconceivable that Markham could have been indifferent to the matter, but neither he nor Lord Baltimore saw fit to mention any such interest.

The two proprietors met at New Castle on May 29, Penn having returned Lord Baltimore's courtesy at their previous conference by riding eight miles below the town to meet his colleague and to escort him to the quarters prepared for him. Once there, Penn became all businessman. He again offered to buy Susquehanna land at Lord Baltimore's price. He was willing to pay, he intimated, in order to avoid controversy; to Baltimore the offer was an admission that Penn had no legal claim whatever. Penn again demanded an immediate response. If Baltimore refused, he said, he would ask the King to intervene in his behalf.[2]

Baltimore was in a quandary. He was not anxious to allow his "ungenerous friend" an outlet to the ocean via his own Chesapeake Bay; knowing that Penn had more friends at court than he had, he was reluctant to refer the matter to London, being, as Penn was very well aware, in difficulty there, facing a loss of his charter through quo warranto proceedings. Remembering, therefore, how Markham had broken off negotiations through illness, Baltimore suddenly announced that he was sick and must go home.[3]

Talbot made the next move, riding into Philadelphia to demand that Penn hand over the Lower Counties to Maryland. Learning that Penn had gone to New York, Talbot called on Nicholas More, now president of the Provincial Council, to surrender the territory. More, of course, refused, so Talbot went back to Maryland, stopping here and there in the Lower Counties to induce the Swedes and Finns who lived there to move to Maryland.

Penn, on returning home, wrote Baltimore a scathing letter, angrily denying the surrender demand, complaining of Baltimore's bad manners in sending a subordinate on such a mission, and protesting at Talbot's attempt to "seduce" the Swedes and Finns. He issued a proclamation forbidding anyone to settle in the Lower Counties between the Delaware and the Chesapeake without his express permission.[4]

Penn then proceeded to mend his political and social fences. In late July he wrote letters to half a dozen noblemen thanking them extravagantly for all that they had done for him and hoping that they would continue their patronage. "I am ill at ease at ceremony and flattery," he said, but he allowed each of the recipients to believe that he was the single individual who had done the most to make the proprietorship possible.[5] He was highly tactful. Quakers did not approve of earthly honorifics, but lest he bruise the ego of any nobleman, he avoided using the "thee" and "thou" of Quaker plain talk, usually addressing them in the third person rather than the second, and being careful to accord each one his proper title.

The sincere gratitude expressed in these letters—Lord Baltimore and other opponents would probably have termed them fawning—was in sharp contrast to another dispatched to the Governor and Council of West Jersey. In this he complained of "great and irreparable damage by some members of your colony." Those critics, he said, had filled England with "noise of wars in Pennsylvania between the inhabitants and Lord Baltimore's people." West Jerseymen had reported that Penn needed a good harbor because "I had no place where ships or boats could come. Of this the 'Change, Coffee Houses, booksellers' shops and country rings thereby discouraging hundreds ready to purchase." He did not suggest what the West Jersey authorities could do about the misconceptions, some of which echo in part what Penn himself had said in talking to Lord Baltimore, but he did seem to intimate that a sort of censorship or a rule similar to that in the Great Law against false reporting might be desirable.[6]

Coupled with his wooing of the "Great and Gracious" King and of the noble lords, all of whom exerted influence in the Council on Trade and Plantations, was a certain amount of propaganda to show how successful his province had become in so short a time. "We have laid out a town," he said, "a mile wide and two miles deep, with 150 very tolerable houses." It was, he added, "the largest town south of New York and already the envy of its neighbors." He did not mention that one could go hunting within a half-mile of the Delaware or that wolves prowled within the greater part of the Philadelphia area.[7]

But Philadelphia, though it had a fair, a well-run market, a ropewalk, a shipyard, and churches for its diversified population, was not the only pride of the province. The countryside was booming, eight hundred houses already built for four thousand people, almost all of whom were young and healthy. Everyone was prosperous. And why not, when a whole deer, bigger, tenderer, and plumper than any venison in England, sold for two shillings, a forty-pound turkey for a shilling, and Indian corn for two and six per bushel? A buyer must, of course, be canny, for prices had risen, and there were instances when Indians had tried to foist a dead eagle instead of a turkey on an unwary purchaser. Now there were strict market rules to punish such sharp practices.

The food was good; fish in abundance and oysters, of which Penn was particularly fond, a good "six inches long." The fruits, vegetables, and grain, Penn reported, were "as good as I have commonly eaten in Europe and, I may say, most of them better." Fresh meat, however, except for the deer and wildfowl, was sometimes a trifle scarce. Farmers were not raising enough livestock for sale, and those who did slaughtered it at "hog-killing time," in October. During the winter people had to rely upon smoked or salted beef, pork, and mutton.[8]

Nevertheless, to live in Pennsylvania was happiness. "The air is serene as in Languedoc, a most fragrant smell of cedar, pine and sassafras." In short, said Penn, "I am fully satisfied with the country," so satisfied, indeed, that he declared, "I must, without vanity, confess that I have led the greatest colony in America than ever any man did on private credit."[9]

Penn was so pleased that, overcoming fears of becoming land-poor, he increased his holdings by buying what was left of John Fenwick's land in West Jersey. The deal was closed on March 23, 1683. The action so pleased the major that when he died, some six months later, his will was found to contain a provision appointing Penn, "my much esteemed friend," his executor and guardian of his grandchildren.[10]

Penn's progress would continue. "With the help of God and such noble friends," he promised Halifax and Sunderland, "I will show a province in seven years equal to her neighbors of 40 years' planting."[11] The promise seemed well grounded. Big ships were coming in from England at the rate of one a week, though not on regular schedule, each carrying a full complement of immigrants. These were the fruits of Penn's intensive land-sales efforts. Welshmen were rimming the city to the west and north and were buying land in the Lower Counties; they had vague hopes of setting up a semi-independent barony. Robert Turner had recruited Scotch-Irishmen to settle on interior lands as far west as the Susquehanna. Benjamin Furly was enlisting people from Krefeld, a textile-manufacturing town in Westphalia just north of Dusseldorf; they intended to settle five of six miles north of Philadelphia in a place that would be known as Germantown. Perhaps it should have been called Dutchtown or New Holland, for the Krefelders' homeland had long belonged to the House of Orange. Though they bought their five-thousand-acre parcel early, in March 1683, they did not appear until October.

Meanwhile, Germans had arrived from Kresheim to settle in the same Pennsylvania area, led by Francis David Pastorius, who had been commissioned to buy a larger area which, his employers assumed, would include a three-hundred-acre dividend within the city limits. Pastorius, a pale, quiet man with an unusually large nose, was, unlike most colonials, a man of remarkable learning. A university graduate, with further training at universities in three different countries, he read and wrote in six languages and was generally reputed to be skilled in law, medicine, theology, philosophy, history, and science. His family name, Schaefer, had been Latinized because he was the shepherd, or the pastor, of a flock.[12]

On arriving in Philadelphia in August, Pastorius could find no house in which to live, so he and his seven servants took up residence in one of the riverfront caves. This, however, was only temporary; with Penn's assistance, he bought a house on Front Street. The assistance thus lent must have been extraordinary, for the purchase price was only £5. Prices at that time were low, but the residence could not have been much more than a shanty over a cave. "The servants I brought with me could have built a far better one in two days had they known how to handle the spade," said Pastorius.[13]

Pastorius made the best of it. He even kept his sense of humor. The next time Penn called, the Proprietor saw a notice scrawled across an oiled-paper window: *"Parva domus sed amica bonis; procul este prophani,"* freely translated as "It's a little house but it welcomes the good. For sinners, no admission." It was only the second occasion, and the last, when Penn was reported to have laughed. The other occasion was when he was told that Sidney and he had quarreled.

His good humor did not carry over into the discussion of the three hundred city acres Pastorius expected to receive. Oddly enough the talk was in French, for English does not seem to have been known at that time as one of the multilingual Pastorius's accomplishments. Penn explained that the offer of a bonus to large-scale purchasers had expired. Even if it had not, three hundred acres would have constituted almost half a square mile, and the entire capital measured only two square miles; it would not have been wise to grant anyone a quarter of the total area.[14]

Nevertheless, the meeting was friendly. Penn invited Pastorius to drop in for dinner twice a week; he need not bother to announce his coming in advance. (No record exists as to how the Penn household staff regarded this arrangement.)

Pastorius enjoyed his new home. The autumn, he reported, was lingering and delightful, but the winter that followed was long and cold. The woods, he added, were "a very Eden of beauty, only cursed with a plethora of rattlesnakes."

Pastorius was a valuable addition to Penn's inner circle, a group which in August would admit Thomas Lloyd, a forty-year-old Welsh physician, and in October would include James Claypoole and Robert Turner when they came over from England. This wholly unofficial cabinet, nearly all of whom were members of the Provincial Council, could be roughly divided into groups, each representative of an important governmental department. Turner, Claypoole, and Nicholas More managed economic and business affairs both in the Council and in their own Free Society of Traders. Pastorius and Thomas Lloyd were excellent administrators, and Thomas Holme and Lasse Cock efficient technicians in their separate fields.

Penn became more and more inclined to follow the counsel of these specialists. As a result, his more advanced theories were sometimes modified in practice, a development that displeased the Assembly. A breach opened between the Proprietor and the lower house, leading in time to the growth of cliques, the conservative followers of the Proprietor and his advisors, and what would today be called the liberals. Still later, a third group, the churchmen, or the Anglicans, would draw away such men as Nicholas More. None of these were political parties in any modern sense, for Penn deplored the rise of what he called factionalism. Divergencies were evident and they were destined to increase.

The cabinet, the Pennsylvania Establishment, served Penn well, especially in calming minority discontent. Lloyd soothed the Welsh by pointing out that though they had not received all their land in one contiguous tract, nor been granted complete self-government, they were to some degree masters of the province. Was not Dr. Thomas Wynne speaker of the Assembly and Lloyd himself first master of the rolls (an important legal office) and later president of the Provincial Council?

Cock, an unofficial "consul" for the Swedes, convinced his people that, as they were not, like himself, traders, they were better off on their larger farms upriver. He did not employ Penn's technique in settling a similar complaint by New Jersey Swedes, whom he mollified by inviting them to an elaborate feast of various delicacies washed down by plenty of choice beverages.

The Pennsylvania settlers, Penn discovered, were, in spite of their varied national origins, very similar in type. The Germans, many of them Pietists and pacifists, were, like his own Quakers, outwardly meek and mild, but they were surprisingly firm in their convictions. Coming from a country where slavery was unknown, they were shocked to find that English colonists tolerated that institution. From the beginning of their settlement they campaigned vigorously against it. Germantown settlers led the American colonies in demanding abolition.

No one ever suspected that the frontiersmen were either docile or inclined to turn the other cheek; they were as stubborn as the Quakers in defending what they knew in their own hearts to be just. Divergencies in beliefs, psychologies, and customs, interacting one upon the other, enriched Pennsylvania's culture to a degree above that of regions settled only by people of a common heritage and of a uniform code. The province would be notable for controversy, but out of it would come progress. The peopling of the province, after the first year or two, by so many professional men, tradesmen, and artisans of different skills and stocks afforded a polish and refinement as well as an economic stability unique in a newly founded colonial community; the mixture accounted for Philadelphia's rapid rise in commerce and in culture.

Penn encouraged the development. Learning that Enoch Flower, one of the grand jurymen, had been for twenty years a Wiltshire teacher, he commissioned Flower to open a school. It was not an elaborate institution, merely a two-room pine cabin, but in it he taught children to read for a fee of four shillings per quarter, plus two shillings more if they wished to learn to write. For £10 they could acquire a complete education, board and washing included. Presumably the rate was intended for upcountry children who could not live too far away from the school, but there was no mention as to where they were supposed to sleep in that small cabin.[15]

Penn must have approved Flower's technique; he did not repeat his usual comment that private tutoring was preferable because schools exposed children to so many evil impressions. Unfortunately, the school did not long continue, because Flower died within a year.

The more Penn saw of his province and the more he reflected upon its possibilities, the happier he became. Though not all its pressing problems were being solved, especially not in the opinion of non-Quakers in London, where, he was told, he remained "a butt for the arrows of malice," he felt that he was succeeding in his Holy Experiment. Yet there was much to worry over. Lord Baltimore remained bothersome. Still insistent on what he regarded as his legal rights, he seemed determined, in spite of the threat of quo warranto, on carrying his case directly to the King. If he did, Penn would be obliged to return to England to defend his own rights.[16]

The fear of imminent poverty also haunted Penn. He calculated that his proprietorship had cost him, in the first year alone, at least £5000 in addition to the £10,577 he had paid out in gratuities. Actually, these costs were offset by £11,000 received from large-scale purchasers and £4500 taken in by his London sales office, so that in reality he broke even on his first year's operations. But Penn, ever the financial pessimist, saw ruin in the future.[17]

Penn held a curious paternalistic attitude toward his people. Both in New Jersey and in Pennsylvania he spoke as though purchasers, after paying full price for their land, were still bound, by love and duty, to care for his support, a support that included his "table, cellar, stable and barge, yacht or sloop." He seems to have thought that he had not really parted with the land but had merely admitted purchasers into his family circle; he would help them and protect them as though they were his children while they, in turn, would care for him as children helped their parents in old age. The feeling may have arisen, and have been nurtured by, the feudal conditions under which he had received his patent and by whose terms he was bound in parceling out the land.

The colonists did not share this view. They, too, had odd misconceptions. They were not as coldly indifferent as Penn sometimes thought. They could not understand why Penn was dependent upon them. He was a rich man, they understood, one of the richest, they believed, in England, the owner of large estates, a close friend of high officials and of the King himself, and therefore close to sources of great income. They, on the other hand, were poor. Except for the handful of prosperous merchants, Pennsylvanians were small-scale farmers. Like most colonials they lived in comparative comfort and they ate well on produce grown by their own labor, but they had little ready cash. Even had they wished to do so, how could they help so great a man as their Proprietor?

Just as Penn, by his carelessness about bookkeeping, exaggerated his losses, so his colonials, in their ignorance of Penn's financial situation, exaggerated his wealth. Inflated rumors spread that the Penns lived luxuriously and that, though notoriously slothful in paying bills, William always had access to money. Penn might complain that his properties were mortgaged to the last penny, but he seemed to have ample funds to publish pamphlets and to subsidize Quaker missionaries.

Penn's illusion probably derived from a misconception of the politico-social relationship. The colonists' impressions arose from inexperience with land ownership; in England they had been urban residents or tenant farmers. Whatever the source, their misconceptions must have been strengthened both by Penn's first-year payment of all expenses and then by his generous refusal, in the second year, to accept the offer of a share in import tax receipts. Penn regretted that refusal. In the third year he intimated delicately that he would like to have the offer renewed, but the Provincial Council and the Assembly failed to take the hint.

Plagued, despite his colonists' misconceptions, by a shortage of ready cash, Penn circularized his "loving friends and tenants" about the quitrents which were part of their purchase price but payment of which had been postponed until 1684. By that time some purchasers, especially the earliest, had honestly forgotten the obligations. Others believed themselves exempt; a few, such as the pre-Penn settlers, thought the requirement did not apply to them. Some professed, with Lord Baltimore's approval, that they were Marylanders and so not subject in the least to William Penn. These last especially angered Penn. He blamed Lord Baltimore for having advised residents of Marcus Hook, on the Delaware below the fortieth parallel, not to pay the taxes. Not seeing any similarity between Lord Baltimore's advice and that which he himself had given two years earlier to Marylanders, he accused Lord Baltimore of stirring up rebellion.

To Pennsylvanians who protested that, in any case, no quitrents would be due for about two months, Penn replied almost apologetically, "You must not take it hard that I press you in this matter, for you know I receive neither customs nor taxes, but maintain my table and government at my own cost and charges, which is what no governor doth besides myself."[18]

The wording was unfortunate. It seemed to imply that Penn would continue to meet provincial expenses and that his people would live untaxed.

25

NEIGHBORLY RELATIONS

MARYLAND TOOK FULL ADVANTAGE OF THE RESENTMENT AGAINST PENN'S CALL FOR QUITRENT PAYMENTS. THE PROVINCES, ESPECIALLY THE LOWER COUNTIES, WERE SHORT OF SPECIE AND NOT AT ALL placated by Penn's willingness to take the tax in tobacco. Colonel George Talbot, Baltimore's nephew, professed sympathy for their distress. He continued to ride up and down through the southern sections of Penn's territory urging Swedes and Finns to move to Maryland. When both Talbot and Lord Baltimore ignored Penn's protests, the Pennsylvania Proprietor threatened stronger action. He would go to London to bring formal charges.[1]

In the belief that some of his minor officials were less than vigilant in policing their districts, either because of cowardice or treachery, he ordered his agents to "lay hard" upon them. "Dismiss from office," he said, "all such as you have reason to believe have been unfaithful."[2]

The order was unnecessary. Only a few of the officials had been disloyal and they more by words than by inaction. Talbot caused much more disturbance than did any of Penn's own people. A hysterical report came up from New Castle announcing that invasion had begun.[3]

"Hast, hast, post hast," the message ran.

It had all happened suddenly. Colonel Talbot had led armed Maryland musketeers to within five miles of New Castle to confiscate the property of all those who refused to acknowledge Lord Baltimore as their rightful overlord. He had opened his campaign by making war on women, evicting a widow, Elizabeth Ogle, from her home. Penn must do something to protect the people; he must act quickly and effectively.

Penn summoned his Provincial Council, told it that an armed party "in a riotous manner invaded the inhabitants of New Castle County," and asked what should be done. Should Talbot "as a quiet traveler, be allowed to pass the country or be arrested for his actions?"[4] Just what Penn meant by "pass the country" is a little difficult to comprehend, though probably it was intended to suggest that the Maryland colonel be permitted to depart unpunished if he agreed to withdraw. Not even a pacifist council, however, was willing to allow an aggressor to escape unscathed; it voted to arrest the intruders.

The order was not executed. Pennsylvania had no military force worth mentioning and its untrained volunteer militiamen showed no enthusiasm for an all-day march in summer heat to fight a Maryland army. Though by this time the Lower Counties had learned that Talbot's force consisted of only three armed men escorting fifteen woodsmen, Mrs. Ogle's neighbors did not rush to her defense. William Welsh, who had sent the message pleading haste, had tried to raise a posse comitatus, but only five or six men appeared. Welsh was courageous enough to charge Talbot with terrorizing the people by breaking the peace of the King and of the Proprietor, William Penn. Unless the Marylanders withdrew at once, he said, they would be jailed as rebels.[5]

Talbot ignored the threat. He set his men to work chopping down the Widow Ogle's trees. He was about to build the log fort that Lord Baltimore had ordered the year before; the lopped-off boughs and branches would make a first-rate breastworks. The posse made no effort to enforce its threats.

Neither did Penn. Instead he waited two months before writing a complaint to the Duke of York. Realizing Penn's helplessness, Talbot reiterated his demand for the entire west bank of the Delaware. When this action drew no response, he invaded another settler's property. Riding up to Joseph Bowle's house, he seemed about to run the man down, but pulled up just in time. "Damn you, you Dogg," he shouted. "You seat under nobody. You have no warrant from Penn nor my Lord. Therefore, get you gone . . . you brazen-faced, impudent, confident dog." (The word *confident* was then used in the sense of presumptuous).[6]

It was doubtless entirely coincidental that four or five days later Penn wrote to the Duke of York, for in the letter to the "Great Prince," Penn mentioned only the Ogle incident, saying nothing of the Bowle affair. Neither did he mention that Talbot had boasted that he would "shorten Penn's territories." He had not yet heard that Talbot had threatened to arrest Penn and his retinue if they should happen to ride into Maryland.

The Talbot tempest ceased as suddenly as it had begun. No formal record gives an explanation. One may guess, however, that Lord Baltimore, worrying whether Talbot's belligerence might give fuel for quo warranto proceedings, called off his nephew. The log fort remained, and from time to time thereafter Maryland made tentative attempts to station men there, but the Widow Ogle and her neighbors retained their property and continued paying taxes to the Penn regime. Probably Lord Baltimore believed that better results could be obtained by lobbying in person with the London bureaucrats.

If so, he and Penn were thinking along similar lines, for Penn was coming to the conclusion that he must return to England to defend his interests. Quo warranto was being threatened against Pennsylvania as well as against Maryland and other colonies. A French ship had been caught violating the Navigation Acts; the very fact that it had been apprehended in provincial waters argued that some local official must have been sufficiently negligent to warrant revocation of the provincial charter. Edward Randolph, the zealous customs supervisor, was flooding the Lords of Trade and Plantations with reports that the people of the Delaware were smugglers cheating the King of his rightful revenue.[7]

Much remained to be accomplished in America but as Penn saw the situation, his personal attention was not essential. Not all the recommendations of the *Laws Agreed Upon* had been enacted, especially those concerning personal behavior, but Penn hoped to see them upon the statute books before he left. He pressed for laws to discourage "enticing, vain or evil sports" and to induce the working people to be more temperate in their drinking. There was need to punish unscrupulous employers who lured bound men from their masters and to penalize servants who shirked their duty. Perhaps it would be well to pass sumptuary laws fixing prices, setting maximum wage scales and forbidding men and women to own more than two suits of clothes. These measures did not require Penn's personal attention, however.[8] Nor was his presence necessary to improve public morals. Though something certainly needed to be done to restrain cursing and blaspheming, or those who were "clamorous, scolding or railing with their tongues," he could accomplish reforms by sending admonitory letters from England.[9]

Some reformers, more enthusiastic than practical, were suggesting that to curb a rising tide of immorality, it might be well to require all young men to marry at a certain age. The agitators did not suggest how, in a province where women were in a distinct minority, wives could be provided for everyone, unless Pennsylvania intended to permit polygamy, enter the bride-importation business, or encourage intermarriage with the Indians. The matter deeply interested Penn. He consistently lamented that human beings paid far less attention to the quality of their offspring than to the breeding of their dogs and horses.[10]

The time was far from ripe for experiments, much less for legislation on such social affairs; it would never be ripe within his lifetime. He could, however, hope for more harmonious relationships among his various types of settlers. Encouraged by the success of Wynne, Cock, and Pastorius in muting the complaints of their fellow countrymen, Penn undertook to become better acquainted with his foreign landowners. For this purpose he undertook a journey to the west. He wished to see the countryside as well; the trip would allow him to meet the Indians, to visit their little villages, and quite possibly to write a report for the Royal Society. Though he had vowed to study the Indian dialects, it is doubtful how much Indian he understood. Pastorius credited him with ability to speak the local language, though before Pastorius himself knew much of it; Lasse Cock, the expert linguist and translator, uttered no such compliments.[11]

Business interests combined with curiosity and scholarship to send Penn westward. Despite his constant complaint of being land poor, he was eagerly enlarging his holdings. He had been steadily acquiring farming rights west and north of Philadelphia and he had reached across the Delaware to buy up Fenwick's interests in West Jersey. He was now coveting Susquehanna areas. At least part of his acquisitive urge sprang from a conviction that Pennsylvania was so attractive that, like England and western Europe, it might within the foreseeable future become overcrowded. A letter from Sir William Petty, an Oxford professor whose clinics he had quite possibly attended, may have inspired that thought. Petty, a statistical economist as well as a medical man and a fellow member of the Royal Society, had warned Penn that world population was increasing too rapidly. The entire globe, Petty predicted, was destined to become as fully populated as England then was.

Penn was not worried; as a patriotic Englishman he was overjoyed. If, as Petty estimated, each human being required four acres of arable land for his support, Penn foresaw that world population would reach its maximum by 1809. "Thus the works and wonders of God's wisdom will be sooner discovered. . . . As people increase, so will philosophers. . . . The King of England having the greater share of the unpeopled Earth, from Nova Scotia to Florida will have a greater share [of philosophers] than he now hath."[12]

Penn would have been pleased if a large proportion of those new philosophers were Indians, since he had a high opinion of the red men. Partly for the information of the Royal Society, much more to increase his own knowledge of these admirable people with whom he would be a neighbor, Penn determined and planned to explore their culture, their environment, and their mode of living on his trip west. He agreed with Pastorius that they were honest, openhearted, and generous toward those who used them well. Their leaders were democratic, always careful to consult their councils before making any important decisions. They were in a large degree communist in the best sense, for "nobody shall want what another man hath."

Penn's partiality toward the Indians was partly attributable to his feeling that they were descended from the Ten Lost Tribes of Israel.

He imagined for them an admirable background, for often he had seen such countenances in London's Jewish quarters. In listening to their talk in council meetings he had been impressed, not only by the extraordinary sweetness and intonations of their accents, but also by the frequency of words that reminded him of Hebrew speech.

It is interesting to note, in passing, that Penn reached his conclusions on Indian psychology and customs on his experiences with their chiefs before he had ever seen an Indian settlement.

Penn did not hurry on his journey among his diverse subjects; he wished to make a thorough survey of the situation. He kept no diary, nor did he disclose too much in letters about the events that he experienced; but it is safe to suppose that he talked with the people of the Welsh tract that began a few miles beyond the Schuykill, with the Pietist Germans who had settled still farther to the west, and with the sprinklings of Scotch-Irish who were beginning to take up land much closer to the Susquehanna. He had no need to probe deeply into manners and customs; having known their kinsfolk in the Old World, he was well at home among them. Here he would be more concerned in hearing their opinions about the way in which the province was progressing and specifically in listening to whatever grievances they might have.

The Indian country afforded novelties. The people of the lower Susquehanna, the so-called Conestogas, were fairly well acquainted with white men, particularly with the Marylanders; but ancient tribal customs had not been wholly forgotten. They usually fished with steel hooks, acquired as part of the purchase price at land sales; but here and there Penn could still see Indians fishing with their hands. The method was to block off a small, shallow creek by making stone dams to imprison the fish. Then by dragging leafy twigs through the water, they drove the fish into pockets from which the Conestogas could snatch them.

Though it was late in the season, Penn saw tiny patches of cultivated land, "ploughed," or rather scratched, by pointed sticks, for the planting of scraggly ears of corn. Small packs of Indian dogs roamed about: the tiny, pointed-eared breed that prior to the coming of the white men had been the Conestoga's only domesticated animals. Here and there, perched on the southern slopes of hills near springs of fresh water, were little villages, clusters of thirty or forty shedlike structures. They were flimsy buildings, seldom higher than the stature of a man, consisting usually of slabs of bark leaning against slanting poles that were often no more than small tree trunks or reasonably straight branches. There was no furniture within; the people slept on reeds or grass spread upon the earthen floor.

To be sure, when Captain John Smith visited the area, in 1608, he found the Susquehannocks, then at their zenith, occupying more comfortable quarters. Several families, each in its own partitioned space, shared long houses, eighty or a hundred feet in length, in which bunks lined the walls. In Penn's time, however, the Susquehannocks had disappeared, virtually annihilated by Iroquois raiders from the north; they had been replaced by the less developed Conestogas.

Fortunately the Conestogas were hospitable. Possibly they had heard of Penn, but whether he came after prior announcement or as a stranger, he was welcomed. They entertained him well, doubtless on venison or fish, for they would have given him the best that was available. They talked with him freely, presumably through an interpreter; it is doubtful whether Penn's grasp of their language was as yet very well developed.

Penn yielded to the missionary impulse that was never very far below the surface of his thoughts; he tried to bring his hosts to a knowledge of the Christian God who had made the heavens and the earth. The Conestogas listened politely, but they were not convinced. Their reply was probably not so fluent and polished as reported, a dozen or more years later, by Johann Kelpius, the Mennonite Hermit of the Wissahickon, but it was direct and forceful.

> You ask us to believe in the great Creator and ruler of Heaven and earth and yet you yourself do not believe and trust Him, for you have taken the land unto yourself which we and our friends occupied in common. You scheme night and day how you may preserve it so that no one can take it from you; yes, you even scheme beyond your life and parcel it out between your children. We believe in God who maintains us and as long as we have this faith we trust in Him and never bequeath a foot of ground.[14]

The verbal exchange was friendly and peaceful. It did not prevent the chiefs from listening to the white men's offer to purchase tracts of land.

The disputes were not serious enough to interfere with traditional Indian courtesies. After Penn had withdrawn to his sleeping quarters, he received a visit from a young lady, a "royal princess," of course, who proceeded to make herself very much at home. Penn was neither shocked nor surprised. The young lady's obvious offers were not unexpected, or unusual. After all, one of the little creeks near the site of Zwaanendael was commonly known as the Whorekill. Though the tender-minded English tried desperately to explain that the name was a corruption of Hoorn-kill, given to the stream in memory of the town in Holland from which the Dutch settlers had come, everyone was well aware that the word commemorated the kindness of Indian girls to foreign sailors.[15]

Penn's moral scruples were too strong for him to accept the invitation; yet if he refused too bluntly, the Indians might consider the rebuff a discourtesy to the tribe. Perhaps he pleaded the rigors of his journey, for not yet having reached his fortieth birthday, he could not excuse himself on account of age. We do know that somehow he managed to maintain his principles without offending his hosts.

Penn's delicacy could not have blocked his progress in buying Susquehanna land, for he found no difficulty in gaining permission to settle on the lower stretches of that stream. When he sought to extend his influence northward, however, he met obstacles. Almost at the very time that Penn was treating with the Conestogas in the south, the tribes of northern Pennsylvania and western New York were appealing to Governor Thomas Dongan of that latter province for protection. "We will not consent," said the Onandagas and Cayugas, "that the Great Penn should settle on the Susquehanna. . . . We have no other lands to leave our wives and children." Pointing out that they had won the Susquehanna "by our sweat," they put themselves "under the protection of the Great Duke of York." Soon after, the Oneidas and the Mohawks followed the Cayuga and Onandaga example.[16]

To protect its Indian protégés and, not incidentally, its fur trade, New York protested to London against what it called Penn's encroachments on the upper Susquehanna. London replied by ordering Dongan to block any such activity. The Crown went further. Not only did it warn Dongan that "Mr. Penn is very intent upon his own interest," but it told Dongan to do everything he could to prevent any joint effort by Pennsylvanians and Jerseymen to extend their influence. Unless he stopped them, said London, "they will push their charters as far as New England."[17]

The injection of New Jersey into the situation puzzled the Americans; there had never been any indication that Jerseymen were in any way interested in the Susquehanna. Thomas Rudyard, now a New York official, knew of no aggression by the province where he had been deputy governor. He had never heard of any New Jersey claim to Susquehanna land, which was separated from New Jersey by ninety miles of Pennsylvania virgin forest. Nor, though William Penn had been a proprietor of both East and West New Jersey, had the Quaker ever suspected such an interest.

Later word from London dispelled the mystery. Early in 1684, it appeared, Dr. Daniel Coxe, a court physician, had bought some New Jersey land, and would later take over what was left of the Byllinge holdings. Apparently he was going about London boasting of discoveries he had made while traveling in America. He had found a huge lake in the north, which he called the New Mediterranean Sea; and from this region, adjacent to Canada, New York, and Pennsylvania, he expected to export one hundred thousand beaver pelts a year. He had himself made plans for this important trade by making friends with the various Indian kings of the area. Such was the basis for the fears that New York would lose its profitable fur trade.[18]

The report was news to Penn. He may have known Dr. Coxe, for both were members of the Royal Society; but he had never heard that Dr. Coxe had ever visited America, much less explored the wilderness. As a matter of fact, he had not; he had remained in London writing *An Account of New Jersey*, in which he described his imaginary adventures.

Thanks largely to Penn's close friendship with Thomas Rudyard, Dongan's close advisor, Penn's relationship with both New York and New Jersey had been cordial and cooperative. Only recently Dongan had paid Penn a visit during which the two governors had discussed plans for an interprovincial postal system, though unfortunately it did not materialize until some time later. The Susquehanna situation must also have been discussed, apparently without serious disagreement and certainly without rancor.

Coxe's loose talk threatened these harmonious arrangements. London, always suspicious of such American provinces as were not under Royal governments, misinterpreted his words to mean that he was trying to set up a huge, semi-independent American dominion. James Drummond, Duke of Perth, and other Scots with interests in New Jersey, feared that he would undermine their influence. Scots and Britons were not, at that time, working hand in hand; but the Duke, then Lord Chancellor of Scotland, persuaded the Royalist bureaucrats that Penn and Coxe were the moving spirits behind the scheme to steal New York's fur trade. The formal Scottish protest did not reach the Council on Trade and Plantations until some time later; but the whispers were circulating that "Master Penn's interest prevails more with him than his pretended unconcernedness with the world." The Pennsylvania Proprietor, the rumors said, was trying to suppress both New York's and New Jersey's rights and privileges in order to increase the trade of the Delaware River. It would be better, the Scots added, for New York to have a flourishing neighbor in East Jersey, even a Scottish neighbor, than "in remoter places" such as Pennsylvania.[19]

Happily, since all three American leaders were men of good will, no open breach resulted on the western side of the Atlantic. Neither Pennsylvania nor New Jersey crossed the New York border; the fur trade flowed in its usual channels. When in 1688 Dongan ceased to be the New York governor, he became Penn's agent for buying Indian land rights on the upper Susquehanna.

While the verbal campaigns were being waged in England, Penn, the unsuspecting "butt for the arrows of malice," was continuing to cultivate Indian friendships. On returning from the Susquehanna, land-purchase agreements in his pocket, he bubbled over with enthusiasm. Everything, he believed, was going well. The Indians were hospitable, much more willing to accept Quakers as neighbors than to have Marylanders close at hand. The land was excellent, much more arable than the valley of the Delaware. Those stay-at-homes who had been skeptical about traveling through the Hundred Mile Forest that they said lay between the Schuylkill and the Susquehanna had been talking nonsense; the terrain, even in the wilderness, was so easily traversed that he could have driven a coach all the way to Conestoga territory.

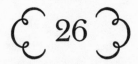

26

AGAIN THE COURTIER

NOT ALL THE MAJOR PROBLEMS OF THE PROVINCE HAD BEEN SOLVED, BUT BY MID-SPRING 1684 THEY SEEMED TO HAVE BEEN REDUCED TO MANAGEABLE PROPORTIONS. THE COUNTRY HAD BEEN SCOUTED, AND governmental machinery was working with reasonable efficiency. Hard specie was still scarce, but the colony was prosperous. Angers had cooled, jealousies been appeased, temperaments calmed, and many misunderstandings corrected. Pennsylvania seemed capable of self-government.

All this was reassuring, and it presaged eventual success, but Penn's personal problems remained. Chief among them was the danger of quo warranto proceedings. The bureaucrats needed only the thinnest of excuses to invoke this means of stripping Penn of his charter, and such excuses were numerous. Minorities whose roots were Swedish, Dutch, or Finnish, or who more recently had been German or Scotch-Irish, grumbled whenever anything went wrong that the English Quakers who controlled the government discriminated against them. That the complaints were minor, and usually ill-founded, was immaterial; the very existence of discontent might be sufficient to cause the cancellation of Penn's charter. Similarly, though the quarrel with Lord Baltimore had subsided, a false move by an underling on either side might cause hostility to flare again. A pirate vessel, suddenly appearing down at undefended Lewes, might raid the town and prove to Penn's enemies that pacifists were incapable of protecting innocent civilians.[1]

Penn was convinced that he must return to England in what his New Castle correspondent would have called "hast, hast, post hast." His apprehension of quo warranto was no minor matter; it was very real. Most American colonies, including those in the Bermudas and West Indies, had either lost their charters or were in grave peril of losing them.

Lord Baltimore was already being challenged; in the course of the proceedings against him, the investigators would certainly bring up the question of who owned the Three Lower Counties.

Penn forehandedly began preparing his defense for the ordeal that was certain to come. Cannily he went to great pains to make it clear that his dispute with Baltimore in no way involved a Pennsylvania claim to sovereignty or to political powers. These, Penn dutifully averred, were Royal perquisites. Lord Baltimore might claim such perquisites but he, William Penn, had no such aim in view; as far as William Penn was concerned all that was at stake was the mere use of the farmlands and the waterways.

Despite his anxiety to defend himself against quo warranto proceedings, Penn could not immediately take ship for England. He had first to find some relief from what he said was Pennsylvania's steady drain upon his pocketbook. He may not have regretted his generous refusal to accept a share of the customs receipts, but he was sorry that the province did not insist upon his taking the money. He was, he reiterated, penniless. The plaint might just possibly have been well founded if his income and expenses from Pennsylvania alone were considered. If a complete balance sheet were drawn up, however, covering all his finances, including his rent-rolls, he would undoubtedly have been much more than solvent. Penn himself cast doubt on his pleas of poverty. At the very time that he was pleading the emptiness of his purse, he was donating to the Society of Friends the stone for its new meetinghouse, together with two thousand feet of boards and three thousand cedar shingles.[2]

To lighten his financial burdens he called Pennsylvania's attention to a New Jersey proposal to tax alcoholic beverages as a means for paying government expenses. Such a step, he said, "will be a trial of affection to me."[3]

Pennsylvania evidenced its love by going through the motions of levying a similar tax. Indeed, it went further by granting Penn a gift of one-third of all assets forfeited to the government. The generosity, however, was only symbolic, since enforcement was immediately suspended "in order to encourage trade." By Penn's account, the net result was that for twenty years the Proprietor did not receive a single farthing.[4]

Yet some of the failure may have been due to Penn himself. As proprietor he was, at least theoretically, entitled to receive quitrents and fees from various sources, including what were described as "incomes from official patronage." Some of these, the quitrents for example, may have been uncollectible; but he still had many thousand virgin acres to sell as well as land once sold and paid for but repossessed because of failure by the purchaser to cultivate or to settle on the property.

For two months the fruitless pursuit of a government payment postponed Penn's return to England. Eventually, a group of sympathizers volunteered to make up a yearly purse of £500, but this, too, proved an empty gesture.[5]

Meanwhile Penn was agitating, with little more success, to reduce alcoholism among the Indians. He tried—and failed—to secure a flat prohibition on wholesale sales of liquor to the tribesmen. The failure, he discovered, was attributable to the willingness of certain merchants, some Quakers among them, to sell large quantities of rum to traders from other provinces who would resell the liquor to the Indians.[6]

By the end of July Penn realized that he could no longer linger in America. Quo warranto investigations were being made into the affairs of Rhode Island, Connecticut, and Maryland. It seemed probable that Pennsylvania would soon be added to the list. Now that he had done all that he could do to guide the province, he must return to England.

Confident that all was well in Pennsylvania, Penn methodically prepared for departure. His leaving would, of course, necessitate the appointment of a deputy to head the provincial government. For this post Cousin Markham, returning from a stay in England, would be again available. Markham, Penn was pleased to note, appeared to be a much improved man. His visit to London had begun most inauspiciously, for soon after his arrival he had been seized with "a violent fit of sickness" in, of all places, the apartments of the King himself. He had been immobilized, as in Lord Baltimore's house, for a month, but happily his luck had turned. He had met a charming lady, the widow of Captain Erven Johnson. Through her strong, successful influence he was restored, as Penn noted, "to a good frame" and was now "more diligent and ready to serve."[7]

For sentimental reasons (Markham was a colleague of Admiral Sir William), Penn might have preferred to appoint his cousin as his deputy, but Dr. Thomas Lloyd seemed better qualified for the position. Everything that Penn had seen of Lloyd as Keeper of the Privy Seal, Master of the Rolls, or President of the Provincial Council convinced him that Lloyd was steady, able, and trustworthy. But he believed that giving any one man too much power led either to arbitrariness or to the slow-moving, gratuity-seeking practices of bureaucrats. Thus he resorted to commission rule.

Penn placed executive control entirely in the hands of the Provincial Council with Thomas Lloyd as chief among the equals and Markham as a sort of administrative secretary. As a further commission, Penn named four men, among them Robert Turner and Nicholas More, neither of them lawyers, as provincial judges. Still another commission, including Thomas Lloyd, was to act as guardian for Penn's nine-year-old son, Springett, the heir to the proprietorship.

Casual observers may have thought it significant that influential James Claypoole was not then included among the top officials. There was, however, no rift between the two men; Claypoole was at the moment too occupied in trying to salvage the Free Society of Traders, which, despite its generous charter, was losing money.

As his personal agent Penn named James Harrison, a member of the Provincial Council. He too was overburdened, his duties ranging from managing Penn's country estate, to cropping the ears of Penn's cattle and branding them with the mark WP PG for William Penn, Proprietor and Governor. He was to keep Penn informed of what was happening in Pennsylvania. In return he would receive news-filled letters to be shared with the legislators and administrators. For all these duties Harrison was to receive his board, lodging, and washing, together with the use of a horse, plus £40 the first year and £50 thereafter.[8]

Even before completing these arrangements Penn wrote what, in the event of misfortune, might be a farewell letter to "My most dear G. Penn."[9]

Being now about to leave this part of the world and ready to come to thee, not knowing how the Lord pleaseth to deal with me in my passage, lest the sea be my grave and the deeps my sepulchre, I write unto thee as my beloved one, the true and great joy and crown of my life above all visible comforts, always valued by me and honored above women. I do most humbly salute and embrace thee with thy dear children.

He then advised her to "live sparingly, have little cumber, teach the children love and humility to the people." He assured her that "my promises to thee be in all fulfilled."

How anyone, least of all Guli's Quaker biographer, could suspect that this farewell letter, and the *Testament* he wrote on leaving England, reveal Guli's shortcomings of character passes understanding; but the feat was accomplished. Guli, the biographer believed, must have been an undue worrier, an unnecessary chider of her servants, and a fusser over trifles, as well as overly casual, unbusinesslike and careless in money matters.[10]

Actually the advice to Guli repeated Penn's customary injunctions voiced to everyone. Together with his fervent hopes that all people should be gentle, kindly, meek, unassuming, and reverent, that they should be hospitable to strangers, should live in love and peace and avoid excesses of all sorts, they comprised the essentials of all his frequent letters to Quaker communities everywhere. Penn was quite as fervent in his farewell message to Thomas Lloyd and the provincial Council.[11]

My love and my life is to you and with you and no water can quench it nor distance wear it out or bring it to an end. I had been with you, cared over you and served you with unfeigned love . . . and now that liberty and authority are with you and in your hands, let the government be upon His shoulders in all your spirits that you may rule for Him whom the princes of this world will one day esteem it their honor to govern and serve in their places.

On August 12, 1684, he boarded the ketch *Endeavor* to set sail for England. As the little vessel with its tall mainmast forward and the much shorter jiggermast aft stood down the river he composed a prayer for the little city he was leaving.[12]

And thou, Philadelphia, the virgin settlement of this province, named before thou wert born, what love, what care, what service and what travail has there been to bring thee forth and preserve thee from such as would abuse and defile thee; my soul prays to God for thee, that thou mayst stand in the day of trial that thy people may be blest of the Lord and thy people saved by His power.

William Penn had been in America just eleven weeks short of two years.

The *Endeavor* made a speedy crossing, reaching the Irish coast in four weeks' time. There the good luck ended. Such strong headwinds set in that the ketch needed fourteen days more to sail to Sussex. On October 6 Penn arrived at the Sussex village of Wonder, from which sailors rowed him up the little Arun River to within seven miles of his home.

Next morning his happiness at being with Guli and his family was interrupted. On sorting out his papers, prior to arguing his case against Lord Baltimore, he saw to his dismay that the Zwaanendael documents upon which he relied to prove his title to the Lower Counties had been left behind. Penn blamed Philip Theodore Lehnmann, his private secretary, for the oversight. The omission was unforgivable, for without the Zwaanendael documents, Penn would be unable to prove that Zwaanendael had been cultivated by a Christian power prior to the date of Baltimore's charter. But why, if they were so vital, had not Penn checked to see if Lehnmann had packed them for him?

Those papers, said Penn, "were the ground of my coming and the strength of all my cause . . . I am here with my fingers in my mouth. . . . Leman can never while he lives repair me this wrong." While Penn did not accuse his secretary of treachery, he did say that Lehnmann could not have done more damage if he had been bribed by £10,000.[13]

A letter rebuking Lehnmann and perhaps dismissing him seems to have miscarried. The secretary either failed to receive it or he ignored it. When, during the winter, Captain Thomas Taylor of the slave ship *Isabella* brought in to Philadelphia a cargo of blacks consigned to William Penn, Lehnmann received them as Penn's broker. He sold the men and, after deducting Taylor's transportation charges and fees for his own services, presumably credited the proceeds to his employer's account.[14]

Penn protested, not because Lehnmann had continued to act as his agent, nor because he had delayed six months before reporting the transaction, but because Philip the German's fees were "lewd and extravagant." (The first adjective was at that time virtually synonymous with base, Penn's more usual epithet.) In his anger Penn ordered Thomas Lloyd to see if Lehnmann could be tried for extortion or fraud, but Lloyd could find no valid evidence.[15]

In the matter of the Zwaanendael documents, however, Penn's good luck helped him once more. Had the Lords of Trade heard the case immediately, according to schedule, Penn would have been obliged to ask for a continuance, which he was sure Lord Baltimore would oppose and which he was not too certain that the court would grant. If, then, the case continued, without the sworn affidavits of aged Dutchmen familiar with Zwaanendael history and without the attested copies of Dutch West India Company records, he would lose his case. Even if the continuance were granted, it would take much time to bring the records over the Atlantic, or even to have copies made in Amsterdam. Moreover, it might be impossible to secure duplicate affidavits; those who had given them were all well over seventy, and might by this time have died.

To Penn's delight, Lord Baltimore himself came to the rescue. Certain that his case was airtight, Baltimore quite accurately believed that this was no time to annoy London by quarrels between rival proprietors. Massachusetts, as well as the other provinces, was under fire; final steps were being taken to annul its charter. As Maryland's violations of the Navigation Acts were notorious, Lord Baltimore thought it wiser to avoid attention as much as possible and asked for a postponement. Penn, as a good diplomat, probably expressed much disappointment at this; but yielding graciously as a favor to his friend and neighbor, he consented to it. He then sent off a message to have those missing papers sent to him as soon as possible.

Baltimore also was lucky. In late October his bellicose nephew, Colonel Talbot, had stormed aboard that oddly named Maryland warship, the *Quaker*, and had refused to eat supper because, he said, it was a fast day. But after the dishes were cleared away, he tried to kiss the captain.[16]

"I desired him to forbear," the skipper said, "because I was no woman." This angered Talbot, who boxed the captain's ears, cursed another officer, and stabbed Christopher Rousby, a Royal customs collector, to death. Had this been known, the Lords of Trade and Plantations would probably have rejected Baltimore's plea for a continuance, in which event Penn would doubtless have lost his province. (As for Talbot, he sought refuge in Virginia, only to be returned to Maryland. He was sentenced to death but was pardoned by the King on condition that he stay away from English territory for at least five years.)

While waiting for his case to be rescheduled, Penn again became a courtier. He did not like the life; but partly for his own interest and partly for that of his fellow Quakers, he found himself lobbying daily. The outright bribery, however carefully described as giving presents, the wirepulling, and the flattery involved were all alien to his nature and to his principles; as a plain speaker, he was averse to the misleadings, the half-truths, and the evasions of politicians. Nevertheless, he was an effective advocate. He was particularly active in working for the release of some thirteen hundred Quakers imprisoned for their faiths.

Daily attendance at court prevented his living at Worminghurst, so he moved up to London. He rented Holland House, a mansion set in gardens near Kensington Palace, that was more magnificent than comfortable. Ghosts wandered freely through the building. Henry Rich, its builder, first Lord Holland, executed for trying to restore Charles I, emerged into the "gilt room" through a secret door, carrying his severed grinning head under his arm. At least three ladies haunted the estate. Luckily Penn did not see the phantoms, else, legend ran, he would have at once dropped dead. So effective was Penn as a courtier that hundreds of petitioners, braving the ghostly dangers, came to the gates each day to beg his intercession.[17]

In the midst of this activity Charles II suffered a stroke. "As the King sat down to shave at 8 A.M. . . . his head twitched both ways." The physicians blooded him and, believing that hot iron, well wrapped in flannel, was an effective treatment, "plied his head with frying pans." He died February 6, 1685.[18]

27

SECRET JESUIT?

On ascending the throne, Penn's good friend James II frankly admitted that, as everyone knew, he was a Catholic. With a majority of his people Protestants and the English laws still discriminating against papists, he was in a difficult position. Short of armed rebellion, however, such as might be raised by his illegitimate nephew, James Scott, the handsome but rather stupid Duke of Monmouth, the new King stood in little danger of serious political or personal attack.

To avoid antagonizing his subjects James acted carefully. Out of preference and policy he steered a conciliatory course. Though he was supposed to have smuggled in a priest to give the last rights to his dying brother Charles, and though he made no secret of his regular attendance at Mass, he was no bigot. He allowed his two daughters to be reared as Protestants and encouraged the toleration of dissenters, chief among them Penn and the Quakers. Cynics charged, of course, that toleration for the Society of Friends was nothing more than a precedent for extending similar freedoms to the Catholics, but there is no solid proof that he was insincere or Machiavellian in his motives.

Penn quite naturally approved the conciliatory moves. For twenty years or more he had been actively urging full toleration. Few knew better than he the urgent need. His work for the Society had shown how grievously some upright worthy citizens—Quakers, Catholics, and unorthodox Protestants alike—had suffered for their faiths. He himself, almost as soon as he had set foot in England, had been charged by Sussex Quarter Sessions Court as "a factious and seditious person who doth frequently entertain and keep unlawful assemblies and conventicles in his dwelling house . . . to the terror of the King's liege people." The Sussex indictment was not pursued because Penn had moved to the haunted house in Kensington,[1] but this removal did not end harassment. In the last weeks of Charles II's life, Penn was twice arrested for unlawful preaching at Westminster. At the very time that he was pleading for the release of thirteen hundred Quaker prisoners he was himself fined more than £20 for participating in unlawful assemblies.[2]

Penn laid such incidents to the overzealousness of local authorities. His acquaintance with the King, his long-time patron and friend, led him to credit James with good intentions. Thus, when the monarch at length agreed to free the prisoners, Penn did not suspect any secret motive. Because James did not open the jail doors immediately but only promised that he would do so after his coronation, some Quakers suspected that the promise was merely a trick to win Quaker support against the rebellion that Monmouth was now seen to be organizing. When Penn, on the other hand, trusted James to keep his word, some accused him of being a tool of the Crown.

Penn was not consciously a tool, but certainly he was a strong supporter of James II. He ordered Pennsylvanians to "avoid indecent speeches" against the King, by which he meant any criticism of James or any show of sympathy for Monmouth. To show its loyalty the province must also immediately acknowledge James as rightful sovereign. Also, as further support of governmental policies and to lessen the possibility of quo warranto, Pennsylvania must scrupulously obey the Navigation Acts.[3]

These were open avowals of Penn's loyalty to James; there were in addition sundry scraps of propaganda popularly ascribed by some to William Penn. These included *The Quaker's Elegy on the Death of Charles, Late King of England*, "written by W.P., a Sincere Lover of Charles and James," and *Tears Wiped Off, a Second Essay of the Quakers by Way of Poetry*, "written in the Sincerity of the Spirit by W.P., a Servant of the Light" both mediocre verse productions that Penn denied having written. "Those who think so," he said, "are as devoid of charity as they are of sense."[4] Penn repudiated both productions. In yet a third publication, *Fiction Found Out*, this one in prose, he asked plaintively why, of all the five hundred or more Englishmen whose initials were W.P., he should be picked out as the author of bad verse.

Penn's faith in James, intensified by his long daily conversations with the King, remained unshaken even when the monarch permitted the bureaucrats to draw up quo warranto writs against all remaining proprietary colonies in America. Penn was certain that his friendship with the King would be ample protection, but it was only the outbreak of the Duke of Monmouth's rebellion in June 1685 that prevented the Lords of Trade and Plantations from bringing the entire seaboard of British North America under Royal control.

That same short-lived uprising, while saving Pennsylvania, plunged Penn into unforeseen, and undeserved, difficulties. After its suppression daily inquisitions of suspected rebels involved certain of Penn's friends. The King's prosecutors used the rebellion as an excuse for punishing critics for pre-rebellion activities. Alderman Henry Cornish, for example, had run some years before in an election for sheriff of London and, in spite of bribery and threats, had won. A few years later, he had been suspected, but not found guilty, of participating in a plot. Now, in spite of Penn's intercessions, he was condemned to death and was hanged in front of his own home.[5]

Penn also pleaded vainly for Elizabeth Gaunt, who "had spent much time visiting the prisons and relieving the wretched," but she was accused of having hidden a fugitive Monmouth soldier. On the testimony of the man whose life she had saved, she was sentenced to be burned. For some unfathomable reason the gentle Penn attended both executions. He watched as "she wrapped the straw around her for burning more speedily and behaved in such a manner that all the spectators melted in tears." Penn reported no special emotion but he did mention that on that night a storm broke out, "as fearful as on the day of Oliver Cromwell's death."[6]

Those rebel soldiers who were not put to death were jailed or sold into a type of slavery. At least one thousand were handed over to various court favorites who were permitted to exact ransoms from the friends of the captives or, failing that, to sell the prisoners into ten-years' bondage overseas. Penn himself "begged twenty of the King," though no record shows their fate.[7]

Not all the victims were soldiers. A teacher at Taunton in Somerset allowed her little girls to go outside to watch Monmouth's troops march by. For this, a hundred children (and undoubtedly the teacher also) were arrested and convicted for rebelliousness. Through the good offices of Mary of Modena, James's Queen, they became the property of the court ladies.

A George Penne of Dorset acted as the court ladies' agent. Loose gossip, motivated possibly by ill-will, questioned whether George Penne the unknown broker was not really William Penn the well-known Quaker. Years later, a biographer of the Duke of Monmouth, failing to check his sources, suggested that no such person as George Penne existed; the broker was, in all truth, none other than William Penn. In an early edition of his famous history no less a scholar than Thomas Babington Macaulay, never a warm partisan of William Penn, gave the error wider currency.[8]

The slander about the Taunton maids broke at a particularly bad moment for William Penn. While the slave-selling story was flooding over London, he had to go to Worminghurst, where Guli was about to give birth to yet another child. Word was coming in from New Jersey that his good friend Robert Barclay was obsessed by a report that Penn was plotting to split New Jersey between Pennsylvania and New York; a year would pass before Barclay really accepted Penn's denials. Word was also spreading that a certain flamboyant Jerseyman who called himself John Tatham was really a renegade Benedictine who had absconded with monastery funds. Penn, who had already warned Thomas Lloyd to be wary of this "subtile, prying, lowly scholar," was being falsely accused of kidnapping this "Tatham" so that Catholics could punish him for defection and embezzlement.[9]

Regardless of whether Tatham (also known as Gray) had actually robbed St. James's Monastery, he was an outstanding Jerseyman. One of Daniel Coxe's attorneys and at one time a New Jersey proprietor, he built himself "a great and stately palace" just across the river from Penn's country estate. The twelve-room house was notable for its collection of five hundred books, one of the largest private libraries in America. His death in 1700 revealed an estate worth £3700.[10]

The recurrent libels and slanders roused such general suspicions about Penn's supposed Catholicism that William Popple, secretary of the Lords of Trade and Plantations, and John Tillotson, who had questioned Penn in the Tower, became disturbed. Unlike those who chattered behind Penn's back, they went straight to William Penn to learn the truth. Penn, of course, once more indignantly denied the rumors. "I abhor two principles in religion and pity those that own them," he said. "The first is obedience upon authority without conviction and the other the destroying them that differ with me for God's sake."[11]

One would like to think that acceptance of Penn's denials by such leaders as Tillotson and Popple would end, once and for all, the common rumors that he was a Jesuit in disguise. The times, however, were not normal. Terror gripped England. Commoners and statesmen alike were certain that any ills affecting the country were the work of malignant plotters. Spaniards, Frenchmen, English witches, all were feared; but more dangerous even than these were Jesuits, an ever present and fiendishly clever secret society, supernaturally crafty, cunningly adroit. Today all this seems ridiculous, but to Penn's contemporaries the dangers were very real.

So deep and wisespread was the fear that even such intelligent individuals as John Tillotson required constant reassurance; Penn found it necessary to remind him that he, Penn, was not among the sly and tricky enemies of the regime. Penn was not alone in being under suspicion; all Quakers were suspect. Did they not refuse, loudly and flatly, to abjure the Pope by solemn oath? Did they not, though facing certain imprisonment, decline to swear allegiance to the King? Did they not refuse to fight against the forces of Catholicism? What better proof was needed of their perfidy? Their pacifism was hypocrisy and cowardice.

Supposedly clear evidence proved Penn a Catholic. A certain William Winchcombe, a graduate of Douai, became a priest under the name Father Penn; who else was this Winchcombe than William Penn who called himself a Quaker? Every bigot was very well aware that the Pope absolved his followers for anything that was done to confound the heretics. Some of the more extreme enemies of Quakerism were certain that Penn and his people kept their hats jammed tight upon their heads lest removal show the shaven pates of Jesuits.[12]

Quaker explanations were too simple, too honest, to be accepted. The general public, accustomed to duplicity, could not believe that any courtier, could be as artless as this William Penn professed to be. His easy access to Whitehall "proved" that some sinister and secret plot was being hatched.

Penn's critics who did not consider him a Jesuit had a less flattering explanation of why he was so welcome at court. If he was trying to win toleration for his Quakers, then, as many people saw it, he must be a stupid Royal tool. Could he not see that toleration for the few English Quakers was a small price for James to pay to gain toleration for so many more English Catholics?

It remained for Lord Macaulay to suggest that Penn was bribed to help the Catholic cause. The historian admitted that Penn was not vulnerable to offers of money "but bribes may be offered to vanity as well as cupidity. . . . He was attacked by Royal smiles, by female blandishments, by the insinuating eloquence and delicate flattery of veteran diplomatists and courtiers." Thus, he was "cajoled into bearing a part in some unjustifiable transactions of which others enjoyed the profits."[13]

Lord Macaulay was vague concerning the exact nature of those unjustifiable transactions, or the ways Penn had helped to bring them about. Certainly he could not have been referring to a decision by the Lords of Trade and Plantations in November 1685 to deny the Lower Counties to Lord Baltimore, nor to the release on March 15, 1686, of Quakers imprisoned for refusing to swear oaths.[14]

The belated liberation of the unfortunate prisoners has sometimes been credited to Penn's publication of *A Persuasion to Moderation*, another of his eloquent pleas for freedom of conscience. "Written by One of the King's Humblest and Most Dutiful Subjects," it reiterated Penn's thesis that, from ancient times, toleration had promoted political and commercial success. As a modern instance Penn cited the rise of Holland, "that bog of the world . . . neither sea nor dry land." To dispel any fear that a multitude of conflicting religions might disrupt the established order, Penn argued that toleration had never yet endangered any government.

The release of the Quakers cheered Penn at a time when he desperately needed comfort. Guli had borne her baby, another Gulielma Maria, but the child, like her elder namesake, was sickly. Despite the supposedly healthier air at Worminghurst, the little girl was not expected to live many months. Throughout 1685 and 1686, Penn was under constant pressure. The warmth of his reception at court pleased him, but it entailed a daily necessity of proving his Protestantism and of defending the administration of his province.

In addition, Penn worried about the state of his finances. His expenses were heavy. The maintenance of two households, at Worminghurst for his wife and children, at Kensington for himself, and the entertainment of the throngs who came there to seek his help, strained his resources. Payments of one sort or another to various officials, either as legitimate court costs or as the unavoidable "presents," drained away a heavy toll. As Quaker leader now that George Fox was failing fast, Penn was obliged to hand out large sums for office expenses, for missioners, for charity, and for loans that would never be repaid. On top of this he complained that he was paying the entire cost of the Pennsylvania government and was receiving nothing in return.

At the same time his sources of supply were drying up. Supposedly his income was derived from Pennsylvania, from England, and from Ireland. Land sales in the province, however, were slowing down and quitrents were not being paid. Constant uprisings in Ireland stopped the flow of rents from Shanagarry. Guli's rich estates continued to produce good crops, but Penn was borrowing heavily with that land as security and some of the land was being sold. Penn had also begun to sell off the timber from the Sussex forests. He was living beyond his means and drawing heavily upon his capital. He might have consoled himself by thinking that in the long run he would be affluent, but for the immediate future he was a loser.

At this juncture, when everything was going wrong, Philip Ford reappeared to present Penn with another bill for back wages and loans, even larger than the one he had given Penn on the latter's departure for America. In the three intervening years Penn had paid nothing to reduce his £2851 debt, nor had Ford foreclosed on his three-hundred-thousand-acre security. Instead, the bill had run on, at the customary rate of 8 percent compounded quarterly, until, as Ford calculated, it now totaled £4293.[15]

As Penn professed to have no money, Ford, whom Penn's apologists have berated for avarice, hardheartedness, and dishonesty, had agreed to wait two years more on the same terms. Thereafter, Penn appears to have disregarded, or perhaps forgotten, the debt, while Ford appears to have remained indifferent, though he continued, at two-year intervals, to submit ever larger bills reflecting the accrued interest. Each time Penn, never questioning Ford's accuracy, merely certified the correctness of Ford's accounts, without bothering to check or even read them.

All in all, what with the misrepresentations, the threats of danger, and the fear of bankruptcy, the first two years of James's reign were anything but happy for William Penn. The Sussex indictment no longer hung over him, but the Westminster authorities for the third time arrested him for preaching, this time doubling his fine to £40.[16]

Years later, Penn reported that, belatedly, the King came to his rescue. "When he came to know the ruin it [the persecution] would cause me and my family," Penn said, "he cried out, 'God forbid that he would ever be the author of such a cruelty.' "[17]

The Royal protection took the form of a warrant "To all Archbishops, Bishops, Chancellors etc.," mentioning the late eminent services of Sir William Penn and the loyalty and good affection of his son, William Penn, signifying the Royal pleasure that "the said William Penn, his family and servants should not be prosecuted and causing all process or proceedings against them to be wholly superseded, discharged or stayed till the Royal pleasure be further known."[18]

In June 1686 Penn took a six-week trip to Europe. Ostensibly he intended to inspect Quaker meetings and to encourage emigration to America. For that purpose he visited the Rhineland and also three tiny Dutch towns. Since he spent more time at the Dutch capital conferring with William of Orange, however, observers quite naturally assumed that the trip's real purpose was diplomatic.[19]

Whether James II sincerely believed in freedom of conscience or whether his real aim was to free his fellow Catholics, there is no doubt of his strong desire to abolish the Test Acts, which disfranchised many citizens and barred them from official position. Since he doubted the willingness of a Protestant Parliament to cooperate, lest Catholics be benefited, he contemplated ending discrimination by Royal decree. As such action, in violation of British custom, would certainly stir opposition, James needed assurance that William of Orange, the outstanding anti-Catholic leader on the Continent, would not intervene on behalf of English Protestants. Possibly Penn the Quaker could convince the Prince that the projected action would help dissenters much more than their adversaries.

If such reasoning dictated Penn's trip, it posed a problem for him. Penn wholeheartedly believed in parliamentary government and James was contemplating what under other circumstances Penn would have considered tyranny. If Penn knowingly went to Holland to further an autocratic action, would he be compromising a deeply held conviction to satisfy a long-cherished desire? Penn's critics had two ready replies, one the well-worn charge of secret Jesuitism, the other the unfair and unkind answer that if Penn was not a stupid man, he must have been well bribed.

As was to be expected, William of Orange approved the granting of toleration, but he balked at the suggestion of repealing the Test Acts. To do so, he said, would imperil the Protestant religion. Moreover, though he gave no details, he would lose all his current revenues from England, together with the inheritance of the English throne by his wife Mary, in the event that King James, her father, died without male issue. Nevertheless, he offered to consent, provided Parliament ratified toleration and the repeal of the Test Acts, and if James would allow Mary, his elder daughter, an allowance of £48,000 a year.[20]

Penn disclaimed any authority to bargain. He was, said Bishop Burnet, then living in exile in Holland, "a great proficient in the art of dissimulation . . . yet we looked upon him as a man employed." Penn offered, however, to forward the suggestion to King James. The latter refused, fearing that the subsidy might be used against him. The collapse of negotiations led Bishop Burnet to sneer at Penn. He "had such an opinion of his own faculty of persuasion that he thought none could stand before it, though he was singular in that opinion."[21]

Penn's failure as an intermediary—assuming that he was an accredited agent—angered Mary, who may have had her heart set on that £48,000 per year; according to a French diplomat it explained her later enmity toward Penn when she and William of Orange ascended the English throne.[22]

If others doubted Penn's success, he himself did not. The Lord, he said, had given him "a great influence and interest with the King, though he modestly added, "not as strong as people generally believed."[23] Penn was not above exerting that influence. While in Holland he met Sir Robert Stuart of Coltness, "a Presbyterian who was not a rebel." Coltness complained that one of Penn's old friends in Ireland had taken his estate. Penn went to the man and demanded that the property be returned. "If thou dost not give me this moment an order for £200 for Coltness to carry him back to his native country and £100 a year to subsist on till matters are adjusted, I will make it as many thousands out of thy way with the King."[24]

Actually, Penn was unable to settle the dispute until after the Glorious Revolution, but at that time Sir Robert received full restitution and a return of all rents that had been withheld from him.

28

VICE RUNS RAMPANT

BAD NEWS POURING IN FROM PENNSYLVANIA LESSENED THE PROPRI-
ETOR'S HAPPINESS. SUPERFICIALLY, EVERYTHING SEEMED TO BE GOING
WELL. PHILADELPHIA BOASTED THREE HUNDRED OR MORE BRICK OR
frame houses, with many more going up, but the growth worried Penn;
he preferred open country where men could see, and be thankful for, the
works of God.

The town was filling up with people, but to Penn's disappointment,
those new immigrants, desirable though they were, did not show the
love, the personal loyalty, that Penn looked for in his protégés. Moreover, too few of them were Quakers.

The town's progress, as Penn had feared, was material, not spiritual.
The City of Brotherly Love concerned itself with business rather than
with mutually helpful benefit. Residents were not cooperating as neighbors should. Though living three thousand miles away across an ocean,
Penn tried to set a good example by lending his workmen to friends who
needed a little extra temporary help, but the policy was not generally
followed. Nor did it work well for Penn; he generously allowed a man
who called himself a sea captain to borrow his sloop, only to have the
fellow return the boat in poor condition, apparently without repairing it
or even offering an apology.[1]

Penn had little trustworthy news as to what was happening in the
province. There were, of course, no professional correspondents in America, and the vast majority of settlers, even those who were literate, wrote
few letters to their English relatives and even fewer to the Proprietor. Occasional messages, sent either by critical malcontents or by
officials who reported success but glossed over failure, gave him his only
information.

He was, of course, obliged to give particular attention to reports sent to the Lords of Trade and Plantations by Royal agents in America. Almost always these men, dedicated to the promotion of Royal control, stressed the shortcomings of proprietary government, particularly the prevalence of smuggling, of piracy, of violation of the Navigation Acts, and of interference with the lawful activities of His Majesty's hard-working representatives.

Penn, the vociferous advocate of high ethical standards, was a special target. Some anonymous female gossipmonger spread the word about Whitehall that Penn, the Quaker, who in England pretended that he would not fight for any cause, was in America a warrior. This pacifist, this preacher of peace, defended his port of New Castle on the Delaware with a battery of cannon. The woman voiced her accusation so loudly and so persistently that even the Society of Friends was moved to question Penn about the matter. Penn answered the charges in detail. Yes, he admitted, there were iron cannon on the New Castle Green, seven of them in fact. They had been there some time, since the Dutch days. They were small and they were old; they were also useless, for some of them rested on broken carriages and the rest lay rusting on the ground. Even in good condition, they would have been of no value in a war, for they lacked powder and shot; neither was there either a militiaman or a regular soldier to make use of them. In short, said Penn, "I am as innocent as any act of hostility as she herself."[2]

It was not as easy to reject his own conviction that Pennsylvania in general and Philadelphia in particular were corrupt places where wickedness and vice ran rampant. He did not blame his Quakers, for they lived quietly in their comfortable houses, attending one or another of their seven meetinghouses and minding their own flourishing businesses. It was the people of the world, the foreigners, the bound men, and above all the sailors, who frequented the taverns and disturbed the peace. With beer at a penny a quart and hard cider even cheaper, they were often drunk; they held indescribable orgies in the waterfront caves.

Actually, it is a little difficult to determine just what was happening in those caves. Penn's strict sense of decorum, his hatred of time-wasting and his condemnation of sports, frivolity, and unproductive play, all of which he grouped as vile and filthy carnal wickedness, led him into overstatement. He lumped drunkenness, loose language, loud talking, brawls, and scuffles into the category of heinous outrages against the laws of God and man. All that is certain is that, to William Penn, his Holy Experiment was being badly besmirched. The *"prophani"* whom Pastorius had warned to stay afar had taken over the caves.

Penn never specified precisely what orgies were celebrated in these caves, other than to call them "sins scandalously and openly committed, facts so foul I am forbid by common decency to mention them." Year after year, almost month after month, he demanded that the city fathers clear the resorts of sin. For one reason or another, the legislators failed to comply, and curiously enough, Penn contented himself by suggesting that liquor licenses issued to hosts in those resorts be revoked.[3]

The Provincial Council paid no attention; it failed, in fact, to hold a single session throughout the winter. When it did meet, it was not to require decency but merely to set aside as cruel and illegal a £10 fine and a lashing imposed on each of three sailors who had stolen a hog worth no more than one pound.[4]

The Assembly, having nothing else to do, impeached Judge Nicholas More for rejecting a jury's verdict and for dismissing a juror. He had gone further; he had, the Assembly alleged, sneered at the Council and had proclaimed, "It would never be good times as long as the Quakers had the administration."[5]

Whoever had drawn the bill of impeachment was a master publicist; he so drafted the charges as to shock the Council, which was to pass upon the matter, and also to recall to Penn's mind his similar experience in the Penn–Meade case. More, however, had Free Society of Traders friends in the upper house. The Council took pity on him because, it said, the man was "under a weak and languishing condition," so it dropped the matter. Penn, too, was in a forgiving mood; he appointed More to a supervisory post. Three years later More died.

Penn was no disciplinarian. Forbearing to chide Council for doing nothing, he urged it to be kind to everyone, especially to the poor and unfortunate. It should be quiet, helpful, and inoffensive; but it should please clean out the caves. Council, accordingly, summoned all cave occupants to clear themselves of any taint of vice or crime; when no one appeared, council took another three-month vacation. Thereafter, nothing was done for a year and then only to pass a resolution urging that Penn's instructions be "persued."[6]

The Council had not been idle, however. Twenty-two-year-old William Bradford, cousin of Andrew Soule of London, the official Quaker printer, had come to town in December 1685 bringing with him a printing press and letters of introduction from Penn and George Fox. The first printer in the Middle Colonies, he announced his intention of publishing a Bible and Samuel Atkin's *Kalendarium Pennsilvaniense*, an almanac. Council favored the project until it discovered that the leading article of the almanac told of "The Beginning of Government in Pennsylvania by Lord Penn." The lawmakers, shocked by a printer's conferring a title of nobility, ordered Bradford to smudge over the offending words. They went further; they instituted censorship by forbidding him to print anything whatever that the Council had not previously approved. They even, by implication, rebuked the Proprietor himself; he had suggested that the Great Law and the statutes be used in schools to teach children how to read, but the Council refused to allow the laws to be printed.[7]

The Provincial Council then proceeded to censor the morals of its

members. It had retained a counterfeiter as a member, but it suspended
another man on the basis of a report that he had been intimate with a
servant girl in his brother-in-law's house. The Council stated that it would
reinstate the man as soon as he proved his innocence, but how, except by
his or the girl's own word, he was to prove his innocence was not quite
clear. However, the Council accepted the assurance of the brother-in-law
that everything was quite all right.[8]

Penn had been trying from afar, through correspondence, to improve
the morals of his people. Even before he left England he had preached to
them: "Till morals and corrupt manners be impartially rebuked and
punished and until virtue and sobriety be cherished, the wrath of God
will hang over nations."[9]

Five developments of widely different nature seriously disturbed the
Proprietor. A number of robberies occurred in Philadelphia; drunkenness became common; both the city watch and the local magistrates
proved careless and inefficient; and the Provincial Council and the Assembly spent more time in factional disputes than on enacting wise legislation. In addition, the city residents indulged in "vice," a catch-all word
that Penn employed to cover almost anything he detested.

He resorted to a variety of methods to save his province from divine
wrath. When exhortation failed he tried a personal appeal. In a display
of what Dean Swift and Bishop Burnet would have called his vanity, he
pleaded with the politicians to take more interest in their work and, at
the same time, to cool their angers. "If they love me, let them love one
another." The Council was not merely to suppress vice but must punish
it. It must not repeat his own mistake of being "too merciful," for, as
Penn underlined, "The repentance of the person is not enough for the
public good."[10]

The injunction to suppress vice and to cherish virtue became a
refrain that for many years ran through Penn's messages to the Provincial Council. Almost always it was accompanied by commands to prod
the law-enforcement agents into more intense activity.[11] "Many eyes are
upon you," he reminded his officials. "Any miscarriage is magnified to a
mountain."[12]

Penn himself was not wholly guiltless in this exaggeration. Though
he professed "not to believe everything that he heard," he was often
much too quick to credit the contents of complaining letters that came
in from overseas. The rigid ethical and moral code to which he scrupulously adhered led him to brand more fallible people as filthy, vile, and
vicious. Such judgments, circulated among courtiers and government
officials, spread misleading ideas about his province. Thus, the Holy
Experiment, far from being looked upon as philanthropic or ethical,
seemed to some to be hypocritical and scandalous. Minor inefficiencies,
overemphasized by Penn himself, were cited as proof of corruption and

incompetence. The misdemeanors in the caves proved flagrant viciousness and crime.[13]

Penn believed in free speech, in what then passed for democracy, and in the absolute necessity of legislation by a popularly elected parliament; but from what he had seen of English politics, he strongly opposed political parties. Decisions should be reached, he thought, as in Quaker meetings, not by mere majorities but by unanimous consent.

To that end, he disliked displays of disagreement. Debate was quite all right, indeed desirable, except when it degenerated into dissension. The public had every right to know the decisions of its rulers; but the steps in reaching those decisions should be withheld from public knowledge. "I beseech you, draw not several ways, have no cabals apart, nor reserve from one another," he urged the Council. "Create with a mutual simplicity an entire confidence in one another. If at any time you mistake, or misapprehend, or dissent from one another, let not that appear to the people. Show your virtues but conceal your infirmities. This will make you awful and reverend with the people."[14]

By coincidence, almost immediately Penn sent to America as his attorney general a brilliant Welsh lawyer, destined to be not only one of the leaders of the colonial bar but a staunch advocate of the political factions Penn detested. David Lloyd, a distant relative of Thomas, had been trained by Sir George Jeffreys, though he certainly did not share that jurist's philosophy. He had transferred from the office of the judge of the Bloody Assizes to the more congenial rooms of Penn's Quaker lawyers. Penn admired his efficiency, especially his skill in drafting land deeds and his expertness in handling quo warranto cases. Possibly there were questions of conflict of interests since Lloyd was retained by such private clients as Dr. Daniel Coxe, the Jerseyman who fathered the New Mediterranean Sea Company; but Lloyd was strictly ethical and acted with perfect propriety.[15]

In politics, however, Penn differed with David Lloyd. The new attorney general led what came to be known as the Anti-Proprietary party, a group composed of upcountry people and less affluent city dwellers as opposed to the conservative city merchants. The confrontation might also be described as the popular Assembly against the so-called aristocrats of the Provincial Council or the unprivileged against the Establishment.

Long before the rift with David Lloyd became visible, Penn was losing faith in the people he had tried to benefit. The province was an expense; it ignored pleas that ranged from indirect suggestions that he would appreciate a little help to broad hints that he needed income for his living expenses.

Penn was deeply hurt at the indifference to his modest needs. Pennsylvania refused to build him a house, to grant him an income, or to pay the quitrents. The province was niggardly. All that he was asking them to contribute was just enought for his "table, cellar, stable, barge, yacht or sloop." To shame the people he let it be known that he would sell the shirt off his back before he would ask for help again.[16]

When Pennsylvania remained unimpressed he reacted angrily, telling his friends as early as November 1686 that he was tempted to return the province to the King, who certainly would replace him with a mercenary governor. "As righteous God is my witness, I have spent thousands more than I have got." No Royal governor would ever do as much for them.[17]

He could not bring himself to take so rash a step. Instead he threatened, most uncharacteristically, to use his powers under his patent "to make them need me as much as I do their supply." In an outburst that he tried to convince himself was not anger but "grieving," he complained at being undervalued and misunderstood. He was hurt that Pennsylvania's public documents failed to mention his name, and worse, that of the King himself. He mourned because his letters were neglected and unanswered and because his appeals for harmony were ignored.[18]

His only recourse, as he saw it, was to cancel the Frame—"dissolve" it—and so withdraw all the liberal privileges he had granted. This, of course, raised the legal question whether the Frame was a gift of grace to be withdrawn at will or an irrevocable contract. To Penn's mind the question did not really matter; if it were a contract, the people had already broken it innumerable times.

Yet, while in private messages Penn severely, and sometimes unduly, criticized his people, he resented even milder criticisms from outsiders. In the same letter wherein he rebuked his officials for dereliction of duty and for quarreling among themselves, he spoke of "giving the lie to vile and repeated slanders cast upon the province."[19]

He could be sufficiently incensed against his colonists to declare that never again would he set foot in a province where he apparently was unwanted, whereas only a few days earlier, he had proclaimed his love for it. "There is nothing my soul breathes for more in this world, next to my dear family's life, than that I may see poor Pennsylvania again."[20]

It was no passing fancy. Two years later he spoke of his desire "to live and die among you. Depend upon it Pennsylvania is my worldly delight of all places on the earth."[21]

29

DECADENCE AND SIN

ESPITE HIS REPEATED THREATS OF SURRENDERING HIS PATENT, AND THUS LEAVING HIS UNGRATEFUL PEOPLE TO CERTAIN UNHAPPY FATE, PENN HAD NO REAL INTENTION OF DOING SO. WHATEVER THEIR faults, however deeply hurt he may have been by the sins and shortcomings of his protégés, he could not bear to cast them loose. He loved them as a father loves his errant children.

Penn displayed his real nature when he expressed his firm intention to live and die in Pennsylvania. He could not go to America at once. Too many problems remained unsolved in England, problems involving Quaker policies, the ever present threat of imminent quo warranto proceedings, the steady drumfire of accusations of secret Jesuitism, financial difficulties, and, perhaps more important to Penn than any of these, the crying need of James II for the support of some important dissenter in furthering religious toleration.

Yet he was strongly tempted to leave for Philadelphia. Lord Baltimore was plaguing him with streams of complaining letters. News came in of yet another Maryland incursion into the Lower Counties, an offense which Penn had supposed had ended with the flight of Colonel Talbot after murdering the King's official. Neither Joseph Bowle nor the Widow Ogle had been again molested, but that log fort illegally built on the banks of Christiana Creek remained and, even worse, was being regarrisoned. Nor was that all. A squadron of forty armed horsemen rode up to John White's place while he was making hay. Their leader, Major Edward English, demanded that White recognize Lord Baltimore as his overlord else the troopers would throw all the hay into the creek. Unlike the rough-spoken Talbot, the cavalry commander, though firm in his demand, was cheerful, even jovial, in attitude. "If thou wilt say, you drunken dog, Ned English, let me cut hay, I will give you leave."[1]

[229]

Whether White recognized that any such request, so improbably suggested in semi-Quaker language, could be construed as formal recognition of Maryland's sovereignty, does not appear upon the record, nor does any statement as to what happened to the hay, but it is recorded that White, like Bowle before him, sent a messenger to ask Penn's Provincial Council what to do.

The Council responded unhelpfully. With no armed forces at its disposal it advised both John White and the province to use no violence against the forty cavalrymen but to "bear with patience" and the King would stop the hostile action.

It was too late for Penn to take any decisive action, but apparently he had some idea of leaving for America. He asked Thomas Lloyd's advice, but added "I aim at Americanizing my family." The intention was not new; he had already shipped, for his family, twenty-five barrels of beef, together with some hundredweight of butter and candles from Ireland. Just why he needed to send food to a fertile province which, as he once said, produced better crops than England did, was not explained. It may be supposed that the provisions were not for his blood kin but for the staff of servants at Pennsbury whom he called his "family." But had that family not been farming the land?[2]

Penn was not happy with the colonial leaders. As yet he had no quarrel with individuals, all of them well-meaning and industrious. Unfortunately, they seemed incapable of reaching the consensus of a Quaker meeting; they divided into factions. Council minutes reveal few details of their differences in formal sessions and nothing whatever of their talk at informal discussions, but it is probable that the business representatives failed to see eye to eye with proponents of the Holy Experiment.

In his strong desire that his people should enjoy self-government, Penn scrupulously stayed above the battle. Even had he wished to intervene, so much time must necessarily elapse between his hearing of a dispute and the receipt of his response that the issue would, in any case, have been long resolved. Necessarily, therefore, his stream of messages to the Council had to be confined to exhortations on the need for mutual understanding and helpfulness, for charity and sympathy toward all, for the repression of vice and the cultivation of virtue. His letters were excellent sermons but poor guides to specific action; each reader interpreted the words to suit his own desires.

Except for such noncontroversial matters as banning tree cutting in the town, Penn seldom dictated any governmental policy; he was content to set forth a principle as a suggestion for consideration by his people. He did, at times, offer an indirect comment, such as after the Council censored the printer Bradford and forbade publication of the laws, he rather pointedly published an abstract of his charter together with the text and comment on Magna Carta. He also defended the right of loyal

English subjects to enjoy the privileges of liberty and the possession of property.

There were, of course, criticisms of his policy, but these Penn brushed aside as due to ignorance if not to prejudice and malice. After his experience in sharing the government of the Jerseys, he considered himself qualified to manage a province overseas. "I know," he said, "how to allow for new colonies; the others don't."[3]

One of Penn's few directions that could be construed as a command involved a proposed action that some might look upon as too adroit. Pennsylvania, alone among the American provinces, was required to bundle up its laws, five years after their passage, for inspection, and possible veto, by the Lords of Trade and Plantation. Legally that period had expired in March 1686, five years after he received his patent, but since for the first few months Penn had retained the Duke of York's Laws, he did not deem it necessary to submit his own legislation until much later in the year.

He held some doubts concerning their reception. Quaker laws were much more liberal than those of England; while the Royal powers were in no way reduced, the popular rights were far more liberal than would be welcomed by the current London regime. The quo warranto movement was growing and Penn feared that his own freedoms might provoke a similar challenge. Nevertheless, before the end of the year he must fulfil his obligation. He had, however, a brilliant idea for avoiding the necessity. He wrote to Thomas Lloyd ordering Council to repeal all laws passed since the start of Quaker rule. Thus, there being no five-year-old laws in force, there would be no need to forward anything for London's scrutiny. After a day or two, perhaps after only a few hours, Council should then repass the measures, with whatever amendments might be desirable. The scheme would thus allow the province five more years before submission would be required.[4]

There was, as Penn saw, a flaw in the proposal; a period must elapse in which Pennsylvania would have no laws in operation, but, if councilmen acted wisely, keeping their mouths shut, the public would not know that any gap existed. Penn's phrase was "to insinuate these [plans] to the wiser only," the information, in other words, to be "discreetly and closely intimidated."

Council refused to consent to Penn's plan.[5]

Two months before the Provincial Council rejected Penn's order to repeal the old laws, he had stripped it of its executive power. The two matters were not connected, for news of the change had not yet crossed the ocean; but Penn had lost faith both in his people and in the institution of democratic parliamentary government. The legislators, and particularly the provincial councillors, were "slothful and dishonorable" in their neglect of duty. Their sessions were disorderly, faction-ridden, and, though Penn did not use the word, conspirational, because privately they conferred with each other outside the legislative halls. Probably they had violated both the charter and the Frame; certainly they had cheated him of property and encroached upon his rights. His publication of a digest of his patent may have been motivated by a desire to make his rights quite clear.

As for the people, "I am grieved to the bottom of my heart. . . . By all hands I understand that debauchery grows to that pitch it almost waves comparison."[6]

The powers taken from the Council went to a five-man commission composed of Thomas Lloyd, John Eckley, Nicholas More, James Claypoole, and Robert Turner, all of them conservatives and the last three, at least, high officials of the Free Society of Traders. Any three of them were empowered, as a quorum, to require the legislature to perform its proper duty under penalty of a dissolution of the Frame "without any more ado." They were to crusade among the populace against the impious, the troublesome, and the vexatious, especially against "the trifling appealers." They were also to invalidate the old laws and then to enact them anew if Council had not already done so.

Simultaneously, Penn named a sort of police commission. Three men, headed by Markham, were to safeguard growing timber, to "forbid windmills as my own royalty," and to protect the Welsh rights to forty thousand acres of contiguous land. They were to punish the man who cut down "the great oak on my son's land against my express orders" and to cancel an illegal land grant to Charles Pickering the counterfeiter and John Gray, alias Tatham, the Benedictine monk. The group was to see to it that Penn received his rents in specie and to prevent any encroachment on the land belonging to the Proprietor or to any of his family.[7]

England, too, provided its share of worries. Philip Ford, after a four-year wait for his 1682 bill to be paid, turned up seeking payment of the debt. This time he asked £5282, representing his original £2851 claim plus accrued interest. The compound interest rate was high, though not abnormal for the times. As usual, Penn acknowledged the validity of the claim. Pleading, as twice before, a lack of ready money, he agreed that if Ford would return in two more years, a total of £6000 would be paid him. Meanwhile, as security, Ford should have a five-thousand year lease, or mortgage, of the province at the annual quitrent of one peppercorn per year.[8]

Penn's anti-Ford biographers have consistently branded Ford as cruel and mercenary because of his perseverence in trying to collect the money owed him (though they fail to lay the same charge against Penn for bringing constant pressure on Charles I to settle the debt owed to Sir William). Without considering the accuracy of the original Ford claim, which Penn reacknowledged at each extension of the bill, the evidence points rather to a remarkable patience on the part of the supposedly sleek, subtle scoundrel said to be encompassing the ruin of a trusting client. Ford was under no obligation to extend the credit, each time at a reduced rate. At any expiration date he could have foreclosed the valid mortgages that he held on Pennsylvania; had Ford so wished he could have deprived William Penn of the entire province.

Penn had also to deal with another perennial annoyance. The ever recurring suspicion of secret Jesuitism, though scotched over and over again, continued to spread. Despite Tillotson's faith in Penn, so frequent and so detailed were the accusations that he again asked for reassurance.[9] Penn again wrote a detailed denial:

> For the Roman correspondence I will freely come to confessions. I have not only no such thing with any Jesuit at Rome (though Protestants may have without offense) but I hold none with any Jesuit, Priest or Regular in the world of that communion. . . . I know not one anywhere. . . . I am a Catholic, tho' not a Roman. I have bowels for mankind and dare not deny others what I crave for myself. I mean liberty for the exercise of my religion. . . . I am no Roman Catholic but a Christian whose creed is the Scripture.[10]

It was a clear-cut statement, but perhaps Penn wrote too cleverly. Undoubtedly Tillotson was reconvinced; but superficial readers, especially if biased or devoid of humor, could have misconstrued his words. Had not Penn admitted that he had freely come to confession? Had he not said "I am a Catholic"? No intelligent man would have misunderstood, but bigots, by the nature of the breed, were highly selective readers, capable of picking out of context precisely what they wished to find. They could have pounced upon his "admissions" to "prove" they had been right. One would like to think that the many denials, corrections, and explanations ended misunderstandings once and for all. Unfortunately, they did not. Some prejudices were so dear to the hearts of those who cherished them that no amount of reasoning, however cogent, could have eliminated them.

The caves, for instance, continued to be viewed by some as haunts of vice, quite possibly because the evils within them had been overstated. Penn had ordered the caves depopulated, cleaned out, and used to house the poor. The Provincial Council was either unwilling to do so or, more probably, did not rate the goings on within them as being as scandalous as did the Proprietor. As late as 1705 Penn was lamenting that in London "much is said of the lewdness of Pennsylvania."[11] Nor was Penn alone in this reporting; his successors, a quarter of a century later, were echoing the cry.

If Penn could not bring himself to be specific about Pennsylvania's vice, others were less squeamish: men like Zachary Whitpain, for instance, who discovered a married lady in what Penn would have been too modest to call a compromising situation. Whitpain was not reticent; he described the offense in detail. It may have been because of that publicity that the aggrieved husband hurried off to Holland, there to write land-sales propaganda for the province he deserted. If no one else appreciated Whitpain's muckraking, Penn's old antagonist Francis Bugg certainly did, even if he did misspell the seducer's name. Neither the issuance, at Penn's insistence, of "a nervous proclamation against vice" nor the revelations of blabbermouths such as Whitpain and his colleague Pentecost Teague proved effective.[12]

Other evils demanded attention: a plethora of speak-easies, rampant bootlegging, far too much public drunkenness. Decadence appeared even among members of the Society of Friends. The province cultivated the black arts, not just common witchcraft but what one monthly meeting called "other sciences": astrology, fortunetelling, palmistry, spiritualism, even the study of patterns formed by casting handfuls of earth upon the ground. These pastimes, even battledore and shuttlecock, were not innocent; they brought, the meeting said, "a veil upon the understanding, a death upon life." Though one man at least was disowned for practicing them, the vogue continued.[13]

Penn opposed improper marriages, by which he usually meant the union of such close relatives as first cousins or of a Quaker to "one of the world." Those who wished to wed irregularly would post the required banns by night at the church or meetinghouse doors and take them down before daylight, thus obeying the letter of the law. This, together with the posting of banns at the worshiping places of people who had never heard of the persons to be married, was, Penn said, the sort of lewdness practiced by the Church of England. A particularly scandalous ceremony where every participant, except perhaps the flower girl, was drunk, filled him with horror.[14]

Nothing but God's wrath was to be expected if this sort of thing continued. The breakdown was, in fact, already evident. Quaker youth were no longer using the appropriate plain language, no longer wearing plain apparel. Quaker tailors, in fact, corrupted youth by making fashionable clothing for them. Youth was misbehaving, taking dancing and fencing lessons (had Penn forgotten his own swordsmanship?), playing noisily in the galleries during meeting, wandering about town on First Day evenings. Why should not parents be required to sit with their children during times of worship and teachers with their pupils so as to admonish them to good behavior?[15]

Nor were the ladies spared. Hair, Burlington Yearly Meeting decreed, should not be "cut back and left out at the brow"; the head should not be dressed high but low, "as becomes women professing godliness and good works." They should rid the house of surplus furniture, remove "great fringes about the valences and double valences and double curtains and many other such like needless things."[16]

When compared with this first-class contemporary testimony, Peter S. Duponceau's rhapsody before the American Philosophical Society in 1821 is most naïve: "No country on earth ever exhibited such a sense of happiness, innocence and peace as was witnessed here during the first century of our social existence . . . when love was not crossed by avarice or pride and friendships were unbroken by ambition and intrigue."[17]

Penn would certainly have wished that it had been so.

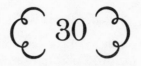

MAGDALEN CASE

FOR AT LEAST TWO DECADES AFTER BECOMING A TRUE AND ABSOLUTE PROPRIETOR WILLIAM PENN STRONGLY INFLUENCED BOTH ENGLISH AND AMERICAN AFFAIRS. IN BOTH AREAS HIS OBJECTIVES WERE THE same, the procurement and preservation of freedom, justice, and equality, but because of special circumstances, he necessarily followed different courses.

For all but two years of that long period he lived in England where, as long as he remained a Quaker, he could not sit in Parliament or hold any office requiring the swearing of an oath. But he could, and did, take an active part in public affairs. Though holding no formal position, he acted as a public defender, an ombudsman, interceding at court for individuals, safeguarding the Society of Friends from persecution, advising the King and various governmental officials. Here he was suave, conciliatory, and persuasive, a Penn who won confidence by his mildness, his open-mindedness, his anxiety to understand an opponent's point of view.

There was, however, another side to William Penn, a characteristic created by his Pennsylvania status. In England he was the advocate for a minority, a minority which, by and large, was not generally approved; in Pennsylvania he was an official with important legislative, executive, and judicial powers. Thus, his methods varied, for, while always gentle and polite, he could, if need be, act more insistently and with authority, even, if necessary, by threatening retaliation against opposition.

In consequence there seemed to be two William Penns, and hence two schools of thought concerning him. Nearly everyone liked him as an individual, for he was generous, eager to please, and anxious to be helpful; but there were those who considered him insincere, even two-faced. The Lords of Trade and Plantations, who as individuals favored him, could not understand why their American agents regarded Penn as hostile to the Crown whereas everyone at court rated him an ardent Royalist. Some colonists, even some Quaker colonists, thought it odd that their Proprietor, who preached sobriety and thrift, seemed to enjoy the gay, and reputedly corrupt, court life they thought he led. And, as always, there was that persistent threadbare rumor that William Penn the Quaker really was a secret Jesuit.

Although he could not hold public office without swearing an oath, rumors persisted that he was about to be awarded one, because he was in daily attendance at court, presumably as a trusted advisor to the King. Since it was known that James had embraced Catholicism it seemed obvious that William Penn had been a secret Jesuit, probably even before the grant of the Pennsylvania charter.

Other critics, unable to think Penn a hypocrite, wrote him down as gullible. William Penn meant well, they admitted, and he was most sincere, but could he not see that he was working not so much for Quaker interests as for Roman Catholic freedom? Penn was himself no Papist, but he was the tool, no doubt unwittingly, of crafty Jesuits.

According to the critics the villain in this subtle scheme was James, King of England. For years, they said, he had pretended a gratitude to the late Sir William. In order to mislead an innocent William Penn. James had been promising that when he came to power he would help the Friends. It was a safe promise, for it required no immediate fulfilment. Penn had confidence in his friend; moreover he was tactful. With a boundary dispute pending with Catholic Lord Baltimore, he did not think it wise to risk angering a king who, as he well knew, did not relish argument, much less criticism.[1]

Penn's acceptance of delay pleased King James. The two men spent long hours together discussing other problems, thus convincing scores of people that Penn's intercession with the King would help advance their case seeking special favor. He earned much gratitude from those whom he was able to assist, but at the same time his activity gave new currency to the persistent rumors that his success was due to his supposed Catholicism.[2]

Persecution of the Friends did, in fact, lessen when those thirteen hundred Quakers were set free. Penn ascribed the release to two publications advocating tolerance. One defended the Duke of Buckingham for having advocated religious freedom; the defense was unsigned, being credited to "a nameless author," but Penn's hand was easily detected. The second, *Persuasion to Moderation*, ascribed to "One of the humblest and most dutiful of the King's dissenting subjects," was believed, by the Quakers at least, to have brought about the delivery from jail.

Penn's enemies made much of a crisis that occurred at Oxford University. In March 1687 the president of St. Mary Magdalen College died. By the terms of the college charter, the fellows had complete authority to choose a new head, but James, intent on favoring Catholics, overrode the regulations and, within two weeks, ordered one Anthony Farmer elected. To violate academic autonomy was a serious enough offense, and the choice was even worse. Magdalen's charter required a president to be a fellow either of Magdalen or of New College, but Farmer was neither; moreover, he was only seven years out of Cambridge, where he had chiefly distinguished himself by disrupting the local dancing school. Nor, though holding an Oxford instructorship, had he spent those seven years in any ivory tower. According to his critics, he was continuing his riotous behavior by habitually returning to college after hours and very drunk. In his nocturnal orgies he had debauched at least one gentleman scholar, had "tossed the Abington town stocks into Mad Man's Pool," and, just the day before his nomination as president, had been drinking until three in the morning trying to seduce a tavern landlady "which, he being a stranger, she permitted him to do."[3]

Oxford, thoroughly Royalist except when its privileges were at stake, rejected Farmer and chose instead Dr. John Hough, prebendary of Worcester and former chaplain to Penn's friend, the Duke of Ormonde.

To settle the conflict James confidently referred the matter to an ecclesiastical commission headed by the Lord Chancellor, Baron George Jeffreys, but even Jeffreys, though a staunch supporter of the King, felt compelled to admit that Farmer was "a very bad man." The commission declared the nominations void.

James, surprisingly restraining his anger at the double rebuff, proposed what he considered a generous face-saving gesture. Instead of Farmer (who thereupon disappeared from history), the fellows of Magdalen should elect Dr. Samuel Parker, Bishop of Oxford. Parker had none of Farmer's weaknesses. An ascetic (at college he had been known as a "greweller" because once a week he mortified the flesh by swallowing nothing but water in which oatmeal had been boiled), he was also a scholar, albeit one who disapproved of Plato, Aristotle, Descartes, and Hobbes. He was well known for his charity, being reputed always to keep £1000 at home in cash to help unfortunates.

Neither Magdalen nor Hough would cooperate. To add to the King's unhappiness, Parker, as Bishop, rebelled against a Royal order to appoint nine Roman Catholics to church positions; he also intimated, and would later announce, that he was not, and never would be, a Catholic.

James, no longer restraining his anger, rushed up to Oxford, "rated Hough and the Fellows in foul language in very angry tone," and warned that unless they did as they were bid they would "feel the weight of a King's hand." When Hough refused to surrender the keys to the college, James had his men break open the door of the room to which Hough had fled and take the keys away by force.

Penn also was, it happened, in the Oxford neighborhood at the moment. In all likelihood they conferred about the Magdalen situation, for Penn interrupted his preaching mission to consult the Oxford leaders. To their delight he seemed to favor their position. They had sworn, he understood, to stand by the Magdalen charter, and while they should have sworn no oaths, they had given their pledge and must observe it. As to the Royal offer, it might bring peace, but both sides must be careful to do nothing underhanded. "Nothing in this world is worth a trick," said Penn. "Nothing is sufficient to justify collusion or deceitful sacrifice." Was there anything that he could do?

There may have been more to all this than either Penn or the Magdalen professors reported. Whether they asked him to mediate or whether he volunteered is immaterial, but apparently Penn suggested that he write a letter to the King on their behalf. James, he led them to understand, misunderstood the situation; turning them out of their positions "would make a great noise and look ill in the world." He delicately suggested that as the King had shown good will by withdrawing Farmer's name, Magdalen might reciprocate by accepting Parker; in the event that they agreed some good position might be found for Hough.

Penn gave no more indication at Oxford than he had in Holland that he was acting for the King; but after the faculty refused his solution an unsigned letter arrived berating the professors for failure to cooperate with Penn, "who, you may be sure, had good authority for what he did." They had rejected "an expedient which, since the King was pleased to propose it, you ought not to refuse it in good manners."

What this letter referred to was left to the professors' imaginations, but other passages were quite clear. The King, the letter said, was much incensed and, being a man "who never will receive a baffle in anything that he espouseth," Magdalen might look for trouble. Quo warranto proceedings were already under way, and as such cases, the writer said, were invariably decided in favor of the Crown, Magdalen would lose its charter. Nor would that college be the only sufferer; its fall would be the signal for the cancellation of other college charters.

As Magdalen had no means of replying to a letter from one whose only identification was "your affectionate servant," Hough led a delegation to call on Penn. The group stressed its loyalty to a King who, Hough said, was "intentionally righteous and just in all his proceedings"; the professors were confident that James would treat them fairly. Penn listened sympathetically, professed himself deeply concerned with Magdalen's welfare, and assured his visitors that he had not written the anonymous letter. When Hough asked for further assistance, Penn turned pessimistic. He would, he promised, do all he could, but the King had now gone too far to turn back. There was, however, still a possible way out. Parker was a sick man; if he should die, Dr. Hough might be appointed to succeed him." What think you of that, gentlemen?"

The professors thought it a bribe. To accept it, Hough replied, would constitute not only what Penn had already called a trick, "a deceitful artifice," but worse, would deliver Magdalen into Catholic control. The Papists, Hough pointed out, already had Penn's own Christ Church College and New College also: "If they get Magdalen they will have the rest."

Penn hurriedly, and emphatically, contradicted him. "That they shall never have, assure yourselves. If once they pressed so far, they will quickly find themselves destitute of their present support." He went on to say, "I hope you will not have the two universities such invincible bulwarks for the Church of England that none but they must be capable of giving their children a learned education. I suppose two or three colleges will content the Papists."

The collegians were very far from convinced. Penn's attitude disturbed them; they did not understand which side he was defending. Penn, the staunch advocate of the classic rights of Englishmen and of the sanctity of agreements, seemed to be telling them to give up the fight. They broke off the conversation and returned to Oxford, resigned to defeat.

They had not long to wait. Quo warranto proceedings, ending precisely as the letter writer predicted in victory for the King, ousted Hough and installed the complaisant Dr. Parker. The new President promptly demanded that his faculty retract their oaths to respect their charter and take new oaths of fealty; when everyone refused, he dismissed them all.

The Royal victory was hollow. Within five months the ailing Parker died and, half a year thereafter, at the outbreak of the Glorious Revolution, James II, in a futile bid to bolster up his popularity, reinstated everyone. In due time Dr. Hough became Bishop of Oxford.

Penn's activities in the Magdalen College case served, of course, once more to spread suspicions of his Catholicism, especially when, in June 1688, he failed to protest vigorously against the trying of seven Anglican bishops ostensibly for "publishing a libel" but in reality for failing to read James's Declaration of Indulgence from their pulpits. Though Penn approved the Declaration (which some people thought he wrote) and so was not too hostile to the trial, the proceedings were conducted in a fashion reminiscent of Sir Samuel Starling's methods. The jury, as in Bushell's case, was ordered locked up, without heat or water, until it reached a verdict acceptable to the King. Penn would have been expected to protest vigorously, even though the case did not concern the

Quakers, but he contented himself with only a mild remonstrance. Penn's critics pounced upon his restraint as proof that his concern for independent juries was insincere and that his real concern was for the triumph of King James the Catholic.[4]

A diarist with the delightful name of Narcissus Luttrell twice reported that, in consideration of his service to the King, Penn was to be appointed a tax commissioner. The rumors were probably unfounded, but in any case, the success of the Glorious Revolution wrecked whatever plans there might have been for any such preferment.[5]

31

FRIENDSHIP SPELLS TREASON

To REWARD THE PENNSYLVANIA PROPRIETOR FOR SERVICES RENDERED, JAMES II DRAFTED A NEW DEED TO MEND PENN'S FAULTY TITLE TO THE WEST BANK OF THE DELAWARE. UNDER THE DOCUMENT'S PROvisions the Three Lower Counties were to be annexed to Pennsylvania.[1]

While the new deed would have corrected an imperfect situation, it might have created an even more curious problem. The State of Delaware would never have existed, but the area enclosed within the Twelve Mile Circle might conceivably have become a thirty-square-mile enclave, an independent entity almost entirely surrounded by the Commonwealth of Pennsylvania.

Penn's optimism over the prospect of a clear title was short-lived. Somewhere between the King's desk and the office wherein the deed was to be engrossed for his signature, the important document went astray. The moment, in November 1688, was most inconvenient. William of Orange had just landed in England bent on dethroning the King. James, fleeing for safety, had no time to locate, much less to sign, the missing deed. His hurried flight cost Penn a clear title to the Lower Counties. Luckily, no one challenged his overlordship during the sixty years that the unsigned document was lost.

Under the new regime of William and Mary, Penn's position was precarious. His Magdalen mediations, his daily visits to the Stuarts in Whitehall, his friendship with King James, and those recurrent suspicions of his supposed Catholicism did not endear him to the new breed of courtiers who replaced the Stuart partisans. William of Orange liked him, though with reservations, because Penn had approved repeal of the Test Acts; but Queen Mary hovered on the verge of hostility. Penn's protestations that, while he liked James as a man and was grateful for favors accorded him, his real loyalties were to England carried some weight, but many William and Mary supporters pointedly avoided him.

Within a month of James's flight to France a squad of soldiers picked up Penn while he was walking in Whitehall. He was charged with no specific offense but was quizzed to discover if he might possibly be a Stuart spy. No witness appeared against him, but neither was he completely cleared; he was released but was told to hold himself in readiness for further questioning.[2]

Penn may thereafter have been imprudent; he may have talked too much. At a small dinner party with the Duke of Arran, his old comrade-in-arms whom he had forced to disgorge property taken from Sir Robert Stuart Coltness, Penn blurted out that King James was mounting a campaign to recover his throne. Someone, perhaps a brother of a noble-man who became one of William and Mary's informants, asked how Penn came by this information and was told that he had received a letter from France stating that James was raising an army in Ireland.[3]

The combination of correspondence with the Catholic country where James had taken refuge, of knowledge of Stuart activities in two foreign lands, and of suspicion of continued friendship with the deposed monarch provided evidence enough to warrant Penn's arrest the very next day. Again he was examined and released, but only under a £6000 bond to appear whenever he was summoned.[4]

Penn promptly wrote to his old associate the Duke of Shrewsbury, one of the seven men who had invited William of Orange to England, asking for his intercession. He professed complete innocence of any wrongdoing: "I do profess solemnly in the presence of God I have no hand or share in any conspiracy against the King [William] nor do I know any that have." He offered, if the new regime would allow it, to retire to Worminghurst, even under a sort of house arrest, until the matter was clarified.[5]

He appealed to the right man. His offer was accepted, and the house arrest was not required. Within a few weeks he was back in London conferring with the rapidly failing George Fox, but in June he was once more called up for questioning. This time he wrote to George Savile, Marquess of Halifax, the Speaker of the House of Lords, a man whom many called the Trimmer, the same epithet sometimes applied to Admiral Sir William. Halifax had helped Penn in the past; would not his benefactor now increase his generosity "in proportion to my unhappiness."?[6]

Either Shrewsbury or Halifax, perhaps both, obtained permission for Penn to remain free on condition that he take no part in politics. Since there was no evidence against him except the imagination of jittery underofficers, the restriction imposed no hardship. Indeed, the whole case against Penn may have resulted from mistaken identity. A few months later a warrant was issued against one John Penn "suspected of treasonable practices."[7]

William Penn faithfully observed his part of the bargain—if there was a bargain—but his quiet life, instead of dispelling suspicions against him, merely intensified them. The years 1690 and 1691 were full of annoyance. Because he was not seen in London, some thought him still in jail; to those who knew him to be free his retirement spelled secrecy, and secrecy was sinister. Again the authorities were alarmed; in June 1690 he "and one Scarlet, another busy fellow, presumably a Quaker" were thrown into the Tower "for some practices against the government."[8]

The detention was short, and Penn immediately went back into his seclusion. His disappearance stirred wild rumors which, in turn, caused yet another proclamation calling for his arrest together with seventeen other conspirators on charges of high treason. When, as was reported, process servers could not find him, new rumors spread. He had escaped from jail, some said, and had fled to Scotland, where, pacifist though he professed himself, he was raising a Catholic army; another version put him in France preparing to lead twenty thousand Frenchmen in an invasion of England.[9]

Even given the sensationalism of the times it is difficult to understand why so many people believed the incredible inventions and even more difficult to know why, a century and a half later, Macaulay accepted them. "It is melancholy to relate," he wrote, "that Penn, while professing to believe even defensive war as sinful, did everything in his power to bring a foreign army into the heart of his own country."[10]

The authorities must have known better but, perhaps to calm the public's fears, once more ordered Penn arrested. The law-enforcers showed a degree of consideration inconsistent with a belief in any real and present danger. They found Penn suffering a stomach upset, so they postponed the arrest until he felt better. When the arrest did take place it was a formality; it involved a two-week surveillance, but there was no trial. Penn, however, disturbed by the constant harassment, unfortunately described himself as "hunted up and down" which gave a false impression that he was a fugitive. At no time were either government officers or his own close associates ignorant of his whereabouts; had the officers really wished to arrest him they could have picked him up without delay. The fact was that as there was no sound case against him, the government did little more than go through motions that would prevent popular hysteria.[11]

As a matter of fact Penn may have been having more difficulty with the Society of Friends than with the law-enforcers. Some associates, including his former co-defendant William Meade, Margaret Fox, and her son-in-law Thomas Lower, were dismayed by Penn's actions in the Magdalen College case. York Monthly Meeting went so far as to inquire if William Penn really was a Jesuit in disguise.

The "evidence" disturbing the meeting was flimsy. Someone told Matthew Webster that Thomas Cooper said that William Penn was a Jesuit. On investigation, Cooper replied that he could not recall having made such a statement to anyone, but that personally he did think Penn a Jesuit because someone had told him that Penn had confessed membership. Cooper then had gone to Penn and asked point-blank if the accusation was true. Penn answered, "How can I be a Jesuit? I have a wife and children." This, said Cooper, proved his guilt.

There was further "evidence" of equal validity. Penn's efforts to repeal the penal code, said Cooper, "would have allowed King James to destroy us all." Besides all this, a man named Barnes had mentioned to him that he, Barnes, had been a fellow student with Penn at St. Omer, the Jesuit seminary.[12]

The Meeting, still unconvinced of Penn's innocence, delegated one of its members to put the question squarely before William Penn. The man, well-meaning but tactless, chose the dinner hour to ask Penn if it was really true that he was a secret Jesuit. Penn threw down his napkin and stormed out of the room.

In view of his troubles his reaction was excusable. For years Penn had been denying that same question. His own people, those who knew him well both personally and by reputation, should have been well aware that the imputation of Jesuitism had no foundation whatsoever. The York questioning, moreover, came at a most unfortunate moment. Penn was being thwarted in almost everything he was undertaking. His Irish lands were yielding only two-thirds their normal rentals. Pennsylvania quitrents that should have brought in at least £400 a year returned "not a farthing, nor the present of a skin or a pound of tobacco." His court costs had soared to some £6000. If he could have lived normally in London a new land-sales campaign could have paid his debts, but rusticated as he was, he had to rely upon agents less efficient and certainly less trustworthy than himself. He yearned to return to America to lead a peaceful life, but he dared not lest, in his absence from England, his opponents should take away his charter.[13]

Amid his personal distresses, Penn had consideration for others. Knowing that his troubles, the arrests, and, even more, the repeated untrue reports would disturb his friends, especially those in America who could not check their accuracy, he wrote a number of what he called "epistles general." "I am innocent of the imputations of Jesuitism, Popery and plots," he wrote on one occasion. "I am well and at liberty," he added later. "My privacy is not because men have sworn truly but falsely."[14]

The rumors continued to mount. On New Year's Day, 1691, a routine Channel patrol caught three men en route to France with letters for King James. Two of the missives, written by William Penn, appeared superficially to be no more than polite inquiries about James' health;

government officials, mindful that when Sir William plotted a Stuart restoration he had used a secret code, suspected that his son was following the example.[15]

Francis Turner, Bishop of Ely, was guilty of a similar correspondence. Turner, a protégé of King James because "his sermons and his graces were short and witty," had, with six other bishops, turned against James when the latter issued a declaration of liberty of conscience. The rift, however, was over policy, not personality, and so, when James was in exile, Turner wrote him two letters of sympathy. Cautiously, he did not sign his name, but his handwriting betrayed him, and so he too was ordered arrested. Unlike Penn, he "kept out of the way" and escaped capture until 1696, when he was exiled. Somehow he escaped this policy also and lived in seclusion until his death five years later.

The multiplicity of charges against him must have thoroughly alarmed Penn. He had been guilty of nothing but imprudence in showing his loyalty to an ancient friendship, the letters expressing only good wishes for continued health and happiness, but those wishes could have been misinterpreted. Certainly they were by Henry Sidney, now the Earl of Romney and an influential privy councillor. In referring to the Channel incident, Sidney told the King, "Mr. Penn is as much mixed up in this matter as anybody." Yet when Penn, in ignorance of this judgment, asked him to explain the situation to the King, Sidney agreed to do so, but only on Penn's assurance, "in the presence of God," that he knew of no plots but that, should he ever hear of one, he would disclose it."[16]

Penn, however, declined politely but firmly to talk freely with Sidney or anyone else except the King and Queen, and not even with them unless assured of immunity. The attitude was difficult to understand. If Penn had nothing to report, there would have been no need for privacy; if he were wholly innocent, no need for any pledge of safety.

King William had no fear of Penn. He was perfectly willing to allow the Quaker to live in peace, but he exacted conditions. Penn must agree to retire from public life, to submit to a modified form of house arrest, and to report any information he might receive. Some said that the King insisted that Penn prove his submissiveness by first rendering the King some sort of service.[17]

As usual, reports conflicted. One version, by an avowed and unreliable critic of William Penn, said that he "as a tacit confession of great guilt ran up a cock loft, at least a chamber four story high, to hide himself." Another had him taking refuge in William Popple's house. Still another, more detailed, related how Penn was brought up from Sussex by a cavalry escort, from which he somehow escaped. He then took a house down by the Thames, the same house, it was said, in which King James had hidden, and secluded himself from everyone except his family and a few close friends. He bored a hole in the doorway through which he would peer to see anyone who knocked for entrance and, if the caller seemed suspicious, could then slip out a back door, jump into a skiff, and row off to safety.

The story had holes, of course. It implied that Penn could run away from horsemen, make his way to London, rent a house without detection, and install himself and his family without causing comment among his neighbors. Not only he but his family must be totally immured lest officials, seeing any of them upon the street, follow them to Penn's hiding place. Nor, if the authorities really desired to arrest him, would they have refrained from shadowing any or all of those close friends. When, moreover, law-enforcement authorities suspect that they know where a fugitive is hiding, they almost invariably guard all entrances and exits to the building. Nevertheless, such was the story related in a London guidebook.[18]

A simpler story, less fantastic but equally untrue, claimed that Penn had got off safely into France. Reports that Penn was a resident at the Stuart court-in-exile at St. Germaine were almost as recurrent as that canard about his Jesuitism, and it was quite as baseless.[19] So, too, was the variant that Guli made yearly visits to carry little presents to the exiled Royal family. Guli, described as "the daughter of a cavalier of good family," was said to have assured King James that, although she considered the Glorious Revolution to be necessary, she was acting from her "inviolable affection of gratitude."[20]

32

BLACKWELL'S ORDEAL

ENN WAS NOT ONLY ACTIVELY INVOLVED IN ENGLAND'S DOMESTIC
TROUBLES; PENNSYLVANIA'S PROBLEMS ALSO CONTINUED TO PLAGUE
HIM. ACCORDING TO THE HIGHLY COLORED COMPLAINTS OF BIASED
correspondents, each of whom had a private ax to grind, the province
was in chaos. As the ultimate authority Penn was supposed to find
remedies that would be efficient, fair, and, above all, speedily applicable.
If he did not do so at once, his informants warned, his colony would
collapse.[1]

Few of the hysterical letters gave specific details of what was happening, but all agreed that colonists were irreconcilably at odds. Royalists opposed Penn's partisans; Anglicans attacked Quakers; farmers
disliked cityfolk; national minorities—Germans, Welsh, Irish, Swedes,
and Dutch—quarreled with one another, though all ganged up against
the English. Everyone, of course, made matters difficult for tax collectors.
Vice and corruption were rampant; criminals terrorized the towns;
pirates ruled the waterfronts. Brotherly love had vanished. Unless
Penn acted quickly and decisively, the Holy Experiment was a failure.
Or so, at least, ran the hysterical reports.

But, some critics admitted, the fault might not be Penn's. Though
Royalists insisted that the Crown should take over Pennsylvania, the real
blame could be traceable to London's laws. Forbidden, as it was, to trade
freely or to manufacture necessities for itself, the province was on the
brink of ruin. The economy was sickly. Specie was scarce and prices
very high for what Pennsylvania must buy, though very low for what the
colony had to sell. Free labor was extremely scarce and, if available, was
inefficient.

From his personal knowledge of most of his correspondents, Penn should have been able to discount the exaggerations and to allow for prejudices, but even had he been free to act, there was little he could do from the wrong side of the Atlantic. His best recourse was to send a new deputy governor with instructions to correct the glaring evils and to restore good government.

By doing so he might lessen the pressures upon himself. He could not conscientiously abandon his pacifist principles or urge others to abandon theirs, but if he appointed a non-Quaker as his deputy, his adversaries in America and the militarists in England would at least understand that he was doing what he could do to be cooperative.

Nevertheless, he was reluctant to allow the government to pass out of Quaker control. On hearing from Dr. Thomas Lloyd, president of the Provincial Council, of general dissatisfaction with political conditions, he asked if Lloyd himself would take the deputyship. Dr. Lloyd, however, declined, as did other Quakers, doubtless because of their pacifist convictions, thus forcing Penn to look elsewhere for a new executive.[2]

Just at this juncture, in the early summer of 1688, a lady brought Penn an inscribed copy of her husband's treatise recommending the issue of paper currency based upon land as its security. She was Mrs. John Blackwell, daughter of General John Lambert. Her parentage did not particularly recommend her to Penn, for Lambert, one of Cromwell's cavalry officers, had been one who opposed sending Admiral Sir William on the West Indies expeditions and, further, had opposed the Restoration. But Mrs. Blackwell and her husband were well known to him; they were fellow landowners in Ireland and had been active in Dublin's Society of Friendship.

Mrs. Blackwell came on a mission; she asked Penn's help in arranging for the presentation of another copy of the treatise to the King. Penn, of course, agreed to do so and, in the course of the conversation, learned that her husband, Captain Blackwell, a cavalry commander, had been working in the financial department of the War Office. At the moment, he was in Boston as a financial consultant.

The information gave Penn an idea. Here was a man, accustomed to command, who knew something of provincial problems. Why not name Blackwell as Pennsylvania's governor? Both by reputation and from personal knowledge he knew Blackwell to be "of high respect as a wise and virtuous man," one who had been in a position to acquire thousands of pounds but who had been noteworthy for refusing the perquisities of office. His appointment would please the militarists and, quite probably, the Royalists; he would also, if necessary, take a firm stand against any hostile neighbors. "I thought," said Penn, "I had a treasure. Not being a Friend, he could better deal with those that were not, to stop their mouths and to be stiff with our neighbors on occasion.[3]

On July 12, 1688, he signed John Blackwell's commission. The new executive was to receive a £200 salary, to be drawn from the proceeds of quitrents paid by the colonists, together with an additional £100 if the inhabitants were willing to grant it to him. Blackwell was to have free use of Penn's Philadelphia house.

Had Penn passed on this background material at once to his people, much difficulty might have been avoided. Instead he sent Blackwell down to Pennsylvania without much advance notice and without telling anyone for almost a year and a half why he had selected this particular official. The neglect almost guaranteed Blackwell's failure.

In appointing Blackwell Penn violated his usual custom. The new-comer was not a Quaker, not a relative, not one of his Irish tenants or even a neighbor, nor was he either a protégé or a relative of Admiral Sir William. He was an active militarist, condemnation enough in a pacifist community; more than that, he had no friends in Pennsylvania, not being known personally to more than one or two at most, nor by reputa-tion to many others. In other than military or bureaucratic activity, he had no experience whatever.

His appointment, moreover, ran counter to provincial custom. In its eight-year history the colony had, at one time or another, seen no less than a dozen deputy governors, but all of them had been Pennsylvania residents, while Blackwell had never even seen the region. The tenure of office of his predecessors had been brief; the average service had been less than seven months. One unfortunate deputy, John Simcock, had not even served a single day; appointed in the morning, he was replaced by noon.[4]

Blackwell, on receiving his commission in November, packed up hur-riedly and started off for his new post. A request to Thomas Lloyd to provide a guide for Blackwell across New Jersey took Lloyd and Phila-delphia by surprise, this being their first intimation that the new deputy, a total stranger, was about to take control. Lloyd, obviously hurt at not having been informed, and perhaps disappointed by Penn's too ready acceptance of his reluctance to take the post, turned against Blackwell from the start. He sent no guide, thus obliging the new deputy to find his own way. The slight soured Blackwell against both Thomas Lloyd and the entire Pennsylvania Establishment.[5]

By no stretch of the imagination could Pennsylvania's welcome be termed effusive. Someone in New Jersey must have directed him to Pennsbury and there his greeting was cordial, but that was by the gardener, the chief servant in attendance, not by anyone in authority. Charles Pickering, the onetime counterfeiter, was also a houseguest there, but professing to be in great haste, he rode off to Philadelphia early in the morning, before Blackwell was ready to leave. Pickering did promise, however, to inform the officials that Blackwell was about to arrive. That promise was also counterfeit, for in spite of his supposed haste, Pickering rode so leisurely that Blackwell overtook him on the road. Presumably they rode to the capital together, though, according to one version, Pickering ignored the new governor.

Philadelphia was equally cold. After inquiring the location of Penn's house, where he was to live, Blackwell rode there, only to be left waiting in the road, the butt of mocking children, because no one living there seemed to know who he was. If the story is true, which seems incredible, Penn had failed to notify the province of the change in administration.

In any case, Blackwell arrived at an inconvenient moment. Markham, who was using the house as headquarters, seems to have been away from home, perhaps down in the Lower Counties, and the house staff was somewhat at a loss. They sent over to Thomas Lloyd's house to ask what they should do. Lloyd found overnight lodging for the governor, but declined to recognize Blackwell's commission. The document, he said, did not bear the proper seal. The Great Seal of Pennsylvania, Lloyd contended, should have been attached, and he, as sole custodian of that seal, had not yet affixed it.

Thus, Lloyd was ranking himself above the Proprietor, for he was requiring the Proprietor to seek his consent for such appointments. Next morning, however, he validated the appointment, allowed Blackwell to move into the Penn house (he found it cluttered), and invited the new governor to dinner.

Lloyd's courtesy was somewhat limited. Blackwell must have told the Keeper of the Great Seal that a meeting of the Provincial Council was to be called; apparently Lloyd did not tell him that a meeting might be difficult to arrange since the Council had not met, except once as a judicial body, for six months. It might not be possible to bring the members together on short notice. At any rate, when Blackwell went over to the meeting place to call the members into conference, he found the chamber shuttered.

Nor did the situation mend. The province accepted its new chief but raised serious questions about him. Why, as a military man with thirty years of service, had Blackwell won no higher rank than captain? Was the promotion failure due to lack of high-placed sponsors or to inability to buy a higher post? Someone in the War Office seemed to approve of him, but was that long stagnation in the captaincy a testimony to military inefficiency or to Blackwell's inability to get along with others? As a career officer he could not expect to be popular with the Society of Friends; nor, as a Cromwellian, would there be enthusiasm for him among Royal agents in the province.

As if these handicaps were not enough, Penn saddled Blackwell with impossible assignments; he was to accomplish what no predecessor had been able to achieve. He was to cancel all legislation enacted during the past five years, something that the legislature had refused to do, and then induce a newly elected legislature to repass the same laws, thus enabling another five-year grace before submitting Pennsylvania laws for London scrutiny. He was to hold a club over both the Provincial Council and the Assembly, by warning, if they were recalcitrant, that Penn would revoke the Frame and so withdraw whatever privileges Penn had thus far granted.[6]

None of this enhanced the province's love, admiration, or respect for poor John Blackwell. Nor was the situation improved when, well after his arrival, Council belatedly received a letter from Penn telling it that Blackwell was under orders to "bear down with a visible authority over vice and faction." The Council held no brief for vice, but to suppress partisanship seemed a direct blow to legislative freedom.

Moreover, having told Blackwell to guide, if not, indeed, to dominate the legislature, Penn then told the Provincial Council that the new man, the outsider, the militarist, was wholly at its mercy. "If he does not please you, he shall be laid aside."[7]

Why Penn issued contradictory orders that insured conflict is inexplicable, particularly as it was virtually impossible for him to arbitrate disputes. Distant as he was, three thousand miles across the Atlantic, he could not know what was happening, nor would he be able to take immediate effective action. Dependent upon correspondents who were very far from being objective reporters, he could not make wise decisions on the basis of their sketchy, highly colored, and contradictory accounts of what had happened. Any advice he could give could not possibly reach America until at least two months after an emergency occurred.

Neither Blackwell nor the Council made much effort to avoid conflict, and even less to understand each other's point of view. Two months after his arrival in the province, both Council and Assembly complained that the Deputy Governor was unkind, harsh, and arbitrary. "If he be not removed it will ruin thy interest. Blackwell was equally antagonistic. The Quakers, he said, were hypocritical. Pretending to be saintly, they were selfish. "Each prays for his neighbor on First Days and then preys upon him for the other six."[8] Actually, the legislators asserted, Blackwell governed by force. Convening sessions in his own house, with an armed guard stationed at the door to overawe the members, Blackwell sat there, rapier at his side, "to command us naked men of the Assembly who have no refuge before the Lord."[9]

The Deputy Governor further antagonized the merchant class by insisting, on Penn's orders, that the Navigation Acts be strictly enforced; unless this were done, said Penn, quo warranto would be invoked. Blackwell went further by suggesting that traders cut their profits. Some of the merchants, and to the popular mind, he implied, nearly all, were buying smuggled goods at bargain rates and selling them at exorbitant prices.

Though the Friends were rapidly losing their almost unchallenged control of Pennsylvania, they still represented, if not a majority of the population, at least a preponderant number of the most influential citizens. While Blackwell intended his strictures to apply to only certain wholesalers, the entire Quaker community considered itself insulted.

Council, still a spokesman for Quaker merchants, responded angrily. Samuel Richardson challenged Blackwell's right to rule. Penn was, of course, the governor, said Richardson, but he had no right to delegate his powers. Blackwell, retorted in what six councilmen, in a joint letter to Penn, termed "factious, mutinous, seditious, turbulent" language.[10]

Thomas Lloyd went further. Accused by Blackwell of having been illegally elected to office, Lloyd proposed that Council fine Blackwell for maladministration. Blackwell retorted by attempts to impeach Lloyd for "crymes, offenses and misdemeanors which were well known to himself, the Governor and divers others." Lloyd, in turn, replied by "sharp and unsavory expressions." Then, when Blackwell, in accordance with Penn's instructions, asked Lloyd, as Master of the Rolls, to provide copies of all legislation then on the statute books, Lloyd refused. He did not, said Lloyd, understand what Blackwell wanted, was too busy to take the time to find out, and, furthermore, not all the laws were available and, if they were, were so badly drafted that no one could really know just what they said. "There is no depending on them," said Lloyd.[11]

Before Penn could return one of his customary recommendations that everyone calm down, avoid factionalism, and live harmoniously, peppery Samuel Richardson, smarting perhaps under the charge of criminality, challenged the Deputy Governor's right to tell him what to do. He spoke so hotly that Blackwell ordered him ejected. Richardson refused to leave. "I was not brought hither by thee and I will not go by thy order. I was sent by the people and thou hast no right to put me out."[12]

Blackwell, in his frustration, burst out in protest against not only the non-cooperative Lloyd but the Quaker Establishment as well. "No person, though ever so respectful, if not under the dialect of a Friend, can have civil treatment or justice done by so high a criminal." The Assembly, he alleged, was no better; it was composed of discontented and highly criminal members, except for one man who, although worthy, had never been properly elected to it. Quite possibly because he suspected that the Proprietor might not see much harm in Quaker attitudes, Blackwell offered to resign.[13]

Richardson was, of course, perfectly correct insofar as his membership was concerned, but his outburst shocked his colleagues. Though they approved his sentiments, they objected to his manners and so voted to eject him, not to please Blackwell but because of breach of decorum. The angry Richardson stormed out, shouting that he didn't care if he never came back; but when Blackwell called a snap election for the next day to fill the vacancy, Richardson changed his mind, announced his candidacy, and won a triumphant reelection. The rejection of Richardson for what, to Blackwell, was the wrong reason, followed by his reinstatement, angered the Deputy Governor. His objections caused a turmoil in the legislative Council sessions, comments which the writer of the minutes softened to "many intemperate speeches and passages happened, fit to be held in oblivion."[14]

They were not held in oblivion by John Blackwell. He wrote a friend, "I do not hesitate to say (and you may tell Mr. Penn so if you see him) that the wild beasts that fill the forests here can govern better than the witless zealots who make a monkey house of the Assembly."[15]

The Deputy Governor, while waiting a reply from Penn accepting his resignation, continued his losing course. In obedience to his instructions, he asked to have the laws repealed. Thomas Lloyd again refused, giving the astonishing excuse that no one in Pennsylvania, including himself as Master of the Rolls, really knew what laws existed, where they could be found, or, if they should become available, just what they meant. If so, Blackwell asked very reasonably, why not repeal them? Think the matter over, he suggested, and return tomorrow to cancel them.[16]

But when Council reconvened the Deputy Governor had another matter on his mind. One of the councilmen, he had learned, had sent a copy of the Frame to the printer's to be published. This, said Blackwell, was very dangerous. Penn, he told an astonished Council, was dead set against publication, a rather remarkable statement in view of the Proprietor's own extensive use of publicity. The offending councilman retorted that not only had Penn sponsored publication of documents basic to English liberties but had suggested using the Frame as a schoolroom text. Blackwell was unimpressed. It was all very well, he explained, for Pennsylvanians to be familiar with the Frame, but for outsiders to know about its contents would be unwise. He ordered the councilman to leave the chamber while Council decided whether to expel him.[17]

Council wrangled as angrily and as pointlessly as it had argued the Richardson case, on one occasion so heatedly that Blackwell, holding sessions in his own house because, he said, the Council chambers were too small and hot, tried to put all the remaining members out. "But divers remained," the minutes read, "and a good deal of confused noise and clamor was expressed at, and about, the Governor's room, which occasioned persons standing by in the streets to stand still to hear."[18] Eventually, when most persons had forgotten what the commotion was all about, Council, instead of repealing the laws, confirmed everything already passed, though neglecting to clarify the meaning.[19]

As though domestic troubles were not enough to pester the province, there were fears of foreign invasion. Sussex, most southern of the Three Lower Counties, sent word that Senecas and Frenchmen were about to invade the lower Delaware. Blackwell, without stopping to wonder how Canadians and New York Indians intended to reach the Lower Counties, called upon the pacifist Council to raise a militia.[20] Council, whether because it considered the rumor absurd, because it would not countenance warfare, or simply because it opposed anything that Blackwell suggested, declined to be stampeded. Even William Markham, he who always kept his arms in readiness, pooh-poohed the rumor. Following his suggestion that everybody stop talking about the supposed dangers lest the talk frighten the women and children, Council advised Blackwell to warn the people against spreading groundless fears. This particular warning against the incursions of red men whom the councilmen called "Sennekers" was, as it happened, premature, but, by odd coincidence, it arrived almost on the very day that the King, three thousand miles away across the ocean, was sending out a call for Pennsylvania to contribute men and money to help repel a French assault from Canada upon New York. The Royal order did not, however, reach Pennsylvania until eight months later.[21]

Blackwell, more at home in the field than in a legislative chamber, urged immediate compliance. When the Society of Friends, opposing war preparation on religious grounds, side-stepped a decision, he sneered that the province was too miserly to incur the cost. The evasion and the tightfistedness sickened him; he yearned to leave the province. It was not a sudden whim. Throughout the whole series of frustrations he had been buoyed by the thought that someday he could escape from Pennsylvania. He could not make up his mind whether Quaker legislators, the local climate, or the myriads of mosquitoes constituted the greatest plague but, as he kept reminding Penn, "I only wait the hour of my deliverance."[22]

December 12, 1689, was the day for Blackwell's jubilation. In a packet of letters just received from England he found the message he awaited. The hour of deliverance or, as Blackwell put it, of redemption, was at hand. Instead of being governor, he was now receiver-general, the quitrent treasurer, whose salary would be paid, as heretofore, from whatever he could collect from un-cooperative colonists.[23]

Blackwell, jubilant over his release from an uncongenial job that he now said he had never desired, boasted that he had held his position despite all that had been done to get him fired and, finally, thanked God that he was rid of it. As far as the otherwise voluminous minutes of the meeting show, not a single councilman uttered a word of farewell as he stalked out of the room. During his year in office no finger had been lifted to provide him with that extra £100 that Penn had intimated might be voted him.[24]

Blackwell's troubles were not over. All winter he did his utmost to collect quitrents only to discover that no one really knew how much was due, who had paid anything whatever, or, if anything had been paid, just what had become of the money. "I have been tried beyond my patience," Blackwell wrote to Penn. "I got not so much as would discharge my horse's standing and ran into debt for every bit of bread I ate."[25]

Philadelphians, he said thereafter, were hypocrites. They preached on First Days about loving their fellow men, but on all other days they broke whatever laws they made. Councilmen talked piously of social service, but they were selfish and egotistic. He returned to Boston, unemployed but happy to be free.

33

LOST AND REGAINED

L ONDON HAD NOT THE FAINTEST SYMPATHY FOR BLACKWELL'S TRIBU-
LATIONS NOR FOR PENN'S PERSISTENT MONEY TROUBLES. NEITHER
PROVINCIAL MALADMINISTRATION NOR THE CONSTANT BICKERING IN
Pennsylvania concerned England in the least, save only as the unrest
added excuses for quo warranto proceedings. The Royal government did,
however, strongly object to Pennsylvania's pacifism.

The criticism was unfair. England had known from the outset that
the Quaker colony would not fight. Though Charles II's original charter
draft had authorized the Proprietor to maintain an army and a navy to
make war upon invaders or national enemies, Whitehall had never any
delusion that the power would be exercised. Pennsylvania, it was clearly
understood, would neither take up arms nor tax itself to pay for warfare.

Nevertheless, since it became evident that the Lower Counties were
not pacifist and since non-Quaker elements in Pennsylvania itself were
increasing both in numbers and in influence, since Penn was mellowing,
and since there were recurrent rumors that the French were moving down
from Canada, the Crown believed it might be safe to test out colonial
sentiment. Accordingly the government, pointing out that New York was
being threatened by Canadians, politely asked all colonies to help their
harassed neighbor.[1]

The appeal marked a change in national policy. London, hitherto
uninterested in intercolonial cooperation, was now bent on setting up an
empire. Accustoming the provinces to work together in the common
interest would, the bureaucrats believed, break down the power of such
proprietors as remained and so facilitate monarchial control; they failed
to foresee that provincial unity might, in time, promote a desire for
American independence.

To the surprise and disappointment of such bodies as the Privy Council, almost every province sent excuses, the tone of the objections being stronger in proportion to their distance from invasion danger. Some provinces were busy defending their own frontiers; others professed to be much too poor. If, said one or two, others were doing nothing, why should they? Most of those who helped gave only promises or, at best, merely token aid.

Pennsylvania realized that any Canadian invaders must first build a fleet to cross the New Mediterranean Sea or else, after fighting New York, thread their way through endless forests. The province failed to become excited. Markham, Holme the surveyor, Lasse Cock, and a few others, professing themselves "in no small terror" at the imminence of French attack, supported the plea to help New York, but all the Provincial Council would allow was permission for them to go up the Schuylkill to see if Indians were restive. Apparently the red men were peaceful, so there was no call to arms. Had anyone inquired why nothing was done, the answer would have been obvious; pacifists had strong religious scruples against war.[2]

The indifference of Pennsylvanians, whose lives and property had not been in the slightest danger, angered the Three Lower Counties. They were vulnerable to pirate raids and there were memories of Maryland aggression. They clamored for a militia. A New Castle man appeared, bearing a commission that he said Penn had issued seven years ago. He vainly offered himself as commander in chief of a defense force.[3]

The rejected demand for protection was only one item in the Lower Counties' unhappiness with the Pennsylvania union. Never more than a peripheral addition to the Quaker province, "territories annexed to Pennsylvania," they resented having no individual identity. As a province of longer standing than Pennsylvania, they considered themselves entitled to seniority but had graciously consented to equality, only to find that as Pennsylvania grew in wealth and prosperity, they were being subordinated. More and more, the residents of the Province, which even lacked a name of its own, talked among themselves about seceding from the union with Pennsylvania.

Everyone looked to Penn for guidance, but he was in no position to afford effective leadership. Officially, as Proprietor and Governor, he could exercise extensive powers, but it had never been practical to rule from a distance and, now that he regarded himself as a persecuted hermit, it was impossible. Nor was this all. Some of his Quaker friends were drifting away from him because of his political activities, and, as usual, he was in financial difficulties. His faculties were as keen and alert as ever, but he was subject to innumerable distractions.

Had he been free to give full attention to the Lower Counties, it is not wholly certain that his mediation would have been as impartial as it would have been in earlier years. Enforced seclusion, after a dozen years of various harassments, had shortened his temper, made him a little testy, induced him to suspect slights and injustices, if not conspiracies, against him. Now that his influence at court had diminished, he was more and more often dropping hints that it still was strong and that one who opposed him might suffer for it. He never resorted to outright threats, but he left no doubt that he had resources not possessed by other men.

The constant bickering, the backbiting, jealousies, tale-bearings, quarreling of the provincial officials sickened him. "Your division has torn me to pieces and opened those wounds that malice gave me," he told Markham and Thomas Lloyd. "Oh friends, I came to you in love, I left you in love with resolutions of returning to you with all that was dear to me in this world. . . . I am a man of sorrows and you augment my grief."[4]

The inefficiencies, discords, and disturbances delighted the Royalists. Wild rumors spread that Pennsylvanians lived under conditions that modernists would call anarchistic. Everything that had happened was exaggerated in the telling. Penn's advice, more hortatory than helpful, for all officials to "love, love, forgive and help and serve one another," while calculated to produce "the happy life of concord," failed dismally to remedy the situation.

The Council steadily refused to mend its ways, continuing to hold out against Royal orders for war appropriations. The issue, said the Pennsylvanians, was a matter of principle; London deemed the refusal not only a defiance of the King's command but a demonstration of the colony's holier-than-thou attitude. New York, which had asked Pennsylvania to send only eighty men, regarded Pennsylvania's inaction as hard-hearted, contemptuous, and niggardly.

The Lords of Trade and Plantations seized the opportunity to recommend to the King that Pennsylvania's charter be vacated, that the Crown assume control and perhaps merge the province with Virginia, Maryland, or New York.[5]

The King in council, though rejecting the suggestion of a merger, unified the war effort in the American theater by placing all provinces from Massachusetts to Maryland under one command. To head the combined force he named Colonel Benjamin Fletcher, veteran of thirty years' military service. Since some of that experience had been in Ireland under the Duke of Ormonde at the time of the Carrickfergus Mutiny, it is not impossible that he and Penn had served together in that campaign.[6]

In any case, Penn failed to welcome him. Instead, he dashed off a letter warning Fletcher to move with exceeding caution. As the Pennsylvania charter had not been legally revoked, the province, insisted Penn, remained his personal property; he held legal title to both soil and government. "I give you this caution," Penn said darkly, "that I am an Englishman," meaning thereby, no doubt, that he would insist upon his rights and hold Fletcher to strict account. He went further, coming close to rebellion by urging Pennsylvanians to resist any aggression that Fletcher might attempt.[7]

Soon thereafter Penn asked his people for financial assistance. Reminding them that the province had already cost him £11,000 and that he had lost the Irish rentals that had once yielded him £1500 yearly, he suggested that one hundred citizens each lend him £100, interest free, to be repaid within four years.[8]

The response was silence. Fletcher sneered openly. "However much they appear his friends," Fletcher said, referring to the provincial leaders, "they stagger when he comes near their pocketbooks. Those that are able want better security and those that are not excuse themselves, saying they would if they could."[9]

It was not much consolation that Fletcher was having no better luck. Though he was the King's personal choice, with strong support from the Lords of Trade and Plantations, Fletcher, who, according to his enemies, had been a barber and an actor before turning soldier, may not have been the best man for his new position. He was a patriotic Englishman and a staunch defender of Royal rights, but a routine soldier with nothing but contempt for the "handful of vermin" who were his enemies. The French and Indians, he complained, would not fight fairly; they skulked behind trees or hid in swamps instead of coming out into the open to be shot. Neither could he understand why the colonists were restless under English rule and so jealous, suspicious, and in some cases hostile toward each other. Though he praised Americans as "noble colonies of British," he had no sympathy whatever for colonial self-government and no skill in what he termed "cajoling an assembly."[10]

Fletcher came to Philadelphia April 25, 1693, intending, in conformity with his commission as captain-general, to enlist troops and to lead them against the vermin. He intended also to dissolve the legislature, to appoint a new council, to hold elections for a new assembly that would have the full powers denied them by Penn's Frame, to cancel laws he considered in conflict with English codes, and to conduct the Admiralty courts that had jurisdiction over the Navigation Acts.

Many of the old Establishment opposed him from the very start. Thomas Lloyd, his first choice as deputy governor, refused to serve, as did most of the former Council. Markham, however, did accept the position of second-in-command, while Robert Turner and Lasse Cock remained as councilmen.[11]

New Castle, if one may believe the minutes of Fletcher's Council, was more co-operative. After holding a council meeting at five o'clock in the morning, he and Markham went down to the Three Lower Counties, where they were greeted by a gunfire salute, "great shouting and joy." It was the same type of celebration for a governor who they hoped would free them from Pennsylvania as they had accorded Penn when they thought he would join them to that province.[12]

Fletcher then proceeded to invalidate both the Frame and the Royal charter. The old laws, he said, were invalid, partly because they had never been properly sealed, more importantly because he found them contrary to English laws. The Crown, he insisted, possessed all powers pertaining to revenue, legislation, warfare, and judicial cases concerning life and death. These powers, which he called "reglia" (he may have meant regalia) could not be alienated. A king, said Fletcher, might lawfully delegate such matters to others but only during his own lifetime; that permission lapsed with the monarch's death. The legislators may not have been men of the wisest, most moral, and best repute as Penn wished them to be, but they certainly were better lawyers than Fletcher. When Fletcher demanded that all laws be repealed because, he said, they were illegal—the same demand that Penn had made, though for a different reason—the Assembly refused point-blank.[13]

Either the Assembly did not believe him or they did not think there was any danger. As good Quakers the assemblymen stood firmly against war. Fletcher gave them no credit for high-mindedness; he thought them miserly, untruthful, and perhaps disloyal. They must choose, he said, whether they considered the province subject to the King or to the Proprietor; they could not hold a dual allegiance. If, he warned, they chose to follow Penn and to reject their Majesties, they must expect to be annexed to New York or to Maryland.[14]

The great stumbling block was, as it had been under Blackwell, the furnishing of men and money to help New York beat back the French and Indians. Fletcher appealed, as had Blackwell, to Pennsylvania's loyalty; the province was in duty bound to heed a sovereign's call for aid. When this argument failed, as it had previously, Fletcher tried to arouse sympathy for fellow Englishmen threatened by a common enemy. When this evoked no response, he tried to terrify the lawmakers. He was, he pointed out, a professional soldier; as such he could see, as any officer might see, that Pennsylvania was vulnerable. Five hundred enemy soldiers, he declared, could conquer Pennsylvania in as little time as it would take to march through the province. When that time comes, he threatened, as it will come, you will beg in vain for help.[15]

In any case, Fletcher questioned their sincerity. They prated of their principles, but was not this merely an excuse for avoiding paying the war taxes that other provinces were paying? They spoke of nonresistance, but, he noted, they took good care to wall their gardens, to lock their doors, and to keep mastiffs around their houses. Why not, then, have forts and soldiers? They talked of charity and philanthropy. Very well, then, why not vote money to clothe naked war victims and to feed the hungry? He did not stress the probability that, though no Pennsylvania money would in his catchy phrase "be dipped in blood," it might be used as bribes to keep the Indians from defecting to the French.[16]

The Assembly, to save face, offered a compromise. (Thus far it had passed but one important law, an act to jail without food or water any Negro gadding about on First Day without a written permit of a master. He was also to suffer thirty-nine lashes, well laid on.) But if Fletcher recognized the Frame, together with the provincial laws already enacted, the Assembly would vote the money he desired.[17]

There was another proviso, not written into the law but thoroughly understood. The money, a tax on property of a penny in the pound, was not in any sense to be used for warfare; as far as wording was concerned, it had nothing whatever to do with New York or with French and Indian invaders. No, not at all. The proceeds of this tax were to be Pennsylvania's testimony to its loyalty to William and Mary, a free-will offering because they wished to show their gratitude to such benign monarchs. They would be completely free to use the money in whatever way they chose.[18]

Fletcher, as their Majesties' representative, supposed that the King and Queen might like to spend the offering to buy uniforms for military officers and perhaps to give a little to various Indian chiefs who might otherwise go over to the French. He did not, however, collect as much as he expected. Though to everyone's surprise heavily Quaker Chester County raised 90 percent of its quota and Philadelphia and Kent at least three-quarters of the amounts due, militarist Sussex turned in less than half. War hawk New Castle and Quaker Bucks gave not a single shilling. The tax, expected to yield £760, actually brought in only half that sum.[19]

Pennsylvania's indifference angered Fletcher. "I never yet found so much self-conceit," he complained. "They will rather die than deal with carnal weapons." When he inquired into the situation elsewhere, however, he discovered that the indifference was not confined to Quaker areas. He asked provincial leaders from as far south as Virginia to attend a New York conference to plan joint warfare against the French only to discover, to his amazement, that few provincials were really interested. Only Virginia, Connecticut, and Pennsylvania sent delegates; the other provinces simply ignored the invitation.[20]

The next year, in 1694, Fletcher tried again to gain Pennsylvania's participation in King William's War. The Assembly, which by this time must have known that by his appeals for food and clothing he really meant troop maintenance, renewed the tax of a penny in the pound and added a new six-shilling levy on the propertyless.[21]

There was a further addition. The first £400 raised by the taxes was earmarked for the salaries of Deputy Governor Markham and of Master of the Rolls, Thomas Lloyd. Whatever was left over should be presented to their Majesties "for whatever they desired."

Fletcher's opinion of the Assembly was never very high; he failed to appreciate its deftness in concealing its surrender. Not all the members were Friends; but like the Quakers, they were, to his mind, insincere and hypocritical. He had no patience with people who would not take an oath but who had no hesitancy in making an affirmation, who would not swear but who would emphasize a statement by making it "in the presence of God," who would not vote money for warfare but who would give it to the King for any use that he might make of it. He also thought that they were playing a trick upon the King, by promising him whatever tax money might be left over after paying those salaries when probably there would be no surplus. With commendable loyalty to his sovereigns, therefore, he protested that the first fruits of that tax should go to William and Mary and whatever was left over to the officials. Better still, let the King and Queen have all the money and trust them, in their well-known generosity, to make the salary payments.

The suggestion failed. David Lloyd, now Speaker of the Assembly, complained that, though Pennsylvania had raised funds to relieve the starving and to clothe the naked, no Pennsylvanian had been present when the gifts were passed out and so the province had received no credit for the aid. Lloyd was careful not to make any direct accusations, but he left no doubt that he suspected that the tax money, in spite of all the promises, really had been "dipped in blood."

Pennsylvania's seeming compliance pleased a London not fully aware of the maneuverings that lay beneath the Assembly voting. Penn took advantage of his opportunity. In July 1694 he begged the Lords of Trade and Plantations to give him back his charter.

Penn's arguments were simple, sound, and true, though not necessarily complete. As a clever courtier he used all the techniques he had learned, pulling all the wires at his command, coloring his pleas to meet the whims and prejudices of those who must pass upon his petition. Pennsylvania, he led them to understand, had seen the light; his people, cooperating with their neighbors, were participating in the common struggle against France. He did not bother to explain that while appropriations had been authorized, as evidenced by the minutes of the legislature, the sheriffs were making little effort to collect the levies.[22]

Somehow the Lords, several of them Penn's personal friends, gained the impression that Penn was promising dutiful obedience to Royal wishes, that he himself was about to go to America to see that soldiers were recruited and defenses put in order precisely as the Lords desired. Penn certainly never said such things in clear and unequivocal terms; but the Lords, believing that he had made such promises, returned his province on August 20, 1694. It had been in Royal hands for thirty months.

Penn reappointed Markham as his deputy. He did not tell his cousin anything about commitments that may have been made to the Lords, but he did drop hints as to specific action that simply must be taken; actions that were not in strict accord with his own philosophy nor with the wishes of his people but which were unavoidable.

> That things are not just now in that posture as you may reasonably desire, you must not take amiss, for neither will the straitness of the times or the circumstances we are in to the Lords of the Plantations permit another method at this time. . . . You know, I believe, as well as I, what has been the main obstacle and is still. . . . We must creep where we cannot go and it is as necessary for us in the things of this life as to be wise as to be innocent. . . . A word to the wise is enough.[23]

Markham thoroughly understood the implications. The legislature, which Fletcher had prorogued in June 1694, did not meet again until February, when Markham officially informed it that Penn was again in power. He passed on, as instructed by Penn, the conditions under which William and Mary had graciously restored Pennsylvania to its proprietor. Whenever Fletcher, as Commander in Chief and Governor of New York, found it necessary to call for help, Pennsylvania would be required to send and to support a force of eighty men. The call was not long delayed. On April 15, 1695, Fletcher asked for the men "or their equivalent in money."

The lawmakers reverted to their former ways. They were perfectly willing to set up a naval patrol off Cape Henlopen to report the presence of any hostile men-of-war, but as to appropriating any money, they would go no further than to levy a tax of one-and-six in the pound, £300 of which would go for Markham's salary, £250 to pay provincial expenses, and whatever balance remained to satisfy government debts. There was, Council regretted, nothing more available; the harvests were bad and some sort of plague was killing off the cattle. Markham, whom Penn believed to be a mercenary man, volunteered to forego his salary; he would rather, he said, "be left out than ignore the Queen's wish," but Council, following its well-worn practice, simply ignored him.[24]

It did not meet again for one full year.

Whatever his critics may have thought, William Penn was consistent. In his youth, to be sure, he had done military service, but in his maturity, after his convincement, he could not resort to force nor dip his money in blood. His conscience would not allow him to order, or even to advise, his agents to take such action; but he had no compunctions against urging them to pay close attention to Royal wishes; he could go no further than to hope that they would please the Crown—a vague direction which both London and the province might interpret as they pleased. On the ground that in such matters Pennsylvania was self-governing, he issued no commands to raise troops or to furnish money for armed activity; neither did he comment specifically on the provincial response.

Penn's record remained clear. Somehow he satisfied the Lords of Trade and Plantations, but not a scrap of evidence indicates any definite promise nor any firm commitment.

Such policies explain why commentators unfriendly to the Proprietor believed him guilty of compromising with his principles, even of casuistry if not indeed a hypocrite.

It was not the first instance of a sort of shiftiness, nor would it be the last.

Most of Penn's difficulties were semantic. He was capable of forthright expression, of declaring precisely what he knew to be eternal Truth, as when he crusaded for liberty of conscience, freedom of religion, the basic rights of man, the gift of honest, popular government, the absolute necessity of righteous living. On issues of less overwhelming importance, however, conduct not dictated by the laws of God, he sometimes evaded anything specific, wrapping his thoughts in cloudy phrases. His court career had taught him the politician's art of conveying an impression without committing himself to a position from which he might later wish to withdraw; thus he could seem to agree with others by resorting to the little nod, the small smile, a slight gesture, a deprecatory shrug (though probably he never descended to the knowing wink). If words were unavoidable he could employ them skillfully, seeding his sentences with weasel words, as when he declared himself ready to grant anything that honest men could reasonably desire for the public good.

Nowhere was this skill better evidenced than when he induced the London bureaucrats to restore his province to him. As a firm pacifist, convinced that God strictly forbade murder, he could never have promised what some of the Lords believed that he had promised: to set up a militia in Pennsylvania, to build forts, and to supply men or money to fight the French and Indians. What he did promise was to see that the Pennsylvania Council and Assembly received the King's commands, that he would insist that they give all due respect to Royal wishes, and that he would do all he could to make sure that the legislators acted properly. If, then, the Lords misunderstood just what he meant, they would have done well to study the English language carefully. He always spoke the truth and nothing but the truth, though not necessarily all the truth.

34

DISCORD BRINGS UNION

DISAPPOINTED BY THE COLLAPSE OF HIS HOLY EXPERIMENT, DISILLU-
SIONED BY THE ALL TOO HUMAN WEAKNESSES OF HIS PEOPLE, PENN
WAS PESSIMISTIC. HIS FINANCES WERE IN POOR CONDITION, HIS
estate reduced, his remaining English and Irish lands heavily mortgaged,
the interest upon them a heavy drain, and for long periods his freedom
of movement was restricted. Even so, he exaggerated his plight, for he
was no longer being persecuted, and as long as he kept clear of active politics, he was not harassed by the authorities. Though in more straitened
circumstances than he liked, he lived in greater comfort than the vast
majority of his contemporaries. With ample justification he considered
himself ill-used, but his enforced seclusion gave him peace and opportunity to plan for the betterment of his province and of the world. That
he could not supervise the execution of the improvements he suggested
was no great loss, for Penn was always more the theorist than the administrator. His counsel was fruitful not only for his day but for posterity.

The province stood in great need of a calm, resourceful mediator like
William Penn. Time and time again, in English and in American colonial affairs, he had quietly, and, in the main successfully, resolved disputes
that could have disrupted harmony. Now in Pennsylvania, in the early
years of the 1690s, his service could have been helpful.

Unfortunately, when ordinarily reasonable people quarreled in the
late seventeenth century, the first casualties were usually courtesy, fairness, and all too often truth. Discord was no novelty among the pacifists,
nor censorship unknown among the passionate Quaker believers in freedom of expression. They stood for tolerance, but to assure conformity,
they set up strict rules of discipline. Stubbornly devoted to liberty of
conscience, they insisted that any Friend should be free to think, to act,

and to speak as he desired, provided only that they remain wholly orthodox. A nonconformist could be "read out of meeting" or disowned, and
thus be thrown into spiritual isolation.

Paradoxically again, excessive conformity might be construed as
unorthodox. Such an individual was George Keith, a stiff-necked fifty-
four-year-old Scot who had come to America after having been imprisoned in Newgate for refusal to swear an oath. Five years later he had
become the first headmaster of the newly established institution later
known as William Penn Charter School. The position paid a £50 salary,
an excellent salary for the times, with the free use of a house, and if he
proved satisfactory and remained longer than a year, he would receive
£120, almost as much as the deputy governor's salary. Students too poor
to pay were to be admitted on free scholarships.[1]

No one denied that Keith was an able teacher, but many criticized his
learning and his methods as pedantic. In both scholastic and religious
matters he insisted on the strict letter of the law, but he differed from the
leaders on just what that letter required. His theology evoked very stringent opposition, especially when he amended the classic doctrines laid
down by George Fox, the founder of the Society of Friends. Orthodox
Quakers, professing a Christianity based upon strict interpretation of the
Scriptures, rejected Keith's acceptance of theories and practices engrafted
upon the teaching of the Apostles. Keith's welcoming of ideas drawn
from historic and dogmatic Christian practices or, worse, from mystics
who believed in the pre-existence and transmigration of souls, shocked
them.

The rank and file of Quakerism neither knew nor cared much about
abstruse and esoteric theory, but the violent branding by Quaker leaders
of Keith as a heretic, and Keith's angry retorts in kind, infected the
Quaker public. Both sides used the unrestrained verbal violence then current; the Society of Friends split into hostile factions.

In defending himself against what he considered unfair personal
attack, Keith went to extremes. He did not hesitate to identify by name
the many individuals whom he accused of hypocrisy: those who openly or
privately, ignored Quaker tabus against vanity and ostentation, those
who took even the slightest action that could be construed as furthering
war efforts. When, therefore, in 1692 a pirate stole a sloop, Keith objected
that the law-enforcement agents, in chasing the thief down the river, were
committing an act of war.

The protest might, in itself, have been ignored as ridiculous, for it
would have permitted thieves to escape punishment, but there were other
incidents, doubtlessly unfairly reported: Keith's insistence on a private
staircase for his own adherents to the meetinghouse gallery, a fistfight
which he described as a gentle stroking of the face "as a nurse would do a
suckling child," the abuse of a speaker as "a nonsensical puppy." Every-

one was well aware that, in the words of one of his critics, he was "a sort of an odd, singular man," but when he condemned the whole Society of Friends for failing to obey St. John's command to "walk in the Light" and then doubted whether the Inner Light was itself sufficient, he went too far.[2]

Philadelphia Yearly Meeting, which had once upheld Keith, reversed itself, without, Keith asserted, hearing him. Two other yearly meetings, Maryland and Barbados, condemned him, not so much, one declared, for his exaggerations as for the manner in which he expressed them.[3]

Though all this time Penn had been in England, Keith insisted that he was the ultimate cause of these decisions. Penn, for his part, declared that he had sought to conciliate the man and had expressed a love for him, but Keith retorted that Penn, a persecutor and a liar, had acted "in a most un-Christian manner, most unjustly and falsely," denying him any sort of hearing, "fair or unfair."

Regardless of the truth or falsity of Keith's charges (and there must have been some basis of fact, else Robert Turner and James Claypoole, among many others, would not have allied themselves with him), he was no match for Penn in the ensuing battle of invective.[4]

Veteran of innumerable verbal mud-slinging contests with people whom he described as filthy, base, and villainous non-Christians, men "whose word and a lie are synonymous throughout America," several of whom were, according to Penn, "the greatest of villains," Penn's retorts were devastating. Linking Keith with "heretics of the deepest dye," Penn alleged that Keith "had stomach enough to lick up even T. Hicks' vomit and wrath enough to spew it out at his quondam Quaker friends." He was, said Penn, "a noisy, froward deserter."[5]

Keith had had quite enough of Pennsylvania, where Quakers cherished "more damnable heresies and doctrines of the Devil" than members of any other Protestant sect. He could no longer tolerate, he said, the "fools, ignorant heathens, infidels, silly souls, liars, heretics, rotten Ranters, Muggletonians" who made up the Society of Friends. He forsook the Society of Friends, had himself baptized an Anglican and, still wearing Quaker costumes, preached in England for the Established Church. Then, in 1702, he returned to America to urge Quakers "in the Queen's name, to return to good old Mother Church."[6]

Some of Keith's followers, unwilling to follow him out of the Quaker movement, set up a separate organization, the Christian Quakers, which continued for more than two centuries before re-entering the main body of the Society of Friends.

For William Penn the rift in Quakerism could not have come at a worse time. He was, as it happened, no longer under close surveillance. In 1693 he had moved with the ailing Guli to Hoddeston, twenty miles from London, not too far from his youthful home at Wanstead.

He was not wholly cleared, however; he still had fences to mend. Little news of the Keithean controversy had reached the general public, but fleeting echoes of his supposed Jacobite and Jesuitical sympathies still circulated, and King William, though he had known Penn for several years, still harbored doubts about his loyalty. Penn's friends Rochester and Sidney disabused the King of whatever misconceptions still remained. They had known Penn, they said, for thirty years and had never known him to do an ill thing. On this assurance, the King, in December 1693, accorded Penn full freedom. Penn had then gone to the Bull and Mouth, taking Springett with him, to reestablish himself in Quaker circles, and so, as far as general repute was concerned, all was well; but he was not entirely free of worry.[7]

Guli did not seem to be improving, and on February 23, 1694, she died, her hand upon Penn's breast. Her last words were, "I never to my knowledge did a wicked thing in all my life."[8]

Penn paid her a magnificent tribute, calling her "the best of wives and women . . . the best in 10,000." She was, he said, "an entire and constant friend, of a more than common capacity and greater modesty and humility, yet most equal and undaunted in danger . . . an easy mistress and good neighbor, especially to the poor . . . neither lavish nor penurious but an example of industry as well as of other virtues."

He did not allow a grief as deep as that under which he had labored at the time of his mother's death to interfere with public duty, though it did prevent his going to America to settle the Keithean controversy. The Worminghurst property, Guli's inheritance and in those years the family's chief source of income, was bequeathed in trust to her three living children, but Penn was allowed living expenses for himself and those minors until they were of age.

Penn's grief was to some extent assuaged by absorption in his writing. He had never ceased to publish, but in recent years the content had been relatively minor, consisting for the most part of reports on Pennsylvania's progress, of routine appeals for tolerance, of prefaces to other peoples' writings or of encyclical letters to Friends meetings throughout the world. Most of these were nobly conceived and display a passionate love of justice and peace; unhappily Penn usually talked about such matters with more spirit than he could put into his writing. In conversing, he was clever, some listeners even said light, but in writing he was wont to unload heavy burdens of authority couched in often turgid prose. Burnet reported, none too graciously, that Penn possessed "a tedious, luscious way that was not apt to overcome a man's reason, though it might tire his patience."[9]

Guli's long illness had caused Penn to write deeper, more philosophical works. Ever since his Oxford days, Penn, like so many other idealists, had been concerned with world unity and peace. Release from routine duties had given him time and leisure to draft a plan more workable than any others that had yet been published.

An Essay Toward the Present and Future Peace of Europe, published in 1692, had proposed, as Sully had done ninety years earlier, an inter-European parliament, including, as Sully had not, the non-Christian Turks and the rapidly rising Russians. These previously outcast nations were each to cast ten votes, as many as France, in the ninety-member parliament, while England must be content with six, since Russia and Turkey, while less economically developed, ruled larger populations. A united Germany, really a revived Holy Roman Empire, would have twelve delegates, more than any other nation. Spain would have ten and a unified Italy six.

The proposed apportionment would have doomed Penn's plan in his own country, and Christian nations would not have willingly ranked themselves below the Turks. Moreover, both Penn and Sully assumed that greedy and aggressive rulers, whom Penn held responsible for causing wars, would tamely submit to judgment by other nations.

The plan, desirable, humane, and even spiritual as it was, contained flaws that almost guaranteed its failure. All decisions of the ninety-man assembly were to require a two-thirds vote, which meant that all the populous and wealthy nations must agree in order to muster the necessary sixty votes: in view of western Europe's bitter rivalries, no unanimity could be expected on any question of importance. It would have been possible, moreover, for such a development as a Turko-Russian entente, unlikely as it would have been, to veto a proposal by collecting eleven votes from minor nations; it was utterly unthinkable that the major powers would permit dictation from the two large countries outside western Europe.

Penn expected no altruism from the diplomats who would comprise the assembly's membership; he did not trust their honesty. To safeguard the records of the assembly, he proposed keeping important documents in a safe too heavy to be carted away that would be secured by as many locks as there were member nations. Whenever it became necessary to consult the records, a delegate from each country must be present, each with his own key, in order that no one would be able to steal or alter the resolutions that had been accepted or rejected. How a violator of an assembly resolution would be dealt with was not quite clear; no doubt Penn trusted that no one would question the decision of a two-thirds majority. Apparently he did not suggest any type of international policing, nor, for that matter, does the word "force" appear.

The plan, while admirable in theory, assumed more rationality, more altruism, and a stronger sense of justice than then prevailed among the European nations. The *Essay* was, however, popular, three reprints being issued during his lifetime. Its effects were lasting. More than a century later, in the midst of the Napoleonic wars, a biographer revived Penn's plan for peaceful coexistence by commenting, "Henri IV [really Sully] showed that it was fit to be done, the United Netherlands that it can be done and Europe, by its incomparable miseries, that it ought to be done." Other flurries of interest stirred when the League of Nations and the United Nations were in process of formation.[10]

It may also have had a contemporary effect in America. It is possible, though not very likely, that Penn's adversary Edward Randolph proposed that all the American colonies under his customs jurisdiction, except Pennsylvania, be united into one district. The exception implied no hostility, for while Randolph suggested that the Three Lower Counties be added to Maryland, he proposed that Penn receive West Jersey in compensation, with East Jersey going to New York. Penn was to become the only proprietor to retain his land.[11]

Whether inspired by Randolph's proposal or on his own initiative, Penn drew upon the *Essay* for the idea that all colonial governors should meet regularly to discuss uniform legislation, extradition of fugitives and criminals, naturalization laws, and the suppression of piracy. The Council on Trade and Plantations, as a result of these pioneer unification proposals, asked Penn to draft a comprehensive plan for achieving unification.[12]

The outcome was a *Brief and Plain Scheme for Union*. It called for yearly meetings of colonial delegates to discuss such common interests as a postal system, a uniform currency, and standard trade practices. Surprisingly, from one who earnestly opposed supplying troops and money for warlike purposes, the scheme included provisions for drafting war necessities if armed conflict ensued. This, however, was not an abandonment of principle but a response to the wishes of his overlords. Penn still insisted that quarrels be mediated as, he said, they were in the Netherlands.

Penn's efforts to promote peace by establishing international and community cooperation came at a time when he feared that he was facing bankruptcy. By his own rather haphazard bookkeeping, and in his customary state of pessimism regarding his finances, he thought he had no money. His income, he believed, was drying up. Long absence from Ireland (he had not seen Shanagarry for a quarter-century) had caused his estates to be inefficiently managed; this, together with the ravages of civil disturbances, had reduced revenues from what should have been his major source of supply. Pennsylvania, he insisted, had sent him nothing for a dozen years but bills for him to pay; there had not been a single penny from quitrents. He had borrowed all he could, mortgaging his property, selling off, before Guli's death, all that he could of Worminghurst's once incomparable stand of timber. He was living on his capital.

35

QUACKS AND WITCHES

EXCEPT FOR THAT TOUCH OF SMALLPOX WHEN HE WAS THREE, THE CHILLS AND FEVER AFTER HIS WINTRY WANDERING IN THE IRISH MOUNTAINS, AND THE SPELLS OF MELANCHOLIA WHEN GULI AND HIS mother died, Penn enjoyed exceptionally good health for nearly half a century. Even these setbacks, except of course the smallpox, may have been less serious than they sound, for the chills and fever abated after he bought himself his little wig, and the grieving left no ill effects except prolonged depressions of the spirits.

Penn's freedom from serious illness testified to an extraordinarily strong constitution, all the more remarkable because he took such little care of it. For years he lived under constant pressure, burdening himself with responsibility both in London and on his innumerable missionary journeys. Even his daily meditation periods were times of tension, not of rest. Penn's relaxation came during his incessant horseback riding in those days when there were but few established coach routes; they afforded plenty of fresh air and exercise to keep him in good physical trim. In buoyant youth he could, and did, throw off any ill effects of pushing himself beyond reasonable limits in all sorts of weather; as he grew older, the strains began to show themselves.

He had thought of prolonging his health by following an Indian precedent. Their chief propensity, he said, was for fevers, the only real illness he himself had suffered since his smallpox, and for that they had a sovereign cure, taxing to be sure, but invariably effective. Having shut themselves up in a tent or cabin, made as airtight as possible and heated by hot stones, they stayed half an hour or so until they were sweating so profusely that they looked as though they had been swimming. Then they burst out of the room stark naked, ran pell-mell to the river, and plunged in, even in the winter, when sometimes they had to break the ice with an ax. Here they dived several times, then, running back to their own wigwams, they wrapped themselves in their woolen mantles, their matchcoats, lay down close to a "gentle fire" until they were dry, and so rose and ate their dinners, seemingly completely cured. Had they borrowed this custom from the early Finnish settlers on the Delaware?[1]

All this, said Penn, he had related to his butler, who was himself suffering from "anguish," whereupon the butler promptly threw off his clothes, ran downstairs, "flounced into a large vessel of hot water," and then ran naked about the garden. The butler outdid the Indians; he repeated the process, then took a swig of brandy, and next morning was completely cured. Not only of ague, Penn averred, but also of deafness. The experiences of the butler and of the Indians thoroughly convinced William Penn; but though he felt feverish on several occasions thereafter, he could not summon up the courage, or the immodesty, to follow their example.[2]

By the opening of the 1690s Penn was needing effective medicament. Plagued by money troubles, worried by insistent Royal demands that he help wage wars, brooding over unfair accusations of Jacobitism, treason, and Jesuitism, disillusioned because his sinful and ungrateful protégés were sabotaging the Holy Experiment, he was in extremely low spirits. By working too hard and taking too little care of himself, he was undermining his health. Added to this had been an eight-months' ordeal, a constant day-and-night ministry to an ailing Guli, even while he himself nursed a five-weeks' fever.

Two Bristol merchants, Thomas Callowhill and Charles Jones, strongly recommended that he restore himself to health through the use of a patent medicine newly created by two German alchemists and marketed in England by a local Quaker, Charles Marshall. This panacea, United Spirit, a mixture of spiritus mundi and spiritus sedativus, blended an opium derivative with a liquid composed of lime dissolved in nitric acid. The mixture was then double distilled until it became "humidity in its pure form," combining the four elements, earth, air, fire, and water, into "the quintessence of the whole."[3]

Either because of its peculiar merit or, more likely because of Penn's confidence in its efficacy, the remedy restored him to health. Perhaps in gratitude, Penn wrote a preface to one of Charles Marshall's books.[4]

The two advisors, Callowhill and Jones, remained very close to Penn, the Callowhill firm having been one of the Admiral's early business partners. Thomas Callowhill's daughter Hannah later nursed Penn back to health. Jones' daughter Mary married Penn's son Billy. A Charles Jones, Jr., who may have been Hannah's brother, operated a slave-trading firm doing business in Pennsylvania.[5]

Perhaps his health was failing. He wrote that he was troubled; whenever he blew his nose he had nosebleed, a symptom that might presage more serious illness, for he was but indifferently well and was not sleeping soundly.[6]

Whether Marshall, his Bristol Quaker friend, was still marketing his panacea, good for "dangerous and acute distempers, as surfeits, grips, fevers, smallpox, pleurisies and the like," does not appear, but it may be that Penn was weaned away by another miracle worker. One William Rowland, author of a *Compleat Chymical Dispensatory*, in Latin and English, offered a nosebleed cure. Rowland, moreover, could cure despondency:

> At the rise of the new moon, take the moss off the skull of a murdered man and hold it [presumably to the nose]. The nosebleed stops miraculously.
>
> If depressed in spirit, go into the garden at the wane of the moon and gather ants. The sharp scent of these ants is wonderfully refreshing to the spirit. If a fit of the ague is coming, gather seven insects, put them in a hollow bean and eat them.—If a child has bruised knees, rub on a mixture made up from a 24-year old redhaired man who was killed.[7]

It is impossible to believe that such an intelligent man as William Penn took such nonsense seriously, but he did tell Hannah that a sovereign way to rid her of her fear of marriage was to swallow purgatives. He himself disseminated medical advice of not much higher scientific value. Asses' milk, "beyond all doctors' skill," sweetens the blood, he assured a friend. So did an infusion of wormwood, camomile flowers, and agrimony, provided they were steeped in good spring water. Hot well water mixed with port helped the vision; "wet a cloth with milk or sack, let it dry, and then apply it hot to the eyes."[8]

Possibly the one recommendation that would receive any acceptance today was Penn's advice that "the precious tea" must not be doused with milk, but drunk "upon its own merit."[9]

None of these precautions, however, spared Penn from getting the gout, that catch-all name for afflictions that plagued so many more men than women. The illness struck him in 1700, confining him to bed just as he was about to entertain several hundred guests, it was to remain with him, in some form or another, for the remainder of his life.[10]

The attack ushered in a succession of mishaps, an injured shin in 1701, an abrasion of the same leg in 1702, together with a fever, the first of a series of strokes in 1704, arthritis of the hands in 1705, followed by a second stroke in the same year. There were to be no further accidents or illnesses for at least four years, but neither would he ever be wholly well again.

Nearly all seventeenth-century people, even intelligent people, believed in witches. Possibly a few daring, unconventional souls entertained an uneasy doubt or two, but once such skeptics opened the Bibles that were becoming an essential feature of every home, all doubts would have been dispelled, for did not the Good Book show convincingly that witches did exist, that they could and did cast spells, and that they brought no good to honest people? The Bible was quite specific; "Thou shalt not suffer a witch to live." As late as 1736 the penalty for witchcraft in England was death.

The fear of witches was a general phenomenon. Sir Matthew Hale, one of the most capable chief justices in English history, a Penn contemporary, assured a jury "that there are such creatures as witches I make no doubt at all; for first, the Scriptures have affirmed as much; secondly, the wisdom of all nations hath provided laws against such persons." A century later, Sir William Blackstone, the great commentator on the English law, declared "to deny the possibility, nay, actual existence, of witchcraft and sorcery is at once to flatly deny the revealed word of God." And John Wesley, after the outpouring of French rationalism, regretted that some people were moving away from a belief in witchcraft; "I am sorry for it—the giving up of witchcraft is in effect giving up the Bible."

The last thing that William Penn would have wished to do was to give up the Bible. But while he believed in witches, he was less frightened by them than were his contemporaries. When, therefore, complaint reached him that two ladies were bewitching Pennsylvania cows, he kept his head. Instead of protecting the public by imprisoning the sorcerers, he ordered an investigation.

Penn, as Proprietor and Governor, sat as judge when Margaret Mattson and Getro (Yeshro) Hendrickson came up for judgment. In view of the Quaker aversion to lawsuits, the proceedings were an inquiry rather than a trial, and before a board of provincial councillors rather than a court, for no lawyers appeared for either prosecution or defense. As both defendants were Swedes whose English was limited, Penn called upon Lasse Cock to interpret for them.[11]

The "evidence" submitted was so farcical that any modern judge would have thrown the whole case out of court if, indeed, it had ever come to trial. One Henry Drystreet attested (being a Quaker he would not swear) that he had been told, twenty years before, that Mrs. Mattson was a witch. Someone's mother had also told him, much later, that twenty cows had been so bewitched that they were giving little milk; the informant did have the grace to say that the bewitching had been done through error. Putting these facts together, Drystreet contended that Mrs. Mattson must have been the culprit. Mrs. Hendrickson, it should be noted, was not implicated in the least.

Though Penn had studied only a short time at Lincoln's Inn, he should have known that hearsay evidence, especially flimsy hearsay evidence twenty years old, is unacceptable in any Anglo-Saxon court; yet he allowed the inquiry to continue. Even so, he should have dismissed the case when the owner of the cows testified that only one of the twenty cows had gone dry and even that one gave no evidence of having been in any way bewitched.

The key witness for what might be called the prosecution then appeared, a Charles Ashcomb, who said that Mrs. Mattson's daughter had told him that her mother was indeed a witch who had put spells on cattle.

As soon as Lasse Cock translated this telling testimony, Mrs. Mattson, who knew no law but did know truth from falsehood, rose in protest. "Where's my daughter?" she shouted. "Let her come and say so."

It was a plea that Penn, with his deep respect for English common law, should have heeded, for all defendants have the right to be faced by their accusers, but Penn, possibly in the hope that the case would collapse of its own weight, failed to call the daughter.

A third, and final, witness dealt another blow to any faint possibility of justice in this hearing; Enoch Flower, the newly appointed schoolmaster, stated that though he had believed Mrs. Mattson guilty, he had served on the grand jury that had indicted her.

If there had been a lawyer for the defense, he would have moved at once for a dismissal of all charges because of insufficient evidence in Mrs. Mattson's case and, even more, because no single word seems to have been said at any time concerning Mrs. Hendrickson's possible guilt. Penn, however, permitted the interrogation to proceed. Possibly he wished to help Mrs. Mattson by asking a sympathetic question or two.

"Art thou a witch?" he said. As was only to be expected, she denied any such activity.

"Hast thou ever ridden through the air on a broomstick?" This time the poor bewildered woman, who, even with the aid of Lasse Cock, may not have understood anything more than the word "broomstick," must have been terrified by fears of hanging or of burning at the stake. She was so flustered that she merely shook her head. Unfortunately, she shook it up and down. "Well," said Penn, "I know of no law against it."

Incredibly, the jury returned a verdict that must be unique in English history. Both defendants were acquitted of witchcraft, as was only to be anticipated, but they were convicted on the charge of being thought witches by their neighbors.

Though almost everything about the procedure had been wrong, Supreme Court Justice William Riddell of Ontario, suggested, two and a half centuries later, that Penn acted wisely in leaving the decision to the councillors. He went on to say that the decision, "though not strictly regular, was a sound common sense verdict wholly justified by the testimony."[12]

"Judge" Penn could not ignore the verdict, but he imposed no penalty; he put each woman under £50 bond to keep the peace. Mrs. Hendrickson's name had been mentioned only at the opening of the trial and at its very close.

Later witchcraft cases received wiser treatment. Six years after the Mattson affair, a worried Bucks County farmer declared that he had heard a neighbor remark, seemingly just as a matter of interest, that he had heard that a witch lived nearby. "And who," he was asked, "is that? And why do you think so?"[13]

"Mrs. Searle," came the answer. "Because she is an ugly, ill-favored woman."

Eleven years still later, in 1701, a strange woman arrived in Philadelphia, where she met, and stayed for a day or two, with a local family. When she took her leave, she suddenly fell ill and, on examination, was found to have several pins stuck in her breast. The incident baffled many, but a local butcher had a ready answer. "Her host and hostess bewitched the stranger."[14]

The matter was inquired into, found trifling, and was at once dismissed.

36

HANNAH TO THE RESCUE

WHILE WRESTLING WITH PROBLEMS OF WORLD PEACE, OF COLONIAL ADMINISTRATION, AND OF HIS OWN FINANCING, PENN FOUND PEACE AND COMFORT. IN THE COURSE OF A PREACHING tour he came to Bristol, the hometown of his grandfather Giles, the merchant-sailor. Here he again met Thomas Callowhill, the import-export broker long active in Quaker affairs; he may indeed have stayed at the Callowhill house on High Street.

For the solution of his personal problems he could have found no more effective help than that offered by Callowhill. A successful businessman, the son-in-law of old Dennis Hollister, pioneer Quaker and retailer of Spanish and African goods brought in by Giles, Thomas was hardheaded and resourceful. He had grown rich, not as so many other Bristol men had done by shipping indentured servants to America, but by canny trading. If anyone could untangle Penn's financial problems, Thomas Callowhill was just the man.

Like all successful businessmen Callowhill looked toward the future. His trading firm was well established; either it or that of his father-in-law, Hollister, with which it had been merged, dated back at least half a century. He had no wish to see it die or pass out of the family. This, however, caused him some concern. Though he and his wife, the former Hannah Hollister, had produced nine children, all but one had died in youth; only a daughter, Hannah, named for both her mother and a deceased elder sister, remained alive.

Callowhill, so the story runs, trained the girl to be a businesswoman. At the dinner table he lectured her on commercial practices, on sources of materials and on markets, on accounting, and on the mysteries of foreign trading. She had a natural aptitude for such matters, he discovered.

When the meal was over and the lectures ended, her mother took her in hand to tell her about household management, the treatment of servants, and how to market efficiently. Her education was not perhaps as intensive as that to which Tish had been subjected, for Hannah had no younger brother to cope with, but she learned enough to assure her success as an efficient housewife.[1]

When Penn, the fifty-four-year-old widower, came to Bristol in June 1695 the brown-eyed Hannah was twenty-four. Though not the striking beauty that Guli had been at that age, Hannah was clever, attractive, and possessed of the marked serenity that Quakers so highly praised. Penn felt an immediate attraction. His preaching commitments did not permit him a long stay in Bristol, but after he left he began a series of letters addressed, oddly enough, to "Dr. Anna Callowhill." The letters were conventional and decidedly noncommittal. An early message brought her a recipe for using dried apples, notable chiefly because Penn pointed out that it came from the kitchens of the Earl of Leicester. Having in this way established his position in life, though certainly no Quaker needed any testimonial for William Penn, he showed his solicitude by telling her how to remedy her eyesight. It was not long, however, before the missives grew more personal. By September, he was writing, "I behold, love and value thee and desire, above all other considerations, to be known, received and esteemed by thee." The tone was quite different from the "o.d.f." letters Guli had received.[2]

Penn's infatuation was no secret; he must have spoken of it freely. He courted Hannah by mail (he had soon learned how to spell her name), sending two or three long letters to each of the short notes he received in answer. He forwarded inscribed copies of his books, told her of his troubles, of Springett's illness, of his sleeplessness, of his occasional nose bleeds. Always he confessed his love. "I love, honor and embrace thee and am, without reserve, entirely thine as thou wouldst have me."[3]

In November 1695, two months after his first clear declaration, the engagement was announced. Soon after, Hannah and William asked their respective monthly meetings to approve the match.[4]

Tongues wagged busily, as was only to be expected when a widower with three children courted a girl of less than half his age. The engagement, it was whispered, crowded on too soon after Guli's death, though that sad event had occurred two years before the engagement was announced. In sharp contrast to the gossipers, however, the ladies of the Penn family were courteous. Margaret Lowther in Yorkshire, Penn's sister Peg, sent Hannah a pot of chocolate. Tish wrote a pretty letter of welcome, saying that she had expected that the engagement would be announced. One or two Penington women sent congratulations. The two monthly meetings, at Horsham near Worminghurst and at Bristol, gave their approval.[5]

Immediate marriage was thought inadvisable. Springett was ill, but his father, detecting what he thought signs of improvement, believed the time would soon come when the boy could travel to Bristol to witness the wedding. The hope was justified. Springett rallied sufficiently to make the journey. When, on March 5, 1696, Hannah and William married, all three of Penn's children, three Peningtons, and Henry Gouldney, Penn's attorney, witnessed the ceremony.[6] Springett died five weeks later.[7]

Hannah promptly took over management at Worminghurst. The arrangements could not have been wholly satisfactory for anyone. Billy and Tish, who now owned the property, were not completely happy at not controlling the inheritance. Tish, while delighted to be rid of domestic duties, may have disliked her reduction in status. Billy, very conscious that he was entering adulthood, would not have been above reminding his father and his stepmother that they were living on his estate by sufferance. Hannah, none too comfortable in a home she had not made, a home where everything reminded her and her husband of Guli, hurried William off to Bristol as often and for as long as she could manage. The absences, and William's ever present need to be in London, meant that Worminghurst no longer continued to be the chief Penn residence.

Soon after the honeymoon Penn hastened to his desk, not to write another of the five religious exhortations he had recently produced, nor another polemic like the castigations he had just administered to Keith and Bugg, not even another program like his *Plea for the Unity of the Colonies*, but to recite a poignant personal tragedy. To what must have been Hannah's dismay, her husband sat down to tell the Quaker world how wonderful his life had been with Guli.[8]

Because Hannah, like any girl in love, must have ached to identify herself with the interests of her beloved, the situation must have been traumatic. If she had asked how the work was progressing, he would have told her, or more likely read to her his pages on how deeply he and Guli had loved each other, what a perfect wife she had been, how she had "so heroically and so willingly sacrificed herself to his religious and public life, saying always, 'Go, my dearest; don't hinder any good for me.'" The not wholly happy bride who had carefully planned to spirit William away from the Guli-ridden influence of Worminghurst may have managed to look pleased and to sound appreciative throughout such an ordeal; but the experience would not have ranked among the happiest moments of her life. Yet if she refrained from asking, William might have thought that she had no interest in what he was doing at his desk.

It is not unthinkable that Hannah sometimes cried a bit, particularly because for twelve full years after the marriage, Penn continued to wear about his neck, day and night, that Spanish gold piece with its memories of Guli.[9]

Hannah gave William Penn the quiet, efficient care that he so badly needed. She protected him against distraction. Even while Guli was alive, even before her long illness, he had been living under pressure. Her sickness and death had burdened him with responsibilities that he had neither the skill nor the temperament to meet; he had been side-tracked into activities which he never enjoyed nor, if truth be told, could well perform. The seventeen-year-old Tish, just at the clothes-conscious age, and her younger brother, the rebellious Billy, were as strange to him as he had himself been to his own father, the Admiral.

Penn needed the relief that Hannah brought him. Pennsylvania was becoming increasingly a burden. Just why the people of the province treated him with such indifference, unless they resented his constant preaching, is difficult to understand; why they regarded him as a messenger boy is incomprehensible. Almost none bothered to send the quitrents that they owed, but they did not hesitate to send bills for him to pay. Philadelphia Monthly Meeting instructed him to look about for a teacher, Penn invited William Sewel but the historian was unwilling to leave Amsterdam. In forwarding Sewel's refusal, couched in Latin, which may have taxed a rusty knowledge of that language—he reminded Pennsylvanians that they had amongst them an admirable candidate in Francis David Pastorius. They followed his advice.[10]

The Americans caused a slight annoyance by reporting the presence, in Lord Baltimore's Maryland, of a weak, sick sailor who called himself William Penn of London; nothing serious developed, but the mix-up of identity somewhat embarrassed Maryland Quakers.

Such annoyances were pinpricks, but their frequency disturbed the peace and quiet Penn required for his meditation and his writing. At odds with their neighbors and themselves, his people seemed bent on self-destruction; the jealousies and backbitings against which he had so often warned had not lessened in the least. It was serious enough to annoy Penn, but, far worse, the situation seemed to London to prove that he was inefficient and that for the best interests of the province, Pennsylvania should be taken over by the Crown.

In spite of a propensity to minimize, if not to overlook, shortcomings in his kinsmen, Penn was forced to realize that Markham, who had served so long and so well, was no longer effective. Advancing years and recurrent illnesses had enfeebled him, making him less decisive, more inclined to shirk responsibility and to procrastinate in making decisions. Letters of complaint pouring into England told of Markham's quarrels with his colleagues, his legislature, and his people. The Lords of Trade and Plantations were being flooded by reports that the Deputy Governor was taking bribes from smugglers and illegal traders.[11]

Markham, of course, denied the charges. The problems, he declared, were not of his making; if anyone were guilty, in the continued violations of the laws concerning tobacco exports, for instance, it was not his responsibility but that of the people of Maryland's Eastern Shore and of the Royal Navy which patrolled the tidewaters and the Atlantic Ocean. Penn did not believe Markham guilty; but, if the accusations were true, he said, he would "heartily" dismiss the Deputy Governor.[12]

Doubts about the integrity of a colonial governor were not peculiar to Pennsylvania. Ship captains, merchants and officials all along the American coast systematically connived to violate the Navigation Acts. Well-bribed customs collectors allowed foreign ships to discharge forbidden cargoes in provincial ports; some, operating their own trading firms, admitted merchandise for those firms without paying duty on the imports. Markham accused the Marylanders of mis-stating the weights and nature of freight, thus cheating the Royal treasury of its rightful revenue. The Lords of Trade and Plantations had been flooded with such complaints but it was noticeable that, among the major American colonies, the fewest number of offenses were charged to Pennsylvania. During the period from 1675 to 1696, the Council on Trade and Plantations considered 183 charges against Massachusetts, 174 against Virginia, 90 against New York, but only 23 against Pennsylvania.[13]

A rebuilt administrative system set up in London seemed at first a good omen for William Penn. Four members of a new Board of Trade, replacing the Council on Trade and Plantations, were old acquaintances. If he relied upon the friendship of the earls of Rochester, Romney, Sunderland and Halifax, however, he was disappointed, for immediately upon taking office, they began investigating his province.[14]

Whether because of pride, indifference or pique Penn would not co-operate. When summoned to appear for a hearing, he returned word that he would not come because he was ill; he arrived a week later than the date when he was expected. When told to produce copies of Pennsylvania's statutes, those which, to avoid any such necessity, he had ordered repealed, he excused his delay on the ground that his steward had died. It is not surprising that when he eventually appeared before the Board of Trade he found the atmosphere quite chilly. After what some observers characterized as virtually a trial he was severely reprimanded.[15]

For these unfortunate occurrences he held the Royal agents in America responsible. "I do expect," he said indignantly, "that those who have been the instruments of raising this smoke against my province will quench that fire which feeds it . . . that a man and his family and his friends should be smothered in a dust malice has raised is scandalous."[16]

The new Board of Trade was not the only group to cause Penn trouble. The London centralizers had created a chain of vice-admiralty courts, special tribunals for maritime affairs, especially the enforcement of the Navigation Acts. These courts, subject only to the High Court of Admiralty, held extensive powers, were not bound by rules of the common law, required no cross-examination of witnesses, and needed no jury. They were entirely free of local interference.

These courts, which Penn held infringed upon his charter rights, ruled that the Delaware was not an inland waterway but a tidal inlet. In any case, the boundaries were the eastern and western shorelines, and, except for areas within the Twelve Mile Circle, conveyed not one drop of river water.

As judge of the vice-admiralty court for the Pennsylvania and Lower County areas the authorities appointed Colonel Robert Quary, former Royal officer in South Carolina. He was destined to be a powerful, and often disturbing, force in Pennsylvania.

Quary did not desire to go to Pennsylvania. From what he had been told about the province he had conceived a poor opinion of it. It was inhabited, he believed, by "a perverse, obstinate and turbulent people who would submit to no laws but their own and who had a notion that no acts of Parliament were in force against them except such as particularly mentioned them.[17] Nevertheless, Quary came to Pennsylvania with a surprisingly open mind. He found that he liked the province; the people, far from being perverse, were "generally very laborious and industrious," and they were admirable farmers.[17]

No American province had less need for importing a distracting influence. At the very moment that London was criticizing Penn, his province was demonstrating its incapacity for good self-government.

Markham, to ease tension within the province, and Penn, to avoid flare-ups among the Royalists, tried manfully to carry out London's requirements; the former with what he would have termed a right good will, the latter reluctantly and in a manner that the Lords resented. When, by Royal command, Governor Benjamin Fletcher of New York made his annual appeal for Pennsylvania to send troops for an intercolonial army, Markham forwarded the request to the Provincial Assembly, which, as usual, would not comply. The province, it insisted, simply could not spare eighty men. The 1695 season had been poor and harvests in the next year promised to be worse. Upcountry farmers were in serious financial condition; they needed every able-bodied man to work the fields. There had been a great mortality of livestock. Even to send delegates to the Assembly had been a hardship, drawing off so many men from their farm duties as to "tend to their utter ruin." The Assembly thereupon adjourned from May until after harvest.[18]

The inaction embarrassed Penn. If, as many people, including Markham, believed, he had led London to suppose that his province would cooperate in the war effort, he ran the risk of losing his colony. If, on the other hand, he ordered his people to comply, he would violate his principles without any guarantee that he would be obeyed. He followed, therefore, a carefully charted course, issuing no demands but urging a friendly councilman to see what could be done to avoid disappointing the King.

The Provincial Council had not waited for instructions. It voted a small amount, not for war or even for preparation for war, but simply "for the King to use as he pleases." The Assembly was not in the least unhappy with this verbal trickery, but, desirous of attaining at least equality with the less liberal Council, refused to approve the measure until Markham granted a new Frame of Government.[19]

Each man was playing a game. David Lloyd must have known that Markham had no power to grant a new Frame; but by having the Deputy Governor write one, the document could be presented to Penn as a *fait accompli* to be accepted by the Proprietor because of his promise to grant anything that his people might reasonably desire. Markham, equally aware of his powerlessness, hoped to keep the Assembly quiet; he may have relied upon Penn to veto the illegal Frame. First, however, he tried to stave off the necessity of yielding. Proroguing the Assembly, he called for new elections, only to find that the new Assembly was even more under Lloyd's control than the old one had been.

Emboldened by this success, Lloyd announced that unless Markham offered a new and, to Lloyd's thinking, better Frame, the Assembly would itself draft and adopt a fundamental law conferring upon the Assembly all the rights it had been demanding. Markham capitulated. He approved a Frame depriving himself, the Deputy Governor, of all power over money matters, commerce, or the courts, except by approval of the Provincial Council, giving the Assembly full rights to draft and originate legislation and to meet and to adjourn at its own pleasure. The new Frame was to remain in force unless Penn disapproved and could not be amended except by a six-seventh vote of the Assembly.[20]

After this victory, the Assembly again granted Fletcher £300 to feed and clothe the Indians, but not until after he had issued another call for help. History repeated itself, for following the well-established custom, the Assembly replied to the second call, "We do not find that we are capable at present to raise any more money."[21]

On this point Penn supported his Assembly. Regardless of whatever promises he had made, or allowed the Lords to think that he had made, he opposed Fletcher's yearly calls for funds. The demands, he said, were too high; the New York Governor was penalizing Pennsylvania because it was more prosperous than his own province.

Nevertheless, Penn was far from pleased by the conduct of his province. Most of his information came from strait-laced Quakers who were shocked by what they called the loose conduct of the public, or from correspondents such as Markham and Robert Turner who detested David Lloyd and his democratic Assembly. The Proprietor's disappointments were not in the least soothed by his failure to receive any remit-

Neither had Markham, or so, at least, he said. Accused of having been bribed by pirates and illegal traders, he replied, "I solemnly declare that I had not the value of a farthing." There had been corruption, he admitted, in Pennsylvania, but that was while Fletcher was in control.

37

PIRATES AND SMUGGLERS

ROYAL OFFICERS AND PROVINCIAL AUTHORITIES CLASHED IN SEVERAL AREAS. DIFFICULTIES SPRANG PARTLY FROM THE CROWN'S INCREASINGLY TIGHT GRIP UPON ITS OVERSEAS PROFESSIONS, A GOAL ATTAINable by using quo warranto. Even had there been no trend toward what we might today call imperialism, the imprecise wording of Penn's patent would have made disputes unavoidable. As the river Delaware and other navigable waters had not been specifically assigned to William Penn or to anyone else, the Crown contended that the river, at least, remained under the King's control, a stipulation that Penn virtually ignored until the Admiralty began to interpret its jurisdiction first to include the shore lines, then the docks and wharves, and finally the important tributary creeks. There were broad hints, also, that the land approaches to the wharves, and even to the minor streams, might be construed as falling under Royal authority.

The situation grew intolerable. Provincial water bailiffs, the local watch, naval officers, and Royal customs collectors each claimed exclusive jurisdiction. Both the admiralty courts and the Pennsylvania tribunals assumed the right to try lawsuits arising from the confused situation. Royal agents, particularly Edward Randolph and Colonel Robert Quary, bombarded London with complaints that Pennsylvania was not only interfering with the work of Crown officials but was both permitting and encouraging violation of the Navigation Acts. These complaints, couched in very strong language, suggested, none too delicately, that Penn's people were allied with smugglers, pirates, and perhaps with foreign agents. If these reckless charges were true, quo warranto would be inevitable, and Penn would lose his province.

The matter, therefore, was very far from academic. No one denied that Parliament had a perfect right to levy customs duties and, under Penn's unique patent, to impose certain other taxes. This, as everyone admitted, implied the stationing of customs collectors, but at just what point did Royal law-enforcement agents take over? Doubtless English officers could prosecute and punish smugglers caught on the ships; but once the goods were landed and hauled inland, who was to police the markets? The Navy would cruise the seas for pirates, but could sailors hunt down pirates in the creeks and inlets? If, as was freely alleged, suspected freebooters were spending what might be pirate gold in city taverns, who was to arrest them and on what charge? Conflict of jurisdiction was everywhere.

In 1696, Francis Nicholson, the newly appointed and very peppery Governor of Maryland, joined Colonel Robert Quary, the Admiralty representative, and Edward Randolph, the customs chief, in promoting Royal interests. They opened war on William Markham. It was not enough that they charged the Deputy with inefficiency; they also accused him of being the bribed tool of smugglers, illegal traders, and pirates. They even, in a sense, made war on Pennsylvania, for they used a Nicholson warship to intercept and search vessels entering or leaving Delaware Bay.[1]

The move amazed Markham, partly because it was Maryland-grown tobacco that formed part of the illegal cargoes Governor Nicholson was trying to find; more because, he said, Nicholson was two-faced. Only recently, said Markham, the Marylander "had embraced me with a kiss" and had given him "all the shows of familiarity," only suddenly to turn against him. "I cannot imagine what has possessed him to drive him into such a rage."[2]

Markham indignantly denied the charges, of course. I have been a slave in this province many years and never saw a farthing of their money. I have done my utmost to prevent false trading."[3]

He had lost none of his spirit. "I wish anyone acquainted with him," he said contemptuously of one detractor, "could have seen him huffing and bouncing when I called him to account. They would have seen him truckle, and as humble as a spaniel dog, but no sooner was he out of town than he fell to reviling me in his base manner." Had anyone said such things to him, said Markham, "I would have been after him and taught him what wood my cudgel was made of."[4]

Markham's protestations apparently satisfied Penn. Though he suspected that his cousin might be a bit too fond of money, Penn trusted Markham. There may have been some question in the Proprietor's mind as to where a man of no visible employment prior to his appointment had found £1000 for purchase of Free Society of Traders stock and still more about the origin of the £5000 Markham had paid for a magnificent estate, but Penn did not believe Markham a pirate beneficiary. Neither did he believe that Markham had followed the example of certain other colonial governors in selling privateer papers, in effect pirate licenses, for £100 per member of a crew.[5]

Yet Pennsylvania's inaction in suppressing piracy and illegal trade did seem suspicious. Markham's explanation was not too convincing. Piracy, said Markham, occurred upon the high seas where he had no police power, and smugglers landed goods in the tidewater creeks over which Nicholson and Quary claimed jurisdiction. If illegal goods piled high upon the stalls of High Street their origin was none of his concern. Though suspicious vessels were clearing for such unlikely ports as those of Madagascar and South Africa, it was not for him to inquire whether the captains were exchanging salt fish, pickled beef, and Pennsylvania wheat for rich Oriental goods pirated from East India Company treasure ships.

Governor Nicholson of Maryland did not doubt Markham's guilt. On learning in 1698 that suspected pirates were in the Delaware Valley he ordered Captain Josiah Daniel to head a 60-man detachment to go up the Bay in small boats to capture them. Daniel found them in New Castle, but when he demanded their surrender, they flashed a commission over Markham's signature constituting them lawful privateersmen.[6]

Apparently they were a jolly lot for they seduced Daniel's troopers with Barbados rum and the famed peach brandy of the Lower Counties into fleeing with them into Pennsylvania. The liberated Pennsylvanians took with them the oars from Daniel's boats. Daniels followed, presumably by road, called on Markham and protested at the loss of his men. When they refused to return with him and Markham gave them shelter, Daniel went back to Maryland, minus his oars, and wrote Markham a letter that blended insult, politeness and humility.

"The worst sailors know how ready you are to entertain and protect all deserters . . . I return my hearty thanks for my entertainment. It was better than I deserved."[7]

The Deputy Governor lacked the courtesy of his late guest. Three weeks later he replied that Captain Daniel's letter was "so indecent that it seems rather penned in the cook room than the great cabin." Unlike Daniel he did not close with an excerpt from a book of etiquette; "I hope I shall not fall into your way lest your treatment be such as I find in the letter."[8]

Edward Randolph also was highly skeptical of Markham's innocence.

All these parts swarm with pirates. They walk the streets with their pockets full of gold and are the constant companions of the Chief of State [Markham]. They threaten my life and those that are active in apprehending them, carry their prohibited goods publicly in boats from place to place for a market, threaten the lives of the King's collectors and, with force and arms, rescue the goods from them.[9]

London summoned Penn to answer the charges. Though, after ten or fifteen years of similar accusations, he must have had an inkling of what was going on, he professed surprise and promised to investigate. He dashed off letters demanding immediate and complete reform and caused proclamations to be issued condemning piracy and smuggling.

Randolph remained unimpressed for he continued to see pirates freely strolling the city streets. He and Nicholson, with Quary's approval, called upon Markham but found him less than cooperative. First Markham denied that either visitor had any authority to punish Pennsylvania pirates, if there were any, whereupon Randolph called him a liar. Then Markham mentioned that since no one had ever told him that such a commission existed, he was under no obligation to honor it. Besides, he said, the so-called pirates had been "very civil" to him.[10]

When one of the law-enforcers impertinently inquired if that civility measured £100 per head and what significance there might be in "a little present" Markham had received from a ship's crew, Markham lost his temper. Again denying that he had ever pocketed a single penny, he threatened to jail his critics.[11]

Randolph made matters very clear. Markham must have known that the only reason Philadelphia Quaker merchants sold foreign goods so cheaply was that the goods had been smuggled. Markham had pirate friends, but that was not the worst of it; he harbored a pirate in his very household. That pirate was his son-in-law. So, inadvertently perhaps but none the less actually, William Penn himself indirectly tolerated and protected pirates.

James Brown, the son-in-law, was a man of mystery, a stranger who had come to town with a story none too easy to believe, or rather with several stories, none of them particularly plausible. He may have been the same James Browne (the name was spelled differently) who had been arrested for piracy ten years earlier in the Carolinas; a companion then had been Robert Quary, now the high-minded judge of the vice-admiralty court. Certainly Markham's James Brown had been captured on a ship upon which, he solemnly averred, he had sailed for months without ever knowing that it really was a pirate vessel. He had boarded that ship a poor man and he had left it rich, but not, he said, because of pirate gold. He had been exceptionally lucky with cards and dice.[12]

If Markham had investigated the stranger's background when Brown asked him for his daughter's hand, he mentioned nothing about it to Penn, nor did Quary give any sign that he had ever known the man. Brown's name cropped up, however, during a sensational trial in London of Madagascar pirates. Quite naturally the Board of Trade asked Penn what he knew about Brown and was told that he was a quiet peaceful farmer in the Lower Counties; as a matter of fact, though Penn was unaware of it, Brown was at the moment cruising off India.[13]

The mix-up, for none of which Penn was responsible, allowed Randolph to lash out at Markham for the latter's "indifferent sense of honesty." Randolph also implicated others. Markham's wife and daughters, he alleged, tipped off Brown and other pirates when they were about to be arrested. Markham's magistrates, moreover, refused to issue warrants, and when, in spite of this, Randolph did arrest the suspects, the sheriff lodged them in such a flimsy jail that the prisoners broke out and ran away.[14]

Penn refused to believe a word of this. He accepted Pennsylvania's assurances that "our magistrates and justices have always been zealous to safeguard the strict laws that we have made." Apparently he did not remember the numerous times he had rebuked their slothfulness.[15]

Penn's faith in Markham's innocence was strengthened because a former Randolph supporter twice testified to Markham's good character. "Notwithstanding the heat between Colonel Markham and myself," he told Penn, "I must do him the justice to assure you that in my judgment no fitter person could be found to govern. . . . I have lived under his government for five years, during all which time his government has been to the satisfaction of the substantial citizens and traders." He implied that he had been induced in the past to give hostile testimony by "a man of passionate temper, of little or no reputation, very indigent."[16]

The situation was bad enough in the early years of the 1690 decade; after 1697 when the Treaty of Ryswick ended eight years of world-wide warfare, hundreds, if not thousands, of privateersmen and sailors on armed merchantmen lost their exciting and highly profitable employment. Resumed trade between Europe and both the East and West Indies, as well as with the rich colonies of the Americas, absorbed many; a large percentage, unwilling to settle down to drab routine, turned their fighting ships into pirate craft or smuggling vessels.

Everyone piously disapproved of piracy, but smuggling could be tacitly condoned; England's Navigation Acts were much too strict to please the provinces, and besides, the smuggled goods were cheaper. Both Royal and local officials preferred, therefore, to charge as many offenders as possible with piracy, the former because it would look well upon their records at home, the latter because it would throw the entire burden of detection and conviction upon the Crown. Moreover, even in a highly ethical Quaker community, a certain glamor clung about a highly successful pirate; for local officials to hang an outstanding neighbor would cause more criticism than a London execution would receive. The early court records of Pennsylvania contain, therefore, more entries of suspected piracy than of illegal trading.

James Brown, belatedly sent to England to stand trial, suddenly disappeared from history after having been convicted; it was supposed, but never proved, that he had been executed. In June 1699, Captain Kidd sailed unexpectedly into Lewes, at Cape Henlopen, bringing with him, it was said, gold and silver plate in sufficient amount to yield each crewman £4000; some estimates reported that he had thirty-five tons of gold aboard. When the inhabitants were rebuked for their kindly reception of the visitors, and for their willingness to enjoy Kidd's shipboard hospitality, they explained, in seeming innocence, that no one had any idea that Captain William Kidd was a pirate.[17]

So many complaints, real or fancied, poured in against Penn's administrators that he protested to his provincial agents that they must not "wink at" illegal trading or "embrace pirate ships and men." London, however, required more drastic action, demanding that he put an immediate stop to all abuses, and as a first step, dismiss William Markham as his deputy.[18]

Penn responded by impressing upon his overlords that Pennsylvania already had strict laws against both piracy and illegal trading, that those laws were strictly enforced—in fact, four of Kidd's men were being held in jail—and that, though Pennsylvania was unquestionably prospering, not one-thousandth part of that prosperity could be traceable to anything illegal. He added, rather surprisingly, that Pennsylvania had always been remarkably law-abiding: "We have never had a spot upon our garments." Only four ships had ever been accused of trading illegally, and on investigation, all four had been cleared of any guilt. Yet Governor Nicholson had dared to criticize the Pennsylvania record, in spite of the fact that Maryland's record was twenty-seven times worse than that of Pennsylvania.[19]

Other critics were suspect. Colonel Quary, said Penn, was too wrapped up in private business ventures, not all of which were above suspicion. He was "the greatest and vilest of Pennsylvania's enemies." Edward Randolph, that "one-eyed gentleman," a man of doubtful honesty, had offered to issue pardons for pirates at £200 a head. As for Francis Nicholson, who was making it his business "to spot holes in our coat and clean up our weaknesses" a former Marylander had called him "the greatest monster ever heard of in these parts of the world and an enemy to God and man." Besides, he was a seducer of young girls.[20]

It was a sweeping condemnation, yet not strong enough to please one worried member of Philadelphia Monthly Meeting. "I have been overcome with passions," he wrote, "and have said in my heart that there was not an honest man in the province except Governor Penn, and that they would go down into the bottomless pit and to the lake."[21]

Only two months later one of the staunchest pillars of the Philadelphia establishment yielded to temptation. A certain Robert Bradenham, reputed to be the pirates' surgeon, had come to Philadelphia with his pockets bulging with what Penn believed to be pirate booty, "624 pieces of Arabian and Christian gold, £414 our money." Given the nature of such haunts as Bradenham was likely to frequent, it would have been foolhardy to carry so much cash on his person or to keep it in his rooms, so Bradenham entrusted his wealth to the care of "the safest vestry he could find." At first blush the Reverend Edward Portlock seemed an odd choice, for the rector of Christ Church had been criticizing Quakers from his pulpit for not making active war against the pirates, but apparently Bradenham knew his man. Portlock may have disapproved of piracy, but he spent much time hobnobbing with the lawbreakers. Penn wrote letters telling how shocked he was at Portlock's behavior, especially "how indecently I found the parson potting and piping" with the pirates, while on Sundays Portlock was attacking them.[22]

Then suddenly, Bradenham and two of his fellow pirates died. Portlock consulted his attorneys, one of them a Christ Church vestryman, and was advised to keep the money and say nothing about it. The clergyman followed the advice. He rushed off to Maryland and then to Virginia, taking the pirate gold with him.

It is difficult to understand why, on the same day that Penn was charging Portlock for absconding with the money, he wrote a friendly letter to Maryland merely announcing that the rector was en route to that province. Though Penn strongly detested Francis Nicholson, he prefaced his news by prescribing medicine for the Governor's illness.[23]

After Christ Church received a new rector, Colonel Quary and his fellow vestrymen struck back at Penn by complaining that Penn and his tools in the Provincial Assembly were persecuting Anglicans. "We have a long time groaned under the miseries and hardships we have suffered . . . exposed to all the miseries imaginable not only from a public enemy but from pirates and Indians." Penn, the complaint alleged, had not only broken his promise of freedom of worship but had taken away the liberties enjoyed prior to his arrival. The complaints were excessive, and nothing whatever was said about Quary's earlier praise for Penn's administration. Neither was there any mention of the Portlock case, nor of the favoritism that had been shown to Bradenham.[24]

38

PROBLEM CHILDREN

WILLIAM AND GULI HAD BAD LUCK WITH THEIR CHILDREN. BORN, OF WHOM FOUR DIED IN INFANCY AND ANOTHER BEFORE WITHIN TEN YEARS OF THEIR MARRIAGE, SEVEN BABIES WERE reaching maturity. One of the two survivors was childless.

In the absence of medical records it is impossible to determine the cause of the high mortality rate, but it is certain that in the seventeenth century childhood diseases were more common and more dangerous than they are today and that infant death rates everywhere were high. Nevertheless, it is a striking fact that in contrast to Guli's misfortunes, five of the seven children of Penn's second marriage lived to maturity. Two of these five died without issue.[1]

Whatever may have carried off Guli's four babies, the survivors enjoyed a very different childhood from their father's. Not for them was a noisy, rollicking, and untidy household; their mother was not irresponsible nor their father a tavern frequenter who spun sailors' yarns and sang bawdy ballads. The Penn children were not brought up to think of their religious duties as a once-a-week appointment.

But as William had rebelled against the customs of his parents, so his and Guli's children reacted against what they were taught. Springett, the first-born son, had given some indication that he might follow his father's footsteps, but though a serious child, there is no record of his having been much addicted to research. Letitia was passive at best, while Billy, unable to endure four hours of Bible reading daily, played the role of prodigal son.

Penn tried to inculcate in his children some sense of order and responsibility, a training missing in his own childhood. Perhaps as a result of his own discomfort on Tower Hill, he firmly forbade frivolity or

unnecessary noise, a tabu that must have puzzled and irked the youngsters but which was essential if the father was to read and meditate
without interruption. The routine was unlikely to appeal to little children; they must have squirmed and wriggled and so drawn down upon
themselves the gentle rebukes and little punishments intended to correct
the misbehavior.

For all of them the economic future was assured, not only by their
shares of the English and Irish rentals but by incomes from vast acreages
in America, by dividends from investments made for them in Free Society of Traders stock, and other business interests.

Thus, at seventeen Springett sailed for Amsterdam to live with
Willem Sewel, the Quaker historian, while taking his shipbuilding lessons.[2] He did not, however, pursue the course laid out for him, for his
bookishness, inherited from his father, diverted him into the Sewel
library where, in addition to studying Dutch and Italian, he delved into
the Latin classics. After only a few months, his health never being good
(he was thought to be tubercular), he returned to England, where he
spent his time trying to correct his brother Billy's waywardness. He
died in 1696, only five weeks past his twentieth birthday.[3]

Letitia, Guli's fifth child but only the second to live longer than a
year, was born at Worminghurst, March 6, 1679. Because her mother
died just before her daughter's sixteenth birthday, Tish, as everyone
called her, had little formal education. Even the private tutoring that
her brothers received was interrupted, in Tish's case, by her responsibilities in caring for Worminghurst's domestic affairs.

Such duties cut short her childhood. Tish, unlike her mother in the
Wanstead days, had no little coach for running about the neighborhood,
even had the rough Sussex roads been as well kept as the Wanstead
lanes. To list, as her father did, two Worminghurst employees as her
personal servants gives somewhat of a false impression; both retainers
spent less time serving Tish than on the routine duties of the estate. But
just because she had neither time nor opportunity for play, she became,
next to her father, the best-trained member of Guli's household.

In one way the remarriage had been a relief for Tish. When Hannah
took over the supervision of domestic affairs, Tish, for the first time in
seven years, enjoyed a normal girlhood. Her mother's illness and her
father's widowhood had burdened her with household chores, depriving
her, to large degree, of the companionship of friends of her own age.
Though Worminghurst had constantly entertained numerous guests,
most of them, to Tish's mind, were old and stodgy. Young folk of the
neighborhood gathered at the Blue Idol, to be sure, but riding to meeting
had been a bumpy, oxcart experience, requiring so much time to go and
to return that little time remained for social life. The move to Bristol
brought more pleasure, because Friars Meeting House was not far distant

from the residence on High Street and because more young people worshiped there.[4]

But now, in 1699, after three years of such relief, her father was talking of moving to Pennsylvania, taking the family with him. Tish was not particularly pleased with the prospect. A young Quaker girl's life was pleasant, though perhaps not so exciting as that of damsels belonging to less demanding faiths. Tish had no strong desire to break off her friendships by moving to a province, which her father often called a wilderness or a desert inhabited by Indians or by rustics who spent all day chopping down trees.

Nor did her brother Billy wish to leave sophisticated London for an indefinite stay in a primitive community where people did not know how to live as befitted a gentleman. The thoroughly spoiled young man, now in the same stage of devotion to fashion and entertainment as his father had professed to be at Versailles and in Dublin, shuddered at the thought of exile among backwoodsmen.

There were parallels in the upbringing of Billy and his father. As small boys both had been left more or less to their own devices, neither having a father's close and constant care. The Admiral had been much away at sea, while the Proprietor was absorbed in missionary work, in Quaker administration, in lobbying, in writing, in meditation, or in colonial activities. Guli, to be sure, was a better disciplinarian than Lady Margaret had been, but Billy, not so studious and introspective as his father, was much less manageable. After Guli's death fourteen-year-old Billy became more or less his own master.

In their early youths, he and his father behaved in strikingly similar fashion. Each began by listening to the wishes of their elders; but Penn, the introvert, could not abide the rollicking of Tower Hill, while his extrovert son resented the dull routine of a household that insisted on so many daily religious services. Penn, the more considerate, may not have enjoyed dressing fashionably, wearing a ceremonial sword, and exchanging chitchat with the socially elite; he said he did so to please his parents, even to the point of considering an army career. Junior, on the other hand, though he must have been conscious of parental displeasure, relished the playboy role.

Though the Admiral had approved and even encouraged his son's frivolities, William Penn the Founder shut his eyes to the boy's irresponsibilities. He was so fond a father, so blinded by affection, that he simply failed to notice any fault whatever in the boy. Just as in Sir William's eyes he himself had never grown up, so to William Penn, Billy remained an innocent child sadly misunderstood.

When Billy was only fifteen, his serious-minded older brother, Springett, predicted that God's punishment would fall on him unless the boy renounced idle companionship. Penn paid no attention, probably thinking that Springett, himself barely out of his teens, exaggerated the situation. There were, besides, pressing problems for Penn to solve; the persecution of thirteen hundred Quakers following the death of Charles II, the turmoil of the Monmouth rebellion, the recurrent charges of Jesuitism, and the boundary disputes with Lord Baltimore. Since Billy would no doubt settle down as he grew older, just as Penn himself had done, Springett's warnings could be disregarded.[5]

That reliance was in vain. The only real restraint on Billy's libertarianism had been that of his elder brother, but that check was very slight and it vanished entirely when Springett died.

Two years later, in October 1698, seventeen-year-old-Billy announced that he was about to marry. It was an irresponsible decision, for except for a few desultory lessons after Springett's death in "the art and mystery" of shipbuilding, he had no training for any occupation, nor, except for a few square miles of undeveloped Pennsylvania land, did he have large independent resources. However, now that Springett was dead, he inherited the greater portion of Guli's estates, and he was confident that, as long as he lived, his father would continue to support him. He had no intention of abandoning his pleasure-seeking life. The lucky lady chosen as his prospective bride was Mary Jones, daughter of Charles Jones, a merchant of Castle Green, Bristol.

For all his high-class London connections, Billy did not become engaged to a sister of one of his social cronies. They may have thought him too young or too unprepared for marriage. Nor did Billy's father display great enthusiasm for the match; the girl was four years older than Billy and, as he would later say, too fond of luxury, too impatient with criticism, and too obstinate in refusing to accept good advice. Besides, she brought with her no substantial dowry. She cost him, Penn said, much more than she contributed to Billy's household.[6]

The Callowhills must have known Mary Jones, at least by sight, for the Jones family was part of Bristol's close-knit Quaker community. Hannah's reaction has not survived the years, but she could not have been displeased. She was not a jealous woman, but she was human, and Worminghurst was full of Guli reminders. There being enough property to share with all Penn's immediate family, she did not mind parting with anything that might carry Guli overtones.

Shortly after Penn's fifty-fourth birthday, Billy and his fiancée asked Bristol Meeting's approval of their marriage. Bristol consented almost immediately to the union of the son of a noted Quaker leader and the daughter of a prominent local Friend, but, for some reason—probably absence from Worminghurst—Billy delayed until New Year's Eve before asking Horsham's approval. The marriage took place January 10, 1699, two months before Billy's eighteenth birthday and the day after Mary's twenty-second. If anyone had qualms about the bridegroom's youth, the feeling was unknown beyond the family circles.[7]

Hannah promptly pointed out that since, by Guli's will, Billy was master of Worminghurst, she and his father would do well to allow the newlyweds exclusive possession. Had Penn realized that Billy had no intention of living in Sussex as a country squire, but would regard the estate merely as a source of revenue while he continued his gay life in London, the Proprietor might have resisted leaving the mansion where he and Guli had been so happy. But, to Hannah's delight, Billy did not make his intention clear, and Penn and Hannah moved away. They went first to Bath where Penn might take the waters; then, on her pleas of homesickness, they went to Bristol. Thereafter, Penn saw Worminghurst only on short visits.

As a helpful wedding present, Penn presented his son and the bride with a pamphlet, *Fruits of Solitude*, a manual of proper conduct toward God and man. The volume, which Penn called an enchiridion, a word he may have borrowed from the Coverdale *Bible*, was obviously not composed at any given time but was the result of years of meditation, containing 556 "maxims," or principles, in sixty-nine categories, on ethics, religion, and righteous living. How much of it Billy read is problematic. If he read the compendium carefully the maxims which probably appealed to him most were those advising against too much reading.

A more practical gift was the settling of a £300 annuity upon Billy. Charles Jones, the bride's father, failed to follow Penn's example. Not until six months after the marriage did he get around to paying the £2000 dowry agreed upon. The transaction was peculiar, since simultaneously, he received from William Penn an identical sum, plus £14 13s, which, said Penn, "clears up various things and balances the books."

It was not the only unusual business arrangement. Jones' neighbor and fellow merchant, Thomas Callowhill—alert to the probability that Billy and Mary would produce offspring and that Penn and Hannah might also have children—sought a sort of insurance against lessened inheritances for Guli's descendants. Within twenty-four hours of the money exchanges between Jones and Penn, Callowhill received a promise that if Penn's second marriage had issue, he, Callowhill, would receive £1500.[8]

Penn and Hannah then turned to planning a trip to Pennsylvania. The better to prepare Billy for his future role as Proprietor and Governor, he urged Billy to go with them, but the boy held back. He gave as his excuse that Mary was pregnant, as Guli had been on the eve of Penn's first voyage. It would be unwise to subject her to the rigors of a transatlantic journey or to ask her to face the ordeal of giving birth in an undeveloped province. Doubtless his concern was genuine, but in any case, the boy had only minimal interest in the knotty problems of finance, labor relations, trading rules, and judicial matters that his father expected him to study. Nor was he concerned with the rivalries of various groups of colonists or with the quarrels between Royal and provincial officers.

As a matter of fact, though Penn wished to have Billy with him in America, he was not unhappy that his son was not ready to go abroad immediately. He over-valued Billy's ability; as he needed a good agent in London, he could rely upon the boy, young as he was, to represent him.

An immediate need was at hand. Philip Ford, who for thirty years had been a trusted employee, had grown increasingly impatient over Penn's delay in settling that long-overdue bill for salary, fees, and commissions due him. Penn had not questioned the accuracy of Ford's bill, but had allowed it to run on until, by 1690, additional entries, plus interests, had swollen the account to over £6300.

With a new type of income tax in force, Ford was not anxious to receive a large cash payment. Again, the two men agreed to let the debt continue, Ford being protected by new mortgages on Pennsylvania land.[9]

Since Penn and Ford trusted each other, they went further. In the event that Penn should be found guilty of treason, he would lose all his property. He therefore "sold" to Ford almost all the land he owned in America, so that if he were convicted, his family would not suffer, for Ford could be relied upon to return the property to Penn's widow and his children. Since Ford received no cash, but leased back the land to Penn, with interest payable in additional acreage, he would evade the new tax on specie.

It was a clever arrangement, but Penn's announcement that he was about to leave for America stirred up the Fords. Philip was ill and Bridget worried that he might die. If so, or if Penn died while still away from England, the Ford claim might not be satisfied by anything but square miles of undeveloped Pennsylvania land.

The Fords turned Penn's courtesy to their advantage. Because Philip was too ill to ride into London from his country house at Islington, Penn rode out to their place to bid the Fords good-bye. His arrival surprised them; they hastily made an excuse to go into another room to hold a whispered conference. On their return, Ford pressed for an immediate payment of the long-standing debt. Penn again professed to have no ready money. Apparently Ford had anticipated the reply, for he proposed that the lease be updated to guarantee the Fords more money. Penn was not unwilling; but as he had left the lease in Sussex, by which he probably meant Worminghurst, some new document would have to be drafted.

Ford had foreseen the necessity; he presented a paper he had written for Penn's signature. According to Penn, Ford gave two rather peculiar reasons. "He, being crazy and I going on so great a voyage, he desired me to do it for mortality's sake." Ford also told Penn that while "he and his wife could rely upon me, they did not know who would come after." The document he wished Penn to sign, a cancellation of the lease and an outright transfer of title to the province, was, Ford said, "for caution and not for execution." He also said, untruthfully, that Penn had examined the accounts and had found them accurate. He may, or may not, have told Penn that this paper that Penn signed, unread, was a power of attorney allowing Ford to sell any American lands "upon such terms as he shall see fit," to represent Penn in court, to manage all Penn's affairs and committing Penn to ratify anything that Ford might do. If Penn had understood the sweeping nature of the powers thus conferred, he must have signed on the assurance that the document was only to be used in the event of his death. Ford did promise that he and his wife could be trusted to keep everything secret and that he would not even mention the matter in his will.[10]

Penn continued to hesitate and Ford grew angry. He must, he insisted, have more money and if Penn would not give any and would not sign the paper, he would bring suit and prevent Penn's sailing. Since the ship was scheduled to weigh anchor within forty-eight hours, Penn capitulated and signed the documents that left Ford in full possession of a deed to all Pennsylvania, free from any lease to Penn.

ℰ 39 ℨ

RETURN TO AMERICA

PENNSYLVANIA REQUIRED A STRONGER HAND THAN WILLIAM MARK-
HAM'S. EVEN IF ONE DISCOUNTED THE MANY FEVERED LETTERS FROM
RANDOLPH AND QUARY AS HEAVILY BIASED, IF NOT COMPLETELY
false, the fact remained that law enforcement in the province was
extremely lax. Ugly rumors alleged Markham's sympathy toward pirates
and the disappearance of quitrent payments, perhaps into his own pockets. Other reports intimated, with as little basis of solid proof, that Markham had sold acreage that was not his own and that he had failed to
credit the proceeds to Penn's account.

Hard as it was for Penn to believe that any of his friends, especially
a kinsman, could intentionally do wrong, his faith in Markham began to
weaken. The man, he realized, had faults, as did all human beings, and
Markham's was a too strong concern for money, but Penn still thought
his deputy completely honest. Any failure in administration, Penn charitably thought, must be due to the deteriorations of age or to increasing
ill-health.

Penn needed a new deputy. He had hoped that his son Billy, now
nineteen, would take over a large share of administrative work, prepara-
tory to becoming Deputy Governor, but Billy was still young and, worse,
too heedless. So, the uncharitable might have said, had Billy's father been
at about the same age, but Billy lacked seriousness, religious zeal, deep
dedication. With the father, diversion was a thin veneer; with Billy it
was reality. As the father remembered his youth he had been, at eighteen,
expelled from Oxford for nonconformity; but Billy's escapades had nothing whatever to do with religion—they were more carnal. Penn trusted
that the boy would settle down, but at the moment he was too immature
to be a governor.

While visiting the Quaker school at Bristol Penn noticed an excellent teacher, a Scotch-Irishman named James Logan. Son of a Latin instructor and brother of a physician, young Logan had gained, even before entering his teens, what was represented as a reading knowledge of Latin, Greek, and Hebrew; the degree of proficiency may have been overstated, but he was later to add a smattering of Spanish, Italian, and French. Although still only twenty-five, he had already taught six years. In addition he was studying mathematics and general science as well as running a coastal shipping business.[1]

Logan was, of course, also too inexperienced to take over as Pennsylvania's governor, though Penn had made worse appointments and would again, but beginning as Penn's secretary, he could be trained to lift some of the administrative burdens from old Markham's shoulders. Penn therefore invited Logan to join him. The recruiting was fortunate; Logan was destined to become one of the most influential colonial statesman of his time.

In the summer of 1699 Penn prepared to sail for America. The departure was certainly unhurried. Although he received clearance from the Quaker meetings in mid-July and, a fortnight later, announced his intention to leave, it was not until August 6 that he preached a farewell sermon. This, however, was only a preliminary, followed a week later by a second farewell. This, too, turned out to be premature, for it was not until August 22 that the Penns boarded the ship *Canterbury*. Even then the Penns and Logans waited in harbor until September 8 before the ship put out to sea. Penn had left his province intending to remain in England for two years; he had been away fifteen.[2]

Hannah was pregnant, as Guli had been in 1682; but Philadelphia was much more developed than it had been in Guli's time, and adequate medical care would be available. Billy had stayed behind, ostensibly because his wife was also expecting a baby in about three months, but more likely because he was reluctant to leave the pleasures of London. Tish, the only other survivor of Guli's children, had joined her father and her stepmother.

Instead of taking with him doorframes for a country mansion as on his previous voyage, Penn brought along a library. Thanks to the decision of the Philadelphia Yearly Meeting in 1690 to subscribe to all books published under Quaker auspices, the province already possessed a sizable collection; but Penn, probably with the assistance of Logan, an astute bibliophile, shipped sixty-eight volumes. Except for *Don Quixote*, all were rather heavy going, for they included the works of Milton, Locke, and Algernon Sidney; the histories of Livy, Suetonius, and Diodorus Siculus; and for lighter moments, the recently published accounts of explorations by William Dampier and Father Louis Hennepin. The works were in Greek, Latin, Hebrew, French, and Italian, as well as in English. Oddly enough for a pacifist, half a dozen dealt with the art of warfare, especially the use of artillery. The technical treatises on agriculture, chemistry, and metallurgy, catalogued in the Pennsbury library in 1702, probably also came with him.[3]

The works, some of which may have been for Logan, were in Greek, Latin, Hebrew, French, and Italian, as well as in English. Oddly enough for a pacifist, half of a dozen dealt with the martial arts, especially the use of artillery.[3]

Penn also imported a stallion Tamerlane. Later report declared the horse a foal of the Godolphin Barb, though that famous sire did not began to cover until 1730.[4]

Because of all the London dockside talk about Pennsylvania pirates, it was not surprising that on his voyage to America the *Canterbury's* captain should have thought himself threatened by buccaneers. He saw a ship upon the horizon and therefore, as a prudent skipper, cleared his decks for action. As in such circumstances noncombatants, especially Quakers, were only encumbrances, he sent Penn and his family to their cabins. Logan, however, stayed on deck. Just how much help he was expected to render is problematic, but at least he was available.

The danger, if it existed, passed. Penn and his family returned to deck. According to a story that Benjamin Franklin credited to Logan, Penn rebuked his assistant for a willingness to take part in warlike action. Logan was said to have replied, "I, being thy servant, why didst thou not order me to come down? Thou was willing enough that I should stay and fight the ship when thou thought there was danger." Though the anecdote does not seem likely, in view of Logan's notoriously quick temper, to have been couched in such intricate language, it does illuminate both Logan's independence and Penn's unwillingness to compel anyone to an action not dictated by conscience.[5]

The voyage proved as comfortable as transatlantic passengers could expect in the seventeenth century. The *Canterbury* sailed past New Castle without stopping and on November 30 arrived at Chester. Penn distributed £6, among the members of the crew.[6]

Hannah, Penn, and Tish became the guests of Lydia Wade, his hostess on his first arrival. She may have been a bit surprised, for though his eventual return had long been awaited, Pennsylvanians had written him warning against his coming at just this time. The summer had been so hot that many people had been sunstruck, mosquitoes had been a plague, and then, in early autumn, an epidemic of Barbados (yellow) fever had carried off more than two hundred people. The warning letter had been sent so late that it passed him on the ocean.[7]

The effects of the epidemic were still evident. Chester rejoiced at the safe arrival of the Proprietor, but he sensed an underlying sadness. The town had "no lofty, airy countenance, no vain jesting or laughing, no witty repartee, no extravagant feasting . . . only pale faces and sunken countenances." Ordinarily Penn would have approved the seriousness and deplored vain jesting, but not under the tragic circumstances that prevailed in Chester.[8]

When, despite the general gloom, Chester planned a welcome ceremony, the luck was bad. A youngster, breaking the express orders of town officials, loaded and was about to discharge a small cannon, possibly one of those left over from the Dutch occupation, but the powder ignited prematurely and the cannon burst, so injuring the boy that his arm had to be amputated. Penn paid the surgeon's fee and cared for the injured youth, but eventually what was described as blood poisoning set in and the lad died.[9]

After four days at the Wade house catching up on provincial affairs, Penn was ready to go on to Philadelphia. Though there was a good road now from Chester to the city, he did not use the luxurious four-horse coach that had preceded him to Pennsylvania, nor ride his fine horse, Tamerlane. Instead, he again took the water route, largely to spare himself and the two women a tiring fifteen-mile ride but also, one suspects, to make a more dramatic entrance into his capital. For Penn, with his keen appreciation of the courtesies due his position, anticipated some sort of civic welcome, not perhaps elaborate as the turf-and-water ceremony of his first arrival at New Castle, but certainly some slight expression of his peoples' loyalty.

He timed his journey to meet their convenience. On this First Day morning, December 3, he believed, most citizens would be at worship close to the center city landing places. By leaving Chester early in the morning he would arrive just at the conclusion of the services, perhaps even a bit earlier so that he could himself drop in at Friends' meeting. If so, after a few words to his fellow Quakers, he could meet others after their own services were concluded. Thus, he could see all his people, tell them of his happiness at their well-being and his hopes for their continued prosperity, and give them an opportunity to welcome him.

As always when traveling by barge, he enjoyed the boat ride. The busy river traffic pleased him; it was mostly local business, to be sure, but a big ship was just coming into port from Bristol, one of the seven vessels, some of them three-hundred-tonners, that had arrived in this one year. He noted how the shore lines, quite unlike the vacant land seen on his first arrival, were dotted with good-sized houses. As he approached Philadelphia, he could see the spire of the new Anglican Christ Church, though probably no one told him that one of the treasures there was the very font from All Hallows Barking in which he had been baptized an Anglican. Gloria Dei, the Swedish Church, was also visible from the river, but the Quaker meetinghouses, more modest in their architecture, did not stand out so prominently. He would also have seen some lordly estates, notably that of Edward Shippen, who kept a herd of deer upon a spacious lawn that ran two city blocks to the river, a lovely lawn that, in warm seasons, glowed with flowers.[10]

Penn was particularly anxious to meet Shippen, famed as "the biggest man who owned the biggest house and rode in the biggest coach in Philadelphia." He had heard much of Shippen, one of the few wealthy New Englanders to become a Friend and who for this reason, according to general belief, had been whipped out of Boston for his faith. Removing to Philadelphia in 1694, he had, within a year, been chosen Speaker of the Assembly and, within another year, been made a provincial councillor and a county judge. Penn and his family were to live in Shippen's Great House until such time as a permanent residence was ready.[11]

The sight of Philadelphia made Penn proud. The town was growing. There were now some two thousand houses, caring for about five thousand people. Though most of the buildings were frame, and a few the log cabins of early days, at least four hundred were new, solid, three-story structures built either of the black-end brick brought in ballast from England or of the red brick baked from Pennsylvania clay.[12]

As Penn had anticipated, a welcoming committee met him at the dock. To his astonishment the group was not made up of influential Quakers, with William Markham at their head; but instead was largely comprised of people whom he had been led to believe would be unfriendly, Colonel Robert Quary being their spokesman. Their greeting was warm and courteous, but its unexpectedness so took Penn aback that, though usually punctiliously polite, he barely acknowledged their good wishes. Then, realizing that the Quakers had not come because they were still at meeting, he hurried to join them. His unexpected entrance—the Quakers had not expected him to come until later in the day—caused considerable stir.[13]

After meeting, Penn visited Markham who, not being a Quaker, had not attended meeting. Though it is highly probable that someone who had been at the dock must have carried word to the Deputy Governor that Penn was in town, Markham explained that he had not supposed that Penn would have journeyed on a First Day. Neither had he ventured to go down to Chester earlier in the week, lest he might find on arrival that Penn had gone to Philadelphia by a different route. It is very possible that Markham was at least a trifle miffed at not having been informed of Penn's plans.

After these calls Penn went over to Shippen's Great House on Second Street near Locust, where Hannah and Tish had preceded him. After the large Shippen family made him comfortable, giving up their best rooms for his accommodation, Penn turned to the task of consulting civic leaders about the province's social, political, and economic conditions.

Most of those he interviewed during the first two or three days were, quite understandably, his partisans and friends. Penn waited for Quary to call, but the latter, having done his duty at the dock, did not appear. "Penn seemed to admire Colonel Quary's distance," which, in other words, meant that Penn wondered why Quary stayed away.

When they did meet, the two men got along much better than either had anticipated, "each man acknowledging some faults of administration." Quary wrote back to London that Penn's arrival promised great changes for the better in the province. "He regrets and abhors what has been done, and assures the King's officers of his favor and encouragement. He is very zealous in promoting all things that doth in any way promote the King's interest." All of which indicates that Penn had lost none of his diplomatic skill.[14]

With so many problems to be solved and so much work to be done, Penn had little time at the beginning of his stay to survey the general state of his province, but even casual observation could teach him much. The aspect of the town pleased him. Philadelphia seemed prosperous. At Samuel Carpenter's Great Wharf stevedores busily loaded outbound ships with meat, grain, barrels of salt fish, and lumber. The ships would return from the West Indies with sugar and molasses to be distilled into rum. Some ships would trade the rum for Negro slaves.[15]

Penn, ordinarily an optimist, sometimes had doubts about the wisdom of such trade; it brought prosperity, to be sure, but the wealth was modifying to some degree the hitherto strict asceticism of Quaker life. Penn himself was not averse to luxury, as long as it was not ostentation nor the chief goal in life. With him, as with very many others, Quaker ethics and their concern for the welfare of others remained as strong as ever; but to some, comforts, even luxuries, were beginning to seem essential. Here, even more than in England, the Quaker garb was plain, though made of rich material; the house furnishings, almost pretentiously simple, were of the finest and most expensive quality. Penn's houseguests, like those of his father, Admiral Sir William, were regaled with choice foods, well cooked and served up in crystal, porcelain, and silver. All this was well enough, as long as Quakers retained their ideals and cared for the less fortunate; but in Philadelphia, as in England, there were too many who were selfish.[16]

There were other disturbing signs. Desirable as all those new houses were, they were encroaching on the open spaces he had wished to leave as breathing places and as fire deterrents. The town was losing its greenery. Worse, housing congestion was beginning to appear. Though large open tracts remained available for building on the outskirts of the settlement, citizens preferred to crowd closer to their neighbors. No slums were visible as yet, except, of course, in those caves along the Delaware waterfront, but a trend was beginning to appear. In planning a green country town, Penn had not envisaged five thousand people living in an urban area of less than half a square mile.

Yet residents were loath to spread out more thinly. Pleasant though it was to fish or hunt wild pigeons within a five- or ten-minute walk to the westward, parents warned their children to stray no farther than a mile or so from the Delaware, lest they be attacked by wolves.

Casual observers would not have detected signs of decay in the flourishing community. They would have been pleased by the new guildhall on High Street and by the noble structure called Clarke Hall, the favored place for social gatherings. They would have flocked to the city center at the proper hour to hear the town crier call out the important current news, or on pleasant evenings, take the air in well-kept public gardens. Probably they would even have approved the "convenient prison," with its pillory and whipping post, as a model of enlightened penology. But Penn, while approving all this except the need for the prison and its appurtenances, would have detected everywhere the signs of subtle corruption always bred by urban life.[17]

"The world," said Penn, "is apt to stick close to those who have lived and got wealth there."[18]

While Penn explored the political and economic situation, Tish enjoyed the social life. It was not exciting, there being nothing whatever in the nature of night life for a properly brought up Quaker girl. Except for gay blades like her brother Billy, life was drab for the young. Even so, Philadelphia offered more distraction than any other place where she had lived. Worminghurst was rural, with its only community life at rather distant Friends meeting, and London life was somewhat restricted. Possibly Bristol presented a little more opportunity for pleasure, but it was by no means wide open, especially not for members of the sedate Callowhill set.

In Philadelphia, William Masters, the boy next door, was interesting and popular, quite obviously the catch of the city. His family was rich, though not outstanding in government or business life; he did, however, have the lure of singularity, his mother being, like Tish's grandmother, an amateur of science. Both Sybilla Masters and Mary Penington Springett dabbled in medical matters, especially the marketing of patent medicines.[19]

Proper Philadelphia maidens set their caps for young Will Masters, discreetly and demurely to be sure, but none the less intentionally and with settled purpose. Tish became, for once, the center of attraction, for was she not the daughter of the first family of the province? Such popularity was new for Tish; she had always been envied for her wealth, but in Philadelphia she was the leader of her peers.

Tish flirted so effectively that gossip spread that she and Will Masters were either engaged or on the verge of being betrothed. They did not go out alone, for there were few places, except the meetinghouse, where nice young people could go alone; but when there was a gathering, Will and Tish somehow gravitated toward each other. Tish enjoyed the situation; it gratified her ego to be preferred above the other girls.

40

TROUBLE SHOOTING

Plenty of evidence proved to William Penn that urban life poisoned human relationships. Rural residents, he believed, were friendly and cooperative, as he naïvely assumed they had been in the best days of Bible times; city folk were competitive, envious, jealous, and selfish, eager to malign their fellows. He had seen such unfortunate developments in London: at court, where schemers connived to undercut each other's influence; in commercial circles, where cheating was accounted cleverness; even among religious people, who slandered one another most unjustly in the name of Christ.

He would have liked to escape to the country, to Bucks County, where Markham had built him a pretentious mansion, but there was too much for him to do in Philadelphia. Always the evangelist, he hoped that his example and his preaching would reclaim a city of vice and raise it to the heights where it might merit its name of brotherly love. As far as material progress was concerned, both the city and the province were prospering, but the social and political malaise, so evident under Blackwell, was reappearing in more virulent form now that Fletcher had departed. Penn's presence and his fatherly care could do much to reinvigorate the Holy Experiment.

There was, he saw, so much to be done. Good conduct and order had to be restored, rivalries and jealousies somewhat cooled; harmony had to be established between the Quakers and the various dissatisfied minorities. Above all mundane matters he must take action to convince the throne and its bureaucrats that he was loyal and obedient.[1]

Whether it was really true, as some knowledgeable Quakers and many uninformed but suspicious people of the world openly proclaimed, that he had recovered his province only by promising to do as he was told is really unimportant; the fact is that Penn's actions after his return gave credit to the story. Rumor had it that the Crown had told him that he must put Pennsylvania "in a posture of defense," that he must have his officeholders promise good behavior by something stronger than an affirmation, that he must take action, if necessary militant action, against pirates and smugglers and shipowners who traded with forbidden ports. All these injunctions had been made before, but Penn, more in innocence than by design, had failed to notice violations.[2]

The bureaucrats were also sternly warning Penn that he could not temporize, that it would not be safe for him to disregard their orders, even if those orders were couched in veiled suggestions, that if he was summoned to appear to answer questions, he would do well to come before the various boards and commissions from whom the orders came. He did not need to be reminded that his position under William and Mary was less secure than it had been under the Stuarts.

It is significant that soon after his return the Provincial Council began sending stiffer legislation to the Assembly. Penn certainly had no love for what would today be regarded as police-state regulations, but he did accept a new requirement that all innkeepers, ferrymen, and boatmen notify the authorities of the arrival of strangers "or other suspicious characters." All individuals must give proper accounts of themselves; the alternative was not spelled out but could have been nothing else than refusal of permission to enter the province or even arrest.[3]

Stricter controls threw much work upon the Council's shoulders. Prior to Penn's return it had been in recess for nearly five months, but one of his first requirements was that it meet weekly, with special meetings at his pleasure, the first of them within forty-eight hours of this announcement.

An early necessity was to correct the libels sent to London by Edward Randolph and other Royal agents. These officials had charged Pennsylvania with tolerating, if not indeed encouraging, piracy and illegal trading, but Penn pointed out that his province had a better record than any competing American colony. "We have never had a spot upon our garments, he boasted."[4]

Pennsylvania had been accused on only twenty-three occasions, less than half the number charged against little New Hampshire.

Nevertheless he thought it politic to reassure the Board of Trade that Pennsylvania was not unmindful of the danger that piracy and illegal trading might occur. Within three weeks of his arrival he issued a strong proclamation against such evils; a week later, the Provincial Council passed even stricter laws. Penn was careful to report such matters to his London overlords.[5]

The Council also tightened the laws affecting local activities. It established a night watch to patrol the town and defend citizens against fires, crimes, or public disorders. It repassed legislation concerning public markets, set standards for the size and price of loaves of bread, even forbade ships lying in harbor to fire their cannon when honoring guests, lest women, children, or visiting Indians be alarmed.[6]

For the encouragement of trade and for the development of the interior, the Council also cleared away stones and stumps in the public road paralleling the Delaware. As this was the highway that Penn would use in traveling to his country home upriver, whenever he did not use his six-oared barge, he thoroughly approved.[7]

He did not anticipate any immediate personal use of the roadway, however. Hannah, on January 6, had borne a son, John, thereafter dubbed John the American. Both mother and child were doing nicely; Penn was especially pleased at the welcome accorded the baby. Pastorius, then teaching school just up the street, assigned eight of his students, all those named John, to write notes of greeting to their namesake. The result, a collection of a hundred paragraphs in English, German, French, and Latin, could not have been solely a student production, but Pastorius put the tributes together in a pamphlet entitled *Onamastical Considerations*, which, thoughtfully, he translated as "Thoughts on Being Gloriously Named." Penn acknowledged the gift, a month later, by sending a letter in Latin to Pastorius's father in Germany, praising his friend as being "sober, upright, wise, pious and of a reputation approved on all hands and unimpeached."[8]

His euphoria vanished as the winter advanced, bringing with it the painful gout, "a distemper easily provoked by the churlish climate or season of the year." Pennsylvania, so highly lauded by Penn, when he was feeling well, as comparable to the Palestine of the Old Testament, he described in early March as "this desolate land." He also complained of fevers and an "ill shin." There were periods when he could neither ride nor walk and when even to use his hands caused pain. Much of the trouble, he believed, was traceable to fatigue due to the long hours spent at his desk, to the tiring rides he made about the province whenever his "gout" permitted, or to the bitterness of arguments with his legislature and his agents. It was an unscientific diagnosis, but Penn could think of no other reason, for at fifty-six he did not consider that he might be growing old.[9]

Except in his youth and in the early days of the Holy Experiment, he had never been overly optimistic. He believed in the essential goodness of mankind if, that is, men followed the teachings of the Scriptures; but with the influx into Pennsylvania of so many non-Quakers and with the corruption of some few members of the Society of Friends by the lure of profit or the prospect of power, he was losing faith in people. Instead of living in harmony, as he had naïvely supposed they would in his provincial Eden, they were contentious and argumentative; all too many of them were tolerant of practices that Penn lumped together under the category of vice.

He was especially hurt at what he considered the ingratitude of almost everyone whom he had tried to help. He could not have forgotten that he had received the province not as a gift, nor as a field for social service, but as a business transaction, an exchange of property to cancel a debt; he could not rid himself of the idea that the Crown was more generous to others than it was to him. Neighbor governors who had done the King less service were receiving, Penn complained, as much as £3000 a year from the Royal treasury, while he, "intently doing the King's business at my own risk," was being ignored.[10]

To Penn it seemed shameful that after he had sold acreage and been paid for it, the people to whom he had been so kind recognized no further obligation to support him. They would not even build him "a pretty box" on his own land to which he might retire to live among them. That "pretty box," as he envisioned it, would, if it were ever built, match the Shippen place in size and luxury.[11]

The legislature, to which he had given a blank check for any laws that thoughtful men might reasonably desire, did not reciprocate. Now and then they went through the motions of voting taxes for his benefit, but almost always they overlooked making provisions for collection of the imposts. If such laws existed no one checked up on the collectors to see if they were executing the laws or, if they knew who was delinquent, if they were punishing the offenders.

The Assembly posed the most difficulty. Regarding itself as the local counterpart of the English House of Commons, it demanded not only equality with the Provincial Council but, as Penn saw it, with the Proprietor himself. Under the domination of David Lloyd, whom Logan characterized as "a man very stiff in all his undertakings, of a sound judgment and a good lawyer but very pertinaceous and somewhat revengeful," the Assembly was more than liberal and democratic; for the times, it could be classed as radical.[12]

To restore the trust and brotherhood that had marked the inauguration of the Holy Experiment would not be easy, nor could it be accomplished overnight. It required not only much time but Penn's daily presence at the scene of action. He could not, therefore, live at Pennsbury, thirty miles from Philadelphia, even if the road to the Falls of the Delaware were cleared immediately, but must reside in Philadelphia, where he could continue in close contact with his legislators and administrators.

Considerate as he always tried to be of others, he could not help realizing that the presence of Hannah and himself, of Tish and the newborn John the American strained the facilities even of Shippen's Great House. He moved, therefore, a few short blocks, to Samuel Carpenter's Slate Roof House at what is now Second and Sansom Streets. This was a wooden structure "with brick trimmings," which, though a dozen years old, was still one of the finest buildings in town, well worth the £80 rental Penn paid for a two-year lease. There, on an estate worth £850, he entertained so lavishly that Lord Edward Cornbury, the eccentric Governor of New Jersey, asserted that Penn's dinners equaled any that he had ever been served in all America.[13]

In accordance with his conviction that good government was not to be assured by good laws alone but depended rather on a climate of good will among all men, he set himself to end the feuds that were disrupting Pennsylvania's peace. His remedy was simple; if only men loved one another, avoided factions, feared God, and heeded the Scriptures, their tensions would relax. There would be differences in men's opinions, but appeals to reason, calm consideration, and an earnest search for truth would teach the proper course to be pursued.

Penn grieved that such a course had not been followed. He had done all he could to please his people. No other governor had been so generous as he in granting whatever right-minded people might reasonably desire; nowhere else had either a proprietor or the Crown required so little in the form of service or of taxes, yet his Pennsylvanians, ungrateful for their blessings, demanded more and more.

Much of the trouble could be traced, he thought, to rivalry between Royal representatives, intent on breaking his charter, and his own officials. Edward Randolph, the seventy-year-old surveyor of customs, and newly arrived Robert Quary, the vice-admiralty agent, were, in Penn's view, working to bring Pennsylvania under Crown control; their aggressions were obvious, extreme, and to Penn's mind grossly unfair. Such hostility was not confined to Pennsylvania, for Lord Baltimore had undergone the same harassment and just across the river, precisely the same conflict was bringing New Jersey to the verge of civil war.

The Royal officials had grievances too. Edward Randolph, whose jurisdiction was nominally New England, was alert to trade practices that might impair customs revenues due the King. Believing himself commissioned to find reasons for extending Royal rule by canceling semi-independent proprietary charters, he took it upon himself to investigate the middle provinces as well. Since 1696 he had been reporting to the Lords of Trade and Plantations that Maryland tobacco was being illegally shipped to forbidden European markets. In multiple reports he revealed the cheating of the King's revenue, the mislabeling of casks and the misstatement of weights.[14]

As long as Randolph confined himself to spying on vessels sailing from the Chesapeake, Pennsylvanians were unconcerned; they may have gloated over Randolph's disclosure of Maryland guilt. The Marylanders changed their tactics, carting the tobacco across the Lower Counties to be shipped from Delaware River ports. Randolph followed, "yapping like a dog," a critic observed, at the heels of the exporters.[15]

Part of the yapping consisted of attacks upon the Pennsylvania gov-

ernment as arbitrary; moreover, it did not require jurors or witnesses in
court trials to swear oaths to tell the truth. Markham, now once more the
Deputy Governor, though not yet approved by the King, not only condoned piracy but befriended buccaneers and had arrested Randolph for
protesting.

Penn twice condemned "Randall" himself as "the greatest offender in
illegal trading." The false weighing charges were, Penn admitted, completely true, but it had been "my one-eyed friend" Randolph who had
instituted the practice, thus defrauding the King of more than £8000 of
customs dues.[16]

Despite the roadblocks set up by David Lloyd and others, Penn tried
sincerely, sometimes perhaps against his better judgment, to follow
London's wishes, not solely because he feared quo warranto but out of
loyalty to the Crown. Because Colonel Quary of the vice-admiralty court
charged Lloyd with acting in bad faith, Penn suspended Lloyd from his
post as attorney general. He saw to it that the falsification of the weights
of tobacco casks came to an end. All this Penn made very sure that
London realized. Just what assurances the Lords had received of Penn's
administration are uncertain but, as he wrote his superiors: "You'll per-
ceive I am in earnest in the prosecution of what I gave you to expect of
me." Randolph and Quary, he repeated, were dishonest. "Some of the
unkindest folks to our government have been the famousest transgres-
sors," Penn declared.[17]

Happily for Pennsylvania Randolph ceased to interfere. Whether
because of illegal trading in Bermuda or because of his caustic criticisms,
the island government sent him to jail. Upon his release Randolph went
back to England where he died in 1702.

On information that must have been sent by Quary, the Board of
Trade complained that Penn had broken a promise not to interfere with
Admiralty concerns. The Pennsylvania officials carefully looked the other
way when a ship arriving from Curaçao unloaded at midnight at a private
dock; they did not notice its arrival until the hold was empty.[18]

Quary feuded with Penn-appointed officials who interfered with the
international trading, shipping, and customs violations that he considered his own sphere of influence. Though he praised Penn for making
honest efforts to root out piracy, to suppress illegal trading, and to protect Royal interests, he resented the presumption of local agents or of
provincial courts in thinking that they, too, should try to police such
matters.

David Lloyd, the young lawyer whom Penn had picked from obscu-
rity in 1686 as his attorney general, was a case in point. Lloyd was no
friend of smugglers or pirates but a brilliant lawyer, one of the best in
the colonies. He had become convinced that Pennsylvania was mature
enough for more self-government. Quary opposed the idea; instead of

strengthening Royal control it would undermine the plan to unite the provinces under the Crown. Incautiously, Lloyd opened an opportunity for Quary to attack him. While objecting to the London government's intrusion into provincial affairs, he brandished an official communication and, pointing to the Great Seal of England bearing William III's portrait, thundered that Pennsylvanians were not weaklings who would be frightened by a baby's picture.[19]

It was a silly gesture and a pointless one, for no stretch of the imagination could confuse the image of fifty-year-old William with that of a small child, but Quary hastened to tell the Committee of Trade and Plantations what had happened; it was, Quary intimated, an insult to the King, if not lese majesty, besides, said Quary, Lloyd had been "irreverend." London thereupon ordered Lloyd dismissed.[20]

As Lloyd's successor, Penn favored the appointment of one Paracletus Parmyter, an attorney and, at the moment, naval attaché to Richard Coote, Lord Bellomont, the Governor of New York. Parmyter's first name was peculiar, but Penn, with his wide knowledge of the Bible, would have recognized it as a title of the Holy Spirit, the Comforter or Intercessor; it was also the name of a convent founded by Abelard of which Héloïse was abbess. Parmyter who was, not surprisingly, Penn's cousin, had been buying wine by the hogshead for Penn, and the Proprietor began a routine investigation to see if he were suitable as an attorney-general. The outcome, a few months later, would provide additional ammunition for Robert Quary.[21]

41

PENNSBURY MANOR

NOWHERE, PENN BELIEVED, WAS URBAN CORRUPTION MORE EVIDENT THAN IN HIS BELOVED PHILADELPHIA. EVEN HAD HE BEEN ABLE TO TOLERATE ITS VICE AND CRIME, ITS HEAVY DRINKING OR THE UNspeakable abominations of its caves, he could not have endured its noise and bustle or the perils posed by those excited horsemen celebrating all occasions by racing up and down the crowded streets, often with their guns blazing. Living in such an environment he could not meditate or write; he needed peace and quiet.

Luckily, Pennsbury, was ready for his Bucks County mansion occupancy. Though about a fifth of the original acreage had been sold off, or given to freed slaves or bound men who had served their terms, 6543 acres still remained. In April 1700, therefore, when spring had come and Hannah was once more able to travel, Penn and his family moved upriver. He kept the Slate Roof House as a town office and a place to stay when he must be in Philadelphia, but Pennsbury was his refuge.[1]

Neither Hannah nor Tish looked forward to living in the country. Hannah expected to be busy managing a household that would lack the amenities of Worminghurst and Bristol. Tish, just past her twenty-first birthday, had serious forebodings. She was not a particularly sparkling belle, but in Philadelphia she enjoyed social prestige by virtue of her father's position. Some of the fruits of this would be lost in sparsely settled Bucks County, nor would she see as much of William Masters, the beau of Philadelphia, with whom she and two other girls had been flirting. In her absence from the city what success would that Penington minx or the too-forward Susannah Harwood be achieving? For they, Tish led her father to believe, violated "faith, truth and righteousness" in their striving for him. Poor Tish! Her company up in Bucks County would be politicians, businessmen, and Indian chiefs who, even if her father did call them kings, would be poor substitutes for William Masters. Girls of her own age probably would be very few.[2]

Nevertheless, the two ladies resigned themselves to Pennsbury. To ride there, carrying a six-week-old baby, would have been impractical, and the calash, a low-wheeled carriage, while excellent for city streets, would have been too light for rough country roads. They went up by river, using Penn's magnificent six-oared barge. It was one of Penn's few prized earthly possessions; "above all dead things," he was wont to say, "I love my barge." Well he might, for it had cost him £15, a sum sufficient to feed a family of six for a full month. As all too often, he was dilatory in paying the boatbuilder.[3]

Hannah and Tish must have been impressed when, on landing at Pennsbury, they walked a broad brick pathway, flanked by rows of poplars, and rising, by two terraces, to a stately sixty-foot-wide mansion that stood, amid gardens, with the forest as a background. Those eighteen rose slips which he had brought with him from England were not yet in bloom, nor were his fruit trees and his walnuts, hawthorns, and hazel trees in leaf, but the gardens were well kept and the lawns a healthy green.

Entering through the door whose frame Penn had brought from England on his first voyage, they found, to their right, the best room and a dining hall, behind which lay the kitchen and a pantry. To the left of the main entrance Penn had a reception room and, off this, an inner sanctum and his library. Mounting to the second floor they found four bedrooms and, above these, more sleeping quarters and an attic.

Penn was less impressed. He had already laid out £2049 on Pennsbury and was expecting to pay some £5000 more, but his builders had skimped on their work. The front of the house, as he had specified, was brick, but the rear was only clapboard. He had paid for solid brick foundations, but the builders had filled in some places with stones and rubble. Moreover, the cistern on the roof leaked badly.[4]

Hannah and Letitia, in white or lavender satin, presided over a sumptuous table. The meats and vegetables were mostly homegrown, and Penn, to be on the safe side, had imported barrels of beef from England. The kitchen gardens, in addition to the more customary vegetables, yielded "sparre grass, parsnips, hartichokes, salatin." Home-brewed beer and cider pressed from Pennsbury apples were the usual beverages, but there was always an abundance of wines, Madeira or Canary; Penn was hopeful that his French and German colonists would produce a drinkable local wine. The Penns liked chocolate, tea, and coffee; for most Pennsylvanians these were novelties. They were expensive, also; a pound of coffee beans cost almost as much as a workman's weekly wage.[5]

The quality of furnishings matched that of the mansion. Ordinarily the Penns ate from pewter plates, but they owned silver in abundance, even eight silver forks, a refinement known since Elizabeth's time in England but rare in most colonial homes. Philadelphia had not yet produced the master craftsmen who would turn out triumphs in mahogany furniture, but Pennsbury had honest oak and walnut tables, fourposters, and comfortable leather or cane seat chairs, or drawing-room seats (satin covered for the ladies, green plush for the men).

Upstairs rooms boasted satin hangings, with here and there striped linens of that Asian silk-wool fabric known as silver camlet. Silk quilts covered the beds, with damask drapes at the windows. Small "rugs" graced the tables and, to the astonishment of visitors, one whole room was carpeted wall-to-wall.

The luxury did not betray a personal extravagance, for Penn's "family" of three adults and a baby, together with his household staff of seven and a number of clerks (Penn called them writers) entailed an average cost, exclusive of homegrown supplies, of less than £3 per day. Even so, some considered that he lived ostentatiously.[6]

They were not so much concerned with his extravagance as with his supposed formality. One of his closest political friends, a leader of the commercial establishment, compared his style of living with that of the Royal court. The ever hostile Francis Bugg reported him as living like the Grand Mogul. You might, were you exceptionally lucky, said Bugg, meet Penn in a carefully arranged audience, but at other times an armed guard kept you at your distance. Whenever the great man deigned to move beyond Pennsbury, the unveracious author averred, Penn was invariably surrounded by an armed bodyguard of his top officials.[7]

Far from repelling would-be interviewers, the Pennsbury neighbors testified, Penn welcomed them. He worked in his study during the mornings, but in the afternoons he roamed his estate, sometimes on his great white horse, sometimes afoot but always alert. He chatted freely with anyone he met. One young man, whom Penn had met on a public coach, recalled, though not with perfect accuracy, that Penn's conversation "was wholesome to the soul, for Penn loved wit and was fond of jest." The description does not sound like Penn, but he made the young man his London agent.[8]

Penn's chief problem lay in staffing this rural retreat adequately. He early realized that he needed a resident manager, a superior steward, one not only capable of carrying out detailed instructions but himself endowed with ingenuity and skill. He was willing to supply such a paragon with a corps of assistants, including a builder, a head gardener, a vintner, even a window sash expert, but good men were hard to find. Some he sent from the Worminghurst estate, others he acquired on the recommendation of friends; but all were to be mature and with successful experience. He would pay them well, give them land as well as wages, and guarantee them employment as long as they wished to stay.

His terms were excellent, but his requirements were so high that he could not take on young men but must enroll older men from whom he could not expect long service. Within the first three years he lost not only his steward, Thomas Fitzwater, but also Ralph Smith, a Scotch-Irish gardener, "well recommended by the best in town, apt to talk but an artist." Smith's term had been surprisingly brief, possibly because he was overburdened. Penn's instructions had been detailed and numerous. "Build fences, level the ground, brick steps, set out a garden. . . . Let a peach be planted between every apple tree. Save all peaches on Indian lands and make a barrel of wine or two and dry the rest, a few preserved when almost ripe, twenty inch wide gravelled walks, handsome steps, make both wine and beer."

The neighborliness and cooperation that Penn expected to find among people of good will in a tolerant community was at once apparent. Major Jasper Harmer, hearing in 1683 that the Proprietor needed help, sent over one of his own workmen, George Booth, with a large chest of carpenter's tools, to lend a hand. Unfortunately, Booth lacked any such warm-heartedness. Instead of reporting for work at Pennsbury, he ran away, taking Harmer's tools with him, and never was heard of more. Thirty years later the Harmer estate suggested that Penn might wish to indemnify the estate for the cost of the tools, but Penn was then in England and may never have known of the request.[9]

Penn had hoped to draw his workmen first from disadvantaged Quakers of his own country, from Europeans of similar religious and social beliefs, and then from the poor or landless of any community. The response to his appeal for immigrants had been so flattering as to be embarrassing. Because of the low rates charged for land, purchasers bought more acreage than single families could cultivate. Extra labor was essential, but with fertile land so cheap and plentiful, free men preferred to work their own farms rather than hire out to others.

Penn's recourse was to indenture labor. Persons who desired to emigrate but who could not pay their passage could go free to America provided they agreed to work a specified time for anyone who would advance the travel costs. Indentured servants, or as the Germans called them, redemptioners, had been common in the Delaware Valley since Swedish times. England had used the system to train apprentices, but Pennsylvania also used it for mature workers, and for a longer period, than did any other colony. Free men and women over twenty-one years of age, in arranging their indentures, could bind themselves to any length of service; though in Pennsylvania, no minor could be so bound beyond his twenty-second birthday. To encourage the practice, Penn allowed a master fifty acres of free land for each redemptioner he imported. The bound man worked to repay his travel costs and his board and keep. Upon completion of his contract, he would receive at least fifty acres for himself; he was also to receive a new suit of clothes, ten bushels of wheat or fourteen bushels of corn as seed for the land, an ax and a hoe, and tools that would enable him to start a small farm of his own. Penn himself gave his own indentured servants at least a hundred acres.[10]

There were, of course, drawbacks to the system. Legally, redemptioners during their period of service were property whose services could be sold, or, as in Booth's case, lent, by one master to another. The indentured servants, occupying a position midway between slavery and freedom, were in addition controlled by laws which a Pennsylvania court later regarded as "exceedingly severe." Since those laws were English laws, however, Pennsylvania was unable to modify them.[11]

Rules provided for discipline of the redemptioners. A servant who ran away, who was unruly, or who tried to evade work was obliged to serve five extra days for each day of insubordination, negligence, or unexcused absence; in addition he worked out any costs of damage his conduct might have caused his master.

On the other hand, the redemptioner received protection. His working hours were set by law, with provisions for good treatment and for rest periods. Servants could lodge complaints which would be investigated and if well founded would result in punishing the masters. If, on the other hand, a protest was unwarranted, the petitioner must serve three extra months.

Penn laid down admonitions for the indentured servants. They must not cheat their masters, rob them, or blacken their reputations. Since he had already counseled all men and women about their responsibilities in social and civic life and about their duty of charity and kindness toward fellow men, he saw no need to repeat his injunctions; but the absence of any mention of employer recommendations opened the door to unfair criticism that William Penn was indifferent to the rights of workmen.

Some employers resented the "tenderness" with which strict Quakers in general, and William Penn in particular, treated their servants. Nicholas, Moore, head of the Free Society of Traders, complained that the province discriminated against employers. He was especially indignant that redemptioners who committed sexual offenses were merely fined or imprisoned. Since bound men rarely had much pocket money, this punishment meant that offenders went to jail, which according to More merely meant that as a reward for their transgression the culprits enjoyed a holiday from work. No one really suffered except the innocent master, who lost the labor that was his due. The legislators may not have sensed the humor in such a situation, but they did amend the criminal code to specify that the jail sentence must be at hard labor. Since this was no more than would have been exacted had the offender returned to his ordinary duties, the master still remained the loser.[12]

Because Penn recruited labor in a hurried, rather haphazard fashion, not all his employees proved satisfactory. There were exceptions, such as John Chandler, who came under a four-year indenture and remained for fifteen before accepting his release. Too many others, in Penn's phrase, were merely so-so. One, Penn complained, could neither plow nor sow; his only redeeming quality was his good nature, though he spoiled the effect of that by his constant swearing. A man hired to be a ranger, neighbors objected, sharpened his hunting skills by shooting their hogs.

Among his best choices was a German-born shoemaker named John Sacher—whose name Penn always spelled Sotcher—and an old friend, Mary Lofty, who had been a lady's maid at Worminghurst but of whom he had lost sight after Guli's death. Penn had, in fact, recommended her to Hannah, but she, while politely admitting that Mary was efficient, had been somewhat less than enthusiastic about anything or anyone connected with Guli's domestic arrangements. Tish, however, joined her father in approving of Mary, and so she was added to the Pennsbury household.[13]

Shortly thereafter Mary and John became engaged, and in October 1701, just before the Penns were to sail for England, they were married. Both Penn and Tish gave wedding presents, Penn a £5 gift well in advance of the ceremony, but Tish delayed seven months before having a £7 chest of drawers sent the happy couple. Tish charged the present to her father's cash account.

After Penn's departure the Sachers took over management of the Pennsbury estate. The assignment pleased Mary more than it did her husband, for John Sacher developed a streak of restlessness. Within six weeks of his appointment as manager he yielded to the appeal of greener pastures, leaving a moping Mary to run the estate. Then he returned for a while, though dreaming of a place of his own, and so went off again to operate a ferry over the Delaware at nearby Bristol. Finally, tiring of that occupation, he returned to Pennsbury, serving there for sixteen more years.

From a distance Penn kept as close an eye as was possible upon the treatment of his bound servants. The Sachers, and James Logan too, were instructed to be "kind to poor Lucy and Dutch," the latter probably a seamstress named Elizabeth Shoemaker or Schumacher. There was also a young lady named Mueller, "the good Dorothy," of whom nothing more is known except that she married one who, before the wedding at least, had been nicknamed "the unhappy German." Unfortunately, there was no further news about his disposition.

There were at least fifteen or twenty other redemptioners, among them, apparently, one Stephen Gould, whose mother was a Penn relative and who was William Penn's clerk and "something of a lawyer." Some of them ran away, but most of them served their time, received their free suits and their promised tools, and so became their own masters. It is remarkable, however, how many of them preferred to stay on at Pennsbury.

Even conceding that the indenture system reduced workmen to semi-serfdom, the life was pleasant, and the labor probably not so taxing as that of an English farmhand. Penn's stewards, being less slave overseers than first among equals, followed Penn's policy of treating subordinates as they would members of the household. Penn, in fact, referred to his staff as "the family."

The indenture system failed to satisfy William Penn in all respects; it seemed weighted against the "servants." That provision, for instance, granting fifty acres at the completion of a contract, was being interpreted as a gift to the master in addition to the fifty acres received as compensation for advancing travel costs. Penn felt that this was double payment, the master having already been reimbursed by the redemptioner's labor. Penn had attempted to remedy the injustice. In drafting, and indeed in printing, the first few copies of *Some Account of the Province*, he had made it clear that the bound man was not to be thus cheated, but pressure of some sort, perhaps from the Free Society of Traders, forced a deletion of the safeguard; later issues of the pamphlet did not carry the protecting passages.[14]

The continued abuse of the land-grant clauses, together with possibility that bound men, if they wished, might easily run off and never be recovered, may be why Penn preferred blacks to indentured white men. "I would have but a little family," he wrote about his Pennsbury work force, "indeed, none but the blacks."[15]

What he enjoyed most at Pennsbury, next to the clean country air and the highly visible "works of God," were his horses, his three brood mares and their colts, his great white gelding Silas, and the "big bull nag" he liked to ride. But why should William Penn, apostle of peace, have named his favorite mount after Tamerlane, who certainly was not a pacifist!

42

BLACKS ARE BETTER

EVER SINCE THE YEAR OF HIS CHIGWELL VISION, WHEN HE WAS ELEVEN, WILLIAM PENN HAD BEEN MORE OR LESS FAMILIAR WITH SLAVES AS INDIVIDUALS AND, AT LEAST SINCE HIS CONVINCEMENT, WITH THE evils of slavery as an institution. But given the conditions of the period, when workmen generally were untaught and exploited, it is not surprising that he failed to realize that the slave's plight was worse than that of the ordinary workman.

Workmen of whatever age, color, or sex in England labored hard and for long hours, often under primitive conditions. Without labor unions, and with no legal right to strike, deprived sometimes even of the right to change their masters, they had little control over their working conditions or their wage scales, no voice in management, and very little opportunity to change their lot. The slave, because he was valuable property, had at least an assurance of some kind of food and shelter, low grade though it might be, but the free laborer had no safeguard against starvation or any assurance of care in his illness or old age. Under such circumstances, the seventeenth-century man, however progressive, farsighted, or benevolent, could think of slavery as an unfortunate but not necessarily evil institution. To be sure, the slave lacked social and political privileges, but so did the great majority of so-called free laborers. The slave in England, moreover, was likely to be a house servant in a reasonably well-to-do household and so accustomed to better living than field hands on an American plantation. Slavery was not completely abolished in England until 1778.

Penn and his fellow Quakers were among the first to call for betterments. Almost a century before Europeans were thinking of slaves as human beings, the Quakers were concerned about their souls. "Negroes and Indians are as much children of God as are their masters," said George Fox in 1657. Only a few years later, Penn was founding colonies where human slavery, instead of being lifelong, was to be limited to a term of years. Penn pioneered in granting to Negroes and Indians all the religious freedoms he accorded to the whites. He looked upon a slave not as the property of a master but as a member of the family.

The Penns acquired their first black while the Admiral was winning Jamaica for the English Crown. This Negro, Sampson, did not, however, remain long with the Penns, for in February 1655 the Admiral traded him to a Barbados merchant in exchange for one Anthony. The Admiral's motive was meritorious, for it placed him somewhat in the role of a missionary; he was en route for England and Anthony "seemed to have a desire to become a Christian." (It was probably Anthony who, four years later, wept so copiously on hearing Thomas Loe's moving sermon at Macroom.) [1]

What happened to Anthony is unclear, but two years later, in 1661, when the Penns were again living on Tower Hill, Anthony was gone, replaced by another Negro, Jack, whose interests were more worldly; he and a fellow black, Mungo, the property of Sir William's crony and benefactor Admiral Sir William Batten, entertained the Tower Hill set by dancing at the strident evening parties.[2]

William's next recorded knowledge of slavery may have occurred when, in 1668, his father and four others invested in a trading venture to the Ivory Coast of Africa. Just what resulted was not widely publicized, but we do know that the ship *Alcana Merchant*, carried a cargo of 367 dozen knives, 27 dozen pottingers, together with some beads and chintz —surely not a full cargo. The captain was to sell or barter the goods. Possibly, since the Royal African Company had not yet monopolized the slave trade, the syndicate may have been planning to take on human freight.[3]

Whatever may have been the purpose, it was not attained; only confusion and contradiction followed. When, years later, Penn went to the court of chancery to clear up matters, he declared that the goods remained unsold and unbartered, yet they had disappeared; there was, he said, a bag of "proceeds" somewhere which had never been delivered to the Admiral or to his friends and which had never been accounted for. He asked the Chancellor to clarify the matter, but thereafter nothing happened.

Penn's personal involvement in slave relationships began with his acquisition of a province. In drafting the Frame of Government for Pennsylvania he was compelled to recognize that slavery had been legal, though not widespread, under the Swedes and Dutch, as well as under the Duke of York. He would have liked to follow a Fox suggestion of 1671 limiting a slave's service to a term of years, but to manumit by a proprietor's edict would have been confiscatory. He could, however, limit future slavery and so, in helping to create the Free Society of Traders, he included that clause allowing freedom to blacks after fourteen years of service, if the slaves to be freed would turn over to the Society two-thirds of the produce grown on lands given them by that organization. It was a high rental, even though the former slave received the land free, but it was liberal for the times, and it was unique.

The terms "slaves" and "slavery" now beginning to convey unpleasant connotations, the Quakers resorted to euphemism. They dropped the objectionable words, substituting the word "servant," which could apply to everyone from the lowliest slave to the highest official serving the Proprietor. Early Pennsylvania records, therefore, place lifetime slaves, term-service slaves, apprentices, and indentured labor in the one all-inclusive category of "servants." As an almost unbreakable rule, all slaves were black, while the great majority of apprentices and bound men were white, but official records do not specify color. The only possible clue is whether the individual had a family, as well as a Christian name. It is therefore difficult, maybe impossible, to determine just when or under what circumstances William Penn acquired a slave. There had been servants in England prior to the Pennsylvania venture, Francis Cooke and Philip Ford for example, but these were neither slaves nor were they indentured; quite probably they were under verbal, but not written, contract. Not that there was, as yet, any revulsion in England against enslavement of what would later be termed undeveloped peoples; many good citizens were in fact convinced that slavery, under benign and considerate masters, evidenced a philanthropic spirit.

William Penn would have shared the view. The soul of a black man was more important than his body. Unlike Benjamin Furly and a very few other extremists, he saw nothing wrong in controlling the labor of workmen, white or black, as long as they were accorded fair and humane treatment; he did insist that every human being, regardless of skin color or social status, was, as a creature of God, equal in God's sight and so entitled to equality among men. A restriction of freedom would be regrettable, but if, as in Anthony's case, it helped bring about a better understanding of true religion, that restriction could be pardoned.

With such a prevalent philosophy and in such a social milieu, it was not surprising that from the outset Pennsylvania countenanced slavery. Everywhere in America farm labor was in short supply and with so much good acreage available at low prices and on easy terms, farm hands were difficult to retain. James Claypoole of the Free Society of Traders, among other Quaker merchants, had been buying blacks from his brother in Barbados. Penn's own business agent in America, Philip Lehnmann, was using the ship *Isabella* in the slave trade. A Bristol firm, headed by Charles Jones, Jr., possibly Billy's brother-in-law, was also interested in sending slaves to Philadelphia.[4]

As early as 1683, Penn himself was buying slaves, some of them from that Captain Nathaniel Allen, who only a year or so earlier had shocked the community by selling a "servant" for six hundred pounds of beef, "with the tallow and hide" plus £6 in sterling. Penn was also selling slaves, among them an expert fisherman for whom he exacted "a full price, for the man will expect it of me."[5]

Penn determined in early 1687 that he would staff his Pennsbury plantation exclusively with black labor under a white overseer. "It was better they was blacks," Penn said of his labor, "for then a man has them while they live."[6]

While Penn was reaching his decision concerning the Pennsbury work force, a tide of antislavery sentiment was rising in his province. Germantown residents, acting in conjunction with a group of emigrants from Cresheim in Westphalia, protested against the buying, selling, and enslavement of human beings, or, as they put it, against trafficking in human flesh. Most of the signers of their protest, the first of its kind in America, were Quakers, but they voiced the general feeling of the little village north of Philadelphia.[7]

Francis David Pastorius, their leader, submitted their protest to their monthly and quarterly meetings. Both bodies approved but took no formal action, because they considered the matter "of too great weight" for them to pass upon; they forwarded the petition to William Penn.[8]

For Penn the situation was embarrassing. Barely a month after the Cresheim protest the *Isabella* had brought in blacks whom Lehnmann had marketed for him. Nor was this all. Though Penn was not at the time aware of it, he was soon to receive another Negro as the bequest of a Quaker from Barbados. Lewis Morris had moved up to New York to establish an estate on what was called Bronck's Land, just north of the Harlem River. He left a slave, Yaffe, to Penn on condition that Penn establish a permanent residence in America.[9]

Penn was living at the time in England and would not return to Pennsylvania for eight years, and then only for a visit, but Yaffe became his property. He was, said Penn, "an able planter and a good husbandman."[10]

Yaffe was one of two favorite slaves. The other was Chevalier, who had arrived at Pennsbury in 1687. They were not the only blacks for whom Penn had a fondness; there were several who, because of length of service, devotion to their work, or fidelity to the Proprietor, had won particular attention; but Yaffe and Chevalier were preferred. The feeling was reciprocated. Try as Penn did to set them free, Chevalier stayed on for more than thirty years, while Yaffe, though he left for a few months in 1703, continued thereafter in Penn's service.

Something of a struggle ensued in Pennsylvania between those who would have abolished slavery and those, such as Penn, who would merely have softened its rigors. Orthodox Quakers would have rejected a suggestion that any connection existed between the abolitionists and the firm stand taken against slavery by the followers of George Keith, founder of the heretical Christian Quaker movement; but there was at least a parallel between them, and taken together, they gave abolition a strong push forward. In 1698, Pentecost Teague persuaded the Friends to condemn the public auctioning of slaves, which so cut into the business of slave trading that it became necessary to express "the sense of the meeting" with a certain amount of deftness. The Friends meeting, accordingly, drafted a letter to their fellow Quakers in Barbados, asking the latter not to send more blacks to Philadelphia because the city, with about one thousand Negro population, was already overstocked. The message did not suggest that Philadelphia merchants or shipowners encouraged the slave trade, but implied that Barbados people were responsible.[11]

Penn had always played an active part in the amelioration movement, his theory being that all would be well if masters and servants alike followed Christian principles. To that end he recommended that servants be welcomed at First Day meetings, with their masters sitting with them, and that a special monthly meeting be set up for Negroes and Indians, the latter to have an interpreter. This suggestion was adopted, but two other Penn suggestions failed. Penn had proposed that a separate township of six thousand acres be created, to be called Freetown, where servants who had worked out their time, and presumably those who had been manumitted, might live together in freedom. It would moreover be well, he thought, if Negro marriages could be regulated, and if special attention could be given to promote the morals, as well as the welfare, of all servants. The Provincial Council approved, but the Assembly, always at that juncture un-cooperative, declined to concur; perhaps because delegates from the Three Lower Counties opposed anything that Philadelphia favored.[12]

Philadelphia's antislavery sentiment, strong among Quakers at least, had exerted such an effect upon Penn that, having pursued his all-black plan so thoroughly that only two white servants remained at Pennsbury, he decided to free all his slaves and to return to his indenture policy.[13]

Differences within the Penn family seem to have delayed action. Letitia was loath to give up the luxury of her personal maid, a woman whom her father described as "a most impudent slut"; Tish may also have been the person who delayed the manumission of another servant whom Hannah charitably regarded as "without integrity."[14]

According to James Logan, Penn, to assure that whatever happened, his slaves would be freed, drafted two important documents which apparently he did not show the family. One, a last will and testament, to be released if he should die, liberated his servants; the other, for possible use if he should live, conferred the same freedom. He entrusted both documents to Logan, with instructions to hold them in confidence until further orders.[15] A new will, written three years later, in 1704, did not contain the emancipation provision.

Though Penn had planned manumission, he had no intention of casting his servants loose; he intended rather to convert them into tenants living on, or close to, his estate, much as his father, the Admiral, had clustered his Navy comrades about him at Macroom and Shanagarry. "Ould Sam," to whom he gave one hundred acres in addition to his freedom, was one of those dependents, as was Sue, once given to Tish, who for some reason, did not accompany her to England. The Sachers were to report on them, especially as to whether they, and some unnamed "black boys," were "beginning to be diligent."[16]

A later black boy would have been Virgil, born in 1713 and a lifelong resident of Pennsbury. Virgil was important not because of any special accomplishment but because long after his death, he was a storm center of argument. Sold in 1733, sixteen years after William Penn's death, to Thomas Penn, by Joseph Warder, whose last name Virgil adopted, he was George Bancroft's "proof" that William Penn, the Quaker, lived and died a slaveholder. Shocked Pennsylvanians indignantly denied the Bancroft charge, pointing out that it was Thomas Penn and not his father who had bought Virgil. The Bancroft statement was, of course, completely true, but not for the reason Bancroft gave.[17]

Soon after Penn's return to England, Pennsylvania's interest in blacks began to falter. Liberal-minded Quakers were dismayed to learn that not all Negroes were paragons. Some absconded, and a few got into trouble with the law, two of them, both named Jack, being arrested in the same month, one for shooting a white man, the other for burning a neighbor's corn crop. Penn himself had an unfortunate experience with a nameless black woman from New Jersey whom he bought, only to find that she cost him more than her purchase price in clothing, medicine, and "entertainment," whatever that meant. Doubtless the incidents were neither more numerous nor more serious than in the past, but in the early days of the eighteenth century, after so much talk about the need for justice to the blacks, their occurrence reversed the tide of sympathy that had been flowing in their direction.[18]

Again a cry rose for restriction of black immigration. The Pennsylvania legislature raised import taxes on slaves from £2 to £20 per head; it tried to buy Penn's support by offering him a share of the income. Penn, however, did not help promote the scheme when it came before the Lords of Trade and Plantation. The Board struck down the tenfold increase and in addition vetoed a further Pennsylvania act barring the importation of any slaves except those who might have been sent abroad by their masters. The vetoed measure had also forbidden the entry into Pennsylvania of any American Indians except those born or "naturalized" in that province. London did not cancel the measure because it restricted the movement of Indians in what had so recently been their homeland but because it conflicted with an Englishman's liberty to move freely within his own country.[19]

43

BESET BY FOES

THE REVEREND EVAN EVANS, WHO SUCCEEDED PARSON PORTLOCK OF PIRATE FAME AS RECTOR OF CHRIST CHURCH, MERITED HIGH PRAISE FOR HIS TIRELESSNESS AS AN ANGLICAN MISSIONARY TO QUAKER Pennsylvania. He was a dedicated worker and unselfish; though his pulpit was in Philadelphia he looked upon his parish as extending fifty miles into the back country, from the village of Oxford, named for his alma mater, to the Three Lower Counties. For a salary of £50 a year, plus any contributions his flock chose to give him, he rode at his own expense throughout southeastern Pennsylvania, founding mission chapels and preaching in Welsh, his native tongue, to win back scores of Welshmen to Episcopalianism.

In his zeal for reformation, the young divine, still in his twenties, listened much too trustingly to vestrymen, such as Colonel Quary, Joshua Carpenter, and John More, three of the four men whom Penn at that time listed as his chief enemies (the fourth was Jasper Yeates). Why Penn failed to include the name of David Lloyd is unclear; Lloyd was a Quaker, but, then, so was Yeates. These vestrymen instilled into their rector a firm belief that Penn, who talked so much about freedom of conscience and of the right of all people to worship as they wished, had actually wiped out the free exercise of religion, "a privilege enjoyed until Penn's arrival." Is it beside the point to note that not one of these pro-testers had been in the province, or for that matter in America, prior to Penn's arrival?[1]

Before the Reverend Mr. Evans had been in Pennsylvania for more than a few months he and his vestrymen signed and sent to the Bishop of London a strong protest against William Penn as a heartless tyrant, a selfish extortionist, and, though they did not use the words, a religious bigot who chose atheists as provincial judges and advisors. They declared:

We have a long time silently groaned under the miseries and hardships we have suffered in the Government. We are exposed to all the
miseries imaginable, not only from a public enemy but from pirates
and Indians. . . . The Government have now made a law that to
write or speak against the Government shall be sedition, of which
they, the Quakers, will be judges, for there is no magistrate of the
Church of England. . . . Our lives, liberties and estates are taken
from us by judges, juries and witnesses not sworn, nor as much as
under the obligation of any test that hath the name of God in it. . . .
Governor Penn resolves not only to continue that uneasy and intolerable yoke and burden under which we have so long groaned under
but is adding more weight to our former misery by making laws contrary to our religious rights and consciences.[2]

This remarkable complaint, accusing Penn of actions wholly foreign
to his nature or to his history, and against which he had consistently
fought for years, can only be ascribed as due to false advisors or to a very
lively imagination. It seems to have been prompted by news that the
Reverend John Keble, a New Castle clergyman, had performed a hasty
marriage service for two servants in violation of a newly enacted law.[3]
For the prevention of bigamy or of secret marriages, both of which seem
to have been increasing in what Penn described as "this licentious wilderness," the new law required banns of intended marriages to be publicly
posted for at least a month in advance. Keble paid no attention to this
requirement. He had, he explained, a higher duty; he owed "a canonical
obedience to marry anyone over twenty-one, not too near in blood and
thrice asked." Nevertheless, the Reverend Mr. Keble was fined £20, a
penalty Anglicans protested both as an excessive punishment and as an
insult to church rules.[4]

Penn's delay, and that of Pennsylvania Quakers, in responding to
the various accusations indicates that the vestry dispatched the letter to
London before disclosing its contents locally. When the news did leak out,
the Quaker reaction was predictable. Penn denied sponsorship of the
requirement of banns; he approved of the idea, he said, but it was a
Nicholson suggestion for an intercolonial marriage law. The fine was
justified because Keble had not only broken the law but had done so
scandalously. To this Penn's friend Isaac Norris thoroughly agreed, adding, rather gratuitously, that Keble's town of New Castle was "a Frenchi-
fied, Scotchified, Dutchified place where quarrelling was raucous."[5]

What to Penn was more important, the rector and vestry of Christ
Church misstated the situation. Far from dominating the province or
oppressing the Anglicans, said Penn, the Quakers were oppressed in their
own land. "The Church people have all posts of profit save one, the
Attorney General. Three of the five counties [actually six] are theirs, but

this is not enough, they must have all. What they do not attempt in state they do boldly in the pulpit, depending on my principle for impunity."[6]

Four years later he was still indignant.

> We went to Pennsylvania to be quiet and safe in our civil and religious privileges, yet we are made extremely uneasy by officious and turbulent persons who, to recommend themselves to the bishops, and especially of London, do us all the despite they can in the name of the Church, though the Church enjoys the same liberty. . . . They desire to be the lords of our labor, have all the employments in their hands . . . a design as barbarous as unjust.[7]

Regardless of Penn's explanations and protests, the Bishop of London preferred to believe the clergyman he had sent to evangelize in Pennsylvania. He asked the Council on Trade and Plantations to veto the obnoxious marriage act; if continued in force, "it will be impossible for anyone but Quakers to live where that law should prevail."[8]

Because such exaggerations had revived the movement to cancel Pennsylvania's charter, Penn felt compelled to return to England to protect his interests. He had, he believed, solid accomplishments to report, especially legislation to check illegal trading and arrests of pirates to be tried at London. Though in military matters his province had not been as cooperative as London had expected, he could show that he had exerted the pressure he had promised. By the skilled presentation of facts, he was confident that blame for incomplete fulfillment would be placed upon his recalcitrant Assembly rather than on his own shoulders.

The return seemed imperative when, on returning from a three-week exploratory trip to the Susquehanna, Penn received word from the Society of Friends in London warning that unless he came back immediately, he and other American proprietors might lose their charters. A bill, the message said, had already been read twice in Parliament, and although it did not seem likely to pass immediately, it would certainly do so in the next session unless Penn was on hand to defend himself.[9]

The danger appeared greater since at the very time he had received the warning his Assembly was balking at supplying military aid for the Crown. On receiving the Royal request, the Assembly, in a pretense of cooperation, had asked him exactly what he wished it to do. As usual, he had evaded a direct answer by replying that the request spoke for itself. The Assembly thereupon protested that though it was loyal and faithful to the throne, the province was still in its infancy, was under heavy expenses and had no money. Since other colonies were doing little or nothing, it could not understand why it should be required to do what others would not do. To forward such a reply to London did not seem wise.[10]

Penn then told the legislators that he must go to England, but since all men were mortal, they should think of what their needs or desires might be. "You will find me ready to comply with whatsoever may render us happy." Look over the laws, he suggested, "propose new ones that may better your circumstances, and what you do, do it quickly," since he hoped to leave as soon as possible.[11]

"I must recommend to your serious thoughts and care the King's letter to me, for assistance to New York of £350 sterling as a frontier Government and so exposed to a much greater expense."

Five days later, the Assembly, appearing in a body, returned a reply. Though it pointedly omitted any expression of regret that Penn was leaving, or any word of thanks for his generous offer, it "humbly presented" a request for certain changes, "some of which in themselves perhaps, might look extravagant." They asked that Penn take the request "in good part."[12]

It hoped that when Penn left he would leave as his representatives "persons of integrity and of considerable known estates," that he would arrange to "absolutely secure and defend us in our estates and properties from himself, his heirs and assigns" and that he would fulfill a number of promises he had made. Among other matters Philadelphia should no longer be "clogged with divers rents and reservations contrary to the first designs and grants." New Castle should be given the thousand-acre commons Penn had promised, and land purchasers should be allowed to cancel their quitrents by lump sum payments. Not a word appeared of any consideration the Assembly might grant William Penn in return.

Penn answered merely that he would think about the suggestions, but he did wish they would pay attention to the King's letter. When he expressed surprise that no changes in the laws had been offered, the Assembly declared that it had "privileges sufficient as Englishmen and were willing to leave the rest to Providence."[13]

Nine days after the Assembly's demands, when Penn had cooled off a bit, he gave a formal answer. He informed them in polite words that much of what they had asked was incomprehensible, that more was none of their concern, and that most of it was, to say the least, unfounded. He also complained that not a word had been said about incursions upon or confiscations of his property. Nevertheless, he added, he had "ever loved them, been kind to them, and ever should continue so, not through any politic design or for interest but out of a most real affection."[14]

He intended the message as a farewell, but remained in Pennsylvania for more than a month. The delay was unintentional, caused by a number of business matters, most of them minor. He had planned to leave in early September, for a short stay only in England, while Hannah and Tish awaited his return to Pennsbury. Neither woman had any desire to remain in Pennsylvania. Even before Penn determined on departure Hannah had apparently been planning to go back to Bristol. About the middle of July at the latest, more likely a month earlier while Penn was finding the Susquehanna country so attractive, she had written her father to expect her early return. By sheer coincidence, the very next day after Tish received her clearance letter from Philadelphia Meeting (Penn and Hannah had received theirs from Falls Meeting near Pennsbury), Thomas Callowhill was writing his daughter that he was daily awaiting her return.[15]

Both women objected strongly to Penn's plan to leave them in America while he took a flying trip to England. Hannah, city born and bred, had only brief experience with rural life, and was not enamored of it. Trained as she had been by her father in business matters, she was unhappy at being little more than a hostess at Pennsbury to visitors who stopped off, often unexpectedly, while traveling between Philadelphia and New York; entertaining Indian chiefs who came for conferences was even less enjoyable. Philadelphia society was more pleasant, probably more so than living in Bristol, for in the capital she met people of many interests, while Bucks County residents were, to put it mildly, dull.

Tish had enjoyed a winter of what in Philadelphia amounted to metropolitan gaiety, and she had flirted mildly with William Masters, but she was seeing little of him now, the thirty miles of separation being too far for him to ride to pay a call. She really did not miss young Masters, she would have protested, and yet, while she was rusticating, she would have felt, illogically, that he had lost interest in her. And who knew what progress her rivals, Susan Penington and Susanna Harwood, might be making with the catch of Philadelphia? She did not care, of course, but. . . . There would be plenty of eligible young men in Bristol.

Even if the need of the ladies for time to prepare for the voyage had not further delayed departure, Penn could not have left immediately. For years the Assembly had been clamoring for a new Frame; the one granted by Markham had never been official. In accordance with his desire to grant whatever his people reasonably desired, the Proprietor wished to gratify them before he left. Not until October 28 did he complete a satisfactory draft.[16]

Satisfactory to him, for close examination revealed that though he granted almost everything for which David Lloyd's Assembly had been asking, he retained more control than in his earlier Frames. He did so with no sinister purpose, no selfish plan in mind; during the twenty years since Pennsylvania's founding, the glow of the Holy Experiment had been somewhat dimmed.

The new Frame disappointed extreme libertarians; it seemed a retreat from the philosophy of the Holy Experiment. Actually, Penn had lost none of his idealism, nor was his loyalty impaired to the liberty of the individual and to what would later be accounted democracy. With advancing age and more intimate knowledge of the nature of human beings, he had less confidence that left to themselves the common people would invariably act with prudence and with altruism. He had not yet swung over to a belief that an elite should govern, nor would he ever do so, but, perhaps after a reading of Polybius, he was beginning to think that the Assembly's popular rule, tempered by the counsel of a wise proprietor, might yield the best results.

First and foremost was a guarantee that liberty of conscience, "according to the true intent and meaning thereof, should be kept, and remain without any alteration, inviolably forever." The popularly elected Assembly gained the right to propose, amend, or repeal legislation, subject to review by a provincial council which, no longer elective, would be chosen by the Proprietor in such numbers and for such term of office as he desired. The Assembly would nominate two men for each public office; the Governor would then choose one of these, but if he failed to do so within two full days, "the top man serves." Other provisions called for yearly elections and for individuals on trial to possess the same rights to counsel and to cross-examine witnesses as the prosecution possessed. The Frame, except for the religious freedom clause, could be amended only by a six-seventh vote of both the Assembly and the Council.

Penn was now ready to depart. Two weeks earlier, by paying 50 guineas, about three times the normal passage rate for three people, he had reserved the entire great cabin for his family's exclusive use. The ship, christened *Dalmahoy*, must have reminded Penn of that Guildford election, a quarter-century in the past, when he had campaigned for Algernon Sidney against Sir Thomas Dalmahoy. Its captain, John Fitch, bore the same name as the skipper who, almost a century later, operated the first steamship in American waters.

Penn's last few days before sailing were somewhat crowded. In addition to his Frame, his "Charter of Liberties," he granted a charter to Philadelphia and another to Chester; he named a council of state to supervise affairs and studied an approved act reorganizing the judicial system. He also executed powers of attorney facilitating the sale of the New Jersey lands he still possessed.[17]

Mindful as always of possible shipwreck, he drew a will giving his blacks their freedom. He bequeathed his English holdings to Billy and Tish, with American lands, and some in Ireland, to Hannah's children, though Billy was to have Pennsylvania acreage, together with the proprietorship. Hannah was to receive £5000 together with one hundred thousand acres for her unborn child if it should be a boy, but seventy thousand if it were a girl.[18]

Doubtless as a result of his legal troubles, and in conformity with Quaker principles, Penn included a strong plea: "Charge my children, as their loving father's last command and desire, that they never go to law but abide by the decision of Friends."

Just as he finished the draft, while a fair copy was being engrossed for his signature, David Lloyd and Isaac Norris, executors of Thomas Lloyd's estate, appealed to Penn to aid Lloyd's widow, Patience; she was, they said, in distress. The call came at an unfortunate moment, when Penn was pressed for time, and from David Lloyd, whom Penn mistrusted and disliked. Mindful of what he considered Thomas Lloyd's mistreatment a dozen years earlier of the newly appointed Governor Blackwell, Penn was cool to the appeal. Forgetful that poor Thomas Lloyd had served nine years as president of the Provincial Council and as deputy governor without receiving a penny of pay, Penn answered sharply, "What I have not received I cannot pay . . . I am, above all the land I sold £20,000 out of pocket for Pennsylvania." He did not believe that he owed more, even though Thomas Lloyd had never had any hand whatever in denying provincial payments to the Proprietor. Penn did, however, instruct Logan to allow Patience Lloyd a £10 annuity.[19]

Not all necessary business was completed when on November 3 the *Dalmahoy* cleared for England. Penn had neglected to name a deputy governor in hopes that his newly created council of state could either perform such duties itself or agree upon a suitable individual to do so, but such were the tensions and disharmonies within that body that no one was selected for the task. While the ship sailed down the river, therefore, Penn, in consultation with James Logan who was riding with him as far as the Capes, pitched upon Andrew Hamilton, a former deputy governor of New Jersey who had been unseated by an antiproprietary faction.

Penn counted on Hamilton's administrative experience as a factor in his favor but failed to take into account any prejudice that Pennsylvania might hold against him as a Scot, a defender of quitrents, an advocate of proprietary government and, as some said unfairly, a suspected friend of pirates. He invited Hamilton to accept the post, an invitation quickly accepted; only eleven days later Hamilton was presiding over the Provincial Council. Since Penn was himself sailing for England, he did not think it necessary at the time to dispatch a formal letter to London asking Royal approbation for the appointment.

Penn then continued on his journey. He was leaving America fully intending to return in a short time, but he was never again to see his province, or any other portion of the New World. He had received his charter in March 1681, but in all the stretch of time since, he had spent no more than three years and eight months in his own province.

44

DARING THE LIGHTNING

FTER A REMARKABLY QUICK PASSAGE, TWENTY-SIX DAYS TO THE
DEVONSHIRE COAST AND TWO DAYS MORE TO PORTSMOUTH, THE
PENNS WERE BACK IN ENGLAND. THE VOYAGE HAD BEEN UNEVENTFUL,
neither pirates nor storms interfering, but just before the ship entered
the English Channel, Penn had the ill luck to scrape his ailing leg, so
that he limped a bit and found it necessary to walk with care lest the
leg ache too much.

As soon as he had landed, Penn rushed to London—it must have been
a painful experience—and lodged again in fashionable Kensington, in
Chatham House near Hyde Park Barracks. Hannah, and probably Tish
also, went on to the Callowhill home in Bristol, where they would stay
until Hannah's child was born.

For a month the leg kept Penn immobilized, unable even to go downstairs. The isolation was fortunate, in a way; although Penn was in
pain, it gave him time to catch up on the news without the necessity of
publicly commenting on his reactions to it.[1]

The news was not pleasing. New Jersey had surrendered its charter.
Penn suspected they had speeded up negotiations in order to complete the
transaction before he had landed. "The weakly haste," Penn thought,
"was an ugly preface" to what might happen to Pennsylvania, for "there
has been villainous work against us."[2]

That villainous work concerned Quary's continuous stream of complaints of Penn's shortcomings as an administrator, his supposed hospitality to Canadian Indians, his alleged interference with the work of the
vice-admiralty, and his requirement that Quary, though a Royal official, post a £2000 bond to insure his efficiency and honesty.

The reiterations irritated Penn and disturbed the Society of Friends.

[335]

William III died on March 8 and was succeeded by his sister-in-law, Anne, the second daughter of James II. She was a High Church Anglican who was prejudiced against dissenters, and Quakers feared that, crediting Quary's complaints, she might permit a revival of restrictions. At Penn's suggestion, therefore, the Society sent her a greeting combining congratulations, a declaration of loyalty, a plea for toleration, and a personal touch: the author identified himself as "the father of the nurse who nursed thy son." Penn's name headed the list of signers, however, the actual father ranking tenth in order. The greeting pleased Anne; she responded by promising protection.[3]

The composition of these congratulations—a much more important diplomatic note than appeared upon the surface—prevented Penn from being with Hannah at Bristol when, on March 9, she bore her second child, Thomas, though it had not interfered with his attending Grace Church Street Meeting the day before. During the first half of 1702, in fact, he was unable to see his family for more than a fortnight all told.

The separation, the continual criticism, the constant care not to alienate some powerful official, the unending leg pains, all affected Penn's naturally cheerful disposition. He was growing suspicious that those for whom he had sacrificed so much, toward whom he had invariably been so magnanimous, were repaying him only by practicing their tricks of Cheat the Governor. He was coming to think of himself as persecuted, not because he was a Quaker, but because he had been too mild and gentle, too forgiving, too readily imposed upon.[4]

More and more often he was lashing back at those who crossed him. Even a casual mention of such names as Quary, David Lloyd, or Randolph caused his temper to flare. Those men he denounced as knaves, liars, and utterly corrupt as, in the cases of Quary and Randolph, not only as defenders of but participants in the illegal trade they were supposed to prevent and punish. Penn admonished everyone to love all others, including, presumably, his enemies, but, being human, he too yielded to his passions.

Usually he was not specific in his accusations, seldom spotlighting just what his foes had done; he mentioned classes of wrongdoing rather than specific instances. Nor was he selective in his identification, his arsenal of invective being limited to such charges as vileness, falsity, baseness, or, most often, villainous behavior. What he lacked in variety he made up for by hyperbole; at least half a dozen opponents were tarred as being "as arbitrary as lives," "the most wicked imaginable," or as "the blackest and most notorious as was ever seen."[5]

He need not be too severely criticized for such outbreaks. Except for his personal appointees, many of them his relatives and all of them his friends, official dispatches from Pennsylvania to the London bureaucracy bore little praise of Penn's contributions and no expressions of gratitude, but instead were filled with reckless reports of failings, probably a majority of them wholly imaginary. Quary was the worst of these hostile commentators.[6]

One of the most damaging of Quary's complaints—Penn called it the blackest—was against Penn's appointment of his cousin Paraclitus Parmyter to succeed David Lloyd as attorney general. Penn was never at his best in selecting legal and judicial personnel, and Parmyter's appointment was certainly vulnerable. He had been tried, found guilty, and sentenced to hang for swindling a widow; on being pardoned for the felony he had "affronted a sheriff," and had then been involved in a tavern brawl wherein the participants flung lighted candlesticks at each other's heads. None of these assertions had ever been denied, nor had anyone ever spoken with enthusiasm about Parmyter's legal qualifications.[7]

Penn had never been closely acquainted with Parmyter. The latter was a Bristol man, but his reputation, after the swindling conviction, was not so good that the Callowhills would have been his close friends; it is unlikely that Penn had seen much of him prior to meeting the man in Governor Lord Bellomont's office in New York. Bellomont, though knowing of the tavern brawl, if not about the swindling, had accepted Parmyter's assurance that his wild oats had been sown and that he had become "very honest and religious." As the post of naval attaché was open and there were no other applicants, Bellomont had taken the man into his service. When Bellomont discovered that Parmyter was in fact, in Bellomont's words, "a most corrupt ill man," he recommended that Penn hire him as attorney general.[8]

Penn, charmed as Bellomont had been by Parmyter's assurances, accepted Bellomont's carefully written "endorsement" at face value, particularly as Parmyter was a cousin, and, while still thus bemused, attacked Quary for maligning the man. Nine months later Penn was finding his cousin "troublesome."[9]

Parmyter was not the only Penn appointee whom Quary disliked. He also hated Deputy Governor Hamilton and favored Jeremiah Basse if only because Hamilton liked him. According to Quary, Basse had an encyclopaedic knowledge of piracy. The proprietary group in other provinces detested Basse, an attitude which only strengthened Quary's support of him. Whether Basse advocated that Penn's New Jersey lands be confiscated is not entirely clear, but Penn was unrestrained in thinking Basse an undesirable, a liar, a friend of that embezzling Benedictine who had been his neighbor at Burlington, a leading member of the ever growing clan whom Penn described as "the greatest of villains." He had also heard, falsely, that Basse had, at one time, been an Anabaptist minister.[10]

Accordingly, when Quary learned that Penn had made Andrew Hamilton, adversary to Jeremiah Basse, deputy governor of Pennsylvania, he vilified Hamilton before the court officials. The news surprised the Privy

Council, for Penn, by protocol, was supposed to have first asked the Queen's approbation of such an appointment, but he had not done so.

Ignoring (if indeed they realized) that Penn had made that appointment just before his ship sailed, and that he had scarcely had time to ask Queen Anne for her approval, the bureaucrats, with Quary's able assistance, believed that the Proprietor was slighting the Crown. It was not the first time he had done so, they complained. As Penn had grown older (he was now past the mid-fifty mark) he had grown more testy, more impatient at being ordered about; he refused to be, in his words, "dictated to." When summoned to explain his right to rule the Lower Counties, he gave no clear, direct answers; instead, he charged his interrogators with bias. To a demand that he show some evidence of ownership of the Lower Counties other than the premature deed given him by the then Duke of York, he flatly refused. "That is all the satisfaction they shall have," he told a friend. The plain fact was he had no better proof.[11]

Penn's failure to draw upon the tact and diplomacy he had once employed so well was most inconsistent with the suave, conciliatory William Penn of his courtier day; it reflected his anger at the "villainous work" that had been used against him.

Not until June 22, 1702, almost half a year after setting foot in England, did he ask Anne's approval of the Hamilton appointment; he had waited until the furor caused by Quary's campaign had subsided. The delay, however, had been a tactical mistake. While the Lords of the Privy Council and of Trade and Plantations may have forgotten about Hamilton, their indignation against Penn was more intense. Piqued that he had waited so long they were ready to deny anything that Penn desired, regardless of whether Hamilton was or was not a Scot and an illegal trader, as Quary had alleged. One of Penn's remaining friends suggested that the Royal approbation might be used as bait to bring William Penn to heel. If the dilatory Proprietor would post a £2000 bond for Hamilton's good behavior, if he would answer speedily and in writing to the questions they had wanted him to answer these last six months, and if he would agree that Anne's approbation would in no way jeopardize her "pretensions" to the Lower Counties, they would allow Hamilton to take office for a one-year probationary period. After that, they would review the matter for final action.[12]

Meanwhile, in America Hamilton had been having troubles of his own. The Assembly, an antiproprietary body, did not like him. When he obeyed Royal orders to ask the province for men and money to fight the French, the Assembly answered precisely as before: it had no money, the people were already taxed too heavily, other colonies were not paying, and the provincial conscience disapproved of dipping money in blood. While the Assembly was taking this firm stand, it also rejected Hamilton's attempt to set up a militia, establish forts, or take any other warlike action.[13]

Poor Hamilton, deluded into thinking that the public would support him, tried to create an independent armed force. Recruiters went about the streets beating drums to enlist volunteers. The public, instead of flocking to the colors, jeered as eligible young men, reluctant to march all the way to Canada to fight the French, failed to respond.[14]

Penn, whose actions had won him slight support in England, rose to the occasion. Fearful of the ill effect his evasions had produced in England, he put aside his strong aversion to supporting military action and actually offered to pay £350 from his own pocket. Where he would have raised the money had his offer been accepted, if his pleas of poverty were well founded, is difficult to ascertain; luckily the New York governor came to his relief by reporting that he no longer needed men or money.[15]

The offer restored Penn to favor at court. Penn's friends, powerful noblemen such as Ormond, Sunderland, Harley, Lord Treasurer Sidney Godolphin, and Lord Rochester, the uncle of Queen Anne, praised his patriotism and cooperation. Penn should have followed his father's example by capitalizing on the friendship of the great; instead he again became sullen and resentful; he continued to ignore or to evade official probings. After more weeks of prodding Penn for answers which he gave grudgingly or unconvincingly, the best his friends could do for him was to declare that they did not think his replies "altogether satisfactory, yet, in order to the dispatch of his business, they are willing to acquiesce."[16]

Penn's intransigent and most untactful behavior may possibly have been triggered by a domestic crisis. Letitia, recovering quickly from whatever heartache the separation from William Masters may have caused her, fell in love again almost as soon as she stepped off the *Dalmahoy*. How or where she met William Aubrey, a Welsh widower and a London businessman, is lost in the shadows of the past, but his courtship was brief and effective. Within two months of the *Dalmahoy's* making port banns were being posted for the marriage.[17]

Whatever favorable opinion William Penn and Hannah may have had of Aubrey as a son-in-law soon disappeared. From the very beginning he seemed less interested in Tish than in her dowry. He scorned Penn's suggestion that he take Pennsylvania acreage in lieu of money. When Penn at last agreed to pay £2000, but could not raise that much in cash, Aubrey reluctantly accepted a promissory note, payable at some indeterminate date, provided Penn paid 10 percent interest; if at any time Penn should fail to pay, the principal would at once become due.[18] Penn described the man as a "tyger." Hannah, less delicately, called him a "muck-worm," an epithet then used for a moneygrubber. Nevertheless the marriage took place in August, six months after the posting of the banns.[19]

Squabbles over Penn's delay in paying off the dowry or the interest caused dissension for many years thereafter, but problems raised by

Billy existed very much in the present. A clever, rather witty youth, at least in his father's estimation, he was tamed neither by parenthood nor by adult responsibilities. A fashionable man about town, supersensitive about what his fellow bloods regarded as their honor and like them a rake who drank too much, he persisted in piling up bills for his father to settle.

Penn conjured up a strange prescription for Billy's wildness. All that was needed, Penn believed, was to send the young man to Pennsylvania, where a committee of ancient Quakers would show the young blade the error of his ways. Why the scheme would work in Philadelphia when it failed in London was not clear. The dismal prospect must have been less than appealing to one accustomed to the gaiety of London, but his father, for once stern with his son, offered no alternative; under no other circumstances would he pay Billy's debts.[20]

Billy, apparently trusting that his father would relent, consented to go overseas, though not immediately. Yellow fever was again raging in America; it would be well to wait until the danger passed. He had certain social obligations to meet, commitments that no gentleman of honor could evade. He must not desert a wife about to give birth to a third child. Travel in winter was notoriously hazardous. Sometime in the spring, if all went well and the London season had ended, he would travel, with his thoroughbreds and his pedigreed hounds, his sporting guns and his fishing tackle, to learn how to become Governor of Pennsylvania. By that time, of course, the bothersome creditors would have been paid off and he could find some other reason for staying in London.

The delay, moreover, would afford a little time for correcting the poor impression which, he understood, Philadelphians entertained of him. He wrote to Logan urging him to tell the people that they were utterly mistaken about him. "I am far different," Billy pleaded, "from what I am represented to be. I love my friends, keep company that is not inferior to me, and never do anything to excess. My dress is all they can complain of, but that but decently genteel, without extravagancy; as for the poking iron, I never had courage enough to wear one by my side . . . I will show you that I have been villainously treated."[21]

Logan, assuming that Billy would soon arrive, tried to improve the Penn finances. The task was difficult, for though the Assembly had voted taxes, the people would not pay, and the Assembly, almost solidly antiproprietary, refused to coerce delinquents. Logan did collect some wheat, only to find that commodity a drug upon the market; ships that he had sent to the West Indies were damaged or sunk by hurricanes, taken by pirates, or, if they reached ports safely, had their cargoes poorly managed by Caribbean agents. Thus, though in spite of Quary's neverending complaints, the Queen was receiving customs duties for goods worth five times as much as when Penn's officials managed matters, the Proprietor was reaping little, if any, profit.[22]

Penn proposed that the Assembly allow him the exclusive right to trade with the Indians for furs. The plan, to be sure, involved a reversal of the firm position he had taken in 1681 against any such monopoly, but there was a great difference between granting the privilege to a Marylander, even a Quaker Marylander, for his sole profit and conducting the enterprise for the mutual benefit of the Indians and the Proprietor. There was much to be said for the proposal, not the least being the ending of any clandestine liquor traffic, but though the Indians seemed willing enough to trade with Penn, the Assembly refused to approve.[23]

Ill luck continued with deputy governors. Penn's delay in submitting Hamilton's name for Royal approbation, his failure to post proper bonds for Hamilton's good behavior, and Quary's opposition combined to delay ratification until after Hamilton had died. After canvassing others for Hamilton's post, Penn "humbly proposed" that the Crown approve William Markham.[24] The nomination, though one more proof of Penn's loyalty to family and to cronies, intensified Royalist hostility. To propose the reinstatement of an official whom Quary branded as a violater of the Navigation Acts, a friend of pirates, and a man whom the Crown had already thrown out of office seemed to London nothing more than sheer contempt for Royal authority. The Crown rejected the nomination out of hand.[24]

Penn proposed an alternative, one John Evans, a young gentleman in his twenties of whom, apparently, no one in authority had ever heard. Quite possibly Penn himself may not have been better informed; to London's request for more identification he curtly replied that young Evans was the "son of an old friend who loved me not a little."[25]

Why the court advisors, already indignant at Penn's evasions and delays, did not resent his attitude is unclear; for whatever reason they confirmed the appointment.

45

LOVE THY NEIGHBOR

TWENTY YEARS HAD ELAPSED SINCE, HORRIFIED BY WHAT HE CON-
SIDERED BLASPHEMY, FILTH, AND WICKEDNESS OF SO MANY CLERGY-
MEN, PENN HAD ERUPTED IN PROTEST. HIS ANGERS HAD LASTED EIGHT
years, but after 1676, he had remained relatively quiet, partly because he
was under a form of probation, more because he was fully occupied with
supervising the activities of the Society of Friends and by his colonization work for New Jersey and Pennsylvania. Save for an outbreak in
1684 against a "conceited and presumptuous" colonist and a mild warning
in the following year against trusting Tatham, the "prying and subtle"
renegade Benedictine, Penn had held his temper in check.[1]

This was the real Penn, a peaceable man who, more than anything
else, loved quiet and meditation. He prided himself on being slow to
anger and on loving even his enemies. He was, in his own words, "swift
to charity" and "apt to be too merciful."[2]

"I am for patience, forbearing, long-suffering and all true moderation,"
he assured one of his closest friends. "I abhor contention, niceties, doubtful disputations."[3]

Over and over again he appealed to his local officers to avoid disputes. "I beseech you, draw not several ways, have no cabals apart, nor
reserve from one another, create in a mutual sympathy, an entire confidence," or as he put it on another occasion, "be not so governmentish."
Since, however, difference of opinion continued on matters of provincial
policy and might, in certain circumstances, even be desirable, Penn
urged his agents to discuss their disagreements privately, lest the public
be disturbed.[4]

In pursuance of this advice both the Provincial Council and the Provincial Assembly barred nonmembers from legislative meetings, publishing only summaries of actions taken but suppressing details of

arguments pro and con. Outsiders might hear that there had been conflicts, but unless a member "leaked" the news, no stranger knew just what had happened.

Penn himself met difficulty in trying to harmonize his theory with his practice. His principles remained unchanged, but the last ten years of the seventeenth century were a very trying time for him. Disputes and misunderstandings with "hungry and mercenary" Royal agents could not be resolved in privacy, for the agents were vocal in their criticisms and their objections had to be countered openly both in England and in America. The flagrant misbehavior of Philadelphians, especially in the caves, was common knowledge, and since the great majority of the offenders were not Quakers, they could not be quietly admonished in the meetinghouses. Penn was saddened by what he considered the selfish and ungrateful actions of colonists whom he had earnestly tried to benefit, but these culprits, too, were beyond the reach of private counselors. The correction of these flaws and the restoration of the hoped-for brotherliness and altruism of the Holy Experiment—if such qualities had ever, at any time, existed—could be achieved only by full-scale reform campaigns conducted openly.[5]

Though an experienced debater on doctrinal details, Penn had little experience in social evangelism. True, he had written copiously advising youth to live simply, prudently, and thoughtfully; but he had devoted little attention to specific details of economic, political, or social welfare, the fields in which his province needed guidance. Nor was he intellectually well equipped for such discussion. When arguing for religious toleration or for the traditional rights of freeborn Englishmen he could draw upon a rich treasury of classic, historical, or scriptural precedents; few, if indeed any, such quotations were applicable to questions of colonial administration. Exhortations to righteous living were effective in an audience of churchmen and Quakers but carried less weight before Royal emissaries, roistering habitués of the waterfront caves, or struggling farmers seeking the abolition of quitrents.

Then, too, William Penn, who should have been hardened to abuse from his opponents, had in his fifties been growing less tolerant of criticism. The self-confidence that had led him in his twenties to challenge the beliefs of older men of more experience, even to his accusing them of impertinence in daring to counteract his own ideas, had become a conviction that he was the beloved, benevolent father to his people. Before he was forty he was certain that his colonists so idolized him that he could calm their internal dissention by urging them, "If they love me, let them love one another." And ten years later he knew very well that England's monarchs, particularly James II and Anne, leaned heavily upon his counsel. One so certain of his own worth would bitterly resent the questioning of his policies by people of less stature.[6]

Just as during the 1670 decade he had lashed out at anti-Quaker opponents, so, thirty years later, he attacked his critics. In so doing he discarded the earlier descriptions of his enemies as blasphemous, anti-Christian, and scurrilous perverters in favor of new adjectives that maligned their personal rather than their doctrinal character.

The shift came suddenly, touched off by charges of deviation in beliefs and practices. In January 1692, Thomas Fitzwater, namesake of the first estate manager at Pennsbury, accused George Keith, a close Penn associate, of denying the "sufficiency of the Inner Light." In denying the accusation Keith struck back sharply by alleging that most Quakers were notoriously indifferent to basic Quaker teachings.[7]

A Quaker reluctance to rake up past disputes ("What good purpose is served thereby?") hampers a full investigation of the serious rift that split the Society of Friends for many years thereafter. Philadelphia Monthly Meeting "disowned" Keith, largely because he ascribed the then current decay in popular morality to Quaker laxity in enforcing discipline. There were, however, deeper reasons not spelled out in official records, particularly a rivalry that sprang up after the death of George Fox in January 1691 over whether Penn or Keith should take over the leadership of the Quaker movement.[8]

Keith based his claim to leadership on seniority. Six years older than Penn, he had been, he pointed out, a Quaker preacher before Penn had joined the Society of Friends, even before he had enrolled at Lincoln's Inn. It was highly improper, Keith contended, for a junior to seek preference over a veteran.

To Penn, who at twenty-four had dared criticize the highly respected Richard Baxter of impertinence, the argument was not convincing. Nor was he moved by the Keitheans' professions of shock at his claim of "immediate Divine inspiration." Penn, they said, had announced that "a Divine Power came upon him so forcible that he knew not whether he was sitting, standing or kneeling." Their comment on this experience, reminiscent of his vision at Chigwell, was curt and final; Penn, they said, was a liar.[9]

Penn replied forcibly and indelicately. Denying a Keithean slur that he and his supporters were "anti-Christians, Saduccees and heretics of the deepest dye," he called Keith a "noisy, froward deserter." Nevertheless, he professed still to love Keith, to hope for his return to orthodoxy and for reconciliation of all the disputants.[10]

Penn's hope was all the more heartfelt because while his message primarily concerned George Keith, it also applied to other longtime trusted friends. Robert Turner, to whom the appeal was addressed, had gone over to Keith's side, as James Claypoole would do later. The news of Turner's defection, Penn mourned, had thrown him into a fever which had lasted five full weeks.[11]

The rift in Quaker ranks occurred at a particularly unfortunate time.

Penn was in distress. The controversy had developed while Guli was mortally ill. Billy, his eldest son, growing into manhood, was developing more into an irresponsible wastrel than into a man of promise. Moreover, though cleared of treason charges, Penn lay under suspicion of both religious and political conspiracy. He was also in financial straits, his province yielding no returns, his Irish estates but little more, and his English lands under heavy mortgages. In addition, he had lost control of Pennsylvania to the militaristic Benjamin Fletcher and had been able to recover his possessions only by promising, after struggling with his conscience, to cooperate in the armed defenses of America. "I am a man of sorrows," he mourned.[12]

The Keithean controversy marked Penn's last major offensive against those who differed with him on religious grounds, an offensive he had once professed as wholly foreign to his nature. His timing was fortuitous; after the dawn of the eighteenth century, he concentrated on personal enemies. Instead of impugning their religious beliefs, his favorite terms of opprobrium became libelous. He branded David Lloyd, leader of the antiproprietary party, as malicious, insolent, crafty, and a forger; he was also named the worst of men and the vilest of the earth. Only a few years earlier he had described David Lloyd as an honest man, the best lawyer in the province.[13]

According to Penn at least three individuals might rightfully be dubbed "the greatest offenders in illegal trade," two of them being the top Crown officials, Colonel Quary and "my one-eyed friend," Randolph.[14]

It was not now enough to call Robert Quary the greatest of villains and the vilest of the earth; he was a virulent viper, the supreme knave. So, too, was Quary's fellow viper John More, who drank toasts to the triumph of sedition. Not only was David Lloyd an unspeakable sinner but so were his followers, the majority of the Pennsylvania Assembly, who, instead of being men renowned for wisdom, sobriety, and integrity, were numbskulls, a pack of brutish spirits, fit only for association with Quary's rude, ungrateful gang.[15]

Penn honestly believed himself fairminded. He assured a worried correspondent that though he was receiving disturbing reports from Pennsylvania, he did not necessarily believe the rumors contained in the letters he received. Yet all too often he uncritically accepted, especially in England, news adversely reflecting on someone he himself suspected or disliked. Distant three thousand miles from his province, with only slight opportunity to check his sources or to hear rebuttals, he could not properly weigh evidence in making judgments and decisions.[16]

The customs of the times, particularly Quaker customs, militated against balanced analyses of situations. Because Quakers, as a rule, restrained their expressions of opinion, taking virtue and honor in human beings as the norm, they often failed to report good actions, for these were only to be expected; in modern terms, such occurrences did not fall within the category of news. In the absence of large and well-developed newspapers and of an efficient postal system, only the startling and the shocking incidents were reported in detail.

Though Penn was an avid reader, he could not be classed as a scholar; he read for nuggets of information but did not invariably carefully assay the ore he found. Thus, on the basis of scanty and unverified report, he condemned his neighbor Governor Francis Nicholson of Maryland as "the greatest monster ever heard of in these parts." In an instance closer to his home, he flared up when the widow and the son of Philip Ford brought suit against him; it was, said Penn angrily, "the blackest and most notorious case ever to come before an English court."[17]

Penn's angry outbursts exerted little effect upon those he criticized. Only in one instance, in 1671, does he seem to have caused a change of heart. Galenus Abrahams, the Dutch Mennonite, who in debating with Penn had been "airy and unstable" and a "virulent and obstinate opposer of the Truth," soon after became, according to Penn, "very loving and tender." With others Penn was less successful. Either because severe and even cruel epithets carried less sting in the eighteenth century than they would today or because Penn's targets were remarkably thick-skinned, his opponents exhibited remarkable tolerance.[18]

For a brief time Penn congratulated himself on bringing his archvillain, Robert Quary, to see the light. Quary did not seem deeply hurt by Penn's outbursts against him, though he did regret that "Mr. Penn's malice and revenge will never cease pursuing me until he ruins me." Though, after three years of Penn's persistent name-calling, Quary thereafter constantly complained of Penn's incursions into areas that Quary held to be Royal preserves, Penn somehow reached the conclusion that "Colonel Quary now seems disposed to favor our affairs."[19]

If any basis existed for this supposition it sprang from Quary's desire to rent Pennsbury as a country retreat; he asked for a seven-year lease, subject to prior termination if Penn should happen to return to Pennsylvania. James Logan, whose antagonism to Quary was less than Penn's, recommended acceptance of Quary's request, and so, only eighteen months after dubbing Quary "a venomous viper," Penn agreed, provided Logan could exact a higher rental.[20]

The armistice did not last. The lease was only a year old when Penn was accusing Quary of maligning him in "vile letters" to the Board of Trade. James Logan did not approve of Penn's renewed hostility to Colonel Quary. "I am sorry to find you so angry," Logan wrote. "I have been very intimate with him and have found good service in it."[21]

In the opening years of the eighteenth century, when the era of debates had ceased, Penn disregarded his own injunctions to conduct his disputes in private and, instead, channeled his criticisms through others, usually James Logan. His opponents, in turn, replied indirectly, Randolph and Quary through the Board of Trade, the Admiralty, or the customs authority. This practice meant that accusations against Penn flooded the desks of officialdom, while Penn's charges received less currency in London. The bureaucrats in consequence heard much more about the deficiencies of proprietary government than about the short-comings of the Royal agents in America.

David Lloyd, the Welsh-born attorney whom Penn had been so happy to recruit, unwittingly supplied the bureaucrats with ammunition. He was forceful and brilliant, completely loyal to Penn's professions of democracy and anxious to promote government by the people on a scale not yet practiced in England or America. Unfortunately for Lloyd, Penn, now that he was shouldering more responsibilities, no longer held such radical opinions.

In his earnest efforts to understand what was happening in his province Penn was victimized by poor and prejudiced reporting. His chief informants were his own highly placed representatives who, in striving to protect Penn's interests and their own, supplied Penn with news that was less than complete and far from being objective. Similarly, the Royal agents forwarded dispatches to their London overlords exaggerating the dissention and maladministration in the province. Since nonpartisans for the most part were not very verbal and in any case were few, the general impression among Englishmen, and even upon Penn, was that Pennsylvania was disorderly, as well as vicious and corrupt.

Brushing aside the fact that David Lloyd had been combating Randolph and Quary quite as vigorously, and, because of face-to-face confrontation, more effectively than Penn himself, the Proprietor believed Lloyd and the antiproprietary party, the majority bloc in the Assembly, were responsible for Pennsylvania's niggardliness and ingratitude.[22]

By the time he was sixty Penn had grown vindictive. He no longer invariably exhibited the idealism that had characterized his younger years. Even his tolerance and pacifism seemed to be wearing thinner. The erosion had long been foreshadowed. Less than a week after first setting foot in America, while professing himself a man of peace, he had added hastily, "But I fear not war." Two years later he was ordering his officials to "lay hard" upon malcontents and cowards who encouraged Lord Baltimore to think that the Lower Counties would support Maryland's claims to Pennsylvania's territory. The Proprietor was famous, and deservedly so, for his fair treatment of Indians, yet he did not hesitate in 1685 to order Thomas Holme to use force against red men who failed to keep their promises.[23]

Although disappointments and injustices in the 1690s kindled Penn's temper, he continued until at least 1694 to believe sincerely that he was patient, forbearing, long-suffering, and notable "for all true moderation." Six years later he was advising his legislature to be slow to anger.

Unfortunately, he did not always set a convincing example. He had not been averse to uttering threats, sometimes veiled, more often open. He had founded Pennsylvania as a haven for the oppressed, yet, as he frankly added, he also hoped for profit. When in spite of various appeals his hopes of a monetary "supply" dimmed, he made it clear that " 'Tis yet in my power to make them [the assemblymen] need me as much as I do their supply. . . . This is no anger, though I am grieved, but a cool and resolved thought."[24]

The William Penn in the opening years of the eighteenth century was not the same Penn who, in the 1670s, had clamored for equality, democracy, and toleration. He still professed the same ideals, continued to write them and to publicize them in the meetinghouses, yet he saw no inconsistency in blasting deviations from the official Truth as laid down by George Fox and himself, nor in believing that Pennsylvania should grant a superior status to himself and members of his family as well as freeing them, and their descendants, from any taxes then or in the future.

The Penn who had prided himself on believing that as all men are equal, earthly distinction was to be deplored, the Penn who had discouraged suggestions that Admiral Sir William should be created Earl of Weymouth, the Penn whose teachings had inspired colonial officials to blue-pencil a careless reference to "Lord Penn," was jealous of his rights and privileges. He had been waging a running battle, a losing one, with provincials who would not support him as their patron, nor pay the quitrents they had promised; he had been victimized by the "Great Game of Cheat the Governor"; he had seen his lands encroached upon, his favorite trees hacked down, his livestock killed by poachers and his horses stolen. He was, to put it mildly, feeling put upon.

When, therefore, East Jerseymen rioted against the proprietary government of which he had once been a part, his sympathies were with the established regime. Without investigating the circumstances too closely, he rushed to the defense of Governor Andrew Hamilton. The rioters, said Penn, were "dishonorable and licentious. . . . It will be hard to find temper enough to balance extremes, for I know not what punishment these rioters do not deserve. . . . If lenitives won't do, coercives should." In more modern terms, if they will not listen to reason, get tough with them.[25]

David Lloyd alone dared suggest that Penn was deceiving himself, that he was believing his own double-talk. Just as, without actually saying so, he had led the Crown to believe that if Pennsylvania were restored to him, he would see to it that the province would raise an army and join the war effort against the French, so he was believing his own statement that he was a man of peace. "How canst thou pretend to be a man of peace and trust when thee acts contrary thereto?" asked Lloyd.[26]

Penn's response reinforced the evidence that the Proprietor's attitudes had changed. He regretted his "confiding, foolish" policy of relying upon and trusting associates. "Browbeat that villainous fellow, David Lloyd," he ordered Logan. And in the same letter he told Logan to "cherish and threaten tenants" as they give occasion. Penn also warned, "Have a care of provoking me too far."[27]

ℰ 46 ℈

RELAPSE FROM GRACE

ALTHOUGH PENN, WITH SEEMING CONFIDENCE, ASSURED HIS FRIENDS THAT HIS HOLD ON PENNSYLVANIA WAS SECURE AND THAT HE WAS SO WELCOME AT COURT THAT QUEEN ANNE REBUKED HIM FOR NOT coming oftener to see her, privately he worried. Shrewd enough to realize that he was not winning but losing friends, not soothing but only sweet-talking his critics, not answering complaints but only evading them, he realized that it was but a matter of time before his tactics would cease to be effective. His surface confidence was only a cover to conceal his uncertainty as to how long he could put off hostile action by the Privy Council or the Board of Trade.

As other American colonies had already lost their charters or, anticipating losing them, had voluntarily become Royal provinces, it was only a question of time before the reiterated complaints of men like Quary would result in Penn's losing Pennsylvania, as well as the Three Lower Counties. By surrendering his charter, Penn believed, he could save more than if it were taken from him. On May 11, 1703, therefore, he offered, "upon a reasonable satisfaction" to withdraw, "saving some few privileges that will not be thought, I believe, unreasonable."[1]

London immediately inquired just what Penn had in mind; Penn, always reluctant to be questioned, waited a week before replying, none too graciously, that he thought he had already made things clear enough. Further requests, over a month's time, elicited no better response, so the Crown commanded that Penn state specifically just what he meant by reasonable privileges. Once more, because of pride or stubbornness, of recklessness or thoughtlessness, of carelessness or of objection to being ordered about, Penn delayed answering. The government had demanded a reply within a week, but Penn made it wait ten days.[2]

By "reasonable satisfaction," it then appeared, he meant receipt of £30,000, a sum equal, he calculated, to the £12,000 debt owed the Admiral in 1660, with simple interest of 4½ percent over the forty-three years since the Restoration. In setting this figure Penn had been generous, for interest rates were almost always higher, sometimes twice as much, and interest was almost always compounded. He seemed to forget, however, that the debt had already been cancelled by the grant of Pennsylvania.

The £30,000 was not all that Penn deemed reasonable. In developing the province Penn had laid out a considerable sum which he variously estimated but never at anything lower than £20,000. To compensate for this expense, he asked the proceeds of a halfpenny tax on each pound of tobacco exported from the province.[3]

There was more. The few privileges which he wished to reserve included all the rights he had been exercising, "all powers, jurisdictions and preeminences granted by patent as lord of the soil and waters, with all incidental courts and offices belonging." He must regain title to the Three Lower Counties. The Queen was certainly to be sovereign over all the land, but she was not to hear appeal cases involving less than £300. She could veto laws, "except some few as I shall object against," and she might name the Governor, provided that she choose him from the two nominees whom Penn would propose to her.

Penn could not have been astonished when the Crown refused to give so much to gain so little, especially since by invoking quo warranto, it could recover everything for nothing.

A stalemate resulted. For Penn, at the moment, the inaction was not unwelcome. The Pennsylvania controversies and money troubles (the Logan trading business was not showing a profit), together with his Quaker commitments had kept him so occupied that, for weeks on end, he had not been out of London, nor seen much, if indeed anything, of his family. The lull in negotiations allowed him, in late July, to run over to Bristol where Hannah, again expecting, was still staying at her father's. Penn was with her when, on July 30, 1703, her third child, Hannah Margaret, was born.

By this time, Billy, having run out of excuses for staying in England, was preparing to leave for Pennsylvania. These last-minute details took time but eventually he boarded ship, leaving behind £200 in debts for his father to settle. In the late evening of February 2, 1704, he and a new Lieutenant Governor John Evans arrived at Philadelphia.[4]

Their reception must have disappointed the two young men. No civic welcome awaited them. The coolness was deliberate. Though the people had no exact knowledge of when they would arrive, it was the usual custom, when a distinguished visitor was expected, for a courier to ride up from New Castle, or even from the Capes, to announce that the guest was on his way, that his ship was in the Delaware sailing north. The news in this case must certainly have been received, but the plain truth was that they had heard too much about the new Lieutenant Governor and the Proprietor's son to be enthusiastic about them.

Of Evans the Pennsylvanians knew only that he was youthful, inexperienced, and on sufferance; there was no special need to celebrate his coming. A crusty upcountry legislator summed up the general feeling of the antiproprietary faction. "He is but a boy, we'll kick him out." Logan tried to pass off the remark by explaining that the lawmaker came from Bucks, "a debauched county where there is scarcely any one man of note, but it was clear that Evans would be working under difficulties.[5]

Logan, under strict instructions to be mentor and substitute father to Billy, guiding hand for Evans, and keeper for both, led them to temporary lodging in his own home. He was to acquaint them with "the factions, the friendly, the sincere, the hollow, the bold, the timid and the weak, whom to countenance and whom to beware of, and whom to gain and use but not trust without good reason." He was to keep an especially close rein on Billy, advising him what company to keep and "how far to go"; he was to forbid his "rambling to New York," and he was to hold the purse strings, allowing Billy only a pound a week.[6]

The arrangement was bound to fail. Both young men resented being under the orders of an underling, especially one so young. Billy would not heed the advice of that committee of aged Quaker councillors picked out to guide him—one member was so old that even Penn described him as barely able to creep about. While Logan lectured about quitrents and taxes, Billy kept thinking of his hunting dogs, and Evans, though more interested in statecraft than his companion, was thirsting for female companionship. It was not long before Billy and the Lieutenant Governor moved off to quarters of their own in William Clarke's Great House at Third and Chestnut streets.[7]

Evans was in financial need. At no time was Penn very responsive publicly to the money needs of other people, but he was particularly brusque with single men who complained of poverty. He had promised Evans £200 per annum, to be collected from government receipts; why should Evans need more?[8]

"It is a poor argument," Penn answered, through Logan, "that because I spent £1000 [a year] that had a wife, child-nurse, three maids and three or four men, a single man must spend £600." Two other royal governors, Penn pointed out, received less; the noble Lord Cornbury only £100 per annum more, though he was the Queen's relative.[9]

The rather pointed desertion did not deter Logan from his duties. He took them to the governor's council, where Evans presided and where Billy had a seat of honor; after one session Billy stayed away for three long months. By then it was spring, so Billy went up with his hunting dogs to Pennsbury to lead the life of a country squire.

Logan believed (on what evidence it is not clear) that his indoctrination had been successful. In what was, to say the least, an over-optimistic report, he told Penn that Billy was a changed man. No longer subject to "those temptations that have been too successful over his natural sweetness," he "seldom fails of drawing love." As for Evans, "The Governor acquits himself to the satisfaction of his and thy friends.[10]

The comment on Billy, made within two weeks of his arrival, was sheer fantasy, while that on Evans, while wholly true, was also wholly misleading, for except for hard-core Quakers, Penn really had few friends left to satisfy, and Evans even fewer. The assessments were goals to be achieved rather than applause for things accomplished.

The Lords again considered Penn's conditions too high a price, and refused his compromise. The rejection disappointed him. He knew that he was losing him former influence, but he had been trying to widen his support by making judicious gifts of little presents, ranging from souvenir bows and arrows to waistcoats of Indian work, fine fur coverlets, and, where necessary, fees for special services. He had been confident that these courtesies would bear good fruit.[11]

He suffered setback also in the province. Pennsylvania had ignored his suggestion that it buy him a house or build him one. Furthermore, it had allowed wholesale fellings of his timber, especially on those acres where black walnuts flourished.[12]

Then, too, some of his former friends were bothersome. Thomas Fairman, owner of the Shackemaxon tract where Indians held council, complained that though for sixteen years he had been at Penn's beck and call, "nay, say at a whistle," the Proprietor had never given him a penny.[12] Penn pleaded poverty. "I think I have convinced him," he told Logan, "that I am one of the poorest men in the province and that my sin has been neglect of myself and not selfishness."[13]

The Fairman case was only one instance of Penn's inability to realize that other people had financial problems. He personally had never gone about with empty pockets, nor had any member of his family ever lacked for bread. It was greatly to his credit that, even from his youth, he had felt strong obligations to assist the poor, but never having lived among the lowly, he knew little of their needs. The best advice he could offer to the poor was to murmur not but patiently to trust the Lord. The counsel was not coldhearted. Penn had a warm, deep, and very real love for his fellow man, but his sympathies were academic, nurtured in the library rather than by actual exposure to the unfortunate.[14]

The plight of Gabriel Thomas was a case in point. Thomas had written a propaganda "history" of Pennsylvania, a pamphlet so glowing in its praise that Penn, unmindful of his earlier disapproval of overblown sales talks, promoted a wide distribution of the work. The pamphlet, Penn declared, was worth at least £20,000 to Pennsylvania.[15] When, however, Thomas asked £100, Penn called him beggarly and base; when the author repeated the request, Penn called him clamorous. After four months, Thomas renewed his appeal only to be dismissed as "a thief sneaking in holes." Penn threatened, if Thomas bothered him again, to have him jailed for life.[16]

So, at least, said Thomas, suppressing the fact that Penn had promised if Thomas dropped his demands and admitted that he had been unjust to the Proprietor, Penn would pay the author's debts and forgive the beggarly appeals. Thomas took a last fling at Penn by accusing him of oppression, but he accepted Penn's offer.

Penn was often short of ready cash, but he was never in poverty; he could not understand the plight of those in real distress. If, then, a needy creditor pressed for payment, Penn thought himself ill-used, the innocent victim of unscrupulous greed. Badgered, bewildered, and hard-pressed as he was, he lashed back, particularly in his later years, in the same terms used by his contemporaries, words that did not then convey as much scorn and insult as they would today.

Penn was growing discouraged. Believing himself vilely used by an ungrateful people, he thought his hopes shattered, his efforts wasted, and himself ignored. Young Deputy Governor Evans, who had gone to Pennsylvania with such enthusiasm for re-invigorating the province, was permitting, if not encouraging, reaction. By knuckling under to the anti-proprietary faction, he had allowed one of Quakerism's most important principles to be undermined, if not indeed abandoned: the province was permitting citizens, who could do so, to give their oaths, rather than to make affirmations. Probably it would do no good, he thought, to protest to Evans, who was not a Quaker, but, as Penn mourned to Logan, "You have given away a most tender point not easily recovered."[17]

There was worse to come. When Lord Cornbury wrote from New York repeating the annual call for Pennsylvania to contribute to colonial defense, Evans had dutifully and vigorously urged the Assembly to comply with the request. He pointed out that it was the Queen's desire; quite possibly he intimated that the Proprietor was not averse to compliance if the money were not dipped in blood, but the Assembly again refused. This time, however, it did not cite religious scruples; instead, it answered somewhat curtly, "We have our own back settlements to defend."[18]

Evans, who had been introduced to his pacifist province as "no soldier but one who hath observed the discipline of troops," whatever that may mean, overrode his Assembly by organizing a Governor's Guard. The move was not popular; certainly not among members of the Society of Friends, only four of whom enlisted; nor among young Royalists, if only because no provision had been made for any pay.[19]

Colonel Quary, whose military experience does not seem to have been much greater than that of Evans, did not spare his scorn. Instead of the ten companies of men whom Evans claimed, Quary had said, there were really only forty men in that "sham defense force," and they were shoeless and stockingless servants or convicts "dragged from jail by great promises of strong liquors." In that powerful array Quary had counted only half a dozen weapons.[20]

Quary did not like the Guard, but Billy adopted it as a plaything. Just as his father had enjoyed marching with the equally ragged Kinsale Foot, so Billy appointed himself drillmaster of this Pennsylvania militia, the first English armed group the province had ever seen. Day after day, when he was not vacationing at Pennsbury or roaming around the province, he was out on Society Hill training his private army.[21]

The daily drills offended not only the Quakers and the Royalists but also David Lloyd's followers; they were angry that they were forced to serve in the city watch while the Governor's soldiers were exempt.[22]

Penn's increasing despondency was deepened because news of these developments reached him not through his agents Logan and Evans, neither of whom had written him for months, but often through opponents who colored their reports to their own advantage. He heard, for instance, that on the night his son and Evans arrived in Philadelphia, John More, his register general, and Colonel Quary spent the evening in a public house, drinking to the success of the Royal government; the report was so worded as to imply that they were celebrating the Crown's eventual takeover of Pennsylvania. Actually, Moore and Quary, longtime colleagues in official life both in South Carolina and Pennsylvania, were, like loyal Englishmen, toasting the Queen, whose thirty-ninth birthday was coming up in just four days. Penn had already stamped More as "a great villain," but this supposed treachery to the proprietary government ended any possibility of preferment; More thus lost any chance he may ever had possessed of becoming attorney general.[23]

Then, too, Evans and Logan both overlooked telling their sponsor that though the Pennsylvania Assembly had voted him a share in taxes that was expected to yield £2000, few steps had been taken to implement the law, and virtually no effort had been made at collecting the impost.[24]

Penn's unhappiness and his resentment showed themselves in a letter to Logan wherein he complained about the trials to which he had been most unjustly subjected. "Oh Pennsylvania, what hast thou cost me? Close to £30,000 more than I ever got by it, two hazardous and most fatiguing voyages, my straits and slavery here and my child's soul almost. . . . In short, I must sell all or be undone and disgraced."[25]

The wail, dispatched to Logan in the spring of 1704, may never have been seen by David Lloyd, but Lloyd, extremely resentful of Penn's complaints, was planning a counterstrike. Unlike Penn, he was not embittered; but he was furious because of Penn's continuous criticism of the province as wicked, decadent, and ungrateful. In early August, therefore, when Billy was evading a spell of torrid summer days by squiring

Lady Cornbury about Burlington, by vacationing at Pennsbury, and by preparing, under pretext of ingratiating himself with the Indians, to go on a jaunt with Evans to Conestoga, David Lloyd struck back.

On the eve of the Assembly's adjournment Lloyd pushed through a resolution to protest the Proprietor's criticism of its actions. Since the legislative body was pressed for time, he had it approve the general idea and appoint a committee to draft the protest and to forward it to Penn in the Assembly's name. As members of that committee he appointed himself as chairman with Isaac Norris, a Penn supporter, and as a neutral, a swing man, Joseph Wilcox, an alderman and owner of a Philadelphia ropewalk. Wilcox, as it happened, did not serve, so Lloyd, without bothering to consult Norris, after the Assembly had adjourned, composed what he called a *Remonstrance*.[26]

The *Remonstrance* accused Penn and his agent Logan of fraud and tyranny, citing as proof all that had been said by anyone, of any faction, against the Proprietor. It denied Penn's repeated statements that he had lost money, saying, instead, that he had really profited by land sales, by receipt of fees and commissions, and by special privileges. It questioned his motives, his integrity, and his inefficiencies. It held the Proprietor responsible for the malfeasance of his subordinates.

Such are the generalities on which Lloyd's partisans and Penn's followers agree, but since few others besides Lloyd's closest friends in America or Penn's even fewer cronies in England ever saw the document, there is wide room for controversy. The stories vary according to the prejudices of the narrator. The Penn side accused Lloyd of holding the *Remonstrance* secret from everyone in America; the Lloyds countered by declaring it a privileged document which should be known only to the Assembly and therefore should not be published. The Penns charged that Lloyd falsely labeled the paper as an Assembly resolution and signed his name illegally as speaker; Lloyd defended the action as having been approved in advance by the Assembly, and said he identified himself as speaker because he had been chosen for that office and remained in the position until officially replaced. Penn's people then asserted that Lloyd had forged the Assembly records in order to give the *Remonstrance* some color of authority. Lloyd flatly denied the charge.

Supposedly the *Remonstrance* was an official Assembly letter intended to be sent to Penn, but, for some unknown reason it was not sent to him but to three anti-Penn Quakers in England. Those three were George Whitehead, a leading Quaker minister; Thomas Lowther, husband of George Fox's daughter-in-law; and William Meade, Penn's co-defendant in the 1670 trial. The key man seems to have been Meade, an associate of Philip Ford. Apparently Lloyd hoped to kindle a backfire in England against Penn within the Society of Friends.

If so, the plan fell through. Fortune rushed, as so often it did, to

Penn's assistance. The ship carrying the *Remonstrance* fell into French hands and was discovered by one of the captured English sailors, who sent it not to those to whom it was addressed, but to Penn himself. Penn read the protest and ordered Logan to expel the "villainous, mischievous and traitorous" Lloyd from Pennsylvania. To provide the necessary evidence Penn forwarded the *Remonstrance* as proof of Lloyd's "forgery." He demanded that Lloyd be arrested for drafting the paper, an action that the prosecutors could not take because the *Remonstrance* was lost in transit.[27]

Penn did not know of the loss until some time later. Not hearing anything about the criminal suit he had ordered filed against the wicked forger David Lloyd, he bombarded Logan with demands for an explanation as to why the man had never been brought to trial.

It may have been just as well that Lloyd never was prosecuted for forgery. The matter would have turned on the accuracy of the records Lloyd, in Penn's view, had altered. To prove that they were accurate and that Lloyd had acted with the knowledge and consent of the Assembly would have required the entire body of legislators to appear and testify, and since the Assembly was Lloyd controlled, the weight of numbers would have been on his side.

Actually, had the English libel laws been stronger, Penn might have brought a similar suit in London against the anonymous author (if he could have been discovered) who had made virtually identical charges against Penn two years earlier.[28]

Penn says it has cost him £20,000 to settle his plantation and that he has not received £500. But he ought to have spoke plain English, that it hath cost him a vast sum to defend his extravagant and illegal acts and proceedings of his government. . . . He has actually received £40,000 and has been benefitted by King's grant of at least £40,000 more. . . . Besides he has reserved 10 manors of 10,000 acres each in the heart of the several counties, which are worth £2000. . . . Next is the Bank, or Front of the city, on which there is a £100,000 improvement, the third part of the yearly rent thereof is his for 20 years. Not to mention imposts, taxes, fines, forfeitures, escheats and licenses, and all the rest of the undisposed lands. Yet he tells the world he has not received £500.

The author is unknown, but David Lloyd would have supported every word.

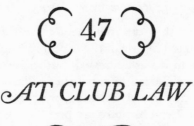

AT CLUB LAW

B ILLY'S CHILDISH PLAYING WITH HIS SOLDIER BOYS ENRAGED THE
WATCH, WHICH HAD POLICE AND FIRE PATROL AS THEIR RESPONSI-
BILITY BUT FEW PRIVILEGES. THEY JEERED AS BILLY DRILLED HIS
troops; the Governor's Guard, none too observant of strict discipline,
returned hard names and insults.

Often in the evenings Billy and his chums, among them the Deputy
Governor, relaxed at Enoch Story's tavern near Christ Church after their
day's labor. It was not the inn of best repute, this drinking place at the
Sign of the Pewter Platter, being chiefly patronized by apprentices and
"servants," none of them entirely wholesome, but young sophisticates
enjoyed the gaiety and raucousness to be found at Story's tavern: the
pleasures that caused the watch to keep it closely eyed for violation of all
those proclamations against "vice" and other misbehavior.[1]

Philadelphia in early September days is traditionally a place of high
and hot humidity, the sort of climate that tries one's patience. It was not
surprising, therefore, that the watch, as it came by, made fun of Billy's
party of young men about town, the macaronis, the fops, and dandies of
the period, or that the highly superior aristocrats responded in kind. A
brawl broke out. As is usual in such disturbances, the facts are not crystal
clear, each side condemning the other for vicious provocation while pro-
claiming its own remarkable self-restraint. What is notable was the difference in political and social status of the contending groups: on the one
side the city watch, largely young men of the working class led by alderman Joseph Wilcox; on the other, Billy, son and heir to the Proprietor,
the Deputy Governor, the Mayor, and the Recorder, the city's chief of
criminal prosecution.

Whoever started the melee, for which each group blamed the other, the tumult and the shouting reached high levels. Because his temper was short after a day-long session of the Provincial Council, where Indians had talked endlessly in an incomprehensible tongue, Billy reacted sharply. Whether he called for pistols, as the watch alleged, cannot be substantiated, for Story would not confirm the charge. Billy alleged that Wilcox punched him in the face, but Wilcox, denied it; he had, he admitted, struck someone but, he said, he had no idea who it might have been. The amateur policemen testified that the Deputy Governor cheered on the tavern set and that both the Mayor and the Recorder had fought against them. Each side denied the other's accusation in this war of words. No one save Billy seems to have been hurt.[2]

City officials, other than Billy's supporters, spoke of arresting him, but Evans quashed all proceedings. Even the Provincial Council considered action against him, the Proprietor's son, but the debate, conducted with Billy in attendance, was mild and scrupulously impersonal. The council minutes reveal little. "There was a——against Mr. Penn," but the charge, if any, was left blank; the reason for it was not mentioned; there was no hint of any action that may have been taken.[3] Billy never attended another session.

The caution exercised by the clerk who wrote the Council minutes was so extreme that he misdated the official records; his extremely understated report of the riot did not appear upon that journal until two full months after the event. Logan also hesitated to inform the Proprietor about the riot; his first letter to Penn after the fracas was written two weeks later and contained only a limited account of the disturbance. If the Council minutes are to be believed, that body had met numerous times before officially hearing of what had happened two months earlier.[4]

Billy himself reacted slowly. Two weeks after that punch in the face he was still planning to remain in Pennsylvania. Except for Pennsbury and the Sign of the Pewter Platter, it was a dull place for a London blade, but the sport was so good that he asked his father to send over his fishing tackle as well as a stallion that had been promised him. Neither had he forgotten a trip to the Conestoga that he and Evans had taken, a visit that included "orgies."[5]

Yet suddenly something changed his mind. Perhaps, though Quakers were usually very considerate about revealing details of personal conduct for which someone had been reprimanded, there may have been criticism of his conduct at Conestoga or at Story's tavern. Whatever the cause, Billy broke away from the Society of Friends, buckled on his sword (though possibly only figuratively), and rushed off to New York, there to catch the man-of-war *Jersey* for England.[6] But not before he had sold a manor he had received only five days before. The sale netted him £850, but Billy did not use it to pay his debts. He left behind two bills for his Conestoga expenses and for "goods for the Indians," a total of over £33. Five years later his creditors were still waiting for the money.[7]

Pennsylvanians voiced no formal resolutions of regret for his departure, but it may be significant that at a subsequent election they chose as Philadelphia's mayor the same Joseph Wilcox who had punched Billy in the face.

Whatever may have motivated the sluggishness in reporting these developments to William Penn, the delay worked to Quary's advantage; it enabled him to give London officialdom the first news of the brawl and of its consequences. Never, of course, had he been hesitant in sending any information that might reflect unfavorably upon Pennsylvania, the Society of Friends, or on William Penn. The colony was insubordinate, even mutinous, contemptuous of the mild suggestions advanced by Royal representatives, notably his own. It was a selfish province, unwilling to cooperate with its neighbors, adamant against contributing to the common defense. Quary had no special love for William Penn, but he did think it shameful that when the Proprietor proposed that one hundred Pennsylvanians each contribute £100 as a loan fund, not one man responded favorably; the total collection amounted to about £27. All this, to be sure, was highly colored in Quary's interest, but as the earliest and sometimes the only news, it exerted a strong influence upon the minds of bureaucratic London.[8]

Doubts about the character of Penn's province increased after London received a Quary letter expressing his gratitude for being appointed surveyor general, a post for which he had applied a year earlier. This was a message again mentioning the riot which, according to the Provincial Council minutes, occurred a fortnight after the Quary letter went off for England.[9]

Quary reported that the brawl had caused:

> very great division and confusion in the government, Quaker against Quaker. The quarrel has been carried so far that the military and civil officers have been at club law. The Quakers have indicted the officers of the militia, not sparing the young gentleman Mr. Penn. . . . The Lieutenant-Governor then put the Queen's order in force, declaring their court proceedings against the militia void. This has incensed the Quakers. . . . Young Mr. Penn is so uneasy with the Quakers that he hath publicly renounced them all, put on his sword and goes home to persuade his father to resign this government. Mr. Penn will now be willing to part with this government on far easier terms; he hath quite lost the end of sending his son over. There was a proposal to raise a considerable sum for Mr. Penn provided he or his son came to settle in a certain unlimited time, in pursuance of which agreement the young gentleman came over, but they are now so incensed against both father and son that they will not advance a penny.[10]

Those sections of Quary's letter treating of Penn's motives and of his future course of action were purely speculative, but because they seemed to be valid reasoning, they influenced the Lords' attitudes in negotiating for the surrender of Penn's province.

Arriving in England on January 16, 1705, Billy drew a bill for £10 on his father for horse hire, and rode two hundred miles to Worminghurst. He sent word to his father that he was home and would come at once to meet him. Not knowing how much his father had heard, he was anxious to present his version of Pennsylvania happenings.[11]

Penn was overjoyed to see his son and to tell him of a new stepsister, Margaret, just two months old. (Billy may not have been so pleased; according to Logan he was jealous of what he regarded as his father's preference for Hannah's youngsters.)[12]

Penn must have been shocked at the sight of Billy's sword, for it is doubtful if the son had written anything about seceding from the Society of Friends or that there had been time enough for messages from any other correspondent to have reached him. They talked for three hours, most of which must have been used by Penn in trying to discover the reason for his son's defection. Billy would not have been anxious to discuss the matter, but the probing did give him an excellent opening for accusing the Quakers, as well as the town watch, for their "mistreatment."

Billy's "going out from the Truth" pained his father, but Penn's paternal blindness to his son's faults, together with an appeal by Logan to "be tender" with the boy—an appeal which told nothing whatever about the rumpus with the watch—induced him to exonerate Billy and to heap all the blame on others.[13]

The sorrow over the defection, the later discovery that Evans, whose character he had highly praised only a few weeks before, had behaved badly on that "lewd voyage to the Susquehanna," and his conviction that the perverse Pennsylvanians had ruined the previously innocent Billy would have been cited by Penn as the reason why, on February 6, he suffered a strange sensation, "a swimming in the head." It was, though Penn did not suspect it at the time, the first of a series of strokes that would eventually kill him.[14]

A further blow afflicted Penn when Billy, a few weeks later, announced his intention of standing for Parliament; to do so revealed his willingness to swear, rather than to affirm, an oath. Penn's acceptance of this breach of one of Quakerism's most important tenets reveals, however, his integrity and his sincerity of belief; much as he disapproved of Billy's willingness, he nevertheless accepted Billy's right to swear if his conscience would permit. Billy, as it happened, lost the election, due, he said, to his opponent's bribes. "I wish it might turn his face to privacy and good husbandry, if not to us," Penn said.[15]

Instead, it turned his face toward a military life. Just as his father before him had sought a post in the Irish command, so Billy applied to his friends, Lord Ormonde among them, to get him a commission. They promised fair both to Billy and to Robert Rooth, but the best offer Billy received was that of a captaincy of a company in the Irish Foot.

Penn was outraged. The offer, he complained, was mean. "He shall go dig potatoes first. He is entitled to a better estate in the kingdom than to take up with so mean an employment." Penn suggested that his son receive a civil employment paying about £600 a year; if that were not available, then he should have £1000 to repay him for two years' fruitless waiting.[16]

Penn gave no reason whatsoever why Billy should receive either a job or an indemnity. The young man's only military experience had been that militia drilling on Society Hill, but then his father had been equally untrained when entering the Kinsale Foot. Nor was there any reason whatsoever for rewarding him for two years' fruitless waiting. But that, again, Penn was willing to try to help him attain a position of which the mature Penn disapproved speaks well for his love for Billy, and even more for his belief that each man's conscience should be respected.

On the other hand, the considerate suppression by Pennsylvanians, of the real facts of Billy's behavior led him to demand special privilege for his boy. In Penn's opinion all men were equal, with no one entitled to favors, but after all, Billy was his son, the heir to the proprietorship. As such, he should not have been dragged by "so rude and base a people" into the common courts. Penn did not say so, but he seemed proud of Billy for having been man enough to tell them that he was above such an indignity. Billy had told him that this was his reason for quitting Pennsylvania.[17]

Similarly, Penn was proud, after hearing "the melancholy story" of the Irish captaincy, that Billy had spurned the offer and, like his father before him, had become a courtier. People in such circles appreciated social position and, therefore, as Penn told Evans, "My son is like to be a somebody here in a while."[18]

Penn was so happy at his son's return that, for the moment at least, he overlooked the fact that Billy was even more careless in his finances than was Penn himself. Before leaving for America, Billy had sold off all the Worminghurst livestock—his father had already stripped it of marketable timber—and had neglected to pay either his taxes or his workmen and thus had shouldered on his father bills amounting to £1000; this at a time when, as Penn lamented, "I was never so low nor so reduced." Billy had repeated the pattern on leaving America; in addition to the Conestoga costs, he had left tradesmen's charges; he failed to mention what had happened to the £850 he had received for selling his newly acquired manor.[19]

The cloak of secrecy that protected Billy did not cover the adventures of Deputy Governor John Evans. When, in 1704, Penn had appointed the young man, he had told the Pennsylvanians that Evans was "sober and sensible," a bookish man. After he and Billy had been a short while in the province, however, reports had drifted in, few at first but then increasing, that the Deputy Governor had changed his character, that he liked the ladies to excess, that he was maintaining a "half wife" in the suburbs, and that he was so intimate with one young lady—one of those, according to report, from whom Tish had lured William Masters—that the dalliance was likely to bear fruit. Evans did what he regarded as the proper thing; he sought out a convict, promised him a pardon if he married the girl, and, like a true gentleman, kept his promise. Then he solaced his grief at losing her by finding a successor. Common gossip said that there were others also.[20]

Evans, not content with these escapades, discovered pressing reasons for frequent trips to the Susquehanna to enjoy Indian hospitality; it was on one of these journeys that he corrupted Billy.

Either Penn did not hear of these adventures prior to being told of the Pewter Platter incident, or did not believe the reports, but after Billy was involved, he reacted sharply. He considered that his honor was at stake. He sent off an angry dispatch to Evans. "As my dependence was upon thy honor, so I never thought myself unsafe in it. But three reports, strenuously improved to my disgrace . . . make me very uneasy."[21]

The reports, one at least from Colonel Quary, detailed other than amorous misdeeds. Evans had encouraged the growth of vice by laxity in enforcing laws against it and, flagrantly, by his own example. He had licensed too many public houses and to unfit persons, "so being not of sobriety and good order." He had been too dramatic and untruthful; when the Assembly failed to respond to gubernatorial, proprietary, and Royal requests to aid other, hard-pressed provinces, notably New York, he had faked reports that invasion was at hand. Astonishingly, William Penn complained that Evans had placed the Lower Counties in jeopardy by not providing arms. "He must be a silly shoemaker," said Penn in a somewhat cryptic remark, "that has not a last for his own foot."

The outburst of anger against Evans did not imply that David Lloyd, "the worst of men," had been forgotten. Soon after that first swimming in the head, Penn had ordered Logan to prosecute him for allegedly forging the *Remonstrance*. Two years later he repeated the demand. "Get the Governor and the best of my friends to bestir themselves and browbeat that villainous fellow," commanded Penn.[22]

⟨ 48 ⟩

TIMES OF STRESS

BRIDGET FORD, IN SETTLING THE ESTATE OF HER DECEASED HUSBAND, DISCOVERED PAPERS SHOWING THAT PENN HAD NEVER PAID OFF THE £2851 WAGE CLAIM SUBMITTED BY PHILIP IN 1682. ORDINARILY, Bridget was a socially minded, charitable woman who had served for years on the Women's Box Committee, which lent money to the needy, even once to William Penn. But with age and failing health, she had become bitter. She thought, with some justice, that a quarter-century was much too long for Penn to put off settling what she considered a just debt. Unless Penn paid her £14,000 immediately, she warned, she would record that conveyance to Pennsylvania that Penn had signed in 1690.[1]

Penn, angered at the ultimatum, refused to pay any such sum as £14,000; the claim, he said, was monstrous, wicked, and insolent. He had paid, he said, at least £8000 to the base, ungrateful Fords, people "worse than the wolf in the fold. They lay hold of the crutch that I gave them," referring to his alleged recruiting of Philip Ford from peddling on the London streets. Nothing, said Penn, could be more villainous than Bridget's demand.

Penn's partisans were, if possible, more indignant; they attacked Bridget and, for good measure, her son Philip, Jr. She was, they said, a bedridden invalid, though only recently she had attended meeting; she was a vixen "addicted to the masculine vices," by which they probably meant she drank too much. Her son, who as yet had taken no part in the controversy, was "as great a scoundrel as either of his parents had he possessed their talents."

Both sides retained attorneys. The case seemed clear. With several signed admissions of debt and various mortgage papers thoughtlessly signed by Penn in Ford's favor, the outcome seemed in little doubt.

Penn's accountants, however, accused his former employee of fraud, of overcharging, of exacting excessive interest, and of failure to credit Penn with various receipts. By their calculations, Penn owed no more than £4303.

This amount Penn offered to pay, but since he had agreed in writing in 1697 to pay Ford £6334, the widow refused to settle for the smaller sum. Rather than go to court, a recourse anathema to Friends, Penn suggested arbitration, but the Fords, though themselves Quakers, refused. This being the second time that the Ford family had gone to law (there had been a similar refusal in 1694, though not in the Penn case) the Fords were read out of meeting.[2]

While the case dragged through the courts young Philip Ford sailed to America, where he sought support from David Lloyd and Robert Quary. Neither accepted the Fords as proprietors, but Lloyd sought votes argued that because of the secret deed Penn was no longer legal governor. Quary insisted that the confusion over ownership proved that Pennsylvania must become a Royal province.

Pennsylvania's turmoil, so much at variance with its professed pacifism, the constant sniping among people who talked of brotherly love; the political, and indeed the social, vices of those who proclaimed the Quaker virtues weakened Penn's position in London. The bureaucrats, once so friendly, increasingly questioned his ability to rule. His failure to resolve the disputes over the Maryland boundary or the ownership of the Lower Counties, the persistence of illegal trading, the breaking of what London regarded as promises to supply military aid, had continued far too long to be tolerated further. Penn's behavior, moreover, alienated some of those who thus far had favored him. They resented his ignoring their suggestions, his reluctance to give speedy and direct answers to their inquiries, his failure to supply provincial laws for their inspection. Nor were they pleased when at last he did supply a partial list of legislation; the wording was too loose, the subjects insignificant. They picked flaws in the failure of the province to post official notices in the churches as well as in the taverns and in the allowing of colonists to manufacture boots, a trade that Parliament had reserved for residents of the mother country. London even found the mild and gentle Quakers much too brutal: "The penalty of standing gagged in a public place five days for scolding is too harsh."

The piling up of complaints, major and minor, was deliberate. The Privy Council, the Board of Trade, and other governmental departments were quite aware of their actions. Knowing of Penn's financial condition and of the confusion in Pennsylvania's leadership, they were bringing pressure on Penn to compel him to come to them to make a bargain. At any time they could have revoked his charter for any number of alleged violations that complaisant courts would judge good cause for quo war-

ranto; they seem to have thought it better tactics to have Penn come
to them, broadbrimmed hat in hand, to beg them to buy him out. The
price that he would ask would be lower than before, and they could then
bargain successfully for still deeper cuts.

They had sound reason for their confidence. Penn had been asking
£30,000 and an impost of halfpence per pound on all tobacco exported.
It seemed a high price for a province which, he had long insisted,
had drained his purse dry without having sent him a single farthing.[3]

The Committee, not surprisingly stunned by Penn's proposals, exhibited no haste in accepting them. Just as it anticipated, Penn lessened his
demands. What he really desired, he said, was exemption of himself and
his descendants from all taxation except customs duties, and, as it would
later develop, some form of recognition of the Penns as persons of special
note in the province. The Lords, however pleased at Penn's reduction of
his terms, sat back, waiting for still greater concessions from the hard-
pressed Penn.[4]

Meanwhile the Fords, particularly the "saucy, insolent and idle"
Philip Junior, persisted in "the blackest and most notorious action any
court ever had before it. Penn said that this was his reward for relying
on and trusting those people that would use him ill.[5]

Penn was blind to the fact that Billy, his eldest son, ranked among
such people. In a fond and thoughtless moment, perhaps when Billy lost
in a bid for election to Parliament, he had promised to make Billy
Proprietor of Pennsylvania. When, therefore, in 1705 Hannah was bearing a third son, Richard, Penn realized that something must be done,
not only for his wastrel son but also to provide for Hannah's growing
brood.

Guli's will had provided well for Billy and Tish; it was understood, but not yet certain, that Hannah's children should have the mortgaged and run-down Irish holdings. If Billy agreed to this, he should
have two-thirds of Pennsylvania, in addition to his Guli inheritance; if
he objected, his share in Pennsylvania would be cut in half and the title
of Proprietor left undecided. In the light of this favoritism it is hard to
understand why Billy believed that Penn preferred the children of his
second marriage.

Billy, uncharacteristically, remained noncommittal. He may have been
obsessed by thoughts of a high adventure bound to make him rich in his
own right. For him, as for his grandfather, Jamaica offered golden opportunity. For at least two centuries Spaniards had sailed the Caribbean,
bringing home cargoes of silver from the mines of Mexico and golden
treasure wrested from the Incas of Peru. Not all of the galleons had been
fortunate. Hurricanes had sunk many a ship, dropping the precious
metals to the bottom of the sea, or pirates had plundered the fleets only
to bury the wealth in island beaches. Sailors returning from the Spanish

Main were retailing romantic yarns in the taverns Billy frequented; they displayed charts that showed just where to dive or dig; they convinced gullibles like Billy that all one had to do was to buy the charts, sail overseas, scoop up the treasure, and revel in luxury forever after.[6]

Billy, his cousin Richard Rooth, and Thomas, Lord Fairfax, a very distant relative through Virginia's Governor Culpeper, organized an expedition. Penn, who should have known better, contributed £300 to carry out a scheme that proved an utter failure.

The unhappy gamble not only cost Penn money that he could ill afford but wrecked whatever harmony still remained within the family. After Richard's birth Penn had brought Hannah back from Bristol to live at Brentford, a fashionable Thames-side resort near Kew Gardens. It must have been a lively household with seven-year-old John the American, five-year-old Tommy, four-year-old Hannah, and baby Richard, but Guli's children stayed aloof. Billy, who should have been grateful for the £300 subscription, would not leave the London fleshpots to live in such a childish atmosphere. Tish could not persuade an angry Aubrey to have anything to do with a man who would throw away £300 on a foolish Jamaica venture when he should have used it, if not to help pay off the dowry, at least to pay the interest he owed on it.

As though money problems, family dissention, and quo warranto threats were not enough to bear, Pennsylvania's actions added to his burdens. Queen Anne, like her predecessors, was asking for monetary help and troop assistance, and again the Assembly, when it did anything whatever, sent out the same worn-out refusals. The provincial leaders, Quary and Governor Evans on the one side, David Lloyd on the other, continued to insult and accuse each other.[7]

Evans condemned Lloyd's Assembly as hypocritical and stupid. "You contend and raise continual scruples about your privileges which have not been attempted to be violated, but seem to neglect your duties. . . . You have been made instruments in the hands of designing men." He issued a double warning. Unless the Assembly made an immediate effort to collect taxes it had approved for Penn's benefit, "the Proprietor will withdraw his care." Unless the Queen received the money for which she asked, she would leave Pennsylvania to the mercies of the French and Indians.[8]

The Assembly remained unmoved. It was, it replied, very sorry for the poor Proprietor, but after all, Penn and his people had equal obligations; Penn had failed to fulfill his promises. As for the Queen's money and the warning of troubles with the Indians, the province stood in no danger; even if it did, there was no money in the treasury.[9]

Logan had no better luck. Asserting that as clerk of council he had received no pay and only £12 in fees, he asked a salary appropriation. Since he had bitterly and consistently assailed David Lloyd and had alienated Evans by dunning the Deputy Governor for board and lodging, he could not have expected either man to rush to his defense, nor did he receive help. To his astonishment, however, the Assembly did vote a property tax of two pence in the pound. Of its estimated proceeds £800 were to go to Evans for his past and current salary. While in a generous mood the Assembly also taxed liquor; it expected the impost to yield £600, of which half would be forwarded to William Penn.[10]

Logan expected Evans to reimburse him but the Deputy Governor simply pocketed the money. Penn's reward was just another empty promise. It made him realize anew that he could not trust his people to be grateful. He recalled with sadness that when, some years before, he had humbled himself to ask that a hundred citizens each lend him £100 for his support, only twenty people in the province had subscribed.

To top it all, he was now being looked upon as "a lurcher of the people," as though he were a petty thief, a rogue, a swindler. "I am a crucified man," Penn wailed, "between injustice and ingratitude there and extortion and oppression here."[11]

Yet he could not bring himself to abandon those unworthy people, the assemblymen who demanded what they called equality with him but who really wanted superiority. He regretted his own failings, a "too kind nature to serve others," a readiness to accept rebuffs and poverty if only he could win their love. "I had rather be poor with a loving people than rich with an ungrateful one," said Penn, but unhappily he was a poor man exploited by his base, ungrateful colonists.[12]

The blame for this misery he laid upon David Lloyd, that mischievous man who must be punished for his forgery and treachery. Penn also wanted to know why those who had so abused Billy had not been punished. "Pray let my son have justice against the authors of that barbarous affront committed upon him," Penn pleaded. "He was my son, the first of the Council, and not rightly within their orders or orb of power or reach . . . I take it as done to myself."[13]

His indignation had some slight basis for extenuation. The friends who kept him informed of Pennsylvania happenings had either toned down the details of Billy's behavior or had omitted any mention whatever of them; they had misled the doting father into thinking that the province was ecstatic over Billy. If he had heard any hostile comment, which is doubtful, he would have dismissed it as vile inventions of his enemies.[14]

A proud father's defense of an unpredictable son is understandable, but Penn's assumption that he and his family were above the law revealed how age, position, responsibility, and such deference as he had received had modified his onetime modesty. The Penn who had disapproved the grant of earthly honors, who had not been unhappy that his father had not received the promised peerage, now coveted aristocratic privilege for his descendants. One wonders whether he would now have objected had an Almanac conferred an honorary lordship upon him.

Evans, loyal to Queen and to Proprietor, schemed to secure a war appropriation from Lloyd's majority in the Assembly. Only some startling development, he reasoned correctly, would change the members' stubborn attitude. With a keen sense of the dramatic, Evans conjured up a plan. Suddenly he announced that an emergency message from the Governor of Maryland warned that a French fleet, loaded with troops, was near the Delaware Capes intent on invading Pennsylvania and the Lower Counties. Logan, highly skeptical that Maryland would have any interest whatever in saving Penn's provinces, suspected that Evans had dreamed up the danger. Evans, however, mounted a horse and, dashing here and there about the capital, summoned all men and boys to muster with their arms.[15]

Panic ensued. The Quakers would not fight, not even in their own defense, but they had no wish to lose their valuables. Gathering up their money and their plate, they hid the silver in wells or sank it in convenient swamps, first making careful note of the location. Some sent their women and children out the new road to Germantown to save them from bloodthirsty invaders.[16]

Logan's disbelief deepened when yet another rumor circulated. Reports came down from Burlington, an upriver town that no French fleet could have reached without having been seen from the Philadelphia waterfront, that the French had come. Logan went up and down the river looking for hostile ships and, seeing none, returned to brand Evans as a liar.[17]

The invasion fear passed with no harm done except to the Deputy Governor's credibility. The general public complained that he had unnecessarily terrified the populace, that he had wasted war materials by handing them out indiscriminately and without keeping records of where they went, and that, by forcing the military to keep useless guard, he had wrecked the troops' morale.

The only people to profit by these antics, other than the volunteers who had been handed guns which they felt no obligation to return, were the inhabitants of the Lower Counties. Their now independent Assembly had voted to build that long-desired fort to defend New Castle; it now made a deal with Evans that if they supported him, he would require ships using the Delaware to clear at New Castle and to pay a tax of a pound of powder for every ton of cargo carried; vessels whose home port was New Castle would pay only a quarter of that amount.[18]

Pennsylvanians protested to the Proprietor against any type of tax laid against them by the Lower Counties, the Quakers among them all the more indignant because the proceeds were earmarked for military purposes. The appeal put Penn in a difficult position. He could not favor one province against another, nor could he permit discrimination. Having led his overlords to think that he would take steps to strengthen defenses, he dared not veto a move in that direction. All that he could do was to put both provinces on an equal footing.

The net result, in Logan's words, was "a great ferment." Lloyd caused the Assembly to impeach Logan for, of all things, "allowing the Lieutenant-Governor to summon Assemblies and dismiss them," a charge which Lloyd, a highly competent lawyer, must have known would not stand up in any trial. For some reason, Logan, "that evil minister," was not even told of the action for at least two months.[19]

The news became public on Christmas Eve and then only by a bulletin posted in a coffeehouse. Logan, wandering into the tavern, saw the paper and, in one of the fits of anger to which he was increasingly subject, ripped it from the wall. For this the Assembly censured him for contempt.[20]

Logan regarded both impeachment and censure as attacks upon the Proprietor. While the Lower Counties people were anti-Penn; they were "men of honor when compared to those vile vipers [the Pennsylvanians] who swell with poison against thee."[21]

Both Evans and Lloyd behaved like schoolboys. Bad feeling broke out anew when the two men attended a conference on court laws. After the meeting had been in progress for some time, Lloyd addressed the chair without rising. Evans, taking this as an insult, rebuked him. As Deputy Governor, Evans said, he represented her Majesty the Queen; to speak without rising was disrespect to the Queen. Lloyd shot back that while Evans represented the Crown, he was spokesman for the people. That answer, Evans charged, constituted lese majesty and sedition. The meeting broke up in confusion.[22]

When the Assembly heard this, it exonerated Lloyd on two accounts. By Penn's Frame, the governor's representative and the speaker of the house were of equal status. But, it added, Lloyd had intended no insult; "he had kept his seat for his ease."[23]

Then it became Evans's turn to challenge rightful authority. A sloop sailed out of Philadelphia with all the proper clearance papers, but it disobeyed the law requiring it to put in at New Castle. Evans, who happened to be in that town, ordered the ship to stop; when it did not, he had the gunners in the fort fire upon it. The ship continued on its course, so Evans chased it in a rowboat. The vessel put in for refuge at Salem, across the river in New Jersey, but Evans followed, boarded the offending vessel, and arrested the crew.[24]

He could not have chosen a worse time to offend a more touchy individual. For a Pennsylvanian to make arrests in another province was bad enough; it just so happened that the New Jersey Governor, the erratic Lord Cornbury, Queen Anne's cousin, was in Salem at the time. No one looked upon him as one of the more lovable characters—Penn believed that he was sent to America merely as an excuse to get him out of England—but he was a person of influence at home and very jealous of his dignity. To offend him might conceivably be construed as something that could be added to a quo warranto indictment.

The affair was settled amicably, the master of the sloop acknowledging his fault, but, though neither the skipper nor Evans, and certainly not Cornbury, were aware of it, Evans was wholly within his rights. Both Salem and New Castle lay within that Twelve Mile Circle which James had conveyed to Penn and Evans was Deputy-Governor over the river waters within that circle. He would have had every legal right to police those waters up to the river's edge though not on a single inch of dry land beyond that edge. None of this hair-splitting had been finally determined at the time of the sloop's seizure, nor would it be until the Supreme Court of the United States handed down its decision more than two centuries later.

Nevertheless the incident gave a final reason for replacing Evans. His amorous adventures had shocked both Logan and Penn. The Assembly detested him for calling it a hypocritical defender of "affrontive behavior." He had become a liability rather than an asset to the Proprietor.[25]

For some time Penn had been vainly canvassing his friends for names of possible successors to Evans. He himself would have preferred Billy; but, as he could discover no support for the idea, he postponed that appointment until Billy had more chance to demonstrate his ability.

Until his successor should arrive, Evans, disgruntled not so much because of his impending removal (like Blackwell, he had gone through quite enough) ; but because of the manner in which Penn was arranging it. He had a little money, amassed from various perquisites, including, as Logan said bitterly, "£112 from me," and he had married a new sweetheart. "He lies buried," Logan wrote, "night and day in the fair Rebecca's arms."[26]

BADGERED AND BEWILDERED

THINGS WERE BREAKING VERY BADLY. PENNSYLVANIA REMAINED A HEAVY EXPENSE. LORD BALTIMORE, ACCORDING TO PENN, WAS BRIBING LONDON OFFICIALS TO SUPPORT HIS CLAIM TO THE THREE LOWER Counties. Penn's business interests in America, two mills and a trading company that he owned in partnership with Logan, were making little money. The Fords were winning in the courts; the Lord Chancellor, though personally friendly, could not overlook the fact that Penn had carelessly signed valid deeds and mortgages and had certified the Ford claims as correct. The best that Penn could hope for was a court order for him to pay or go to jail.

To Penn's surprise, no less an adversary than Colonel Robert Quary brought a ray of sunshine. The two men had been unjust to one another, trading accusations of bad faith and broken promises. The Proprietor, Quary had said, was maliciously bent on ruining anyone who disagreed with him; especially, of course, Colonel Quary. Penn also, said Quary, had been an intolerant persecutor of the Anglicans. The sweeping condemnation was deliberately exaggerated, but it was more specific than Penn's customary retorts that critics were villains.

Yet, in the midst of Penn's troubles with the Fords, and only four months after he had unfavorably likened Quary to a snake, Quary suddenly turned friendly. Cynics might suspect that Quary's overture for peace was somehow influenced by his desire to rent Penn's plush house at Pennsbury, but Penn was so happy that Quary "now seems disposed to our affairs" that he did not analyze the vice-admiralty judge's motives.[1]

While Penn welcomed the friendship in one of his rare instances of restoring a former great villain to favor, he exercised some caution. "If

[372]

you think it to my advantage to have him enter the Council," he told Evans, "I should be also, and to be first or second to show he is reconciled." Apparently Evans did not think it wise to put Quary in the high position that Billy had held, nor even to include him in the tight little group of provincial councillors, for Quary's name never appeared on the roster of those attending meetings.[2]

Logan was more friendly, but he too was canny; realizing that the house was in such poor condition that if it were not repaired and reoccupied it would "soon go to decay," he agreed to Quary's terms with one exception; the rent must go to £40.[3]

The year's delay between Quary's desire to rent and the completion of negotiations was probably traceable to the extensive rehabilitation that Pennsbury received at Quary's expense.

The Fords continued to be troublesome. Bridget and her son, Philip Junior, brought suit for £20,000. The amount astonished everyone; Sir Simon Harcourt, a brilliant young barrister who would, in time, become Lord Chancellor, explained that the sum represented the original debt, plus additional arrears of salary and commissions, together with certain unpaid loans, all at compound interest over a quarter-century. Penn's attorneys, Gouldney and Springett, called for detailed accounts which the Fords were unwilling to yield until required to do so by the Court; their reasons for objecting became obvious when Penn's accountants discovered errors, overcharges, and failures to credit Penn with payments he had made. All these, the Penn side contended, reduced the actual debt to about £4300.[4]

Penn would have settled for this amount but the Fords, hopeful that if they carried the case into chancery they could get much more, would not agree. Penn thereupon revived another argument, invalid in court but which, Penn hoped, would exert a psychological effect; he pointed out that Philip Ford had died leaving an estate worth £23,000. "I never heard of a rich steward who was an honest man," Penn had said.[5]

Chancery upheld the Fords in principle but refused to approve the claim for £30,000, whereupon the Fords agreed to settle for £7600 in full payment for the debt and for their mortgage on Pennsylvania, provided £3000 was paid immediately. Penn declined the offer. He fumed at the necessity of giving the Fords anything; for that matter, he did not have that much money. A group of friends, headed by Lord Treasurer Sidney Godolphin, repeated an offer to lend him the necessary amount, but Penn preferred to go to debtors' prison.[6]

On January 7, 1708, while Penn was preaching at Grace Church Street Meeting, bailiffs arrested him and took him to the Fleet.[7] Technically, he was in jail, but more accurately he was under a sort of house arrest, for he enjoyed "the freedom of the rules," which meant that by posting bail he could live almost anywhere within the prison neighborhood in any style that he preferred. Years earlier, when first confined to the Tower, he had scorned Thomas Rudyard's proposal that he purchase special treatment, but with age he had become more compromising in such matters; he was not now a martyr for the cause of freedom of conscience. Other than inability to move about London as he pleased; he could read and write without supervision, order whatever meals he wished, invite friends to dinner, even hold meetings.[8]

Hannah, unfortunately, could not be with him. She was again at Bristol with her children, trying vainly to nurse the dying five-year-old Hannah Marguerite back to health.

The detention could not have been very widely publicized. A month after the arrest the Lords, apparently unaware of the situation, were complaining of his failure to appear before them. Penn regretted that he could not come immediately but promised to call upon them as soon as he was free.

Though the bureaucrats had not been told of his plight, certain high-placed friends knew of it, among them the powerful John Churchill, Duke of Marlborough, and his wife the former Sarah Jennings. So, oddly enough for a man of peace, did some of the more important army officers. They seemed to have Penn's confidence. Somehow knowing of Penn's dissatisfaction with the flighty Deputy Governor Evans, they recommended to Penn a possible successor who seemed to meet Penn's needs.[9]

Their choice was, of course, a soldier, one Captain Charles Gookin, for whose "morals, experience and fidelity" Penn himself could vouch, since he had known the captain forty years. Gookin lacked family relationship to the Penns, nor had he served with Admiral Sir William, but the Gookins had lived at Shanagarry ever since 1670; Penn had leased them land when Charles was only six.

Penn's acceptance of the Captain's availability reflected his conviction that anyone of good family who had been a neighbor and a Shanagarry tenant must necessarily be an appropriate selection. Gookin's grandfather had lived in Ireland since the days of James I, and the father, Daniel Gookin, had been an outstanding colonial official in America, one who had shown a special interest in the welfare of the Indians.

Otherwise, Penn knew relatively little of the man. He was, of course, a soldier, a veteran of the Flanders fighting in Lieutenant General Thomas Earle's command. Though Earle and Marlborough both spoke well of him, neither provided many details of his accomplishments. The omission did not bother Penn; as usual, he set greater store upon personality than upon any other consideration except previous connections with the Penns, and, as the Captain seemed a quiet, thrifty man, "of easy temper and not voluptuous," well trained in giving orders and in obeying them, Penn was much impressed. Besides, he was "a pretty nice mathematician," just as Markham had been. Above all, perhaps, he delighted Penn by professing a desire to devote the rest of his life to Pennsylvania. "He intends, if not ill-treated, to lay his bones as well as substance there," Penn told his friends.[10]

London, still intent on pushing Penn into compliance with bureaucratic desires, used his application for approval of the Gookin appointment to extort another declaration that the Queen's approval of Gookin as Deputy Governor would in no way weaken her claim to possess the Three Lower Counties. They phrased the admission, as they always did, in such a way that Penn did not actually recognize that her title was superior to his own, but neither did she "resign her pretension" to the area.[11]

Gookin then left for his post. He was to face the same dreary round of asking the province to supply men and money for the wars, and was to receive the same refusals, and undergo the same frustrations as his predecessors. The strain would, in time, affect not only his health but even his sanity.

Penn's friendship with the Marlboroughs yielded very practical advantages, not the least being that Lady Sarah Churchill's intimacy with Queen Anne allowed him direct access to the monarch. Penn made good use of his opportunities, such that the jealous Colonel Quary complained to the Board of Trade. "Mr. Penn is free to fill the heads of his friends with strange tales of his extraordinary great interest at court, so that Her Majesty's officers of the Admiralty and Customs are but so many bumpkins." The plaint echoed past grumblings that Penn was not above reminding adversaries that he had better connections than they at the seats of power.[12]

It may well be that Penn's renewed activity at court inspired a revival of his poetic efforts. Just as Penn at Oxford had praised in verse the dead Duke of Gloucester and as someone with the initials W.P. had written an elegy for Charles II and a welcome to his successor James, so a William Penn produced a poem, *Deborah and Barak*, to celebrate the achievement of a military man who forged a Grand Alliance to put down the despot Sisera. The identification of Barak with Marlborough and the close similarity between the prophetess Deborah and Queen Anne, the Mater Patriae, was not forced, or was France specified as the realm of a more recent Sisera, but the comparisons were obvious for those who wished to see them.

The Marlborough influence allowed Penn to draw trained administrators and, in one or two instances, deputy governors from a pool of experienced officials. Most of them were military men, people whom Penn, as a pacifist, would otherwise not have been able to meet, but his use of them as influential advocates in the London bureaus implied no weakening of his antiwar principles. He was, in every respect, opposed to using violence to settle disputes; he had nothing but contempt for those who, through greed or selfishness or for the satisfaction of their vanity, brutally imposed their will upon weaker neighbors. But not all military men were vicious, and there were times when even unscrupulous tyrants might have humanitarian impulses. The trained military officer, moreover, was likely to be practical, resourceful, and efficient, a leader who could both direct and cooperate; in other words, an able administrator.

For that matter, though Penn was never put to the test, there might be times when warfare could be condoned: to repel an invader, to right a wrong, to recover land or property unjustly seized by an aggressor. Such exceptions, however, posed serious difficulties, for no warmonger would be without a plausible excuse for opening hostilities.

The thin and often indistinguishable line between legitimate defensive war and a false pretense of a justified conflict posed difficulties for William Penn, as it did for many another Quaker. He would not resort to arms nor urge others to fight when he himself would not, but neither would he stand in the way of those whose consciences impelled them to resist. In consequence, he was often misunderstood by his own people, who questioned his Quakerism, and always by his opponents, who called him insincere or hypocritical.

Whether Penn won freedom from the Fleet because of Marlborough intervention or because the courts trusted that he would pay the £7600 upon which he and the Fords had agreed, it was necessary for him to rely upon his friends for help. Rich as he was in undeveloped virgin land, he had, as usual, little ready money. Again as usual, friends rushed to the rescue. At Gouldney's suggestion a coterie of admirers, including Thomas Callowhill, scraped together the necessary sum. To guarantee the return of their money, and to discourage further hostile action by the Fords or, for that matter, by any one else, Gouldney had Penn sign a long lease on Pennsylvania. Thus the province would be spared for Penn and for the Society of Friends.[13]

A week after the Fords accepted payment, thus allowing Penn to leave the Fleet, Gouldney and Springett completed arrangements for the sale of Worminghurst. This, too, posed a problem, for while Penn drew a small annuity from the property, the title was in Billy's name. Since the playboy had no wish to live as a country squire and since the sale price would pay off his debts and leave him with a little nest egg, he agreed to sell.[14]

Penn's agents sold the estate for £6000, a tidy profit over the purchase price. He had already cleared £2000 from the timber sales, and Billy had made a little money from selling off the livestock. The sale resulted in both father and son being, for once, out of pressing debt. Unfortunately, the relief did not long endure.

Penn must have deeply regretted severing his ties with Worminghurst and with the Blue Idol Meetinghouse, which he had brought into being. He must have recalled those happy First Day oxcart rides to service and his uncomfortably narrow chair in the corner of the Blue Idol from which he could see Guli across the room. True, he had seldom attended the Blue Idol in the dozen years since Guli's death, but up till now, there had never been a need to make an irrevocable farewell.

Seldom in his life, and almost never in these later years, had Penn been noted for his tact in personal relationships, but one hopes he did not bother Hannah with such reminiscences. She, for her part, was too wise a woman to let him know that her regret at losing all connections with Worminghurt was less poignant than was his own.

Penn's chief concern was now the future of his family. What would happen to Hannah and their five small children if he should die? No help could be expected from the grasping Aubrey, clamorous for Tish's unpaid dowry, or from Billy, the wastrel son. The Callowhills could not be expected to support their daughter and her small children. There being so little expectation of getting much revenue from Pennsylvania, the only course open, as the practical-minded Logan kept reminding the Proprietor, was to accept the best terms available for surrendering the charter.[15]

London, in view of Penn's difficulties, showed no haste in reaching an agreement on the sale. The Lords of Trade and Plantations willingly enough verified Penn's title to Pennsylvania, though not to the Three Lower Counties; a clear title would help the Crown quite as much as it would help Penn, but they saw no need to raise their offers for the purpose. Both he and the Lords knew well that he must cut his asking price, which was what Penn meant when he wrote his friends that he "must consider more closely of my own private and sinking circumstances." The Lords were in no haste to buy him out; the longer they delayed the better bargain they could drive.

As always in times of stress, Penn resorted to the meetinghouse. The decision to resume active preaching—he had never really abandoned the practice—coincided, as it happened, with a belief that he must change his residence. The deaths of two daughters had convinced him that Brentford was as unhealthy as Rickmansworth, and so he had been casting about for some region where the air was better. Twenty or thirty miles west of London, at Ruscombe, he rented a comfortable house. It was four or five miles from Reading Meeting; he would be driven there in his "chariot." Here he would live the rest of his life. Years later, this same region, if not the same house, would be one of Benjamin Franklin's homes; he is said to have written part of his *Autobiography* there.[16]

Penn had first preached at Sun Lane Meeting near Reading just before Christmas 1708. His visit must have roused memories, for this, a generation earlier, had been one of the Quaker communities most torn by the Story–Wilkinson dissension. It had taken a leading part in the

women's movement for equal rights. John Wilkinson's followers had forbidden women to hold separate meetings; when the ladies defied the
order, the men swarmed into the building, spread themselves out upon
the floor, and refused to let the women enter. Just how their refusal
was supposed to block the women's demands for separate meetings
was not quite clear. Penn, mediating the causes for the dispute, had
ruled against Wilkinson's "heresy"—a strange word for Quakers who
believed in liberty of worship—but Reading's men, rejecting the decision,
continued, the women complained, to shut them out in the cold and
snow.[17]

Sit-down strikes were no longer being conducted at Sun Lane, but in
spite of Penn's best efforts to bring about a settlement, the division still
remained. Since he would not join the men in their refusal to allow their
wives and daughters into meetings, he allied himself with the pro-female
group who met on London Street in Reading. The separation lasted five
years after he moved into the large, quaint house he occupied opposite
the Anglican church.

Despite the rift, Penn was happy in his new home. Less active than in
the past, for he was sixty-five and showing signs of age, he yet managed to
visit nearby meetings and to preach frequently. He spent long hours in
his library or at his desk writing, somewhat less polemically than in his
younger years, a series of prefaces for various Quaker works and, a major
work, a memoir of that Sir Bulstrode Whitlocke, who long ago had told
him of the Gustavus Adolphus-Oxenstjerne project for a peaceful colony
of free consciences. As Quakerdom's leading theorist and its most experienced man of political affairs, he held frequent conferences. It was obvious, however, that he was slowing down.

James Logan noticed the change. He had just come from America full
of indignation against a David Lloyd Assembly that had slandered him
without granting him an opportunity for explanation or defense. Two
days before the 1709 election, Logan alleged, the Assembly had sent
Deputy Governor Gookin a *Remonstrance* loaded with calumnies with
which, Logan complained, "I have been most injuriously loaded." The
Remonstrance, posted like other attacks in the public houses, was particularly objectionable because, after having issued it, the Assembly had
at once adjourned so that Logan had no opportunity for rebuttal. When
the Assembly reconvened, Logan asked for a hearing on the various
charges only to be told, falsely, Logan said, that Gookin refused to permit
it.[18]

❧ 50 ❧

REVERSION TO PEACE

FOR MORE THAN THREE YEARS AFTER THE 1712 ATTACK PENN RE-
MAINED PHYSICALLY WELL BUT UNABLE TO CONCENTRATE, SOMETIMES
NOT EVEN ABLE TO SPEAK. HE COULD GET ABOUT WITH ONLY SLIGHT
assistance, on at least one occasion going down to London. More often,
he went to Bath for longer stays to drink the strengthening waters, a
quart or so each day. Now and then he attended Reading Meeting,
though not to preach. Travel over the rough roads tired him. After June
Monthly Meeting, 1715, he ceased to make the trips to Reading; by the
end of the year he was immobilized at Ruscombe.[1]

Doubtless he was not so senile as some biographers described him. No
trustworthy evidence indicates that he chased butterflies like a small child
or took an infantile pleasure in running from room to room, or in standing by the great windows wondering at the snow and rain. At worst,
he had fallen into what Thomas Story called a state of innocency, a condition in which his understanding was, in Story's words, suspended.[2]

Hannah pampered him. Solicitous about a swelling in the legs, she
worried about a possible return of his paralysis—she called it palsy—and
was relieved when told, probably incorrectly, that it was nothing more
than a recurrence of his gout. Settling him in a comfortable chair, she
brought him orange wine and the lemon-flavored brandy that he preferred to all other stimulants.[3]

Her outward cheerfulness kept William and her household in good
spirits. To hold the family together, to rear a household of teen-agers
and youngsters while battling their demanding Uncle Aubrey and step-
son Billy, who consistently evaded his responsibilities, to manage a heavily mortgaged estate while nursing an ailing husband, to be almost
simultaneously at Ruscombe with the family, in Bristol smoothing out

her parents' affairs, or in London consulting with her advisors—all this seemed too great a hardship for the highly capable Hannah Penn. Yet somehow her practicality enabled her to solve each problem as it arose.

The need had vanished, she reasoned, for training her sons for public service; she was confident that negotiations for the sale of Pennsylvania would be successfully concluded. She started the older boys in business careers by apprenticing John the American, a sufferer from rheumatic fever, to the head of the Callowhill textile firm. When John, lonesome the first time away from home, became despondent because of the exile, she cheered him by a stream of letters. She counseled Thomas, who wavered between studying medicine and following John into the dry-goods business; eventually she indentured him to London with the injunction "Mind your books, do as your master orders and learn two chapters of the Bible every day by heart." She kept in close touch with Tish, whose life with Aubrey could not have been entirely happy.[4]

By tacit consent, Hannah exercised greater authority in the management of Penn property than was really allowable under the strict letter of contemporary law or custom. She was to be Penn's sole executor, it was generally understood; during his incapacity, considerate officials permitted her to anticipate her legal assumption of that role. When Penn's signature was needed on a document, they winked as she put a quill into the hands of her ever smiling but totally uncomprehending husband; they looked the other way as she guided his fingers in signing his name. Their cooperation may have resulted from her willingness to fee officials so that papers "would more readily slip through their hands."

She was anxious to be rid of Pennsylvania. It is doubtful whether she had ever really shared her husband's confidence that the province could become Utopia; that vision, seen by Penn a score of years earlier, had faded from his own mind before Hannah came into his life. She cherished no illusions that a province, cursed by thirty years of jealousy and strife, could be rebuilt into a community of saints living happily in the spirit of the Scriptures.

Reports from the provinces dismayed her. Though Penn had come to discount highly exaggerated complaints, Hannah was more credulous. Not realizing that David Lloyd sincerely believed the principles that he professed, she branded him the evil spirit that his enemies declared him to be. She trusted Logan, but she was shaken by his opponents' violent criticisms. Not having her husband's knowledge of Gookin's abilities, she credited those who looked upon him as "a hopeless misfit, stupid, overbearing, jealous, avaricious, subject to recurrent fits of insanity." Expecting that her two chief agents in America, Gookin and Logan, would work harmoniously, she was taken aback when the hot-tempered Logan reported that Gookin, "the weakest animal that was ever called a Governor," was ignoring him.[5]

Now that Hannah needed money for household expenses and to pay off Tish's dowry, London agreed to her reduced asking price. In March 1714, the Crown offered £12,000, payable over four years, which included, as a down payment, £1000 given the Penns in advance. Hannah, after consulting with her Quaker advisors, Henry Gouldney and Thomas Story, and with her attorney, Herbert Springett, Guli's relative, readily accepted.[6]

Complications blocked the sale. Hannah held no valid power of attorney. Though the government was perfectly willing to accept a deed signed by Penn as Hannah guided his fingers, Billy, Aubrey, and some of the mortgage-holders objected; they thought their prospects endangered. Hannah suggested that the government compensate them by lands in the West Indies, St. Kitts, for example, but those sugar acres were too valuable for the Crown to yield.[7]

Someone in the friendly Earl of Oxford's government suggested that the objections be circumvented by an Act of Parliament, but unfortunately, at that juncture Oxford's administration was overthrown, as was that of his successor, the equally friendly Earl of Halifax; they were succeeded by the Earl of Shrewsbury, formerly Penn's friend but now a Tory. The sale was not only postponed; it was never completed. Hannah was obliged to scrape together £1000 to repay the advance. The Penn title to his province remained alive until the American Revolution.

Meanwhile, Queen Anne had died, bringing the Hanoverian George I to the throne. The change weakened Gookin's influence, his Marlborough backing now being less formidable. Hannah, recognized informally if not in full legality as Penn's guardian, thus managed, in 1716, to dismiss her unpredictable governor. He had held the longest rule of any of Penn's deputies, eight years in one term as against a cumulative seven years for Markham's three tenures and five for John Evans.

To replace Gookin, Hannah nominated thirty-six-year old William Keith, a man who, despite his youth, had had more executive experience than had any other deputy since Hamilton. He may have been a relative of George Keith, the Christian Quaker—they came from the same area in Scotland—but George had died in 1716, the year before William's appointment, and if there was any close kinship between them, it is unlikely that Hannah, a good Quaker, would have made the appointment. William Keith's chief attribute was an ability to work harmoniously with warring factions. His gracious manner and his fine appearance, in contrast to the roughness of some of his predecessors, charmed the Pennsylvania leaders.

Pennsylvania greatly needed a man of suavity and tact. The province had been growing rapidly, its population having increased sixfold during the previous thirty years. The growth to more than sixty thousand people had been foreseen, but few had suspected that the influx would have left the Quakers so outnumbered as to deprive them of control. No one had anticipated that a projected agricultural Utopia would have become an urban commercial community or that Anglicans would direct policy. Keith, as it happened, was himself a Churchman.

The Crown consented to his appointment, but only on condition that the Penns once more agree that approval of Keith as Deputy Governor of Pennsylvania and the Three Lower Counties in no way diminished the King's claim of ownership of those Lower Counties. He took the oaths of office May 31, 1717 as a supporter of the Assembly against the proprietary party and served until 1726 in an administration longer than Gookin's. Two years after taking office he proposed a stamp tax on the colonies, a proposal rejected at the time but revived, with unhappy consequences, in 1765.[8]

The Crown's insistence on requiring the Penns to confess their weakness of title to the Three Lower Counties did not escape attention. John Gordon, seventh Earl of Sutherland and Lord Lieutenant of Northern Scotland, claimed that the new King, George I, owed him £20,000; he asked that it be paid off by a grant of the Three Lower Counties. Luckily, Charles Spencer, Earl of Sunderland, son of Penn's Oxford classmate, was Lord Keeper of the Privy Seal and blocked the progress of the application. Later Sutherland tried again, this time asking for "certain islands in Delaware Bay," as did Gookin who apparently had recovered his sanity, but both applications failed. The Board of Trade took the opportunity to declare that, as the New Jersey grants ended at the east bank of the river while Penn's possession began at the western shore, the islands belonged to the Crown. When, by the American Revolution, all Royal territories came under United States jurisdiction, the dividing line between New Jersey and Delaware was set at midstream, except for that area within the Twelve Mile Circle which James, when Duke of York, had granted to Penn.[9]

Amidst all these distractions Hannah gave Penn the gentle nursing which gave him the relief he so badly needed. Though at times he seemed comforted, if not, as she optimistically believed, almost well, he usually existed in a state of semiconsciousness. On a few occasions he suffered what Hannah described as "a little fit," which must have been a series of minor strokes.[10]

At about midday, July 28, 1718, Penn suddenly had alternations of chills and fever. Hannah sent for a physician, who pronounced the symptoms unimportant and insignificant. Hannah was not so sure.[11]

Her fears were justified. On July 30 she wrote Logan, "My poor Dearest's last breath was fetched this morning between two and three o'clock."[12]

Joseph Besse, his first English biographer, embroidered the account. After noting Penn's "continual and gradual declension for about six years," said Besse, "his body drew near to its dissolution, and on the 30th day of the 5th month, in the 74th year of his age, his soul, prepared for a more glorious habitation, forsook the decayed tabernacle."[13]

Large numbers of Quakers attended the funeral, arriving at Ruscombe late in the evening for a solemn ceremony. "Our coming," said Thomas Story, occasioned a fresh remembrance of the deceased, and also a renewed flood of tears from many eyes. A solid time (of worship) we had together, but few words among us for some time, for it was a deep baptizing season and the Lord was near . . . As the Lord had made choice of him in the days of his youth for great and good services, had been with him in many dangers and difficulties of various sorts, and did not leave him in his last moment, so He was pleased to honor this occasion with His blessed presence and gave us a happy season of His goodness to the general satisfaction of all.[14]

On August 5, William Penn was laid to rest in the burial grounds at Jordan's. His body, encased in a lead coffin, was placed to the right of that of Guli, her mother, Mary Springett Penington, being on her left. At her death in 1727, Hannah was interred in the same grave as her deceased husband.[15]

Behind these graves, under magnificent beech and linden trees, lie the bodies of five Penn children, four by Guli and an infant by Hannah. These are the graves of Letitia and Springett, John the American, and his sister Margaret, who married Thomas Fraeme. Of the other Penn children, Billy died abroad, two years after his father's death. An unnamed daughter, who may have been born in 1683, is said to be buried at the Blue Idol, and the remaining children either on their own estates or at Stoke Poges (scene of Thomas Gray's "Elegy"), which Thomas Penn purchased in 1760.

On hearing of the death of Brother Onas, their protector and friend, Pennsylvania's Indians sent Hannah a message of condolence, together with a gift of skins and furs with which to fashion garments suitable for the thorny wilderness of care through which she, as a widow, must thereafter travel.[16]

Penn's will, drafted in May 1712, by Robert West and offered for probate November 4, 1718, was not the perfectly crafted document that two such legal experts as West and Penn might have been expected to produce, perhaps because both men had recently experienced what physicians, in the parlance of the time, described as paralytic attacks. It contained what Logan assumed were blunders due to haste.[17]

In accordance with previous understandings, the American lands were divided, half going to John, Hannah's eighteen-year-old eldest son, the other half going to his three younger brothers, Richard, Thomas, and

Dennis, with right of survivorship. Because of their youth, however, they were to be guided by two long-time friends, Robert Harley, Earl of Oxford and Mortimer, and William, Earl of Paulet. Harley's selection was not surprising, for he had long been a confidential advisor to Penn, but that of Paulet was rather unexpected, since he had not been publicly active as a close associate—the only other connection recorded had been as a member of the family from whom Penn and Guli had rented Basing House.

The entrusting of the Pennsylvania government to the four boys, under the supervision of the two noble lords carried no slight to Hannah, for this was a matter of statecraft and government with which she was relatively unfamiliar. In more material affairs she was to be executrix of the Penn estate; she was also to receive a £300 annuity. Unfortunately, the codicil bequeathing the annuity had not been properly witnessed. She was also disappointed because Penn's personal property, upon which she had counted to meet current expenses, was eaten up by the payment of outstanding debts.

Billy, having already been amply provided for by Guli's will, received only the Irish lands, a bequest which he so much resented as to lead him to contest the entire will; his children, Springett and William Penn the Third, together with Hannah and her children, received more generous treatment.[18]

The self-exiled Billy, whom she characterized as "the indiscreet son who, for several years, had been hastening to his own destruction," unexpectedly turned up. Unhappy at learning that while he was to inherit the proprietary title, the soil would go to Hannah and her children, he contested the will; by separating the administration from the ownership of Pennsylvania, he contended, his father had invalidated the entire instrument. He, and he alone, Billy believed, should be the rightful owner of both Pennsylvania and of the Three Lower Counties. By thus appealing to the primogeniture principle, whereby in English law of former times the eldest son inherited all real property to the exclusion of his brothers and sisters, Billy sought to nullify one of his father's pet reforms, the abolition of primogeniture in Pennsylvania.[19]

Though nothing was left to Billy, he was not faring too badly. He was already amply provided for by Guli's will. His three children were now to have Shanagarry and what was left of the Springett estates, which, it was estimated, would bring in about £1500 per year, though the ownership would be in their names and not in his. The children, and Letitia, too, were each to have ten thousand acres in Pennsylvania.

One biographer, indeed, made a gallant attempt to show that Billy, instead of being discriminated against, was really being made the major beneficiary of Penn's will. "It must be remembered," it was said, "that until a year or two before the will was drawn Pennsylvania had not yielded a shilling a year, and that, when the will was made, only about £500, so that Penn thought he was settling the best estates upon Guli's children." But on the other hand, by 1712 the Springett lands had either been sold or so heavily mortgaged as to be of little value.[20]

If there was any discrimination, Billy had brought it upon himself. During his father's long illness, while Tish and Hannah's children had been solicitous in their attendance, Billy had remained aloof, "almost a stranger," as a commentator remarked. He had been missing, also, from his own home. He had left his wife and family—a desertion which his father would not have strongly criticised—but in utter disregard of Hannah's burdens, Billy had sent his children to Ruscombe for her to look after. He had then virtually disappeared from Ruscombe's knowledge. The hopes that Penn had entertained that Billy would reform had entirely vanished.

Perhaps because of William Aubrey's abrasive behavior, he gave Letitia a rather peculiar bequest; she was to have "whatever my wife thinks of it." Tish, in addition to her more material inheritance, was to receive a sentimental remembrance, Penn's cherished Spanish medal, the coin Guli had prized so highly and which, after her death, Penn always wore about his neck.[21]

The London authorities had refused to commit themselves on the question of which master Pennsylvania should obey. Though they approved of Keith as deputy, they suggested that the time was near when the province should be restored to Royal control.

To cancel the charter was not a simple process. Though the major problems were settled, both the Penns and the Crown agreeing that £12,000 was a fair price, doubt remained as to who had power to sign the necessary papers. While the courts deliberated, Billy died somewhere in France, in late June 1720. His death, at forty, did not halt proceedings.[22] Springett Penn, his nineteen-year-old son, proclaimed himself heir-at-law. Springett, a year younger than John the American, had for eight years been living under Hannah's protection, but the rewards to be gained by breaking his grandfather's will outweighed any gratitude he may have felt.

A year and a half after Billy's death Hannah suffered "a fit of the dead palsy." The stroke did not affect her mind, as it had her husband's, but it left her physically weak. Other misfortunes befell the family. John the American was seldom in good health, and Dennis, her youngest boy, died of smallpox soon after his mother's illness. Hannah did, however, live to hear, in December 1726, the courts at last dismiss all contests against Penn's will. She died a week later.

Thereafter, her three surviving sons, John, Thomas, and Richard, administered the province as true and absolute proprietors. They retained control until the outbreak of the American Revolution.

NOTES

INTRODUCTION: *Man of Paradox*

1. See Appendix A.
2. *The Chronicle* (Gloucester, England), October 6, 1845, reporting the exhumation of Admiral Penn's body.
3. "Franklin, Benjamin" (really Richard Jackson), *An Historical Review of Pennsylvania* (London, 1759), 14.

   For Franklin disclaimer of responsibility, see his letters to Isaac Norris, March 19 and June 9, 1759, in Carl Van Doren, *Benjamin Franklin* (New York, 1938), 284. The serpent–dove relationship was suggested by *Matthew* 10–16.
4. Hull, William T., *William Penn: A Topical Biography* (New York, 1937), 309.
5. See, among others, *More Work for George Keith* (London, 1696). To Governor and Provincial Council, January 10 and 22, 1703.
6. Bugg, Francis, *Ulmorum Acherons: History of Penn's Conversion from a Gentleman to a Quaker* (London, 1682). For a report on this book's exhibition at Independence Hall, see *Philadelphia Evening Bulletin*, May 12, 1913.
7. Shepherd, William R., *History of Proprietary Government in Pennsylvania* (New York, 1896), 185.

   See also Norman H. Mason, 42 *General Magazine and Historical Chronicle* (1944), 481–90.
8. Sutcliffe, Robert, *Travels in Some Parts of North America* (London, 1811).
9. Watson, John F., *The Annals of Philadelphia* (Philadelphia, 1830).
10. To George Whitehead et al., 1668; also, to William Burr, 1674.
11. See Appendix E.
12. *Philadelphia Inquirer*, December 21, 1973.

CHAPTER 1: *Self-Reared Child*

1. See Appendix B.
2. Hepworth Dixon, who was not infallible, quotes Hugh David as having so informed Robert Proud. In *N & Q*, First Series, No. 84, June 7, 1854, 45.

3. Frequent Giles references in *CSP*, Barbary, 1630–87. Consul appointment, November 30, 1637.

4. Material on George and on William Penn, father of the Founder, unless otherwise credited, is from Granville Penn, *Memorials of the Professional Life and Times of Admiral Sir William Penn* (2 vols., London, 1833). Hereafter cited as GP.

5. Albert Cook Myers, *Early Life of William Penn* (Moylan, Pa., *n.d.*), 24–25.

6. 2 *Duke of Portland, MSS.*, HMC, 54.

7. Clarendon, Edward Hyde, *The History of the Great Rebellion and the Civil War* (London, 1888), passim.

8. *PD*, passim.

9. *Parish Register*, All Hallows Barking. The font in which William Penn was baptized was transferred in 1697 to Christ Church, Philadelphia, where it is now in use.

10. *PD*, September 25, 1660; August 1, 1667.

11. "Black Monday," March 29, 1652. The outcome was a charge that the Admiral embezzled captured treasure. Years later Penn was completely cleared. Cf. 2 GP, April 14–21, 466–92.

12. Codicil to Penn will of October 8, 1706.

13. Admiral's petitions: December 15, 1653; September 1, 1654; October 16, 1655. Imprisonment: September 20 to October 30, 1655.

14. Cromwell to Penn, December 1, 4, and 20, 1654. 2 *Portland MSS.*, HMC, 88–89.

CHAPTER 2: *Lonely Visions*

1. To Anna Maria Van Schurmann, September 13, 1677.

2. Page, William and J. H. Round, *History of Essex* (London, 1907), 2: 504.

3. *Great Case of Liberty of Conscience*, 1673.

See also: to George Whitehead, 1668; to William Burr, 1674.

4. Aubrey, John, *Brief Lives*, ed. by Oliver Lewis (London, 1958), 274.

5. Stott, G., "Early History of Chigwell," 52 *Essex Review* (1953), 4–14.

See also Smith, E. Fell, *History of Essex* (London, 1907), 2: 544.

6. Saltmarsh, John, *Sparkles of Glory* (London, 1627).

7. To Van Schurmann, September 13, 1677.

8. Hodgkin, L. V., *Gulielma, Wife of William Penn* (New York, 1947), 3–30.

See also: to Mary Pennyman, November 22, 1673, and to Whitehead, 1668, and Burr, 1674.

9. Penney, Norman, *Experiences in the Life of Mary Penington* (Philadelphia, 1910), 74–76.

10. *CSP*, Ireland, 1642–49, passim.

11. 14 *JCAHS* (1908), 105–16; 50 (1949), 31–39.

12. *Account of His Convincement*, MSS. at Friends House, London, attributed to Thomas Harvey, who said he had heard it from William Penn about 1700. The question has been raised whether this William Penn was the Founder or his son. 12 *JFHS* (1935) 22–26. See also Acts 17:104.

13. To Van Schurmann, September 13, 1677.

14. *CSP*, Ireland, Series 4, 449.

See also J. T. Collins, 51 *JCAHS* (1946), 96–107.

15. 1 *Ormonde MSS.*, passim.
16. O'Suilleabhain, Sean, 50 *JCAHS*, 71 *f*.
17. Harben, Henry A., *A Dictionary of London* (London, 1918).

    See also Stapleton, Alan, *London Lanes* (London, 1930).
18. PD, July 5, 1662; November 9, 1663; November 6, 1665; June 6, 1667; September 22, 1668.

CHAPTER 3: *Scholar and Gallant*

1. Schachner, Nathan, *The Medieval Universities* (New York, 1938), 230.

   See also Newcombe, L., *University and College Libraries in Great Britain and Ireland*, (New York, 1927), 160.
2. *No Cross, No Crown; New Witnesses Proved Old Heretics.*
3. *Truth Exalted.*
4. Penn to Father, May 6, 1665.

   Epicidea (Oxford, 1660). Later published in *European Magazine and London Review*, April, 1790.
5. Wood, Anthony A., *Athenae Oxoniensis* (London, 1691), 2: 105–54.
6. Ibid.
7. Besse, Joseph, *Abstract of the Sufferings of Friends* (London, 1753), 2: 569.
8. To Robert Turner, April 2, 1681.
9. *Short Testimony Concerning Josiah Coale*, 1671.
10. *Journal, 1677; Truth Exalted; New Witnesses.*
11. *Journal, 1677.*

    Gough, John, *History of the People Called Quakers*, (Dublin, 1790), 2: 214.

    See also *PD*, January and February 6, 1662.
12. The only volume ever specifically mentioned in this connection is Henry Stubbs's *A Light Shining Out of Darkness*, first published in 1659, which Penn is said to have "edited," when he was a 15-year-old freshman.
13. To Anna Maria van Schurman, September 13, 1677.
14. To Sunderland, July 28, 1683.
15. Croese, Gerardus, *Historia Quakeriana* (Amsterdam, 1696), 41.
16. *No Cross, No Crown.*
17. Sturgis, Samuel Booth, *The Huguenot Source of Penn's Ideal of Religious Tolerance* (Philadelphia, 1956).
18. Unknown to Sir William, April 23, 1683.

    See also: to William Burr, 1674.
19. GP, 612–16.
20. Robbins, Caroline, "Algernon Sidney's 'Disclosures Concerning Government': Textbook of Revolution," *William and Mary Quarterly*, vol. 4, no. 3 (July, 1947), 267–98.

CHAPTER 4: *Worldly Glory Fades*

1. *PD*, August 24, 1664; September 13, 1665.

   See also Captain P. Gibson, in GP, 616.

   See also *Ah, Tyrant Lust*, 1664.
2. Ringrose, Hyacinthe, *The Inns of Court* (London, 1909).

   See also *Records of Lincoln's Inn*, I: 205.
3. Wood, Anthony À., *Athenae Oxoniensis* (London, 1721), 2: 1050.

4. Bell, W., *Lincoln's Inn: History and Traditions* (London, 1947), 41.
5. Wood, *Athenae*, 2: 1050.
6. See *Oxford English Dictionary*, entry under "municipal."
7. To Admiral, April 23, 1665.
8. To Admiral, May 6, 1665.
9. *No Cross, No Crown.*
10. *PD*, October 20, 1667.
11. GP, 2: 296.
12. *PD*, November 9, 1663.
13. Robinson to J. Williamson, December 23, 1671. *CSP*, Domestic (1669–71), 40.
14. Details of the Irish visit not otherwise credited are from *My Irish Journal*, November 22, 1670.

    See also Gilbert, Sir John, *Ancient Records of Dublin.*
15. To Friends, in Holland, July 13, 1677.
16. Shannon to Penn, August 20, 1667.

    See also Admiral to Penn, April 9, 1667.
17. Orrery to Admiral, May 29, 1666.

    See also Admiral to Penn, July 30, 1666.

    See also Admiral to Orrery, August 7, 1666, GP, II, 430–33.
18. To Robert Harley, July 14, 1706.
19. To Thomas Harvey, 1700 (?), 32 *JFHA*, (1935), 22–26.

    See also Rutty, John, *History of the Quakers in Ireland* (London, 1756), 96, 116–17, 124.
20. Orrery to Penn, November 5, 1667.
21. Besse, Joseph, *Abstract of the Sufferings of the People Called Quakers* (London, 1753), 2: 3.
22. Admiral to Penn, October 12, 1667.
23. Gough, John, *History of the People Called Quakers* (Dublin, 1790), 2: 217.
24. Ibid, 221.

    See also: to Anna Maria Van Schurmann, September 13, 1677.

CHAPTER 5: *Tower Prison*

1. Dutch attack, February 21, 1667.
2. *XI Journal,* House of Lords, 285; *XII ibid.* 227–28.
3. *No Cross, No Crown.*
4. *FI*, September 18, 1944, reporting an oral tradition in Pennsylvania.
5. "Fragments of an Apology for Himself," *Memoirs*, III, HSP, Part 2, 235–42.
6. *Answer to a Vain Flash*, February 1668.
7. *A Guide Mistaken*, 1668.
8. *Sandy Foundations Shaken*, 1668, Part I.
9. *PD*, February 12, 1669.
10. Evelyn, John, *Diary* (London, 1859), January 3, 1669.
11. Warrant for arrest, December 2, 1668.

    See also *Newsletter*, December 7, 1668.

12. *Newsletter*, December 12, 1668.
13. Bruce, John, *Observations Upon Penn's Imprisonment in the Tower, 1668* (London, 1853), 185.

    See also Dixon, William Hepworth, *William Penn: An Historical Biography* (Philadelphia, 1851), 62.
14. Besse, Joseph, *Abstract of the Sufferings of the People Called Quakers* (London, 1733), I: 9–10.
15. Mortimer, R. S., "Penn and His Printer," 46, *JFHS* (1954), 64–65.
16. Cooke visit; December 24, 1668, 9 *CSP*, Domestic, Entry Book, folio 30, 96.
17. To Guli, December 28, 1668.

    See also 1 Besse, *Abstract*, 6.
18. Will dated January 20, 1669.
19. Admiral to Privy Council, March 31, 1669.
20. To Stillingworth, January 4, 1669.
21. To Arlington, June 19, 1669.
22. Lewis, Edwin O., *William Penn, Lawyer* (Philadelphia, 1959).
23. *London Newsletter*, July 28, 1669.

CHAPTER 6: *Love and Duty*

1. Besse, Joseph, *Abstract of the Sufferings of the People Called Quakers* (London, 1733), passim.
2. To Penington, October 17, 1668. Loe died October 5.
3. 42 *Edinburgh Review* (July 1813), 444 *f.*
4. Swift, Jonathan, *Prose Works* (London, 1902), X: 356.

    See also Burnet, Bishop Gilbert, *History of His Own Time*, ed. by M. J. Routh (6 vols., Oxford, 1823), 139–40.
5. October 6, 1669.
6. Unless otherwise credited, details of the trip to Ireland are drawn from *My Irish Journal*.
7. Affidavit to Chancery, January 30, 1705.

    See also: to Friends, November 18, 1705.
8. *Suffering of Friends in Bucks*, September 4, 1665; January 27, 1666. MSS. in Friends Library, Euston Road, London.
9. Ford, *Account Book*, 1672.
10. Aubrey, John, *Brief Lives*, ed. by Oliver Lewis, (London, 1958).
11. Harris, J. Rendel, *The Finding of the* Mayflower (Manchester, 1920).

    See also *The Friend* (London), August 6, 1920.

    See also *Christian Science Monitor*, February 24, 1955.
12. John Gay to Penn, July 23, 1670.

    See also *CSP*, Ireland (1669–70), 84, 201–2, 328.
13. *BFHA*, Philadelphia (1925), 37.
14. To an Unknown from Dublin, November 1, 1669; February 12, 1670.
15. George Fox to Henry Sidon, May 25, 1677.

    See also: to James Harrison, March 18, 1685.
16. Admiral to Penn, April 29, 1670.
17. April 29, 1670.

18. J. T. Collins, "The O'Heas of Cork," 51 *JCAHS* (1946), 106.
19. Lord Broghill (brother to Orrery) to Penn, May 18, 1670.

CHAPTER 7: *For English Rights*

1. Guli to Penn, July 16, 1670.
2. John Gay to Penn, July 23, 1670.
3. Robinson, Ralph M., *The Penn Country and the Chilterns* (London, 1929), 28–29.
4. Elizabeth Bowman to Penn, July 16, 1670.
5. Inventory in *Penn MSS.*, Forbes Collection.
6. John Rouse to Sarah Fell, August 15, 1670, in John Bardy, *Letters of Early Friends,* vii, (London, 1841), 177.
7. Stephens, Sir James, *History of the Criminal Law of England* (London, 1883), 373.
8. *People's Ancient and Just Rights Asserted* (London, 1670). Formerly attributed to Penn, but disclaimed by him, at least in part. This is the Quaker report of the Penn–Meade trial. Starling replied in his *Answer to a Tedious and Scandalous Pamphlet* (London, 1670). Cf. Caroline Robbins, "The Papers of William Penn," 93 *PMHB*, 3–12.
9. To Admiral Penn, September 6, 1670.
10. 36 *English Reports*, King's Bench Division, Easter Term, 26 Carolus II.

    See also 89 *English Reports*; 66 *State Trials; Vaughn's Reports,* 135.
11. Death: September 16, 1670. Will proved: October 6, 1670. Deathbed speech, GP, 2: 562–64.
12. Cartwright, B. F., *Pictorial History of St. Mary's, Redcliffe* (London, 1963).

    See also: to Navy Commissioners, December 2, 1670.
13. William Sewel, *History of the Rise of the People Called Quakers* (London, 1795), 2: 295–97.
14. To Pepys, November 4, 1670.

    See also: to P[—]M[—], Vice Chancellor of Oxford, November 9, 1670.

    See also: to Parliament, 1670.
15. Sewel, 2: 295–97.
16. Ellwood, 2: 238.
17. In Holland, July 28 to September 15, 1677; in Germany, September 16 to October 20, 1677.

    See also Hull, William I., *William Penn and the Dutch-Quaker Migration to Pennsylvania* (Swarthmore, 1935), 193–95.
18. Schotel, D. J. "A Dutch Blue Stocking and Quaker of the 17th Century," 207 *Edinburgh Review*, (1908), 358–77.

CHAPTER 8: *Freedom to Think*

1. *Great Case of Liberty of Conscience,* 1670.
2. To Orrery, November 9, 1667.
3. To Guli, December 28, 1668.
4. To John Sobieski, August 4, 1677.
5. To Tillotson, January 29, 1667.
6. To Tillotson, January 29, 1667.

7. *England's Great Interest in the Choice of This New Parliament*, 1679.

8. Shannon to Penn, August 20, 1667. See for "girl who thinks thee mad," John Gay to Penn, July 23, 1670, *CSP Ireland* (1669–70), 202.

9. Bassett, John S., ed., *The Writings of Col. William Byrd of Virginia* (New York, 1901). It should be noted that Byrd was not born at the time of the supposed scandal and that he did not write of it until 20 years after Penn's death. He gave no corroboration, perhaps because there was none.

10. Fox to Penn, August 28, 1674.

11. To James Logan, February 24, 1703. Lehnmann was Penn's private secretary, 1672–1685.

12. Ford, *Account Book*, 1672, 81.

13. January 9 to March 17, 1673, *Register of Quaker Births*. Richard died, April 1, 1673.

    See also 9 *Essex Parish Register*, Chichester.

14. Muggleton debate, December 15, 1672.

CHAPTER 9: *Overseas Opening*

1. Whitelocke, Sir Bulstrode, *Journals of the Swedish Embassy* (London, 1772).

   See also Preface to revised edition of Whitelocke's *Memorials of the English Affairs From the Beginning of the Reign of Charles I* (London, 1713).

2. Carter, Edward C., and Clifford Lewis, "Sir Edmund Plowden and the New Albion Charter," 33 *PMHB* (1959), 150–79.

   See also Preface to revised edition of Whitelocke's *Memorials of the English* Turner, *Some Records of Sussex County* (Philadelphia, 1909), 285–88.

3. Harder, Leland, "Plockhoy and His Settlement at Zwaanendael, 1663," 3 *Delaware History* (1949), 150; 5 *MA* (1667–87), 410–16.

4. Groff, "Lost Settlement," entries of January 9–11, 1682.

5. Cullen, Virginia, *History of Lewes, Delaware* (Lewes, 1956), 14–15.

6. Duke of York's Grant, June 24, 1664, reaffirmed February 5, 1674, *Salem #1* (New Jersey Historical Society), 1–8.

7. Cf. United States Supreme Court *Reports*, February 5, 1934, 291: 61.

8. Andrews, Charles M., *Colonial Period in American History* (4 vols., New Haven, 1937), 3: 138 *n.*

9. Clement, John, "William Penn: His Interest and Influence in West New Jersey," 5 *PMBH* (1881), 313–33.

10. March 6 and 14, 1674, Leaming, Aaron and Jacob Spicer, *The Grants, Concessions and Original Constitutions of the Province of New Jersey* (New Brunswick, 1858), 64 *f.*

    See also New Jersey Concessions, February 20, 1665, 1 *NJA*, 8–14, 28–43.

11. Jones, Edson S., "The Salem County Historical Society," *Salem Sunbeam*, December 28, 1906.

    See also Stewart, Frank H., *Major John Fenwick* (Woodbury, N.J., 1939).

12. Johnson, Robert Gibbons, *John Fenwick: Historical Account of the First Settlement of Salem* (Philadelphia, 1839), 37.

13. Edwards, Irene, 47 *JFHS* London (1935), #1. Loan repaid 1678, *Report*, Women's Box Committee, London Monthly Meeting Records, vol. 2.

14. To Byllinge, January 20, 1675.

See also: to Fenwick, January 30, 1675.
15. Quinpartite Deed, July 1, 1676, 1 *NJA* 205–19.
16. Trustees appointed February 9, 1675.
17. Ogilby, John, *America* (London, 1671).
18. *Description of the Province of West New Jersey*, July 1676. Fenwick's proposals, 6 *PMHB* (1882), 86–90.
19. Salem Deeds, 1 *NJA*, 186–87.
20. The description is from Francis David Pastorius's *Positive News From Pennsylvania* (Philadelphia, 1684), but the conditions apply to all transatlantic vessels of the time.
21. John Spooner rebuke: *Minutes*, Salem Monthly Meeting, August 6, 1676.
22. 1 *NJA* 193.
23. Roger Pedrick to wife, June 14, 1676, Stewart, Frank H., *Major John Fenwick* (Woodbury, New Jersey, 1939), 8.
24. A broadside, possibly by Fenwick, echoing John Ogilby's *America* (London, 1671).
25. Clement, John, "A Sketch of William Biddle and Thomas Biddle," 14 *PMHB* (1890), 364–86.

See also 12 *New York Colonial Documents*, 579.

CHAPTER 10: *Come, Ye Oppressed*
1. 1 *NJA* 56–57.
2. *Present State of West Jersey.*

Cf. the overblown praise in "Beauchamp Plantagenet's" *Description of the Province of New Albion: A Direction for Adventurers with a Small Stock to get two for one and good Land freely and all Servants Laborers and Artificers to Live Plentifully* (London, 1648).
3. *Brief Account of the Province of West Jersey*, London, January 1765.

See also *A Further Account of New Jersey*, 1676.
4. Pomfret, John W., "Edward Byllinge's Proposed Gift of Land to Indigent Friends," 61 *PMHB* (1937), 88–92.
5. Newcombe, L., *University and College Libraries in Great Britain and Ireland* (New York, 1927).

See also Smith, H.F. Russell, *Harrington and His Oceana* (Cambridge, 1914).

See also: to Sir John Rhodes, October 1693.
6. Preface to Pennsylvania *Frame of Government*, 1682.

See also: to Provincial Council, April 1, 1700.

See also: To Robert Turner, April 12, 1681.
7. To Algernon Sidney, October 13, 1681.
8. Abstracts of letters from "later on former testimonies from the inhabitants of New Jersey and other eminent persons," London, 1681.
9. *Description of the Province of West New Jersey* (London, July 1676).
10. Woody, Thomas, *Quaker Education in the Colony and State of New Jersey* (Philadelphia, 1923), 192–93.

11. Pomfret, John E., "Proprietors of the Province of East New Jersey," 77 *PMHB* (1953), 251–93.

    See also: to John Penniman, November 18, 1677.

CHAPTER 11: *Squire in Sussex*

1. To Sheriffs, May 3, 1671.
2. *Truth Rescued From Imposture*, "a brief reply to a mere rhapsody of lies, follies and slanders . . . by a professed enemy to oppression, W.P.," March 1671.
3. To Edward Terry, January 29, 1673, "The Skulker in Holes."

    See also *New Witnesses Proved Old Heretics*, John Reeve and Ludovici Muggleton accused of "ancient whimsies, blasphemies and Heresies," 1672.

    See also *More Work for George Keith*, 1692, schismatic and trouble-maker.

    See also Hyde, James, "The Muggletonians . . . ," *New Church Review* (1900), 7: 215–27.
4. To John Morse, February 2, 1673.
5. *Invalidity of J. Faldo's Vindication.* "By W.P., who loves not controversy for controversy's sake," 1673.
6. To Faldo, January 20, 1675.
7. Sylvester, Matthew, *Reliquiae Baxteriana* (London, 1697), Part 3, 174.
8. To Baxter, October 6 and 11, 1675.
9. Births: February 28, 1674. Deaths: May 15, 1674 and February 24, 1675. *Quaker Records*, Somerset House.
10. Lower, Mark A., *A Compendious History of Sussex* (London, 1870), 2: 229.

    See also Horsfield, Thomas Walker, *History, Antiquities and Topography of the County of Sussex* (London, 1835), 2: 191.
11. Wood, Anthony À., *The Life and Times of Anthony A. Wood*, ed. by Andrew Clark (5 vols., Oxford, 1892–1900).

    See also *Quaker Records*, Somerset House.
12. Bill of Complaint, *Chancery Proceedings*, January 29, 1695, 50: 114.
13. *Christian Discipline in Good and Wholesome Order* (Birmingham, 1751), a broadside compiled from various sources for family guidance.
14. Lane, Jane, *Titus Oates* (London, 1949).
15. February 9, 1676,, 10 *CSP* (1675–76), 379.
16. Hull, William I., *William Penn: A Topical Biography* (New York, 1937), 412.
17. To Earl of Middlesex and Dorset, 1680.

    See also Passport to Holland: June 15, 1693, 4 *CSP*, Domestic, 182.
18. Cadbury, Henry J., in *Journal of George Fox*, ed. by John L. Nickalls (Cambridge, 1952), 718.

CHAPTER 12: *Crusade in Europe*

1. Incidents of the journey unless otherwise credited are from *Travels in Holland and Germany, 1677*.
2. Hull, William I., *William Penn and the Dutch-Quaker Migration to Pennsylvania* (Swarthmore, Pa., 1935), 212–13.

3. October 9 and 11, 1677.
4. To Earl of Middlesex and Dorset, November 17, 1677.

See also: to John Penniman, November 18, 1677.

5. November 16, 1677, *Minutes*, Meeting for Suffering, I: 39–40.
6. Ford, *Accounts*, October 28, 1678.
7. *To the Children of Light in This Generation*, London, November 4, 1678.

CHAPTER 13: *Charm a Deaf Adder*

1. *Epistle to the Children of Light in This Generation*, 1678.
2. *Minutes*, Meeting for Suffering, February 20, 1678.
3. March 22, 1678.
4. To Peter Hendricks and Jan Claus, November 27, 1679.
5. *Journal*, House of Commons, October 31, 1678.

See also Thomas Rudyard to George Fox, November 2, 1678.

6. *CTB*, March 7, 1679, VI: 126–27; Canceled, ibid., April 30, 1681, VIII: 131.
7. *Records*, Dorking and Horsham Monthly Meetings, March 6, 1679.
8. Bugg, Francis, *Ulmorum Acherons, or The History of William Penn's Conversion from a Gentleman to a Quaker* (London, 1682).
9. Algernon Sidney to Benjamin Furly, August 16, 1678.
10. *England's Great Interest in the Choice of This New Parliament*, 1679.
11. Sidney's Accounts of the Guildford Election in Collins, Arthur, *Letters and Memorials of State* (London, 1746), I: 150–54.

See also Blencoe, R.W., *The Sidney Papers* (London, 1825).
———— *Diary of the Times of Charles II* (London, 1843), I: 114–20.

12. Hull, William I., *William Penn: A Topical Biography* (New York, 1937), 216.

CHAPTER 14: *Passport to Peace*

1. *CSP,* Colonial America (1677–80), #1373, 544.
2. To Lord Romney, September 6, 1701.
3. Preamble to patent for Pennsylvania, *PC* 17–26.
4. To Earl of Middlesex and Dorset, August 27, 1701.

See also: to Robert Harley, February 9, 1704.

See also: to Hugh Roberts, December 6, 1689.

5. To Romney, August 27, 1701.
6. *CSP* (1677–80), #1544, October 10, 1680.
7. To Harley, February 9, 1704.
8. To Robert Turner, March 5, 1681.
9. To Lords of Trade and Plantations, January 22, 1681.
10. Patent to Pennsylvania, 1 *PC* 17–26.
11. Oldmixon, John, *The British Empire in America* (London, 1744), I: 182–83.
12. To Board of Trade, August 14, 1683.
13. Werden to Governor Sir Edmund Andros, May 12, 1681.

See also: to Lord Hyde, February 5, 1683.

14. Maryland Patent, June 20, 1632, 1 *MA*.
15. Penn resignation: April 1, 1683. Pomfret, John E., "Edward Byllinge's Proposed Gift of Land to Indigent Friends," 61 *PMHB* (1937), 88–92.

Auction: February 1, 1682. Pomfret, John E., "Proprietors of the Province of East New Jersey," 77 *PMHB* (1953), 251–93.

16. Baltimore agents to William Blaythwaite, June 23, 1680, *CSP* (1677–80), 554.

CHAPTER 15: *Freedom for the Asking*

1. Robbins, Caroline, "Algernon Sidney's 'Discourses Concerning Government': Textbook of Revolution," *William and Mary Quarterly, 3rd Series,* 4: 284.

For Barillon see Dalrymple, Sir John, *Memoirs of Great Britain and Ireland* (London, 1790) I: 357–58.

2. King's order, April 2, 1681.
3. Swift, Jonathan, *Prose Works,* ed. by Temple Scott (London, 1902), 7: 120.
4. April 8, 1681.
5. Ibid.
6. To Robert Turner, April 2, 1681.
7. Ibid.
8. Claypoole to Samuel Claridge, September 10, 1681, in "James Claypoole's Letter Book," 10 *PMHB* (1886), 188.
9. Claypoole to Samuel Claridge, July 26, 1681, Ibid., 190.
10. Claypoole to Edward Claypoole, 1682, in Nash, Gary B., "The Free Society of Traders and Early Politics of Pennsylvania," 89 *PMHB* (1965), 153.
11. To Turner, August 25 and September 7, 1681.
12. To Sidney, October 13, 1681.
13. To an unknown, July 1681, *Penn MSS., Domestic Letters* in HSP.
14. Guli's son Billy born March 14, 1681.

CHAPTER 16: *Planning Perfection*

1. Cummings, Hubertus M., "William Penn of Worminghurst Makes His First Sales of Land in Pennsylvania," 30 *Pennsylvania History* (1963), 265–71.
2. *True Protestant Mercury,* June 10, 1681.

See also: to John Aubrey, June 13, 1683.

See also: to Free Society of Traders, August 12, 1683.

See also: to Earl of Arran, January 9, 1684.

3. Wright, Louella M., *Literary Life of the Early Friends* (New York, 1932).

See also Wright, L.M., "William Penn and the Royal Society," 30 *BFHA* (1941), 8–10. Herrman's map: London, 1673. Dutch map: by Visscher, Amsterdam, 1655.

4. *Brief Account of the Province of Pennsylvania* (London, 1681).
5. Nash, Gary B., "The Free Society of Traders and Early Politics in Pennsylvania," 89 *PMHB* (1965), 147 ff.
6. Pomfret, John E., "The First Purchasers of Pennsylvania," 80 *PMHB* (1956), 137–63.
7. Mason, Norman H., "Miss Philadelphia," 42 *General Magazine and Historical Chronicle* (1940), 481–90.
8. Prideaux, Humphrey, *The Old and New Testaments Connected in the History of the Jews* (London, 1760).
9. August 1, 1701, 2 *PC,* 22.

CHAPTER 17: *Quo Warranto Threat*

1. Bieber, Ralph Paul, *The Lords of Trade and Plantations*, 1675–96 (Allentown, Pa., 1919).

   See also Harper, Lawrence A., *The English Navigation Laws* (New York, 1909).

   See also Hoffenden, Philip S., "The Crown and Colonial Charters," 15 *William and Mary Quarterly* (1953), 297–317.

   See also George Hutchinson to Penn, March 18, 1683.

2. Hall, Michael Garibaldi, *Edward Randolph and the American Colonies* (Chapel Hill, N.C., 1960).

   See also Randolph to Robert Southwell, January 29, 1684, in Toppan, Robert H., *Edward Randolph* (Boston, 1899), IV: 45.

3. *PD*, August 6, 1666; September 15, 1667; April 28, 1688.

4. To Markham, October 18, 1681.

5. To Markham, April 20 and October 28, 1681.

6. Markham to wife, December 7, 1681, in Buck, William J., *William Penn in America* (Philadelphia, 1888), 35.

7. Commission: September 30, 1681.

8. Beef: 1 *PC*, 63, March 20, 1683.

9. *True Protestant Mercury*, June 10, 1681.

   See also Claypoole to Claridge, July 12, 1681, in "James Claypoole's Letter Book." 10 *PMHB* (1886). Claypoole changed his forecast to "next spring" in a later letter, September 16, 1681.

10. Lord Baltimore to William Blaythwaite, March 11, 1682, in "Narrative of Proceedings Between Lord Baltimore and Captain William Markham," 5 *MA*, 374–78.

11. 5 *MA*, 377–378.

12. 5 *MA*, 374–80.

13. Mobilization Day was September 26, 1682.

14. Nicasis letter, October 18, 1651, *Portland MSS.*, HMC, 13th Report, Part 2, 70.

15. Admiral to Cromwell, September 1, 1654. Admiral's petition *CSP*, Domestic (1654), 351. Cromwell's approval 2 *GP* 19, September 1, 1654.

CHAPTER 18: *Drift to the Right*

1. Nash, Gary B., "The Free Society of Traders and Early Politics of Pennsylvania," 89 *PMHB* (1965), 147 *f*.

2. Charter of Free Society of Traders, March 25, 1682, 5 *PMHB* (1881), 37–50.

3. 11 *PMHB* (1887), 175–80.

4. Lady Margaret died at Walthamstow, March 4, 1682. Will probated March 15, 1682.

5. 19 *PMHB* (1895), 297–306.

   See also Preface to *Frame*.

6. *Frame*, 1 *PC*, 29–42, April 25, 1682.

7. *The Great Law*, 1 *PC*, 43–57, December 4–7, 1682.

8. 19 *PMHB* (1895), 297–306.

9. Rejoinder to Sidney, October 13, 1681.
10. Markham to Governor Benjamin Fletcher, May 20, 1696.
11. *Laws Agreed Upon in England*, May 5, 1682.
12. Barnes, Harry Elmer, *Evolution of Penology in Pennsylvania* (Indianapolis, 1927), 54–55.

CHAPTER 19: *Rule by Amateurs*

1. Chandler, Charles Lyon, 215 *Journal*, Franklin Institute (Philadelphia, 1933), 445–53.
2. *Minutes*, Thakeham Meeting, 5th Month, 1682.

See also Sanville, Florence M., "The Cross at Little Thakeham," *FI*, November 16, 1957, 743–44.

See also Dransfield, Frank, "The Blue Idol Meeting House," *Sussex County Magazine* (April 15, 1969), 247–48.

See also McLean, David, "Sussex and the United States," *Sussex County Magazine* (1930), 125–35.

See also Marsh, E. Harold, "The Blue Idol at Coolham," *The Friend* (London, November 5, 1909), 750–51.

3. Hough, Oliver, "Captain Thomas Holme," 19 *PMHB* (1895), 415–21.

See also Cooper, M. S., 23 *Transactions*, Cumberland and Westmoreland Antiquarian and Archaeological Society (1923) New Series, 78 *f*. Holme sailed April 18, 1682.

4. To Crispin, October 18, 1681.
5. To Crispin, September 30, 1681.
6. To Holme, August 8, 1685.
7. June 23, 1682.
8. To James Logan, July 23, 1701.
9. To Thomas Lloyd, 1685.
10. 1 *PC*, 59, March 12, 1683.

See also Markham to Penn, October 5, 1686.

11. Colonel Nathaniel Utie's raid, September 8, 1659.
12. August 12 and 24, 1682.
13. 206 *United States Reports* (April 1907), 550.

See also 291 *United States Reports* (February 1934), 251–85.

CHAPTER 20: *Westward to Utopia*

1. To Logan, July 23 and August 12, 1701; February 24, 1703; January 24, 1713.

See also Logan to Penn, January 24, 1713; July 5, 1714.

See also: to executors of Thomas Lloyd, August 12, October 27 and 29, 1701. Lloyd died in 1694.

2. The confused and protracted case of the Ford debt is impossible to document, resting, as it does, on Penn's memory of private conversations held a score of years before and on unsubstantiated claims by Ford's heirs who were not present at the conferences. The best available reconstruction of events is William R. Shepherd's *History of Proprietary Government in*

Pennsylvania (New York, 1896), 281 *f.* The worst is probably William Hepworth Dixon's highly prejudiced *William Penn: A Historical Biography* (Philadelphia, 1851).

3. To Logan, June 10, 1707.

4. August 26, 1682. This document, sometimes described as Penn's confession of debt and a deed to Pennsylvania, seems to have been a power of attorney for use in case of Penn's death either at sea or while in America. If the debt was real it was remarkable that Ford did not use this authority to withdraw the money due him from Penn's funds in his possession.

5. Dixon, *William Penn*, 188, 275; Shepherd, *Proprietary Government*, 185.

6. *A Vindication of William Penn* (London, February 12, 1683) replying to an item in *London Gazette*, January 15, 1683.

7. James Claypoole to Benjamin Furly, March 13, 1683, "Claypoole Letter Book," 10 *PMHB*, 188 *f.* Claypoole may have misdated his letter.

See also Guli to Margaret Fox, April 3, 1683.

8. *Testament to His Wife and Children*, August 4, 1682.

9. Material relating to voyage of the *Welcome* unless otherwise credited is drawn from "Narrative of Richard Townsend," published in Robert Proud's *History of Pennsylvania* (Philadelphia, 1797–98). The inventory of foodstuffs, etc., however, is from Dixon, *William Penn*, 195.

10. Buck, William, *William Penn in America* (Philadelphia, 1888), 65.

11. Anecdotes of the voyage are from Watson, John F., *The Annals of Philadelphia* (Philadelphia, 1830).

12. Neill, Rev. Edward Duffied, "Rev. Jacob Duche," 2 *PMHB* (1878), 58 *f.*

13. Dixon, *William Penn*, 201. A more trustworthy source is *Records*, New Castle County, folio 92, 11.

14. Robert Wade to wife, April 2, 1676, in *A Further Account of West Jersey*," (London, 1676).

15. Jasper Dankaerts' visit, November 22, 1679.

16. Ashmead, Richard, *History of Delaware County, Pennsylvania* (Philadelphia, 1884), credits the name Chester to Thomas Pearson, December 10, 1682, who believed "most of the inhabitants came from Chester, England."

CHAPTER 21: *Seeds of Unrest*

1. To Lord Baltimore, November 2, 1682.

2. November 8, 1682; call for election November 20.

3. Markham purchases, July 15 and August 1, 1682. Keith, Charles P., *Provincial Councilors of Pennsylvania* (Philadelphia, 1883), 3.

See also Buck, William, *William Penn in America* (Philadelphia, 1888), 111–12.

4. "Treble island"; Clarkson, Thomas, *Memoirs of the Life of William Penn* (London, 1813), 126. Sand and gravel: "Girard" in *Philadelphia Evening Bulletin*, June 7, 1940.

5. Clarkson, *Memoirs of the Life of Penn*.

6. Session opened December 4, 1682.

Myers, Albert Cook, speech at Chester, May 21, 1932.

7. *Conditions and Concessions*, July 11, 1681.

 See also *Laws Agreed Upon in England*, May 5, 1682.
8. December 7, 1682.

CHAPTER 22: *How To Treat Minorities*

1. *Conquest of Granada* (1669–70), Part I, Act I, Scene I.
2. To Free Society of Traders, August 16, 1683.
3. To Henry Savile, July 20, 1683.
4. To Free Society of Traders, August 16, 1683.
5. To Crispin, September 30 and October 16, 1681.
6. To Emperor of Canada, January 21, 1682.
7. To Indians, October 18, 1681.
8. Ibid.
9. To Crispin, September 30 and October 16, 1681.
10. Oldmixon, John, *British Empire in America* (London, 1741).

 Duponceau, Peter S. and J. Francis Fisher, "History of the Celebrated Treaty of Shackamaxon, 1682," 3 *Memoirs*, HSP, Part 2, 145–99.

 Ford, Philip, *A Vindication of William Penn* (London, February 12, 1683), "Published in sincerity by him who is a lover of truth but a hater of falsehood."

 Stone, Frederick D., "Penn's Treaty With the Indians," 6 *PMHB* (1882), 217–38.

 Watson, John F., "The Indian Treaty," 3 *Memoirs*, HSP, Part 2, 130 *f.*
11. Mrs. Preston, in Watson, John F., *Annals of Philadelphia* (Philadelphia, 1830), I: 121.
12. Cullen, Virginia, History of Lewes, Delaware (Lewes, 1956), 15.

 See also Groff, George G., "A Lost Settlement on the Delaware," *Some Records of Sussex County* (Philadelphia, 1904), 285–88.
13. To Free Society of Traders, August 16, 1683.
14. Watson, "The Indian Treaty."
15. To Lord Sunderland, July 28, 1683.

 1 *PC*, 105, May 10, 1684; 1 *PC*, 147–53, July 25, 1685.
16. Holme to James Harrison, February 8, 1685, in *Pemberton Papers*, HSP, I: 7.

 Holme to Friends, February 18, 1685, Ibid.: 7.
17. To Holme, August 8, 1685.
18. Francis David Pastorius to parents, March 7, 1684, in Sachse, Julius F., *Letters From Germantown* (Philadelphia, 1903), 2.
19. 1 *PC*, 147, 154, July 21 and September 17, 1685.

CHAPTER 23: *Baltimore Confrontation*

1. To Friends in Maryland, May 3, 1673.

 See also Fox to Penn, August 28, 1674.

 See also *Minutes*, London Meeting for Suffering, November 11, 1676 and December 16, 1677.

2. Patrick Falkoner to Maurice Trent, October 28, 1684 in Scot, George, *The Model of the Province of East New Jersey* (Edinburgh, 1685), 196.

See also: to Lord Baltimore, January 6, 1683.

3. Proud, Robert, *History of Pennsylvania* (Philadelphia, 1797), I: 209 n.

For "homing gentry," see 1 *PA* 385–86.

4. King to Lord Baltimore, August 19, 1682.
Reports differ on what occurred at this conference. The Maryland version is in 5 *MA*.

5. Ibid.

6. The Pennsylvania account is in 1 *PA*.

7. To Free Society of Traders, August 16, 1683.

See also: to Culpeper, February 12, 1683.

8. 1 *PC*, 88, March 10, 1683.

9. 1 *PC*, 59–60, March 15, 1683.

10. Dr. Thomas Wynne elected March 13, 1683, 1 *PC*, 59.

11. 1 *PC*, 61–62, March 20, 1683; 1 *PC*, 68–69, March 26, 1683.

12. To James Harrison, November 7, 1686.

13. 1 *PC*, March 20, 1683.

14. Smith, George, *History of Delaware County* (Philadelphia, 1862), 75.

15. Penn Letters and Ancient Documents Relating to Pennsylvania and New Jersey, in APS Library.

16. To Jasper Yeates, February 5, 1684.

17. 1 *PC*, 69, March 29, 1683.

18. To James Logan, September 14, 1705.

19. 1 *PC*, 74, May 23 and 25, 1683.

CHAPTER 24: *The Loving Tenants*

1. Baltimore to Talbot, March 19, 1683, *Calvert Papers*, Maryland Historical Society, 709.

2. 5 *MA*, May 29, 1683.

3. Baltimore to William Blaythwaite, December 7, 1683.

4. To Baltimore, October 31, 1683.
Proclamation: October 18, 1683.

5. To Marquis of Halifax, Earl of Rochester, Lord Keeper of Privy Seal North, Henry Sidney and "An Unknown Gentleman," July 24, 1683.

6. To the Government of West Jersey, June 6, 1683.

7. To John Aubrey, June 13, 1683.

8. To Free Society of Traders, August 16, 1683.

9. To Halifax, February 9, 1683.

See also: to Sunderland, July 28, 1683.

10. Stewart, Frank H., *Major John Fenwick* (Woodbury, N.J.), 1939.

11. To Sunderland, June 14, 1683.

12. Pennypacker, Samuel W., "The Settlement of Germantown," 9 *PMHB* (1880), 1–41.

13. Turner, Beatrice, "William Penn and Pastorius," 57 *PMHB* (1933), 56–90.

14. Ibid.

15. 1 *PC*, 91, December 26, 1683.

16. George Hutchinson to Penn, April 18, 1683.
17. Ford, *Account Books*, 1683.
18. To "Loving Colonists," September 16, 1681; August 11 and November 9, 1683.

CHAPTER 25: Neighborly Relations

1. To Talbot, December 5, 1683.
2. To Agents, April 2, 1684.
3. William Welsh to Penn, April 5, 1684.
4. 1 *PC*, 104–5, April 7 and 8, 1684; 1 *PC* 115, June 3, 1684.
   1 *PC*, 113, June 3, 1684.
5. Welsh to Penn, April 5, 1684.
6. To Duke of York, June 8, 1684.

   See also 1 *PC*, 114–15, June 11 and 12, 1684.
7. French ship (Scottish built), 1 *PC*, 91, 122–23, October 14, 1684. The incident caused Penn to be fined £53, December 15, *Calendar of Treasury Books* (1681–85), Part 2, 1455.
8. 1 *PC*, 93, January 17, 1684.
9. Epistle of Penn and other Quakers, May 27, 1675.
10. 1 *PC*, 91, January 7, 1684.
11. Pastorius to parents, March 7, 1684. Penn himself, in a letter to the Free Society of Traders, August 16, 1683, says he will study Indian so as not to be dependent on interpreters.

    See also Sachse, Julius F., *Letters from Germantown* (Philadelphia, 1903), 171.
12. Sir William Petty to Penn, August 14, 1682.

    See also Petty to Sir Robert Southwell, September 19, 1685, in Lansdowne, Marquis of, *The Petty-Southwell Correspondence* (London, 1928), 155 f.
13. To Free Society of Traders, August 16, 1683. Subsequent material on the Indians, unless otherwise credited, is to this source.
14. Kelpius, Johann, in Pennypacker, Samuel W., *The Settlement of Germantown* (Philadelphia, 1899), 252.
15. The Indian princess story is in John Oldmixon, *The British Empire in America* (London, 1708), 2: 308. Oldmixon asserts that Penn related the story to him personally.
16. New York Indians protest Penn's attempt to purchase the Susquehanna, August 2, 1684, 1 *CSP* (1681–85), 673.
17. Sir John Werden to Governor Thomas Dongan, March 10 and August 27, 1684, in 1 *CSP* (1681–85), 680; 3 *New York Colonial Documents*, 340–41.
18. Zimmerman, Albright C., "Daniel Coxe and the New Mediterranean Sea Company," 76 *PMHB* (1952), 86–96.
19. Earl of Perth et al. to Earl of Sunderland, in *CSP*, Domestic (1684–85), 126.

CHAPTER 26: Again the Courtier

1. De Valinger, Leon, Jr., "The Burning of the Whorekill," 74 *PMHB* (1950), 73–79.
2. *Minutes*, Philadelphia Yearly Meeting (1682–1714), 4.

3. To Turner, March 31, 1684.
4. To Logan, August 27, 1703.
5. May 30, 1684, *Isaac Norris Papers*, HSP.

   See also Shepherd, William R., *History of Proprietary Government in Pennsylvania* (New York, 1896), 78–79.
6. 1 *PC*, 105, 116, May 10 and July 25, 1684.
7. Markham to Penn, March 27, 1684.
8. To Harrison, August 15, 1684.
9. To Guli, August 6, 1684.
10. Hodgkin, L.V., *Gulielma, Wife of William Penn* (New York, 1947), 187.
11. To T. Lloyd et al., August 4, 1684.
12. To James Harrison, August 15, 1684, dated from Lewes.
13. To Harrison, October 7, 1684.
14. Lehnmann to Penn, May 29, 1685. Ship had arrived November 21, 1684.

    See also William Haig to William Frampton, Jr., June 10, 1685.
15. To T. Lloyd, August 15, 1685.
16. 11 *CSP* (1681–85), 735–36, October 31, 1684.

    See also 12 *CSP* (1685–88), 213, July 15, 1686.
17. O'Donnell, Elliott, *Ghosts of London* (New York, 1933), 116.
18. To T. Lloyd, March 16, 1685.

CHAPTER 27: *Secret Jesuit?*

1. *Quarter Sessions Order Book, Sussex* (1679–85), January 13, 1685.
2. *Records*, Middlesex County, Preface, lxi-lxiv, January 26 and February 17, 1685.

   See also *Minutes*, London, Meeting for Suffering, 4: 219, December 3, 1684.
3. To Thomas Lloyd, March 16 and 17, 1685.

   See also 1 *PC*, 132, May 11, 1685.
4. Hull, William I., to A. C. Myers, January 6, 1933. Forgetful of *Epicidea*, of *Our Holy Triumph*, and of *Ah, Tyrant Lust*, Penn declared, "I pretend not to poetry at any time." (These were not the only verses attributed to Penn but not acknowledged by him. The Dutch edition of Willem Sewel's history of the Quakers contained a poetic tribute to Josiah Coale supposedly composed by William Penn. It does not appear in the English editions.)
5. To James Harrison, October 25, 1685.
6. Burnet, Bishop Gilbert, *History of His Own Times*, ed. by M. J. Routh (6 vols., London, 1833), 1: 649.
7. To Harrison, October 2, 1685.
8. Sunderland to Mr. Penne, February 13, *CSP*, Domestic, 2 James II, 11.

   Roberts, George, *The Life of the Duke of Monmouth* (London, 1844), 243.

   See also Macaulay, Thomas Babington, *A History of England* (London, 1848), 2: 645–48.

   See also 6 *N & Q for Somerset and Dorset* (1905), 353–54.

   See also George Penne to Privy Council, November 25, 1687, *Acts of Privy Council, Colonial* (1680–1720), 2: 605.
9. Barclay to Penn, September 10 and October 9, 1685.

   See also *Acts of Privy Council, Colonial (1680–1710)*, 2: 245.

10. Bisbee, Henry H., "John Tatham, alias Gray," 83 *PMHB* (1959), 253–64.

    See also Given, Lois V., "The Grand and Stately Palace," Ibid., 265–70.
11. To Tillotson, November 22, 1685.
12. *N & Q*, 6th Series, V: 516, June 30, 1888.
13. Macaulay, *History of England*, 504.
14. 12 *CSP* (1685–88), 320.
15. Shepherd, William H., *History of Proprietary Government in Pennsylvania* (New York, 1896), 185–89.
16. 164 *N & Q*, June 3, 1933, February 19, 1686.
17. To Lord Romney, September 6, 1701.
18. Warrant, March 9, 1686, *CSP* (1686–87), 62.
19. Holland trip, June 11–July 26, 1686.
20. d'Vaux, *Ambassades*, in Bibliothèque Royale, Paris, V: 48.
21. Burnet, *History of His Own Times* (London, 1833), 3: 139–40.
22. Strickland, Agnes, *Lives of the Queens of England* (London, 1840–49), 2: 39–40.
23. To Harrison and Turner, April 9, 1687.

    See also Quary to Board of Trade, December 7, 1702, 24 *PMHB* (1900), 61–80.
24. Janney, Samuel M., *The Life of William Penn* (Philadelphia, 1852), 273.

CHAPTER 28: *Vice Runs Rampant*

1. To James Harrison, November 27, 1685.
2. To Stephen Crisp, February 28, 1686.
3. Sins scandalous: To Friends in Philadelphia, September 5, 1697.

   Shut the caves: July 26, 1685; April 24, September 25, November 25, 1686; January 21, September 17, October 21, 1687; June 5, 1688, etc.

   Cancel licenses: July 26, 1685; September 8, 1694.
4. 1 *PC*, 132, September 23, 1685; 1 *PC*, 58–59, March 12, 1685; 1 *PC*, 165, January 9, 1686.
5. 1 *PC*, 55–59, March 12, 1685; 1 *PC*, 165, January 9, 1685; 1 *PC*, 136–39, May 12 and 15, 1685; 1 *PC*, 148, August 19, 1685; 1 *PC*, 154, November 17, 1685.
6. 1 *PC*, 199, April 2, 1687.

   See also: to T. Lloyd, March 28, 1688.
7. 1 *PC*, 165, January 9, 1686.
8. 1 *PC*, 176, 180, May 10 and 12, 1686.
9. 1 *PC*, 222, May 10, 1688.
10. To Provincial Council, May 14, 1685; to Phineas Pemberton, October 26, 1685. But see September 11, 1691 and April 2, 1698.

    See also: to Provincial Council, August 19, 1685.
11. To Magistrates, July 26, 1685; to Provincial Council, August 19, 1685; to Harrison, December 14, 1685.
12. November 17, 1687.
13. To Harrison, September 8, 1687.
14. To Thomas Lloyd, June 6, 1687.
15. Appointed April 24, arrived July 11, 1686.
16. To Harrison, September 23 and November 7, 1686.

17. To Harrison, October 28, 1687.
18. To Harrison, January 28, 1687.
19. To Provincial Council, December 22, 1687.
20. To Harrison, November 7, 1686.
21. To Harrison, September 23, 1686.

See also: to T. Lloyd, March 28, 1688.

CHAPTER 29: *Decadence and Sin*

1. 1 *PC*, 189, August 5, 1686.
2. To Harrison, April 24 and September 23, 1686.

See also: to Thomas Lloyd, September 21, 1686. The use of the word "Americanize" in this letter may have been the first use in the English language. The Oxford English Dictionary cites no such use before 1816.

3. 1 *PC*, 165, January 9, 1686.

See also: to Officers of Government, October 21, 1687.

See also *The Excellent Privilege of Liberty and Property* (Philadelphia, 1687).

4. To T. Lloyd, September 21, 1686.
5. Council rejection April 2, 1686, 1 *PC*, 171.
6. To Markham et al., February 1, 1687, 1 *PC*, 206.
7. To Provincial Council, February 1, 1687, 1 *PC*, 206.
8. Shepherd, William R., *History of Proprietary Government in Pennsylvania* (New York, 1896), 187.
9. Tillotson to Penn, April 29, 1686.
10. To Tillotson, January 29, 1687.

See also Birch, Thomas, *Life of Dr. John Tillotson* (London, 1752), 135–41.

11. To Governor John Evans, September 30, 1705.
12. Bugg, Francis, *News From Pennsylvania* (London, 1703), 123–24.
13. *Minutes*, Concord Meeting, April 2, 1697.
14. To Governor Lord Bellomont, October 8, 1700.
15. Plain language, *Minutes*, Burlington Monthly Meeting, September 21, 1698.

Plain dress, *Minutes*, Philadelphia Monthly Meeting, April 26, 1700 and July 25, 1701.

Rowdy youth, *Minutes*, Philadelphia, July 26, 1700; January 3, 1701; October 27 and November 28, 1707; November 28, 1708, etc.

Games and Pastimes, *Minutes*, Philadelphia, March 6, 1699; August 6, 1701; March 26, 1706.

16. *Minutes*, Burlington, April 28, 1700; August 28, 1701.
17. June 6, 1821 in Watson, John Fanning, *Annals of Philadelphia* (Philadelphia, 1830), I: 207.

CHAPTER 30: *Magdalen Case*

1. To T. Lloyd, March 16, 1685.
2. Croese, Gerard, *General History of the Quakers* (London, 1696), II: 41.
3. Unless otherwise credited, all material on the Magdalen College case is from Bloxen, Rev. John Rouse, *Magdalen College and King James II* (Oxford, 1886).

4. *State Trials* 4: 262–82.
5. Luttrell, Narcissus, *A Brief Historical Relation of State Affairs, September 1678—to April 1714* (Oxford, 1857), I: 453, 461.

CHAPTER 31: *Friendship Spells Treason*

1. Rodney, Superior Court Justice Richard S., "Early Relations of Delaware and Pennsylvania," 54 *PMHB* (1930), 209–40.
2. *CSP*, Domestic, Warrant Book, 35: 95, December 10, 1688. Penn was released December 13.
3. Singer, Samuel W., *Diary of Lord Clarendon* (London, 1828), February 25, 1689.
4. Warrant for Penn's arrest, February 27, 1689, 1 *CSP*, 163.
5. To Shrewsbury, March 1, 1689.
6. To Halifax, June 28, 1689.
7. Warrant for John Penn, October 26, 1689, 1 *CSP*, 651.
8. Luttrell, Narcissus, *A Brief Historical Relation of State Affairs, September 1678 to April 1714* (Oxford, 1857), I: 553, June 29, October 24 and 28, 1690.
9. *London Gazette*, July 21, 1690.
10. Macaulay, Thomas Babington, *A History of England* (London, 1848), 4: 1998.
11. Janney, Samuel M., *The Life of William Penn* (Philadelphia, 1852), 368–69.
12. York Monthly Meeting, August 1690. William C. Braithwaite to A.C. Myers, October 1916.
13. To Thomas Lloyd and James Harrison, December 27, 1687.
    See also: to William Popple, October 24, 1688.
14. To Provincial Council, December 30, 1689.
    See also: to Friends, September 30, 1690 and May 30, 1691.
15. 2 *CSP*, 228, January 5 and 20, 1691.
16. Sidney to King, January 20 and February 27, 1691, *CSP*, Domestic 282–83, 288.
    See also: to Sidney, April 22, 1691, 4 *Memoirs*, HSP, Part 2, 192–95.
17. Sidney to Penn, November 7, 1691, *ACM Collection*, 68: 219.
18. Wheatley, Henry and Cunningham, Peter, *London, Past and Present* (London, 1891), 601.
    See also Bugg, Francis, *The Pilgrim's Progress From Quakerism to Christianity, together with a Remedy Proposed for the Cure of Quakerism* (London, 1698), 88–90. A variant title, also London, 1698, and probably a second edition, reads *The Pilgrim's Progress from a Gentleman to a Quaker.*
19. Harley, Robert to Sir Edward Harley, September 15, 1691, *Portland MSS.*, 14th Report HMC, 474.
    See also Luttrell, Narcissus, *A Brief Historical Relation of State Affairs September 1678–April 1714* (Oxford, 1857), 2: 234.
20. Strickland, Agnes, *Lives of the Queens of England* (London, 1840–49), 6: 1878.

CHAPTER 32: *Blackwell's Ordeal*

1. Material in this chapter not otherwise credited rests upon Wainwright, Nicholas Biddle, "Governor John Blackwell," 74 *PMHB* (1950), 157–62.

2. To Thomas Lloyd, December 30, 1689.

3. To Hugh Roberts, December 6, 1689. *Penn MSS.*, 1, APS.

4. Martin, John Hall, *Bench and Bar of Philadelphia* (Philadelphia, 1876).

5. Blackwell to T. Lloyd, November 11, 1688.

6. To Blackwell, August 14 and September 25, 1689.

7. To Pennsylvania Commissioners, September 11, 1688.

8. Blackwell to Sir Thomas Hartley, April 9, 1689, Buell, Augustus C., *William Penn: Founder of Two Commonwealths* (New York, 1904), 225.

9. Samuel Carpenter, et al. to Penn, February 24, 1689.

10. Ibid.

11. Lloyd to Provincial Council, April 8, 1689, 1 *PC*, 277.

12. 1 *PC*, 268, 270, April 1 and 3, 1689.

13. Ibid.

14. April 8, 1689, 1 *PC*, 277.

15. Blackwell to Sir Thomas Hartley, April 9, 1689.

16. 1 *PC*, 135, 275–76, February 7 and April 6, 1689.

17. 1 *PC*, 277–78, April 9, 1689.

18. 1 *PC*, 294, May 20, 1689.

19. 1 *PC*, 296, May 23, 1689.

20. Sheriffs and Justices of Sussex, Delaware to Council, April 2, 1689, 1 *PC*, 277.

21. Royal order, April 18, 1689, received October 1, 1 *PC*, 301.

24. 1 *PC*, 312–14, January 1, 1690.

23. To Robert Turner, October 4, 1689.

24. 1 *PC*, 312–14, January 1, 1690.

25. Blackwell to Penn, January 11, 1690.

CHAPTER 33: *Lost and Regained*

All references for this chapter not otherwise credited are to entries in *Minutes of the Provincial Council of Pennsylvania*, vol. 1 (1 *PC*).

1. Shrewsbury to Penn, April 13, 1689, 302.

    See also Leisler, Jacob, New York, to Thomas Lloyd, April 2, 1690, 302.

2. April 24, 1690, 334–35.

3. Peter Alrichs, May 13, 1690, 337.

4. To T. Lloyd and Markham, September 11, 1691, in 33 *PMHB* (1909), 423–26.

5. October 12, 1691, 13 *CSP*, #1820, 89–92.

6. Fletcher commissioned October 21, 1692, 145–54.

7. To Friends in Philadelphia, December 5, 1692.

    See also: to Fletcher, December 5, 1692.

8. To Friends in Philadelphia, February 4, 1693.

9. Buck, William, *William Penn in America* (Philadelphia, 1888), 212.

10. May 16, 1693, 399–400.

11. May 1, 1693, 369.

12. May 17, 1693, 401–3.

13. May 24, 1693, 415.

14. May 24, 1693, 415.

15. May 17 and 31, 1693, 403, 437.
16. May 16, 1693, 399–400.
17. July 11, 1693, 381.
18. May 16, 1693, 400.
19. May 29, 1694, 462.
20. Fletcher to William Blaythwaite, June 12, 1693. *New York Colonial Documents*, 4: 31–32.
21. May 29 and June 26, 1694, 463–64, 469–70.
22. July 14, 1694, *Diary*.

    See also August 1 and 3, 1694, 13 *CSP* (1693–94), #1181; text of the restoration, August 20, 1694, 473–74.
23. March 26, 1695, 473.

    See also: to Markham, November 24, 1694, 474–75.
24. September 27, 1695, 493–95.

CHAPTER 34: *Discord Brings Union*

1. *Minutes*, Philadelphia Monthly Meeting, July 26, 1689.
2. Henry Gouldney to Robert Barclay, February 28, 1695.

   See also Keith, George, *The Trial of Peter Bass* (London, 1693).

   See also *John* 1: 7.
3. *Minutes*, Philadelphia, May 26, 1692; Burlington, September 12, 1692; Barbados, March 6, 1693.

   See also Jennings, Samuel, *The State of the Case* (London, 1693).
4. April 1793; "George Keith's Journal," *Collections*, New York Historical Society (1851), 537.
5. *More Work For George Keith* (London, 1696).
6. Budd, Thomas, *A Just Rebuke to Several Lyes, Calumnies and Slanders: Some Account of Quaker Politics* (London, 1693).
7. Rochester, Ranelagh, and Sidney to King, November 25, 1693. A memorandum drafted by Penn at Hoddesdon, December 11, 1693 and noted by ACM, volume 60.
8. *Account of the Blessed End of Gulielma Penn and Springett Penn* (London, 1699).
9. Burnet, Bishop Gilbert, *History of His Own Times* (London, 1833), 693.
10. Clarkson, Thomas, *Memoirs of the Life of William Penn* (London, 1849), 130.
11. Randolph to Commissioners of Customs, October 16, 1695, *CSP, America* (1693–96), 2237.
12. Board of Trade to Penn, December 11, 1696.

CHAPTER 35: *Quacks and Witches*

1. Floyer, Sir John, *History of Cold Bathing* (London, 1702).
2. To Dr. Edward Baynard, September 1702.
3. Thompson, C.J.S., *The Lure and Practice of Alchemy* (London, 1932), 226–27.
4. Marshall, Charles, *Sion's Travelers Comforted* (London, 1714). The publication was six years after Marshall's death at 61.

5. William Haig to William Frampton Jr., June 30, 1685. *Bristol and Philadelphia Letters 1671–89*, HSP 2532.
6. To Hannah Callowhill, December 6, 1695.
7. *Philadelphia Evening Ledger*, October 13, 1923.
8. To Hannah Callowhill, December 6, 1695.

See also: to Governor Nicholson, December 31, 1700.

See also: to Ambrose Galloway, December 20, 1709.

9. To Hannah Callowhill, December 20, 1709.
10. To Logan, July 23, 1709.
11. Inquiry: February 27, 1684, 1 *PC*, 95–96.

See also Gummere, Amelia Mott, *Witchcraft and Quakerism* (Philadelphia, 1908), 8–9.

12. Riddell, Chief Justice William, "Pennsylvania and Witchcraft," *Journal of Criminal Law and Criminology* (1927), 411.

See also Burr, George Lincoln, ed., *Narratives of the Witchcraft Cases, 1648–1706* (New York, 1914), 88.

13. September 10, 1690. *Minute Book,* Common Pleas and Quarter Sessions Court, Bucks County 1684–1700, 219.
14. 2 *PC*, 15, May 21, 1701.

CHAPTER 36: *Hannah to the Rescue*

1. Drinker, Sophie Hutchinson, *Hannah Penn and the Proprietorship of Pennsylvania* (Philadelphia, 1956), 4.
2. To Hannah, June 28 to September 10, 1695.
3. To Hannah, December 17, 1695 to February 14, 1696.
4. Banns asked November 11, 1695; certificates granted January 11 and February 4, 1696.
5. Tish to Hannah, October 12, 1695.

See also Peg to Hannah, January 2, 1696.

6. *Quaker Registers*, Bristol.
7. April 10, 1696.
8. *Account of the Blessed End of Gulielma Penn and Springett Penn* (London, 1699).
9. Codicil, October 8, 1706, to will of October 20, 1705.
10. Sewell to Penn, August 2, 1696.
11. To Council on Trade and Plantations, November 1, 1697.

See also Robert Snead to Sir John Houblen, September 20, 1697, *CSP* (1697–98), 613–15.

12. 1 *PC*, 550–51, May 19, 1688.
13. Daniels to Markham, March 9, 1698, in *CSP* (1697–98), 43 *f*.
14. Markham to Daniels, March 30, 1698, Ibid.
15. To Council on Trade and Plantations, November 1, 1697; March 6 and August 6, 1701.
16. August 8, 1695.
17. Quary to Board of Trade, June 19, 1700 in Ames, Herman V., "Pennsylvania and the English Government," 24 *PMHB* (1900), 61–80.
18. 1 *PC*, 480–81, June 29, 1695.

19. 1 *PC*, 492, September 19, 1695.

    See also 1 *PC*, 507, November 3, 1696.

20. 1 *PC*, 506–7, October 30, 1696, 1 *PC*, 426–27, May 31, 1693.

21. 1 *PC*, 509, November 7, 1696.

    See also 1 *PC*, 429, June 1, 1693.

22. 1 *PC*, 610; May 31, 1700.

CHAPTER 37: *Pirates and Smugglers*

Unless otherwise credited all references to footnotes 1 to 11 inclusive are to be found in *Collection of Papers Relating to Piracy in Pennsylvania* 15 *CSP, America* (1697–98), 43–98.

1. To Council on Trade and Plantations, May 6, 1697.
2. Markham to Penn, March 1 and April 27, 1697, in Myers Collection.
3. Markham to Penn, February 13, March 1 and May 1, 1697, in Myers Collection.
4. Markham to Penn, April 24, 1697, in Myers Collection.
5. Randolph to William Popple, April 25, 1698.
6. Quary to Penn 1697. (Letter carries no identification of either day or month, but is published in 15 *CSP, America,* November 27, 1697.)
7. Daniels to Markham, March 9, 1698.
8. Markham to Daniels, March 30, 1698.
9. Randolph to Board of Trade, February 12, 1698.
10. Captain Robert Snead to Sir John Houblon, September 20, 1697.
11. Depositions of Thomas Robinson and Captain Robert Snead, in Randolph to Board of Trade, April 26, 1698, and Randolph to Popple, May 12, 1698.

    See also Markham to Penn, February 10 and 24, 1697, May 1 and August 6, 1698, in Myers Collection.

    See also Francis Jones to William Penn, November 13, 1697.

12. Randolph to Council on Trade and Plantations, April 25, 1698.

    See also Richard Coote, Earl of Bellomont, "Report on the Examination of James Brown," May 25, 1700.

    See also Clayton, Thomas, "Civil and Ecclesiastical Affairs in Pennsylvania in 1698," 13 *PMHB* (1889), 220.

    See also Ramsay, David, *History of South Carolina* (Charleston, 1809), passim.

13. Pennsylvania Assembly to the King, August 10, 1698, 1 *PC*, 528–29.
14. Randolph to Popple, April 25 and May 12, 1698.
15. Pennsylvania Assembly to the King, August 10, 1698, 1 *PC*, 528–29.
16. Francis Jones to Penn, August 10 and November 13, 1697, in 16 *CSP, America,* 23–24, 97–98.
17. Quary to Council on Trade and Plantations, June 6, 1699 (raid was April 1), in 17 *CSP, America,* 274.

    See also Luke Watson to Provincial Council, 1 *PC*, 3, August 31, 1698.

    See also Earl of Bellomont to Council on Trade and Plantations, September 21, 1698.

18. King disapproves of Markham, August 31, 1699, *Acts of Privy Council* (1630–1720), 1 *PC*, 758.
19. To Charlwood Lawton, August 18, 1701.
20. Gerard Slye to Penn, June 27, 1698, 23 *PMHB* (1899), 400–1.

    See also Slye to Sir James Vernon, May 26, 1698, in 16 *CSP*, America, 97–98.
21. Davis, Thomas, recantation in *Minutes*, Philadelphia Friends Meeting October 16, 1700.
22. To Sir James Vernon, December 30, 1700.

    See also: to Council on Trade and Plantations, December 31, 1700, in 18 *CSP*, America, 772–73.
23. To Nicholson, December 31, 1700.
24. Christ Church Vestry to Council on Trade and Plantations, January 28, 1701, in *CSP*, America (1701), 57–58.

CHAPTER 38: *Problem Children*
1. See Appendix C.
2. Passport to Holland December 12, 1695.
3. Hull, William I., *William Penn: A Topical Biography* (New York, 1937), 49.
4. Lucas, Edward V., *Highways and Byways in Sussex* (London, 1904).
5. Hull, William I., op. cit., 49.
6. To Logan, July 8, 1707.
7. Approval asked of Friars Meeting, October 24, 1698; granted November 21. *Minutes*, Bristol Monthly Meeting.
8. July 19, 1699, *Egmont MSS.*, HMC, #2668, folio 3.
9. Penn's account of his arrangements with Ford, August 23, 1699, are in his *Statement of Transactions with Philip Ford*, submitted to the courts September 7, 1706. *Penn Papers: Ford vs Penn*, HSP.
10. Ibid., August 23, 1699.

CHAPTER 39: *Return to America*
1. See Tolles, Frederick B., *James Logan and the Culture of Provincial Pennsylvania* (Boston, 1957).

    See also Cooper, Irma Jane, *Life and Public Services of James Logan* (New York, 1923).
2. Luttrell, Narcissus, *A Brief Historical Relation of State Affairs, 1678–1704* (6 vols. Oxford, 1957).
3. Tolles, Frederick B., *Meeting House and Counting House* (Chapel Hill, 1948), 145.
4. Fairfax Harrison, Washington, to Albert Cook Myers, October 6, 1932.
5. Tolles, *James Logan*, 13. Benjamin Franklin reported that James Logan himself told him of the Penn–Logan conversation. *The Autobiography of Benjamin Franklin* (First American edition, 1818), Chapter 8.
6. Penn's *Cash Book*, 7–8.
7. Robert Wade to Penn, November 11, 1699.
8. To Secretary Vernon, March 10, 1700.
9. See also *Cash Book*, December 10, 1699–February 1700, passim.

10. Tolles, *James Logan*, 43.

See also Leach, Josiah Granville, "The Colonial Mayors of Philadelphia," 18 *PMHB* (1894), 410–28.

11. Scharf, J.T., and T. Westcott, *History of Philadelphia* (Philadelphia, 1884), I: 301, 497.

12. Perry, Rev. William Stevens, *Historical Collections of the American Colonial Church* (Hartford, 1870), 211.

See also Drinker, Edward, *Philadelphia Gazette*, April 20, 1788. Presumably an eyewitness account by a man, aged 102, who died November 17, 1782.

13. Buck, William, *William Penn in America* (Philadelphia, 1888), 230.

14. Ward, Townsend, "South Second Street and Its Associations," 4 *PMHB* (1880), 51–59.

See also Tolles, *Meeting House*, 87–91.

15. Quary to House of Lords, March 6, 1700, *House of Lords MSS. (1699–1702)*, 4: 323–26.

See also: to Secretary of State James Vernon, February 26, 1700.

See also: to Commissioners of Customs, February 28, 1700.

16. Quary to Board of Trade, March 6 and April 10, 1700, in *CSP*, #169 and #300.

17. Tolles, *Meeting House*, 87–91 and Ward, "South Second Street and Its Associations," 51–59.

18. *A Testament for his Wife and Children*.

19. Needles, Samuel H., "The Governor's Mill and Globe Mill," 8 *PMHB* (1884), 279 f.

See also Logan to Penn, September 6, 1702.

See also Billy to Logan, August 18, 1702.

CHAPTER 40: *Trouble Shooting*

1. To Secretary Vernon, February 26 and March 10, 1700.

See also: to Board of Trade, February 17 and April 22, 1700.

2. To Commissioners of Customs, February 28, 1700.

See also Board of Trade to Penn, August 4, 1699.

See also: to Commissioners of Customs, February 28 and April 22, 1700.

3. 2 *PC*, 15, February 18, 1700.

4. To Commissioners of Customs, May 7, 1700.

5. To Commissioners of Customs, February 28, 1700.

6. 1 *Colonial Records*, 586, August 7, 1700.

7. 1 *Colonial Records*, 587, September 11, 1700.

8. *Register*, Philadelphia Quarterly Meeting, January 28, 1700. One copy only survives, in German Society of Philadelphia. See *Philadelphia Evening Bulletin*, July 27, 1933.

See also: to Melchior Adam Pastorius, February 20, 1700.

9. To Governor Lord Bellomont, January 11, 1700.

10. To Logan, July 23, 1700.

11. To Logan, April 1, 1703.

12. Logan to Billy, September 25, 1700.

13. Ward, Townsend, "South Second Street," 4 *PMHB*, 51.
14. Randolph to Commissioners of Customs, October 16, 1695, in Publications of the Prince Society (Boston, 1909), 507–11.

    Penn's answer, March 7, 1696, 22 *CSP* 1693–96, #2237.
15. Hoffenden, Philip S., "The Crown and the Colonial Charters," 15 *William and Mary Quarterly*, 3d Series (1958), 306.
16. To Charlwood Lawton, August 18, 1701.
17. To Robert Harley, April 20, 1700.
18. To Board of Trade, April 28, 1700.
19. Quary to Board of Trade, June 19, 1700, in Ames, Herman V., "Pennsylvania and the English Government 1699–1704," *PMHB* (1900), 61–80.
20. See Quary to Board of Trade, June 19, 1700.
21. To Governor Lord Bellomont, June 4, 1700.

CHAPTER 41: *The Pennsbury Manor*

1. Survey, March 13, 1700.
2. To Logan, September 6, 1702.
3. *Penn MSS. Journal*, January 3, 1701.
4. To Logan, July 23, September 3, 1700; September 14, 1705.
5. Proud, Robert, *History of Pennsylvania* (2 vols., Philadelphia, 1797–98), I: 206.
6. Buck, William J., *William Penn in America 1681–1701* (Philadelphia, 1888).
7. Isaac Norris to Daniel Zachary, August 30, 1700. Isaac Norris *Letter Book, 1699–1702*.

    See also Bugg, Francis, *News From Pensilvania, The Friend* (Philadelphia, 1833), 221, HSP, 399–450.
8. Fisher, Joshua Francis, "The Private and Domestic Habits of William Penn," 3 *Memoirs*, HS Penn (1836), 57–104.

    See also Buck, *Penn in America*, 228.
9. 19 *PA* 2nd Series, 553, April 6, 1703. The event occurred in 1683.
10. Herrick, Cheesman A., *White Servitude in Pennsylvania* (Philadelphia, 1926).
11. Respublica vs. Keppele, 2 Dallas, 198.
12. 1 *PC*, 61, March 16, 1683.
13. To Hannah, January 28, 1696.
14. Cf. Harvard University Library's early copy.
15. To Governor Blackwell, September 25, 1689.

CHAPTER 42: *Blacks are Better*

1. Release by Samuel Drew, February 25, 1655. *Duke of Portland MSS.*, HMC II: 90.

    See also *Account of His Convincement*.
2. *PD*, March 27, 1661.
3. To Francis, Baron Guildford, Lord Keeper of the Privy Seal, December 1, 1684.

4. James Claypoole to Edward Claypoole, June 27 and October 11, 1682, in James Claypoole's "Letter Book," 10 *PMHB* (1886), 188 f.

See also Lehnmann to Penn, May 29, 1685.

See also William Haig to William Frampton, Jr., June 30, 1685. "Bristol and Philadelphia Letters, 1671–89," *MSS.* HSP.

5. 1 *PC*, 63, March 20, 1683.

See also: to Harrison, July 11, November 20, December 10, 1685.

See also: to Phineas Pemberton, February 8, 1687.

See also: to Governor Blackwell, September 15, 1689.

6. To James Harrison, October 25, 1685.

7. April 18, 1688.

8. Binder–Johnson, Hildegarde, 55 *PMHB* 145–56.

See also Kelsey, Rayner W., 21 *BFHA* (1932), 28–30.

See also *The Friend*, Philadelphia, March 13, 1844, 125–26.

9. Lehnmann to Penn, May 29, 1688.

Will dated February 7, 1690; probated October 23, 1690.

10. To Logan, April 1, 1703.

11. Turner, Edward Raymond, "Slavery in Colonial Pennsylvania," 25 *PMHB* (1911), 141–51.

See also *Minutes*, Philadelphia Monthly Meeting, September 30, October 16, 1698

12. *Minutes*, Philadelphia Monthly Meeting, October 24, 1698; March 25, 1700. Freetown: September 27, 1701.

13. To Governor Blackwell, September 25, 1689. Logan to Penn, October 2, 1702.

14. Hannah to Logan, October 3, 1705.

See also *The Friend*, 18 (1848), 353.

15. Logan to Hannah, May 11, 1721.

Will dated October 30, 1701.

16. To John and Mary Sotcher, October 12, 1705.

17. Bancroft, George, *History of the United States* (Boston, 1858), 2: 401–2.

18. April 25 and 28, 1701.

To Governor Hamilton, April 27, 1701.

19. Tax acts: June 7 and November 27, 1701; January 12, 1706; September 8, 1709; February 28, 1711; January 7, 1712.

CHAPTER 43: *Beset by Foes*

1. Vestry to Bishop of London, January 21, 1701, in 19 *CSP*, America (1701), 57–58.

2. To Governor Evans, August 2, 1703.

3. To Council on Trade and Plantations, June 8, 1702.

4. To Charlwood Lawton, December 21, 1700.

Keble deposition, September 9, 1701, in 20 *CSP*, America, 378–79.

5. Testimony to Council on Trade and Plantations, June 8, 1702.

See also Isaac Norris to Daniel Zachery, January 29, 1701.

6. To Charlwood Lawton, December 10, 1700.

   See also: to Robert Harley, February 9, 1704.
7. To Robert Harley, February 9, 1704.
8. December 9, 1701.
9. Susquehanna trip, June 2–26, 1701.

   George Whitehead et al. to Penn, June 4, 1701.

   Bill introduced April 24, 1701.
10. 2 *PC*, 29, 31, August 2 and 6, 1701.
11. 2 *PC*, 35, September 15, 1701.
12. 2 *PC*, 37, September 20, 1701.
13. 2 *PC*, 43, September 29, 1701.
14. 2 *PC*, 46, October 7, 1701.
15. Thomas Callowhill to Hannah, September 28, 1701, in Buck, William J., *William Penn in America, 1681–1701* (Philadelphia, 1888), 382.

    Tish certificate, Philadelphia, September 27, 1701; Penn and Hannah certificate from Falls Meeting.
16. 2 *PC*, 56–60, October 28, 1701.
17. 2 *PC*, 54–55, October 25, 1701.
18. To Logan, November 14, 1701.
19. David Lloyd and Isaac Norris to Penn, October 29, 1701, in *Penn MSS.* 36, Friends House, London.

    See also: to Logan, October 29 and 31, 1701.

CHAPTER 44: *Daring the Lightning*

1. To Robert Harley, January 31, 1702.
2. To Pennsylvania Government, January 11, 1702.
3. *Minutes*, Kent Meeting for Suffering, April 17, 1700.

   Petition to Anne, June 3, 1700.
4. To Logan, September 5, 1700.
5. Quary's complaints to Council on Trade and Plantations, March 31, April 20, and June 23, 1702, in 20 *CSP*, America (1702), passim.

   See also William Popple to C. Lawton, April 16, 1702, in 20 *CSP*, America (1702), 226–28.

   See also Penn to Council on Trade and Plantations, April 25, 1702, and June 23, 1702, in 20 *CSP*, America (1702), 276.
6. See, for instance, Quary to Board of Trade, June 17 and November 14, 1700; March 31 and December 7, 1702.
7. Quary produced Bristol records showing (1) swindle of widow, October 8, 1689; (2) forgery, March 18, 1693; (3) sheriff, July 18, 1698; (4) brawl, April 29, 1700.

   See also: to Logan, June 4, 1702.
8. To Bellomont, July 4, 1700.

   See also: to Council on Trade and Plantations, December 22, 1703, April 29 and June 23, 1702.

   See also: to Logan, December 7 and 22, 1703.
9. To Logan: September 16, 1704.

10. *New Jersey Colonial Documents*, 288.

See also 11 *NYCD*, 778; 18 Ibid., 34.

See also: to Lawton, December 10, 1700, and July 2, 1701.

11. To Logan, March 28 and July 28, 1702.

12. Petition to Queen, April 17 and June 22, 1702.

One-year approval, November 11, 1702, 2 *Privy Council, Colonial*, 519.

13. 2 *PC*, 77–78, November 17 and 18, 1702.

See also Logan to Penn, December 1, 1702.

14. Logan to Penn, December 1, 1702.

15. April 20 and June 18, 1702.

16. Council on Trade and Plantations to Penn, December 1, 1702, in 20 *CSP*, America (1702), 765.

17. Banns, *Minutes*, Horsham Meeting, June 29, 1702.

18. Dowry agreement, August 18, 1702, *Letters attorney* #2 (1701–2), Land Office, Harrisburg, Pa.

19. Hannah to Penn, December 27, 1703, in Drinker, Sophie Hutchinson, *Hannah Penn and the Proprietorship of Pennsylvania* (Philadelphia, 1958), 21.

20. Billy to Penn, February 15, 1704.

21. Billy to Logan, August 18, 1703.

22. Logan to Penn, April 29, 1703.

23. To Logan, February 2, 1703.

24. To Council on Trade and Plantations, July 2, 1703.

25. To Queen Anne, July 6, 1703.

See also: to Logan, August 27 and December 7, 1703.

CHAPTER 45: *"Love Thy Neighbor"*

1. To Jasper Yeates, February 5, 1684.

To Thomas Lloyd, March 16, 1685, against one "Gray," really John Tatham.

2. To Provincial Council, August 19, 1685.

See also: to Robert Turner, February 27, 1694.

See also: to Assembly and Council, June 7, 1700.

3. To Provincial Council, August 19, 1685, and January 6, 1687.

4. Ibid.

5. To Charlwood Lawton, May 18, 1701.

6. To Phineas Pemberton, October 25, 1685.

7. Thomas Fitzwater, January 29, 1692, cited John 1: 7–9, *Minutes*, Philadelphia Monthly Meeting.

8. *Minutes*, Philadelphia Monthly Meeting, June 24, 1692.

9. Winder, Henry, *The Spirit of Quakerism Laid Open* (London, 1696), 30–31.

10. *More Work for George Keith*, 1696.

See also: to Robert Turner, June 11, 1694.

11. To Robert Turner, November 9, 1692.

12. To Thomas Lloyd and William Markham, September 11, 1691.

13. To Logan, June 10, 1701; January 10, 1703; March 2, 1706; June 10, 1707; September 11, 1708; February 27, 1709.

See also: to Charlwood Lawton, July 2, 1701.

See also: to James Harrison, June 4, 1702.

See also: to Pennsylvania Government, January 10, 1703.

See also: to Governor Evans, September 30, 1705.

See also: to Randolph, March 7, 1696.

Note: The addressees were not the gentlemen libeled, but the recipients of messages libeling others.

14. To Robert Harley, April 20, 1700; August 18 and 27, 1701.

See also: to Logan, June 24, 1702.

See also: to Pennsylvania Government, January 10, 1703.

15. On Quary: to Pennsylvania Government, January 10 and December 4, 1703.

See also: to Governor Evans, September 30, 1705.

See also on Pennsylvania Assembly: to Logan, March 1, 1704, and October 14, 1709.

16. To Provincial Council and Assembly, June 7, 1700.

17. Nicholson: Gerard Slye to Penn, June 27, 1698, 23 *PMHB* (1899), 400–1. Ford suit: To Friends, November 18, 1705.

18. Galenus Abrahams: Hull, William I., *William Penn and the Dutch-Quaker Migration to Pennsylvania* (Swarthmore, Pa., 1935), 8.

19. Quary to Board of Trade, July 25, 1703, in 21 *CSP*, America (1702–3), #950.

See also: to Governor Evans, February 7, 1706.

See also: Logan to Penn, March 2, 1707, and January 28, 1708.

See also: to Logan, July 8, 1707.

20. Logan to Penn, March 2, 1707, and January 28, 1708.

See also: to Logan, July 8, 1707.

21. To Logan, September 11, 1708.
Logan to Penn, February 3, 1709.

22. To Logan, January 2, May 10, 1705.

23. Logan to Penn, October 27, 1704.

See also: to Logan, September 14, 1705.

See also: to Provincial Council, April 2, 1684, and August 8, 1685.

24. To James Harrison, November 7, 1686.

25. To Andrew Hamilton, April 3, 1701.

26. David Lloyd to Penn, July 19, 1705, in Franklin Papers, Library Company of Philadelphia.

27. To Logan, May 10, September 14, and October 7, 1705; February 9 and 26, 1706; June 10, 1707; October 14, 1709.

See also: to Friends, November 15, 1705.

See also Logan to Penn, February 3, 1709.

CHAPTER 46: *Relapse From Grace*

1. To Council on Trade and Plantations, May 11, 1703, in 21 *CSP*, America, 426.
2. Council on Trade and Plantations, June 9, 1703, summons Penn to report within a week, in 21 *CSP*, America, 490.
3. To Council, June 18, 1703, in 21 *CSP*, America, 509–10.
4. Billy and Evans arrived February 2, 1704, 2 *PC*, 115. Billy's letter to his father announcing his arrival was dated February 18. The delay was probably attributable to the lack of an earlier ship sailing.
5. To the Council on Trade and Plantations, July 8, 1703, in 21 *CSP*, America, 541.

   See also to Logan, August 27, 1703.

   The "crusty legislator," William Biles, was reported by Logan to Penn, July 4, 1705.
6. To Logan, January 4, 1701. Logan's cash book reveals that he obeyed instructions but, unfortunately, he paid Billy biweekly. The young man apparently regularly exceeded his allowance in the first few days so that, until the next payday, he ran up bills.
7. To Logan, April 8, 1704.
8. Logan to Penn, May 26, 1704.

   See also Isaac Norris to Jonathan Dickinson July 28, 1704. Isaac Norris *Letter Book*, HSP, 170.
9. Tolles, Frederick B., *James Logan and the Culture of Provincial Pennsylvania* (Boston, 1957), 45.
10. To Logan, April 3, 1703.
11. To Logan, February 20 and March 28, 1704.
12. Thomas Fairman to Penn, reported in Penn to Logan, July 23, 1701.
13. To Logan, July 23, 1701.
14. *Fruits of Solitude.*
15. Gabriel Thomas to Council on Trade and Plantations, August 10 and November 24, 1702; January 24, 1703, in 21 *CSP*, America (1702–03), #1183.
16. Thomas to Council, January 24, 1703, *Colonial Office* #1261–62.
17. To Logan, April 8, 1704, but the Queen-in Council, January 21, 1703, had ordered oaths or solemn affirmations, and because of this, many court operations had been halted in Pennsylvania. Lokken, Roy N., *David Lloyd, Colonial Lawmaker* (Seattle, 1959), 135.
18. King's order, January 19, 1701; Queen's order, May 3, 1703; 2 *PC*, 29, 114.

    See also Governor Cornbury to Pennsylvania, May 1, 1704, 2 *PC*, 136.

    See also Council's refusal, May 9, 1704, 2 *PC*, 189.
19. Logan to Penn, May 26, 1704.
20. Quary to Council on Trade and Plantations, in Ames, Verman V., "Pennsylvania and the English Government, 1699–1704," 24 *PMHB* (1900), 61–80.
21. Tolles, Frederick E., *James Logan and the Culture of Provincial Pennsylvania* (Boston, 1957.)
22. 2 *PC*, 155 and 211, July 11, 1704, and August 23, 1705.

23. To Logan, March 1 and 22, 1704.

See also: to Evans, March 5, 1704.

24. 2 *PC*, March 22, 1704, 122.

25. To Logan, early spring, 1704.

26. *Remonstrance* dated September 1, 1704, 9 *Memoirs*, HSP, 331–32, 338–39. Council reports first hearing of it was November 10, 1704, 2 *PC*, 181.

See also Franklin Papers, Library Company of Philadelphia, X: 11.

27. To Logan, September 14 and February 9, 1706.

28. *Reflections on the Printed Case of William Penn, Esq.* (London 1702), 9–10.

CHAPTER 47: *At Club Law*

1. 2 *PC*, 164, September 15, 1704.

2. Quary to Council on Trade and Plantations, October 15, 1704, in 22 *CSP*, America, 281–87.

3. 2 *PC*, 160–61, September 15, 1704.

4. 2 *PC*, October 3, 1704 and 2 *PC*, 175, November 2, 1704.

5. To Logan, September 16, 1704.

6. Quary to Council on Trade and Plantations, October 15, 1704, in 22 *CSP*, America, 353.

See also Logan to Tish, November 8, 1704.

7. Isaac Norris to John Askew, October 9, 1704, in Norris, *Letter Book* #2.

See also *Penn MSS. Ledger*, November 28 and December 10, 1704; January 3, 1705; August 20, 1709.

8. Quary to Board of Trade, October 13, 1704, in NJA 3: 317.

9. Quary to Council on Trade and Plantations, May 30, 1704, in 22 *CSP*, America, 353.

10. Quary to Council on Trade and Plantations, October 15, 1704, in 22 *CSP*, America, #605.

11. To Logan, January 16, 1705.

12. Logan to Penn, December 8, 1704.

13. Logan to Penn, September 22, 1704.

14. To Logan, February 6, 1705, and May 3, 1708.

15. To John Oldmixon, May 10, 1705.

See also: to Logan, May 10, 1705.

16. To Robert Harley, July 14, 1706.

17. To Logan, September 17, 1705.

18. To Evans, September 22, 1705.

19. To Logan, February 24 and December 7, 1703.

See also *Penn MSS. Journal*, November 28, 1704.

20. To Logan, May 3, 1708.

21. To Evans, May 15 and June 10, 1707.

See also Janney, Samuel M., *The Life of William Penn* (Philadelphia, 1852), 496.

See also Tolles, Frederick B., *James Logan and the Culture of Provincial Pennsylvania* (Boston, 1957), 44–45.

22. To Logan, June 10, 1707.

CHAPTER 48: *Times of Stress*

1. To Logan, February 7 and March 2, 1706.
2. *Minutes*, London Monthly Meeting, December 26, 1705.

   See also *Minutes*, Six Weeks Meeting, February 14, 1706.
3. To Council on Trade and Plantations, May 11, 1703, in 5 *Colonial Papers*, *HMC* #28–29.
4. To Board of Trade, June 18, 1703, and June 2, 1705.
5. To Friends, November 18, 1705.
6. To Logan, March 26, 1706.

   See also: to J. and C. Dickinson, March 6, 1706, in 2 *Penn–Logan Correspondence*, ed. by Deborah Logan, Logan *Letter Books*, HSP, 111–12.

   See also: Dickinsons to Penn, February 8, 1707, in 2 Ibid., 172–74.
7. Logan to Penn, December 12, 1705.
8. 2 *PC*, 193–95, 335–40, May 11, 1705, and February 15, 1707.

   Queen's requests, June 7, 1703, January 29, and May 30, 1704, 2 *PC*, 89, 114. Cornbury request, 2 *PC*, 159, May 4, 1704.

   Refusal, 2 *PC*, 181–82, May 9, 1704.
9. 2 *PC*, 200–5, May 26, 1705.
10. 2 *PC*, 220, December 4, 1705.
11. To Logan, May 10 and September 14, 1705.
12. To Logan, September 21, 1705.
13. Ibid.
14. To Evans, September 22 and 30, 1705.
15. 2 *PC*, 249, May 14, 1706.
16. Samuel Preston to Jonathan Dickinson, May 19, 1706, Logan *Letter Books*, HSP.

    See also 2 *PC*, 317, June 26, 1706.
17. Logan to Penn, May 28, June 12, 1706.
18. March 31 and May 12, 1702.
19. Logan to Penn, December 20, 1706.

    See also 2 *PC*, 357–65, March 4, 1707.
20. Tolles, Frederick E., *James Logan and the Culture of Provincial Pennsylvania* (Boston, 1957), 66.
21. Logan to Penn, December 20, 1706, and March 4, 1707.
22. 2 *PC*, 340–48, 351–55, February 24, 1707.
23. 2 *PC*, passim, February 20–June 1707.
24. Logan to Penn, May 5, 1707.
25. Logan to Penn, June 24, 1708.
26. Logan to Penn, September 1 and November 8, 1708.

CHAPTER 49: *Badgered and Bewildered*

1. To Evans, February 7, 1706.

   See also: to Logan, March 2, 1707.
2. To Evans, February 7, 1707.
3. Logan to Penn, June 23, 1707.

4. To Court of Chancery, May 1707.

   See also Isaac Norris to Richard Hill, November 29, 1707, Isaac Norris *Letter Book*, HSP.

5. To Friends, November 18, 1705.

   See also: to Logan, May 3, 1709.

6. Ibid.

7. Isaac Norris to Richard Hill, November 29, 1707.

   See also: to Chancery, October 5, 1708.

8. Norris to Hill, January 10, 1708, in Isaac Norris *Letter Book*, HSP Ibid.

   See also Norris to Joseph Pike, February 11, 1708.

9. Norris to Pike, March 25, 1708. Ibid.

10. To Logan, May 3, 1708.

   See also Earle and Marlborough to Queen, March 25, 1708; Isaac Norris to Joseph Pike, Norris *Letter Book* (1706-09), 162.

   See also: to Norris, Samuel Carpenter, Thomas Story, et al., September 28, 1708.

   See also Luttrell, Narcissus, *A Brief Historical Relation of State Affairs, September 1678, April 1714* (6 vol., Oxford, 1857), 6: 837.

11. To Anne, May 20 and July 2, 1708.

12. To James Harrison, April 9, 1687.

13. Lease to Gouldney and Callowhill, October 7, 1708, in Rawle, William Brooke, "The General Title of the Penn Family to Pennsylvania," 23 *PHMB* (1899), 601-68.

14. Billy sells to James Butler and Dr. Henry Penrice, November 22, 1707, in Hull, William I., *William Penn: A Topical Biography* (New York, 1937), 55.

   See also: to Logan, May 18, 1708.

15. Logan to Penn, September 15 and December 20, 1706, June 14, 1709.

16. Treacher, Llewellyn, "Some Notes on the Parish of Roscumbe," *Berks and Oxon. Archeological Journal* (April 1906), 54.

17. Faber, Mrs. M.A., "William Penn and the Society of Friends at Reading," 11 *PMHB* (1887), 37-49.

18. Logan to Henry Goulding, December 19, 1713, Logan Papers X: 13, HSP. 7 *PA*, 2nd Series, 28.

CHAPTER 50: *Reversion to Peace*

1. Hannah to Thomas Penn, May 11, 1715, in "Letters of William Penn," 33 *PMHB* (1909), 430.

   See also Hannah to Logan, February 27, 1715, in Drinker, Sophia Hutchinson, *Hannah Penn and the Proprietorship of Pennsylvania*, 69.

2. Story, Thomas, "An Unpublished Letter of Hannah Penn," 4 *JFHS* (1907), 136-37.

3. Hannah to Story, February 15, 1716 and January 29, 1716.

4. Hannah to Thomas Penn, May 11, 1715, 33 *PMHB*.

5. Tolles, Frederick B., *James Logan and the Culture of Provincial Pennsylvania* (Boston, 1957), 117.

6. July 17 and September 9, 1712, 10 *Calendar of Treasury Books* (1708–14), 235, 360.

See also "The Case of William Penn: Report of Surrender Negotiations," 32 *CSP*, America, November 29, 1720, 208 f.

7. *Acts of Privy Council*, March 20 and June 5, 1714, 6: 348, 616.

See also Hannah to Logan, April 2, 1715.

8. *Acts of Privy Council*, March 30 and June 5, 1714, 6: 616.

See also similar disclaimer, 35 *CSP*, America, March 1, 1726, 201.

9. October 25, 1715, Gipson, Lawrence Henry, "An Anomalous American Colony," 27 *Pennsylvania History* (1960), 144–64.

See also similar disclaimer as to islands, 33 *CSP*, America, May 17, 1722, 69.

10. Hannah to Logan, October 13, 1712, to Thomas Penn, May 11, 1715; Hannah to Logan April 8, 1716.

11. Hannah to Thomas Story, July 28, 1718.

12. Hannah to Logan, July 30, 1718.

13. Besse, Joseph, Preface to *Collection of the Works of William Penn* (London, 1726).

14. Story, Thomas, "An Unpublished Letter of Hannah Penn," 4 *JFHS* (1907), 36–37.

15. Story, Alfred, "The Grave of William Penn," 64 *Harpers Monthly Magazine* (1882), 637.

See Appendix F.

16. Hannah to Logan, March 12, 1719.

17. Will dated May 27, 1712, in 1 *Memoirs*, HSP (1826), with comments by Simon Clement to James Lloyd, 212–26.

18. Hannah to Thomas Story, September 14, 1718.

19. Report to the King by CSP "On Affairs in Pennsylvania," September 8, 1721, 32 *CSP*, America, 418–20.

See also Hannah to "Sonne Penn" (Billy), January 13, 1719.

20. Dixon, William Hepworth, *William Penn: An Historical Biography* (Philadelphia, 1851), 336.

See also Lipscombe, William, *History and Antiquities of Buckinghamshire* (London, 1847), which gives place and date of Billy's death as Liege, June 23, 1720.

21. Hannah to Logan, June 29, 1720, says Billy died "about three weeks ago at either Calais or Lille."

Appendixes

APPENDIX A: PORTRAITS OF WILLIAM PENN

OF THE HALF-DOZEN portraits, two busts, and various statues purporting to represent William Penn, none is unqualifiedly accepted as authentic. Only three paintings at most have even the faintest claim to having been produced by contemporaries of the Founder. Though it is possible that he sat for his portrait in Ireland, the original painting of a young man in armor has been lost. Three existing copies, two in England and another owned by the Historical Society of Pennsylvania, though dated 1666, are now known to be eighteenth-century productions. There is some basis for the belief that when Penn was in France, at nineteen, he sat for a miniature by Samuel Cooper, but the suggestion is contested.

The three other best-known likenesses—the Benjamin West portrait of a treaty signing at Shackamaxon, the thirty-seven-foot statue raised to the top of the Philadelphia City Hall in 1894, and a more recent statue, three times lifesize, at the Pennsylvania Capitol at Harrisburg—are idealizations produced years after the Founder's death. Though based upon the best research available at the time of their production, these three memorials are shot through with imagination.

The West portrait, commissioned for £420 by the Penn family in 1773 when West was president of the Royal Academy, was purchased in 1851 for £500 from Granville John Penn, the Founder's great-grandson, and is now in Independence Hall in Philadelphia. The treaty it celebrates was probably not signed at either the time or place commonly ascribed for the ceremony; moreover, the painting contains anachronisms in costume and includes among the spectators James Logan and Thomas Lloyd, neither of whom was in America at the time of the supposed treaty. Though one old lady who professed to have seen Penn at Shackamaxon (her recollections were fallible) described him as the "handsomest, best-looking man she had ever seen," West drew him, at thirty-eight, as a fat old man.

The twenty-six-ton City Hall bronze, modeled in 1893 by Alexander Milne Calder, does not purport to be an authentic likeness, but it does present a tall, vigorous man of about Penn's age at the time of his first arrival in Philadelphia. Accurate in dress and style, it is probably the best-known landmark in the city.

Nor does the two-ton bronze by Janet de Coux, cast in Mexico for the Pennsylvania State Capitol, pretend to exact portraiture. Miss de Coux depicted Penn as a young man, hatless and posed as though in imminent movement. Superimposed in low relief on the left breast of a mid-seventeenth-century Quaker coat is a small figure, Free Man, symbolizing Penn's insistence on liberty.

Two small color chalk portraits by Francis Place, a lawyer turned artist, are now believed to represent William and Hannah, though it was once supposed that they portrayed the Founder's parents. Formerly the property of Robert Surtees, the author of *Jorrocks*, they were purchased in London in 1957 by the Historical Society of Pennsylvania. Undoubtedly they are of the Penn period, but the identification is not yet firmly established.

Greater credence for accuracy is given a small ivory bust carved nine years after the Founder's death by Sylvanus Bevan, a Quaker apothecary of London. According to an anecdote reported by Benjamin Franklin, Lord Cobham of Stow planned to set up in his gardens a number of statues of eminent British leaders. Lacking an authentic portrait of Penn, he inquired among his friends if any such existed. While still searching, he received one day an unsolicited package that arrived anonymously and without any word of explanation. Opening the package, he found therein the Bevan bust. Cobham, who Franklin said had known Penn intimately, at once cried out, "Whence comes this? It is William Penn himself." The bust was used as the model for a large statue in the Stow garden.

James Logan eventually acquired the original bust and, with the bulk of his library, bequeathed it to the Library Company of Philadelphia. The original was lost in a fire in 1831, but one duplicate exists in the Historical Society, next door to the Library Company building, and another in England. Pierre Eugene Du Simitière made an engraving in 1770 based upon the Bevan bust.

Franklin also heard of an alleged Penn portrait that showed the Founder wearing whiskers. He doubted the picture's authenticity, partly because Quakers of the time opposed painting as betraying vanity and pride, and partly because the picture was on boards, a practice not current during Penn's adult lifetime. Subsequent opinion has held that Franklin's skepticism was entirely justified.

A lead statue, cast for Francis Dashwood, Lord Despenser of High Wycombe, stands in the grounds of the Pennsylvania Hospital in Philadelphia. Short, heavy-set, and ill-proportioned, it may be the work of John Bacon, winner in 1769 of the first gold medal for sculpture ever awarded by the Royal Society. Many coats of black paint have obscured the brightness of the original bronze. As Lord Despenser intended to mount the statue on the roof of his saw mill, the statue looks downward as though to observe the activities of Despenser's Hell-Fire Club and of his Society of Dilettanti, both of which met in the grounds that had been landscaped into the form of a woman's body.

According to one not-too-well-authenticated story, the statue eventually was sold to a plumber for its lead. Another story has it placed indoors at Stoke Poges. Wherever it may have been, John Penn, the Founder's grandson, presented it to the Hospital in 1804.

A heavy gale in 1850 toppled the statue, an event that stirred considerable speculation as to how even a heavy wind could blow over a leaden statue, but investigation showed that corrosion had destroyed the support of one foot. The statue was fitted out with a high heel and a reinforced sole, similar in form to the footgear he had worn in France, and was replaced on its feet.

An iron statue graces the Penn Mutual Life Insurance Company building on the site of the old Walnut Street prison in Philadelphia.

In 1935, after considerable prodding by Albert Cook Myers and Charles Francis Jenkins of the Historical Society of Pennsylvania, William Penn was admitted to New York University's Hall of Fame. He is represented by a bronze bust designed by Alexander Stirling Calder, son of the sculptor who produced the giant City Hall statue.

A portrait of William Penn and another of Guli, painted on glass and reproduced in engravings, were once believed authentic, but both the costumes and style of painting suggest that the likenesses are eighteenth century.

Another possible likeness appears in Egbert van Heemskerk's painting *A Quaker Meeting*, which purported to show Penn, George Fox, and other leaders worshiping in 1677 either at Rotterdam or at the Bull and Mouth in London. The identifications, however, are highly questionable.

SOURCES

Francis J. Dallett, "A Penn Portrait at Holker Hall," 91 *PMHB* (1967), 393.

Frank M. Etting, "The Portraiture of Penn," 12 *Scribner's Monthly* (1876), 1–7.

Benjamin Franklin to Lord Kames, January 3, 1760, *Papers of Benjamin Franklin*, Ed. by Leonard W. Labarre (New Haven, 1961), 249–50.

William Isaac Hull, "Egbert van Heemskerk's 'Quaker Meeting,'" 27 *BFHA* (1938), 17–33.

R. Pearsall Smith, *Mss.* at Friends' House, Euston Road, London, parts of which appear in John W. Graham's *William Penn: Founder of Pennsylvania*, (New York, 1910), 239.

R. Norris Williams, "The New Penn Portraits," 82 *PMHB* (1957), 347–50.

STATUES

Thomas G. Morton, *History of the Pennsylvania Hospital* (Philadelphia, 1897), 331–35.

Francis R. Packard, Some Account of the Pennsylvania Hospital (Philadelphia, 1938), 92–93.

Paul H. Smith, "William Penn's Other Statue," 95 *PMHB* (1971), 521–24.

APPENDIX B: THE PENN ANCESTRY

BASICALLY A LONELY man whose forte was loyalty, Penn almost hungered for relatives. Kinship meant much to him; he felt compelled to account for any or all of his kin.

Of these there were many. By his own etymology any family which in ancient times had lived near a headland or a hill might bear the name of Penn; he assumed that all such were at least collateral descendants of a common ancestor. Whether that ancestor was Welsh, Norman, or Saxon was unimportant, for in Buckinghamshire there was a certain Penn Manor where the three lines merged. That land, the property deeded by William the Conqueror to one de la Penne, had somehow slipped from the family's possession into that of Chacombe Priory of Northamptonshire, but three centuries later, by sheer coincidence, it had been restored to the Norman heirs and thus became the seat of Penns of Penn.

The restoration was by Edward VI, who gave the manor and the right to nominate the vicar to his foster mother, Sybilla Hampden, who had nursed him. By this time she had married David Penn, descended, it was said, from a Welsh warrior who also had been rewarded with land in this same neighborhood.

Thus the Penns of Penn became united with the ancestors of John Hampden, but the connection is not easily traced. The donation was supposedly to Sybilla, David's wife, but David has been identified with one John Penn, not a relative, who was Henry VIII's barber-surgeon. Nor was this all; John the Barber was confused with John, the eldest son of David and Sybilla. Furthermore, Sybilla had supposedly been governess not only for Prince Edward but also for his sisters, Mary and Elizabeth. So she would have had the rare distinction of training three future rulers of the kingdom, but as Princess Mary was seventeen years older than her sister and twenty-one years older than Edward, the triple tutorship may readily be questioned.

The link between the Penns of Penn and William Penn the Founder is also weak. No documentary proof has been discovered nor, for that matter, do surviving records join these Penns of Penn with either Wales or the Conqueror, much less the Saxons. Nonetheless, Penn the Founder firmly believed that the Penns of Buckinghamshire were his kinfolk, and when in later years, the Quaker had gained wide renown, so did the Penns of Penn.

David and Sybilla had a daughter and three sons. One child, William, became a monk at Glastonbury, that St. Mary's monastery credited, on very fallible guesswork, with associations with King Arthur, Joseph of Arimathea, and the Holy Grail. Just why Monk William renounced his vows, if he ever took any, and why he was rewarded for it when Henry VIII suppressed the monastery is not explained. According to the legends, this was how the Penns first came to Gloucestershire. It would seem more reasonable to think that if there had been a Monk William at Glastonbury he would have been descended from a Welsh line.

William Penn the Founder did not question the Monk William story, nor did he for a moment question the Penns of Penn relationship. After all, an unbroken succession of six Williams, culminating in himself, was to him strong argument. Evidently he did not know that David's will, while mentioning six children, said nothing about a son William. John Penn, David's eldest son, did christen one of his own boys William, but this child was born in 1578, long after Glastonbury was abandoned. Nor could John's William have been a monk, else why should John enjoin him in his will "to order himself honestly, give up his lewd ways and be ruled by the executors as to the choosing of a wife"?

To counterbalance Lewd William, the Founder noted that an unidentified young woman of the Bucks line, one who delighted in wordly pleasures, reformed while on her deathbed. Having seen a vision of the Lord Jesus in the garb of a plain countryman, she demanded that all lace and other finery be stripped from her garments.

And then there was Sybilla, the tall, lean ghost in a long, gray gown who, with lanky arms outstretched, haunted the manor house.

SOURCES

James Coleman, *A Pedigree and Genealogical Note of the Most Highly Distinguished Family of Penn* (London, 1871).

Thomas Gilpin, *Pedigree of the Penn Family* (Philadelphia, 1852).

Thomas A. Glenn, "Wills of the Penn Family," 17 *PMHB* (1893), 57–58.

George W. Marshall, *Pedigrees of the Knights of England, Charles II—Anne,* (London, 1873).

Oliver Frederick Gillilan Hogg, *Further Light on the Ancestry of William Penn* (London, 1964).

Gilbert Jenkins, *A History of the Parish of Penn* (London, 1937).

Horace Mather Jenkins, *The Family of Penn, Founder of Pennsylvania* (Philadelphia, 1899).

J. Henry Lea, "Genealogical Gleanings Contributing to a History of the Family of Penn" 14 *PMHB* (1899), 52–53, 425–26.

William H. Shaw, *The Knights of England* (London, 1910).

John Jay Smith, "The Penn Family," 5 *Lippincott's Magazine* (1870), 149–62.

APPENDIX C: THE PENN FAMILY

ON APRIL 4, 1674, William Penn married Gulielma Maria Postuma Springett, (February 1644–February 23, 1694), daughter of Sir William Springett and Mary Proude Springett, later Mary Proude Penington.

William and Gulielma had at least six children quite possibly seven. Of these, four died in infancy and another before coming of age. Two children married but only one had issue. The children were:

Gulielma, February 23, 1673–March 17, 1673

William, a twin, February 28, 1674–May 15, 1674

Margaret (or Mary), a twin, February 28, 1674–February 24, 1675

Springett, February 25, 1676–April 10, 1696

Letitia, March 6, 1679–April 14, 1746 (married, / _ust 20, 1702, William Aubrey [d. May 21, 1731]. The marriage was childless.)

William, March 14, 1681–June 23, 1720 (married, January 12, 1699, Mary Jones of Bristol [1677–1703]. They had three children, Gulielma Maria [November 10, 1699], Springett [February 10, 1701], and William 3rd, [March 6, 1703].)

An unnamed daughter may have been born March 13, 1683, if so, she died in infancy. The only authority for this possible child, other than local gossip at Worminghurst, stems from a letter, dated March 13, 1683, from James Claypoole to Benjamin Furly, now at the Historical Society of Pennsylvania.

All descendants of William Penn and Guli trace their ancestry through William Penn 3rd, whose daughter Christiana married Peter Gaskill of Bath. Their children adopted the name Penn-Gaskill.

William Penn's second marriage, March 5, 1696, was to Hannah Callowhill, daughter of Thomas Callowhill of Bristol and his wife, the former Hannah Hollister. They had seven children, of whom four lived to maturity. The children were:

John, the American, January 28, 1700–October 25, 1746. Died unmarried.

Thomas, March 9, 1702–1775. Married Lady Juliana Fermor, daughter of the Earl of Pomfret. They had eight children, of whom four died young. The male line became extinct in 1844.

Hannah Margaret, July 30, 1703–February 4, 1708.

Margaret, November 7, 1704–1751. Married Thomas Freame. They had one child, a daughter, whom they named Philadelphia.

Richard, January 17, 1706–1774. Married Hannah Lardner. They
had four children, the male line becoming extinct in 1863.
Dennis, February 26, 1707–1722.
Hannah, September 5, 1708–January 24, 1709.

APPENDIX D: PENNSYLVANIA PUBLICITY

OF ALL AMERICAN colonies, those of the Delaware River Valley were by
far the best advertised. Real-estate salesmen covered both the British
Isles and Western Europe. Promotional brochures praising the climate,
the beauty of the landscape, the fertility of the soil, and the peacefulness
of the region circulated widely.

The earliest descriptions were fantastic. In 1641, Sir Edmund Plowden, holder of a patent to all land lying between Sandy Hook and Cape
May westward to the Pacific, published *A Direction for Adventurers in
New Albion*, a Catholic colony projected for the east bank of the Delaware; it promised settlers earthly pleasures greater than any to be found
in any of the palaces of Europe.

One Beauchamp Plantagenet, who professed himself the descendant
of kings but who may have been Plowden himself, produced, seven years
later, *Description of the Province of New Albion*. He laid less stress on
baronial courts; they would not be needed in "the fairest country that
a man might see, where angels in the guise of birds sang matins, prime
and evensong, where it was always day and moderate and neither hot
nor cold." Unfortunately, disillusioned colonists, seeing no angels in the
trees and suffering under temperatures that were arctic in the winter
and tropical in July, not only murmured against Plowden but marooned
him upon most unfriendly shores. His patent lapsed.

Major John Fenwick, inspired by John Ogilby's *America*, a guidebook by a former dancing master and theatrical manager, waxed ecstatic
in his own book, *Proposals for Planting a Colony of New Caesarea, or
New Jersey*. "If there be any terrestrial Canaan it must certainly be here
where the land floweth with milk and honey."

Penn himself wrote prolifically, though carefully avoiding overstatement. Either from his own quill, or at his direction, five propaganda
pieces appeared in the year 1681. He must have been forehanded in
their preparation, for one, *Some Account of the Province of Pennsilvania*,
a ten-page leaflet, circulated within a month after the King signed the
Pennsylvania charter.

Within that short period, it is interesting to note, Penn's reluctance about self-advertising had vanished. He soon became reconciled to the "immodesty"; the *Account* uses the name "Pennsylvania" freely and without apology or explanation.

Four months later, in July, the first of three *Brief Accounts* supplemented the preliminary version. He also prepared, but did not immediately publish, *Certain Conditions and Concessions*, his agreement with early purchasers about the type of government and laws under which they would live.

It was, in a way, unfortunate that these arrangements circulated, at first, only by word of mouth. Energetic salesmen apparently did not feel too tightly bound by the exact terms; it may even be that Penn himself, in perfect innocence, left upon some of his subscribers impressions that they later misunderstood or failed to remember accurately. The resultant confusion between purchasers and certain provincial officials as to just what was bought and under precisely what conditions later led to considerable dispute.

APPENDIX E: THE MATHER HOAX

On April 28, 1870, the *Easton* (Pennsylvania) *Argus* alleged that in 1682 Cotton Mather disclosed a plot to sell Penn and a hundred other Quakers into slavery.

According to the article, one of the most notorious hoaxes in American history, on September 15, 1682 Mather wrote a letter to John Higginson, a Salem clergyman of strong anti-Quaker prejudices, stating that the Massachusetts General Court, the legislature, had voted secretly to intercept the *Welcome*, seize the Quaker passengers, and send them to Barbados to be exchanged for rum and sugar. The letter, it was said, was found in a chest of papers deposited at the Massachusetts Historical Society by one Robert Greenleaf, of Malden.

Scholars immediately denounced the pretended letter, *Ye Scheme to Bagge Penn*, as a forgery. Samuel Abbott Green, librarian of the Society, denied the existence of any such paper; he also said that no one had ever heard of the "Mr. Judkins of the Massachusetts Historical Society" who was said to have discovered the document. William Frederick Poole, founder of the well-known *Index*, who only a year before had defended Mather against charges of complicity in the Salem witchcraft trials, pointed out discrepancies. Mather supposedly had described Penn as the chief "scampe," a word that was not used until more than a century after the date of the false letter. Not only was Judkins unknown, but no one had ever heard of the Captain Malachi Huxett of the brig *Porpoise*, who was supposed to intercept the *Welcome*, or of Robert Greenleaf. Mather, who was only nineteen at the time of the imaginary letter, never signed his name, as the forger signed it, "yours in the bowels of Christ." And how was anyone in America supposed to know that the *Welcome* was at sea? It sailed only two weeks before the date of the letter.

According to Poole, James F. Shunk, editor of the *Easton Argus,* confessed to the invention. It was, Shunk said, written to expose "the skeletons in New England's closet" because he resented the excessive Yankee claims that they alone had carried on the struggle for freedom in America.

Notwithstanding the complete demolition of *Ye Scheme to Bagge Penn*, the hoax continues to be resurrected every four or five years.

SOURCES

Shunk's *Easton* (Pennsylvania) *Argus*, April 28, 1870, cited as "authority" a faked letter supposedly from Cotton Mather to John Higginson, dated September 15, 1682. The canard was picked up by several American newspapers, including the *Chicago Tribune* of May 23 and the *New York World* of May 31, 1870.

William F. Poole, who had seen the story in the *Tribune* published a strong condemnation of the story as a hoax. In the *Boston Evening Transcript* of June 1, he asserted that he had received a letter from Shunk admitting the fabrication stating that he "was proud of it." A later writer, David Franklin Barbee, in 1 *BFHS* (1907), 87–90, questioned Poole's accuracy, pointing out that no such letter had ever been produced; this criticism was repeated in 42 *BFHS* (1953), 66. It was also included in a Barbee article in 27 *Tyler's Quarterly Historical and Genealogical Magazine* (May 1946), 180–81.

The same false report of a plot to kidnap Penn appeared in England in E.D. Neill's *English Colonization of America* (London, 1871). It was immediately challenged by William Henry Whitmore, editor of *The Historical Magazine* and of *The New England Historical and Genealogical Record* (8 *N & Q*, 4th Series, September 9, 1871, 202–3).

Subsequent revivals of the Mather hoax have surfaced in the *Philadelphia Public Ledger* and *Philadelphia Evening Bulletin* of September 20, 1927 and in the *Philadelphia Inquirer*, June 5, 1964. The first two were protested by Albert Cook Myers two days later; *the Inquirer* corrected its report within a week.

Refutations of the story have frequently appeared. As early as 1870 Samuel Abbott Green, librarian of the Massachusetts Historical Society, exposed the fabrication (12 *Proceedings of Massachusetts Historical Society*, 328ff).

Clifford K. Shipton, librarian of the American Antiquarian Society, 28 *Tyler's Quarterly Historical and Genealogical Magazine* (1946–47), 662–65, answered Barbee. Richard Dean Hathaway, "Ye Scheme to Bagg Penne," 10 *William and Mary Journal* (1953), 403–21, and Louis Weeks, "Cotton Mather and the Quakers," 89 *BFHS* (1970), 24–33, refuted later revivals of the Shunk invention.

APPENDIX F: THE GRAVE OF WILLIAM PENN

IN 1871, John Wien Forney, publisher of the *Philadelphia Press*, proposed that the remains of William Penn be brought to the city for reburial. Reinterment in a magnificent mausoleum in Fairmount Park should be, he suggested, a principal feature of Philadelphia's observance, in 1882, of the bicentennial of its founding. The move, Forney reminded his readers, would fulfill the Founder's wish that his bones should rest in Pennsylvania. England, Forney was sure, would raise no objection, for the Jordan's burial site, long unmarked, was overgrown with weeds, was unknown to most Englishmen, and was generally neglected.

To those who might contend that Penn should lie among his fellow countrymen, Forney replied that many of Britain's most famous sons were buried not among their kinsfolk but in Westminster Abbey. He also mentioned that the sarcophagus of Alexander the Great was not in Macedonia or in Greece but at Constantinople.

The proposal was opposed not so much for the reasons Forney anticipated as because of family rivalries. Descendants of Penn's first marriage, most of whom lived in Britain, disliked the idea of having Penn rest in America among several of Hannah's descendants; it would be cruel, they protested, to move Penn from Guli's side, and from Hannah's, away from Jordan's, a site they said that he had selected. One man, recipient of a British Government pension granted in lieu of lands confiscated from the Penn estate at the time of the American Revolution, feared the loss of his annuity. Quaker meetings in the Jordan's neighborhood objected that the transfer would involve "the pomp and circumstance of a state ceremonial." Though Queen Victoria was not unfavorable, it was reported, the powerful *London Times* raised the point that Philadelphia was unworthy of the honor because the city was notoriously indifferent to its historical landmarks.

The Forney editorial had little immediately effect, but in 1881, the

Pennsylvania Legislature passed a joint resolution favoring the reburial. Governor Henry M. Hoyt appointed George Leib Harrison, a Philadelphia industrialist, to go to England, at his own expense, to arrange details. Harrison, bearing credentials not only from the Commonwealth of Pennsylvania but from Philadelphia City Councils, Secretary of State James G. Blaine and James Russell Lowell, then the American Minister to the Court of St. James, strove earnestly but could not gain success.

By that time, moreover, enthusiasm even in America had died down. The *Press* itself, originator of the idea, confessed, "No tears will be shed over the failure of a project which has never had any considerable support."

SOURCES

Henry J. Cadbury, "Guli Penn's Grave," 76 *PMHB* (1952), 326–29.
Jack Caudle, "The Grave of William Penn," 50 *JFHS* (1962), 9–14.
George Leib Harrison, *The Remains of William Penn* (Philadelphia, 1882).
Alfred Story, "The Grave of William Penn," 54 *Harper's Magazine* (1882), 62–67.
The Times, London, July 20, 1881.

APPENDIX G: COMMEMORATIONS

THE FIRST FORMAL commemoration of William Penn's services appears to have been General Peter Stephen Duponceau's address to the American Philosophical Society at Philadelphia, June 6, 1821. Duponceau, an international lawyer, lavished praise on Penn, comparing the Founder favorably with Lycurgus, Solon, and Romulus. As a distinguished historian, he did not hesitate to assert that Penn had brought into being the very utopia which had been planned.

"No country on earth," said Duponceau,

ever exhibited such a scene of happiness and peace as was witnessed here during the first century of our social existence—those patriarchal times when simple, yet not inelegant, manners prevailed everywhere among us, when rusticity was devoid of roughness and polished life diffused its mild radiance around, unassuming and unenvied, when society was free from the constraint of etiquette and parade, when love was not crossed by avarice or pride and friendships were unbroken by ambition and intrigue. This was the spectacle which Pennsylvania offered.

This heaven on earth, Duponceau added, had continued to flourish into the time when he himself arrived from France, a boy of seventeen, just before the winter at Valley Forge.

Three years later eighteen prominent Philadelphians, among them John Fanning Watson, the annalist, gathered in Letitia Court, at an inn built on the supposed site of a Penn official residence, to toast the Founder on the 142nd anniversary of his arrival in America. Seated in Penn's walnut cane-seated chair, while other celebrants sat in chairs made from the wood of the fallen Treaty Elm, Duponceau repeated the gist of his Philosophical Society address, this time adding Numa Pompilius and Confucius to the roster of Penn's peers. The party was gay, as well it may have been after the downing of thirteen formal toasts, including one to Hannah. Mention of Guli was omitted, no doubt, through oversight.

The most fantastic commemorative celebration occurred on October 20, 1882, when the bicentennial of Penn's coming was celebrated by a special pageant. No effort was spared to make the affair memorable, in spite of the unwillingness of the Historical Society to participate—it said the date was wrong. A Danish bark, fitted up to represent the *Welcome*, came up the river under tow, bringing a company of people dressed to represent Penn and other leading Quakers. As the *Welcome* approached the city, Penn took a stand in the bow, gazing fixedly at the shore, while his companions, in a semicircle behind him, held a pose, arms outstretched, pointing toward his landing place. Warships of the North Atlantic Fleet roared a salute, the *Welcome* answering with its own little cannon. Meanwhile the ship's crew, "extremely picturesque in their petticoat trousers, huge boots, striped jerseys and pirate caps, ran up and down the shrouds. A watching crowd ashore, dressed as Dutchmen, Swedes, and Indians, cheered lustily."

Immediately upon Penn's arrival, he was taken to an improvised Blue Anchor Inn for a drink and was then escorted to a reviewing stand where he watched a parade of five thousand members of the Improved Order of Red Men, forty-five hundred members of the Catholic Total Abstinence Societies, brigades of old time firemen, innumerable Germans, and most impressive of all, according to the reporter for *The New York Times*, the associated butchers of the city.

The parade lasted three hours and a half. In the evening there were fireworks, notable for pyrotechnical portraits of Penn, Washington, Lincoln, and the murdered President Garfield. The climax showed a fireworks representation of Niagara Falls.

Until the outbreak of the Civil War, the Historical Society of Pennsylvania had held elaborate dinners now and again, at various places in the Commonwealth, always on November 8, which it insisted was the proper anniversary of Penn's arrival. In 1882, having boycotted the

October pageant, it revived its old custom. The toasts were less numerous than in Duponceau's day, there being toasts only to Penn, the Three Lower Counties, the Laws Made by Penn, Religious Freedom, the Eighth of November, the Interior of the Province, and Pennsylvania's Place in the Federal Union.

Homesick Pennsylvanians living in California observed the bicentennial by a dinner which, if the menu is to be accepted at face value, was certainly unparalleled in history. They ate through a feast in Santa Barbara that included Petroleum Soup, Boiled Pig Iron, Coal and Iron Hash, Keystone Dumplings, and Anthracite Pie.

To commemorate Penn's establishment of a local government, Philadelphia staged a Founders' Week celebration in 1908. The actual date, supposedly the 225th anniversary of Philadelphia's founding, was somewhat arbitrarily chosen, for it coincided with no known Penn activity in the area, nor with any particularly outstanding event in Penn's career —even by the old calendar his birthday fell a week later.

William Penn was virtually ignored in a program designed to advertise Philadelphia's progress through the years. He did receive tribute as an advocate of religious liberty, and he appeared, though briefly, in a historical music-drama given nightly on the University of Pennsylvania's athletic field, but after this token recognition attention centered on Pastorius and the Germans, on an Italian memorial to Giuseppe Verdi, on the placing of a tablet at the site of Comte de Rochambeau's 1781 encampment, and on parades by the Knights Templar and the Improved Order of Red Men. The week had begun by the ringing of all church bells in the city at six o'clock on Sunday, October 4, and was closed by horse races on Saturday afternoon. Throughout the week American and foreign warships sailed up and down the Delaware, firing innumerable salutes to Philadelphia's progress. The climax was reported to have been a historical pageant of forty floats and five thousand characters noted in Philadelphia history; it was heralded as "the first of its kind in any American city and on a much larger scale than any ever produced in England or in Continental Europe."

The Pennsylvania Society of New York, in 1911, offered a more lasting tribute. Charles Follen McKim, the distinguished Chester County architect who headed the firm of McKim, Mead and White, had long desired to honor Penn's memory; he arranged for a commemorative tablet to be placed in All Hallows Barking, the Anglican church where Penn had been baptized. McKim died before completing his tribute, but two years after his death the Society finished the project.

Philadelphia's observance in 1932 of the 250th anniversary of the founding of the province avoided the flamboyance of its predecessors. Under the direction of Albert Cook Myers, a program was presented consisting of an address by Frank Aydelotte, president of Swarthmore

College, and of radio broadcasts of messages from President Hoover, the Queen of the Netherlands, the kings of Sweden and Great Britain, the governors of Pennsylvania, Delaware, and New Jersey, and the mayors of London, Deal, New Castle, Chester, and Philadelphia. A three-act pageant-play *Thou Philadelphia*, written by Eleanor Price, depicted Penn's activities in the province.

As part of the observance, bronze memorial tablets were erected on the sites of the Blue Anchor Inn, Penn's Philadelphia and Chester residences, the Friends' Meetinghouse, where the provincial assembly first met, and at "Solitude," the home of John Penn, the last colonial governor. A tablet was also placed in memory of Guli.

The observances were capped by the presentation to the Commonwealth of Pennsylvania of Penn's house and grounds at Pennsbury. An innovation was the sale of a special commemorative stamp, two hundred thousand of which were sold in Philadelphia alone.

SOURCES

New York Times and *Philadelphia Press*, October 25, 1882.
William M. Matos, ed., *Philadelphia: Its Founding and Development*, Official Founders' Week, Philadelphia, 1908.
A. R. Biggs, *All-Hallows Barking and the Memorial to William Penn* (New York, 1911).
Philadelphia Public Ledger, October 28, 1932.

APPENDIX H: WRITINGS OF WILLIAM PENN

OVER A FIFTY-YEAR span Penn published more than one hundred fifty titles. The average of three publications a year seems more impressive, however, than it really was, for most of the issues were slim and the press runs small. John W. Graham estimated Penn's literary output at 1586 closely written manuscript pages totaling approximately one and a half million words. By current publishing practice, this would equal about one thousand printed pages.

Penn holds no high rank among the masters of English style. His sentences were heavy and involved, his grammar not impeccable, his point of view objective. During his earlier years, at least, virtually his entire output was written to defend Quakerism against its critics and detractors, but his writing was more hortatory than persuasive, more polemic than appealing. Following the Amyraut example, reinforced by Lincoln's Inn training, he relied heavily on precedent, bludgeoning his readers by the weight of authority, passages from the Bible, from the Church fathers, or from the Greek and Roman classics.

He was capable of more effective writing. In his *Fruits of Solitude*, for example, he wrote more than 550 maxims, tersely composed, dealing with sixty-nine different topics—he termed the book an enchiridion, or manual of guidance. Now and then, as in *No Cross, No Crown*, he lapsed into recounting a small measure of personal experience; these ventures, dealing with such matters as his Chigwell vision, his supposed expulsion from Oxford, his being turned out of doors, may not have been completely accurate in all details, but they served their purpose.

Penn's two volumes of travel experiences, in Ireland and on the continent, and his letters to the Free Society of Traders on the Pennsylvania Indians and on the fauna and flora of the province, evidence a keen ability to observe and to report. It is unfortunate that he did not pursue this type of writing; his proposals for universal peace and for a union of the American colonies were so far in advance of his era that it is a pity that he did not devote more time to discussing government and international politics.

Most of all, one regrets that little in his writing shows any trace of that agreeable and spirited temperament of which Jonathan Swift spoke or of the light, gay touch which he reportedly displayed as a young man in Dublin's Society of Friendship before he was convinced of Quakerism. These qualities, if exercised, would have enlivened his pages, and, had he only written more about himself and his experiences, would have made for fascinating reading.

THE MORE IMPORTANT WRITINGS OF WILLIAM PENN

VIRTUALLY ALL PENN *MSS* defend the principle of universal peace, freedom of conscience, and toleration of religious beliefs and practices differing from one's own. Equally, they uphold what Penn considered the ancient rights of free Englishmen, the rights to liberty, ownership of property, justice, and the dignity of the individual, as well as the equality of all men under the King and before the Lord.

Inclusion of a publication in any of the subjoined categories does not therefore imply the denial of any just and ancient privileges belonging to other categories.

1. Toleration.

    Nov. 1667. To Earl of Orrery.
    1668. *No Cross, No Crown: A Discourse showing the nature and the discipline of the holy cross of Christ and that the denial of*

self and daily bearing of Christ's cross is the alone way to the rest and kingdom of God. To which are added the living and dying testimonies of many persons of fame and learning both of ancient and modern times in favor of this treatise.

July 1, 1669. To Lord Arlington.

June 14, 1672. To The Friends and People of the United Netherlands.

1672. *Epistola Consulibus Emdense cum Senatus Dantisci.*

Dec. 12, 1674. To Friends in Netherlands and Germany.

1675. *England's Present Interest Discovered.*

1675. *The Continued Cry of the Oppressed.* By the author of *England's Present Interest Discovered.*

Aug. 4, 1677. To the King of Poland: *A Call to Repentence.*

Nov. 4, 1678. *Epistle to the Children of Light in This Generation.*

1679. *The Great Case of Liberty of Conscience, once more briefly debated and defended by the authority of reason, scripture and antiquity which may serve the place of a general reply to such late discourses as have opposed a toleration.*

Nov. 20, 1681. *A Brief Examination of the State of Spiritual Liberty.*

1682. *Some Sober and Weighty Reasons Against Prosecuting Protestant Dissenters.*

1688. Three Letters tending to demonstrate how the security of this Nation lays [*sic*] in the abolition of the present penal laws and tests and in the Establishment of a Universal Liberty of Conscience. Anon.

1689. *The Reasonableness of Toleration.*

Feb. 20, 1698. To the Czar of Muscovy.

2. Peace

1693. *Essay Toward the Present and Future Peace of Europe. By the Establishment of a European Dyet [sic], Parliament and Estates.*

Feb. 7, 1697. *Plan for a Union of the Colonies.*

3. Civil Liberties.

1670. *Some Seasonable and Serious Queries Upon the Late Conventicles, against the Express Word of God.* Anon.

1687. *The Excellent Privilege of Liberty and Property, being the birthright of the free-born subjects of England.*

1688. *The Great and Popular Objection against the Repeal of the Penal Laws and Tests briefly stated and considered, which may serve as an Answer to several late Pamphlets upon that Subject.* By a Friend to Liberty for Liberties' Sake.

4. Administration of Justice.

Aug. 6, 1670. *Exceptions to the Proceedings of the Court at the Old Bailey, London, Sixth Month 1670.*

Sept. 1670. *The Peoples' Ancient and Just Rights Asserted in the Trial of William Penn and W. Mead against the most arbitrary proceedings.*

Feb. 5, 1671. *Bill of Injustices Detected and Re-statement of Trial* [sic] *at the Old Bailey.*

1671. *Truth Rescued From Imposture, or a brief reply to a meer* [sic] *rhapsody of lies, folly and slander but a pretended answer, writ and subscribed by Samuel Starling.* By a Professed Enemy of oppression, W.P.

5. Governmental Policy.

1675. *England's Present Interest Discovered.* Anon.

1679. *England's Great Interest in the Choice of This New Parliament.* Philanglus.

1681. *The Great Question: How Far Religion is Concerned in Policy or Civil Government.* Philo Britannicus.

1681. *One Project for the Good of England.* Philanglus.

1685. *Persuasion to Moderation to Church Dissenters.* By One of the Humblest and Most Dutiful of the King's Dissenting Subjects.

1688. *Advice in the Choice of Parliament Men.*

1692. *Just Measures.* By a Lover of the Truth and Them.

6. Indians.

Aug. 16, 1683. To Free Society of Traders.

1937. The above, enlarged and annotated, appears also as Albert Cook Myers' *William Penn: His Own Account of the Delaware Indians* (Moylan, Pa.), 1937.

7. American Publicity.

1676. *Description of the Province of West Jersey.*

1681. *Some Account of the Province of Pennsylvania.*

1682. *The Frame of Government of Pennsylvania, Together with Certain Laws Agreed Upon in England.*

1682. *Brief Account of the Province of East Jersey.*

1682. *Draft of a Charter of Liberty, with Notes by Benjamin Furly.* MSS. in HSP.

1684. *Information and Direction for Such Persons as are Inclined to America.*

Dec. 12, 1685. *Further Account of the Province of Pennsylvania.*

1690. *Some Proposals for a Second Settlement on the Susquehanna.*

8. Travels.

1670. *My Irish Journal.*

Sept. 1671. *A Trumpet Sounded in the Ears of the Dutch.*

1694. *An Account of My Journey into Holland and Germany in 1677.*

9. Family Life.

1682. *A Testament for his Wife and Children.*
1693. *Fruits of Solitude in Reflections and Maxims.*
1699. *Fruits of a Father's Love, Being His Advice to His Children Relating to their Civil and Religious Conduct.* (First published in 1726.)
1699. *An Account of the Blessed End of Gulielma Penn and Springett Penn.*
Sept. 3, 1699. Epistle of Farewell to Friends.
1702. *More Fruits of Solitude.*
1836. Publications of *A Fragment of an Apology for Himself 3 Memoirs*, HSP, Part 2, 233–42.
Personal *MSS.* at the HSP:
Something Begun Toward a History of My Life: Account of My Life Service since Convincement. A Vindication of Myself from the slanders of wicked men.

10. Quaker Beliefs and Practices.

June 24, 1661. *A Declaration From the Harmless and Innocent People of God* (Not by Penn).
1667. *The Spiritual Base*, By a University Pen.
July 10, 1668. To a Young Person of His Acquaintence. "Deny all ungodliness and worldly lusts and live soberly, righteiusly and godly. —no sports, plays or entertainments. No idle talking or vain jesting."
1672. *A Serious Apology for Friends.*
1672. *A Discourse on the General Rule of Faith and Practice.* Anon.
1672. *The Spirit of Truth Vindicated.*
1674. *The Christian Quaker and His Divine Testimony Vindicated.* In Two Parts. The First, more General, by W. P., the Second, More Particular, by George Whitehead.
1675. *A Treatise on Oaths, Containing Several Weighty Reasons Why the People Called Quakers Refuse to Swear.* By William Penn and others.
1677. *Tender Counsel and Advice By Way of an Epistle to all Those Who Are Sensible of Their Day of Visitation and Who Have Received the Call of the Lord.*
Aug. 10, 1677. To the Churches of Jesus Throughout the World.
Nov. 4, 1678. To the Children of Light in This Generation.
1682. *Answer to a False and Foolish Libel.*
1687. *A Letter Containing Some Reflections on a Discourse Called "Good Advice" to the Church of England, Roman Catholics and Protestant Dissenters Upon Three Letters From a Gentleman in the Country.*
1696. *Primitive Christianity Revived in the Faith and Practices of the People Called Quakers.*

1698. *A Defense of a Paper Called "Gospel Truths," Against the Exceptions of the Bishop of Cork's Testimony.*

1699. *A Brief Account of the Rise and Progress of the People Called Quakers, in which their Fundamental Principles, Doctrines, Worship, Ministry and Discipline are Plainly Declared with a summary relations of the former Dispensations of God in the World, by way of Introduction.*

11. Non-Quaker Sects.

Feb. 5, 1668. *An Answer to a Vain Flash.* Enclosing a pamphlet [which] carrieth with it not one sound and handsome proposition, being only filled with unnecessary excursions and idle ramblings and prophanely [sic] and vain, wanton jestings, looseness, debauchery, jeer and immodest abuse."

Jan. 23, 1671. *A Seasonable Caveat Against Popery.*

1672. *New Witnesses Proved Old Heretics, Ancient Whimsies, Blasphemies and Heresies.* (Ludovici Muggleton and John Reeve.)

1672. *A Winding Sheet for Controversies Ended.* Anon.

1681. *The Oaths of Irish Papists.*

1681. *Protestant's Remonstrance Against Pope and Presbyter.*

1685. *A Defense of the Duke of Buckingham's Book of Religion and Worship from the Exceptions of a Nameless Author.* By the Pennsylvanian.

1699. *Just Censure of Francis Bugg's Address to Parliament Against the Quakers.* Anon.

Sept. 11, 1674. *Naked Truth Needs No Shift, or An Answer to a Libellous Sheet, "The Quakers' Last Shift Found Out."*

12. The Hat Honor.

Oct. 11, 1672. To William Mucklow, "Pulling off the hat is a mark of respect to God, not to be shown any mortal."

1673. *Answer to "The Spirit of the Hat"* by A. Alexander. By a True Witness to the One Way of God, W.P.

13. War By Pamphlet.

1668. *Sandy Foundations Shaken*: A Reply to Thomas Vincent's *The Foundation of God Standeth Still.*

1669. *Innocency With Her Open Face.* Presented by Way of Apology for the Book entitled *Sandy Foundations Shaken.*

1670. *Truth Exalted. A short but Sure Testimony against those Religions whose faiths and worships have been formed and followed in the darkness of apostasy.*

Feb. 19, 1670. *A Letter of Love to the Young Convinced: God's Controversy Proclaimed to the Nation.* Signed by "Your younger brother and fellow traveler in the Kingdom of God and Patience of Jesus, our Lord."

Feb. 1670. *A Guide Mistaken and Temporizing*: A Brief Reply to a book by Jonathan Clapham entitled *A Guide to the True Religion*.

June 29, 1671. *A Serious Apology for the People Called Quakers Against the Malicious Aspersions, Erroneous Doctrines and Horrid Blasphemies of Thomas Jenner and Timothy Taylor*.

1672. *Wisdom Justified by Her Children: Answer to the Ignorance and Calumny of H. Halleywell*. Anon.

Quakerism a New Nick-Name for Old Christianity. Answer to a book entitled *Quakerism No Christianity* by John Faldo.

1672. *The Spirit of Truth Vindicated against that of Error and Envy Unseasonably Manifested in a Late Malicious Libel*.

1672. *Plain Dealing With a Traducing Anabaptist*. (John Morse) anon.

1673. *Jeremy Ives Sober Request Proved False, Impertinent and Impudent*.

1673. *Several Tracts Apologetical Against Injurious and Calumnious Opposition*.

1673. *Invalidity of John Faldo's Vindication: a Return to John Faldo's "Reply."*

1674. *Counterfeit Christian Confronted Against the Vile Forgeries, Gross Perversions, Black Slanders, Plain Contradictions and Scurrilous Language of Thomas Hicks*.

1674. *Urim and Thummin, the Apostolical Doctrines of Light and Perfection Maintained Against the Opposite Plan of Samuel Groville a Pretended Minister of the Gospel*.

1675. *Saul Smitten to the Ground: Dying Remorse of a late Living Enemy, Matthew Hyde*.

1676. *The Skirmisher Defeated: Answer Upon John Cheyney, A Skirmish Upon Quakerism*.

1681. *An Exalted Distraphas Reprehended*. Penn was one of several to write against the Spirit Truth manifested in William Rogers' scandalous book, *The Christian Quaker Distinguished*. From a report by Richard Snead, Feb. 12, 1678 to William Penn.

1692. *New Athenians No Noble Bereans*: A reply to charges against Friends in the *Athenian Mercury* June 4, 1692.

1696. *More Work for George Keith*.

1675. *The Spirit of Alexander the Coppersmith: The Devil's Champions Defeated*.

1675. *Judas and the Jews: Truth Cleared From Scandals* Anon. Rejoinder to a nameless reply, *Tyranny and Hypocrisie Detected*.

14. Biographies

1668. *Words in Earnest: Thomas Loe's Dying Words*.

1671. *Short Testimony Concerning Josiah Coale: Books and Divers Epistles of the Faithful Servant of the Lord*.

1694. *Introduction to the Journal of George Fox*.

1709. *Preface* to Sir Bulstrode Whitelocke's *Memorials of the English Affairs*.

1710. Preface to the *Journal* of John Banks.

15. Poetry.

> 1660. *Epicidea Academia Oxoniensis: Obitum Celissimi Principe* Henrici Duci Glocestrensia M DC LV.
>
> 1664. *Ah, Tyrant Lust.*
>
> 1685. *Tears Wiped Off, or The Second Essay of the Quakers By Way of Poetry.* Written in the Sincerity of the Spirit by W.P., a Servant of the Light.
>
> 1685. *The Quaker Elegy on the Death of Charles, Late King of England,* Written by W.P., a Sincere Lover of Charles and James.
>
> April 1685. *Fiction Found Out* "In disavowing the two poems above," Penn wrote "I that pretended not to poetry at any time."
>
> Jan. 6, 1933. William I. Hull, of Swarthmore, wrote Albert Cook Myers that a poem on Josiah Coale, believed to have been written by William Penn, appeared in the Dutch edition of Willem Sewel's *History of Quakerism,* but was not included in the English edition.

APPENDIX I: PENN BIOGRAPHIES

WILLIAM PENN HAD been dead for a century before he became the subject of a full-length biography. Two Hollanders, one as early as 1695, had paid tribute to his ministerial services, and during the eighteenth century three compilations of his writings had appeared, one of them with a somewhat idealized sketch of his career, but as an individual Penn remained more a legend than a personality.

Part of the explanation lies in the then current belief that incidents of private life had no place in a report of public service, that a leader should be rather judged by what he did than by the motives that impelled him. The Society of Friends was not alone in believing that, in stressing principles, character, and good works, no extraneous elements, and especially no human frailty should be permitted to intrude.

Thus, the first two sketchers of Penn's career, Gerard Croese and Willem Sewell, both of Amsterdam, concentrated almost entirely on Penn's life as a Quaker missioner. While they mentioned other services, they did so chiefly to make clear his sufferings for his conscience. Joseph Besse, who published a collection of Penn's writings in 1726, prefaced his work by a chapter about Penn's career; it was the first such publication in English but it said little about Penn as a man. Similarly, when in 1797 Robert Proud, the schoolteacher-historian, published a history of Pennsylvania, his opening chapter praised Penn the Founder, but it too was stilted and uninformative.

It remained for Thomas Clarkson to produce the first full-length Penn biography in 1813. Interestingly enough, he was neither a Quaker nor particularly interested in Pennsylvania; as an Anglican deacon and an antislavery advocate, he was drawn toward Penn because of Quaker opposition to the slave trade. He wrote a pedestrian book, reminiscent of its predecessors, but because of its uniqueness the two-volume biography ran through several edditions. A rival author published a belated review in 1851, condemning Clarkson as "profoundly unacquainted with history" and as "ignorant of two-thirds of the facts now known about Penn."

If Clarkson borrowed heavily from authors whose copyrights had long expired, he was himself the victim of similar pilferings while his own copyright still ran. Mrs. Mary Robson Hughs did not identify her sources, save only as "the usual authorities," but she had the assistance of Peter Stephen Duponceau of Philadelphia and she had access to some, at least, of the Penn-Logan letters.

Mason Locke Weems, famous inventor of the cherry-tree fable, produced the first American biography of William Penn in 1820. It was not a great book, for Weems did not lavish the same flame and spirit on Penn as he had been pouring into recent publications about God's vengeance against murderers, gamblers, adulterers, and duelists, but he did rank Penn with such other American heroes as Washington, Franklin, and Francis Marion.

The bicentennial of Penn's birth passed without much special notice, but in 1848 Thomas Babington Macaulay raised a storm of protest by attacking Penn's integrity. Clarkson had recently died, at eighty-six, but a long foreword of defense was included in a new one-volume edition of his work. W. Hepworth Dixon, editor of the *Athenaeum*, who had so disapproved of Clarkson, used thirty-nine pages of his own imaginative biography to rebut Macaulay. Samuel McPherson Janney, a birthright Quaker who had only recently sold his girls' boarding school to devote his life to social service, wrote an entire new life of Penn, using numerous original sources, among them manuscripts at the American Philosophical Society and the Historical Society of Pennsylvania; in fifteen pages he demolished Macaulay's "evidence."

For over half a century after the anti-Macaulay campaign, biographers showed little interest in Penn. Except for a brief unimportant pamphlet in 1873 and an undistinguished "life," commemorating the bicentennial of the founding of Philadelphia, no more Penn biographies appeared until 1904. In that year, Augustus C. Buell, publicist for the leading private builder of warships in America, produced *William Penn: Founder of Two Commonwealths*. Though Buell on the whole flattered Penn, he avoided over-effusiveness; rather, he sometimes found Penn timorous and despondent. He was among the first of the more comprehensive biographers to pay much attention to Penn's colonial activities.

Three "lives" appeared between 1907 and 1910; of these only that of John W. Graham, college president and novelist, was outstanding, and this because of his clarification of chronology and his study of Penn portraiture. ,

Another publication lull ensued after the appearance of the Graham volume, not because of any lack of interest in Penn's career, for both popular magazines and scholarly journals ran articles on special facets of the Penn story, but because biographers were preparing for the 250th anniversary of the Holy Experiment—there would be seven new volumes during this 1930 decade, plus a number of reissues.

Word had also spread that Albert Cook Myers, a local historian of the Philadelphia area, was preparing a fifteen-volume definitive *Life and Works*. Myers, in an introductory volume intended for purchase "only by approved individuals and institutions," asserted that he had "searched the world in an earnest endeavor—with the utmost personal sacrifice, even to the hazard of life"—to learn every available fact about William Penn. Unfortunately, he died before completing more than a few slim monographs. His notes and manuscripts were kept under seal at the Chester County Historical Society at West Chester, Pennsylvania.

By far the best of the Penn biographies since Janney's volume—a work which in 1930 a Quaker historian declared "can never be superseded"—are the two volumes compiled half a dozen years later by William Isaac Hull of Swarthmore College. Professor Hull's careful and judicious comparisons of previous historians and his analyses of their comments marked a high spot in scholarship.

Of the twenty-five major Penn biographies, good, bad, and indifferent, few have ever presented a rounded picture of the great Quaker leader. In the early days they concentrated attention on his religious activities and since their material was drawn from his published work, which slackened in his later years, they minimized his personality and almost wholly excluded his social and political contributions. Oddly enough, though more than half the biographies were written by Americans, most of them, based as they were on secondary sources, ignored more than passing references to Penn's colonial activities. Up until the present century, when biographies dealt at all with Penn's secular activities they were more concerned with refuting unfair criticism than with recounting Penn's positive achievements.

Though every biography professed to admire Penn's high ideals, some writers of more recent times tend to regard him as at least slightly tainted by hypocrisy. Others put him down as honest and well-meaning but as the somewhat gullible tool of the unscrupulous Stuarts. A few praise his influence on the building of American democracy, but there are those who, suspecting that his principles were eroded by disillusion, dismiss his idealism as barren. He is criticized also for vacillation, for changing his mind when circumstances shifted, and, though more in the distant past than in the present, for opportunism. None of these criticisms, most of them subtly implied rather than expressly stated, are justly made. Recent trends toward studying special facets of Penn's career do much to rescue Penn from the libels of the less well informed.

BIOGRAPHIES

Beatty, Edward E.O., *William Penn as a Social Philosopher* (New York, 1939).

Besse, Joseph, *A Collection of the Works of William Penn, to which is Prefaced a Journal of His Life With Many Letters and Papers Not Before Published* (London, 1726).

Brailsford, Mabel Richmond, *The Making of William Penn* (London, 1930).

Bronner, Edward B., *William Penn's Holy Experiment* (New York, 1962).

Buck, William J., *William Penn in America* (Philadelphia, 1888).

Buell, Augustus C., *William Penn: Founder of Two Commonwealths* (New York, 1904).

Clarkson, James, *Memoirs of the Private and Public Life of William Penn* (London, 1814).

Comfort, William Wister, *William Penn, 1644–1718: A Tercentenary Estimate* (London, 1944).

―――― *William Penn's Religious Backgrounds* (Ambler, Pa., 1944).

―――― *William Penn and Our Liberties* (Philadelphia, 1947).

Dixon, W. Hepworth, *History of William Penn, Founder of Pennsylvania* (London, 1851).

Dobree, Bonamy, *William Penn, Quaker and Pioneer* (New York, 1932).

Dunn, Mary Maples, *William Penn: Politics and Conscience* (Princeton, 1967).

Fisher, Sydney George, *The True William Penn* (Philadelphia, 1900).

―――― Joshua Francis, "The Private and Domestic Habits of William Penn," 3 *Memoirs, HSP* (1836), Part 2, 65–104.

Graham, John W., *William Penn, Founder of Pennsylvania* (New York, 1916).

Grant, Mrs. Colquhoun, *Quaker and Courtier: The Life and Work of William Penn* (New York, 1907).

Gray, Elizabeth Janet, *William Penn* (New York, 1938).

Hayes, A.L., *Biographical Sketch of William Penn* (Lancaster, Pa., 1873).

Hughs, Mary Robson, *The Life of William Penn, abridged and adopted to the use of Young Persons* (London, 1822).

Hull, William Isaac, *Eight First Biographies of William Penn: In seven languages and seven lands* (Swarthmore, Pa., 1936).

―――― *William Penn: A Topical Biography* (Swarthmore, Pa., 1937).

Illick, Joseph Edward, *William Penn's Relations With the British Government* (Philadelphia, 1963).

―――― *William Penn the Politician* (Ithaca, 1965).

Janney, Samuel MacPherson, *The Life of William Penn With Selections from his Correspondence and Autobiography* (Philadelphia, 1852).

Jenkins, Horace Mather, *William Penn: His Character and Career* (Wilmington, Del., 1883).

Lawton, Charlwood, *A Memoir of Part of the Life of William Penn, 3 Memoirs, HSP* (1836), Part 2, 213–31.

Myers, Albert Cook, *William Penn's Early Life in Brief* (Moylan, Pa., n.d.).

Peare, Catherine Owens, *William Penn* (Philadelphia, 1957).

Pound, Arthur, *The Penns of Pennsylvania and England* (New York, 1932).

Roberts, Lucy B., *William Penn: Founder of Pennsylvania* (New York, 1910).

Spence, Mary Kirk, *William Penn: A Bibliography* (Harrisburg, Pa., 1932).

Stoughton, John, *William Penn, the Founder* (London, 1882).

Vulliamy, Colwyn, *William Penn* (New York, 1934).

Weems, Mason Locke, *The Life of William Penn, the Settler of Pennsylvania, the Founder of Philadelphia, One of the First Lawgivers in the Colonies, now the United States, in 1682* (Philadelphia, 1836).

Index

453